EIGHTH EDITION

Terrorism and Homeland Security

Jonathan R. White

Grand Valley State University

WADSWORTH
CENGAGE Learning

Australia • Brazil • Japan • Korea • Mexico • Singapore • Spain • United Kingdom • United States

WADSWORTH
CENGAGE Learning

Terrorism and Homeland Security,
Eighth Edition, Jonathan R. White

Editor in Chief: Linda Ganster

Acquisitions Editor: Carolyn Henderson Meier

Assistant Editor: Casey Lozier

Editorial Assistant: Casey Lozier

Media Editor: Ting Jian Yap

Brand Manager: Liz Rhoden

Director, Brand Management: Kim Russell

Market Development Manager:
Michelle Williams

Director, Market Development Manager:
Mandee Eckersley

Art and Cover Direction, Production
Management, Text/Photo Research, and
Composition: PreMediaGlobal

Manufacturing Planner: Judy Inouye

Rights Acquisitions Specialist: Roberta Broyer

Design and Cover Image illustration:
© PreMediaGlobal

For product information and technology assistance, contact us at
Cengage Learning Customer & Sales Support, 1-800-354-9706.

For permission to use material from this text or product,
submit all requests online at **www.cengage.com/permissions.**
Further permissions questions can be e-mailed to
permissionrequest@cengage.com.

Library of Congress Control Number: 2012949730

Student Edition:

ISBN-13: 978-1-285-06196-2

ISBN-10: 1-285-06196-9

Loose-leaf Edition:

ISBN-978-1-285-06226-6

ISBN-1-285-06226-4

Wadsworth
20 DAVIS DRIVE
Belmont, CA 94002-3098
USA

Cengage Learning is a leading provider of customized learning solutions with office locations around the globe, including Singapore, the United Kingdom, Australia, Mexico, Brazil, and Japan. Locate your local office at **www.cengage.com/global.**

Cengage Learning products are represented in Canada by Nelson Education, Ltd.

To learn more about Wadsworth, visit **www.cengage.com/Wadsworth**

Purchase any of our products at your local college store or at our preferred online store **www.cengagebrain.com**

Printed in the United States of America
3 4 5 6 7 16 15 14 13

Dedicated to:

Wendy Wenner and Gayle Davis—for making it all work

JONATHAN WHITE is Professor of Interdisciplinary Studies in the Brooks College of Grand Valley State University, Allendale, Michigan, and a Senior Research Associate for the Institute for Intergovernmental Research, Tallahassee, Florida. He holds a Ph.D. in Criminal Justice and Criminology from Michigan State University and a Master of Divinity from Western Theological Seminary. He teaches classes on religious terrorism, radicalization, and jihadist violence for the State and Local Anti-Terrorism Training (SLATT) program of the United States Department of Justice, Bureau of Justice Assistance. He also taught at the FBI Academy in Quantico, Virginia, and worked with several foreign police agencies and the United States Department of State Anti-Terrorism Assistance program.

BRIEF CONTENTS

CONTENTS

PART 2 International Terrorism: National and Ethnic Movements   135

6 Long-Term Separatist Terrorism   137

11 Al Qaeda and Jihadist Networks   274

PART 4   Domestic Terrorism and Homeland Security   307

12   Domestic Terrorism   309

13   An Introduction to Homeland Security   333

PREFACE

Terrorism is always in transition. Organizations change, groups transform structures, and new issues arise. As the United States has ended one conventional war and winds down another, domestic extremist violence is on the rise. The world economic crisis has presented Europeans with resurgent revolutionary threats and the potential for endemic ethnic and immigrant trouble. The al Qaeda ideology has spawned franchise organizations from the Pacific Rim to western Africa. The Middle East has experienced revolutions and the election of religious conservatives. A holocaust, unrecognized in much of the world, continues in Africa. Drug violence and economic injustice continue in Central and South America. Any text that tries to capture and summarize the changing nature of terrorism within the volatile world climate is quickly outdated.

Professors who have used previous editions of this book have asked for changes and updates to this text. In addition, they have offered valuable critiques, suggestions for additional material, and corrections of factual errors. Many of the requests for revision have focused on reorganization of the first section and the consolidation of historical material throughout the book. I have written the Eighth Edition of *Terrorism and Homeland Security* to address the changes in international and domestic terrorism. The book has also been revised to meet the needs of the professors who use it in the classroom.

The purpose of the book remains the same. It is designed to introduce criminal justice and other social science students to the field of terrorism and homeland security. The book is also designed to provide a pragmatic background for the law enforcement, intelligence, and military communities. It is a basic, practical introduction for people who will or already do face the threat of terrorism. Many theories, polemics, and models are summarized and compared, but readers will find no grand theory. The purpose is to expose readers to a vast array of issues, campaigns, theories, and opinions.

As stated in the previous editions, issues surrounding terrorism are emotionally charged. Therefore, the information in this text is presented from a variety of positions. The purpose is to explain various points of view without taking sides. Students are exposed to differing interpretations of issues that have spawned heated controversies, and they are asked to engage issues in critical thinking exercises at the end of each chapter. Hopefully, the text presents enough information to allow students to make informed decisions.

Overview

This text is arranged to enhance student learning. Part I deals with basic background. It begins with a chapter on the history of terrorism. The decision to begin with a historical overview was based on numerous requests from a variety of users. Chapter 2 focuses on the social structure of terrorism, and Chapter 3 is about structure and financing. The discussion of terrorist finances has been increased, again to meet requests from instructors. The remaining chapters in Part I deal with the media, gender, tactics, and force multipliers.

Part II deals with international terrorism from ethnic, nationalistic, and separatist perspectives. Chapter 6 discusses long-term separatist movements. It focuses on Ireland, the Basque region of Spain and France, and Sri Lanka. The chapter also contains a discussion of reactionary terrorism against separatist groups in Spain. As requested by professors, much of the historical material on Ireland has been reduced and placed in the first chapter. Chapter 7 follows with examinations of short-term anticolonial movements in Cyprus, Kenya, and Algeria. Repression is examined once again, only the discussion focuses on official governmental policies instead of illegal groups. The chapter continues in this manner with examinations of separatist terrorism in Russia, Turkey, and China. It concludes with a discussion of endemic terrorism in Africa.

Chapters 8 and 9 focus on the Middle East. Chapter 8 provides historical background and current information for understanding the region. In essence, it serves as a reference for students. Information also includes the confused meaning of the term "Middle East," a general background to Islam, and a summary of other issues such as the Iranian Revolution. Chapter 9 discusses the question of Israel and Palestine. The major groups, issues, and policy controversies are covered here. Although some groups are based in religion, all of the regional terrorist organizations are presented from nationalistic and ethnic positions. The conflict regarding control of Israel and Palestine has many religious issues, but local groups fight for control of national identity.

Part III is devoted to religious and ideological terrorism. Chapter 10 covers violent revolutionary extremism. It examines revolutionary movements in Uruguay, Colombia, Peru, Greece, Iraq, and Nepal. It includes a section on revolutionary theory and illustrations from the history of revolutionary terrorism in Europe. The chapter also contains a discussion of counter revolutionary death squads. Chapter 11 moves to the international jihad. It begins with a discussion of al Qaeda's history and operations, and ends by examining the evolution of the internal jihad. The focus is updated to reflect the al Qaeda franchise and related religious movements such as the Haqqani network in Pakistan.

Part IV has three purposes: to discuss domestic terrorism, homeland security, and future trends. Chapter 12 focuses on domestic terrorism, including the expansion of violent anti-government groups and the controversies over homegrown terrorism. Material on the sovereign citizen movement has been added. The next three chapters focus on homeland security. Chapter 13 is designed to discuss basic issues, and Chapter 14 discusses how law enforcement deals with these issues. Chapter 15 focuses on civil liberties, legal controversies, and other constitutional issues. The book closes with an examination of future issues. Gleaned from emerging trends, there are discussions of the future directions of homeland security and foreign policy.

New to this Edition

There are several changes that apply to all chapters in the Eighth Edition. These changes specifically reflect requests from the instructors teaching the course. They include:

- Enhanced pedagogy to drive enhanced student understanding:
  - The chapter summaries are now matched to specific chapter-opening objectives.
  - The length and degree of coverage in each chapter has been balanced to equalize weekly study assignments.

- Key words have been revised for clarity.
    - The extensive discussion of the definitional debate has been reduced and replaced with an historical summary in the first chapter.
    - More contemporary examples of terrorism are included throughout.
- The book has been reorganized and structured to meet the needs of students in a 15-week course.
- Each chapter is introduced with a crucial current event related to the chapter.
- Chapter Take Aways have been added just before the objective summaries; these Take Aways highlight the chapter's thesis and offer generalized conclusions as a counterpoint to the bullet-point chapter summary.

Chapter-by-Chapter Changes

Each chapter has specific changes, additions, deletions, and new features; they are summarized as follows.

Chapter 1 Defining Terrorism in Modern History

New Material

- Chapter introduction is based on changes in U.S. criminal justice and national security policies in the wake of terrorism.
- The early experiences of terrorism are grouped together from the French Revolution through the formation of the Irish Free State.

Revised Material

- The discussions of definitions is reduced.
- Early historical material reorganized and moved to this chapter.
- The historical discussion of Ireland from the ninth century through the eighteenth century is de-emphasized.
- New emphasis on the Irish Republican Army as it emerged from Republican movements in the late nineteenth century through independence in the early twentieth century.
- Reorganization sets the stage for explaining historical developments in specific cases later in the text.

Chapter 2 The Social Underpinnings of Terrorism

New Material

- Discussion of alienation.
- New discussion of the debates about radicalization.

Revised Material

- Enhanced and updated discussion of radicalization.

Chapter 3 The Organization and Financing of Terrorism

New Material

- Sidebar summarizing methods of financing terrorism.
- Added information on Mexican drug links to Hezbollah.
- Discussion of money laundering.
- Black Market Peso Exchange.
- New art work on money laundering.

Revised Material

- Added information on terrorism financing.
- Financial section reorganized as requested by professors using the text.

Chapter 4 Terrorism and the Media

New Material

- Discussion of gender stereotypes and the media.
- The media's influence on homeland security.

Revised Material

- Liberal and conservative critiques of reporting; both sides discussed.
- Discussion of the media as a weapon.

Chapter 5 Gender Roles, Tactics, and Force Multipliers in Terrorism

New Material

- Discussion of the tactical impact of women on terrorist operations.
- Discussion of the national counterterrorism strategy and gender.

Revised Material

- Expanded discussion of tactics.
- Updated cyberterrorism to include catastrophic attacks.

Chapter 6 Long-Term Separatist Terrorism

New Material

- Discussion of the ETA peace declaration in October 2011.
- Analysis women in the Sri Lankan peace process.

Revised Material

- Reorganized and expanded discussion of ethnic and nationalist violence.
- Refocus on modern issues in Ireland.
- Expanded evaluation of the impact of peace in Sri Lanka.
- Updated analysis of activity in the Tamil diaspora.

Chapter 7 Nationalistic and Endemic Terrorism

New Material

- Discussion of Boko Haram.
- Discussion of Joseph Kony.

Revised Material

- Revised material on the Lord's Resistance Army.

Chapter 8 Background to the Middle East

New Material

- Discussion of the Iranian nuclear program.

Revised Material

- Streamlined coverage based on feedback from outside reviews.

Chapter 9 Israel and Palestine

Revised Material

- Increased emphasis on current threats rather than history.
- Historical threats have been categorized to enhance student understanding.

Chapter 10 Revolutionary, Counter Revolutionary, and Religious Terrorism

New Material

- Coverage of Anders Breivik and the 2011 Norway shootings.

Revised Material

- Updates of revolutionary terrorist groups.
- Rearranged the format and organization of the chapter; it moves from revolutionary models to Tupamaro-style groups, Maoist groups, European left- and right-wing groups, through death squads.
- Eliminated historical discussion of Japan and cut historical material on the Tupamaros.

Chapter 11 Al Qaeda and Jihadist Networks

New Material

- Attacks in France.
- Death of Osama bin Laden.
- Addition of the Haqqani network.
- Death of Anwar al Awlaki.

Revised Material

- Reorganized around the al Qaeda franchise.
- Eliminated descriptions of Iraq and Afghan wars.
- Increased discussion of networks.

Chapter 12 Domestic Terrorism

New Material

- Section on the sovereign citizen movement.
- Typology of extremism.

Revised Material

- Chapter reordered according to a typology of extremism.
- Sections on lesser-known groups from the twentieth century deleted.
- Revised section on homegrown terrorism.
- Revised section on anti-abortion violence.

Chapter 13 An Introduction to Homeland Security

New Material

- Discuss of the creation process of fusion centers.
- Added governmental and academic critiques of the homeland security network.

Revised Material

- Streamlined 9/11 section as requested by reviewers.
- Updated intelligence processes.
- Added discussions of RICs, HIDTAs, and ATF gun intelligence centers.

Chapter 14 Law Enforcement and Homeland Security

New Material

- Case study of DOJ-DHS rivalry.
- Coverage of law enforcement investigations of terrorism.

Revised Material

- Added information of dysfunctions in bureaucracy.
- Added information on the proper evaluation and management of organizations.

Chapter 15 Homeland Security and Constitutional Issues

New Material

- Emerging research among criminologists on the intelligence system and civil liberties.
- Summary of the 2011 extension of the Patriot Act.

Chapter 16 Security, Terrorism, and the Future

New Material

- Franchising al Qaeda's ideology.

Ancillaries

A number of supplements are provided by Cengage Learning to help instructors use *Terrorism and Homeland Security* in their courses and to aid students in preparing for exams. Supplements are available to qualified adopters. Please consult your local sales representative for details.

For the Instructor

Instructor's Resource Manual with Test Bank. Newly updated by Vanessa Escalante of L.A. College International, the manual includes learning objectives, key terms, a detailed chapter outline, a chapter summary, discussion topics, student activities, media tools, and a newly expanded test bank. The learning objectives are correlated with the discussion topics, student activities, and media tools. Each chapter's test bank contains questions in multiple-choice, true-false, completion, essay formats, and new scenario-based questions with a full answer key. The test bank is coded to the learning objectives that appear in the main text, and includes the page numbers in the main text where the answers can be found. Finally, each question in the test bank has been carefully reviewed by experienced criminal justice instructors for quality, accuracy, and content coverage. Our Instructor Approved seal, which appears on the front cover, is our assurance that you are working with an assessment and grading resource of the highest caliber.

The manual is available for download on the password-protected website and can also be obtained by e-mailing your local Cengage Learning representative.

PowerPoint Slides. From Babette Protz of the University of South Carolina, Lancaster, these handy Microsoft PowerPoint slides, which outline the chapters of the main text in a classroom-ready presentation, will help you in making your lectures engaging and in reaching your visually oriented students. The presentations are available for download on the password-protected website and can also be obtained by e-mailing your local Cengage Learning representative.

Lesson Plans. From Robert Cadigan of Boston University, the Lesson Plans bring accessible, masterful suggestions to every lesson. The Lesson Plans includes a sample syllabus, learning objectives, lecture notes, discussion topics, in-class activities, a detailed lecture outline, and assignments. Lesson Plans are available on the instructor website, or by e-mailing your local representative.

ExamView® Computerized Testing. The comprehensive Instructor's Manual described above is backed up by ExamView, a computerized test bank available for PC and Macintosh computers. With ExamView you can create, deliver, and customize tests and study guides (both print and online) in minutes. You can easily edit and import your own questions and graphics, change test layouts, and reorganize questions. And using ExamView's complete word-processing capabilities, you can enter an unlimited number of new questions or edit existing questions.

WebTutor™ on Blackboard® and WebCT®. Jump-start your course with customizable, rich, text-specific content within your Course Management System. Whether you want to web-enable your class or put an entire course online, WebTutor delivers. WebTutor offers a wide array of resources, including media assets, test bank, practice quizzes linked to chapter learning objectives, and additional study aids. Visit www.cengage.com/webtutor to learn more.

The Wadsworth Criminal Justice Video Library. So many exciting new videos—so many great ways to enrich your lectures and spark discussion of the material in this text. Your Cengage Learning representative will be happy to provide details on our video policy by adoption size. The library includes these selections and many others.

- *ABC® Videos.* ABC videos feature short, high-interest clips from current news events as well as historic raw footage going back 40 years.

- *Cengage Learning's "Introduction Criminal Justice Video Series"* features videos supplied by the BBC Motion Gallery. These short, high-interest clips from CBS and BBC news programs—everything from nightly news broadcasts and specials to CBS News Special Reports, *CBS Sunday Morning*, *60 Minutes*, and more—are perfect classroom discussion starters.

Criminal Justice Media Library. Cengage Learning's Criminal Justice Media Library includes nearly 300 media assets on the topics you cover in your courses. Available to stream from any web-enabled computer, the Criminal Justice Media Library's assets include such valuable resources as: Career Profile Videos featuring interviews with criminal justice professionals from a range of roles and locations, simulations that allow students to step into various roles and practice their decision-making skills, video clips on current topics from ABC® and other sources, animations that illustrate key concepts, interactive learning modules that help students check their knowledge of important topics, and Reality Check exercises that compare expectations and preconceived notions against the real-life thoughts and experiences of criminal justice professionals. The Criminal Justice Media Library can be uploaded and used within many popular Learning Management Systems. You can also customize it with your own course material. You can also purchase an institutional site license. Please contact your Cengage Learning representative for ordering and pricing information.

Careers in Criminal Justice Website. *Can be bundled with this text at no additional charge.* Featuring plenty of self-exploration and profiling activities, the interactive Careers in Criminal Justice Website helps students investigate and focus on the criminal justice career choices that are right for them. Includes interest assessment, video testimonials from career professionals, résumé and interview tips, links for reference, and a wealth of information on "soft skills" such as health and fitness, stress management, and effective communication. Ask your rep about the state-specific Careers in Criminal Justice Website, which features information that pertains to any individual state.

For the Student

Coursemate. Cengage Learning's Criminal Justice CourseMate brings course concepts to life with interactive learning, study, and exam preparation tools that support the printed textbook. CourseMate includes an integrated eBook, quizzes mapped to chapter learning objectives (updated for the current edition by James Blair of South Texas College), flashcards, videos, and EngagementTracker, a first-of-its-kind tool that monitors student engagement in the course. The accompanying instructor website offers access to password-protected resources such as an electronic version of the instructor's manual and PowerPoint® slides.

CLeBook. Cengage Learning's Criminal Justice eBooks allow students to access our textbooks in an easy-to-use online format. Highlight, take notes, bookmark, search your text, and, for most texts, link directly into multimedia. In short, CLeBooks combine the best features of paper books and eBooks in one package.

Current Perspectives: Readings from InfoTrac® College Edition. These readers, designed to give students a closer look at special topics in criminal justice, include free access to InfoTrac College Edition. The timely articles are selected by experts in each topic from within InfoTrac College Edition. They are available free when bundled with the text and include the following titles:

- Cyber Crime
- Victimology
- Juvenile Justice
- Racial Profiling
- White-Collar Crime
- Terrorism and Homeland Security
- Public Policy and Criminal Justice
- Technology and Criminal Justice
- Ethics in Criminal Justice
- Forensics and Criminal Investigation
- Corrections
- Law and Courts
- Policy in Criminal Justice

Acknowledgments

The following reviewers provided valuable insight and criticism. I would like to thank:

Lee Ellen Ayers—Southern Oregon University
Erick Barnes—University of Detroit–Mercy
Phillip Cohen—San Jacinto College North
Salih Hakan Can—Pennsylvania State University–Schuylkill Campus
Theodore Darden—College of DuPage
Michael T. Eskey—Park University
Gardel Feurtado—The Citadel
Donald V. Haley—Tidewater Community College
Charles Hantz—Danville Area Community College
Daniel R. Kempton—Northern Illinois University
Nathan Moran—Midwestern State University
Melissa Ricketts—Shippensburg University
Vaughn P. Shannon—Wright State University
Albert Sproule—DeSales University
Michael C. Walker—Passaic County Community College

I would like to thank special members of the editorial and production staff: Carolyn Henderson Meier, Marie Desrosiers, and David Heath.

Disclaimer

Much of the work for this book was completed while I was working with the State and Local Anti-Terrorism Training (SLATT) program. SLATT is a Bureau of Justice Assistance (BJA) program managed by the Institute of Intergovernmental Research (IIR) and the Federal Bureau of Investigation (FBI). The material in this book does not necessarily represent the positions of BJA, IIR, the FBI, or any entity of the United States Department of Justice.

Terrorism in Historical and Social Contexts

CHAPTER 1

Defining Terrorism in Modern History

Hoberman Collection/Glow Images

LEARNING OBJECTIVES

After reading this chapter, you should be able to:

> Explain the reason *terrorism* is difficult to define.

> Summarize the impact of context on definitions of *terrorism.*

> Explain the impact the Enlightenment on democracy and potential revolutionary thought.

> Summarize the origins of modern terrorism from the Enlightenment through the Napoleonic wars.

> Explain why terrorism became defined as a revolutionary activity after the European experience in 1848.

> Define socialism, anarchism, and communism.

> Summarize the differing meanings of terrorism in Russia from the Peoples' Will through the Lenin and Trotsky.

> Summarize the early history of the Irish Republican Army.

> Define *selective terrorism* as used by Michael Collins.

ecretary of Defense Leon Panetta announced a new strategy for national defense in 2012. For decades American military preparedness had been based on the axiom that U.S. armed forces should be able to fight two independent major wars while maintaining a strong continental defense. The United States fought two regional wars in the early part of the twenty-first century, and both involved guerrilla warfare and terrorism. Panetta, under President Barack Obama's direction, ordered a military streamlining with an emphasis on countering changing aspects of conflict. A few years earlier, President George W. Bush reorganized the U.S. government and the Federal Bureau of Investigation. The new Department of Homeland Security and the FBI were charged with protecting the country from a form of unconventional war: terrorism.

Defining terrorism, conflict, and war is not an academic exercise. The manner in which terrorism is defined will help shape American law enforcement and national security policies in the coming decades. This is not a new concept. The definition of terrorism changes over time. Changes in the Department of Defense, the Department of Homeland Security, and the FBI have been partially prompted by the way we define terrorism at this point in history.

The Difficulty with Definitions

social construct: The way people view reality. Groups construct a framework around a concept, defining various aspects of their lives through the meanings they attribute to the construct.

academic consensus definition: A complex definition based on the work of Alex Schmid. It combines common elements of the definitions used by leading scholars in the field of terrorism.

Terrorism is difficult to define. It is not a physical entity that has dimensions to be measured, weighed, and analyzed. It is a **social construct;** that is, terrorism is defined by different people within shifting social and political realities (Schmid, 1992). The term has spawned heated debate because it is nebulous and pejorative. As a result there are many definitions of terrorism and no single accepted understanding.

Some scholars have opted for a simple definition stating that terrorism is an act or threatened act of violence against innocent people for political purposes (Laqueur, 1987, 1999). Some nations have criminalized terrorism, defining it as a violation of law (Mullendore and White, 1996). Alex Schmid (Schmid and Jongman, 2005, pp. 1–38, 70–111) tries to synthesize various positions in an **academic consensus definition.** Schmid says most definitions of the term have two characteristics: (1) Someone is terrorized and (2) the meaning of the term is derived from the terrorists' targets and victims. Many victims of government violence claim that repression is terrorism, while governments tend to define terrorism by the violent situations they face (Bady, 2003). There is no standard meaning of *terrorism*.

H. H. A. Cooper (1976, 1977b, 1978, 2001) first approached the problem by stating there is "a problem in the problem definition." We can agree that terrorism is a problem, but we cannot agree on what terrorism is.

Definitions Influenced by Social Context

social context: The historical, political, and criminological circumstances at a given point in time. The social context affects the way terrorism is defined.

The **social context** surrounding the term *terrorism* influences how it is defined. Consider the following examples and the differing meanings of *terrorism*:

A. In early 2010 a colleague returned from a U.S. State Department Anti-Terrorism Assistance program in Jordan. He was working with 27 Jordanian police officers, 12 Christians, 12 Muslims (all Sunnis), and three agnostics. They never argued about religion, but they were appalled when he outlined the operational methods of Hezbollah. The reason: The Jordanian police officers vehemently stated that Hezbollah was not a terrorist organization. It was a militia fighting the Israeli Defense Force. Hezbollah is a Shi'ite group, but that made no difference to the Sunni Muslim, Christian, and agnostic police officers. In their minds Hezbollah was a legitimate militia resisting Israeli aggression.

B. Many Lebanese have a similar view. Israel keeps a close eye on militant activities in Lebanon, routinely violating Lebanese airspace with fighter jets. The Lebanese view these actions as a form of terrorism. They have no capability to fly over Israel, but Israel can use its superior military power against Lebanon (Croft and Heller, 2010). Therefore, many Lebanese believe Israel to be the true source of terrorism. They believe the Israelis use their superior military might to subjugate the Arabs within and around their borders.

C. Israel would hardly agree with such an assessment, citing its experience with conventional war and terrorism since 1948. In February 2010, for example, an Israeli soldier sat in a jeep at a checkpoint on the West Bank. A Palestinian police officer pulled beside him in another vehicle, walked over to the soldier, and stabbed him in the chest. The police officer fled, and the soldier died of his wounds (Lappin, 2010). Most Israelis would literally cite thousands of similar examples and claim that these are examples of terrorism. Flights over Lebanon are merely self-defense against enemies who have vowed that they will not stop fighting until the state of Israel is destroyed.

D. The definition becomes even more complicated in war zones. In Afghanistan, North Atlantic Treaty Organization (NATO) forces are fighting two major enemies, a loose association of central Asian fundamentalist Muslims called the Students, or the Taliban, and another terrorist group known as al Qaeda. News reporters, politicians, and military officers often lump the two organizations into a single group of terrorists, but there are profound differences. Al Qaeda operates as an international terrorist group while the Taliban form divergent regional militias and use **selective terrorism** to support guerrilla operations. More importantly, the theological tradition of the Taliban differs from al Qaeda's infatuation with a violent interpretation of a twentieth-century militant Egyptian theologian. Linking the two organizations under the single umbrella of terrorism results in a profound misunderstanding of the Afghan war (Christia and Semple, 2009).

E.   On November 5, 2009, U.S. Army Major **Nidal Malik Hasan** went on a shooting spree at Fort Hood, Texas, killing 13 people. There were many reports that Hasan had embraced radical Islam and that he had decided to attack his fellow soldiers as part of a global jihad against the West (Simpson and Gorman, 2009). A former high-ranking intelligence officer immediately called this an act of terrorism, yet many government officials stated that it was the act of a mentally deranged soldier (Sherwell and Spillius, 2009). In this case, even the country victimized by murder seemed unable to decide on a definition of terrorism.

selective terrorism: A term used by Michael Collins during the Irish War of Independence (1919–1921). Collins did not launch indiscriminate terror attacks. Rather, he selectively targeted the British military, the police force it sponsored, and the people who supported the United Kingdom.

Nidal Malik Hasan: (b. 1970) an American soldier of Palestinian descent. Hasan was an Army psychiatrist who apparently White became self-radicalized, embracing militant Islam. He went on a shooting spree at Fort Hood, Texas, on November 5, 2009, killing 13 people and wounding almost three dozen others. He was wounded, arrested, and charged with several counts of murder.

Definitions of Terrorism Are Based in History

Entire nations change their approach to national security, intelligence, and law enforcement depending on the way terrorism is defined, a process evidenced by recent changes in American defense and law enforcement policy. And this is not a new trend: When the term *terrorism* was first introduced in Western history, governments adjusted their policies based on the way they defined the threat.

Terrorism did not begin in a vacuum. Many Americans became acutely aware of modern terrorism after the first World Trade Center bombing in 1993 and after the bombing of the federal building in Oklahoma City in 1995. Yet modern terrorism began decades, even centuries, before these events. Terrorism, at least from the Western perspective, grew from the French Revolution (1789–1799), and the word was originally used to describe the actions of a government, not of a band of revolutionaries. Terrorism developed throughout the nineteenth century, changing forms and ideology. The meaning of terrorism changed in the twentieth and twenty-first centuries as well. As Christopher Hewitt (2003, pp. 23–45) observes, the definition of terrorism and anti-terrorist policies changes with political tides. The political atmosphere, in turn, changes with history.

 Self-Check

> Why is terrorism difficult to define?
> What does Cooper mean by a problem with the problem definition?
> What examples illustrate contextual meanings of *terrorism*?
> How is the definition of terrorism based in history?

The Origins of Terrorism in Western History

The meaning of terrorism has changed with political tides in Western history. Social revolutions were based on ideas from an eighteenth-century intellectual movement. Terrorism began as government repression in France, but the term was transformed to refer to guerrilla tactics in the Napoleonic wars. By the middle of the nineteenth century, the word was used to describe the actions of revolutionaries. Nationalists copied revolutionary tactics in the early twentieth century, and the meaning of terrorism came full circle when Communists in the Soviet Union used terrorism to subjugate the population.

Social Revolution and the Enlightenment

The people of the European Middle Ages did not think that they were living in the Middle Ages, just as samurai of the Tokugawa (1603–1868) shogunate did not think that they were living in feudal Japan. In contrast, many Western people living in the eighteenth century believed that it was a time of historic change. Historians often call the eighteenth century the Age of Reason or the **Enlightenment**. Jonathan Israel (2001, pp. 23–29) says that there is reason to use the title *Enlightenment* even though the age was full of contradictions, inconsistencies, and political turmoil. Europe had been exhausted by the carnage of the Thirty Years' War (1618–1648). To preserve peace, several rulers agreed to tolerate different sects of Christianity within the same realm. During the Enlightenment, theology, Israel says, lost its monopoly on providing answers to all human questions. This gave rise to science and a new age of discovery. The deductive logic of the former age was gradually replaced by empirical observation. The late 1600s and early 1700s proved to be an enlightening time.

Europe and America experienced tremendous economic, political, and social change during this time. Many people, especially intellectuals and the middle class, dared to question the assumptions of the past. They used the term *enlightenment* to describe this time. Dorinda Outram (1995, p. 31) says *enlightenment* meant many things in the 1700s, and one of the definitions involved changes in the approach to political power. Before the Enlightenment, a large segment of the European population was tied to a class of nobles, and smaller groups of people were part of emerging trade and professional classes or free farmers. During the Enlightenment, many Europeans began to question how they were governed, and they sought to increase the political power of the lower classes. Questioning differed around Europe. For example, Christopher Clark (2006, pp. 163–174) points out that Prussian farmers, despite the modern stereotype of Prussian militarism, limited the power of nobles to demand their services during the Enlightenment. They worked for greater autonomy, refusing to serve when nobles were abusive. James Melton (2001, p. 45–46) demonstrates that evolving legal authority in England began to limit the power of the monarch, and the French questioned the authority of their king even more directly. The forces of change during the Enlightenment brought a new way of thinking about citizenship. Ordinary people came to believe that the state existed to protect everybody, not just the nobles. The nobles and other people who held power were frightened by this line of thinking.

The Enlightenment was an international intellectual movement. Although diverse in political opinions, the philosophers of the Age of Reason produced a common idea about government. They believed that governments should exist to protect individual rights and that the best form of government was democracy. The philosophers argued that citizens had rights and that government's duty was to protect those rights. Common people were to control the government under a social contract, or constitution, that spelled out the rights of citizens and limited governmental power. The Enlightenment brought an increased demand for democracy. Such thinking produced tension between the ruling class and the governed, and some of the tension spilled into violence.

The American Revolution, 1775–1783

Americans living in British North America believed that Great Britain was evolving toward a government that would protect rights and property. Yet many American

Enlightenment: An eighteenth-century intellectual movement following the Scientific Revolution. Also called the Age of Reason, the Enlightenment was characterized by rational thought and the belief that all activities could be explained.

colonists also believed that those basic rights were being denied to Americans. By 1775, American talk of democracy moved from intellectual circles to the streets and eventually to the battlefields. The war began in April 1775 when colonists clashed with British soldiers in Lexington, Massachusetts, and again a few hours later in Concord. The British launched an offensive in Boston to stop the rebellion, but the Continental Congress formed an army. The Second Continental Congress declared independence from Britain on July 4, 1776. The British tried to fight on several fronts at the same time. Although the British were frequently successful, American forces remained in the field. The Continental government formed important alliances with France, Spain, and the Netherlands. In October 1781, a major British force surrendered at Yorktown, Virginia. The British army evacuated most of its troops in 1782, and Great Britain and the United States signed a peace treaty in 1783.

The American Revolution was important in Europe, but it was viewed primarily as a "conservative" revolution. Theodore Draper (1996) sums up current thinking about the origins of the Revolutionary War: Great Britain had been quite happy to grant local autonomy to several of the American colonies. They were responsible for civil functions, law enforcement, and local affairs. Individual colonies held quite a bit of power. Great Britain cared little about day-to-day administration and would have found it difficult to manage it had it chosen to do so. Draper believes that a simple understanding between Britain and the colonies emerged. Americans were to assist in the maintenance of the empire, serve as loyal subjects, and contribute to military ventures when needed.

By the mid-1700s America's economic and population expansion threatened Britain. As it tried to exert control, Draper argues, Britain faced an increasing number of people who wanted the democratic rights of English citizens. The desire for independence came late in the war, and it was not at first supported by a majority of Americans. In 1783, the locus of power moved from London to the new capital of the United States, Philadelphia, and most American leaders (with notable exceptions, such as Thomas Jefferson) perceived the United States to be a British-style democracy without Britain. The birth of the United States was an evolutionary process, but when seen within the context of traditional European power struggles, it was viewed as both a defeat for Great Britain and the formation of an Enlightenment democracy.

The revolution did bring about profound change, even though it was conservative. The United States *was* like Great Britain without a monarchy. Democracy was no longer an idea inside the debate circles of Enlightenment philosophers; Americans created a republic based on a representative democracy. It did not change the class structure, but it was a democracy. That idea set the imaginations of some Europeans on fire.

The Enlightenment and the birth of democracy gave rise to two paradoxes. The first deals with the relationship between democracy and terrorism. F. Gregory Gause III (2005) points to a variety of studies about this relationship, and he comes to a depressing conclusion: Terrorist attacks occur more frequently in democracies than in countries with any other form of government. Citing State Department statistics between 2000 and 2003, Gause finds that of nearly 530 attacks, almost 390 occurred in countries practicing full or limited democracy. The democracy factor would come into play in the nineteenth century and continue into the twentieth (see *Another Perspective: Terror and Democracy*). The second paradox appeared much more rapidly. Partially inspired by America's revolution and directly motivated by class inequity and the Enlightenment, French revolutionaries poured into the streets of Paris in 1789. Their actions brought a new meaning to the word *terrorism*.

The French Revolution, 1789–1799

The French Revolution was based on the same enlightened principles as the American Revolution, but it took a very different and much more deadly tone. During

✦ ANOTHER PERSPECTIVE

Terror and Democracy

Many terrorism analysts believe that terrorists need democratic states to function. Totalitarian states, they argue, make it impossible to engage in covert activities. Terrorists need freedom of speech, freedom of thought, and freedom of action. Jenny Hocking takes the opposite view. In reaction to a terrorist attack in Bali, Indonesia, in 2002, the Australian government followed the path of the United States, Hocking says. Political rights have been trampled in the name of the war on terrorism. A counterterrorist network invades civil liberties in Australia, and the Australian Intelligence Security Service has been given permission to pry into the lives of law-abiding citizens. Terrorism is a threat, but overreaction to it also threatens democracies. The internment of terrorist suspects without charge or trial is a greater threat than terrorism.

Source: Hocking, 2004.

Estates General: An assembly in prerevolutionary France consisting of all but the lowest class. The Estates General had not been called since 1614, but Louis XVI assembled them in 1789 in response to demands from the Assembly of Notables, who had been called to address the financial problems of France. Radical elements in the Estates General revolted, and the disruption led to the French Revolution.

National Convention: Elected in 1792, it broke from the Estates General and called for a constitutional assembly. The White Convention served as the major legislative body of France until it was replaced by the Directory in 1795.

Committee of Public Safety: Assembled by Maximilien Robespierre (1758–1794) to conduct the war against invading monarchal powers, it evolved into the executive body of France. The Committee of Public Safety initiated the Reign of Terror.

the 1700s, French merchants and manufacturers were able to accumulate vast wealth from business profits, but they were not adequately represented in the feudal hierarchy of the French ruling class. Nobles and the clergy paid no taxes, but workers, the new middle class, and the poor did. In 1789, King Louis XVI called an Assembly of Notables of the **Estates General**, because only the Assembly had the authority to raise taxes. Unfortunately for Louis, the Estates General gave way to a National Assembly, and the new legislative body revolted. The revolt took a more radical turn when the National Assembly dissolved and formed an assembly to create a new government in 1791, a government based on class revolution. The monarchies of Europe declared war on France to stop the revolution, and the king tried to flee to join the other monarchs. He was captured and eventually executed by the revolutionary government. The radical revolution continued. A **National Convention** was elected in 1792, and it appointed a **Committee of Public Safety** in 1793. Controlled by radicals, the Committee of Public Safety executed thousands of nobles and clergy at the same time that France managed to stave off invading monarchies. Executions spread from Paris to the countryside. A new government formed in 1795, but France remained in political and economic chaos. In 1799, a middle-class general, Napoleon Bonaparte, returned from a disastrous expedition in Egypt and took over the government, ending the revolution. The French Revolution had been extremely bloody, and it was the first revolution in the modern sense of the word.

The American Revolution transferred power from the British upper classes to American upper classes. In France, power was transferred *between* classes. If America represented a long-term evolutionary process toward democracy, France represented a radical shift in the power structure. Not only did European governments take notice, but the nobles and their upper-class supporters feared for their way of life and their very lives. They mobilized their armies to stop the French, subjecting Europe to war for 20 years.

The Reign of Terror

The term *terrorism* appeared during this period. Edmund Burke, a noted British political philosopher of the eighteenth century, used the word to describe the situation in revolutionary Paris. He referred to the violence as the **Reign of Terror**, and he used the word *terrorism* to describe the actions of the new government. Members and associates of the Committee of Public Safety were called terrorists by French nobles, their families, and sympathizers. From 1794 to 1795, the French

Reign of Terror: The name given to the repressive period in France, 1794–1795. The revolutionary government accused thousands of French nobles and clergy of plotting to restore the monarchy. Executions began in Paris and spread throughout the countryside. Large mobs attacked and terrorized nobles in rural areas. Summary executions (executions on the spot without a trial) were quite common.

Spain in 1807: The Peninsular War (1808–1814) began when Spanish and French forces divided Portugal in 1807. Napoleon, whose army entered Spain in 1807, attempted to use his forces to capture the Spanish throne in 1808. British forces under Sir Arthur Wellesley, later Duke of Wellington, joined Spanish forces White loyal to the king of Spain and Spanish partisans to fight the French.

government conducted 17,000 legal executions. Some scholars estimate that there were 23,000 additional illegal executions (Tilly, 2004). Class violence ripped through France as middle- and working-class revolutionaries tore power from the hands of the social elite and the state-sponsored Roman Catholic Church. But as the government consolidated power, the would-be democracy gave way to Napoleon Bonaparte and military authoritarianism. Hundreds of thousands more would die.

Guerrillas and the Spanish Peninsula

In the Napoleonic Wars, the meaning of *terrorism* started to undergo a subtle transformation. Napoleon invaded **Spain in 1807,** and his army would face a type of threat that it had not experienced up to that point. Small bands of Spanish partisans began to attack French troops. Frequently armed and supported by the British army, the partisans attacked the French in unconventional manners. They could not gather and face a French corps on a battlefield, but they could murder off-duty soldiers, attack supply columns, and engage in hit-and-run tactics. The Spanish called the partisans patriots, but the French referred to them as terrorists. Thus, the meaning of *terrorism* shifted away from governmental repression to the resistance of some people to governments. This definitional transformation would continue through the nineteenth century (Tamas, 2001).

Guerrilla warfare did not originate in Spain, but it was particularly savage there. It served as an asymmetrical method of resisting the French revolutionary army. It began a decade before the invasion of Spain when armed citizens loyal to the king fought against the French Revolution. It continued in Spain, and David Bell (2007) says that it came to full fruition when the 1812 French invasion of Russia failed. The massive French army was decimated by Russian guerrillas during its retreat from Moscow during the winter of 1812–1813. Few armies could resist Napoleon in the field, but groups of disbanded soldiers and armed citizens were another matter. Bell believes that this signaled an ideological transformation in the meaning of war. Whether his thesis is correct, one aspect of his argument is certain: These guerrilla movements helped to set the stage for terrorism.

Self-Check

> What role did the Enlightenment play in political thought?

> How did revolution differ in France and in the United States?

> How did the French Revolution have a major impact on terrorism?

> How did the meaning of *terrorism* change from the French Revolution through the Napoleonic Wars?

1848 and the Radical Democrats

The meaning of *terrorism* changed in Western minds essentially because of the nature of European violence in the 1800s. The French Revolution did not bring democracy; it brought Napoleon. The Napoleonic Wars continued until 1815, and then a new international order emerged. Although democracy continued to grow in the United States and in the United Kingdom, royalists reasserted their power in the rest of Europe. Under the surface, however, democratic ideas continued to grow. These ideas led to further political struggles and demands for freedom.

The democrats of the early 1800s were not united. Most of them believed in middle-class democracy, and they were reluctant to take to the streets if a legislative process was available. They believed that they could create constitutional monarchies and evolve into a system of democracy as the United States had done. The main objective of most European middle-class democrats from approximately 1815 to 1848 was to obtain constitutions to ensure liberty. Several of the German states began writing constitutions, but they were thwarted by monarchal forces and decisively defeated between 1848 and 1849. Austrian and Russian monarchs simply controlled all governmental processes. In the wake of failure, disgruntled democrats began to speak of nonlegislative avenues for change.

radical democrats: Those who tried to bring democracy to all classes. They sought a more equitable distribution of wealth throughout all economic classes, believing that concentrated wealth and class inequities prevented societies from becoming truly democratic.

Radical democrats demanded immediate and drastic change. They were not only interested in developing constitutions but also wanted to distribute evenly the wealth created by trade and manufacturing. Many **socialists**, including a group of socialists called **communists**, argued for centralized control of the economy. **Anarchists**, sometime allies and sometime foes of the socialists, sought to reduce or eliminate centralized government. The wealthy owners of industry, known as capitalists, were politically powerful, and many people from the middle class prospered when capitalist enterprises expanded. The capitalists opposed all forms of socialism and anarchy. Radical democrats felt that the capitalists were little better than the royalists. The radical democrats wanted all people to be equal, and they argued that democracy should be based not only on freedom but also on economic equality. This meant that the class structure and distribution of wealth had to be reorganized. This frightened the newly emergent capitalist and middle classes in the same way the French Revolution had scared European royalty. The radical democrats called for class revolution.

socialists: Radical democrats who sought wealth equality in capitalist societies. Some socialists sought governmental guarantees of living standards. Others believed that the state should control industry and divide profits among all members of society. Others believed that people would form cooperative relationships on their own with no need of a government.

The revolution came in 1848. The conservative system established by governments after the Napoleonic Wars was antidemocratic. As constitutional movements failed in many countries, people grew restless. Parisians took to the streets in February 1848, and they overthrew the government. Many people in other European capitals followed suit, and by autumn almost every major European country had experienced unrest or revolution. In some cases, as in Berlin in Prussia, the army came to restore order. In other cases, such as France, a new republic was proclaimed. The middle class saw some gains, but most workers did not.

communists: Socialists who believed in a strong centralized economy controlled by a strong central government. Their ideas were summarized in *The Communist Manifesto,* written by Karl Marx and Friedrich Engels in 1848.

Governmental control was slowly restored in Europe between 1848 and 1849, but new class awareness and unrest emerged. The 1848 revolutions fostered working-class distaste for the distribution of wealth and power. George Woodcock (2004, p. 81) says that the 1789 French Revolution ushered in a new class structure, but it also resulted in a new economic system—capitalism—and a centralized state. The conservative system after 1815 tried to restrain the middle class as a new group of wealthy capitalists displaced the nobility. In 1848, radical democrats revolted but failed to change the system. Craig Calhoun (1989) adds that the 1848 street revolutions demonstrated that common people were aware of economic tensions, even if they were not able to change the social structure. In this sense, the issues of 1848 were an extension of the class revolution of 1789. The rebels were defeated in the street, and they moved underground.

anarchists: Those in the nineteenth century who advocated the creation of cooperative societies without centralized governments. There were many forms of anarchy. In the popular understanding of the late nineteenth and early twentieth centuries, anarchists were seen as violent socialist revolutionaries. Today, anti-globalists calling themselves anarchists have little resemblance to their earlier counterparts.

This underground movement, Michael Burleigh (2007) writes, signaled the beginning of modern terrorism. It started with the nation-state and the French Revolution, and organized governments used terrorism far more effectively than revolutionary groups. Yet, Burleigh says, secretive revolutionary groups formed the nexus of modern terrorism after 1848, a transformation that took place in Western Europe. Claudia Verhoeven (2009), on the other hand, moves the point of origin further east. She argues that modern terrorism began in Russia. Though Russia experienced its first terrorist campaign in the 1870s, several small groups organized individual cells a decade earlier. This, she concludes, represents the origin of modern terrorism. Regardless of geographical location, Burleigh and Verhoeven make the same point: When groups went underground after 1848, terrorism as it is known today came into its infancy.

Socialists

Three strains of radical democrats coalesced after the failed revolutions of 1848: communists, socialists, and anarchists (Figure 1.1). Socialists wanted to completely

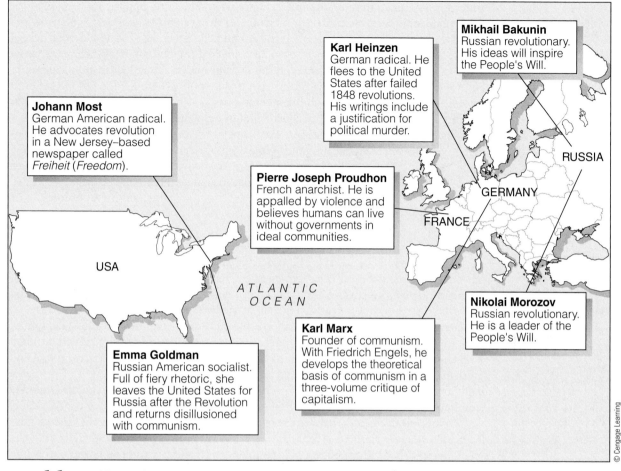

FIGURE **1.1** Anarchists and Socialists

democratize society and assume control of industrial production. They believed that a strong state would ensure that profits from industry were distributed in an egalitarian manner. Communism represented a particular form of socialism, advocating a strong centralized government, the elimination of all classes except the working class, and a complete state monopoly over all forms of industrial and agricultural production. Socialists and communists agreed that wealth was not a private matter. It belonged to all workers. Although many socialists embraced communism, communists denounced socialists who failed to advocate for strong state controls. Many socialists emphasized democracy over the centralized power of communism (see Levin, 2003). The radical democrats believed political power should be held in common. Their concept of socialism was especially popular among some groups of displaced workers. Unfortunately, the upper and middle classes frequently believed terrorism and socialism were the same thing (A. Roberts, 2002).

One of the chief spokespersons and intellectuals in the socialist camp was the founder of communism, Karl Marx (1818–1883). He finished a PhD in philosophy in 1841 and moved to Paris shortly thereafter. He met Friedrich Engels and formed a lifelong friendship. He outlined theories of socialism in several writings, including a three-volume critique of capitalism. Marx believed that social structure is arranged by the material circumstances surrounding existence. Humans shape the environment through work and even produce more than they need. Marx referred to this extra production as *surplus*. In medieval societies, nobles controlled the surplus production of peasants, but control shifted to capitalists with the end of the Middle Ages. Marx and Engels claimed that the capitalist economic system exploited the lower classes for the benefit of others. He called for a change in the system.

Despite the many labels applied to him and the derogatory statements of his enemies, Karl Marx was not a terrorist. Marx referred to "revolutionary" change, but he never clarified what he meant by revolution. Further, he did not advocate political bombing or assassination. In fact, on most occasions he publicly condemned it. He believed socialism was to be a reflection of democracy, not violence. A massive seizure of power by the general population might be justified, but individual acts of murder were not.

The process of democratization was slow, however, and some of the radical democrats began to feel violent revolution was the only possible course of action. A few radical democrats went underground, choosing subversive violence as a means to challenge authority. They became popularly known as terrorists because they hoped to achieve social revolution by terrorizing the capitalist class and its supporters.

Anarchists

Anarchists shared many ideas about the egalitarian nature of society with the socialists, but they disagreed on the function of the state. The term *anarchy* was not new. It originated several hundred years earlier, when Greek philosophers spoke of eliminating governments, but the nineteenth-century anarchists were also concerned with the distribution of wealth. This frightened the upper classes, which already associated socialism with terrorism. Pierre Joseph Proudhon (1809–1865) was one of the advocates of modern anarchism. His political activities eventually landed him in a French prison, but Proudhon was not a man of violence. He called for the extension of democracy to all classes, to be accomplished through the elimination of property and government. Property was to be commonly held, and families living in extended communes were to replace centralized government.

Proudhon disagreed with Karl Marx and other socialists about the role of government. Most socialists saw centralized government as a necessary evil. Like the democrats, the socialists believed government had to exist to protect the individual rights of citizens. Communists took the role of the state further, insisting on a strong central government. Proudhon, on the other hand, believed that all government was evil. Proudhon had revolutionary ideals, but he was a man of peace. He believed that anarchy would develop peacefully as people learned about the structure of governments and the capitalist economy. Not all of Proudhon's disciples were of the same peaceful bent. They came to see themselves as revolutionaries, and they would have growing influence on terrorism in the second half of the nineteenth century.

Violent Anarchism

Despite the rhetoric, both the socialists and anarchists engaged in more talk than action after the 1848 revolutions. Both groups debated the efficacy and morality of violence, and most of the people who called for revolution spoke of mass action, not individual violence. Walter Laqueur (1999, p. 12) says that the socialists and anarchists rejected terrorism on practical and theoretical grounds. Practically, terrorism could not promise strategic success, and many of the revolutionary theorists rejected violence in general. Marxists and anarchists favored strikes, demonstrations, and other mass actions.

Richard Jensen (2004) also believes that the initial calls in history for revolution cannot be associated with terrorism. Even though socialists and anarchists disagreed about the path for creating a new society, they avoided violence. Those who advocated violence usually did so only rhetorically; however, this changed in the 1880s as anarchists began assassinating heads of state. The media sensationalized anarchist events, leading people to conclude that anarchism was a vast international conspiracy of terror. By 1880, the press and politicians had collapsed all forms of socialism into the generic term *anarchism*, and anarchists were deemed terrorists in popular opinion.

How did this change occur? Jensen says that several factors merged to create a culture of terrorism among some members of the anarchist movement. He outlines some of the reasons, and other researchers have identified a number of factors (Laqueur and Alexander, 1987; Laqueur, 1999; Epstein, 2001; Woodcock, 2004; Clutterbuck, 2004; Grob-Fitzgibbon, 2004). Taken together, these factors reveal a pattern in the transformation of some anarchists from rhetoric to violence.

The first cause for transformation can be found in the growing numbers of people attracted to the movement. Proudhon rejected violence, but new followers brought conflicting ideas. As debates grew more intense, no single view seemed to define either socialism or anarchism. Sometimes the debates caused splits inside the movement and various camps formed. The anarchist movement contained a variety of political viewpoints, and some schools of thought favored violence over peaceful social change.

Economic change also influenced the anarchist movement. Just as wealth had shifted to capitalists in the early and mid-nineteenth century, so new entrepreneurs consolidated economic power in the last decades of the 1800s. This fostered new alliances and realignment with middle-class political parties. Proudhon and other anarchists spoke of an evolution toward communal socialism, but the new political structure effectively blocked peaceful change. Middle classes, the **bourgeois,** dominated the political scene in Western Europe and America, and their interests tended to coincide with the interests of capitalists.

Economic consolidation was accompanied by social stress. Labor movements attempted to foster an international relationship among workers from all countries. Hundreds of anarchists flocked to Paris, voicing their approval of the labor movement. As some anarchists turned to violence, journalists and politicians viewed all forms of labor violence as a manifestation of an international anarchist conspiracy against capitalism. In central and eastern Europe, police cracked down on revolutionary activity, creating a two-fold cycle. Each repressive measure sent more revolutionaries to the west, where violent activities continued, and anarchist violence intensified in central and eastern Europe to retaliate for governmental crackdowns.

Nationalistic factors also influenced the growth and spread of violence after 1880. Although many people viewed anarchism as an international conspiracy, it emerged differently in each country. Spanish anarchism involved artisans and skilled workers who were displaced by economic shifts. They had difficulty attracting urban workers to their movement because the living standards of industrial wage earners actually improved. Italian anarchism was tied to internal struggles for national unification, and French anarchists were inevitably caught up in the Franco-Prussian War of 1870–1871. Germany and Austria witnessed the growth of internal police to protect the **Hohenzollerns** and **Hapsburgs,** and the remainder of central and eastern Europe saw increased political repression. Despite—or maybe because of—repression, Russia gave birth to a revolutionary anarchist group. The United States and the United Kingdom experienced increased rhetoric, labor violence, and social unrest. The common factor in all countries was murder. Anarchists championed political assassination.

The importance of assassination cannot be overemphasized. It was propaganda by deed, the ultimate expression, as Alex Schmid (Schmid and Jongman, 2005, pp. 21–25) called it, of political frustration. Violent anarchists wanted to send the message that no industrialist was safe and that the capitalist order would crumble under the philosophy of the bomb. Governments, journalists, and the population in general believed the message, supporting overactive measures against anything that remotely resembled left-wing violence. This trend would last well into the twentieth century. In addition, assassinations were not simply abstractions. Police officials, politicians, royal leaders, and presidents were killed by anarchists from Russia to the United States between 1880 and 1900.

The final factor influencing the adoption of violent action was the invention of dynamite. Alfred Nobel blended explosive material with chemicals, cotton, and

bourgeois: The middle class. *Bourgeoisie* (plural) in Marxist terminology refers to tradespeople, merchants, artisans, and other nonpeasants excluded from the upper classes in medieval Europe. Marx called the European democracies after the French Revolution bourgeois governments, and he advocated a democracy dominated by workers.

Hohenzollerns: The ruling family of Brandenburg and Prussia that ruled a united Germany from 1871 to 1914.

Hapsburgs: The ruling family of Austria (1282–1918), the Austro-Hungarian Empire (1437–1918), and the Holy Roman Empire (1282–1806). Another branch of the family ruled in Spain (1516–1700). Reference here is to the Austrian royal family.

refined clay to produce an explosive 20 times more powerful than black powder. To be sure, the power of dynamite was often overestimated. One anarchist claimed that ten pounds of it could sink a battleship. But dynamite gave an individual or small group a psychological edge. For the first time in history, a small group had a technological force multiplier that allowed it to launch a major attack. Rhetoric gave birth to propaganda by the deed, but dynamite fostered the philosophy of the bomb.

Rhetoric, Internal Debates, and Action

By 1880 various groups of left-wing revolutionaries came to be known as anarchists in the popular mind. This was partially due to simplification and sensationalism in the press, but it also resulted from internal debates in the socialist movements. The debate began when Marx separated from Proudhon. Marx believed that Proudhon's vision of cooperative, nonauthoritarian communities was an unachievable utopian ideal. Marx called for worker control of industry and a strong, centralized state dictatorship. This initial split resulted in further fragmentation in the left-wing movement and the eventual endorsement of violence.

Pyotr Kropotkin (1842–1921), a Russian prince turned anarchist, continued to advocate for an evolutionary pattern. George Woodcock (2004) says Kropotkin and other nonviolent anarchists saw themselves as part of a tradition dating back to prehistory. Kropotkin believed humanity existed between two competing tendencies—cooperation and authoritarianism. Cooperation involved mutual aid and altruistic humanitarianism. Kropotkin called it the creative spirit of the masses. It is evidenced in the emergence of tribes, villages, and trade guilds—all created, according to Kropotkin, without legislation. Authoritarianism competed with this cooperative tendency. Humans tended to arrange themselves in hierarchies and give authority to their leaders. Kropotkin stated sarcastically that this tendency began with witch doctors and rainmakers and ended with military bands. Woodcock says Kropotkin believed that every period in human history was dominated by the tension between cooperative anarchy and authoritarianism. He rhetorically called for revolution, but abhorred violence. The forces of history worked against the interests of centralized government, and Kropotkin believed that human cooperation would dominate the final period of human existence.

Mikhail Bakunin (1814–1876) rejected Kropotkin's nonviolent anarchy, calling for "propaganda of the deed." Barbara Epstein (2001) says Bakunin vehemently disagreed with advocates of peaceful change. Revolutionaries could not use the state as an instrument of emancipation because it was inherently oppressive. The state must be destroyed, and its destruction would come when masses of people recognized that they were being exploited by the state. Anarchists could not attach themselves to an authoritarian structure in the way Marxists and some socialists did. Bakunin encouraged bombings and individual assassinations as a means of awakening the masses to reality. After spending ten years in prison following the 1848 revolutions, Bakunin championed Proudhon's ideas of international revolution, according to Richard Jensen (2004).

At this point, a new trend arose. Karl Heinzen (1809–1880), a radical German democrat who embraced anarchy, came to the United States after the 1848 revolutions failed in Europe. Benjamin Grob-Fitzgibbon (2004) believes that Heinzen sat at a pivotal point, where modern terrorism can be directly related to the past. Grob-Fitzgibbon criticizes theories that terrorism was linked to the anarchists and other radical democrats. They were assassins at worst, he argues, not the forerunners of modern terrorism, with its indiscriminate killing. Heinzen was different because he advocated political murder—murder that could be arbitrarily distributed through society. Walter Laqueur (1999, p. 13) believes that Heinzen's theories were relatively insignificant until Johann Most (1846–1906) published Heinzen's writings in a radical newspaper, *Freiheit* (*Freedom*), in New Jersey. Most, a German born in Augsburg, immigrated to the United States in the late 1800s. Like Heinzen, he did not believe that capitalist societies would change peacefully. He advocated terrorism in

Freiheit and called for violent action, the best form of propaganda. The philosophy of the bomb was the method for communicating such propaganda, according to Most. Grob-Fitzgibbon believes that this philosophy represents the beginning of modern terrorism. Laqueur (1999, pp. 11–12) agrees.

Heinzen and Most represent an important transition in the history of Western terrorism. Terrorism began with a group of radical revolutionaries conducting mass executions in the name of the French government. There was a subtle shift in meaning as Spanish partisans terrorized French troops with irregular tactics after the 1807 French invasion of Spain, and the meaning changed further as anarchists, socialists, and communists were labeled terrorists. Despite the label, nineteenth-century anarchists were not terrorists (see Laqueur and Alexander, 1987; Laqueur, 1999, p. 13; Grob-Fitzgibbon, 2004). In a Canadian television interview cited by Grob-Fitzgibbon (2004), David Rapoport, a noted authority on the development of modern terrorism, argued that the anarchists of the nineteenth century were a far cry from modern terrorists. When the anarchists engaged in violence, it was targeted toward either a specific person or a group. It did not involve striking innocent people who had little to do with a cause.

Selective and nonselective destruction became the point of differentiation between "old" and "new" terrorism in the late 1980s and early 1990s. Walter Laqueur (1987, p. 91) argues that modern terrorists are more ruthless than their historical counterparts. Not only does Laqueur believe that the historical terrorism was mainly rhetorical; he also points out that anarchists were extremely selective about their targets. He cites one case in which an anarchist refused to toss a bomb at a Russian official because he was afraid he would injure innocent bystanders. Laqueur notes that this sensitivity is hardly typical of modern-day terrorists. He says modern terrorism has been typified by indiscriminate violence and the intentional targeting of the civilian population. Modern terrorists strike at governments by killing their citizens. They strike airliners, buses, and other targets containing innocent noncombatants with no vested interest in the outcome of a political struggle. Modern terrorists come from another tradition, engaging in the sensationalized murder of innocents (Scheuer, 2006).

Grob-Fitzgibbon (2004) and Jensen (2004) offer competing evidence for this view. They point to Heinzen and Most as progenitors of mass terrorism. They argue that Sergey Nechaev (1847–1882), a Russian anarchist who even murdered a fellow revolutionary, was absolutely ruthless. He cared nothing for innocent victims, and his purpose was to kill. Laqueur admits that some of the anarchists were violent, but he still draws a distinction. Nechaev and others advocated murder, but they did not conduct attacks that resulted in massive innocent casualties. In this sense, new terrorism—as practiced in the late twentieth century—differs from the old terrorism of the nineteenth century.

Isabelle Duyvesteyn (2004) says that the distinction between old and new terrorism involves a false dichotomy. She believes that modern terrorism is directly related to past practices. If there is a new terrorism, she argues, it needs to be confirmed by rigorous testing and the presentation of evidence. No such evidence has been produced. The label "new" should be applied only on the basis of historical research. In addition, it is necessary to conceive of terrorism in the same rational form across time if comparisons are to be made. In other words, to differentiate between old and new terrorism, the term must have the same meaning today as it did in 1848. Using the labels "old" and "new," she concludes, does nothing to clarify contemporary problems.

Anarchism and Nationalism

If the 1800s witnessed the growth of anarchism, it also saw the growth of nationalism in the West. As anarchists called for an end to government, nationalistic organizations demanded the right to self-government. Many nationalists adopted the tactics of the anarchists to fight the foreign powers occupying their lands. Nationalistic groups throughout Europe turned to the philosophy of the bomb, and nationalist terrorists began to follow the pattern set by the violent anarchists.

Nationalistic groups did not view themselves as terrorists. They believed that anarchists were fighting for ideas. Nationalists believed that they were fighting for their countries. Anarchists were socially isolated, but nationalists could hope for the possibility of greater support. Governments labeled them terrorists, but nationalists saw themselves as unconventional soldiers in a national cause. Nationalists believed that they were fighting patriotic wars. They adopted only the tactics of the anarchists, not their ideology.

The nationalistic Irish Republican Army (IRA) grew from this period. Unlike anarchists, the IRA did not reject the notion of governmental control; rather, the IRA wanted to nationalize it. The IRA believed Ireland was entitled to self-government. Their weakness relative to the government's power caused them to use the terrorist tactics fostered by the anarchists. In the twentieth century, other nationalistic groups in Europe followed the example of the IRA. (See Chapter 6 for the development of terrorism in the IRA.)

Though two distinct positions had emerged, it is not possible to completely separate nineteenth-century anarchism and nationalism. Grant Wardlaw (1982, pp. 18–24) sees a historical continuity from anarchism to nationalistic terrorism. Richard Rubenstein (1987, pp. 122–125) makes this point by looking at contemporary anarchist and nationalistic groups. Rubenstein says that the stages terrorists must go through to employ violence are similar for both types of terrorism; the moral justification for anarchist and nationalistic terrorism is essentially the same. J. Bowyer Bell (1976) gives an excellent example of the links between the anarchist and nationalistic traditions in examining the IRA. Since 1916, the IRA has been permeated with socialist revolutionaries and with nationalists who reject some aspects of socialism. While the two sides have frequently been at odds, both groups are heir to the same tradition. Modern nationalistic terrorism has its roots in anarchism. Both traditions formed the framework of modern European terrorism.

Terrorism in the modern sense came from violent anarchists in the late 1800s. The anarchists were based in Western Europe, but they carried their campaign to other parts of the world. The most successful actions took place in Russia before the 1905 and 1917 revolutions. Anarchist groups assassinated several Russian officials, including the czar. Anarchism also spread to the United States. In America, it took the form of labor violence; American anarchists, usually immigrants from Europe, saw themselves as linked to organized labor. The anarchist movement in America did not gain as much strength as in Europe, and American anarchists were generally relegated to industrial areas. Right-wing extremism was not part of the anarchist movement, but by the mid-twentieth century, right-wing groups began to imitate tactics of violent anarchists.

Lindsay Clutterbuck (2004) states that most analysts believe that modern terrorism derived from the blend of anarchism and nationalism in Russia after the assassination of Czar Alexander II in 1881. She argues that the major influence came from early twentieth-century Ireland. Both issues will be examined here. This chapter ends with a discussion of revolutionary Russia, and Chapter 6 contains a summary of violence in Ireland.

Dynamite and Revolution

It is not possible to transport the values and attitudes of one period of history into another, but it is possible to examine current events through historical analogy. Before discussing revolutions in Russia, one footnote should be considered. The nineteenth-century anarchists caused a panic, and their activities were sensationalized by the press. Richard Jensen (2004) says that the fear caused by dynamite and random explosions had a negative psychological effect on Europeans and Americans. People feared anarchism, and they believed that anarchists were involved in an international conspiracy designed to topple Western governments. Shortly after the turn of the twentieth century in the United States, Jensen notes, Theodore Roosevelt claimed that every aspect of national policy sank to insignificance when compared to the need to suppress anarchy.

ANOTHER PERSPECTIVE

Noam Chomsky Examines Terrorism and Morality

Noam Chomsky (2002) approaches terrorism with two critical questions: (1) How should terrorism be defined? and (2) What is the proper response to it? He says that the problem of defining terrorism is complex, but there are many straightforward governmental responses. Almost all of these definitions cast terrorism within a moral framework; that is, terrorism becomes a criminal act where innocents are victimized. These circumstances require a government to act; yet, the response frequently evokes a paradox. Governments define terrorist acts as immoral, but they tend to respond by acting outside the bounds of morality. They justify their actions by citing the original immoral act of a terrorist group.

Chomsky finds this approach unacceptable. The same moral framework that allows a society to define an illegal act as terrorism requires that the response to terrorism be conducted within the bounds of morality. Terrorism, Chomsky says, is something "they" do to "us," and it is never about what "we" do to "them." Citing just-war doctrine, Chomsky says the response to terrorism cannot be terrorism. A moral truism states that any illegal activity is immoral no matter how a state wishes to justify its response to an event.

The definition of terrorism provides a moral constant. For example, if an official definition states that terrorism is the use of violence against innocent people to change political behavior, a state is morally obligated to live within the bounds of this definition. It cannot use violence against innocents to force its political will. If terrorism is a crime, the response to it must not be criminal if the response is to be morally legitimate. The contradiction comes, Chomsky concludes, because the United States operates within a moral definition of terrorism only when its own interests are served. As a result, oppression, violence, and illegal actions are rarely defined as terrorism when they are condoned by the United States or its allies.

Yet the anarchists failed, and it was due neither to police nor to other governmental action. Barbara Epstein (2001) says that the anarchists attempted to ally with the labor movement, but labor leaders could not support random violence. George Woodcock (2004) adds that the anarchists were simply out of touch with the forces of history. They lived at a time when state power and industrialization were centralizing. He believes that anarchism was not revolutionary; rather, it was a reaction to economic consolidation and the centralized state. He notes that anarchism was strongest where industrialization was weakest.

If Woodcock is correct, industrialized states ironically feared anarchism more than did agrarian states. As anarchism and labor violence grew from 1880 in the United States, fear of anarchism increased. Events such as the assassination of President McKinley in 1901, the Russian Revolution of 1917, and the Boston police strike and Red Scare of 1919 alarmed many Americans. As fear increased, Attorney General A. Mitchell Palmer, known as the "Fighting Quaker," took extra-constitutional measures in the name of defending liberty from the anarchists. He repressed radicals and violated the civil liberties of many Americans. To be sure, anarchist violence was a threat. In addition to random violence, radicals conducted a bombing campaign in 1919, but this hardly threatened to topple the U.S. government. Most historians believe that Palmer overreacted (see Cole, 2003). It might be wise to wonder, in the wake of 9/11, whether there are contemporary parallels to his overreaction.

Self-Check

> Describe the various schools of revolutionary thought in the mid-nineteenth century.
> Why did governments refer to these movements as terrorism?
> How did these revolutionaries differ from the Enlightenment revolutionaries?

Terrorism and Revolution in Russia: 1881–1921

Joseph Stalin: The dictator who succeeded Lenin. Stalin solidified communist control of Russia through a secret-police organization. He purged the government of all suspected opponents in the 1930s, killing thousands of people.

Vladimir Lenin: The Russian revolutionary who led a second revolution in October, bringing the communists to power. Lenin led the communists in a civil war and set up a dictatorship to enforce communist rule in Russia.

Vladimir Putin: (b. 1952) a former KGB officer and second president of the Russian Federation from 1999 to 2008. He began serving as Russia's prime minister after the end of his presidential term.

The historiography of the Russian Revolution and the fighting that took place afterward have changed drastically since the collapse of the Soviet Union. Histories written during the cold war tended to be either pro- or anti-Communist. As documents and archives became available to Western writers in the past few years, views of Russia changed and new histories and biographies emerged. Sheila Fitzpatrick (2001) views the revolution from a perspective that begins with revolt and ends several years after the rise of communism as **Joseph Stalin** (1878–1953) purged and executed his enemies in the 1930s. Robert Service (1995) concludes a three-volume biography of **Vladimir Lenin** (1870–1924) with a picture of a ruthless man who forged policy by force of will. Service's Lenin is a man who was not interested in power for its own sake and who genuinely wanted to create a better socialist state. Confrontations forced him to compromise in the end. Katerina Clark (1998) presents the tremendous cultural shifts from 1913 to 1931 by focusing on St. Petersburg from late czarist times until Stalin consolidated power. Christopher Read (1996) divides his the era into two periods—the collapse of czarist Russia and the building of the new socialist order. Service (2005) brings another perspective, completely rewriting the history of Russia from the fall of the czar to the rise of **Vladimir Putin.**

At the time of the revolution, however, the West viewed the communist state with horror. They equated communism with anarchism and revolution. Class revolution became a reality in Russia, and the West feared that Russia would export revolution through terrorism. Late-nineteenth-century Russia differed significantly from the other great powers of Europe. Class distinctions between nobles and peasants were virtually the same as they had been before the French Revolution, and Russian peasants were beset by poverty. Industry had come to some of Russia's cities, but Russia's economic and governmental systems were not adequate to handle the changes. Czar Alexander II (ruled from 1855 to 1881) vowed to make changes in the system, but when he attempted to do so, he found himself in the midst of revolutionary terrorism.

The Peoples' Will

Three groups in Russia after 1850 felt that they could reform and modernize the Russian state, but they disagreed about the ways to do it. One group, whose views Czar Alexander shared, wanted to modernize Russia from the top down. Another group, the intellectuals, wanted Russia to become a liberal Western democracy. Violent anarchists took another path. They believed that Russian problems could be settled through revolution. Narodnaya Volya (the People's Will) advocated violent socialist revolution. When it launched a campaign of revolutionary terrorism in the 1870s, it faced confrontation with conservative elements such as the church, police, and military. Members of the People's Will came to believe that it was necessary to terrorize these conservative organizations into submission.

The motivations behind the People's Will evolved from Russian revolutionary thought. According to Laqueur (1999, pp. 15–16), the philosophy of anarchist terrorism in Russia was embodied by Mikhail Bakunin and Sergey Nechaev. Their revolutionary thought developed separately before they met each other in the 1860s, when they formed an intellectual union. Both spoke of revolt against the czar, and both endorsed violence as the means. Yet, even in the nation that would experience a violent anarchist campaign and eventually a communist revolution, Bakunin and Nechaev basically stuck to rhetoric.

Although they were ideologically linked to anarchism in Western Europe, they were distinct from their Western supporters. Russian anarchists were writing for a general population in the hope of sparking a democratic revolution. Laqueur says that their significance lies in their influence on later revolutionaries and the violence and assassinations those later revolutionaries committed. They were not radical revolutionaries in Laqueur's view.

Sheila Fitzpatrick (2001, pp. 19–21) presents a different view. Russian economic progress dominated the last part of the nineteenth and early part of the twentieth centuries. The problem was the attitudes of peasants and industrial workers. According to Marx, agrarian peasants did not have enough motivation to join the proletariat in revolution, but Fitzpatrick says that Russia was different. Revolutionary sympathy was high among the peasantry, giving them a closer relationship with many urban workers. Revolutionary rhetoric and writings had touched the lower classes, but Russian economic prosperity had not. The lower classes were receptive to revolution, although as Christopher Read (1996, p. 294) illustrates, no single theme dominated the revolutionaries until it was imposed by the state under Lenin.

Regardless of the debate, the writings of the Russians were powerful. Nechaev (reprint 1987, pp. 68–71) laid down the principles of revolution in the "Catechism of the Revolutionary." His spirit has been reflected in writings of the late twentieth century. Rubenstein compared the "Catechism" to Carlos Marighella's *The Minimanual of the Urban Guerrilla* and found no essential differences. Both Laqueur and Rubenstein believe that Nechaev's influence lives on. Bakunin (1866, pp. 65–68) believed that the Russian government had been established on thievery. In "Revolution, Terrorism, Banditry" he argues that the only method of breaking the state's hold on power is revolt. Such rhetoric did not endear Nechaev and Bakunin to the czar, but it did make them popular with later revolutionaries. Laqueur (1999) concludes that such revolutionary pronouncements correctly belong with Russian expressionist literature, not terrorist philosophy.

These philosophies guided the People's Will. They murdered the police chief of Moscow and went on a campaign of bombing and murder. In May 1881, they succeeded in striking their ultimate target: They killed Czar Alexander II. Ironically, this brought about their downfall. The People's Will was eliminated, Alexander III (ruled from 1881 to 1894) ended all attempts at reform, and revolutionaries went underground. Nicholas II (ruled from 1894 to 1917), who succeeded Alexander III, was a man who would be toppled by revolutionary forces.

Czar Nicholas and the Revolutions of 1905 and 1917

Nicholas faced his first revolution in 1905, after his army lost a war to Japan. In addition to losing the war, Russia was consumed with economic problems and bureaucratic inefficiency. A group of unemployed workers began demonstrations in St. Petersburg, and some enlisted men in the Russian navy mutinied. Their actions were brutally suppressed by Nicholas's army and police forces, feeding the spirit of revolution that burned below the surface. Russian revolutionaries needed another national disaster to create the atmosphere for revolution. It came in 1914, when Russia entered World War I (1914–1918).

By 1917, the Russian people were tired of their economic woes and their czar. In February, a general strike in St. Petersburg turned into a revolution. Unlike 1905, the Russian army joined the workers, and a new Russian government was formed. They envisioned a period of capitalist economic expansion that would save the beleaguered Russian economy. **Workers Councils (or Soviets)** were established in major Russian cities.

Workers Councils (or Soviets): The lowest-level legislative body in the Soviet Union following the October Revolution. *Soviet* is the Russian word for "council."

The primary mistake of the February revolutionaries was that they kept Russia in the war, a decision unpopular with the Russian people. This had two immediate ramifications. It created unrest at home, and it inspired the Germans to seek a way to remove Russia from World War I. The Germans found their answer in Vladimir Ilyich Lenin. Lenin orchestrated a second revolution in October 1917 and removed Russia from the war.

Lenin and Trotsky

The Russian Revolution utilized terrorism in a new manner, and this had an impact on the way people viewed terrorism in the twentieth century. Lenin and one of his

Leon Trotsky: A Russian revolutionary who led foreign affairs in Stalin's government and later became the commander of the Red Army. He espoused terrorism as a means for spreading White revolution. He was thrown out of the Communist Party for opposing Stalin and was assassinated by communist agents in Mexico City in 1940.

lieutenants, **Leon Trotsky** (1879–1940), believed that terrorism should be used as an instrument for overthrowing middle-class, or bourgeois, governments. Once power was achieved, Lenin and Trotsky advocated terrorism as a means of controlling internal enemies and as a method for coping with international strife. Russia was very weak after the revolution. It faced foreign intervention and was torn by civil war. By threatening to export terrorism, Lenin and Trotsky hoped to keep their enemies, primarily Western Europe and the United States, at bay.

With their threat, Lenin and Trotsky instilled the fear of communist revolution in the minds of many people in the West. To some, terrorism and communism became synonymous. Though the Russians, and later the Soviets, were not good at carrying insurrection to other lands, Western leaders began to fear that communist terrorists were on the verge of toppling democratic governments. Despite Lenin and his successor, Joseph Stalin, having the most success with another form of terror—murdering their own people—fear of communist insurrection lasted well into the twentieth century, and some people still fear it. Even as the Soviet Union tottered into dissolution, Western analysts still saw terrorism through the lens of Western–Soviet confrontation (see Livingstone and Arnold, 1986; Sterling, 1986). Former CIA analyst Michael Scheuer (2006, pp. 20–23) believes that this perspective hinders the ability to comprehend terrorism today.

In fairness to analysts of the cold war, Lenin's victory and subsequent writings have inspired terrorists from 1917 to the present. Although communist terrorism was not part of an orchestrated conspiracy, it did influence behavior. Some terrorists scoured the works of Lenin and Trotsky, as well as other Russian revolutionaries, to formulate theories, tactics, and ideologies. Although not a simple conspiracy of evil, this influence was real and remains today.

Self-Check

> How did revolutionary thought develop in czarist Russia?
> Describe the two revolutions under Nicholas II.
> How did Lenin and Trotsky influence the direction of revolutionary thought?

Outdated History?

Michael Scheuer (2006, pp. 20–23), former director of the CIA's bin Laden unit, believes that the focus on history is often misplaced. There are two types of terrorist experts, he contends—retired governmental and military officials and informed commentators. The latter group is made up of academics and journalists. Scheuer believes that these people are far from experts because not only do they fail to understand history but they are also stuck in a time frame. Media consciousness about terrorism developed and grew in the 1970s. Two issues dominated terrorism: the cold war and violence around Israel and Palestine. Expertise about terrorism came from studying both the emergence of theory, with its roots in the West, and the anticolonial movements associated with the early part of the cold war. Terrorism was a historical phenomenon, an outcome of confrontations growing from the influence of Western history. Ideological groups such as the Baader-Meinhof Gang or the Red Brigades came from political battlefields. Nationalistic groups, such as the Puerto Rican Armed Forces of National Liberation (FALN) or the Basque Nation and Liberty (ETA), were motivated by patriotism, but they also centered on leftist agendas. The anti-Western attitude of Palestinian groups like Hezbollah and the Abu Nidal Organization was tinged with a left-wing philosophy and a style of operation similar to their counterparts in ideological and nationalistic movements. Western expertise was honed over two decades, from 1970 to 1990, Scheuer says, and it has very little to do with terrorism today.

Jihadist terrorism comes from a different tradition. It does not rely on political and theoretical developments in the West, and although jihadists frequently embrace the cause of the Palestinians, they do not seek to establish an independent Palestinian state or replace a destroyed Israel with a new Arab country. They come from a religious tradition dating from the twelfth century in the Western calendar, and they operate in a manner far different from terrorist groups in the late twentieth century. Expertise on the old-style groups is not applicable to the jihadists, Scheuer concludes. So-called terrorism experts are outdated. They are stuck in the past and examine modern terrorism through a perspective "yellowed with age."

Consider these issues in terms of future developments:

- Unlike most criminals, terrorists study the past to develop tactical models. Is there merit in studying the history of terrorism? If so, what is the time frame for beginning such study?
- Does the history of terrorism teach lessons across cultures? Are there certain aspects of terrorism that remain constant across time and location?
- How is the form of twenty-first-century terrorism different from its previous manifestations? How is it similar?

Selective Terrorism and the Birth of the Irish Republic

In August 1969, the British army was ordered to increase its presence in Northern Ireland in an effort to quell a series of riots. Although the army had maintained bases in Northern Ireland for some time, rioting in Londonderry and Belfast was suddenly far beyond the control of local police and the handful of British regular soldiers stationed in the area. On August 18, 1969, British army reinforcements began arriving, hoping to avoid a long-term conflict. Their hopes were in vain. The meaning of terrorism in Ireland changed with history. Unlike revolutionary France, Europe in 1848, and the differing forms of terrorism in Russia, terrorism in Ireland developed over a number of centuries (Lee, 1983).

The Irish have never ruled their island as a single political entity, and they have experienced some type of foreign domination since a series of Viking incursions in A.D. 800 (Costigan, 1980; and Cahill, 2003). The Vikings were driven out in the eleventh century, only to be replaced by invading Normans in the twelfth century (Simms, 2000). England began to colonize the northern part of Ireland in the late 1500s. This not only brought conflict between the colonizers and the colonized, it created a direct collision between Protestants and Catholics (Bradshaw, 1978; O Corrain, 2000; Curtis, 2000, pp. 16–18, orig. 1936; and Herren and Brown, 2002). Finally, after the United Kingdom was formed in 1801, Ireland was literally absorbed by Great Britain (see Cronin, 1984; Foster, 2001, pp. 134–172). This last act created a new type of Irish person, the *Republican*, a citizen wanting to be free of the British in a *Republic* of Ireland.

The Early Irish Republican Army

By the twentieth century, the struggle in Ireland had become a matter of the divisions between Unionists, people who wanted to remain in the United Kingdom of Great Britain and Ireland, and Republicans, people who wanted independence. A host of other conflicts were associated with this confrontation, but the main one was the Unionist–Republican struggle. The Unionists often had the upper hand because they could call on support from the British-sponsored police and military forces. The Republicans had no such advantage, and they searched for an alternative.

Costigan (1980) believes that the Republican military solution originated when the Irish Republican Brotherhood (IRB) formed in the 1850s. Support came from exiles and emigrants around the world. Irish Catholics had emigrated from their homeland to America, Australia, Canada, and New Zealand, but they never forgot the people they left behind. Irish immigrants in New York City created the Fenian Brotherhood as a financial relief organization for relatives in the old country. After the American Civil War, some Irish soldiers returning from the U.S. Army decided to take the struggle for emancipation back to Ireland. Having fought to free the slaves, they believed that they should continue the struggle and free Ireland. They sponsored a failed revolt in 1867, and others launched a dynamite campaign in London a decade and a half later. Although the IRB pledged to work peacefully with Charles Stewart Parnell, it gradually evolved into a revolutionary organization.

J. Bowyer Bell (1974) has written the definitive treatise on the origins and development of the Irish Republican Army (IRA). He states that it began with a campaign of violence sponsored by the IRB in the late 1800s. Spurred on by increased nationalistic feeling in the homeland and the hope of home rule, the IRB waged a campaign of bombing and assassination from 1870 until 1916. Its primary targets were Unionists and British forces supporting the Unionist cause. Among their greatest adversaries was the British-backed police force in Ireland, the **Royal Irish Constabulary** (RIC).

Royal Irish Constabulary (RIC): The police force established by the United Kingdom in Ireland. It was modeled after the London Metropolitan Police, but it represented British interests. After the Free State was formed, the RIC became the Royal Ulster Constabulary (RUC). In turn, the RUC gave way to the Police Service of Northern Ireland (PSNI) as part of Irish and British attempts to bring peace to Northern Ireland after 1995.

The activities of the IRB frightened Irish citizens who wanted to remain united with Great Britain. For the most part, these people were Protestant and middle class, and they lived in the northern counties. They gravitated toward their trade unions and social organizations, among them the Orange Lodges, to counter growing IRB sympathy and power. They enjoyed the sympathy of the British army's officer corps. They also controlled the RIC.

The Fenians of the IRB remained undaunted by Unionist sentiment. Although Irish Unionists seemed in control, the IRB had two trump cards. First, IRB leadership was dominated by men who believed each generation had to produce warriors who would fight for independence. Some of these leaders, as well as their followers, were quite willing to be martyred to keep Republicanism alive. In addition, the IRB had an organization. It not only served as a threat to British power; it also provided the basis for the resurgence of Irish culture.

The Easter Rising

At the turn of the century, no person embodied Irish culture more than Patrick Pearse (1879–1916). The headmaster of an Irish school, Pearse was an inspirational romantic. He could move crowds to patriotism and inspire resistance to British policies. He was a hero among Irish Americans, and they sent hundreds of thousands of dollars to support his cause. He told young Irish boys and girls about their heritage, he taught them Gaelic, and he inspired them to be militantly proud of being Irish. He was also a member of the **Supreme Council of the IRB.** When the possibility of home rule was defeated in the British parliament, Republican eyes turned to Pearse.

Supreme Council of the IRB: The command center of several Republican terrorist organizations, including the Irish Republican Army, the Official Irish Republican Army, and the Provisional Irish Republican Army. The name was transposed from the Irish Republican Brotherhood.

By 1916, the situation in Ireland had changed. The British had promised home rule to Ireland when World War I (1914–1918) came to an end. Whereas most people in Ireland believed the British, Unionists and Republicans secretly armed for a civil war between the North and the South. They believed a fight was inevitable if the British granted home rule, and each side was determined to dominate the government of a newly independent Ireland. Some Republicans were not willing to wait for home rule.

With British attention focused on Germany, leaders of the IRB believed that it was time for a strike against the Unionists and their British supporters. At Easter in 1916, Patrick Pearse and James Connolly (1868–1916) led a revolt in Dublin. Pearse believed that the revolt was doomed from the start, but he also believed that it was necessary to sacrifice his life to keep the republican spirit alive. Connolly was a more pragmatic socialist who fought because he believed a coming civil war was inevitable.

The 1916 Easter Rising enjoyed local success because it surprised everyone. Pearse and Connolly took over several key points in Dublin with a few thousand armed followers. From the halls of the General Post Office, Pearse announced that the revolutionaries had formed an Irish republic, and he asked the Irish to follow him. The British, outraged by this treachery, in their view, in the midst of a larger war, sent troops to Dublin. The city was engulfed in a week of heavy fighting.

Whereas Pearse and Connolly came to start a popular revolution, the British came to fight a war. In a few days, Dublin was devastated by British artillery. Pearse recognized the futility of the situation and asked for terms. Bell (1974) points out the interesting way Pearse chose to approach the British: He sent a message using a new title, commanding general of the IRA, to the general in charge of the British forces. The IRB had transformed itself into an army: the IRA.

If Connolly and Pearse hoped to be greeted as liberators, they had greatly misjudged the mood of Ireland. Popular opinion favored home rule, but many Irish people believed it would come without a fight, Britain granting it at the end of the war. Paul Bew (1999) says that the republican political party had not captured the public's imagination earlier. Had the British played to Irish sympathy, they might have stopped violent republicanism. Their actions, however, virtually empowered **Sinn Fein**. The British handed down several dozen death sentences for the Easter Rising. Hundreds more people received lengthy prison sentences. Pearse became an Irish legend. Standing in front of a firing squad, he gave an impassioned plea for Irish independence. Connolly, who had been badly wounded, was tied to a chair and placed before a firing squad. Public sympathy shifted to the rebels.

Sinn Fein: The political party of Irish Republicans. Critics claim it represents terrorists. Republicans say it represents their political interests. Despite the debate, Sinn Fein historically has close connections with extremism and violence.

ANOTHER PERSPECTIVE

State Repression

Edward Herman (1983) says terrorism should be defined in terms of state repression. During the cold war the United States supported several Latin American dictatorships because the dictatorships were anticommunist. These governments, with some of the worst human rights records in history, routinely jailed, tortured, and executed political opponents. The United States not only ignored the repression but funded the activities and trained the repressive military and police forces. When the amount of human suffering from these dictatorships is compared to violence caused by insurgent terrorism, the pain caused by modern terrorism shrinks to insignificance. The "real terror network," Herman argues, is found in repressive government. University of Virginia sociologist Donald Black (2004) summarizes the paradox evident in Herman's earlier work. Counterterrorism, he says, is more violent than terrorism.

Two important people managed to escape the purge. Eamon de Valera (1882–1975) received a prison sentence instead of death because of questions about his nationality. He had been born in New York City and brought to Ireland at an early age. Michael Collins (1890–1922), who was in a cell where prisoners slated for execution were being segregated from those selected for internment, walked to the other side of the cell and found himself among the internment group. It saved his life. De Valera would emerge as a revolutionary and political leader, and Collins would become the leader of the IRA.

The Black and Tan War (1920–1921)

Sinn Fein, the political party of Irish republicanism, continued its activities in spite of the failure of the Easter Rising. When World War I ended, many of the Republicans were released. There were several moderates in Ireland, represented by the Parliamentary Party, and they sought to reopen the issue of home rule. They believed that this was the only nonviolent way to approach the Irish question. Bew (1999) says that the moderates were also willing to cede the northern province, Ulster, to the Protestants who wished to remain united with Great Britain. If the Protestants were forced into a united Ireland, they reasoned, violence would continue.

Bew believes Sinn Fein took advantage of the moderate position and championed the cause of a united Ireland. The ideologues of republicanism expressed themselves in extremist terms. They not only rejected home rule but demanded a completely **free state** devoid of any British participation in Irish politics. For Sinn Fein, anything but a united Ireland was out of the question. The British government also vacillated. Conservatives, especially the military officer corps, were reluctant to abandon the North either to home rule or to an independent Ireland, whereas others sought to solve the Irish problem with some sort of home rule. Bew argues that Sinn Fein moved into the arena by discrediting the Parliamentary Party. Moderation fell by the wayside as extreme republicanism increased.

Free State: The name given to the newly formed Republic of Ireland after Irish independence.

Selective Terror

Michael Collins was appalled by the amateur tactics of the Easter Rising. Revolution, he believed, could be successful, but it would not develop from a popular uprising. It needed to be systematic, organized, and ruthless. After being released from prison in a general amnesty, Collins studied the tactics of the Russian People's Will and the writings of earlier anarchists and terrorists. Collins developed a strategy called "selective terrorism." Devising a plan that would later influence terrorists as diverse as the proto-Israeli group Irgun Zvai Leumi and Ernesto "Che" Guevara's communist revolutionaries in Cuba, Collins reasoned that indiscriminate terror was of no value. Random or large-scale attacks would alienate public opinion. Conversely, launching an attack and waiting for the population to spontaneously rise to rebellion was equally futile. To be effective, terrorism had to selectively and ruthlessly target security forces and their symbols of authority.

After months of planning, recruiting, and organizing, Collins launched a new form of the IRA. He began by gathering intelligence, learning the internal workings of British police headquarters, and obtaining a list of intelligence officers. The first attacks were devastating. Using the information from the extensive preparation, Collins's men ambushed off-duty police and intelligence officers and murdered them. He then began attacking police stations. IRA terrorists would emerge from a crowded sidewalk, throw bombs and shoot police officers, then melt back into the crowd before authorities could respond. A master of strategy, Collins continued a campaign of terror against Unionists and the RIC.

The British responded by sending a hastily recruited military force, called the Black and Tans because of their mismatched uniforms, and Ireland became the scene of a dreadful war. Each side accused the other of atrocities, but murder and mayhem were the tactics of each. The conflict became popularly known as the Tan War or the Black and Tan War.

Separation and Independence

Meanwhile, home rule had not been forgotten by more moderate groups. Politicians in Britain and Ireland sought to bring an end to the violence by formulating the steps to grant Irish independence. The main stumbling block was the North. Protestant Unionists were afraid of being abandoned by the British. In 1921, the situation was temporarily solved by a treaty between Britain and Ireland. Under the terms of the treaty, Ireland would be granted independence and the northern section, Ulster, would remain under British protection until it could peacefully be integrated into Ireland. Southern Ireland became the **Free State**—the Republic of Ireland. The majority of people in Ireland accepted the treaty. Michael Collins also accepted the treaty, but the IRA did not.

When the treaty between Ireland and Britain was ratified in 1921, a civil war broke out in the newly formed republic. Michael Collins led the Irish Army, while his former colleague Eamon de Valera took the helm of the IRA. The IRA fought

Irish governmental forces, claiming that Irish independence had to extend to all Irish people. They rejected British control of Ulster. De Valera campaigned against his former colleagues and eventually orchestrated the murder of Michael Collins.

For their part, the British wanted nothing to do with the civil war in the southern areas. They tightened their hold on Northern Ireland and bolstered its strength with a new police force, the Royal Ulster Constabulary (RUC). The northern Unionists were delighted when the British established a semiautonomous government in Northern Ireland and gave it special powers to combat the IRA. The Unionists used this power to gain control of Northern Ireland and lock themselves into the British orbit. Ireland became a divided country (see Foster, 1989, pp. 431–465; Laffan, 1999).

 Self-Check

> How did the IRB evolve toward militancy?
> How did the Easter Rising impact republicanism?
> What is the meaning of "selective terror," and how did Collins employ it?
> The Black and Tan War led to partial independence and future violence. Why?

CHAPTER TAKE AWAYS

The United States has changed national security and law enforcement policies based partially on the way it defines terrorism. This is a situational definition, however, because the meaning of terrorism changes through history. The ideas behind modern democracies were contained in the Enlightenment, giving birth to revolutions in the American colonies and in France. Terrorism was a product of the class-based revolution in France, and the term described the actions of the government. It would go through many changes in meaning until it once again was used to describe government repression. Many of the chapters in Part 2 will summarize recent regional histories to show how the definition continues to fluctuate.

OBJECTIVE SUMMARY

- The term *terrorism* is a social construct and not a physical entity. Furthermore, the term is pejorative because it evokes a variety of politically charged responses. The way terrorism is defined often has life or death consequences.
- *Terrorism* is defined within social and political contexts, and it means different things in different time periods. The meaning even changes within a historical time frame as contexts change. This is the primary reason that no single definition of terrorism will ever be successful.
- The eighteenth-century Enlightenment provided the intellectual climate to support modern democracy. The ideology spawned revolutions in the American colonies and France, but the French Revolution brought a new government that ruled by the fear of terrorism. The French would change the meaning of the word again by calling Spanish guerrillas terrorists.
- European governments and capitalists came to fear class revolution as a series of uprising swept across Europe in 1848. After governments restored order by the use of force, they remained leery of groups calling for economic equality and full democracy. A small minority of the radical democrats called for violence and terrorism. People with political power began to label all types of activism as terrorism whether it was violent or not.
- Socialism refers to controlling an economy by direct democracy and utilizing economic profits to ensure the well-being of citizens. Anarchism is a philosophical concept originating in ancient Greece. In the eighteenth century anarchists generally disavowed the power of national governments. Some anarchists were

violent, engaging in bombing and assassination. Communism in its ideal form is socialism where economic production and profits are owned and distributed by workers.

- Modern revolutionary terrorism is closely associated with a series of revolutionary activities that began with the People's Will and continued through the Russian Revolution. After the communists seized power, they returned to the practice of the French revolutionaries and used terrorism to maintain political power.
- Irish revolutionaries fought for independence for several centuries. The Irish Republican Brotherhood was created in the mid-nineteenth century. They soon adopted the tactics of the 1848 revolutionaries, waging a campaign of terror that culminated in the Black and Tan War.
- *Selective terrorism* was a term used by Michael Collins after the failure of the Easter Rising. His intention was to target specific government officials and supporters. He sought to terrorize them until they accepted IRA terms.

Critical Engagement: Definitions and the Future

The Bush Administration reorganized the federal government in response to terrorism, and the Obama Administration changed the Department of Defense's mission partially because of terrorism. Apart from policy ramifications and academic debates, the definition of terrorism is important for the future. The world may be experiencing a radical change in the way nations conceive of the idea of war, and this will impact criminal justice systems, international relations, notions of international sovereignty, and the use of military force. David Bell (2007) illustrates this in a work entitled *The First Total War*.

Bell argues that total war came with the 1789 French Revolution because Europeans dominated international understandings of the nature of conflict, and their notions about war changed with the fall of the French monarchy. He believes that the age of Catholic and Protestant religious wars, from the early sixteenth century to the middle of the seventeenth century, ushered a new paradigm into European politics. Religious wars were too destructive, but political wars had their purposes in the everyday practice of European politics. In the new paradigm, war was limited to specific political objectives. The purpose of war was to maintain the dominant political system, and to shift power within the system. In the rare instances when nations sought to eliminate other countries, such as Maria Theresa's policy against Frederick the Great in the Seven Years' War (1756–1763), the political goals were to maintain social and political systems, not to replace them with another set of values.

The key to understanding this type of war, Bell believes, was two-fold: It was normal and limited. Nobles left courtly life to engage in the adventures of war. They were part of society, not apart from it. Far from professional, they were expected to be poets, dandies, and wits. Although lower classes suffered more under this system, nobles, peasants, and the middle classes identified with their counterparts in enemy countries. Peace was abnormal because it interfered with the natural political competition among various national interests. This limited paradigm did not threaten the political or social structure of Europeans or their empires. Bell says this changed in 1789.

The French Revolution and the rise of Napoleon brought a new mindset. The change came for a number of reasons. A movement toward religious and intellectual pacifism began to assume that peace was normal and that war was an aberration. Shifting political and social structures in France transformed the distribution of political and economic power. Some social groups, such as loyalist French peasants in the Vendee region of revolutionary France, felt their existence was threatened. They sought to destroy revolutionary forces, and revolutionary generals responded in kind with massacre and murder. Ironically, since people came to believe that war was abnormal, military force was to be employed with maximum violence to eradicate the enemy that caused war. Even though technology remained relatively constant, the new paradigm radicalized the nature of war. It was aimed at the elimination of an enemy and the enemy's political and social structure. It was waged to build national character with heroic self-sacrifice. In Bell's interpretation, this evolved into total war.

If Bell is correct, his thesis may well be important for understanding the definition of *terrorism* and the future. Bell maintains that war changed between 1789 and 1815, and that we are experiencing a similar change today. We are confused, however, because we face changing conflict within the framework of total war. Victor Davis Hanson (2000) and Thomas Barnett (2005 and 2006) use different evidence, but come to a similar conclusion. Unlike the shift during the French Revolution, technological changes imply that the total war can destroy a significant portion of the planet and even threaten human existence. In addition, technology makes terrorism possible. (See Donald Black's explanation of social geometry, discussed in Chapter 2.)

Consider these issues in terms of future developments:

- If war and conflict are normal, should policies be aimed at eliminating terrorism or controlling it?
- Is terrorism a single concept, or does it change with the political and social circumstances of each cause?
- If the nature of war is changing, what factors support the interpretation of terrorism as a military problem? What factors suggest that it is a problem for law enforcement and criminal procedures?

KEY TERMS

Social construct, p. 1-4	Estates General, p. 1-8	Socialists, p. 1-10	Workers' Councils or
Academic consensus	National Convention,	Anarchists, p. 1-10	Soviets, p. 1-19
definition, p. 1-4	p. 1-8	Communists, p. 1-10	Leon Trotsky, p. 1-20
Social context, p. 1-4	Committee of Public	Bourgeois, p. 1-13	Royal Irish
Selective terrorism,	Safety, p. 1-8	Hohenzollerns, p. 1-13	Constabulary, p. 1-22
p. 1-5	Reign of Terror, p. 1-8	Hapsburgs, p. 1-13	Supreme Council of the
Nidal Malik Hasan,	Spain in 1807, p. 1-9	Joseph Stalin, p. 1-18	IRB, p. 1-22
p. 1-5	Radical democrats,	Vladmir Lenin, p. 1-18	Sinn Fein, p. 1-23
Enlightenment, p. 1-6	p. 1-10	Vladmir Putin, p. 1-18	Free State, p. 1-24

The Social Underpinnings of Terrorism

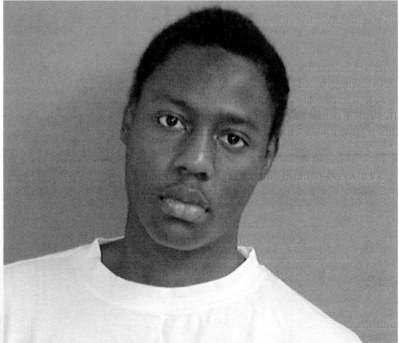

ZUMA Press/Newscom

LEARNING OBJECTIVES

After reading this chapter, you should be able to:

> Outline differing approaches for understanding social reality.
> Define the elements of netwar.
> Describe terrorism as a religious process.
> Define practical criminology as used by security forces.
> Describe the differences between terrorist and criminal behavior.
> Explain the reason terrorists and counter terrorists need to justify violence.
> Summarize studies of the ways terrorist violence is justified.
> Describe three views on the profiling debate.
> Outline differing points of view about radicalization and alienation.

Omar Farouk Abdulmutallub was sentenced to life in prison for attempting to detonate a bomb on a Northwest passenger plane in 2009. He expressed no remorse at the time of his sentencing three years later, only stating a willingness to wage his version of holy war. One day later, Amine Elkalifi was arrested by FBI agents for allegedly trying to explode a suicide vest bomb at the White House. According to the Associated Press (Pickler and Brumfield, 2012), Elkalifi was convinced that the "War on Terrorism" was a "War on Islam." Authorities became suspicious in 2011 when Elkalifi began expressing these views to his acquaintances. He expressed a desire to kill himself in a suicide bombing in Alexandria, Virginia. Undercover operatives from a Joint Terrorism Task Force were able to successfully investigate the case and supply Elkalifi with inert weapons. The questions that often puzzle counterterrorism officials and social scientists are, Why and how are people motivated to such extremes?

Terrorism is a social activity. That means it is organized by groups of people who define social reality and either sustain or change their beliefs. Even when a person takes action individually, some type of social process is behind the person's definition of reality. People who use terrorism are motivated by some cause, and all of them have varying levels of commitment to their respective group. Hardcore ideologues believe deeply in their causes, and they remain committed throughout their lives. Prison sentences, negotiations, concessions, and even the threat of death rarely reduce the attachment such people feel toward their group's purpose. At other times, criminals become involved in terrorist groups for economic gain, and they have a low level of commitment to a cause. Some people simply enjoy the thrill of terrorism. Spirituality has also entered the picture. In recent years, a lot of young men have joined terrorist organizations in the name of religion, and young women have followed their example. Finally, many people join groups out of a sense of social justice. This ranges from people who experience an intense social crisis, such as the violent death of a loved one, to those who are alienated by Western economic and social dominance of the world. Terrorism is the result of a long-term social process that takes place on many different levels. Social structures and actions are the foundation of terrorism.

Terrorism as a Social Process: Two Frameworks

social process: As used in this discussion, social process is the way individuals and groups structure themselves, interpret reality, and take action based on those interpretations.

meaning: The subjective interpretation people give to events or physical objects. Meanings are developed by individuals and groups, and different meanings can be attributed to the same event or physical object because the definitions are always influenced by interpretation. Social scientists in this tradition believe that meanings cause actions.

meaning framework: The definitional boundaries for a particular social meaning. Individuals and groups create boundaries around their experiences and perceptions, and they define issues within them. Meaning frameworks are the social boundaries surrounding those definitions. Juergensmeyer sees the clash between modern values and traditional culture as one of the reasons for terrorism. Religious terrorists look at the modern world and reject it. This world is evil in the meaning framework of religious terrorists, and they refuse to accept the boundaries of the secular modern world.

Terrorism is a **social process**. It involves groups of people forming associations, defining social realities, and taking actions based on the meanings given to those realities. Unlike many other social processes, terrorism is violent, and it is conducted in situations where violence is not expected. The social process is influenced by individual psychological interpretations of group members. Individuals take actions within associations, applying an individualized understanding of reality and reacting to environmental stimuli and motivators. Many social scientists explain behavior as a group process taking place inside a social construct or as a multilevel mixture of constructs operating within the same time frame. This methodology has been used by modern historians when they seek to understand the dimensions of interpreting an event. Analysis of group behavior is a favorite domain of sociology and criminology, and many of their techniques are used in political science, social psychology, and other disciplines in the social sciences.

Although there are many approaches to the study of social explanations of group behavior, two schools of thought dominate the scholarly literature on terrorism. One group tends to focus on the meaning of activity; the other school looks at the structure of action. Both approaches enrich efforts to explain terrorism from a vantage point emphasizing security, and they can be moved from theory to practical application.

The Meaning Framework

Many social scientists study group behavior by looking at the **meaning** of actions. The German tradition of sociology was very important in the search for social meaning, and some social scientists study behavior as if they are looking at scenes in a play or movie. Others came to see the study of life as a dramatic series of actions filled and driven by meaning (for examples, see: **Goffman**, 1959; **Schutz**, 1967; Manning, 1976, pp. 21–37; Kahan, 1997; Roberts, 1999; Wexler and Havers, 2002; Edgley, 2003, pp. 141–172; McCormick, 2007; Nelson, 2009). Social scientists who study group and individual behavior from this perspective believe the way we interpret the world motivates the actions we take.

When this method is used to study terrorist organizations, it can be called a **meaning framework**. Theories about terrorism in the meaning framework focus on the interpretation individuals and groups give to the actions of others as well as their own actions. Researchers also examine the circumstances in which the subjects define their roles. Mark Juergensmeyer (2000, pp. 216–229) uses this approach to study the impact of religion on terrorism. Violent religious movements and the organizational structures they create are rooted in the ways certain groups of people view reality. Michael Arena and Bruce Arrigo (2005, pp. 11–48) study meaning by looking at the ways terrorists look at symbols to develop their concepts of self. On a more applied basis, retired DEA agent Gregory Lee (2005) uses a meaning framework to develop a method of classifying terrorist organizations. His purpose is to assist law enforcement officers in conspiracy investigations. Eli Berman (2009) examines the internal interpretations and publicly projected meanings to examine the emergence of religious terrorist groups.

Historians often use this methodology. Bernard Lewis (2002) examines the rise and demise of the Ottoman Turks, the last great Islamic empire, in the face of Western expansion and colonialism. He argues that trouble between Islam and Western modernity can be attributed to the meanings each group attributes to historical change. Middle Eastern Muslims tend to search for a lost ideal, whereas the West embraces modernity. If this thesis is applied to the formation of terrorist groups, one would expect to find militant organizations forming within parts of the Islamic world based on the rejection of Western ideals. Indeed, many researchers have come to this conclusion (see R. Wright, 1986, 1989; Armstrong, 2000b, pp. 32–60; Rubin and Rubin, 2002, pp. 3–6; Lewis, 2003a).

Samuel Huntington (1993, 1996) makes the same argument about cultural perceptions, and Thomas P. M. Barnett (2005) advances a similar point when examining economic competition in the modern world. Huntington believes that a new political order emerged at the end of the cold war, and future conflicts will take place between the world's major civilizations. Barnett believes that the world is divided into three economic groupings, and conflict will be based on the distribution of wealth. Both political scientists argue that the social meanings groups of people give to the world explain political behavior.

The point here is not to critique social scientists who use meaning frameworks but to demonstrate that some sociologists, historians, economic analysts, and political scientists embrace a similar assumption. Social action is based on social meaning. When applied to terrorism, terrorist organizations are the result of subjective meanings, and any strategy designed to confront and destabilize terrorist organizations must include an aggressive effort to introduce alternative meaning frameworks.

The discussion so far has been limited to theory, but it can be directly tied to practical problems. Malcolm Nance (2003, pp. 47–59), perhaps inadvertently but very effectively, advances a **theory of action** while dealing with the practical aspects of counterterrorism in *The Terrorist Recognition Handbook*. In Nance's analysis, terrorists take action out of an ideological desire for social change. He implies that all terrorists are unhappy with the state of the world, and they are motivated to change it.

theory of action: A social science theory that assumes human beings take action based on the subjective meanings they attribute to social settings.

Nance makes no effort at all to discuss any type of social science theory, yet his entire practical guide assumes that terrorism results from the meanings terrorists apply to the modern world. This assumption is the foundation of his discussion of the rise of anticolonialism, trouble in the Middle East, state-sponsored terrorism from Libya (in the 1980s and 1990s) and North Korea, and all aspects of domestic and international terrorism. Tactically, counterterrorism involves specific steps to prevent violence and deconstruct terrorist groups. Strategically, it involves countering ideas

---

From the Meaning Perspective . . .

> Events and structures are created, sustained, and changed through social interpretations.

From the Structural Perspective . . .

> Social structures provide the framework for defining an event.

FIGURE **2.1** Meaning vs. Structure

with alternative interpretations of reality. Nance is a veteran of the American intelligence community with no apparent interest in social theory, but his step-by-step manual is grounded in the meaning framework.

The Structural Framework

Another social science tradition seeks to avoid subjective meanings when examining events. This methodology maintains that human societies need to accomplish certain functions, so they create organizations to do that. Organizations develop according to the needs of a society, or indeed any group of people.

Such organizations take predictable actions, or functions (**Parsons**, 1951; Martindale, 1965; Schmaus, 1999; Tetlock, 2002). The approach to understanding terrorist behavior by looking at the way organizations function can be called a **structural framework**.

Donald Black (2004) approaches terrorism from this vantage point. Black argues that explaining terrorist behavior is comparable to explaining any other aspect of human action. Groups do not organize and take action based on the meanings people attribute to the world. All groups, including terrorist organizations, take action because they belong to a **structure** that operates for a specific purpose. Black calls this **social geometry**. Groups take actions based on their relationships with other groups. Terrorist groups move to strike governments, and governments have structures that strike back. Groups are not violent, Black says; the structures that contain them may be.

Black thinks many analysts do not understand terrorism because they search for social and political meanings to find the root causes of conflict. Scholars are often particularly weak in their understanding of terrorism because they focus their attention on descriptions of violent groups and individuals. The structure and movement of groups explain terrorism. Terrorism develops when a group with inferior power moves against a superior group, inducing mass civilian casualties.

Terrorism was rare in the past because geography would not allow it to develop. For example, people exploited by a European colonial power in 1870 had no ability to strike Europe and kill massive numbers of civilians. Modern technology has changed this situation by shrinking distance and providing weapons. Black sees the process of terrorism as violent self-help, and terrorists organize in quasi-military units fighting outside the norms of war and criminal law. Some scholars believe that Black's methodology can be translated into procedures both to explain terrorist organizations and to protect citizens from terrorist attacks (Howden and Ryan, 2009).

Structural Approaches and Netwar

There are other structural approaches to terrorism, and one of them has caused security specialists to recast their approach to terrorism. They believe terrorists are united through networks. Vito Latora and Massimo Marchioni (2004) state that terrorist organizations are complex systems that can be modeled mathematically and projected by computer simulations. Meaning frameworks have little to do with understanding terrorist behavior from this standpoint. According to Latora and Marchioni's thesis, terrorist organizations are structured in the same manner as communication and transportation systems. This means they are composed of networks that move in patterns—for example, patterns of telephone lines or highways—to particular critical points, or nodes.

Latora and Marchiori's position reflects a new theory in modern warfare called **netwar** (see Arquilla and Ronfeldt, 1996). According to this theory, sub national criminal, terrorist, or revolutionary groups organize themselves in a network of smaller

structural framework: The idea that social constructs are based on systems that provide order. The systems are social structures that accomplish functions necessary to survive. Human activity occurs to accomplish the functions required to maintain the social structure of the system.

structure: The manner in which a group is organized and its purpose. Social scientists from this tradition feel that a group's structure and purpose cause it to act. They also believe that groups are created for specific functions.

social geometry: As used by Donald Black, the social space occupied by a structure and the direction in which it moves.

netwar: One network fighting another network.

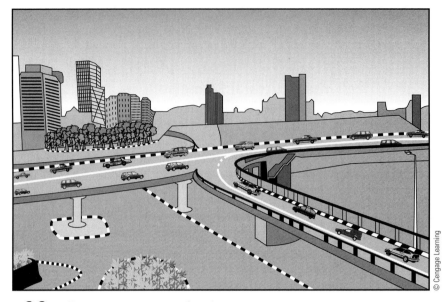

FIGURE **2.2** Traffic Pattern as a Network
The traffic pattern on the highway is akin to a network, and the crucial intersections, merge ramps, and expanded traffic lanes are nodes.

nodes: In counterterrorist or netwar discussions, the points in a system where critical components are stored or transferred. The importance of a node is determined by its relationship to the network.

logistical structures, groups, or command posts. Any point where information, weapons, or personnel are gathered or exchanged is called a **node**; the node is the critical target for counterterrorist operations. Latora and Marchiori argue that once an organization is modeled as a network, the nodes will appear as movement is monitored. If the node is destroyed, the network is disrupted.

To understand this approach to terrorist organizations, consider the traffic pattern in a major city. If you monitor cars moving through the city at rush hour, you will soon find critical points where traffic must keep flowing or the city will become locked in a traffic jam. The traffic pattern on the highway is like a network, and the crucial intersections, merge ramps, and expanded traffic lanes are nodes (see Figure 2.2). If vehicles begin clogging at a node, traffic slows or comes to a standstill at many points in the network. Notice how this differs from organizational models based on meaning. In the netwar metaphor, a vehicle does not take action based on the meaning it attributes to the network. When the network is disrupted, a driver cannot operate a vehicle effectively no matter how the environment is defined. Disrupting terrorist networks has the same effect on terrorist operations.

Researchers at Sam Houston State University in Huntsville, Texas, used a structural model to track terrorist organizations throughout the world (Ward and Hill, 2002). Avoiding a meaning framework, they identified more than 500 violent groups engaged in subnational violence. Using public information, they created a database that tracked 21 types of events with a multiplicity of variables. The structures that emerged from their research were defined by the events and variables. The effort resulted in a comprehensive picture of terrorist violence.

 Self-Check

> In what way is terrorism a social process?
> Describe the differences between meaning approaches and functional approaches when examining terrorism.
> Compare and contrast examples of meaning approaches and functional approaches.

Terrorism as a Religious Process: Anthropological and Sociological Approaches

According to Marxist theories, the conventional wisdom of modern societies, and some schools of science, modernization should lead to the decline of religious identification (see Dawkins, 1998; Wilson, 1999). Ironically, the opposite seems to be true. Tanja Ellingsen (2005) says two primary reasons account for the continued influence of religion. First, religion has always been an important factor in the history of humanity. There is no reason to believe that it will fade as technology grows. Second, modernization tends to break down communities, families, and social orientation. People seek a deeper meaning to their lives. After conducting an empirical study of the influence of religion on terrorist violence, Ellingsen says the world is not witnessing a resurgence of fundamentalism; rather, people have had deep religious feelings all along. Religion continues to hold sway in people's lives, and she argues that her findings demonstrate that its impact on terrorism is more important than political and economic factors.

Susanna Pearce (2005) uses an empirical analysis of religion to examine social science, theological, and historical analyses of religion and terrorism. She believes that strong religious beliefs increase not only the likelihood of religious conflict but also the intensity of fighting. Violence results when sacred traditions are threatened, and the cosmic consequences of failure mean that victory is the only option available to the faithful. **Eschatology** plays a major role because messianic warriors in the endtime correct the heresies of the past and fight for the ideal divine order of a deity. Pearce believes that empirical findings demonstrate that terrorism is partially a religious process.

Anthropologist Marvin Harris (1991, pp. 437–453) believes that human beings have experienced two types of religions: killing and nonkilling religions. Killing religions developed during the food-gathering cycles of preagrarian and early agricultural societies, and they were premised on a deity helping the community in times of crisis. In the killing religions, gods slaughtered enemies. Harris says these beliefs gave way to the nonkilling religions because the older, killing religions did not, in fact, protect early villages from the ravages of war and natural disasters. The nonkilling religions embraced enemies and developed elaborate theologies to justify violence as a last resort. The nonkilling religions appeared in order to try to transcend everyday experience. Harris says the irony of the human experience is that nonkilling transcendence is often transformed into a militant ideology designed to protect a state or other social group by rationalizing the use of violence as a last resort. Why does this happen?

Jessica Stern (2003b) answers this question by stating that people around the world are returning to their religious roots as a means to escape the complexity of modern life. People have too many choices, she says. All the choices bring confusion, and most people want to escape confusion. Returning to old, established patterns of earlier generations, frequently the truths of their traditional religions, people confused by modern complexity seek to ground their lives. Unfortunately, old truths in one society may collide with the truths of another society. This is especially the case when one group believes it is under attack. When mythological truths compete, violence often results.

People use stories to explain deep truths beyond the immediate world, and terrorist groups build their own mythologies to justify their actions through stories. Stern believes stories change the nature of terrorist organizations, and they help to produce different group organizations and styles. Some organizations center on rigid structures. Other groups grow when insecure people gather around a strong personality. Some groups are informal, and everybody in the group has a leadership function. Some loners loosely affiliate with a group but tend to act on their own. Criminals

eschatology: (pronounced es-ka-TAW-low-gee) A Greek word used to indicate the theological end of time. In Judaism and Christianity, it refers to God bringing creation to an end. In some Shi'ite Islamic sects and among Christians who interpret biblical eschatological literature literally, believers contend that Jesus will return to lead a final battle against evil. Other major religions also have end-time theology.

flock to other associations. Stern says the most successful groups operate with a variety of different styles of subgroups.

Individuals come to a group, according to Stern, because they believe they have been called to the story of an entire people. They join a cosmic struggle, a holy cause. New recruits each take a separate path to terrorism, but they are usually motivated by the organization's sacred story. Most sacred stories emphasize self-sacrifice and even death. As a result, many new terrorists seek a path of martyrdom, sometimes facing grave dangers and other times intentionally committing suicide to destroy cosmic enemies. Another path involves developing some type of specialty, and many are motivated to become mighty warriors. Thinking of ancient heroic stories, such as those about the mythic Greek Hercules, illustrates Stern's point. Hercules was half human and half god, and he had strength far beyond that of any mortal. Upon his death, Zeus, the king of the gods, placed Hercules in the heavens as a constellation. This type of myth serves as a model for the ultimate warrior. In a similar way, stories about warriors who sacrifice themselves can be used to justify self-sacrifice or suicide.

Many times people become disillusioned with leaders who fail to live up to mythical standards, and they leave the group but remain sympathetic to the cause. Stern says those who become leaders originally join a group because they believe in the myth, but after a time the lifestyle produces the need for professional behavior, and the group must face professionalization of the leadership, that is, the emergence of a professional terrorist. In other words, the power of the myth becomes less important and the day-to-day job of terrorism grows. Terror for the sake of terror becomes a way of life, and peace threatens the leader's livelihood.

To maintain the power formally given by the sacred story, leaders develop internal enforcement mechanisms. Rewards are given and withheld to encourage correct behavior within the group. When ideology breaks down, leaders may find themselves in alliances with enemies. At this point, the behavioral patterns of religious terrorists cease to matter. They eventually become long-term professional leaders who know only one kind of work. They are professional terrorists for sale to the highest bidder.

Stern also believes that religion helps to produce the "lone-wolf avenger," a person striking out with an ideology but no group. An individual lone-wolf avenger needs to find some type of justification for his or her actions, and religion provides the perfect path. Stern says lone-wolf avengers have a special, narcissistic relationship with their deities. In essence, they create a god in their own image. They become the ultimate loners, and Stern demonstrates that they are the most difficult type of terrorist to deter or detain.

Mark Juergensmeyer (1988, 2003, 2009) spent many years examining the issues surrounding religious terrorism. In *Terror in the Mind of God*, he approaches several militants from different religious traditions around the world. After extensive interviews, he categorizes their discussions to find commonalities. The findings are based on the meanings his subjects attach to modernity. In Juergensmeyer's research, terrorism is created by the meanings subjects attach to social situations. This produces a common pattern in religious terrorist organizations. If Juergensmeyer is correct, groups form as like-minded individuals gather to reject modernity, select a course of action, and violently embrace their interpretation of tradition.

Believers must identify with a deity and believe they are participating in a struggle to change history. And this struggle must be a cosmic struggle; that is, the outcome of the struggle will lead to a new relationship between good and evil. When they feel the struggle has reached the critical stage, violence may be endorsed and terrorism may result. The call to violence, Juergensmeyer argues, is a call to purify the world in a holy war that eliminates the nonbeliever and the incorrect interpreters of tradition. The lines of battle are clear and positions cannot be compromised. Such a war allows only one way of thinking: Those people who do not stand with the holy warrior are evil. If the holy warrior falls in a losing cause, the warrior becomes a martyr for hope. If the warrior is successful, it is a victory for the deity. The holy terrorist is victorious either by killing the enemy or by dying in the struggle (see *Another Perspective: Religion and Ideology*). Juergensmeyer (2009) argues that this process is not simply part of terrorism. It has embraced many modern nationalistic movements, and militant religious imagery is used to reinforce mainstream political concepts. At the same time, it is attractive to those who reject the mainstream because it provides sacred justification for rejecting the norms. Secular nationalism was a rallying cry to many emerging states in the mid-twentieth century. It promised individual liberation, political freedom, and the fruits of modernity. But these promises failed in many parts of the world, especially in areas that were formerly controlled by European colonial governments. Religion emerged as a suitable alternative to secular nationalism, and militant groups were quick to embrace the sacred to justify rebellion. Religious terrorism is a manifestation of a larger social movement.

Eli Berman (2009) takes a different approach to religious terrorism. He argues that it is possible to understand religious terrorism by looking at the economic factors that cause groups to prosper and grow. Despite their utilization of sacred stories and cosmic mythologies, they are hardly religious at all. They are neither motivated by rewards in the afterlife nor inspired by the ideals expressed by their religion. They are effective when they provide social services to their members. The internal economic dynamics of a religious terrorist group are the key to its success. It has very little to do with theology.

Berman argues that his findings have important implications for security specialists. First, religious terrorists are lethal. He uses raw numbers of casualties, as given by the U.S. Department of State from 1968 to 2007, to demonstrate that religious terrorist groups killed more people with fewer attacks than secular terrorists. (Statisticians might criticize this approach by pointing to the inordinate numbers of casualties caused by the September 11, 2001, attacks in the United States.) Berman says the numbers point to a simple fact: Religious terrorists are deadlier than their secular counterparts. Logic seems to indicate that counterterrorism programs should focus on radical ideologies. Reduce the violent rhetoric and the level of terrorism goes down.

This is not true, says Berman. There are only a few religious terrorist groups in the world, and they are extremely difficult to organize. Many of them have no staying power. This finding leads to the second factor for security forces. Berman believes there are 20 active religious terrorist organizations in the world: Eighteen of them are based in Islam, and less than a dozen are very effective. Rather than attempting to counter a religious ideology popular among angry young people, Berman says counterterrorist policy should be aimed at studying the internal ability of a selected group to operate effectively. They hold together, he says, because they are economically able to care for their members and potential constituents. They also keep members from defecting because they create and maintain strong social and economic bonds. Security should be based on examining what religious terrorists do rather than on what they say.

ANOTHER PERSPECTIVE

Religion and Ideology

David Rapoport believes that religion has influenced terrorism because of eschatological expectations. Belief in end-of-the-age theology and the coming of a deity serves to justify violent behavior. Although this seems to separate religious and political terrorists, Rapoport argues that the two sets of behavior are similar. Political ideology plays the same role for political terrorists as eschatology does for religious ones. There is little difference in behavior between secular and religious terrorists, and both types of terrorists are intensely dedicated to a cause. Ideology and eschatology differ, but the behavioral outcome is similar.

Source: Rapoport, 1984.

Self-Check	

> Why would some social scientists examine terrorism from a religious perspective?
> What role do sacred stories and narratives play in religious violence?
> How does the confrontation between good and evil motivate religious terrorists?
> Are the beliefs of religious terrorists more important than the internal operations of the group?

Terrorism as Practical Criminology

CesareBeccaria: (1738–1794) One of the founders of the discipline of criminology. His work *Of Crimes and Punishments* (1764) is the classic Enlightenment study of the discipline.

There are two branches of criminology in the practical world of criminal justice. When using the word *criminology* in an academic setting, images of psychological and sociological theories appear in the minds of researchers and teachers. This is classic criminology, tracing its origins to **CesareBeccaria** and using the most modern theories of individual and group behavior. When the word is mentioned in a law enforcement agency, a different image appears. Practical criminology focuses on the common actions of lawbreakers. Police officers are not as concerned with theories of criminality as they are with the practical aspects of criminal behavior. They want to know what criminals do so that they may deter them from committing a crime or catch them after the crime is committed.

The purpose here is to consider this second branch of criminology, the applied actions in crime prevention and apprehension. This distinction is important because, although terrorists commit crimes as they struggle for a cause, they differ from ordinary street criminals. Terrorists have organizational structures, belief systems, and motivational values that separate them from ordinary criminals. Law enforcement personnel must recognize the differences between typical criminal behavior and terrorist activity if they want to prevent crime and apprehend criminals. Law enforcement officials are frequently the first governmental agents on the scene of a terrorist incident. If they fail to recognize that the scene may be something more than an ordinary crime, they may well miss the point of the investigation. For example, should malicious destruction of property always be classified as a simple misdemeanor or felony? If someone unlawfully enters a farm, destroys cages, and frees the animals, is this simply malicious destruction? Many law enforcement officers would answer *yes*, but consider the Animal Liberation Front (ALF). In instructions to members and sympathizers, the ALF advocates the systematic destruction of farms that produce fur for clothing. Their website gives potential recruits tactics for the most effective destruction of mink farms (formerly, www.nocompromise.org/alf/alf.html.

One of the issues that has dominated the discipline of criminal justice over the past few decades is the debate about the academic function of the discipline. Some scholars favor a theoretical approach to the field, while others believe that professors with previous professional experience are better suited to address the discipline. This debate takes place not only takes place on college campuses, but in the workaday world of criminal justice as well.

Professionals—tend to focus on criminological findings with crime fighting results.

Professionally oriented social scientists—tend to conduct studies that will help professionals reduce crime.

Theoretically oriented social scientists—tend to focus research on increasing the body of scientific knowledge regardless of application.

In reality, all three approaches are necessary and valued. Each "type" of criminology has a valid purpose.

FIGURE **2.3** Theory vs. Practice

See http://www.animalliberationfront.com/index.html). If a deputy sheriff or state trooper happens on such an attack, it will probably be classified as malicious destruction of property even though it may well be part of a larger operation.

To counter such tendencies in law enforcement, the FBI has created local terrorism task forces—Joint Terrorism Task Forces (JTTFs)—around the country. In theory, this allows the FBI to coordinate law enforcement resources in the face of domestic terrorism and to expand investigations. Internationally, the FBI also provides investigative resources when Americans are victimized by terrorism in other countries. Yet the fact remains that individual patrol officers are usually the first people to arrive on the scene of a terrorist incident. They must recognize the traits of terrorism to begin the investigation. Terrorist investigations do not follow the pattern of most criminal investigations because terrorists seldom behave like normative street criminals. D. Douglas Bodrero (2002), the former commissioner for the Department of Public Safety in Utah and a former member of the International Association of Chiefs of Police Committee on Terrorism, offers a comparative analysis between terrorist behavior and that of ordinary criminals. Bodrero argues that typical criminals are opportunistic. This means that criminals tend to be impulsive. Most street criminals do not plan their crimes extensively, and they react to easy opportunities on the spur of the moment. Criminals are usually not committed to a cause. Even career criminals do not believe in crime as an ideology or religion. Crime is just a method for obtaining goods. Because of this lifestyle, criminals tend to be self-centered and undisciplined. Except for a small proportion of career criminals, ordinary street criminals are untrained. Their goal is to obtain cash or goods and get away.

Bodrero and most police officers base crime prevention and apprehension strategies on these assumptions about street criminals for one simple reason: They work. By protecting (or hardening) targets, denying opportunity, and conducting aggressive patrols, many ordinary street crimes like burglary can be suppressed (W. Harris, 1998). In addition, making police an extension of the community can reduce crimes that seem to defy suppression, such as domestic violence (Trojanowicz et al., 1998). By using criminal intelligence files to keep track of known felons, criminal associations, and crime patterns, police suppress criminal activity. Police search for hangouts of local criminals, they know their friends and family, and they maintain sources of information about suspicious activity. These procedures not only serve as the basis of community policing; they are the essence of criminal investigation.

Bodrero (2002) says terrorist behavior differs from standard patterns of criminal behavior because terrorists are highly motivated and loyal to a particular cause. Whereas ordinary criminals are opportunistic, terrorists are focused. They may select targets of opportunity, but the target has a symbolic value. Terrorists use crime to make a symbolic statement about a political cause.

If criminals are uncommitted and self-centered, terrorists find strength in a cause and the ideology or religion behind the cause. They are supported by an organization and sent on a mission. They are team oriented even when they act as individuals. For example, suicide bombers do not act alone; their preparation involves teamwork. Being part of something greater than themselves becomes the basis for action. Even in the case of lone wolves, the ideology is all-consuming. They might act alone, but deep-seated beliefs cause loners to feel that their actions are part of the vanguard of a movement. Terrorism is an organizational process whether support is real or implied through ideology (Schweitzer, 2000; Khashan, 2003; Kaplan et al., 2005; Azam, 2005).

Ideology and religion are not limited to suicide bombers; they also influence individuals who will become terrorists for a single event. For example, Buford Furrow entered a Jewish day care center in August 1999 and began shooting people. He was a lone wolf, or what is called a "berserker." He had no extensive logistical network or support organization. Yet Furrow was consumed by an ideology of hate and a religion that demonized Jews. He was not an uncommitted opportunistic criminal acting alone. He was an agent of an ideology on a divine mission. Again, as Bodrero (2002) indicates, this is not the pattern of typical criminals. Bodrero says that criminals are undisciplined, untrained, and oriented toward escape. Terrorists are exactly the opposite. They have prepared for their mission, they are willing to take risks, and they are attack oriented. Lone wolves might be untrained, but they are prepared and attack oriented.

In summary, terrorists and criminals exhibit practical behavioral differences. These include:

1. Criminals are unfocused. Terrorists focus their actions toward a goal.
2. Criminals may live in a criminal underworld, but they are not devoted to crime as a philosophy. Terrorists are dedicated to a cause.
3. Criminals will make deals to avoid punishment. Terrorists rarely cooperate with officials because they do not wish to betray their cause.
4. Criminals usually run when confronted with force. Terrorists tend to attack.
5. Criminals strike when the opportunity to do so is present. Terrorists strike agaist symbols after careful planning.
6. Criminals rarely train for crime. Terrorists prepare for and rehearse their operations.

These differences influence the ways criminal intelligence is gathered and the process of criminal investigations. Terrorism investigations involve long-term observation, informant development, and evidence collection. It usually involves a lengthy process of piecing together elements of a complex criminal conspiracy (see Lee, 2005; Dyson, 2008).

The significance of Bodrero's argument can be measured in the investigative response to terrorism. When investigating a crime, police officers can take advantage of the behavioral characteristics of typical criminals. The most hardened criminals will usually act in their own self-interest, and they will make deals to receive a lesser sentence. When searching for a fleeing felon, law enforcement officers find it productive to question known associates and keep family and friends under surveillance. These tactics do not work in countering terrorism. Law enforcement, military, and security officials need to focus on ideology, group and individual behavior, and sharing information over broad geographical regions to successfully investigate terrorism.

Self-Check
> What is "practical criminology"?
> Why do investigators use practical interpretations of criminology?
> What are the differences between terrorists and criminals?
> How do these behavior differences impact investigations?
> Could terrorists avoid criminal behavior? Why or why not?

Justifying Terrorism

Every person who uses force must seek to justify it. As the amount of force increases, the need to justify it becomes greater. Deadly force demands the greatest amount of justification. When a person threatens to kill or does kill another person, he or she must feel it was right to do so.

When a person engages in violent activity on the state's behalf, the government unveils its most sacred symbols and rituals to reward the person. Warriors need such rewards. Terrorists have the same need for social approval, but they rarely obtain it because their actions are not sanctioned by the governments they attack. They are routinely condemned by the population at large. Even when citizens approve of the cause associated with terrorism, they are reluctant to embrace and endorse the methods of mayhem. Terrorists must, therefore, look outside normative social channels to gain approval for their acts.

The terrorist group becomes the primary source of social reality for individual terrorists. It provides social recognition and reinforcement for its members. Like soldiers, who undergo a similar bonding process during basic training, potential terrorists join groups for varied reasons: They may be sympathetic to the cause, or they may simply be social misfits. The terrorist group reshapes identities and provides a ticket to social acceptance.

For social acceptance to work, however, the terrorist group must be isolated from mainstream society. Richard Cloward and Lloyd Ohlin's (1960) study of American urban youth gangs provides an analogy. The gang is a self-referential group in a world gone awry. By rejecting the norms of the urban environment, the gang is made free to create its own norms. Israel's experience with Arab suicide bombers has shown that terrorists go through the same process. A terrorist must be isolated before beginning a mission, interacting only with others who are directly involved in the mission. During this period, the terrorist is constantly indoctrinated in the importance of the mission and reminded that the goal is more important than human life. Suicidal terrorists are often housed together so that they can continue reinforcing each other. Like gang members, terrorists must enter a world of their own reality.

Research on Motivation and Justification

One of the current weaknesses in terrorism research is the lack of quantitative and qualitative behavioral studies. Randy Borum (2004) says that researchers have come to the conclusion that there is no standard rationale for justifying behavior. He says it is profitable to distinguish three different phases of self-justification: reasons for joining the group, reasons for remaining, and reasons for leaving. Jeff Victoroff (2005) agrees that a multiplicity of factors are used to justify violence, but he does not believe current research is comprehensive. Both Borum and Victoroff call for more behavioral research.

One promising approach is to study the relationship between behavioral and economic factors. After examining terrorism in 127 countries from 1968 to 1991, one study suggests that terrorist groups form because members are unhappy with the economic status quo. Terrorists exhibit a collective frustration about poverty, whether they are themselves impoverished or not, and believe violence is justified to redress denial of economic opportunity. Increased access to economic activity decreases the level of violence; in contrast, decreased opportunities in high-income countries increase the probability of terrorism (Blomberg, Hess, and Weerapana, 2004).

Jerrold Post (1987, 2008; Kruglanski et al., 2008) believes there is no single terrorist personality but that terrorists do follow similar behavioral patterns. The most important pattern has to do with group and individual acceptance. Terrorist groups are very much like criminal groups in having been rejected by mainstream society. The group becomes the only source of social reward because of its members' isolation. Terrorists reinforce one another. Post says this pattern holds true across cultures.

The individuals who are attracted to terrorist groups are as much outcasts as the organizations they seek to join. Post believes this results in an us-against-them mentality. The constant reinforcement of antisocial behavior in terrorist groups produces conforming behavior inside the organizations, although strong leaders may not conform and may splinter the group. According to Post, the rejection of external authority results in the acceptance of internal authority because behavior must be reinforced somewhere.

Some researchers have begun to ask how the perception of social and political events leads to the justification of violence. In one study researchers found that members of al Qaeda were able to find solace by appealing to an idea of universal morality (Halvercheid and Witte, 2008). Other researchers conclude that both terrorists and those engaged in counterterrorism justify their actions in terms of larger social issues (Findlay, 2007; Reiff, 2008). Potential terrorists are motivated to join groups through religion, ethnicity, nationalism, or ideology (see Lutz and Lutz, 2008, pp. 69–215).

Self-Check

> Why do people seek to justify violence?
> What do empirical studies about the process of justification reveal?
> How does the perception of injustice motivate terrorists and counter terrorists?

Classification Systems: Can the Terrorist Personality Be Profiled?

Frederick Hacker (1976) introduced a general theory of individual terrorist behavior, and others followed. As studies proliferated, the typical terrorist was thought to be a young, unmarried, middle-class male with some university training and an understanding of left-wing political philosophy (Russell and Miller, 1983, pp. 33–41). Unfortunately, this described millions of people, most of whom were not terrorists. Continued study failed to enhance the profile of a typical terrorist, causing Andrew Silke (2001) to lament that researchers still knew very little about terrorism.

Attempts to find psychological profiles of terrorists continue in the twenty-first century. Two psychologists, Ervin Staub and Clark McCauley, believe that certain types of people are drawn toward terrorist groups. Staub states that terrorists come from three types of social groups: those who identify with a suffering group, those who respond to suffering in their own group, and alienated individuals who find purpose by joining a terrorist group. McCauley sees four types of personalities: revolutionaries drawn to a cause, people who wander among terrorist groups, people who have a sudden conversion experience, and people who are attracted by peers (Kershaw, 2010; see also Staub, 2002; McCauley, 2010).

profiling: A practical criminological process designed to identify the behavioral attributes of certain types of criminals.

Many law enforcement agencies, including the Behavioral Science Unit in the FBI, have attempted to develop practical models for **profiling** terrorists based on individual psychological characteristics. They employ a variety of techniques and have become more sophisticated in using behavioral science against many forms of criminality (Turvey, Tamlyn, and Chisum, 1999). Agencies also attempt to assess the level of potential threats, and violent political extremists usually represent the most dangerous threat.

A practical example of such classification systems comes from the United Kingdom. Police officials there make practical decisions based on profiles of terrorists and the classification of each incident. When faced with an act of terrorism, the local ranking police official makes an assessment of the event. If it is classified as a criminal activity or the result of a mentally deranged individual, the local police commander handles the incident. If the commander deems the action to be the result of political terrorism, the central government is informed, and the incident is handled on the prime ministerial level. In addition, if the level of the threat is sufficiently high, the matter may be referred to the national government.

Although such profiling has practical applications in law enforcement, the larger question remains: Is it possible to profile the terrorist personality? The question has spawned a heated debate. One side claims that profiles cannot be developed because terrorism changes with historical events. The other school believes profiles can be developed, but they must measure a variety of factors.

Rejecting Terrorist Profiles

Walter Laqueur (1999, pp. 79–104) says that no one can develop a composite picture of a terrorist because no such terrorist exists. Terrorism fluctuates over time, Laqueur argues, and the profile of the terrorist changes with circumstances. There can be no terrorist mosaic because there are different types of terrorism. Laqueur says we can be sure that most terrorists are young, but their actions and psychological makeup vary according to social and cultural conditions.

Laqueur (1999) believes that other group characteristics can be discerned through the type of movement. Nationalistic and separatist groups are aggressive, and their actions are characterized by horrible violence. Such violence may or may not be the result of psychological inadequacies. In democracies, Laqueur says, terrorists tend to be elitists. Nationalistic movements produce terrorists from the lower classes, but religious terrorists come from all classes. Individual and group profiles are the result of political and social conditions.

In the final analysis, Laqueur believes it is impossible to profile a terrorist personality because terrorism is not the subject of criminology. In the past, he says, perfectly normal individuals have opted to engage in terrorism as a rational political statement. Terrorism is a political phenomenon different from ordinary crime or psychopathology.

Several researchers agree with Laqueur. Randy Borum (2004, p. 37) states that there is no single terrorist personality and that terrorists represent a variety of physical types. He further states that the word profiling has so many different meanings that it has become virtually useless. Furthermore, if terrorist groups learn that members are being profiled, they select an operative who does not match the profile. If terrorist prevention rests on profiling, Borum concludes, it is doomed to failure.

Proponents of the impossibility of profiling also look at specific types of terrorism and terrorist groups. Robert Pape (2003) finds that suicide bombers come from several different backgrounds and that there is no single description of them. Marc Sageman (2004, pp. 66, 81–91) finds that the social process of becoming a terrorist may have a pattern, but there is no pattern of psychological disorders (see *Another Perspective: Using a Group to Profile*). RohanGunaratna (2002) states that al Qaeda operatives came from several countries and had differing ethnic backgrounds. With so many variables, critics believe that profiling is impossible.

Proposing a Multivariate Profile

Jeffrey Ian Ross (1999, pp. 169–192) offers an alternative view. Rather than attempting to delineate an individual profile, Ross says it may be possible to conceptualize terrorism in a model that combines social structure with group psychology. He believes that such a model is necessary for policy makers to develop better counterterrorist responses.

Ross believes that five interconnected processes are involved in terrorism: joining the group, forming the activity, remaining in the campaign, leading the organization, and engaging in acts of terrorism. He says that many analysts have attempted to explain terrorism based on these concepts, but they fall short because there is no model of terrorism. Rather than simply trying to profile the typical terrorist, Ross tries to explain how social and psychological processes produce terrorism. The model offers a great deal of promise.

Two factors are involved in the rise of terrorism at any point in history. The first centers around social structure. Structural factors include the way a society is organized, its political and economic systems, its historical and cultural conditions, the number of grievances citizens have and their mechanisms for addressing grievances, the availability of weapons, and the effectiveness of counterterrorist forces. Ross says that modernization, democracy, and social unrest create the structural conditions that facilitate terrorism. In Ross's analysis, urban areas produce the greatest potential for unrest and the greatest availability of weapons. When governments fail to address social pressures in these areas, the likelihood of terrorism increases. When counterterrorist intervention fails, the amount of terrorism is likely to increase.

ANOTHER PERSPECTIVE

Using a Group to Profile

Marc Sageman changes the entire debate on profiling behavior by shifting the unit of analysis from the individual to the group and engaging in empirical study. Rather than looking for a social or psychological factor that would remain constant in changing social space and time, Sageman began looking at radicalized members of al Qaeda. Using public sources and the biographies of 172 militants, he found a common behavioral pattern in al Qaeda. The terrorists were almost exclusively male and were radicalized in the West. Most of the men were mentally stable, and they came from middle-class—sometimes wealthy—families. They had no history of violence, and few of them had arrest records. There is no evidence to show that they were recruited by a sinister network or that they were brainwashed by militant ideology. These future al Qaeda members were lost and lonely. They joined with a small group of other isolated men and began the path to radicalization. In a sense, members of the group fell in love with each other, and radical ideology or religion played only a minor role in their decisions. Group loyalty was their most important factor. Radicalization came when members of a group tried to outdo each other in zeal for al Qaeda. According to Sageman, each group was "a bunch of guys." He finds psychological parallels in the world of religious revival and cults. Sageman, who comes from both the medical and intelligence worlds, finds that it is possible to create profiles. The unit of analysis should be a particular group, not individual terrorists.

Source: Sageman, 2004.

Next, Ross believes structural factors interact with the psychological makeup of potentially violent people to produce terrorism. He says several schools of psychology can be used to explain violence, but none is adequate to explain terrorism. As a result, he identifies five psychological and other factors involved in the development of terrorism: facilitating traits, frustration/narcissism–aggression, associational drives, learning opportunities, and cost–benefit calculations.

Psychological factors change constantly and interact with each other. Facilitating traits include fear, anger, depression, guilt, antisocial behavior, a strong ego, the need for excitement, and a feeling of being lost. Ross says that the more of these traits a person exhibits, the more likely it is that the person will engage in terrorism. Frustration/narcissism–aggression means that a person has suffered a blow to the ego and reacts hostilely. Frustration refers to aggression channeled toward another person or symbol. Ross believes that high frustration may result in terrorist acts. This, in turn, interacts with structural factors to cause more violence. Associational drives are developed in group settings. Ross believes that when potential terrorists perceive benefits from particular groups, they tend to join those groups. Once inside, violent behavior is likely to increase because the group's acts of terror reinforce it. The existence of groups that engage in acts of terrorism creates an environment for teaching terrorism to others. As learning opportunities increase, Ross says, the amount of terrorism increases. Finally, violence takes place after a cost–benefit analysis. In other words, terrorists evaluate whether the cost of an attack is worth the result.

Although not a typical profile of a terrorist personality, Ross's ideas explain the transformation of terrorism across history and provide social and psychological indicators of terrorism. Ross believes certain psychological factors interact with social factors to create a climate conducive to terrorism. Laqueur (1999) says a profile cannot be obtained because terrorism is a political activity, but Ross counters by demonstrating both political and psychological factors.

Paths and Routes

John Horgan (2008), director of the International Center for the Study of Terrorism at Pennsylvania State University, has taken the profiling debate to a new level. He argues that many psychological approaches have mistakenly focused on the root causes of terrorism and the search for criminological profiles of terrorist behavior. These methods, he argues, miss the point. Rather than searching for the "roots of terrorism," Horgan believes researchers should search for the **routes to terrorism**. In other words, Horgan is concerned with the psychological processes that lead people to terrorist groups, the issues that keep them in the group, and the support for people who want to leave.

The psychology of terrorism is complex, but the process of becoming a terrorist involves three distinct phases. In the first phase, a person must decide to become a terrorist, and this is followed by a decision to remain in a terrorist group. Both of these decisions return to the arguments about justifying violence, but there are points where people decide that they can no longer accept terrorism. Horgan believes this leads to a third process, disengagement—the behavior of people who decide to abandon terrorism. These pathways to terrorism are more important than searching for a definitive profile of terrorist behavior.

If Horgan is correct, his research suggests that a more effective approach to profiling is to identify actions and policies that may help prevent the desire to join or remain in a group. It also suggests a need to understand and support the factors involved in deciding to leave a group. This approach moves the debate about profiling into another arena. Horgan asks researchers to focus on the psychological process of radicalization.

routes to terrorism: As used by John Horgan, refers to the psychological and social factors that motivate people to join and remain in terrorist groups.

 Self-Check

> Do patterns of behavior exist in terrorist groups?
> If so, how could this be used to develop a profile of terrorist behavior?
> If not, why is it difficult or impossible to profile terrorist behavior?
> Is it more profitable to focus on factors that motivate terrorists to join, remain, and leave terrorist groups?

Radicalization: Mixed Opinions

radicalization: As used in this context, refers to the psychological process of adopting extremist positions.

violent radicalization: Refers to the process of adopting extremist positions and engaging in violence based on a new set of beliefs.

alienation: Happens when an individual or group becomes lost in the dominant social world. A person or group of people is alienated when separated from the dominant values of society at large.

One of the psychological and social issues surrounding terrorism is **radicalization**. This is the process that changes a person's socially acceptable behavior into terrorism. John Horgan (2009, p. 155) states that many researchers and security experts are looking at the process of radicalization, but they miss the point. It is unrealistic to assume that programs or policies can prevent radicalization, and most of the people who hold radical views are not violent. **Violent radicalization** is the problem of terrorism, Horgan believes. Movement toward violence is a psychological process influenced by peer groups and terrorist causes. In other words, it is a social and psychological path. Brian Jenkins (2009) believes that since it is process, people moving toward violent radicalization exhibit observable signs. Family members, peers, and people closely associated with an individual may witness the behavioral changes. If this is true, others may observe them, too.

Another concept closely associated with radicalization is **alienation**, a term used in several branches of the social sciences, as well as in other disciplines such as theology. Many sociologists define alienation as a process by which an individual or group becomes separated from the values, norms, and mores of the dominant social world. This leads to self-estrangement. The concept was initially popularized by Karl Marx's work on economic alienation, and many sociologists of the nineteenth and twentieth centuries expanded his approach, focusing on concepts like social isolation, lack of meaning, and normlessness.

Many terrorism analysts began looking at radicalization and alienation in the first part of the twenty-first century; their focus tended to be on individuals attracted to Islamic extremism. Some researchers found that individual decisions were less important than the social-psychological patterns of an entire group. Members of groups became radicalized together. A clique of friends moved collectively toward terrorism, and individual identities were absorbed and redefined when the clique joined a terrorist movement (Borum, 2004; Sageman, 2004, pp. 152–156; Horgan, 2005, pp. 80–105). Further analysis indicated that paths to radicalization developed differently for different causes and different types of groups. Ethnic, nationalistic, political, and religious terrorists were radicalized in a multitude of ways (Post, 2007).

Research on radicalization and alienation is controversial. Many prominent analysts and social scientists believe that radicalization is a social process with behavior that can be observed and modeled. In addition, most of these analysts believe that alienation is part of the radicalization process. Other researchers maintain that radicalization may be a social process, but many aspects of human behavior are the results of social processes. These researchers maintain that radicalization is a broad category that offers little useful information. There are so many commonalities between the social processes associated with alienation and radicalization that many critics believe the topics are too broad to produce practical results. Both of these points of view merit further consideration.

Research in Group Processes

A number of researchers believe that members of terrorist groups go through decision-making processes while they are being violently radicalized (Sageman, 2004, pp. 152–156; Borum, 2004; Ryan, 2007; Post, 2008; Hoffman, 2009; Rinehart, 2009; Kershaw, 2010; Ganor, 2011). Research in the area has been expanding over the past decade, and there are many emergent findings. One position maintains that radicalization can be understood as a process of socialization: It is the result of learning to engage in radicalized violence (Wilner and Dubouloz, 2011). Case studies provide rich data to determine individual paths (Ganor, 2011; Vidino, 2011). Another area of growing research is the process of de-radicalization. Although more data is needed, some preliminary findings suggest that if a person can go through a process of radicalization, the person can reverse the path and become de-radicalized (Gunaratna and Ali, 2010; Horgan and Braddock, 2010). Empirical evidence is still emerging, however, and our knowledge of radicalization is incomplete (Dalgaard-Nielson, 2010).

Marc Sageman (2004) was one of the first analysts to suggest that radicalization could be modeled and observed. Sageman presents radicalization as a six-step framework. It starts with alienated young men who find other groups of alienated young men. They "discover" religion as a way of giving meaning to their lives. Terrorism enters the equation if the newfound religious orientation turns to violence. Regardless, it remains difficult to join a terrorist group. They must meet a broker, an activist who knows actual terrorists, and be accepted by an actual terrorist group.

Sageman's framework applies to groups of males, but radicalization also occurs among women. Some recent research suggests that women are attracted to religious study groups as a social outlet in traditional cultures in which they are not given the same opportunities as men. The group gives them a means of social expression and acceptance apart from the male-dominated culture. Radicalization depends on the nature of a study group and the beliefs of dominant males in their lives. If these groups and dominant males emphasize militancy, the women in a study group may become radicalized toward religious violence (Ali, 2007; International Crisis Group, 2009). Paradoxically, women who struggle against a male-dominated culture may reject radicalization as an expression against a male-dominated ultraconservative religious culture (King, 2009).

Summarizing Sageman's Model

STEP 1 Alienated young man

STEP 2 Meets other alienated young men and forms bond

INTERIM They become a "Bunch of Guys"

STEP 3 Groups gravitate toward religion

INTERIM They outdo each other in zeal in order to express love for the group

STEP 4 Religion interpreted in militant terms

INTERIM Most groups stop at this point

STEP 5 Militant group meets terrorist contact

STEP 6 Militants join terrorists as a group decision

Johnny Ryan (2007) maintains that there are behavioral commonalities as groups move toward violence. Radicalization is the result of "Four Ps": persecution, precedent, piety, and perseverance. He believes that these four concepts present a single interpretive framework that can be used to understand militant rhetoric and violent behavior. Ryan does this by comparing militant Islamic groups with Irish Republican militancy. He argues that both types of groups feel they have been persecuted, and that both groups have experienced this over an extended period of time. The history of persecution presented a precedent for resisting the persecutors. Violence became a righteous or almost sacred action of devotion for both Republicans and Islamic militants. Ryan believes both ideologies have continued over time, and each generation is called upon to make new sacrifices.

The message of radicalization is recognizable and based on experience. Ryan says that al Qaeda and its associated networks explain revolutionary theory in an ideological manner similar to the IRA. Both Republican and Islamic militants present historical grievances to prove that revolutionary violence is the only alternative to an unjust system. He believes that radicalization cuts across cultures. It can be understood by the formula of heroes and martyrs, grievances against the superior power, and utopian goals that are articulated in the revolutionary message. It is an observable process and can be used to explain violence.

Other researchers have come to the conclusion that there is no single process of being radicalized, but that radicalization can occur in a variety of ways. John Horgan (2009) finds that radicalization occurs as individuals make decisions within the group. These observable points can be found when an individual decides to join a terrorist group, when the group moves from rhetoric to violence, and when individuals make the decision to either stay with or leave the group.

Michael King and Donald Taylor (2011) say that radicalization is a process that is not specifically applicable to any national, political, religious, or ideological group. They examine several models in an attempt to find commonalities in research findings. Beginning with Marc Sageman and Sageman's subsequent work with the New York City Police Department (discussed previously), King and Taylor believe that some form of deprivation or alienation takes place in the initial steps of the model. Steps toward radicalization are a logical response to feelings of alienation.

King and Taylor also believe three other models dominate the research field in radicalization. The first model focuses on social and economic deprivation and the resentment resulting from it. Deprivation leads to blaming an outside group for the group's situation, and the outside group is demonized. This provides an opportunity for violent radicalization.

The second model is based on long-term learning. As in the previous model, a group feels that it is victimized. In other words, they feel deprived because they can never hope to live as well as the group that is victimizing them. Some members of the group eventually seek to understand the reason they are deprived. The answers lead to resentment, and the process is exacerbated when the group has religious goals or is seeking a religious explanation for deprivation. In this model, a group's orientation is refocused and radicalization is learned over a period of time.

A third model maintains that radicalization is the result of psychological interpretation of events. Individuals in deprived economic circumstances gravitate toward one another and generally resent the position of a superior group. They develop options to attack what they see as unfair treatment. Aggression eventually emerges if the group becomes morally outraged and develops a solidified sense of injustice. Once the group takes a terrorist action, the radicalization process is completed.

King and Taylor combine all the models to suggest three areas for further study. The first area is to seek to understand how people react to relative deprivation. A second factor involves understanding how a group interprets its identity. This means that researchers need to locate and describe social processes involved in creating subjective reality. The final area involves personality types. King and Taylor believe it is necessary to understand why people exposed to the same social environment react in different ways—most of them do not engage in terrorism.

Groups in Prison

Recent reports suggest that groups are being radicalized in prison, and Mark Hamm (2007) has conducted the definitive study of prison radicalization in the United States. The process in prison usually involves a charismatic leader who gathers a number of individuals in an entourage. A leader will often target selected prisoners for a group, or will dominate new inmates, intimidating them until they join the group. Hamm maintains that recruitment is similar to procedures used by street gangs.

Terrorists also use recruiters who are not incarcerated. This is most frequently associated with religion, and the person who recruits and radicalizes potential terrorists may bea visiting chaplain. A chaplain has access to prisoners and may claim freedom of religion while delivering a radical message. Hamm says militant chaplains also distribute radical literature in the form of religious works.

Most of the people who enter prison have to adjust psychologically to the loss of freedom, constant monitoring, and threatened violence from other prisoners. This frequently leaves a new inmate, especially people in prison for the first time, in a state of crisis. Recruiters for a radical cause often recognize differing types of crises, and they try to bring individuals to the radical cause with strategies that match the psychological state of the person they hope to entice.

Hamm found five common patterns of converting people to violent radical causes. The first contains people in crisis, who will respond to religious overtures for emotional support. A second type involves people seeking protection in the prison

---

PRISON RADICALIZATION—Mark Hamm's research for the National Institute of Justice concludes that inmates are recruited and radicalized in a number of ways:

Crisis Convert—joins a radical group as a result of a personal crisis

Protection-Seeking Convert—seeks a group out of fear

Searching Converts—have been exposed to religion, but seek deeper meaning while in prison

Manipulating Converts—are controlled by a strong member inside a group

Free-World Converters—result from chaplains outside of the system who spread literature and preach radicalization

Source: Hamm, 2007.

FIGURE **2.4**

environment. These people will convert because the radical group offers safety. The third group of potential converts—Hamm calls these people searches—have had little exposure to religion, and they are fascinated by both the multiplicity of religious expressions inside prison and the feeling of belonging among members of the group. The fourth personality is common in prison. It involves manipulating people for personal gain. Finally, Hamm classifies chaplains from the outside as free-world recruiters.

Behind almost every conversion, according to Hamm, lies a friendship or kinship link, but sometimes a new inmate simply meets somebody in the yard and converts to a new faith. Radicalization tends to take place among two factions and three major groups. The first faction involves various Muslim groups who use cut-and-paste versions of the Quran, and the second group centers around white supremacy. This results in three major groups: (1) Islamic extremism, (2) Christian extremists who use selected biblical passages to justify their views, and (3) white supremacists who have adopted the Norse pantheon of Odin, Thor, Frida, and the other gods and goddesses (Martin, 2007; Hamm, 2009).

Patterns of prison radicalization in other countries seem to follow patterns similar to those uncovered by Hamm, but the level of the threat they represent varies. In central Asia, the prison systems are deteriorating, and it is difficult to monitor outside religious leaders who make visits to inmates. Militant Islamic missionaries use this situation as an opportunity to radicalize individuals. Militant converts are growing inside central Asian prisons, threatening to further disrupt correctional operations. In addition, individuals seek to join other militant groups outside the prison after they are released. Prison radicalization is a growing threat in central Asia (International Crisis Institute, 2009).

The United Kingdom, on the other hand, has experienced similar missionary activity, but it does not present as great a problem (Gartenstein-Ross, 2009). At this point, researchers know that radicalization takes place inside prison, but there is not enough evidence to indicate how dangerous the threat is.

Individual Radicalization

There is evidence to suggest that radicalization is not always a group process, or at least that it involves individual reflection whether a group plays a role or not. Post's (2007) research shows that individual psychological and sociological factors create the framework for interpreting reality. The influence of social structure serves as the major background for interpreting reality for most individuals. Post says that ideology is transferred from generation to generation within this framework, and he believes that traditions of radicalization are passed in this manner.

Earlier research by Martin van Creveld (1991) and Thomas P.M. Barnett (2005) reinforces the pattern presented by Post. Radicalization tends to happen with individual interpretation of larger actions. The probability of individual radicalization increases when a relatively weak group feels that its existence is threatened and that it has been victimized by a superior power. Feelings increase if the superior group dominating the threatened group is believed to be morally depraved. These situations create the social and psychological conditions for a person to become radicalized. All social conventions pass by the way and the radicalized victim comes to believe that terrorism is the only weapon for the weak to use against the strong.

Alienation and radicalization are the results of social and psychological interpretations of reality. Interpretations of reality involve social meaning and structure, the ability to move as described in Black's social geometry, and narratives created through social identity. In fact, the individual interpretation of reality and the process of becoming a terrorist tie most of the theories presented in this chapter together. All types of criminology help to explain the processes of individual radicalization because the social sciences focus on the complexity of human behavior, and practical criminology gives security forces a tactical view of the challenges they face.

Cases of Radicalization

Concrete examples provide illustrations of radicalization. Bruce Hoffman (2009) and Boaz Ganor (2011) have used case studies to explain radicalization in Europe. Individual cases in the United States may also be used. **Umar Farouk Abdulmutallab** tried to destroy a Northwest airliner as it entered American airspace after a six-hour flight from Amsterdam on Christmas 2009. He attempted to detonate explosives hidden in his underwear. Passengers noticed Abdulmutallab's suspicious behavior as the plane neared Detroit, and he was subdued after trying to light the explosives. An American intelligence official assessed the incident by concluding that local issues in the Middle East had driven Abdulmutallab to a global act of terrorism (Dickey, 2010).

Abdulmutallab's story illustrates the complexity of radicalization. He would seem to have been a poor candidate to fall under the influence of Arabian militants. Born to a wealthy Nigerian family, he received an elite education and went to the United Kingdom to complete boarding school and college. Yet he felt alone and isolated. Raised with a set of tolerant Islamic values, his experience in London challenged his concept of right and wrong. He was alienated. He eventually found solace on militant websites and gravitated toward radicalism. Falling under the influence of a militant preacher, Abdulmutallab eventually joined a militant group in Yemen and began the attempted suicide mission (Hosenball, Isikoff, and Evans, 2010; *New York Times*, 2010).

In another instance, **James W. von Brunn** walked into the United States Holocaust Memorial Museum in Washington, D.C., on a summer day in 2009. He began shooting, sending frightened tourists scrambling for cover. He was wounded by security guards, but not before he fatally wounded Stephen T. Johns, one of the officers trying to stop him. It was not the first time von Brunn had encountered law enforcement. He tried to take the Federal Reserve Board hostage in 1981, and was sentenced to prison for the attempt. Von Brunn wanted to wage war on the federal government.

Von Brunn's radical development did not take place in a vacuum. He had a long history of being a loner and a white supremacist. According to news reports, he consumed information from neo-Nazi groups, and he believed that Jews were in league with nonwhite races to destroy white Americans and Europeans. Von Brunn developed antigovernment, racist, and anti-Semitic views over decades, maintaining a hate-filled website after his release from prison. He attacked the Holocaust Museum as a final act of rage (Stout, 2009; Wilber, 2010).

James von Brunn's life had the makings for success. Born in the Midwest, he was strong, good-looking, and educated. He entered military service in the Second World War, and returned to enter advertising in New York City. He married into an established East Coast family in 1951, and seemed to be on his way to a successful career. Unfortunately, there was another side to von Brunn. He hated Jews with a militant passion. His hatred abated during the war, but it increased after moving to New York City. He began writing about his views, growing increasingly bigoted against both Jews and nonwhites. It eventually cost him his marriage, but not his deeper journey into anti-Semitism (Ruane, 2009).

The reasons for von Brunn's radical descent into hatred are not clear, but there were influences in his life that seem to have spawned an individualized journey into bigotry. He belonged to a German–American friendship group in the late 1930s that served as a front for the Nazi Party. After his divorce, according to the *Washington Post*, he traveled a path into deeper paranoia and virulent anti-Semitism. This eventually led to his attempted attack on the Federal Reserve Board in 1981. After being released from prison, he developed even stronger beliefs and began writing and managing a website. Two years before the museum attack, the only son from his first

Umar Farouk Abdulmutallab: (b. 1986) According to a federal indictment, smuggled a chemical bomb and chemical igniter in a syringe onto a Northwest flight from Amsterdam to Detroit on December 25, 2009. He was born into a family that practiced Islam but became radicalized while attending school in the United Kingdom. He was allegedly trained by terrorists in Yemen, who supplied the explosive compound.

James W. von Brunn: (1920–2010) An American white supremacist and anti-Semite. He entered the Holocaust Museum on June 10, 2009, and began shooting. He killed a security officer before he was wounded and subdued. He died in federal custody while awaiting trial.

marriage committed suicide. In 2009, he apparently decided he had had enough and that the government and the Jews were going to pay (Ruane, 2009).

Omar Hammami:
(b. 1984) An American leader of Al Shabaab, under the name of Abu Mansoor al-Amriki.

The various paths to radicalization are not very clear. **Omar Hammami** was one of the coolest kids in his Alabama high school. He came from a loving family with a Muslim father and a Christian mother. Both parents kept their faith, and Omar was baptized in a Southern Baptist church. He dated the most popular girls in his high school and seemed destined for success. Yet Omar felt alone and began searching for his Islamic roots. His Syrian father began taking him to Friday prayers, and Omar became engrossed in a deep internal conflict. He did not know if he was Christian or Muslim. He came to a radical conclusion (Elliot, 2010).

The conflict in Somalia has caused a number of second- and third-generation Somalis to go through a process similar to Hammami's journey. A group of promising young men from Minneapolis have abandoned their promising futures to search for their Somali roots. Some of them have turned to militancy by actually going to Somalia and joining a jihadist group called **Al Shabaab**. Omar understood this decision. His identity conflict ended when he embraced a violent, intolerant form of Islam. Shocking his Muslim father and Christian mother, Omar abandoned his family and future to become a commander in Al Shabaab. He fights and makes jihadist recruiting videos under his nom de guerre, Abu Mansoor al-Amriki (Elliot, 2010).

Al Shabaab: (also known as the Harakat Shabaab al-Mujahedeen, the Youth, Mujahedeen Youth Movement, and Mujahedeen Al Shabaab Movement) Formed as a militant wing of a federation of Islamic courts in Somalia in 2006. Its senior leadership is affiliated with al Qaeda.

Commonalities in Radicalization

In the examples of Abdulmatallab, von Brunn, and Hammami, there are several common forms of behavior. First, it is interesting to note that the three men all came from well-to-do, middle-class environments. *The New York Times* reports that most international attacks against the United States in the twenty-first century have come from well-educated terrorists from the middle class (Mackey, 2010). Gerald Post (2007) argues that such regularities are common to the radicalization process. All three men became deeply angered and filled with moral indignation. This was reinforced by identifying with a victimized group and the desire to violently redress grievances. They were alienated from mainstream thought as they expressed anger, and they sought to address their situations by doing something meaningful. Finally, there was some type of event that triggered their decision to take violent action.

Recall that Brian Jenkins (2009) believes there are common behavioral patterns associated with radicalization. These patterns may be observed by family members, friends, and other associates. If Jenkins is correct, this would suggest that there is some merit in identifying the behaviors associated with radicalization and in training security personnel to search for and recognize them. This is not to suggest that the National Counter terrorism Center is incorrect in its proposal that security and law enforcement agencies have a broader mission than counter terrorism and that indicators may be valuable to such agencies.

For example, assume that you are the chief of a mid-size American police agency of 120 personnel. Your officers have recently been trained in the six-step model gleaned from Sageman. Recall that this is: (1) alienated youth, (2) join other alienated youths, (3) they seek orientation in religion, (4) their religion is militarized, (5) they encounter an actor who knows terrorists, and (6) the actor introduces them to the terrorists and they join. Because there are differing paths to radicalization, there are more models, but we will use this model for illustration.

Assume the training has taken place and your officers are looking for these behavioral patterns during investigations and routine patrol operations. If this happens, you would soon be receiving field contact information and reports that identify alienated young people and the groups they join throughout your jurisdiction. This would help identify potential problems in schools, communities, and other organizations. It would also help to identify potentially harmful directions in which alienated young people could move, such as gangs or other criminal groups. Although the original purpose was to gather information on terrorism, the overall result produces a more comprehensive picture of your community. It is part of a concept known as Total Criminal Intelligence, which will be discussed in the last section of the book.

With 120 personnel, department budgets, and community safety, you have many problems in your jurisdiction. The probability of terrorism in your jurisdiction may be low, but if it happens, its impact will be critical. In addition, the media, citizens, and elected officials will ask you what you did to prevent it after the event has occurred. By training officers to recognize the signs of radicalization, you will have taken a proactive step before an incident and have another tool that allows for better deployment of resources because the process gives you a more strategic view of the community (see Saupp, 2010).

Empirical research suggests that even though radicalization resembles other forms of behavior, there are some distinct issues involved. In religious radicalization, people exhibit distinctive forms of behavior, and these may appear in any sequence (Gartenstein and Grossman, 2009). They adopt rigid, literalist interpretations of religion. They trust only selected radical sources of theological information, and they tolerate no deviance from their interpretation. These patterns can be seen across many religions (White, 2010).

When Islam is involved, there are other behavioral indicators. People being radicalized accept the idea of the "clash of civilizations," and they believe that the West is at war with Islam. They selectively interpret government actions to prove the point. They also aggressively and vehemently attempt to convert other Muslims to their point of view, and publicly denounce those who will not follow them. They either break away from mainstream mosques or join an organization that supports their interpretation of religion. Finally, they begin adopting traditional forms of dress (Gartenstein and Grossman, 2009).

Eli Berman's (2009, pp. 30–35) suggestion about violent groups is also worth noting when security forces are dealing with terrorism. The number of terrorist groups is rather small, while the number of radicalized people is very large. The key to counterterrorism is to focus radicalized individuals when they try to join the militant group. John Horgan (2009, p. 155) complements this idea with another tactic: It is virtually impossible to control all the factors that may radicalize a person, but there are points when terrorists want to leave the organization. It is important to know how to extricate people. They might always be radicalized, Horgan points out, but if they are not engaged in violence, they are not terrorists.

Research Criticized

Not everybody believes that research in radicalization and alienation will produce valuable knowledge. The National Counterterrorism Center (2010, p. 133), a federal agency created in 2004 to integrate all information gathered on international terrorism, officially says that this type of information does not help analysts understand the process of radicalization. Indicators of radicalization reflect experiences and behaviors seen in all people. In addition, people who are radicalized are motivated by local issues, and radicalization is so diverse that its myriad sources are difficult to discern. Therefore, the so-called signs of radicalization are really only signs of human behavior. According to the National Counter terrorism Center, there is little need to study the processes of radicalization.

Mark Sedgwick (2009) complains that there is no consensus about the definition of radicalization. Many researchers use the term, but it is used in a variety of different contexts. Security experts see radicalization as a problem for law enforcement, while those concerned with eliminating relative economic deprivation seek to integrate minority groups into the dominant system. On a grander scale, foreign policy experts look at radicalization as a problem created by networks of groups, schools, and national or regional ideologies. All of these contexts are different, and each approach has its own set of assumptions and research agendas. Sedgwick believes that the term "radicalization" simply confuses everybody. He proposes a solution: Abandon the use of the word as an absolute, definitive concept.

Chetan Bhatt (2009) believes radicalization is associated with alienation. He looks at Muslim populations inside the United Kingdom and argues that Western governments seek to integrate and assimilate immigrant populations. This poses a problem because many immigrants choose to maintain their native identity, including political and religious affiliations. This does not represent a path toward political violence; however, it does indicate a rejection of Western norms. It is possible to argue that continued identification with traditional values is a form of purposeful alienation. The new country's values and norms are rejected, while the old country's ways are incorporated in a different society.

Bhatt compares Pakistani militia movements and immigration of central Asians into northwest London. The issue does not appear to be alienation. Bhatt argues that the Muslim community is exposed to a wide array of militant thinking, and this thinking may impact the subsequent decisions of young people to support militant groups or to take violent action. Militant ideology is not the main source of the decision to engage in violence; rather, the growth of international organizations to train paramilitary fighters is the source of militancy. The primary culprit is the intelligence agency of Pakistan. By supporting militant groups that use terrorist tactics, Pakistan has created new associations between international paramilitary groups and Muslim immigrants in the United Kingdom. Militancy is not a result of alienation; it is a conscious decision to maintain national identity and sacrifice for a greater cause.

Frazer Egerton (2011) states that the common perception of the Salafi–jihadist movement is related to alienation. Yet writers in this field seldom define what they mean when using the term alienation, and the term is generally under-theorized and over-applied. The discussion of alienation, he asserts, is intuitive but unsubstantiated. One of the common approaches, he argues, is to look at structure. It is commonly assumed that young Muslim males, aged 15 to 30, are alienated from social structures and as a result, they are frustrated and are attracted to violent ideologies.

In other versions of structural alienation, young males are seeking meaning and they move toward religion to find that meaning. As a young man becomes more and more involved in religious activities, he moves toward radical interpretations of the religion and subsequently to violence. A variant of the religious journey involves the relationship between economic deprivation and terrorist violence. This version of structural alienation maintains that poor economic conditions alienate young men from society and lead them to take out their frustration in violence. Another popular version of structural alienation involves ethnic exclusion. Proponents of this theory maintain that when people are excluded from normative society due to their race or ethnicity, they respond with violence.

Egerton concludes that while such theories are attractive and are used to explain terrorist violence, they are overly generalized. For example, very few people respond to alienation with terrorist violence. In addition, most religious behavior, even fervent, intolerant religious beliefs, do not lead to terrorism. Egerton suggests that social scientists avoid using the term. He says that the concept of alienation is nuanced and complex. It exists in degrees, and is manifested in several different ways. To suggest that someone is alienated is to ignore the complexity of human behavior. Researchers will obtain more fruitful results by examining militant ideology and finding the concepts that attract followers.

Self-Check

> What is the process of radicalization?
> How do various scholars model radicalization?
> What commonalties appear in examples of people who were radicalized?
> What are some limitations on knowledge gained from studies of radicalization and alienation?

CHAPTER TAKE AWAYS

Terrorism is a social process and it can be studied with the same methods used by social scientists. One method is to search for meanings behind actions. Another way to analyze terrorism is to look for structures. Black's social geometry shows movement within structures, and the netwar metaphor represents a practical application of this technique. Researchers who believe that modern terrorism has been changed by religion look for meanings that drive actions. Security forces use both methods, searching for practical behavior clues that can be used against terrorists. They often search for the ways that terrorist behavior differs from normal criminals, and they seek understanding the ways terrorists justify violence. Some researchers have tried to model terrorism by profiling terrorists or looking for models of radicalization and alienation.

OBJECTIVE SUMMARY

- Social scientists examine actions from a variety of perspectives, and this impacts the way researchers look at terrorism. Some analysts look at the manner in which groups attach meanings to actions. Another accepted method is to look at the social structures that support action.
- Netwar is a structural method for examining terrorism. The analogy assumes that terrorism takes place within a network of social connections. Actions take place at nodes, or connections in the network. The goal of counterterrorism is to disrupt the network.
- Scholars and analysts who use religion as a way of examining terrorism use meaning and structural frameworks. They believe that religion influences behavior. It does so by placing terrorism within the context of a sacred story giving new meanings to the actions a group takes or the social structures supporting the organization.
- Law enforcement, intelligence, and military communities use both meaning and structural approaches to understand terrorism. Security forces do not look for theories about behavior. They look for practical results to neutralize terrorism. Therefore, they approach criminology from a practical perspective.
- The behavior of criminals and terrorists differs. Criminals tend to be unfocused and not dedicated to a cause. Terrorists are focused and dedicated. Some analysts believe that religious terrorists are more dedicated than political terrorists.
- All people, including terrorists, must feel that they are justified in their behavior. Socially, terrorists are justified by the use of group reinforcement, ideology, and symbols.
- Some scholars believe that terrorist behavior cannot be profiled because it fluctuates with historical, political, and social circumstances. Others believe that profiles are possible if social factors are matched to a behavioral profile.
- Some scholars have developed models of alienation and radicalization. They believe that models help researchers to understand terrorism. Models differ, but social alienation seems to be a common element among models. Other researchers believe that terms like radicalization and alienation are too broad.

Critical Engagement: The Edges of Radicalization

Scott Helfstein (2012) argues that radicalization is the result of ideological beliefs gradually merging with social definitions of reality. In a study for the Combating Terrorism Center at West Point, he states that understanding the process of radicalization may impact the ability to produce a terrorist profile. In the past, profiling models were attempts to categorize behavioral characteristics. His study suggests that the study of the interaction between social and ideological behavior may produce a theory that would have practical results for counterterrorists.

Very few people are motivated to take violent action while they are in isolation. Instead, they are radicalized through social interaction. Ideology is important at the beginning of the process because it reinforces an individual's interpretation of social reality. As an individual moves closer to terrorist violence, the group's reinforcement of an individual's actions is crucial. Once a person accepts violence and becomes part of a violent group, the need for external validation is minimized because the group itself is reinforcing violent attitudes among its members. Helfstein calls this self-serving extremism.

He concludes by saying that our approach to radicalization and profiling has been incorrect. Rather than trying to counter an ideology or list the psychological characteristics of a terrorist, it is important to look at both the ideological and social processes surrounding radicalization. Radicalization takes place because an individual becomes involved in a group where social standing is increased and self-interest needs are met. While he calls for further empirical research, Helfstein'sstudy suggests that radicalization takes place because a violent group meets the social needs and enhances the prestige of its members and potential recruits.

Consider these issues in terms of future developments:

- If Helfstein is correct, can the social factors causing people to join violent groups be modeled?
- How could the focus on profiling be shifted from mapping individual psychological traits to isolating the ideological and social indicators that make membership in a violent group attractive?
- If it is possible to recognize these indicators, what types of intervention might prevent an individual from joining a violent group?

KEY TERMS

CHAPTER 3

The Organization and Financing of Terrorism

AP Photo/Gregory Bull

LEARNING OBJECTIVES

After reading this chapter, you should be able to:

> Summarize rural, urban, and insurgent models of terrorism.

> Trace the evolution of terrorist organizational structures.

> Discuss the challenges involved in leading a terrorist group.

> Describe the issues involved in terrorist financing.

> Describe legal and illegal sources of income.

> Explain the ways funds are disbursed in an underground economy.

> Describe the hawala system.

> Summarize views on the political economy of terrorism.

> Outline the manners in which drugs and terrorism overlap.

In January 2012 special forces from the Mexican army conducted a helicopter raid on a ranch in northern Mexico. During the raid the government captured many workers for the Sinaloa Cartel, one of the country's most deadly drug trafficking organizations. The special forces also shot and killed the regional leader of the cartel. The Sinaloa Cartel is not a terrorist organization, but its activities are closely related to terrorism. It has turned some areas of Mexico into a virtual shell state, that is, an area where the official government cannot effectively rule. The cartel also uses the same underground networks used by terrorists. In addition, cartel members use terrorist tactics as they operate. Since the cartel represents a threat to both Mexico and the United States, it has become associated with the term narcoterrorism. Operating in an underground economy, it is a traditional organized crime syndicate, yet it is connected inside a network that includes terrorism. The tremendous profits from the sale of illegal drugs can also be used to finance terrorism. As you examine the organization and financing of terrorism, you may conclude that it is difficult to differentiate between the Sinaloa Cartel and terrorist organizations in Central and South America.

Terrorist organizations evolve over time. Terrorists need to move, develop more effective and daring tactics, create new structures, and modify communications to avoid detection. They also need resources, logistics, and financing. Organizations that do not change when security forces develop their own networks of information can be eliminated. Two factors interact with change: the organization's structure and its finances. These factors, in turn, are influenced by the strategic philosophy of a particular movement, a philosophy that can be historically modeled. Accordingly, security forces need to understand the principles of a group's strategy and tactics, the way it is organized, and its support mechanisms.

Many of the organizational traits of terrorism are unique to a particular campaign, but there are broad patterns behind the particularities. It is important to understand the idea motivating the group. For example, does it view terrorism as a selective tactic, or is the strategy to terrorize an entire population? Security forces also need to map the internal workings of a group and identify members and key personnel. In the twenty-first century, several governments have come to realize that open, accountable financial systems can be used to track the fiscal systems of terrorism, but a deeper understanding is necessary. Financial investigators are trained to uncover money laundering and movements of large amounts of goods and currency. Terrorists, however, do not operate that way.

Strategic philosophy, organizational structures, and financing are important when trying to understand, prevent, and investigate terrorism. This chapter explores these topics within the context of changing terrorist networks.

Models of Terrorism

The first wave of modern terrorism appeared in Africa and Asia after 1945. For the next 20 years, nationalistic rebellions broke out against Western colonial powers in struggles for independence. Some of the movements involved long guerrilla wars in which terrorism was used as a tactic to support a general movement. After roughly 1965, ideological terrorism brought a more urban model, employing terrorism as a strategy because no other weapons were available. Religious terrorists began employing the same urban model in the 1980s. Yet something else had been happening. Anticolonial movements in places like Kenya and Algeria were based on nationalistic revolts. This was nothing new, but tactics were evolving. By the twenty-first century, a new model of insurrection seemed to have evolved.

These three models—rural, urban, and insurrection—represent general trends from 1945 to the present. Since terrorism is dynamic, the models are generalizations. They do not represent a rigid classification system that defines a movement, but they do illustrate shifts in the strategy and tactics of terrorism. These models help to explain the evolution and practice of contemporary terrorism, and they embody the philosophy behind particular types of terrorist movements.

Guerrilla Warfare and Rural Terrorism

Guerrilla war is an age-old phenomenon. Several nationalistic rebellions after World War II were based on guerrilla war, including the long campaign that toppled the Chinese government in 1949. Mao Zedong (1893–1976) inspired both fellow communist and nationalistic revolutionaries, but the Cuban Revolution from 1956 to 1959 captured the minds of left-wing ideologues. They came to view guerrilla war as a statement of struggle against capitalist powers, and terrorism had a special role in this revolution (see Wickham-Crowley, 1992, pp. 51–59).

The Cuban Revolution did not create guerrilla warfare, but it popularized it throughout the world. Despite only one other guerrilla movement having succeeded in overthrowing an established government—the Nicaraguan Sandinistas

FIGURE **3.1** Central America and the Caribbean

in 1979—guerrilla war is the preferred method of fighting among Latin American revolutionaries. Unlike the model for urban terrorism, the guerrilla model began with a successful structure, then moved toward a theory (see March, 2005; O'Connor, 2006).

The process began in the hills of Cuba. The Cuban revolutionary leader Fidel Castro tried to seize power in 1956, but he was soundly defeated. Retreating to the rural regions of Cuba, he surrounded himself with a ragtag group of revolutionaries, including a friend, **Ernesto "Che" Guevara** (1928–1967). Guevara was born in Argentina in 1928. After earning a medical degree at the University of Buenos Aires, he turned his attention from medicine to the plight of the poor. He believed poverty and repression were problems that transcended nationalism, and revolution was the only means of challenging authority. He served the regime of Guatemala in 1954 but fled to Mexico City when communists were purged from the government. There he met Castro.

Guevara immediately impressed Castro, and the two worked together to oust the Cuban military dictator Fulgencio Batista (1901–1973). After failing to seize power in 1956, Castro began to meet secretly with rural partisans. Castro organized a command-and-support structure, enlisted partisans, and formed regional guerrilla forces. As Castro's strength grew, he moved to more conventional methods of warfare and triumphantly entered Havana in 1959. Throughout the campaign, Guevara had been at Castro's side.

Ernesto "Che" Guevara (1928–1967): Fidel Castro's assistant and guerrilla warfare theorist. Guevara advocated guerrilla revolutions throughout Latin America after success in the Cuban Revolution. He was killed in Bolivia in 1967 while trying to form a guerrilla army.

Guevara: On Guerrilla Warfare

Inflamed with revolutionary passion, Guevara completed a work on guerrilla warfare shortly after Castro took power. Far from theoretical, it can be deemed a how-we-did-it guide. Translated copies of Guevara's *Reminiscences of the Cuban Revolutionary War* appeared in the United States as early as 1961, but the book did not enjoy mass distribution until the end of the decade. It describes both Guevara's evolution toward Marxism and the revolutionary process in Cuba, and it details the

Cuban guerrilla war:
A three-step process as described by Che Guevara: (1) Revolutionaries join the indigenous population to form guerrilla *foco*, as Guevara called them; (2) small forces form columns and control rural areas; and (3) columns unite for a conventional offensive to overthrow government.

structure and strategy of Castro's forces, as well as the guiding philosophy of the **Cuban guerrilla war**. Guevara also outlines the revolutionaries' methods of operation and principles of engagement. With the advantage of hindsight, it makes a stirring description of how victory was achieved.

Guerrilla revolutions based on the Cuban experience are typified by three phases, each designed to progress from and complement the previous one. In phase one, Guevara-style revolution begins with isolated groups. In phase two, the isolated groups merge into guerrilla columns. The final phase brings columns together in a conventional army. The goal of the strategy is to develop a conventional fighting force, or at least a force that renders the conventional opponent impotent. Although Guevara's work focused specifically on the Cuban experience, it had two important effects. In Latin America and to revolutionaries there, in particular, Guevara became an icon. In addition, guerrillas throughout the world studied the guide and copied the tactics used during the revolution (see Burton, 1976, p. 70; J. K. Clark, 1988; Asprey, 2002, pp. 698–710; Taber, 2002, pp. 25–37).

Terrorism plays a limited role in Guevara's guerrilla framework. Although Guevara's focus was on the countryside, he saw the need for small urban terrorist groups to wage a campaign of support. These actions, however, should be extremely selective; their purpose is to keep governmental forces off balance, terrorizing them in their "safe" areas, never letting them relax. The main purpose of terrorism is to strike at the government's logistical network; a secondary purpose is to demoralize the government. Terrorism is a commando-type tactic.

Debray: Expanding Guerrilla Warfare

The theory of guerrilla war came after the appearance of Guevara's work, and it was popularized by a French socialist named Régis Debray. In *Revolution in the Revolution?* Debray (1967) summarizes his concept of Latin American politics. He writes that the region has one dominating issue: poverty. Poverty threads through the entire fabric of Latin American life and entwines divergent cultures and peoples in a common knot of misery. Poverty is responsible for the imbalance in the class structure, as the wealthy cannot be maintained without the poverty of the masses. Debray sees only one recourse: The class structure must be changed and wealth redistributed. Because the wealthy will never give up their power, revolution is the only method of change.

Debray's prime target was the United States. Behind every power in the south stands the United States, according to his thesis. Debray held the United States responsible for maintaining the inequitable class structure, and he shared the common Marxist belief that North American wealth caused Latin American poverty. It was quite logical, therefore, to target the United States.

As did Frantz Fanon, Debray continually talked of revolution. He saw little need for terrorism, however, and he minimized the role of urban centers in a revolt. Debray believed revolution was essentially an affair for poor peasants, and it could begin only in a rural setting with regional guerrilla forces. Terrorism had no payoff. At best, it was neutral, and at worst, it alienated the peasants needed for guerrilla support. According to Debray, for a revolution to work, it needed to begin with guerrillas fighting for justice and end with a united conventional force. Terrorism would not accomplish this objective.

Urban Terrorism

The model for modern urban terrorism was intellectually championed by Frantz Fanon (1925–1961). Born on Martinique in 1925, Fanon studied medicine in France and became a psychiatrist. When Algeria revolted against French rule in 1954, Fanon was sent to Algiers, the capital of Algeria, to work in a mental hospital. His experiences there caused him to side with the rebels. Fanon believed the pressures caused by exploitative imperialism were the primary causes of mental illness in Algeria. He produced two works, *The Wretched of the Earth* (1982) and *A Dying Colonialism* (1965), as a result of his Algerian experiences. He died of cancer in 1961, a year before the Algerian War ended, unable to play a leading role in revolutions; his thought, however, was strongly imprinted on Africa, Asia, and Latin America (see University of Singapore, 2007).

In *The Wretched of the Earth*, Fanon indicts colonial powers and calls on all the colonized to practice terrorism. He writes that Western powers have dehumanized non-Western people by destroying their cultures and replacing them with Western values. Even when Westerners are not present, they are represented by a native middle class that embraces Western values and turns its back on the general population. Native culture is forgotten by the middle class as native intellectualism is replaced by Western traditions. The masses end up suffering a perpetual identity crisis: In order to succeed, they are forced to deny their heritage. Fanon argues that the natives can follow only one course of action: revolution.

To be sure, Fanon was no Gandhi. His only argument was for violent revolt, including guerrilla warfare and acts of terrorism. He claimed decolonization was destined to be a violent process because it involved replacing one group of powerful people with another group. No group would willingly surrender power. Therefore, according to Fanon, achieving freedom was inherently violent. Political action and peaceful efforts toward change were useless. Only when oppressed people recognized that violence was their only alternative would they be assured of victory. Fanon saw guerrilla warfare and individual acts of terrorism as tools of revolution. Guerrilla war was the initial method of revolt because third-world revolutionaries could not mount direct, conventional campaigns at the beginning of their struggles. Fanon's concept of guerrilla warfare was based in rural revolution, but urban terrorism would become the major weapon rendering colonial administration impotent.

Terrorism was to be limited to specific acts. Fanon argued that terrorism should not be used against the native population in general. Like communist Chinese revolutionary leader Mao Zedong, he believed it would alienate potential supporters. Instead, he proposed two targets for terrorism: white settlers and the native middle class. The purpose of terrorism was to terrorize Westerners and their lackeys into submission. Individual murders, bombings, and mutilations would force the white settlers to leave the country and frighten the native middle class away from their colonial masters. Brutality would be the example. It would bring on governmental repression, but this would only cause more natives to flock to the terrorist cause.

Fanon's ideas flourished in Latin America, but they came with a twist. Beginning in Brazil, some revolutionaries believed cities would be the focus of Latin American revolution, and they embraced Fanon's idea of urban terrorism. They felt a revolutionary could create the context for an impromptu general uprising through the use of spontaneous violence. Directly reflecting Fanon, these revolutionaries believed terrorism could communicate with the people and infuse them with the spirit of revolt. The foremost proponent of this idea in Latin America was **Carlos Marighella** (1911–1969; see O'Connor, 2006).

Carlos Marighella (1911–1969): A Brazilian communist legislator and revolutionary theorist. Marighella popularized urban terrorism as a method for ending repression and eliminating U.S. domination of Latin America. He was killed in a police ambush in São Paulo in 1969.

Carlos Marighella and the Urban Model

Marighella was a Brazilian legislator, a leader of the nationalistic Communist Party, and eventually a fiery revolutionary terrorist. He was killed by Brazilian police in an ambush in São Paulo in 1969. In two major works, *For the Liberation of Brazil* (1971) and *The Minimanual of the Urban Guerrilla* (1969), Marighella designed practical guides for terrorism. These books have had more influence on recent revolutionary terrorism than any other set of theories. Marighella wanted to move violence from the countryside to the city, and although his call to terrorism was politically motivated, his model was apolitical. He designed a method for organizing a campaign of terror that, for the past 40 years, has been employed by groups ranging across the political spectrum—from the Japanese Red Army to the Freemen of Montana.

Marighella believed the basis of revolution was violence. Violence need not be structured, and efforts need not be coordinated among groups. Violence created a situation in which revolution could flourish. Any type of violence was acceptable because it contributed a general feeling of panic and frustration among the ruling classes and their protectors. Marighella's most original concept was that all violence could be urban-based and controlled by a small group of urban guerrillas. From Brazil, this concept of revolution spread throughout the world.

The hierarchy of Marighella has been replaced by uncoordinated activities in many groups, but Marighella might have been satisfied with this, since his four-stage model did not require coordination. Urban terrorism was to begin with two distinct phases: one designed to bring about actual violence and the other designed to give that violence meaning. The violent portion of the revolution was to be a campaign employing armed revolutionary cells to carry out the most deplorable acts of violence. Targets were to have symbolic significance, and although violence was designed to be frightening, its logic would remain clear with regard to the overall revolution. That is, those who supported the revolution would not need to fear terrorist violence themselves (see Moss, 1972, pp. 70–72; Marighella, 1969; Smith and Damphousse, 2002, pp. 6–13).

The terror campaign was to be accompanied by a psychological offensive to provide peripheral support for terrorists. The psychological offensive would not only join students and workers in low-level challenges to governmental authority; it would also be used to create a network of safe houses, logistical stores, and medical units. In essence, the supporting activities would carry out standard military support functions.

A campaign of revolutionary terrorism in an urban setting could be used to destabilize governmental power. A psychological assault would convince the government and the people that the status quo no longer held. They would come to feel that the terrorists were in control. When this situation developed, Marighella believed, the government would be forced to show its true colors. With its authority challenged and the economic stability of the elite eroded, the government would be forced to declare some form of martial law. This would not be a defeat for terrorism but rather exactly what the terrorists and their supporters wanted. Governmental repression was the goal of terrorism at this stage.

This view might appear to be contradictory at first glance, but there was a method to Marighella's madness. Marighella believed the public supported governmental policies because they did not realize the repressive nature of the state. The terrorist campaign would force the government to reveal itself, thereby alienating the public. With no place else to turn, the public would turn to the terrorists, and the terrorists would be waiting with open arms. As the ranks of the urban guerrillas grew with the rush of public support, Marighella believed, the revolutionaries would gradually abandon their terrorist campaign. Their efforts would focus more and more on the construction of a general urban army, one that could seize key governmental control points on cue. When the urban army had reached sufficient strength, all its forces would be launched in a general strike.

Marighella's theory has only one weakness: It does not work. Even so, several terrorist groups have, unfortunately, used it to organize murder throughout the world. Marighella writes that the purpose of the urban guerrilla is to shoot. Any form of urban violence is desirable because a violent atmosphere creates the political environment needed for success. Terrorism could be used to create that environment, and terrorism could be employed with minimal organization. Therefore, terrorism is to be the primary strategy of the urban guerrilla.

Marighella (1969) outlines the basic structure needed for an urban terrorist group in the *Minimanual of the Urban Guerrilla*. The main operational group of a terrorist organization should be the firing group. Composed of four to five terrorists each, several firing groups are needed to construct a terrorist organization. They can join as needed to concentrate their power, but their small size ensures both mobility and secrecy. For Marighella, the firing group is the basic weapon of the urban guerrilla.

In a single theory, Marighella provides the justification for violence and the organizational structure a small group needs to begin killing. Unlike Fanon, Marighella endorsed violence for the sake of violence. Terrorists operating in this way use terrorism as a strategy. It is the only type of attack they can launch. Guerrillas are capable of other types of operations. Therefore, terrorism becomes a tactic for guerrillas. Globalization, modern communications, and new weapons technology allow subnational groups to wage another type of campaign, an insurrection. Some military theorists believe this is a third model of terrorism.

An American Understanding of Insurgency

Due to negative experiences in Vietnam, the U.S. military resisted incorporating counter insurgency tactics in training and operations. Many officers vowed never to enter another war without having a visible enemy and clear-cut objectives (Cassidy, 2006, pp. 99–100; see also Beebe, 2006). Given experiences in the twenty-first century, some American military officers have reversed this position, concluding that guerrilla war and various forms of modern terrorism have changed the nature of subnational conflict. They are seeking to recover an American tradition of success in battling insurgency (Cassidy, 2006, pp. 105–112; and see detailed example in Lin, 2000).

The focus on insurgency and counter insurgency is due to a small group of officers who began looking at military failures during the Vietnam War. They were not convinced that the United States would only be able to select wars with front lines and an identifiable enemy in the future (see Cebrowski and Barnett, 2003; Barnett, 2005). One of these officers was a young colonel who was completing a doctoral dissertation on counter insurgencies at Princeton University; he would eventually command the counter insurgency in Iraq before being promoted to full general. General David Petraeus completed a detailed study of France's strategy in the Algerian insurgency and found that a French officer, David Galula (1919–1967), had outlined an alternative method for countering terrorism. Many officers were in agreement, and more joined the ranks after the 2003 American invasion of Iraq (see Galula, 1964).

According to the emerging doctrine developed by this group of officers, insurgencies represent a new mix of operations and tactics made possible by sweeping technological changes and globalization. This can be illustrated by a failed attempt to detonate a car bomb in New York City's Times Square on May 1, 2010. Faisal Shazad was an American of Pakistani descent. Apparently angered by American military actions in Pakistan and Afghanistan and dispirited by economic woes, Shazad allegedly traveled to Pakistan, received training from militants, and returned to the United States to plant a bomb, according to the *New York Times* (2010). His actions matched Donald Black's theories perfectly (see discussion in Chapter 2). He was a disgruntled person with the ability to cross internal borders, and he had the technology, albeit deficient, to launch an attack.

Compare this situation to the British experience in Afghanistan in the nineteenth century. When the British launched military operations in Afghanistan in 1842, an attack like Shazad's could never have happened. It would have taken months or years for a Pashtu warrior to reach London, and he would have had no idea what to do even if he made it there. He would have lacked the technology to launch an attack. The world is different today. Globalization, travel, and technology changed all the rules. These factors also make a new type of insurgency possible (Green, 2007).

Insurgencies differed from terrorism prior to globalization, and they require an innovative response, according to the officers who believe in counter insurgency doctrine. It is impossible to fight insurgencies with military tactics designed for guerrilla war or terrorism, even though insurgents use guerrilla and terrorist tactics. Insurgents control information, operate with global communication, incorporate technological weapons, and require few personnel. If they are modeled as guerrillas or terrorists of the past, an insurgency will be viewed as a law enforcement and military problem. It is much more complicated (Petraeus and Mattis, 2006).

Security forces operate at a disadvantage during an insurgency. Insurgents require few personnel, but a security force needs to be massive. In addition, the job of a security force is to do much more than enforce laws or exercise deadly force. They must form partnerships with a host of other agencies and nongovernmental organizations and coordinate efforts to create social stability. Soldiers trained to use deadly force find themselves performing many other jobs. Ironically, the military mission focuses on not shooting (Petraeus and Amos, 2006, pp. 1–24).

The nature of counter insurgencies is paradoxical (Petraeus and Amos, 2006, pp. 47–51). For example, security forces have to follow the model of community policing. They need to be highly visible and embedded in neighborhoods. This places military forces at risk. In other words, creating a secure environment for military forces is counter productive. In addition, the use of force may increase the power of insurgents. The Times Square bomber, Shazad, and many other people in the Muslim world are incensed at American drone attacks in Pakistan, attacks which effectively kill terrorists and insurgents fighting against America and its allies in Afghanistan (Sanger, 2010). It is thus better to let the local government do something poorly than to have foreigners do it more efficiently. Insurgents can be defeated with economic growth, social stability, and a working infrastructure (Wojdakowski, 2007).

Insurgencies developed, according to Petraeus and Amos, at the end of the cold war. When the United States and the Soviet Union stopped propping up weak governments to maintain the balance of power, various tribal, national, ethnic, and religious insurgencies began growing in the vacuums left by the superpowers. Technology and weapons helped many of these insurgencies grow, and instantaneous communications and travel provided a means for creating large networks of support. The new political atmosphere made the rise of organizations like al Qaeda possible.

Insurgents depend on social and support networks, according to Petraeus and Amos. This implies that counter insurgency operations must also be based on networks of various organizations. These networks, in turn, are supported by a narrative, a story that justifies and sustains the insurgency. Recall Jessica Stern's comments, cited in Chapter 2, about the importance of a story. The narrative becomes the path to action, and if networks function by the power of a story, security networks need their own story to counter the power of an insurgency. The comprehensive nature of network to network confrontations suggests that the insurgency model will be one of the dominant factors in the future of terrorism.

Self-Check

> How is terrorism used in the rural guerrilla model?

> How does terrorism change in Marighella's urban model?

> How does the *Minimanual* prepare urban groups for terrorism?

> What factors are responsible for changes in terrorism at the end of the Cold War?

Changing Dynamics and Structures

The invention of dynamite was one of the two most important developments in the history of modern terrorism. It gave small groups of violent people a powerful tool. The other development dealt with the deployment of power, that is, the formation of tactical groups. Terrorists must organize in the same manner as any other rational human group, and they have to operate in secret. The first such organizations were created in Ireland in the early 1900s during the struggle for independence. Michael Collins, leader of the Irish Republican Army (IRA), studied revolutionary tactics from the eighteenth and nineteenth centuries and developed a method of isolating small units of terrorists. He called the small units **cells**. Each cell had its own mission, and it operated without knowledge of other cells in the area. This method of organization re-emerged after World War II, and it dominated the structure of terrorism until the 1990s. After that time, many large terrorist groups developed more dynamic methods of organization.

cell: The basic unit of a traditional terrorist organization. Groups of cells form columns. Members in different cells seldom know one another. In more recent terrorist structures, *cell* describes a tactical group dispatched by the network for selected operations.

The Evolution of Cells

James Fraser, a former counter terrorist specialist in the U.S. Army, discusses two aspects of the organization of terrorist groups: the structure of the organization and its support. According to Fraser and Ian Fulton (1984, pp. 7–9), terrorist groups are necessarily designed to hide their operations from security forces, and so analysis is difficult. Still, certain organizational principles are common to all terrorist groups. Groups employ variations of command-and-control structures, but they are frequently organized in the same pattern no matter what causes they pursue.

pyramid: An illustration of the way terrorists organize themselves into hierarchies. It is an analogy showing a large base of support culminating in a small group of terrorists at the top.

The typical organization is arranged in a **pyramid** (Figure 3.2). It takes many more people to support terrorist operations than to carry them out; therefore, the majority of people who work in terrorist organizations serve to keep terrorists in the field. Thus, the most common job in a terrorist group is support, not combat. According to Fraser and Fulton, the hierarchical structure of terrorist groups is divided into four levels. The smallest group, at the top of the pyramid, is responsible for command. As in military circles, leadership makes policy and plans and provides general direction. Other researchers have often pointed out that the command structure is not as effective as in legitimate organizations because of the need for secrecy. The command structure in a terrorist organization is not free to communicate openly with its membership; therefore, it cannot exercise day-to-day operational control.

The second level of Fraser and Fulton's hierarchy is the active cadre, the people responsible for carrying out the mission of the organization. Depending on the organization's size, each terrorist in the cadre may have one or more specialties. Other terrorists support these specialties, but the active cadre is the striking arm of the terrorist group. After the command structure, the cadre of active terrorists is the smallest organization in most terrorist structures.

Below the active cadre is the second largest and the most important level of a terrorist organization: the active supporters. These people are critical to terrorist campaigns. Any group can carry out a bombing or kidnapping, but maintaining a campaign of bombings and kidnappings takes support. Active supporters keep the terrorists in the field. They maintain communication channels, provide safe houses, gather intelligence, and ensure that all other logistical needs are met. This is the largest group actively engaged within the organization.

FIGURE **3.2** A Pyramid Organization

The last and largest category is the organization's passive supporters. This group is extremely difficult to identify and characterize because passive supporters do not actively join terrorist groups; they simply represent a favorable element within the political climate. When a terrorist group can muster political support, it will have a relatively large number of passive supporters. When its cause alienates the mainstream, passive support dwindles. Passive support complements active support.

Most terrorist groups number fewer than 50 people as active supporters, cadre, and command and are thus incapable of mounting a long-term campaign. Under the command of only a few people, the group is divided according to specific tasks. Intelligence sections are responsible for assessing targets and planning operations. Support sections provide the means necessary to carry out an assault, and the tactical units are responsible for the actual terrorist action.

Larger groups are guided by the same organizational principles, but they have major subunits capable of carrying out extensive operations. In especially large groups, subunits have the ability to act autonomously. Large groups have the tactical units and the support sections to conduct terrorist campaigns.

Anthony Burton (1976, pp. 70–72) describes the basic structure of subunits. Terrorist organizations have two primary types of subunits: the cell and the column. The cell is the most basic. Composed of four to six people, the cell usually has a specialty; it may be a tactical unit or an intelligence section. In some organizations, the duties of tactical cells vary with the assignment. Other cells are designed to support the operations (Figure 3.3).

Groups of cells create columns, semiautonomous conglomerations of cells with a variety of specialties and a single command structure. As combat units, columns have questionable effectiveness. They are too cumbersome to be used in major operations, and the secrecy demanded by terrorism prevents effective cooperation among columns. Their primary function is combat support because elements in a column can be arranged to support the tactical operations of cells.

Although both Fraser and Fulton's work and Burton's analysis appear to be dated, the structures they outlined are still applicable to terrorist groups. Patrick Seale (1992) finds the same type of structure when examining the Abu Nidal group, which was sponsored by many states in the Middle East and Europe. Reuven Paz (2000) sees similarities with the organization of the Islamic resistance movement Hamas. Religious terrorists, such as Aum Shinrikyo in Japan, also copy the group model (Brackett, 1996). The only terrorists who do not follow typical organizational models are individual terrorists who operate without a group.

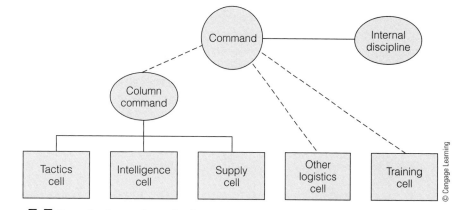

FIGURE **3.3** Terrorist Group Organization

Newer Models: Umbrella Organizations and Modern Piracy

umbrella: A group that shelters, supports, and inspires smaller terrorist groups. The RAND Corporation refers to this as a hub.

Around 1982, new types of organizational styles developed from the pyramid, and organizational transformations continue today. The first change came with the birth of the **umbrella** organization (Figure 3.4). In this type of organization, several small pyramids gather under a sheltering group that manages supplies, obtains resources, creates support structures, and gathers intelligence. The umbrella organization does not become directly involved in terrorism, claiming to be a legitimate organization representing a political cause. The sheltering group convenes periodic meetings with sympathizers, suppliers, and terrorist leaders, thus allowing terrorists to resupply, select targets, and plan. The sheltering umbrella disassociates its activities from violence, casting a blind eye when the semiautonomous pyramid groups take action.

The actions of Unionists and Republicans in Northern Ireland illustrate the operation of the umbrella. Both sides maintain legitimate political organizations to campaign either for continued relations with the United Kingdom or for unity with the Republic of Ireland. Paul Dixon (2004) argues that much political activity is conducted as a public drama to hide other activities. A number of researchers claim that violent paramilitary groups have operated under the umbrella of legitimate organizations for decades, while the open political party—the umbrella—continually denies any connection to terrorist violence (see Hastings, 1970, pp. 40–56; Winchester, 1974, pp. 171–180; Lee, 1983, pp. 59–97; Dunn and Morgan, 1995).

virtual organizations: Associations that develop through communication, financial, and ideological links. Like a network, a virtual organization has no central leadership.

chain organizations: Temporary associations of diverse groups. Groups in a chain come together for a particular operation and disband after it is over.

Researchers from the RAND Corporation (Arquilla, Ronfeldt, and Zanini, 1999) identify several other new types of organizational styles that emerged in the 1990s. **Virtual organizations** are created through computer and information networks. **Chain organizations** involve small groups linked by some type of communication and whose members periodically cooperate. A hub organization has a centralized group with semiautonomous groups supported in other regions. Centralized hubs have developed to manage or support individual cells, and they operate much like umbrella

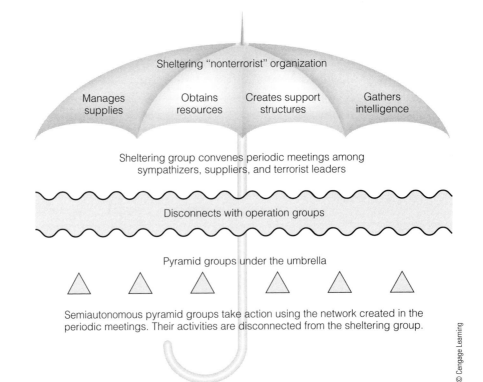

Sheltering "nonterrorist" organization

Manages supplies

Obtains resources

Creates support structures

Gathers intelligence

Sheltering group convenes periodic meetings among sympathizers, suppliers, and terrorist leaders

Disconnects with operation groups

Pyramid groups under the umbrella

Semiautonomous pyramid groups take action using the network created in the periodic meetings. Their activities are disconnected from the sheltering group.

© Cengage Learning

FIGURE **3.4** The Umbrella Organization

groups. However, the most important new style of organization identified in Arquilla, Ronfeldt, and Zanini's and other research is the terrorist network.

The network's structure can range from simple to complex (Arquilla and Ronfeldt, 1996, 2001; Arquilla, Ronfeldt, and Zanini, 1999; Sageman, 2004, pp. 137–174). A complex all-channel network is composed of groups, logistical systems, and overlapping relationships among groups, individuals, and technology. The second concept in the network is the node. A node can refer to any critical function in the network, and this can range from a group to support systems, such as a bomb-making factory or a cybercafé. The network is a series of nodes held together through communication.

The RAND approach reveals the structure of networks. They involve terrorist, extremist, criminal, and disruptive-activist groups. The key to **networks**, according to this approach, is their ability to operate in a technological setting. Operations are characterized by the dual nature of the network. Violence takes place on two levels: organized small groups and disruptive violence arising from demonstrations. Another characteristic is the structure of the group. It is not a traditional hierarchy; it is a network. Members can be quickly assembled even though they operate from diverse locations, and group structures are temporary, designed to fit a particular situation. They appear seemingly from nowhere, strike, and return to obscurity. RAND refers to this as the ability to swarm.

One of the changes in network functions began appearing in Europe around 2004. The *Times* (2009) of London captured this subtle change in an article examining links to terrorism from the United Kingdom to Somalia and Pakistan. Many experts thought that terror networks operated exclusively by the power of the network. As bombings took place in London and Glasgow, an interesting twist in the power of terrorist networks appeared. It was possible to create a hub or umbrella inside the network. In other words, a command group can recruit, train, plan, supply, and launch an attack within a network with minimal links to the home group (see Figure 3.5).

networks: Organizations of groups, supplies, weapons, and any structure that supports an operation. Much like a traffic system or the World Wide Web, networks do not have central leadership, and they operate under a variety of rules.

Umbrella Groups and Pirates

Gal Luft and Anne Korin (2004) worry that such practices may soon be seen on the high seas. Arguing that most people incorrectly assume that piracy is an activity of the past, they note that incidents of piracy have doubled in the past decade. Today's

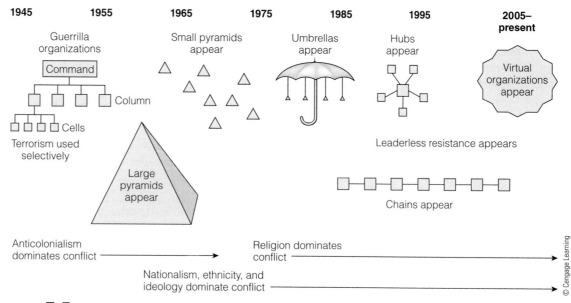

FIGURE **3.5** Timeline of Organizational Styles

pirates are armed with global positioning systems, satellite phones, machine guns, rockets, and grenades. Most of them currently work for organized crime syndicates, but Luft and Korin warn that international terrorists could take note of the rise and success of piracy. If their thesis is correct, organized crime provides an ideal model for terrorists: a seemingly legitimate business (the sheltering organization) provides cover for pirates (the pyramid organization) while denying all connection with illegal activities. Today's piracy is already conducted under an umbrella. In reality, the legitimate business is the front for an organized crime group. The business group, in turn, denies any affiliation with crime, and it shelters the pirate groups operating under its shield. Terrorists need merely copy the model.

By 2005, terrorist networks in the Horn of Africa had established links with maritime pirates. Somalia had been gripped by internal and external struggles for the previous decade and a half. Anarchy dominated the region as various militias vied for control of the government, including foreign militia and jihadist groups. As economic chaos continued, local fishermen and unemployed militiamen found that they could obtain large payoffs by seizing ocean freighters and releasing them for ransom. Realizing the potential profits and opportunities to attack international targets, jihadist groups began moving into pirate coves. They either formed alliances with pirates or took over their operations (Schroeder, 2010).

An article in *Military Technology* (2009) reports that attacks began to increase in 2008 and increased throughout 2009. These actions started drawing media attention and demands for a response. With the rise of an international consensus against piracy, warships from several nations moved into the area, but there was little agreement on what they should do. Some simply observed, while others cruised to make a show of force. Shipping companies shared in the confusion. Some advocated placing armed guards aboard ships or incorporating nonlethal defense measures such as high-pressure water hoses. Others believed that defensive measures placed crews in jeopardy, and maritime insurance agencies were loath to have armed guards aboard ships. Regardless, the United States, France, China, and Russia began to respond with force in 2009.

Although some nations have employed their naval forces, the problem of piracy is endemic to the political struggle in Somalia. Piracy off the coast of the Horn of Africa is caused by the multifaceted conflict in Somalia and the attendant breakup of legal authority and social systems. Although jihadists are involved, the complete identity of Somali pirates and their locations are not known. Some people have taken to piracy because fisheries have been destroyed by toxic wastes; others see themselves as protectors of their communities. In early 2010, several nations signed an agreement to work cooperatively against maritime terrorism and piracy, and warships from the United States, Europe, and China have regularly patrolled the area. Some shipping companies have employed armed guards and others have employed nonlethal systems to secure ships. These measures respond to the symptom, but prevention of piracy will likely not occur until order is restored in Somalia (Baniela, 2010).

Self- Check

> Describe the structure of terrorist cells immediately after World War II.
> What changes in organizational styles have influenced the ways terrorists organized themselves?
> What is a terror network?
> How do hubs function in terror networks?
> How is maritime piracy related to terrorism?

Managing Terrorist Organizations

Whether groups organize in a traditional pyramid, an umbrella, a hub, or even a virtual organization, it is possible to chart the structure of even the most secretive groups. Any student could probably make a fairly accurate diagram of most terrorist groups after taking an Introduction to Management class. Terrorist leaders face operational problems and seek to solve them with the same strategies taught in such a management class. Terrorist leaders also have special organizational problems.

The first problem is the need for secrecy. This dominates the operational aspects of terrorism and leads to a variety of problems that open organizations do not encounter. Ironically, although secrecy is the greatest strength of the terrorist organization, it also is the basis of its greatest weakness. Terrorism demands secrecy, and secrecy prevents effective communication. Sometimes a terrorist group's work is so secret that even the members do not know what they are doing.

Because the necessity for secrecy is so great in any type of terrorist organization, subgroups are usually allowed a relatively high degree of autonomy. Terrorism is a decentralized affair, and the larger the group, the greater the degree of decentralization. This is not the most desirable kind of organization, but it is an operational necessity. Terrorists know a centralized structure is easily infiltrated and destroyed by security forces. One well-placed informant can destroy an entire centralized organization.

Decentralization offers relative security: Very few people know many other members of the organization. This approach affords great protection but difficult administration. The organization of the Provisional IRA illustrates the problem. The IRA is organized like most large terrorist groups. It is governed by a Supreme Council whose members are drawn from IRA battalion or column commanders. Column commanders are responsible for a number of cells, which in the IRA are frequently called by military names such as platoons, squadrons, and companies. The command of the IRA, however, has problems that emanate from secrecy and decentralization.

On paper, the organizational chart looks extremely logical. In practice, that logic is modified by the need for each unit to be protected from discovery. This means members of various cells and columns usually have no idea who other members of the IRA are and what they are doing. They get their orders from one person, and that person supposedly represents the Supreme Council. This paves the way for potential splintering or, at the least, misunderstandings. It is easy to see why the IRA is difficult to manage.

To prevent factionalism and excessive autonomy, terrorist commanders turn to internal discipline for control. In essence, commanders continually threaten to terrorize the terrorist organization. However, internal discipline can become a major factor in the demise of a terrorist organization. There are two opposing dynamics at work—one pushing for cohesion and cooperation through fear and the other pulling for autonomy through decentralization and secrecy. Sometimes, attempts at discipline backfire. For example, when leaders try to punish errant members by assassination, they may themselves become the target of disgruntled followers. As a result, large terrorist organizations frequently find themselves splitting.

Another problem of terrorist management is that of gaining immediate tactical support for operations. As Fraser and Fulton (1984) suggest, the most important element of a terrorist campaign is the number and structure of active supporters. Without active supporters, launching a campaign is impossible. Although the press has frequently portrayed terrorist leaders as secretive plotters controlling hidden armies of true believers, in reality terrorist leadership must exert itself to develop and maintain active support. The majority of their time is spent creating networks of active supporters, not launching headline-grabbing operations.

Marc Sageman (2004, pp. 171–173) believes that operations are managed by the social organization of networks. Examining militant Salafi structures associated with the al Qaeda movement, Sageman finds four major clusters, or nodes, connected by a central staff cluster. Friendships and social relations form the communication and managerial nexus of the organization. These relations are enhanced by cliques within the group. Al Qaeda and its affiliates thrive because command is decentralized in the network. The one exception is Jamaat Islamiyya, a militant religious group in Indonesia still organized around the concept of cellular hierarchy. Hierarchies are more difficult to manage because power is concentrated, making them more vulnerable to counter terrorist techniques.

The formation of command structures within networks creates a method for overcoming some of the difficulties inherent in managing terrorist organizations. This is difficult to create in a stable social setting, but relatively easy to do in areas where a government cannot exert its authority. Jayshree Bajoria (2010), a member of the Council on Foreign Relations, argues that this explains the rise of command structures in the tribal areas of Pakistan. With the government of Pakistan unable and sometimes unwilling to exert authority in its **tribal areas**, several differing organizations have been able to establish their presence in the border region with Afghanistan. Because they are isolated and protected, they can develop command structures. This facilitates better control of attacks.

Command and control from Pakistan has mixed results. In July 2005, terrorists carried out the first suicide attacks in Western Europe when three young men detonated bombs in separate trains on the London Underground. A fourth bomb exploded on a bus. The investigation revealed that the attack was linked to Pakistan (Storm and Eyerman, 2008). Interestingly, the young men were part of a large Pakistani community in the United Kingdom, and this may explain the effectiveness of the command structure. When another young man tried to detonate a bomb in Times Square in New York City five years later, the plot failed even though he allegedly received training in Pakistan. Even when a hierarchy is created inside a network, this does not necessarily ensure that cells or individuals can be managed effectively.

tribal areas: Refers to Federally Administered Tribal Areas (FATA) in Pakistan along the Afghan border. Seven different Pashtu tribes have control of the region by agreement with the central government.

Group Size and Length of Campaign

Regardless of the behavioral aspects of terrorist organizations, the size of a group affects its ability to operate over time. Large groups last longer than small ones. Ted Robert Gurr's (1988a, pp. 23–50) analysis of group size demonstrates that larger groups are more effective than smaller groups over time, although most terrorist actions involve only a few people who generate more noise than injury. Terrorism is short-lived because it seldom generates support.

Thus, the ultimate conundrum for terrorist groups: Terrorists need to create a large following to conduct a lengthy campaign. However, terrorism almost always involves violence by an unpopular political fringe movement. Therefore, terrorist are hard-pressed to form a large constituency to support the campaign. If they do, then they must move away from the political fringe, and fanatics are reluctant to do that (see Hewitt, 2003, pp. 69–80).

There are methods for getting around this problem. Terrorist groups may find state sponsors (Livingstone and Arnold, 1986, pp. 1–10). In the 1990s, it became popular to speak of failed states, regions of lawlessness where criminal and terrorist organizations can thrive. Small groups operating in failed states exhibited staying power in the first decade of the twenty-first century (Napoleoni, 2003, pp. 11–28). A network may give a small group an opportunity to participate in a larger campaign (Scheuer, 2006, pp. 65–68). Today, it is also important to consider the religious and ideological factors that hold international networks together. In the initial stages of radicalization, an ideology is one of the most important factors attracting recruits to a small group (Helfstein, 2012).

A terrorist campaign promises the greatest opportunity for success, but political revolutionary and radical groups do not have the popular appeal needed to gain support for their activities. As a result, many terrorist activities remain isolated and do not grow into a campaign. Terrorists seldom offer serious challenges to authority. Gurr believes large groups became large because they have embraced popular political issues. Only a few groups have been able to adopt popular positions since 1945.

✅ **Self-Check**

> What special problems separate terrorist organizations from other groups?
> How are these problems similar to ones managers in any organization face?
> How does a group's size impact its ability to operate?

Financing Modern Terrorism

Capone discovery: A term used by James Adams to explain the Irish Republican Army's entry into organized crime.

When modern terrorism began to emerge after World War II, security forces frequently concentrated on investigative measures, military force, and tactics to counter the terrorism. Financing was often overlooked. This type of thinking changed by the 1980s as security forces came to realize the crucial role that money played in terrorist operations. In Northern Ireland, law enforcement officials and terrorism analysts realized that the IRA made a **Capone discovery;** that is, it developed an organized crime network to finance its operations (Adams, 1986). A decade later American analysts demonstrated that Middle Eastern terrorists were raising funds in the United States through grocery coupon fraud (Kushner and Jacobson, 1998). Other investigators found legal businesses laundering millions of dollars for terrorist organizations (Navias, 2002). Many terrorist organizations began using petty crime, money laundering, and the transfer of illegal contraband to finance operations (Hinnen, 2004).

Awareness of the importance of financing evolved slowly, partly because of an inherent contradiction in the cost of a single terrorist event when compared to the cost of a campaign. Stated simply, a terrorist operation does not cost a lot of money, but the overall budget for a campaign is quite high. The *Economist* (2003) reports that terrorism is cost-effective in terms of the causalities and destruction terrorist events cause. Events like the 1995 Oklahoma City bombing or the multiple bomb attacks on trains in Madrid in 2004 cost only a few thousand dollars. A single attack like the 2009 Fort Hood shootings might only cost a few hundred dollars. Yet, as Neil Livingstone and David Halevy (1988) explain, it takes a lot of cash to run a terrorist group for any length of time. For example, 9/11 was inexpensive, but holding al Qaeda together cost several thousand dollars per month (L. Wright, 2006, pp. 168–169). After 9/11, analysts began more thorough investigations to find out how terrorists raised, laundered, transferred, and stored funds (Levitt and Jacobson, 2008, p. 13).

Financial Information as an Investigative and Intelligence Tool

When security officials began to believe that money trails would prove to be the best tool to use against terrorism, they equated terrorist organizations with drug gangs and organized crime. Conventional wisdom suggested that terrorist groups could be dismantled simply by "following the money." There were arguments for waging "financial warfare" by freezing assets and tracing the funds used by terrorist groups (Navias, 2002). The U.S. government endorsed this approach, arguing that counter terrorist investigations should focus on sources of financing and mechanisms to transfer money (National Strategy for Combating Terrorism, 2006, p. 7). These financial approaches took the position that campaigns were expensive and that attacks on terrorist financing would reduce incidents of terrorism.

This approach was too simple. It assumed that terrorists would act only in the legal, formal economy. In reality, terrorists participate in underground criminal networks that are relatively immune to financial regulations. So-called financial warfare would not be effective because terrorists do not respond to formal controls (Basile, 2004). Experience in Canada suggested that financial investigations against terrorists was ineffective (Montpetit, 2008) and that anti-financial measures in the arsenal of counter terrorism did not appear to work, at least on the surface.

As criticism of counter terrorist financial investigations increase in the media and among the public at large, security forces came to realize that the nature of money trails in terrorism was misunderstood. Many people assumed that terrorists operated like drug networks; but that was not the case (Giraldo and Trinkhunas, 2007, p. 293). Whereas an intensive financial investigation of money laundering networks could result in the successful prosecution of an international drug ring, the same tactic did not work against terrorist groups. This was true even with large international networks. Counter terrorist specialists and investigators came to realize that financial investigations could be used as a tool in a process, but investigations of the flow of funds by themselves would not stop terrorism.

Drug dealers and organized criminals require massive organizations to collect and launder large amounts of money. Terrorists do not operate like that. Terrorists do not launder money frequently; as noted earlier, it takes relatively little money to launch an individual terrorist operation (Liu, 2012). Traditional financial investigations are not effective against terrorists because of the limited amounts of money required for a terrorist operation, but when financial transactions become one aspect of larger investigative or intelligence operations, they help to provide a comprehensive picture. Terrorists do need money, and they get it by both legal and illegal methods. If financial information is added to evidence gained by other investigative techniques, it can provide a more comprehensive picture of terrorist activities (Levitt and Jacobson, 2008, p. 15).

Terrorist networks operate much like a business franchise, although transactions frequently take place in the underground economy. Money is moved across international borders. Therefore, financial investigations are conducted internationally and require international agreements to stem the flow of money. As result, one aspect of counter terrorism involves tracing money and using the information with other intelligence to produce a comprehensive picture of terrorist operations (Williams, 2007, pp. 77–82; Levitt and Jacobson, 2008, p. 15).

John Cassara (2006) argues that America has stalled in its efforts to fight terrorism because law enforcement agencies have not used sufficient forensic accounting tools. It is possible to track terrorists' money laundering, cash purchases, banking accounts, and stock and business investments. Cassara also argues that tracking money can create better intelligence—criminal intelligence and national security intelligence. Mapping the financial activities of suspected groups and individuals gives intelligence a comprehensive focus. **Forensic accounting** can be used to solve crime and to gain information.

forensic accounting: An investigative tool used to track money used in illegal activities. It can be used in any crime involving the exchange, storage, or conversion of fiscal resources.

Illegal Funding Methods

Terrorists raise money by a variety of legal and illegal means. Some of the illegal methods include running criminal enterprises, engaging in the drug trade, conducting illegal business activities under a legal cover, smuggling money, illegally transferring money, and a variety of other methods. Middle Eastern terrorists engage in smuggling and document fraud. Document fraud raises money for terrorist organizations and provides terrorists with false identification. In central Asia terrorist organizations trade illegal arms, launder money, and distribute drugs. Latin American terrorism is tied to drug production and public corruption. In the United States, domestic terrorists engage in fraud schemes and robberies to finance political violence (Mili, 2006).

expropriation: A term used by Carlos Marighella for armed robbery.

Raising money for illegal operations is nothing new. The Brazilian terrorist-philosopher Carlos Marighella argued that "urban warfare" begins with a campaign of **expropriation**—that is, robbery (1969, 1971; see also Burton, 1976). Terrorists around the world use a variety of criminal methods to raise funds. Violent activities involve kidnapping, extortion, and robbery. Less violent methods include fraud, larceny, smuggling, dealing in contraband, forgery, and counterfeiting (Nance, 2003; Williams, 2007, p. 77). Interpol estimates that counterfeiting and intellectual property theft is responsible for $200 billion in illegal profits in the United States alone, doubling to $400 billion when the international community is included. This involves pirated CDs and DVDs, counter feit clothing, and stolen computer software (Noble, 2008). Counterfeiting and fraud are common practices among the American extremist right (Pitcavage, 1999a, 1999b, 1999c).

Domestic extremists are not the only violent fanatics who raise funds in the United States; international terrorists also engage in fraudulent activities in America. From approximately 1981 to 1986, the Abu Nidal Organization engaged in various criminal activities in Tennessee and the St. Louis metropolitan area to generate funds (E. Harris, 1995). Hezbollah ran cigarettes from North Carolina to Michigan and used some of the profits to fund operations in Lebanon (*United States of America v. Mohamad Youseff Hammoud, et al.*, 2002). There are a variety of schemes across the country using baby formula. American baby formula is treasured throughout the world because of its nutritional value. Terrorists sometimes steal formula and use illegal distribution networks to raise money (Clayton, 2005). In Cincinnati, law enforcement officers broke a ring of convenience stores that were selling stolen goods to finance terrorist organizations (Coolidge and Prendergast, 2003). Police in Dearborn, Michigan, arrested two men for making false identification papers for Middle Eastern groups (U.S. Immigration and Customs Enforcement, 2005).

The Internet has become a tool for fraud. Terrorists use online activity in identity theft and in gaining access to bank and credit card accounts. They also sell items at Internet auctions. Security fraud is another method of raising funds. For example, a group might buy a large amount of stock in a company that is fairly inactive. They then fill the web with stories of new products, new technology, or some other item that will cause the company's stock to increase. As the stock value increases, terrorists sell the stock at an inflated price even though the company has seen no real increase in value. Before the stock drops back to its normal level, the terrorists make a huge profit. This process is known as "pump and dump," and it is frequently used by dishonest stock speculators and other criminals (Hinnen, 2004).

Terrorists use extortion and protection rackets to raise money. Terrorist organizations force legitimate businesses and other people to make payoffs to avoid being attacked. Loretta Napoleoni (2003, pp. 27–28) reports that the Shining Path of Peru taxed farmers for protection. Rebels and death squads in Colombia did the same. Zachary Abuza (2003b) says similar tactics are used in Southeast Asia. In essence, Abuza concludes, terrorists use the same fund-raising techniques that criminals have used for years, in addition to their unique methods of gathering money.

Stolen vehicles also play a role in fund-raising (Sallot, 2006). North American cars, especially SUVs, are attractive to terrorists. When used as car bombs, they can pack more explosive power than a smaller vehicle. They can also be used to raise cash. A stolen SUV can be sold in the Middle East or central Asia for nearly $100,000.

Examples of illegal fund-raising extend to all forms of crime. At the heart of illegal activity is fund-raising, and terrorists have learned that crime can pay. Traditional crimes, especially large embezzlement schemes in the global economy, represent a source of income for small groups as well as large organizations (Labeviere, 2000, pp. 54–55; Napoleoni, 2003, pp. 203–205; D. Kaplan, 2005). After raising funds, terrorists frequently spend them in underground networks to support operations.

Tobacco has become an important source money for terrorist organizations. By 2012 al Qaeda in the Islamic Maghreb (AQIM) had become the primary source of income for the al Qaeda network (Rogers, 2012). AQIM achieved this prominent position by smuggling cigarettes. David Cid, director of the Memorial Institute for the Prevention of Terrorism, says that cigarettes are easy to buy and easy to smuggle. They can also be counter feited. The Afghan Taliban produces millions of fake Marlboros and distributes them through Afghanistan and China. The Irish Republican Army raised an estimated $100 million over a five-year period by smuggling cigarettes. The Kurdish Workers Party raises money by taxing cigarettes as they cross the border. Many of the drug smuggling routes in North America have been used for cigarette smuggling. Drug detection methods don't work against cigarettes, and penalties for illegally possessing cigarettes are much lighter than those for possession of drugs (Wilson, 2009).

Legal Methods of Raising Funds

Terrorists do not limit their financial activities to underworld networks and illegal revenue sources. Many groups engage in legitimate business activities to raise and distribute money (Navias, 2002). Activities include soliciting contributions, operating businesses, running nongovernmental organizations (NGOs), creating charities, using wire transfers, forming or using banks, and using informal money transfer systems. Sometimes people smuggle large amounts of money across international borders. At other times foreign workers send money back to organizations in their home countries. One terrorist group legally raises the money through normal employment (National Strategy, 2006; Levitt and Jacobson, 2008; and Montpetit, 2008).

According to several researchers (S. A. Emerson, 2002, pp. 183–219; Ehrenfeld, 2003, pp. 21–22; Napoleoni, 2003, pp. 111–179), charities have been involved in funding terrorism. Data from national and international law enforcement sources agree with these findings (Scott-Joynt, 2003; Isikoff and Hosenball, 2004; U.S. Department of State, 2004b). Many people who contribute to charities do not know they are supporting terrorist organizations. Others believe the efforts they are supporting are not terrorist operations but legitimate military operations. Zachary Abuza (2003b, p. 93) writes that terrorists often set up a phony charity or skim the proceeds from legitimate organizations. Either way, charitable funds are frequently diverted to terrorist groups.

✓ **Self-Check**

> How do financial tools impact investigative and intelligence functions?

> What are some of the common illegal methods of funding terrorism?

> What types of legal activities fund terrorism?

Networks and Systems

David Carter (2009) points to an important characteristic of terrorist organizations. When terrorists move goods, people, weapons, money, or contraband, they must do so in underground networks. It is not possible to build a network overnight; they develop only through long-term trust. This means, Carter concludes, that terrorists use existing criminal networks for logistics, including financing activities, and they are vulnerable to intelligence-gathering activities. Even researchers who disagree about the stability of networks see the importance of the underground economy (Biersteker and Eckert, 2007). Even if illegal economic routes are not stable, money still flows through a network. The examination of underground economic systems shows links among people and groups.

The FBI estimates that the underground economy produces $500 billion per year. An underground economy requires secret institutions, and terrorists have found various enterprises for hiding money (Maier, 2003). Rachel Ehrenfeld (2003, pp. 10–30) says that terrorists run banks and create phony companies to launder or hide their funds. They also engage in secret transactions and form alliances with organized crime.

Friedrich Schneider (2002) says the underground economy and its ties to crime are so important to terrorists because all the transactions remain hidden. Organized criminal and smuggling networks have long had the means of hiding money through seemingly legal transactions. Terrorists take advantage of these networks. Schneider believes that terrorism has become a big business. Terrorists not only move funds but also smuggle stolen goods and contraband. As mentioned earlier, document fraud and forgery are money-raising activities.

Terrorism is linked to organized crime throughout the world, and in some cases it is almost impossible to distinguish between terrorist and criminal activity. Tamara Makarenko (2002) says that Russian organized crime groups trade weapons for drugs in Colombia. She also finds that both terrorists and criminals take advantage of political instability in regions like central Asia and the **Triborder region** in South America (around the common border of Argentina, Brazil, and Paraguay; Figure 3.6). In the Middle East and Southeast Asia, terrorists and criminals kidnap for profit. She believes that terrorist and criminal organizations have grown into global enterprises.

The **globalization** of crime and terrorism has created opportunities for vast profits in the diamond trade. African diamonds, or "conflict diamonds," are obtained illegally and sold in an underground network. According to Global Witness (2003), a British human rights organization, al Qaeda spent ten years moving into unregulated

Triborder region: The area where Brazil, Paraguay, and Argentina join. The major city is Cuidad del Este.

Globalization: A common global economic network ideally uniting the world through production and international trade. Proponents believe it will create wealth. Critics believe it creates corporate wealth and increases distance between the rich and poor.

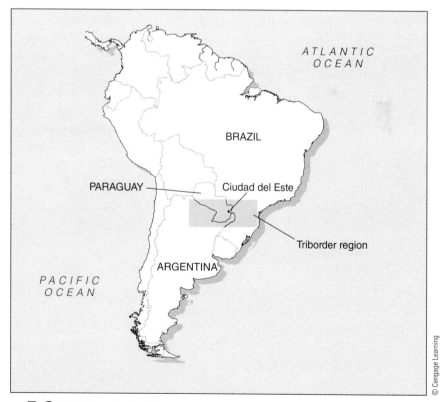

FIGURE **3.6** The Triborder Region

The Triborder region is the area in South America where Paraguay, Brazil, and Argentina have a common border. Quite a bit of criminal activity takes place in the region, and the Paraguayan city Ciudad del Este is particularly known for its lawlessness. The region is also home to more than 20,000 Middle Eastern immigrants. Hamas, Hezbollah, and other terrorist groups have been known to frequent the area.

diamond trading in West Africa. In the early 1990s, it infiltrated legitimate trading centers to establish a base. After success in mainstream trading, al Qaeda slowly and quietly switched from legitimate trading centers to underground criminal networks. Then, taking advantage of weak governments and regulations in Africa, it established its own international trading network. The new system allowed al Qaeda and allied jihadist groups to make tremendous profits while providing a ready-made network to hide and launder money. It should be noted that the 9/11 Commission (2004, p. 171) examined claims about al Qaeda's involvement in the diamond trade and came to a different conclusion. The commission found no evidence that diamonds were used to support al Qaeda. Global Witness disagrees and believes it has presented evidence of al Qaeda's activities.

Hidden Transfers

It is hard to trace some money because it is hidden in underground networks or in informal transfers. The Money Laundering Threat Assessment Group (2010) explains that organized crime and drug networks use extensive money-laundering systems. Criminal groups will launder money several times, converting illegal income to another form of funds and further laundering it by other means. Empirical research shows that terrorists do not usually go to these extremes. While terrorists use the same networks and channels as organized criminals, they do not launder their money extensively. This means they usually convert money in one step, such as converting cash into a money order or wiring cash to a group's financier. Terrorists also launder significantly less cash than organized crime or drug networks. One empirical study involving almost 200 money-laundering techniques indicated that the maximum sum of money for organized criminals was $69 million, while the maximum amount for the terrorist cases involved $4.8 million (Liu. 2012).

Black Market Peso Exchange: A method for converting illegal profits in U.S. currency to Colombian pesos in an effort to hide the illegal funds. Terrorists have frequently used the system, although they launder less money than organized crime or drug networks.

One common method for laundering drug money from Colombia is known as the **Black Market Peso Exchange**. Terrorists, especially the Revolutionary Armed Forces of Colombia (FARC), have used this network, although not as much as drug

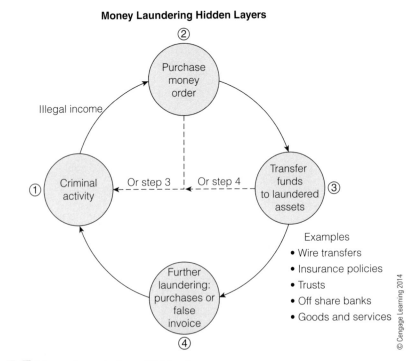

FIGURE **3.7** Money Laundering – Hidden Layers

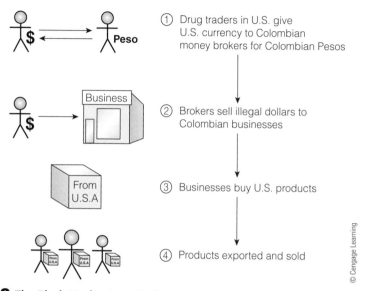

FIGURE **3.8** The Black Market Peso Exchange

dealers. In the Peso Exchange drug dealers sell their products in the United States and accumulate large amounts of U.S. currency. Unlike terrorism investigations, law enforcement officers are well versed in disrupting drug networks simply by following the path of such money. As a result, the dealers need to find a way to hide the cash. They do so by selling the money to brokers in Colombia, who pay the dealers in Colombian pesos. The money brokers, in turn, take the illegally gotten U.S. currency and buy consumer goods in Colombia. These goods are marketed and sold in Colombia and, through exports, even back in the United States. The drug dealers end up with "clean" Colombian pesos, and the U.S. currency accumulated from illegal drug sales is hidden from formal audits. When terrorists use the Peso Exchange, they follow the same procedures, though laundering less money (Money Laundering Threat Assessment Working Group, 2010).

Many international terrorist groups move money through an ancient trading network called the **hawala system**. The system originated several hundred years ago in China under the name of Feng Chin, or "flying money." Today, it is primarily used in Pakistan and India, though there are hawala dealers around the world. It is a legitimate means of transferring money without using money or moving actual funds across international borders, although it may violate currency transfer regulations in some countries. It is a network based on long-term trust relationships and the knowledge that each dealer is impeccably reliable for all debts (see *Expanding the Concept: Advantages of the Hawala System*).

Several hundred years ago central Asian merchants were frequently robbed of the gold and silver they carried in caravans to pay for goods. They developed a system of noncash exchange as a result. Rather than carrying money, caravan leaders would visit merchants and pay for goods with a promissory note. When the caravan reached its destination, the leader sold his goods and the distributors would pay the caravan leader with promissory notes. The leader returned home, presented the note, and the local chit dealer paid the debt. The system worked because the dealers honored the promises. As long as people trusted each other, each chit was worth silver or gold, and merchants, caravan leaders, and others could thus travel without money. The hawala system is one version of this ancient practice (Jamwal, 2002; Schramm and Taube, 2002; Sharma, 2006).

hawala system: A system of exchanging money based on trust relationships between money dealers. A chit, or promissory note, is exchanged between two hawaladars, and it is as valuable as cash or other traded commodities because the trust between the two parties guarantees its value.

Advantages of the Hawala System

- Money moves with no record.
- Money crosses international borders with ease.
- It is based on trust, and long-term trusting relationships are in place.
- Money can easily be bartered for contraband.
- No tax records exist.

Today's hawala system works much as the old system did (Figure 3.9). Imagine that Asadullah Kahn lives and works in Los Angeles. He is an American citizen, but his parents live in Peshawar, Pakistan. Asadullah wishes to assist his parents, so he regularly sends them money. It is difficult, however, to get funds into Pakistan, and it is even more difficult to move them across the North-West Frontier Province to Peshawar. Postal service is frequently unavailable, and parcel services can take months to deliver a package. Therefore, Asadullah goes to a local jewelry store because he knows the owner is a *hawaladar*, a hawala dealer. Asadullah gives the hawaladar $500 and tells him that he wants it delivered to his parents. The hawaladar subtracts a small fee, usually 1 or 2 percent, and sends word to a hawaladar in Peshawar that Asadullah sends his parents the balance. Asadullah's parents visit the Peshawar hawaladar and he pays them the promised money. No money actually moved from Los Angeles to Peshawar, but Asadullah's parents received nearly $500. The system works because the hawaladars in Peshawar and Los Angeles implicitly trust each other. They know the debt will be honored (see U.S. Department of the Treasury, 2003).

Change the imaginary scenario a bit and the impact on terrorism can be demonstrated. In the revised situation, imagine that Asadullah is not a hardworking son seeking to support his parents but an operative for the Lashkar-e-Taiba, a Kashmiri terrorist group. Asif, Asadullah's contact in Peshawar, needs $500 to buy AK-47s.

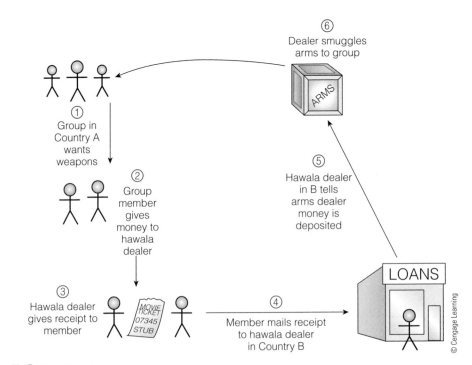

FIGURE **3.9** The Hawala System

After raising funds in the United States, Asadullah visits the hawaladar, hands over $500, and asks the hawaladar to get the money to Asif. The Peshawar hawaladar gives Asif the money, not knowing its use. Asif buys the weapons and delivers them to contacts in the Lashkar-e-Taiba. There is no record of the transaction, and no way to trace the flow of funds. The hawala system was not established to support terrorism, but it hides transactions in the modern world of international banking (Sharma, 2006).

Hezbollah as an Example

Hezbollah can serve as an example of the complexity of terrorist financing (Levitt and Jacobson, 2008, pp. 65–68). It uses all types of sources for funding, and it moves money in underground networks and laundering systems. Most of Hezbollah's funds come from state funding, with Iran acting as the principal sponsor. Hezbollah receives an estimated $200 million per year from Iran. There are numerous Lebanese Shi'ites dispersed throughout the world, and Hezbollah receives quite a bit of money in direct donations from members of the Lebanese diaspora. Charities and other front organizations around the world also serve as a base for funding. One charity forwarded $50 million a year to Hezbollah before its activities were stopped by law enforcement.

Hezbollah also relies on criminal activities in Lebanon and in other countries. One of the main sources of illegal income inside Lebanon is an extensive protection racket. Legitimate businesses are forced to pay a "Hezbollah tax" in order to ensure that their property will not be damaged and that their personnel are not harmed. Hezbollah is also involved in narcotics trafficking and cigarette smuggling in North America and Africa. The organization is so complex that it even manages legitimate businesses, and it controls branch offices for international wire services. Finally, the group is so well funded that it is able to finance other terrorist organizations such as Hamas and the Palestinian Islamic Jihad (Levitt and Jacobson, 2008, pp. 65–68; Chalk, 2012).

✓ Self-Check

> What impact do underground financial networks have on terrorism?
> Describe three hidden or informal fiscal exchange systems.
> How does Hezbollah embody the financing of terrorism?

The Political Economy of Terrorism

The financial aspects of terrorism have influenced the changing nature of the international economy. After the collapse of the former Soviet Union in 1991, the United States became the world's only superpower. Promoting an economic system that emphasized international production, trade, and consumption, American economic policies focused on reducing the trade barriers between nation-states. Some countries have prospered under globalization of the world economy, but others have grown weaker and poorer. Globalization is based on the belief that international trade barriers should be removed so that commerce and industry can develop in an international free market. Terrorism has taken hold in some of the areas left behind in the rush toward globalization, and this has changed the nature of terrorist financing (see Barber, 1996, pp. 48–49).

Loretta Napoleoni (2003) examines this process, formulating a new theory about the financing of terrorism. Agreeing with Adams's early findings and other studies that found links between organized crime networks and terrorism, Napoleoni goes far beyond a summary of the immediate circumstances. In *Modern Jihad* she argues that terrorism has evolved as an economic entity. The fall of the Soviet Union and subsequent

new economy of terrorism:
A term used by Loretta
Napoleoni to describe
the evolution of terror-
ist financing from the
beginning strategies of the
cold war to the present.
Economic support and an-
titerrorist policies interact
to form the new economy.

globalization have produced what she calls the **new economy of terrorism**. Napoleoni says that the origins of the new economy of terrorism grew from the cold war (1945–1991). As Bruce Hoffman (1998, pp. 43–65) says, colonial revolts began at the end of World War II (1939–1945). Napoleoni (2003, pp. 11–28) sees this as the beginning of a macroeconomic shift. Western nations began to use underground methods to fund their struggles in the colonies, and revolutionaries sought their own sources of money. The origins of the new economy of terrorism can be traced to anticolonial revolts.

To demonstrate the birth of this new economy, Napoleoni turns to France. After World War II, when France was still a colonial power in control of many foreign lands, nationalists revolted against French rule all over the world. In Vietnam, the revolutionary nationalists were called the Vietminh. Although they had international communist backing, the Vietminh needed money. They muscled their way into opium production, sold the drugs, and used the profits to keep their guerrillas in the field.

Ironically, France tried the same concept. When the war against the Vietminh became politically unpopular, the French government found it difficult to finance military operations. Napoleoni says the French took over opium profits and used them to finance the war. As a result, drug trafficking became one of the primary methods governments used to finance activities during the cold war.

Napoleoni says that as the cold war developed, the Soviet Union and the United States fought each other by proxy; that is, they did not fight each other directly. The Soviets used allies to attack countries loyal to the United States, and the United States used its friends to attack Soviet-backed countries. Napoleoni believes that modern terrorist groups evolved from these surrogate conflicts, and that they looked for ways to become independent from both superpowers. The desire for autonomy led terrorist groups to join criminals in an underground economy.

Napoleoni cites several examples to support this idea. She says a radical Marxist group in Peru, the Shining Path, turned to the drug trade in northern Peru, regulating drug production to fund their activities. The Revolutionary Armed Forces of Colombia (FARC) went a step further and joined the Colombian drug trade. Militant Palestinians went in another direction, using robbery and extortion to raise funds. The IRA started diverting funds from American charities before turning to organized crime. Napoleoni says these sources of financing fueled most of the terrorist activities of the 1970s and early 1980s.

failed state: An area
outside a government's
control. Failed states
operate under differing
warlords, criminal groups,
or competing governments.

shell state: A political
situation where a
government nominally
controls its own state but
where large regions are
either anarchic or under
the control of others.
A government is unable to
enforce law or provide for
other forms of social order
in a shell state.

The ETA (a separatist group in Spain) changed the structure of terrorist finance. Instead of seeking links to an underground economy, ETA tried to gain control of the economy. They forced Spanish businesses out of the Basque areas of northern Spain and weakened the entire state. The Basque region became a **failed state**, a place where Spain could no longer exert power. When this happened, ETA established an illegitimate economy in a **shell state**. It paid salaries to terrorists, provided for the families of fallen members, and even ran a pension system for retired terrorists. ETA was successful because the Spanish economy failed in the Basque region, leaving the area in a hopeless political mess. ETA was strong enough to enforce stability.

The new terrorist economy can be understood from the example of ETA. Napoleoni believes that globalization has created pockets in the world where failed or weak states are left to govern with little economic or political power. Terrorists and criminal groups grow in such places, running their own underground economies and providing some form of political stability because they are strong enough to resist the state. Illegitimate groups form a shell state, an organization that acts as a government in a place where the government is not strong enough to act.

As globalization increased, according to Napoleoni, it not only created economic vacuums where shell states could form but also fueled the growth of a global underground economy. It provided illegal trade routes for drugs, arms smugglers, contraband dealers, and human trafficking. Terrorist groups funded themselves through these activities, and they could not exist without them.

Napoleoni believes that modern terrorism is an international force supported by groups in shell states that continually change both their organizational structures and political goals to maintain income from an international underground economy. They hide their economic views with religious rhetoric or patriotic slogans, but their most important objective is to raise funds. Without funding, a terrorist group cannot exist. The prime goal of a group, then, is to maintain its finances. Napoleoni concludes that powerful groups even become strong enough to invest in legitimate markets, and in some instances they move so much money that they affect the global economy.

Complementing Napoleoni's work is a model developed by Mario Ferrero (2002), who argues that modern radical Islamic groups use violent activity as a means of providing economic stability. Jihadist groups cannot keep outsiders away or fire slackers for being unproductive. Numerous recruits flock to training camps and meetings, including people who are less than totally motivated. The slackers threaten stability by using a group's limited resources. To control this, jihadists increase rhetoric and violence to drive all but the most loyal members away from the group. This leaves enough resources to support the true believers.

Jeanne Giraldo and Harold Trinkunas (2007, pp. 7–11), of the U.S. Naval Postgraduate School, suggest that the political economy of terrorism is related to failed states and areas where governments cannot exert political control over their own territory. This has resulted in autonomous terrorist groups with their own funding sources. The terrorism generated by such groups is not related as much to a new style of terrorism or religious motivation as it is to their ability to generate funds. They control their economic circumstances, and funding creates violence.

Like Napoleoni, Giraldo and Trinkunas believe that the old Marxist groups were constrained by their sponsors. Unlike Napoleoni, they do not see the long emergence of a political economic system through the evolution of cold war financing. They believe that the key is self-sufficiency. Financial and political autonomy allows terrorists to operate without the constraints of a sponsor. Further, by participating in the global economy, they can function much like a government, controlling the flow of cash, goods, and services.

If these macroeconomic theories of terrorism are correct, they have meaning for the nature of counter terrorism. Many criminologists believe that crime can be reduced when potentially deviant groups have a vested interest in the economic structure of society. Macroeconomic theory suggests that counter terrorism policies should be aimed at providing the world's peoples with economic stability, opportunity, and participation in the mainstream economy (see Barnett, 2005, p. 49). Economic policies to counter terrorism would thus involve supporting states in danger of failure, providing opportunities for people to participate in and benefit from economic systems, and eliminating underground economic networks. When a state fails and a terrorist group creates its own shell state, the group has no incentive to participate in legitimate economic enterprises. As Benjamin Barber (1996, p. 299) says, when economic globalization threatens the ability of ordinary people to meet their needs, they will find other ways to survive. Indeed, this reflects Napoleoni's thesis. Poverty does not cause terrorism, but economic and political failures may result in a shell state where terrorism can be organized and funded.

 Self-Check

> What is a macroeconomic theory?

> How does it apply to terrorism?

> What political assumptions must be made to see the logic of a macroeconomic theory?

Narcoterrorism

narcoterrorism: A controversial term that links drugs to terrorism in one of two ways: Either drug profits are used to finance terrorism or drug gangs use terrorism to control production and distribution networks.

A heated issue surrounding the discussion of terrorist financing is the relationship between terrorism and drugs. The term **narcoterrorism** refers to groups using either terrorist tactics to support drug operations or drug-trade profits to finance terrorism. Rachel Ehrenfeld championed the concept of narcoterrorism in her early works, and she recently expanded on the idea (Ehrenfeld, 2003). According to her research, terrorists are involved in the international production and distribution of drugs; indeed, she believes that the narcotics trade is one of their primary sources of money. The U.S. government tends to accept this position, but it is nonetheless extremely controversial.

The Link between Drugs and Terrorism

Steven Casteel (2003), an executive with the Drug Enforcement Administration (DEA), told a U.S. Senate committee that terrorism and the drug trade are intertwined. Organized criminals, smugglers, and drug dealers naturally linked up with terrorist groups, he says, because all these organizations move in the same circles. Like Napoleoni, he believes that globalization has intensified this relationship. He says that the relationship between drugs and terrorism has been in place throughout history.

David Adams (2003), reporting for the *St. Petersburg Times*, says that Hezbollah and Hamas use the Latin American drug trade to raise funds. He writes that U.S. military units have tracked their activities in South America, and the military is concerned about the large amount of money involved. According to the U.S. Central Command, hundreds of millions of dollars have been raised in Latin America. The military's prime concerns are the Triborder region, the Venezuelan island of Margarita, and the areas controlled by FARC in Colombia. The DEA agrees with this assessment. An official from the U.S. Department of State puts it succinctly: Whether it is from Latin America or elsewhere, terrorist groups are financed through drugs. This is demonstrable, not debatable (J. P. Walter, 2002).

Other governments also believe that terrorism and drugs are linked. The French Ministry of Defense issued a report stating that drugs are the primary currency used to finance international terrorism. The French government points to the Shining Path and FARC to show the influence of cocaine. The ministry claims that radical Islamic groups get most of their money through the drug trade in central and Southeast Asia. Afghanistan is the primary source of heroin in Europe, and the profits from these drug sales fund all international Islamic terrorist groups (Chouvy, 2004). Officials in India believe that Lashkar-e-Taiba and al Qaeda have smuggled drugs and other contraband through Africa, central Asia, and Eastern Europe (*Times of India*, 2003). According to many in the Indian government, militant Islamic groups are funded by the drug trade.

Joshua Krasna (1997) takes the argument to another level. He says that if people are willing to expand the definition of national security beyond the framework of military defense, drugs pose a security problem. Defining security as social safety, Krasna says that the drug trade threatens political and economic stability by disrupting society. The drug trade limits the ability of legitimate governments and increases the power of insurgent and terrorist groups. Terrorists, for their part, use drugs not only to exploit the social safety concerns of their enemies but also to fund terrorist activities.

Nothing illustrates Krasna's point better than the unfortunate situation in Mexico. Seven major drug trafficking organizations dominate the political landscape in northern Mexico. Officially labeled drug trafficking organizations by the United States government, these drug cartels bring a high level of criminality to the U.S.–Mexican border. Violence spills over into Arizona and Texas, and the cartels have directly influenced urban gang activity in Los Angeles, Chicago, New York, Dallas, and San Francisco. Another alarming trend is the link between one of the groups, Los Zetas, with Hezbollah. This has spawned concern over an emerging link between drug trafficking and terrorism. Los Zetas uses Hezbollah in West Africa to launder drug profits while Hezbollah uses the payoffs from Los Zetas to finance terrorist operations. There is speculation about an even closer link between Los Zetas and Iran, as some analysts believe that the drug cartel may have been involved in an assassination plot against the Saudi ambassador to the United States in late 2011 (Chalk, 2012).

Narcoterrorism Controversies

Not everyone accepts the link between drugs and terrorism. Some people argue that terrorists may use drugs as a source of income, but they also use several other illegal activities to raise money. Selling drugs is only one method, and the drug problem is not caused by terrorism. Other people believe that the use of the term *narcoterrorism* is an attempt to take political advantage of the fear of terrorism. If drugs and terrorism come to mean the same thing, it will be easier to take actions against drug dealers. Critics believe that combining the drug problem with terrorism confuses two different issues.

The 9/11 Commission (2004, pp. 171–172) dismisses the idea that drugs were linked to al Qaeda's attack on New York and Washington, D.C. There is no evidence, the commission writes, that indicates bin Laden used underground drug networks or narcotics trafficking to support the September 11 attacks. The Taliban used narcotics trafficking to support itself in Afghanistan, but bin Laden used a network of donors based in Saudi Arabia and the Gulf States.

In the same article in which he explains narcoterrorism, Adams (2003) acknowledges the critics. He points to skepticism about the military and DEA assessment of Latin America. Many critics believe these organizations have overstated the problem. Other people point to misunderstandings. Terrorists are not necessarily linked to the drug trade even when they appear to be involved with drugs. Many Arabs live in the Triborder region, and they support Hamas and Hezbollah. Just because drug traders flourish in this region does not mean that either the Arabs or the terrorist groups are associated with drugs.

David Kaplan (2003) says the financing of militant Islamic groups has very little to do with the drug trade. Based on a five-month study for *U.S. News & World Report*, Kaplan blames Saudi Arabia for funding the spread of an intolerant form of Islam. Violent intolerance, he says, spawned the rise of terrorist groups, and the sect most sympathetic to an intolerant version of Islam comes from Saudi Arabia. Charities are responsible for the bulk of terrorist financing, he believes, and the money funds radical mosques, militant schools, and Islamic centers that support the jihadist movement. Saudi money can be traced to violence in Algeria, Bosnia, Kashmir, the West Bank, Gaza, Indonesia, Somalia, and Chechnya. The spread of militant Islam is not about drugs.

Pierre-Arnaud Chouvy (2004) does not agree with the position of the French military. He argues that the term narcoterrorism is too vague to describe either drug traffickers or terrorists, and it does not help address either problem. The problem with drugs involves supply and demand. Western Europe and North America provide ready markets for drug use. Typical Afghan farmers fight to survive. They produce opium, the base for heroin, because it is a cash crop. Western Europe has the demand, Chouvy says, and Afghanistan has the supply. Opium production has nothing to do with terrorism. Narcoterrorism is a convenient term for the French government to use, appealing to public emotions and giving the police more power.

Civil libertarians are especially critical of attempts to link terrorism and drugs (TalkLeft, 2003). Agreeing with Chouvy, they see the attempt to link narcotics and terrorism as a ploy by states. If terrorism were to disappear, the drug trade would remain. But if governments link drugs with terrorism, they can reinvent the meaning of crime. Drug dealers will become terrorists, and a frightened public will grant the government expanded powers to combat drugs. In addition, courts more readily grant search warrants and wiretaps against terrorists. Civil libertarians often believe governments want to define drug pushers as narcoterrorist kingpins in an effort to increase their own power.

Michael Scheuer (2006, pp. 42–44) takes the middle ground in the debate over narcoterrorism. In an examination of Osama bin Laden, Scheuer writes that the analyses of al Qaeda's use of heroin to finance jihad range from believable to fantastic accounts. Some reports of the narcotics connection are true, some are simply asserted without evidence, and a great deal of propaganda is obviously false. Nevertheless, the narcotics trade in Afghanistan makes billions of dollars. It would be naïve, Scheuer concludes, to assume that bin Laden has not been able to take advantage of some of those funds.

Self-Check

> Define the two elements of narcoterrorism.
> What arguments support the idea?
> Why do some analysts reject the idea of narcoterrorism?

Chapter Take Aways

Terrorist organizations are as complex as any other social organization designed to accomplish a mission. They are hampered in their effectiveness due to the secret nature of their operations. Most organizations are designed either to support guerrilla movements or to operate as a terrorist movement. The former use terrorism selectively, the latter simply terrorize as a strategy. All groups require funding. This has caused some analysts to focus on the fiscal aspects of terrorism, believing that terrorists used money in the same way as other organized criminals. Investigations have revealed that the money trail in terrorism differs from the flow of funds in other criminal enterprises because of the special structure of terrorist operations. However, it is important to understand the financing of terrorism because it is an important intelligence tool.

OBJECTIVE SUMMARY

- Modern terrorism can be characterized by three overlapping models. A rural model is associated with anticolonial guerrilla war, and an urban model emerged from ideological terrorism. The insurgent model combines both approaches and associates them with networks, technology, and globalization.
- Organizational structures evolve over time. Hierarchies gave way to umbrella or hub organizations. Terrorism continued to develop into leaderless networks. Failed states have given terrorists the ability to create a hub or umbrella organization within a network. In addition, modern piracy is related to organized crime; however, in the Horn of Africa it has become linked with terror networks.
- Leading a terrorist group is difficult due to the need for secrecy, decentralizing the organization, and factionalism. Operational efficiency is affected by these factors, as some groups operate alone in a network and others work with command-and-control systems. Large groups or networks are more effective than smaller ones outside a network.
- Analysts have slowly developed an appreciation of the importance of terrorist financing. Today, it is commonly assumed that good counter terrorist policy involves strategic efforts to deny fiscal resources to terrorists. One group of analysts and scholars believes that a financial strategy against terrorism will reduce

violence. Another group argues that this approach is too simplistic because terrorists operate in an underground economy immune from formal governmental sanctions.

- Terrorists raise funds by a number of legal and illegal methods. Illegal methods include robbery, counterfeiting, fraud, cigarette smuggling, extortion, kidnapping, and a variety of other criminal activities. Terrorists also raise money through legal operations. They divert funds to support terrorist operations. Charities and business operations are the most frequent legal activities.
- Funds are disbursed in an underground economy or through traditional money laundering activities. These include hidden money transfers such as the hawala system and the Black Market Peso Exchange. They also smuggle cash, launder money, convert it to consumer products, or keep the money or goods within the organization.
- The hawala system is based on an old method merchants used to exchange money without risking transport of actual cash. It is based on agents who exchange promissory notes. Today, some terrorists use this system to fund operations.
- The political economy of terrorism involves groups that have the ability to act autonomously in shell states and failed states. Becoming a *de facto* government power, they control the movement of money, goods, and services.
- There is a debate about the relationship between illegal drugs and terrorism. Proponents believe that terrorists use drugs to finance operations, and they use the term narcoterrorism to describe this activity. Opponents argue that governments use the term to increase their own power by defining common criminals as terrorists.

Critical Engagement: Drug Economies and the Future—The Complication of Drug Violence in Mexico

The narcoterrorism debate is far from abstract. Different drug cartels are in daily conflict with Mexican authorities. They have divided the country into spheres of influence, and they rule by intimidation, violence, and murder. Drug-related murders were counted in the thousands in the early twenty-first century, and the first mass graves from drug executions began to appear in 2004. Cartels control large areas of the U.S.–Mexico border, they use the profits to corrupt police agencies and government officials, and they openly attack police agencies and military forces. Cartels torture and murder their victims, leaving mutilated bodies as a warning to others (Katel, 2008).

The struggle in Mexico is not classified as terrorism, but it certainly exhibits aspects of the urban and insurgent models. In addition, drug crime and official corruption are so widespread that parts of Mexico are, and the entire government may become, ungovernable. If that were to happen, the area would be open to any terrorist group. In October 2009, former U.S. drug czar Barry McCaffrey told Congress that the problems in Mexico are enormous. The theme of his testimony was a warning. The United States cannot have a 2,000-mile border with a failed state (Kellner and Pipitone, 2010).

The drug problem in Mexico is related to the demise of two cartels in Colombia in the 1990s. As drug routes through the Gulf of Mexico were closed, Colombians began moving drugs through Mexico. At first, they paid Mexican criminals to protect and transport the drugs; eventually they let the Mexicans gain control. This spawned a number of drug cartels. By 2000, they were making tremendous profits (González, 2009).

The money taken in by the cartels is astounding. In 2009, U.S. intelligence officers believed it was as high as $18 to $38 billion annually. For comparison, Google made $17 billion in the same time frame. Two cartels, the Sinaloa Cartel and the Gulf Cartel, dominate the others. The Gulf Cartel grew dramatically in the 1990s, and it incorporated deserters from the Mexican Special Forces in a group called *Los Zetas*. By the twenty-first century, they provided security for the Gulf Cartel, but they wanted much more (Kellner and Pepitone, 2010). After a crackdown by the Mexican government in 2003, the Sinaloa Cartel formed an alliance with several other cartels in the north, while the Gulf Cartel formed its own alliance with smaller drug gangs and Los Zetas. The result was chaos (González, 2009).

Mexico is engaged in a three-way internal conflict that threatens the ability of local and federal governments to rule effectively. The alliances of drug cartels are fighting each other and the Mexican government. Victims are tortured, murdered, and mutilated. Their heads or disfigured torsos are dumped in public venues as a warning to all who might oppose them. Some cartels have also conducted extensive extortion and kidnapping campaigns against wealthy Mexicans (González, 2009).

Violence is fueled by the money from drug sales in the United States. Mexican criminals with millions of American dollars bribe officials, infiltrate all levels of government, and bring police officers into their organizations (Kellner and Pepitone, 2010). They also arm themselves with weapons from the United States. An estimated 90 percent of the weapons used by the cartels are purchased in the United States within 50 miles of Mexican border. In addition, the cartels have established operations in 48 American states (González, 2009).

The situation in Mexico reflects several issues in this chapter. It suggests that criminal terrorism could be modeled from political frameworks. It also demonstrates the effectiveness of command structures in criminal organizations that use terrorist tactics, and it certainly presents an economic model based on drug trade. If Mexico

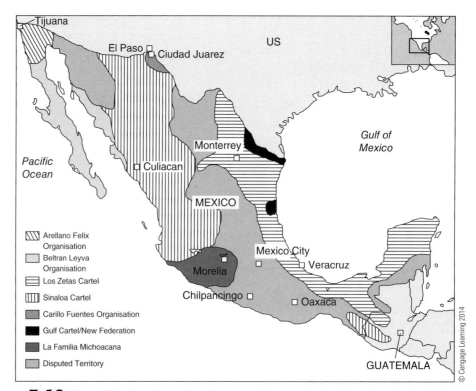

FIGURE **3.10** Map of Mexican Drug Cartels

becomes a shell or failed state, terrorists will establish bases much closer to the United States than those in the tribal areas of Pakistan.

Consider these issues in terms of future developments:

- Does narcoterrorism exist or is it simply a means for government to create more power by equating criminals with terrorists? If you answer the first part affirmatively, how does it compare with political terrorism? If you answer the second part affirmatively, why would this be harmful, given the state of affairs in Mexico?
- The issues in Mexico go far beyond law enforcement. What types of policies in both the United States and Mexico might stabilize the situation?
- If Mexico becomes a failed state, what implications might this have on the future of terrorism in the rest of North America?

KEY TERMS

Ernesto "Che" Guevara p. 3-56	Umbrella, p. 3-64	Forensic accounting, p. 3-70	Hawala system, p. 3-75
Cuban guerrilla war, p. 3-57.	Virtual organizations, p. 3-64	Expropriation, p. 3-71	New economy of terrorism, p. 3-78
Carlos Marighella, p. 3-58.	Chain organizations, p. 3-64	Triborder Region, p. 3-73	Failed state, p. 3-78
Cells, p. 3-62.	Networks, p. 3-65	Globalization, p. 3-73	Shell state, p. 3-78
Pyramid, p. 3-62	Tribal areas, p. 3-68	Black Market Peso Exchange, p. 3-74	Narcoterrorism, p. 3-80
	Capone discovery, p. 3-69		

Terrorism and the Media

CHAPTER **4**

Kathy deWitt / Alamy

LEARNING OBJECTIVES

After reading this chapter, you should be able to:

> Discuss the role of the media in constructing social reality.

> Explain the tension between security forces and the media.

> Describe how the media can be viewed as a weapon.

> Explain how news frames are used to present a story.

> Describe the special relationship between terrorism and television.

> Explain how the Internet has impacted terrorism.

> Summarize various positions regarding bias in the news media.

> Define the contagion effect.

> Debate the issues of freedom of the press and censorship.

James Oliver Rigney, Jr. (October 17, 1948–September 16, 2007), whose pen name was Robert Jordan, began publishing a massive fantasy series entitled *The Wheel of Time* in 1990. Sadly, he passed away in 2007, but the 14-volume series is scheduled to be completed by Brandon Sanderson. The books tell stories of a world where demons fly, women weave special powers from a mythical city called Tar Valon, young men and women seek their destinies, and good forces battle evil for control of creation. Of course, the series is the product of Rigney's imagination, yet the books contain quite a bit of truth about the human experience. One theme that occurs over and over throughout the series is the way tales are passed by word of mouth. Readers are allowed to experience men and women struggling against evil through the eyes of the main protagonists. After the confrontations, the story spreads through fictional kingdoms and the stories change. By the time they are told for the fifth, sixth, and seventh times, the stories do not resemble the original narrative. This is the way human beings share stories, and not merely the product of entertaining fiction.

On May 2, 2011, commandos from the U.S. Navy's elite SEAL Team Six landed in a compound north of Islamabad, Pakistan. Their target was one of the most infamous terrorists of all times, Osama bin Laden. The raid was successful. Shortly after the raid President

Barack Obama called President George Bush to give him the news. A few minutes later President Obama came on the major networks and announced that Osama bin Laden was dead. Then the stories of the stories started to spread. Military experts and former commandos first appeared on cable television to give "authoritative" accounts of the raid. Network news broadcasts and nationally syndicated newspapers expanded stories of the raid the following day, complete with illustrations and graphics. The White House released an official version of the raid. A few days later a SEAL publicly contested the official version, and television producers began focusing on documentaries to explain what "really" transpired. Within weeks there were several versions of the story about the death of the world's most wanted terrorist.

Events become stories in literature and in day-to-day life. Most stories are forgotten, but some of them are repeated. Twice-told stories evolve into sagas, and sagas change to legends. The *Wheel of Time* series demonstrates this process through literary fiction. The many versions of Osama bin Laden's death arose in the world of electronic mass-mediated information. Almost everyone who had a version of the story tried to get an account of the incident publicized, including al Qaeda. While this is the manner in which humans have always transmitted their stories, the process develops much more rapidly in the world of modern mass communication. Both security forces and terrorists want their version of the story publicized, and each side wants to control the media environment for one simple reason: The various media are not and cannot be neutral; they are a weapon.

The Media and the Social Construction of Images

news media: As used in this text, refers to television, radio, and print journalism. It also refers to newer sources on the Internet, including news reporting services, the blogosphere, website pages, and propaganda broadcasts.

Jeffery Ian Ross (2007) raises several important points about the relationship of terrorism to the **news media**. In essence, many criminologists and analysts discuss it, but there remains much to be learned. Terrorism requires interdisciplinary research techniques because it involves so many aspects of the human experience, and its relationship with the media has not been fully explored. While there are a number of studies about terrorism and the media, they tend to refer to the same scholarly sources. Ross concludes that the range of publications and research adds very little new knowledge.

Ross believes that there are several areas in need of new research but that we do know something about the relationship between the media and terrorism. First, as discussed in Chapter 2, meanings are socially created, and Ross demonstrates that reporting is part of the social construction of terrorism. Second, terrorists are aware of the power of the media and seek to manipulate their message through it. Third, while the media enhances the power of terrorism, it does not cause it. Finally, terrorists will increasingly use the Internet to communicate as the relationship between the media and terrorism grows stronger in the future.

While more interdisciplinary research is needed, Ross is quite correct about the issues around terrorism and the media. Terrorism involves symbolic communication, usually aimed at an audience far beyond the immediate victims of violence. Alex Schmid and Albert Jongman (2005, p. 21) write that terrorism is designed to communicate specific messages to a select audience. Nancy Snow (2006) points out that terrorism is such an effective communication device that governments respond by trying to send their own messages through the media. Communication develops in three primary manners. The first, and most obvious, involves the reporting of terrorist events. Media exposure magnifies events, campaigns, and causes, and both terrorists and governments attempt to manipulate reports so that they are portrayed in a favorable light. This is especially true as it applies to television, but it is applicable to all news reporting. Second, the media plays a major role in creating the social definition of terrorism. It can, for example, globalize a local event or personalize a global event on a local level. Third, the World Wide Web has become a conduit for propaganda and communication. In any form, terrorism sends a message.

Some scenes have become all too familiar. A hooded member of Black September stands on a hotel balcony in Olympic Village. Elsewhere, a hijacker forces an airplane pilot to stick his head out the cockpit window while the hijacker fires a pistol into the air. On the Internet, a fanatic stands behind a blindfolded and rope-bound hostage, reading a religious proclamation claiming that the innocent hostage represents evil. After the proclamation, the terrorist kicks his hostage to the floor, pulls out a long knife, and slowly beheads the hostage while crying out, "God is great!" Scenes like this play out time and time again on television, on the Internet, on radio talk shows, and in newspaper stories and pictures. The meaning of terrorism is socially constructed, and the media provide a large part of the interpretation (Munson, 2008).

Popular Media Misconceptions

Everybody in the public eye wants to use the media to his or her advantage; interest groups, including governments and terrorists, compete for favorable labels and images. Daya Thussu (2006) states that the United States' perspective on terrorism has dominated the international media since 9/11. This is due to the media's ability to create and sustain the social image of terrorism. Thussu refers to this power as mythmaking, and the myths circulated by television news shape the worldview of those who watch. Such myths and misconceptions are presented far beyond the West, and they have defined social reality after 9/11 in many parts of the world. If social constructs are created by collective definitions, the power of the media helps to define the boundaries of those constructs.

According to Thussu, the media's presentation of terrorism is dominated by several simplified stories presented and re-presented on 24-hour cable news networks. This type of reporting leads viewers to believe that terrorism is the result of Islamic radicalism, and it results in other falsehoods and misconceptions in the minds of viewers. Viewers are encouraged to accept a few isolated, simple facts about complicated issues and to accept misappropriated labels. Every event is portrayed in a moralistic tone.

Islam suffers from cable news simplifications. Viewers are encouraged to believe that radicalism defines Islam and that all Muslims believe exactly the same thing. There is no difference between Hezbollah, Hamas, and al Qaeda. In fact, the religious radicals have replaced the Soviet Union as a cold war rival to the West, and the only way they can be confronted is to respond with military force. Not only is Islam defined by radicals, but reports gradually demonize the entire religion. When Muslims appear, they are described with negative labels, such as "radical cleric," "violent Wahhabi," or "Islamic militant."

Other myths become subtly incorporated as the larger image takes shape, and they are not limited to religion. When reporting on terrorism in general, the media exaggerates the threat of weapons of mass destruction. They also use simple catchphrases or accept the simplifications that politicians use to popularize a point. Phrases like "broken borders" and "war on terrorism" create images that become reality after they are used again and again. Thussu (2006), critical of American counterterrorist policy, feels media myths distort the issues surrounding terrorism.

Topics selected for coverage distort images, and unselected topics go unnoticed. Steven Chermak and Jeffrey Gruenewald (2006) found this was true in reporting on domestic terrorism after a content analysis of stories in American newspapers. David Altheide (2007) says that the United States "discovered" international terrorism after the attacks of September 11, 2001. Media coverage of terrorism, however, focused on fear and sensationalism. As a result, one of the main issues concerning terrorism, the change in American foreign policy, did not receive the same amount of coverage. Politicians, Altheide argues, transformed the link between America's fear of crime to America's fear of terrorism, and the media increased this fear. As a result, the United States took the lead in countering international terrorism, but the media did not analyze that aspect of the story. That is, American foreign policy changed, but this generally went unreported and unanalyzed.

Many media analysts criticize reporting that is sympathetic to governmental positions, assuming that the media's job is to present alternatives to official actions. Some critics point to issues such as reporters embedded with military units and stories that rely on senior law enforcement or military personnel as their only sources. For example, the Israeli press was criticized for not opposing the government's decision to target terrorist leaders for assassination. Media analysts have also criticized the American press for writing reports favorable to security forces (see Korn, 2004; Rozen, 2009; Steuter and Wills, 2010). Sometimes it seems that the media's job is to uncover the hidden "truth" behind a policy and insist that government officials follow the wisdom of the press. Such media representations may place security forces at risk.

Roberto Valdeon (2009) argues that reporting about terrorism in Spain has framed the struggle with the Basque Nation and Liberty (ETA). According to his research, Spanish journalists tend to capture the violence behind terrorist activities, but international journalists tend to look at the ETA in a different light. They tend to refer to the ETA as "separatists" instead of "terrorists." For example, although the international media reports the pain and ensuing chaos after ETA bombing attacks, many times they refer to the attack as part of the Basque *separatist* movement with ETA *separatists* conducting the attack. Valdeon examines the nuances of language, but the argument can be taken further. Since terrorists are so dependent on the media to expand their aura, such softening of terminology may prolong a conflict and place security forces at risk. Despite claims of objectivity and the public's "right to know," when the news media make a report, they automatically become part of the story. Reporting about terrorism cannot be neutral.

Tension between Security Forces and the Media

Although some scholars believe the media favors governments, police and security forces frequently find themselves at odds with this media power (see Nacos, 2002). On the one hand, they compete for favorable media coverage. On the other hand, governments exhibit a strong disdain for the press because media social constructions often run counter to governmental objectives and policies. Paul Wilkinson (1997) argues that governments seek to harness the power of the media for social control. For example, in hostage situations, security forces are responsible for the fate of the victims. Reporters often do not focus on the security mission of such incidents because they are under tremendous pressure to be first with the story, and they have their own agendas when reporting the story. As a result, Wilkinson concludes, law enforcement and military goals often conflict with the goals of the reporters.

Whereas Thussu concludes that the social meanings created by news segments favor governmental policy, security forces come to the opposite conclusion. Within everyday police or military operations it is not uncommon to hear many statements criticizing the media. Chiefs of police and military commanders generally do not respect or trust media figures or reporters, and their attitudes are reflected by line personnel. Specialized command units are often created within police agencies to portray a favorable image to reporters, and U.S. military forces include public relations units when they go to war.

Police and security forces officially represent the social order, and they are charged with maintaining governmental authority. They see themselves as servants of the public interest in the United States and other Western democracies. In addition, they believe they make decisions for the public good. They perceive themselves to be the forceful extension of democracy. They think reporters are only trying to gather sensationalistic stories. Practitioners understand the reality of media coverage and seek to limit and control coverage (Parent and Onder, 2001). Scholars like Douglas Keller (2006) think this may be somewhat ironic because media reporting generally favors security forces.

embedded reporters:
Refers to reporters who
placed inside military
units during a combet
operation.

Police and military forces frequently try to take advantage of the media's ability to define social reality. For example, in the 2003 invasion of Iraq, the Pentagon invited print and electronic journalists to join combat units. They were known as **embedded reporters**. The military assumed that this would lead to better control of news reports. The results were partially realized. When compared to the free coverage during the 1991 Gulf War to oust Iraq from Kuwait and the subsequent enforcement of no-fly zones in northern and southern Iraq from 1991 to 2003, reports submitted by embedded journalists to their editors were more favorable to American military units. After editing, however, published reports did not exhibit more favorable general coverage (Pfau et al., 2004).

The Media as a Weapon

The late Richard Clutterbuck once concluded that the media was similar to a loaded gun lying in the street. The first person to pick it up got to choose how to use it. Governments see the media as that loaded gun. If they pick it up, as by embedding reporters, they can use it to their benefit. Police executives and military officers are frequently trained in media manipulation. They want to make skillful use of the weapon when they pick it up.

Terrorists also recognize the power of the media as a weapon. Ayman al Zawahiri, a leader of al Qaeda, views the media as one of the tools in al Qaeda's arsenal. First, any attack, especially if it is sensational, can dramatize the struggle. Major attacks draw major media coverage, and although the reports are not favorable among the enemy audience, they play well with sympathizers of al Qaeda. Second, Zawahiri can turn to his own media relations group. When he ran Egyptian Islamic Jihad, Zawahiri relied on a suborganization devoted to public relations; since joining al Qaeda, he continues to rely on such an organization. Third, Zawahiri uses his own writings to justify terrorism. He writes books and pamphlets, playing on sympathy for Muslims victimized throughout the world. Finally, along with other jihadists, he uses the Internet (Aboul-Enein, 2004).

Counterterrorist researchers from the Combating Terrorism Center at West Point find that literature from violent extremists frequently reveals important information about their organizations and strategies (Brachman and McCants, 2006). Steven Corman and Jill Schiefelbein (2006), from Arizona State University, examine literature from militant Islamic groups to determine their media strategies. Their analysis shows that jihadists are keenly aware of the media's ability to influence the social construction of reality. Jihadist texts reveal three media strategies. First, they seek legitimacy for their movement, especially wanting to justify acts of violence to other Muslims. Second, they want to spread their message and increase sympathy for their militant interpretation of religion. Third, their opponents, both the West and Muslims with a different interpretation of Islam, are targeted for intimidation.

✓ Self-Check

> How do media outlets construct an image?
> Describe the tension between security forces and the media.
> How can the media be turned into a weapon?

News Frames and Presentations

Although communication scholars debate the definition, David Levin (2003) says reporting patterns are packaged in segments called **news frames**. The purpose of a news frame is to assemble words and pictures to create a pattern surrounding an event. The news becomes a symbolic representation of an event in which the audience is allowed to participate from a distance. Television and other media spin the event so that it can be translated into the understanding of popular culture. They use rhetoric and popular images to set the agenda, and the drama becomes the hook to attract an audience.

news frames: Visual, audible, or written packages used to present the news. Communication scholars do not agree on a single definition, but news frames generally refer to the presentation of the news story. They contain a method for beginning and ending the story, and they convey the importance of characters and actions as the story is told.

News frames form the basis for communicating symbols. Karim Karim (2001, pp. 18–19) says the news frame creates a narrative for understanding a deadly drama. Characters are introduced, heroes and villains are defined, and victims of violence become the suffering innocents. The people who produce the frame provide their interpretation to the audience. Because the news frame exists within the dominant political context of the producers, it is not necessary to expend a great amount of energy on propaganda. The audience has been indoctrinated by journalists and mainstream reporters who present governmental officials as protectors and terrorists as villains. The news frame provides the "correct" symbolism for the consumer.

Simon Cottle (2006) believes that news frames help "mediatize" the presentation of terrorism; that is, they shape the way an event is communicated. The news frame is used by all media, but it is especially applicable to television. The news frame, although intentionally used, is one of the least understood aspects of broadcast journalism because its complexity goes unnoticed. Discussions of news frames usually focus on a specific story, or they involve reducing ideas to common elements. Actually, Cottle says, selecting from among the different styles of news frames presents an issue in a particular fashion. The classic approach in television is the **reporting frame**. It is usually short and designed to provide the latest information. Although facts and figures are presented, the story fails to focus on context or background. It is superficial, reducing reality to violent actions and reactions, while the underlying causes of conflict are ignored.

reporting frame: The simplest form of a news frame. It is a quick, fact-driven report that summarizes the latest information about a story. It does not need to contain a beginning or an end, and it assumes that the consumer understands the context of the facts.

Types of Frames

Other frames complement the reporting frame, according to Cottle. A dominant frame presents a story from a single point of view. An authority figure or institution defines the story in this type of frame. Closely related is the conflict frame, which presents a story frame with two views, each side having experts or witnesses to support a position. A contention frame summarizes a variety of views, and investigative frames champion the role of the press as the protectors of democracy. Cottle identifies other frames designed to serve the community, enhance collective decision making, and enrich social understanding of an event (see *Expanding the Concept: Communication Frames*). Frames can also campaign for a single interpretation of an event or provide in-depth coverage beyond the shallowness of a reporting frame. Finally, Cottle says, television news presents a mythic frame, which reinforces deeply held values. This frame is frequently used to depict those people who have sacrificed their lives for a cause. The combination of all these communication frames complicates the presentation of the news on terrorism.

EXPANDING THE CONCEPT

Communication Frames

Simon Cottle (2006) says that news frames are complex because they are composed of a variety of communication frames. Terrorism is reported within the following types of frames:

- Reporting frames: superficial, short, and laced with facts
- Dominant frames: one authority's view
- Conflict frames: two sides, with experts
- Contention frames: a variety of positions
- Investigative frames: exposing corrupt or illegal behavior
- Campaigning frames: the broadcaster's opinion
- Reportage frames: in-depth coverage with background
- Community service frames: information for viewers
- Collective interest frames: reinforce common values
- Cultural recognition frames: a group's values and norms
- Mythic tales frames: hero stories

Source: Cottle, 2006.

Ambiguous Stories and News Frames

News frames give the story a structured meaning, but sometimes a story defies structure. The frame is centered on getting viewers' attention, presenting information, and revealing the results. What happens when the results are inconclusive? Frank Durham (1998) answers this question by looking at the crash of TWA Flight 800, a passenger airliner that exploded over the Atlantic Ocean shortly after taking off from JFK Airport in New York City in 1996. Durham believes that the news frame works when a report is based on sources with definitive explanations of an event. There were no solid answers in the TWA crash, however, and no authority could emerge with a definitive story on the crash. Durham tracked reporting in 668 stories from the *New York Times* for one year following the explosion. Dominant news frames emerged, but all were proved incorrect.

Durham concludes that ambiguity destroys the ability to create a sustainable news frame. Reporters covering TWA 800 expected to find facts that would reveal a logical cause. They looked to terrorism, a missile strike, and finally mechanical error. In the first months following the crash, neither facts nor logical conclusions pointed to an answer. As a result, Durham says, the *New York Times* could not produce a news frame for the story.

Durham's conclusion might have an interesting effect on understanding terrorism. If terrorism is reported in well-defined news frames, both the media and the consumer will assume that there is a political beginning, a violent process, and a logical end. If there is ambiguity about the story, however, the method by which reporters gather the story and present it becomes the story because there is no logical conclusion. Currently, most media outlets report terrorist events within the logic of a well-defined frame (see Althaus, 2002). When violence is ambiguous and continual, the frame loses meaning, and terrorism is reported as an endless cycle of violence. As Leon Uris (1977, p. 815) writes in *Trinity*, a novel about Anglo-Irish conflict in Ulster, there is no future in Ireland, just the cycles of the past. Cycles may not be amenable to news frames.

Beating the War Drum

Regardless, the news frame is a powerful instrument. It gives the media outlet covering an event the power to define it. Douglas Kellner (2002) knows that terrorism attracts attention, but he is critical of America's typical news frame. After September 11, Kellner says, American television presented only one news frame, patterning the attack as a clash of civilizations and suggesting that only a military response would stop future attacks. The militants behind the strike responded in the same manner with diatribes filled with simplistic anti-Americanisms, and American and international news frames defined their reports of al Qaeda within the boundaries of militancy.

Rather than examine the complexity of the issues, Kellner says, television beat the war drum and called in a variety of terrorism experts who reflected the single view. Radio was even worse, engaging in sensationalistic propaganda. The process did not stop with news reporting. One national network broadcast patriot war movies after several days of news coverage. Whether **postmodern** or not, news frames simplified the cause and pointed to one logical solution: war. A military solution may well have been the proper answer to 9/11, but news frames presented no other option.

The media also offered long-term extensive coverage of military actions in Iraq and Afghanistan. It can be argued that images of suffering and death change public perceptions. The media brings stark images into American homes. Even if there is a bias to support American foreign policy—and most policy makers would vehemently argue there is not—access to new types of digital media can expand perspectives. For example, if the news frames of cable television present one ideal, there are a variety of other interpretations available in other media (Zimmerman, 2007). Perhaps the focus should be on audiences. Consumers who do not want to understand

postmodern: Describing the belief that modernism has ended; that is, some events are inexplicable, and some organizations and actions are naturally and socially chaotic and defy explanation. A postmodern news frame leaves the consumer thinking there are many possible conclusions.

other perspectives or who choose not to be informed might be more responsible for misunderstanding terrorism than the commercial news organizations framing a story.

Beating the Wrong Drum

While some scholars have argued that the various media have taken an uncritical look at U.S. military actions in the first part of the twenty-first century, other scholars suggest that the media have the wrong focus. Brigitte Nacos, Yaeli Bloch-Elkon, and Robert Shapiro (2010), do not question the media's focus on counter terrorism, but they do suggest that the focus is improperly centered on military and law enforcement action overseas. These actions are important, but domestic actions are just as important. The problem is that the media have virtually ignored domestic security issues.

The public depends on the mass media for information about issues. In turn, public perceptions formed by news stories frequently set the agenda for political policies. There is a strong correlation between the issues that the public thinks are important and the actions taken by political leaders. Communication scholars argue that one of the most important roles for the free press in a democracy is to make sure that critical issues stay in the news. At the same time, heightened competition for audiences creates an atmosphere in newsrooms in which shocking and dramatic information trump complex stories dealing with non-sensational issues. In other words, attacks against known terrorist leaders in Yemen or Pakistan draw more attention than mundane congressional hearings on port security. This concerns Nacos and her colleagues.

Nacos's study of several hundred news accounts in the first decade of counterterrorist action after 9/11 reveals that the American news media did not believe there was a need to focus on domestic security. The media's main focus was on perceived threats overseas. For example, Nacos and her colleagues examined all of the terrorism stories on ABC News, CBS News, and NBC News during a 39-month period. The three networks aired a total of 85 stories concerned with homeland security. During the same time frame the networks ran 373 stories dealing with the threat of terrorism. Most of the stories about security were aired after some type of public security breach. The researchers believe their findings indicated television's preference for sensational events.

The danger in this reporting is not in beating the war drum. The threat of terrorism is real and it demands some type of response. While some scholars are quick to condemn any type of military action or the use of deadly force in response to political violence, Nacos and her colleagues did not question the necessity to act with force. Their focus was on the national security agenda as portrayed by media reporting. There is a need to examine the threat, they argue, but the need for domestic security is just as important. By not analyzing the complex factors needed to secure the American public, the media has deemphasized homeland security. The researchers conclude that this is a dangerous situation.

Terrorism and Television

Benjamin Barber (1996, pp. 76–83) analyzes the problems of news frames and popular images on television in *Jihad vs. McWorld*. The title suggests that he is examining the world of the jihadists, but in fact he is looking at global economic inequities and the resulting ideologies that drive people into different systems. Instead of moving people to discuss problem solutions, Barber believes, the media flourishes on one overriding factor: entertainment. He humorously calls the 24-hour news networks the **infotainment telesector**.

The infotainment telesector is not geared for depth; it is designed to create revenue. "News" becomes banter between a news anchor and a guest, and debates devolve into shouting matches between controversial representatives. Issues are rarely discussed. Hosts perpetually interrupt their guests or provide answers to their own

infotainment telesector: A sarcastic term to describe cable news networks. It refers to news organizations producing stories to entertain their audiences under the guise of presenting objective information.

questions. Coverage of many shows is driven by a pleasing personality who either lacks intellectual depth or does an excellent job hiding it. Morning news shows are full of interviewers who discover issues obvious to the rest of the world and who shake their heads in wonderment when common knowledge is revealed.

These contexts of the infotainment telesector and the desire to beat the other networks have a negative effect on homeland security. Documents are leaked, confidential plans are unveiled, and vulnerabilities are exposed. Terrorism is made more horrific to create better drama. News film is constantly replayed, giving the illusion that attacks are repeated time and time again. News hosts spend time interviewing reporters from the field who speculate on the facts surrounding an event. This leads to a dilemma for policy makers. Freedom of the press is guaranteed in the First Amendment to the Constitution, but television coverage frequently becomes part of the story it is covering.

Over the years several studies have pointed to the close relationship between terrorism and television. H. H. A. Cooper (1977a) was one of the first analysts to point to the issues, explaining that terrorist acts were **made-for-TV dramas**. Abraham Miller (1982) published one of the first books on the subject, pointing out that television brought terrorist events into our homes. More recently, Yassen Zassoursky (2002) says that television and the Internet give terrorists an immediate international audience. Gadt Wolfsfeld (2001) says acts have become so graphic and sensational that they grab media attention. In one of the best standard-setting studies, Alex Schmid and Jany deGraaf (1982) say that the relationship between terrorism and the media is so powerful that Western democracies may need to take drastic action and even implement censorship.

David Levin (2003) says that the purpose of television news coverage is to keep the audience primed with emotion and excitement. News organizations use a standard drama pattern to accomplish this. It is designed to keep the viewer tuned to the station. The attention-getting theme is the essence of the drama.

A drama pattern is constant in any unfolding event. On-the-scene reporters send reports back to the anchor, who calmly sits at the desk gathering information, sometimes asking urgent questions to clarify issues for the audience. The hidden meaning of the report intimates that the station has crucial information on "breaking news," and members of the audience need to know it. The anchor is the authority figure who is able to process information for the viewers. Reporters are the researchers sending the latest information back from the scene. The overriding message of the drama is "stay tuned." It is the pattern of Greek tragedy, and it works for television—whether covering the weather, terrorism, election results, or *Football Night in America* (see *Expanding the Concept: TV Drama Patterns*).

made-for-TV dramas:
Refers to news stories that will keep viewers' attention. H. H. A. Cooper was among the first analysts to recognize the drama that terrorism presented for television.

EXPANDING THE CONCEPT

TV Drama Patterns

What makes a good news drama?

Change: The situation is changing and the outcome is unknown.

Information: The latest news and breaking news about the situation is on *this* station.

Stay tuned: You must keep watching; the best is yet to come.

Expertise: Only this station is qualified to explain the situation.

On-the-scene reports: Reporters are there telling you what is happening, even when they do not know.

Control: The anchor controls the information from the studio, giving you a vicarious feeling of control.

Participation: You are allowed to vicariously participate in the event.

Money: The station breaks away to sponsors but promises even more drama after the commercial.

End of the Western Monopoly

al Jazeera: An international Arabic television network.

Control of the drama pattern was held in a Western monopoly until recently. New networks such as **al Jazeera** and al Arabia have challenged the West's—especially the American—hold on international news. If there is an effect from 24-hour cable news slanted toward a particular interpretation, new national perspectives influence it (Gilboa, 2005). In addition, localized networks present other perspectives and definitions of terrorism. Judith Harik (2004, pp. 160–161, 189) points out that Hezbollah has learned to do this by projecting a positive image on Lebanese national television. She says Hezbollah took advantage of **al Manar** television, Lebanon's network, as the Israelis withdrew from Lebanon and again during the **al Aqsa Intifada.**

al Manar: Hezbollah's television network.

al Aqsa Intifiada: An uprising sparked by Ariel Sharon's visit to the Temple Mount with a group of armed escorts in September 2000. The area is considered sacred to Jews, Christians, and Muslims. Muslims were incensed by the militant aspect of Sharon's visit.

Al Manar television presented a sympathetic view of the al Aqsa uprising, and Hezbollah was quick to take advantage of al Manar's 24-hour coverage. The method of reporting was the key to success. The news was interspersed with inspirational religious messages. Hezbollah was able to get al Manar to focus on Hezbollah's role in the Intifada and to run programs on its former glories. In an effort to demoralize the Israelis, al Manar broadcast pictures of Israeli casualties and ended with the question: "Who will be next?"

Power came in the form of visual images. Harik believes al Manar television helped to elevate Hezbollah to heroic status. She cites one example whose effect swept through Lebanon: Faced with heavy fighting in a West Bank village, Israeli forces withdrew. The Israeli Defense Forces (IDF), using Israeli mass media, denied it had abandoned the village. Al Manar presented another view. When the Israelis withdrew, Hezbollah fighters entered the village along with Palestinian mujahideen. Hezbollah raised its flag over the village, and someone took a picture. As the IDF was denying it had retreated, al Manar showed the village with the Hezbollah flag flying high overhead. Hezbollah achieved a media victory.

Television makes the viewing audience participants in a terrorist attack. Viewers have short- and long-term psychological damage after seeing terror attacks on television, and it shapes anxiety and attitudes. Anat Shoshoni and Michelle Sloan (2008) measured the reactions of 300 university students in Israel after they had been exposed to terrorist violence on television. Looking at levels of anxiety and anger, they wanted to see if attitudes and perceptions of the enemy and the willingness to accept negative group stereotypes would be affected. Unlike the immediate experiences of anxiety and anger, attitudes are generally formed over a long period of time.

The experiment began with a survey to measure anxiety and attitude. After the survey, students were shown two seven-minute video clips, one of a terrorist attack and the other of nonterrorist violence from the same group, and they conducted a second set of measurements. As they had expected, Shoshoni and Sloan found that anger and anxiety increased, but they also saw that long-term attitudes changed within the same time frame. In other words, the violent vignettes not only increased short-term fear; they were also responsible for fear and anxiety long after the students viewed the videos.

Television seeks drama, and terrorism provides an unfolding dramatic event. Tyler Cowen (2006) argues that terrorism is a spectacle that has a focal point, various actors, and a storyline. Television news coverage works well with such spectacles. Dramatic moving shots can be played over and over, while in-depth analysis gives background to an eager audience. Terrorist leaders need the unfolding drama, too. It allows them to motivate followers and increase control of an organization.

Televised Gender Stereotypes

Television also impacts the way women are viewed in terrorist organizations. Although women have played significant roles in modern terrorism and have frequently assumed positions of leadership, television tends to portray women as minor figures in the male-dominated occupation. Brigitte Nacos (2009) finds that television depicts female terrorists in a manner similar to the way women politicians are portrayed. Terrorist organizations use typical gender clichés that are, in turn, captured and restated in television reporting. The result is that women are cast in supportive and nurturing roles devoid of any personality characteristics required for tough political action. Television generates the same stereotypes for female terrorists and politicians.

Nacos presents several images created by television news frames. She discusses the "physical appearance" frame, which focuses on the way a woman looks in front of the camera. The "family connection" frame is used to create the appearance of a "typical housewife." The "terrorist for the sake of love" depicts a lovelorn female entering a life of terrorism due to her relationship with her male companion. The "women's lib" frame paints a picture of a nontraditional woman seeking to define herself in a more masculine role, as does the "tough as men—tougher than men" news frame. Finally, news frames also depict women as bored, frustrated housewives out of touch with reality.

The result of such depictions, Nacos concludes, is that television misrepresents the threat of terrorism by misstating the dangerous role that female terrorists play. Instead of looking at the actual activities of women, they are portrayed with gender stereotypes. The traditional method of framing female politicians has weakened in recent years, Nacos says, but the same is not true for the images of women terrorists. As a result, women are able to use their television-generated image to avoid detection. Gender-biased reports weaken our ability to respond to terrorism.

✓ Self-Check

> What is a news frame?
> How are news frames used to cover terrorism?
> Describe the relationship between terrorism and television.

The Internet and Terrorism

The Internet impacts news coverage of all events and often exceeds the ability of the established media to report an event. It is also used for communication, propaganda, reporting, recruiting, training, and as a tactical weapon. Either side can directly control information or hack into opponents' websites. Both sides can mine data and gather intelligence. The Internet can be a weapon, and either side may use it effectively. Terrorists have learned to use it on several levels.

Todd Hinnen (2004) says that the Internet is used most frequently as a communication device and that sending unsecure e-mail is the most common usage for terrorists. Unsecure e-mail is easy to penetrate, and evidence from it is frequently used in criminal prosecutions. Hinnen cites charges against a Colombian terrorist group for arms trafficking based on evidence gathered from e-mail. Terrorists, aware of the dangers of unsecure e-mail, use a variety of methods to hide communications. One way, Hinnen writes, is to give an e-mail account's password to several members of a group. A member can then draft a message, but never send it. Other members log on, read the draft, and then delete it after all have viewed it. Because the message is never sent, there is no e-mail record. A second method involves setting up a secure website, such as terroristgroup.com, with its own e-mail server. All members of a terrorist group would receive an address, such as jsmith@terroristgroup.com. If e-mail stays exclusively within the secure site, it is difficult to trace.

Terrorists understand the power of the Internet. They run their own websites, and they sometimes hack into existing sites to broadcast propaganda videos. Yassen Zassoursky (2002) says that these abilities enhance the power of terrorist groups, and he believes that the Internet's communication capabilities allow terrorist groups an opportunity to attack the global community. Sonia Liff and Anne Sofie Laegren (2003) reinforce Zassoursky's thesis by pointing to Internet cafés. They say that cybercafés enhance the Internet's striking power because they make communication untraceable.

steganography: Refers to embedding a hidden encoded message on an Internet site.

Steganography is frequently said to be one of the Internet's greatest vulnerabilities in light of criminal and terrorist communication. The process refers to embedding hidden information in a picture, message, or another piece of information. The process is not new. A Roman general once shaved the head of a slave, had a secret message tattooed on the slave's head, and waited for the slave's hair to grow back. When the message was covered, he sent the slave to the recipient with instructions to shave the slave's head (Lau, 2003). Obviously, the Internet presents possibilities for faster communication, and it does not present the risk of permanently displaying the message if the messenger goes bald! A steganographic message can be encrypted, placed in plain text in a hidden file, or sent on a covert channel (Westphal, 2003). There are numerous potential purposes for using steganography in terrorism. It could be used to hide communications, steal information from security forces or an organization within the critical infrastructure, or provide opportunities for electronic attack (Wingate, 2006).

There are two positions on the steganographic threat to the United States. Stephan Lau (2003) says one position claims that steganography is used by terrorist groups to communicate and launch cyberattacks. After 9/11, for example, media reports claimed that al Qaeda was hiding information in steganographic images. Some believe that it will be used in denial-of-service attacks or to deface websites. Lau takes the other position, claiming that fear of steganography is the stuff of urban legends. Although steganography programs are readily available and difficult to detect or counter with security hardware, programs offering statistical analysis of data contained in any Internet transmission readily reveal irregularities and the location of a hidden image. Entrepreneurs are marketing these programs to corporations and governments, but Lau believes the threat is not in the hidden image. He says that there is no evidence to show that the use of steganography by terrorists is a threat. The real threat, Lau argues, is the American government's enhanced ability to decipher private communications based on a threat that does not exist.

In the areas of propaganda, reporting, and public relations, the Internet has been a boon for terrorist groups. It allows terrorist groups to present messages and to portray images that will not appear in mainstream media. Paul Wilkinson (2006, pp. 144–157) says that terrorists have always used some medium for communication. In the past, it ranged from tavern gossip to handbills. Thus, it is logical to assume that the Internet serves the same purpose, now literally at the speed of light. Major terrorist groups run websites to present alternative views. For example, before its demise in 2009, the Liberation Tigers of Tamil Eelam (LTTE) ran a news service called EelamWebsite (http://www.eelamwebsite.com). Violent single-issue groups use the website for propaganda as well (see *Expanding the Concept: As Sahaab versus al Hurra*).

Salafi movement: Used by orthodox Muslims to follow the Prophet and the elders of the faith. Militants narrow the use of the term and use it to justify violence. The Salafi movement refers to those people who impose Islam with force and violence.

The Internet can also be used for recruitment and training. Abdul Bakier (2006b) finds Salafi jihadists using websites and e-mail to make training manuals available. The World Wide Web has become more important as growing numbers of females join the **Salafi movement**. One blogger, who identified herself as the mother of Osama, claims that the Internet gives women the opportunity to become *mujahidat* (female holy warriors). Bakier finds some sites specifically aimed at recruiting or retaining females. Other sites encourage suicide bombings. Discussion groups examine tactics and provide basic weapons orientation, and some militant scholars provide in-depth theological apologias to justify religious violence. One site has an entire first-aid course to deal with battlefield wounds. Bakier finds more and more groups using recruiting sites.

EXPANDING THE CONCEPT

As Sahaab versus al Hurra

Al Qaeda's media campaign has proved difficult for the United States to counteract. Al Qaeda's underground video network, known as As Sahaab, wages an effective propaganda campaign using the Internet. Evan Kohlmann (2005), an NBC terrorism analyst, explains the process. Local camera operators film studio sequences of a propaganda statement or live-action footage of mujahedeen along the Pakistan–Afghanistan border. The footage is edited on a computer, dubbed or subtitled, and handed over to an Internet group called al Fajir, which posts links to the clip in Arab chat forums. (Ironically, most of these forums are hosted in North America.) Television networks pick up the broadcasts. Western networks heavily edit them, but, on networks like al Jazeera, they sometimes appear as full-length broadcasts, according to the Discovery Times Channel (2005). In its own media offensive, the United States launched al Hurra, an Arabic-language 24-hour satellite station, in early 2004. The results have been disappointing. One prominent Arab writer called the $62 million project the American *Pravda*, after the communist news organization in the former Soviet Union (Cochrane, 2004). The Discovery Times Channel agreed, stating that most Arabic-speaking viewers distrust the news produced by al Hurra. In essence, a few thousand dollars invested in website cams, PCs, and video software have made more of an impact than a multimillion-dollar television enterprise. The United States has yet to capitalize on the Internet for spreading propaganda.

Sources: Kohlmann, 2005; Discovery Times Channel, 2005; Cochrane, 2004.

The Internet is also used in target selection, reconnaissance, and, sometimes, as a tool to support an attack. Maps, satellite imagery, and diagrams provide ready-made intelligence sources. Stephen Ulph (2006a) sees terrorists increasingly using Internet searches to find economic targets. He believes this trend is notable because terrorists across the globe can unite and research a particular target in a matter of minutes. He also finds terrorist groups attracted to data mining. One terrorist training manual points out that it is possible to gather information on enemy targets simply by using the Internet. Ulph (2006b) also sees the Internet as a potential weapon. Terrorists want to take hacker warfare to their enemies. Groups post methods to steal passwords and instructions for breaking into secure areas. There are instructions on systems and denial-of-service attacks, as well. As a logistical tool, the Internet can also be used to assemble people for a violent action. Clearly, the Internet has become a weapon in many arsenals.

There is another side to the story. Security forces also use the Internet, and they do so effectively. Researchers have access to databases, government reports, and other information. Security forces also monitor websites and chat rooms (Wright, 2008). New laws in a number of countries have given law enforcement and intelligence agencies the authority to monitor Internet content for criminal activity, although such surveillance is controversial in Western democracies (Brown, 2009). Law enforcement networks in the Regional Information Sharing System (RISS) have the ability to share criminal investigative information, and they provide local, state, and federal law enforcement with secure communications. The Internet can thus be used against terrorism and other forms of criminal activity.

Self-Check

> How do terrorists use the Internet to communicate?
> What is the value of Internet propaganda?
> Is the Internet a potential weapon for terrorism? Why or why not?

Issues in the Media

Because the media is so powerful, the way issues are reported and communicated is hotly debated. For example, Fox News claims to be "fair and balanced." Critics maintain it is not, but supporters believe that it presents objective reports. National Public Radio

(NPR) reporting is debated in the same manner, except that critics believe that NPR has a liberal bias. Such debates are not easily resolved, and the arguments favoring one side or the other are frequently full of opinions rather than hard evidence. Before leaving the discussion of the media, it would be helpful to review some of these issues.

Liberal and Conservative Biases in Terrorism Reporting?

Most mainstream media claim objectivity when presenting information about terrorism. They know governments and terrorists are trying to manipulate news stories, so they seek an ideal—objectivity. Many reporters believe that it is their job simply to tell the truth. They seek to be fair and balanced, as Fox News claims to be. These assumptions are naïve, according to former CBS employee Bernard Goldberg (2003, pp. 103–114). All news comes with a slant, and reporters are expected to create news frames reflecting their outlet's orientation. For people outside the newsroom, the debate is intense. At one end of the spectrum, critics claim that the media has a liberal bias. Critics fume, claiming that the print and electronic media are inherently anti-Western and anti-American (see Bozell, 2005; Anderson, 2005). These critics claim reporters are sympathizing with terrorism at worst or undermining the government at best.

Pundits and other nonscholars attack this position. They claim that the media has been taken over by conservatives. Conservative talk show hosts and guests banter about pseudo-facts, reinforcing right-wing ideology. Guests are invited on these programs only to be bombarded with conservative ranting. The critics claim that the news media is dominated by bullies and hatemongers who seek to silence any voice but their own. Reporting on terrorism cannot be objective in such a format—it is designed to create fear and limit individual freedom (see Anderson, 2005; Willis, 2005).

Is there bias in the coverage of terrorism? Some scholars think so, but it is much more subtle and complicated than the writers of popular diatribes believe. Rather than joining the debate by measuring the amount of conservatism or liberalism in news content, Daniel Sutter (2001) analyzes the economic aspects of news production. He asks, What incentives would generate a bias, and why would a profit-making entity risk losing an audience? One of Sutter's answers comes in the form of an analogy. Suppose the public is composed of 600 television news viewers who are liberal, moderate, or conservative. By statistical distribution, 300 viewers would fall in the middle, or moderate, category. The remaining 300 would divide equally between liberals and conservatives. A news organization, as a profit-making entity, has an incentive to attract the largest possible audience. If the news moved either to the right or left, it would be threatened with the loss of mainstream viewers. Sutter sees no incentive for a liberal or conservative bias. Or does it have a bias that is neither liberal nor conservative? (See *Another Perspective: Media Ownership*.)

ANOTHER PERSPECTIVE

Media Ownership

Edward Herman (1999) focuses on the social construction of reality and political bias when he examines the media, but not from the perspective of most critics. The bias is economic, he says, and it is dominated by multinational corporations. The American media is part of a vast propaganda machine promoting the values and goals of business corporations. He conducts case studies examining advertising, ownership, and content to demonstrate the point. Stories affecting corporate profits are manipulated in a positive way. Dictators are portrayed as moderate or benign when they favor corporate investments and profits, even as the same leaders repress or massacre their own citizens. Newspapers use catchphrases such as "free trade," "third world elections," and other simplifications to hide the powerful economic forces behind political action. The political bias is neither liberal nor anti-American; it is based in its market orientation.

There is a caveat in his logic, Sutter admits, because some media organization owners would be willing to sacrifice profit to stand for a political position. In addition, some journalists will insert their own feelings into a story even when these feelings do not reflect the owner's position. These factors are countered by trends in the profit-driven media. First, if the entire media were to exhibit a bias, one owner would need to have a monopoly on all media outlets. One company can afford to take a position, Sutter says, but the entire industry will not. Second, journalism is a profession. Work is reviewed and approved by editors and reviewed by colleagues. Individual bias is readily identified, but each journalist or reporter thinks and presents news separately. This process prevents an overall bias in the industry. Third, as news organizations expand, there will be pressures for a bias to develop special audiences among liberals and conservatives. Yet the media will remain market-driven, and the entire industry will not take up the biases of a limited, specialized audience. Finally, news organizations are increasingly led by boards and groups of owners driven by the desire to make money. They do not have the incentive to introduce bias that alienates their mainstream viewers.

David Baron (2004) takes a different approach, suggesting that bias appears on two levels: the individual discretion of the reporter collecting information for a story and the public's desire to watch or read the most captivating story. Small portions of a reporter's individual bias may slip into the story, but the corporation presenting the news will limit it. The business wants the greatest number of viewers, hence revenue, it can attract; therefore, it keeps reporters focused on captivating issues. The organization also wants to tailor the report to the beliefs and values of the audience. Therefore, there is very little incentive for bias. The one exception deals with reporters' salaries. Less objective news appealing to a specialized, politically biased audience can mean lower overall wages for reporters. Baron says that reporters who frame stories within a political bias do not need critical thinking and discernment skills. Therefore, station managers can pay them less and increase profits. There is a risk in this process, however, because bias may lower consumption, resulting in less income and lower profits. News corporations want to avoid risk and will keep major biases out of their stories.

Tim Groseclose and Jeffrey Milyo (2005) come to a different conclusion, stating that the American media has a liberal bias. Using multiple variables, Groseclose and Milyo selected a variety of media outlets, including newspapers, magazines, and television and radio news shows, to study. They limited their study to news items, eliminating editorials, commentaries, book reviews, and other opinion pieces from their study. They then selected think tanks and research organizations those media outlets used to provide information, guidance, and evaluation on governmental programs and policies. Next, they divided Congress into liberal and conservative members, and counted the numbers of times liberals and conservatives cited a think tank. Finally, they compared the number of times each selected news source cited the same think tank and compared this to the congressional numbers. They concluded that the news media cited the think tanks referenced by liberal members of Congress more than they cited the think tanks referenced by conservative members. Groseclose and Milyo concluded that the American news media has a strong liberal bias.

Fouzi Slisli (2000) is not concerned with a liberal or conservative orientation; instead, he focuses on the use of pejorative labels. He believes adjectives introduce bias into the news. Citing sensationalism and failure to conduct in-depth reporting, Slisli says that the American media is full of oversimplifications and stereotypes (see *Another Perspective: Stereotypes and Media Reports*). The media plays to the lowest level of understanding among its viewers. Large groups of people are lumped together in news reports with no intention of examining complexities. False categories are created to further simplify issues.

David Levin (2003) examines the reporting of peace processes, intimating that it has the problems of simplification, the inability of the audience to understand complexities, and a network's desire to attract an audience. The news is aimed at particular audiences, and different organizations approach audiences in a variety of ways. Information and education stations approach the news differently than do 24-hour cable news networks that focus on entertainment and emotions. It is difficult to explain sufficiently well the nature of the conflict, the various political positions, internal fighting within governments and terrorist organizations, and other issues surrounding attempts to bring peace to areas such as Sri Lanka, the Basque region of Spain, Israel and Palestine, and Ireland. Many people prefer simplicity and entertainment. Thus, many news programs and some networks search for an unreflective audience, playing to the most susceptible members of the audience. Some producers even attempt to find a supermarket-tabloid audience by searching for the lowest common denominator among them, that is, people who want to be spoon-fed and entertained. These shows exploit emotions, favor sensation over facts, fail to examine issues in depth, and place entertainment value above information.

ANOTHER PERSPECTIVE

Stereotypes and Media Reports

Are American television reports on terrorism objective? Fouzi Slisli (2000) answers with a blunt NO! Citing sensationalism and failure to conduct in-depth reporting, Slisli says that large groups of people are portrayed without depth in American television. Terms such as *fundamentalist*, *radical cleric*, and *terrorist* are used by reporters who either fail to understand issues or sensationalize their reports.

Source: Slisli, 2000.

Information networks approach the same issues with different objectives. They seek to educate their audiences. Their shows are thoroughly researched and focused on the complexity of information. Their purpose is to inform, and they seek an audience that wants to reflect, criticize, and analyze. They will introduce the intricacies of competing interpretations of information and accept ambiguity as normal. When trying to bring peace to an area plagued by political violence and terrorism, subtlety and complexity are the norms.

Richard Miniter (2005) shifts the argument to accuracy. He states that the media used to have a conservative bias, but now it has tilted toward liberalism. This is not the problem, however. The issue for the media is that it is spreading incorrect information about terrorism. He identifies 22 misconceptions about terrorism accepted as truth by most newspapers, magazines, and broadcasters. The myths come from a variety of sources, including honest mistakes in reporting, American and foreign government disinformation, and contrived leaks. Although the myths are accepted by much of the media and the public, they obfuscate terrorism because they are untrue (see *Another Perspective: Miniter's Media Myths*). Miniter is an investigative journalist, and he cites many credible sources. Other investigative journalists citing other credible sources disagree with some of his findings (for example, see Gordon and Trainor, 2006; Ricks, 2006).

critical media consciousness: The public's understanding of the media and the way stories are presented. A critically conscious audience would not simply accept a story presented in a news frame. It would look for the motives for telling the story, how the story affected social constructs and actions, and hidden details that could cause the story to be told in another way.

There is another type of conservatism beyond popular definitions and classical political science definitions. Some institutions provide social stability and preserve the status quo of social structure (see Manning, 1976, pp. 102–103). The media may be playing this role far beyond exhibiting a liberal or conservative bias. Todd Fraley and Elli Roushanzamir (2006) say that the current conditions of subnational and supranational violence are shifting and distorting all media presentations of violence, including terrorism. They sadly conclude that the mass media is spreading more propaganda than news in a world dominated by media corporations. The flow and amount of information, however, could serve to raise the awareness of news consumers, creating a new **critical media consciousness**.

News consumers need to develop analytical abilities that look beyond the news frame and examine the issues behind terrorism and other political events. If they do, Fraley and Roushanzamir believe, political freedom will expand throughout the world. If consumers remain at the current level of understanding, corporations will continue to remain in charge of mass media outlets, and emerging subnational and supranational groups—such as multinational terrorist organizations—will fight for control of emerging media. If the established media only stabilizes the existing social order, this will result in polarization with other forms of media, such as the Internet.

The Contagion Effect

copycats: Refers to people who imitate other criminals after viewing, hearing, or reading a story about a crime. A copycat copies the targets and methods of another criminal.

Some analysts are not as concerned about the content of press coverage as they are about its role in spreading terrorist violence; they wonder if media coverage inspires more terrorism. There are many vehement opinions, but this issue reintroduces the problem described by Jeffery Ian Ross (2007). Research indicates that the media do not cause terrorism, but the effects on areas such as crimes by **copycats** are unclear. There is definitely a need for further research.

⁂ ANOTHER PERSPECTIVE

Miniter's Media Myths

Richard Miniter says that popular images, conservative and liberal views, and urban legends are popularized through the media. Many of these media-based "truths" cannot stand the test of investigation. A selection of myths follows.

The Myth	The Truth
In an e-mail, Lt. Col. Oliver North allegedly warned Senator Al Gore about Osama bin Laden.	North was testifying to another senator about Abu Nidal, a Middle Eastern terrorist.
Former Soviet Union backpack nuclear devices have been stolen by al Qaeda.	The weapons appear to be secure and are more difficult to steal than popularly believed.
Jihadists are most likely to infiltrate from Mexico.	Canadian media has little respect for the abilities of Canadian police and intelligence services, and jihadist sympathizers operate a strong lobby in Canada. Miniter says the evidence indicates that jihadists will come from the north.
Conservative media personalities argue that political correctness keeps us from targeting via racial profiles terrorists who travel by air. If we could use racial profiles, we could identify terrorists.	Racial profiling does nothing to single out terrorists within ethnic groups. Comparing air travelers with a comprehensive terrorist knowledge base would work, but civil libertarians, both liberal and conservative, prevent that.
Liberal media personalities claim that the defense contracting company Halliburton made tremendous profits in Iraq.	Halliburton has shown little profit from Iraq, both for investors and for conspiracy theorists.
A popular Internet and Arab-media myth states that Israeli intelligence warned Jews to avoid the World Trade Center on September 11, 2001.	Although the exact number is unknown, hundreds of Jews died in the 9/11 attack, including five Israelis.

Miniter believes that all media serve as a source of disinformation. The primary reasons are sloppy reporting, editors who fail to check facts, and rumors that are accepted as truth. People gravitate to belief in conspiracies as a result.

Miniter says that the American government can help stop disinformation by making its reports readily available and by releasing the entire transcripts of officials' interviews before items are reported in the news.

Source: Miniter, 2005.

Most of the studies on media-induced contagion are dated or focus on areas other than terrorism. Several years ago Allan Mazur (1982) studied bomb threats in the nuclear industry. His study compared bomb threats against nuclear power plants with the amount of press coverage the plants received. He began by noting that news reports of suicides increase the actual number of suicides, and he wondered whether he might find a similar pattern in the nuclear industry. He found that the number of threats proportionately matched the number of news stories. When coverage increased, bomb threats increased. Conversely, when coverage decreased, bomb threats decreased.

One of the first criminal justice scholars to study media contagion was M. Cherif Bassiouni (1981); he felt that media coverage had several contagious effects. He found that media reports promoted fear and magnified threats. This caused fear to spread. The media also influenced the way terrorists selected their targets: to spread violence, terrorists selected targets for maximum publicity. From this standpoint, terrorism was contagious: Media-reported terrorism caused more terrorism.

If Bassiouni was correct, that meant that images influenced behavior. A few years later, research suggested that media images produced emotional behavior, but not in ways that were completely predictable. When exposed to violent images, some people felt immediate sympathy for the victims. They responded with facial grimaces and accompanying body movements. As other images were presented, viewers reported that they felt their level of anxiety and emotion increase. At that point, several different things happened. Some people became angry; others simply turned away (Tamborini, Stiff, and Heidl, 1990). Images influenced behavior, but they did not seem to cause violent behavior contagiously.

More recent research indicates that the effects of media exposure are even more complex. Many researchers believe that the fear generated by media reporting is contagious (Altheide, 2006). When the anthrax attacks that followed the suicide bombers of September 11 were first reported, anxiety soared. As time went on, however, even when the story was extensively reported, anxiety levels were reduced (Berger, Johnson, and Lee, 2003). In addition, news reports did not seem to cause further anthrax attacks. Other findings demonstrate that media reports might inspire a person to engage in terrorism, but so do stories from friends and families (Weatherston and Moran, 2003).

There may be a contagious relationship between a terrorist event and the level of violence in later events. On March 11, 2004, terrorists set off a series of bombs on commuter trains in Madrid. The attack was intended to kill as many people as possible in a spectacular fashion. Ana Lisa Tota (2005) believes that this type of attack is a side effect of mass media reporting. International terrorists have come to understand that their attacks must be spectacular in order to achieve international coverage. In this sense, the level of violence is contagious.

Some researchers believe that if a contagion effect exists, it might be used to counter terrorism. Reports covering effective policing project images of social and political order. Steven Chermak and Alexander Weiss (2006) found this to be the case when examining community policing. News agencies projected positive images of law enforcement efforts and community responses. The same principle could apply to security forces responding to a terrorist attack. Media coverage would show police officials on the scene restoring order and helping victims. This is a positive image that works against terrorism. Yet the story must still be presented. Chermak and Weiss found that after initial reports on successful community policing, reporters moved on to other stories.

It is possible to reach conclusions about the contagion effect in areas outside of terrorism, and one conclusion is that the contagion effect is unknown. Barrie Gunter (2008) has conducted an in-depth historical study of the influence the media has on social aggression and violent behavior. Concern about the impact of images of violence began with movies in the 1920s, and it continues today. Gunter says a variety of researchers approach the topic with a multitude of methodologies, but there are problems inherent in the decades of study. Most models assume that media violence is linked to negative behavior. That model may be acceptable to policy makers, Gunter argues, but it is not acceptable to social scientists.

Other problems in media-induced violence appear with differing methodologies. First, the causal variables are unknown. Researchers do not know, and cannot control, other factors other than the media that might be responsible for violent behavior. Second, consumers may prefer media violence as entertainment while never accepting violent behavior in their everyday life. Third, causal relationships are often oversimplified.

longitudinal studies: In social science, these studies involve examinations of the same subjects over long periods of time.

Gunter concludes that studies of the relationship between behavior and media violence need to be **longitudinal studies**. They need to concentrate on multiple variables and realize that the impact of the media does not take place in a vacuum. Despite the large number of studies, current evidence is not conclusive, and it is often couched in political catchphrases. If Gunter is correct, the contagion effect of the media on terrorism should be examined in the same framework. Currently, very little is known.

✷ ANOTHER PERSPECTIVE

Wilkinson's Analysis of the Media

Paul Wilkinson argues that terrorists must communicate their efforts and they use the media to do so. He concludes the following about the relationship between the media and terrorists:

- Terrorists and the media have an interdependent relationship.
- Terrorist groups have an underground communication system, but they need the mainstream media to spread their messages.
- Mass media serve as the terrorists' psychological weapon by creating fear and anxiety.
- Terrorists may trap the media into spreading their message.
- The media may inadvertently shift blame for an incident from terrorists to victims or governments.
- Governments benefit when media sources portray the savage cruelty of terrorist groups.

Source: Wilkinson, 1997.

Censorship Debates

Debates over censorship arise because many people assume that acts of terrorism are induced by reckless media coverage and that media outlets provide terrorists with information. This again raises Barrie Gunter's point about utilizing inconclusive selective evidence. For example, the leader of one media watchdog group says that long-term exposure to media violence causes violent behavior and insensitivity toward victims. He says that the Surgeon General, the American Medical Association, and the National PTA know this to be true (Klite, 2000). Although he advocates internal self-regulation, his logic explains the thought behind censoring the media. The common wisdom is that media coverage of terrorism is harmful; therefore, it must be censored.

Paul Wilkinson (1997) believes that governments face three choices when it comes to maintaining freedom of the press and combating terrorism. A popular position is to assume a laissez-faire attitude. This hands-off approach assumes that market forces will determine the norms. A second choice is censorship, meaning that a governmental agency would have veto power over news reports. A final choice is to let the press regulate itself. Wilkinson says that reporters would not behave in an irresponsible manner if they knew what they could do to avoid aiding terrorists. He notes that governments and security forces seldom provide direction for news organizations (see *Another Perspective: Wilkinson's Analysis of the Media*).

The arguments about censorship are heated and deal with core issues of democracy. At the center of the debate is the right to free speech and the essential question: Does free speech necessitate media access to information? The media answers in the affirmative, claiming that the public has a right to know. Critics respond that free speech does not imply unlimited access to information. There is a right to speak; there is no right to know. In another sense, the censorship debate also focuses on truth or factual information. Because terrorists and governments understand that media images are important in terrorism, they both spend great amounts of energy trying to manipulate the media . Regardless, when a democratic government openly censors information, democracy is threatened. Manipulating the media and withholding information are very different from governmental control of the press (see Cram, 2006; Ross, 2007; and Weimann and von Knop, 2008), .

Looking at actions shortly after the United States started its war on terrorism, Doris Graber (2003) summarizes both sides of the argument. She argues that freedom of the press is crucial during times of national crisis, but that is when the media is most vulnerable. She believes that people who seek increased censorship do so by developing strategic arguments based on sloganeering and knowledge of select audiences. These efforts are attempts to manipulate people into supporting censorship by using verbal tactics to make arguments that it seems illogical to disagree with. Officials in the Bush Administration augmented this process by withholding information and encouraging lower-ranking officials to do the same. The Democrats supported this policy up to the 2002 elections.

Graber says several arguments were used in favor of censorship. The first was national security, a powerful excuse used in times of emergency. According to this position, information must be controlled to ensure the survival of the state. Another position was to claim that the public wanted the information withheld. Democratic Senator Joseph Lieberman voiced his support for controlling information, claiming that the American people overwhelmingly supported these governmental efforts. According to this logic, America was fighting a new type of war and some form of censorship was required. Other arguments asked Americans to behave patriotically. Ultimately, governmental officials claimed that they were asking for restraints, not censorship.

According to Graber, mainly journalists presented the anti-censorship view. They cited a variety of governmental mistakes and misdeeds, all hidden under the cover of national security. They condemned governmental officials who fought against the **Freedom of Information (FOI) Act**. They also argued that terrorism was essentially a war of information. Instead of trying to silence sources, the government should focus efforts on getting out the facts. Finally, every governmental clampdown cast officials in a bad light. The anti-censorship camp reserved its harshest criticism for media outlets that decided to self-censor as a service to the government.

Freedom of Information (FOI) Act: A law ensuring access to governmental records.

Graber concludes that arguments for and against censorship in times of crisis are as old as warfare. They will not be resolved in the current struggle with terrorism. She also offers her own opinion. The United States is fighting for freedom and democracy, and only an informed public is capable of successfully defending liberty. Editors, she argues, should hold back information to protect citizens and security forces, but those decisions belong to the media, not the government.

Gabriel Weimann (2008) argues that two issues come into play when debating government regulation. First, terrorists use the media, but they have access to their own forms of communication. One of their main tools is the Internet. Second, many analysts have focused on the problem of cyberterrorism, and that emphasis needs to shift. The major problem with the Internet, Weimann says, is the way it is used every day. Terrorists maintain hundreds of websites and use the Internet for research and communication. Counterterrorism should be aimed at learning how terrorists use the Internet and devising methods to thwart their effectiveness.

Weimann says governments may be tempted to censor or regulate the media in the name of security, but this is a dangerous course of action. The foundation of Western democracy is based on free speech and communication. Censorship, regulation, and gathering data from communication threaten the basis of democracy. It does not take much imagination, he says, to see the harm that invasive government operations might have. In the end, censorship could do more to damage freedom than the terrorist attacks themselves.

Self-Check

> Describe issues that affect the way reporters approach terrorism.

> Can terrorism be contagious? Why or why not?

> What might happen if news about terrorism is censored?

CHAPTER TAKE AWAYS

Television and other media shape the way we view terrorism. This creates quite a bit of controversy about the role of the media in reporting terrorism, and it frequently pits reporters against security forces. All sides try to manipulate the media because of its extensive power. This means that there is extensive competition to present a point of view and a news frame, leading to charges of biases from all sides. This is especially true in television because terrorism is a made-for-television drama. Some scholars have called for limited censorship because the media is so powerful.

OBJECTIVE SUMMARY

- Media stories help impact the ways consumers construct social reality. Images of terrorism are frequently simplified, skewing social constructions. A number of scholarly works focus on terrorism and the media, and most agree that reporting magnifies the power of terrorism.
- This frequently creates tension between security forces and the media. Law enforcement and other security forces represent the power of social order, and they are responsible for maintaining governmental authority. Media outlets feel that they are responsible for informing the public and providing a check on governmental power. Despite these differences, media reports tend to show security forces in a favorable light simply because they show them responding to an emergency.
- Both terrorists and security forces seek to manipulate the media by using it as a weapon. In addition, terrorists have found that they can directly control the media by creating their own information outlets. This can backfire because terrorist propaganda frequently contains important intelligence information that can be used by security forces.
- News frames shape stories about terrorism. They set the stage for the story, introduce the characters, give a narrative of the action, and either provide a conclusion or lead consumers to a variety of conclusions.
- There is a special relationship between terrorism and television. Terrorism has a close relationship with television because it provides an unfolding drama. Television news reports are often designed to entertain and excite audiences. Some critics maintain that television reporting focuses more on entertainment than information. New international outlets often provide sympathetic views of terrorism.
- The Internet has a complex relationship with terrorism. It can be used like other media to report an event, but it has many other functions including serving as a means for communication, propaganda, recruiting, and training. It can also be

used as a tactical weapon. Information on the World Wide Web can be used for sending embedded messages and as a tool to support an attack.

- Some media commentators believe that there is a liberal bias in television news reporting. Others feel that conservative views dominate the airwaves. There are some networks on cable television that cater to particular political audiences, and they adjust their reports to match the opinions of their viewers. Gender roles are also shaped by the way terrorism is covered. The power of media has prompted some security experts to call for censorship when reporting about terrorism.

- Because many news consumers experience an event only through the media, all forms of media play an important role in the social construction of reality by the ways they provide information.

Critical Engagement: Images, Control, and the Future

In *The Packaging of Terrorism*, Susan Moeller (2009, pp. 130–133) makes a crucial point about the power of media images. They define how we perceive the world. Firefighters responding to chaos or raising an American flag over the ruins of the World Trade Center convey a powerful message about the U.S. government, and when blended with shots of al Qaeda in the hills of Afghanistan, they say a lot about an enemy as well. Images also present media outlets with several issues, including the ways to cover live terrorists attacks, how to respond to terrorism, and how to use video created by terrorists. The resulting images change diplomatic relations, foreign policy, the powers of government, and the course of history.

Perception of images defines the way violence is interpreted. Brigitte Nacos (2008) says that the press has always been interested in reporting violence; but the multitude of television channels, radio stations, and large media conglomerates understand their audiences' lust for shocking stories and sensationalized violence. Terrorism must be reported in a free society, but, she asks, how far should it go? Should there be limits on reporting?

Sensationalism is rampant. After terrorist bombings in Madrid killed nearly 200 people in 2004, one national news magazine ran a picture of mutilated bodies on its front cover. Television stations showed the same explosive attacks over and over again until one or two explosions took on the aura of an artillery barrage. Nacos cites other incidents, such as a leading newspaper's account of a terrorist video in which a weeping victim from the West is beheaded by a knife-wielding jihadist. Regarding another video of a beheading, she criticizes a reporter's description of a terrorist video as if it were a movie review. These graphic images and descriptions should not be reported by responsible journalists, Nacos concludes.

In the past, media outlets were bound by national borders. This has changed with the growth of networks like al Jazeera and al Manar. Media outlets now compete in a global market, and Nacos says these factors give terrorists an upper hand. For example, Nacos refers to a 2002 takeover of a Moscow theater by Chechen terrorists. When the takeover was complete, the Chechens delivered a prepackaged video tape, but not to Russian television networks. They presented it to the Moscow bureau of al Jazeera. Although the Russians censored their own networks, Russians and everyone else watched the drama unfold on global networks.

The Internet has made the situation more complicated. Terrorists now operate with their own media advisors and production centers. Al Qaeda created the Global Islamic Media Front and launched its own weekly Internet television show. The show featured a news anchor and reports from Afghanistan, Iraq, Gaza, and Sudan. If media outlets do not show horrific violence, Nacos concludes, terrorists will broadcast it themselves.

Consider these issues in terms of future developments:

- There is a debate about censorship, but will censorship control the images of terrorism as they are presented in the media? Will internal broadcasting standards have any impact?
- How will terrorists continue to use the Internet as a source of propaganda? Should censorship be introduced on the Internet because of this?
- Images of terrorism increase anger and anxiety. Would images of security forces responding to terrorism create different feelings? How might politicians take advantage of emotions evoked by images of terrorism?

KEY TERMS

news media, p. 4-87

embedded reporters, p. 4-90

news frames, p. 4-91

reporting frame, p. 4-91

postmodern, p. 4-92

infotainment telesector, p. 4-93

made-for-TV drama, p. 4-94

al Jazeera, p. 4-95

al Manar, p. 4-95

al Aqsa Intifada, p. 4-95

steganography, p. 4-97

Salafi movement, p. 4-97

critical media consciousness, p. 4-101

copycats, p. 4-102

longitudinal studies, p. 4-104

Freedom of Information (FOI) Act, p. 4-105

Gender Roles, Tactics, and Force Multipliers in Terrorism

LEARNING OBJECTIVES

After reading this chapter, you should be able to:

> Summarize the tactics of modern terrorism.

> List and describe four force multipliers.

> Discuss historical and current roles of women in terrorism.

> Outline the tactical importance of female terrorists.

> Define the types of threats posed by technological terrorism.

> Explain the effects of biological, chemical, and radiological weapons.

> Characterize the possibility and possible outcomes of nuclear terrorism.

> Discuss the role of the media as a force multiplier.

> Summarize transnational economic targeting in the tourist, energy, and transportation industries.

> Summarize theories of suicide bombing.

The Center for American Progress (Sofer and Addison, 2012) raised the alarm about an unaddressed problem in counterterrorism. The role of females in terrorist groups is increasing around the globe, but the new U.S. strategy for countering terrorism makes no mention of the problem. In fact, the issue of women in terrorism is not even discussed. This is ironic because the number of female suicide bombers has been increasing in recent years, and terrorist groups are expanding recruitment efforts to attract women.

The Center says the threat is not new. Secular groups have been using females for decades, and the Kurdish Workers' Party (PKK) used women in 76 percent of its attacks in the last two decades of the twentieth century. Religious groups soon followed suit. The first known female suicide bomber struck in April 1985 when a young Muslim woman drove a truck laden with explosives into an Israeli army convoy. The Pakistani Taliban and al Qaeda formed female suicide cells after the first female suicide bomber struck in Pakistan in 2010.

It should be noted that the use of women in terrorist attacks does not constitute a tactical change. The same basic tactics of bombing, ambush, robbery, assassination, kidnapping, and hostage taking remain the same. The organizational structures are also relatively constant. The change is due to the expanding roles of females in terrorist organizations, especially in male-dominated conservative movements. It is also impacted by stereotypes. Society at large casts women in nurturing roles, often unwilling to see them performing nontraditional tasks in both legal and criminal organizations. Feminist criminologists have been aware of this problem for decades, but it is new to the media. As a result, when women strike, the attack receives greater attention and the media becomes a force multiplier.

The Tactics of Terrorism and Multiplying Force

Although it is difficult to define terrorism, it is not difficult to summarize terrorist tactics. To begin with, Ian Lesser (1999, pp. 8–10) suggests that terrorism is defined by a situation, and it changes with each new situation. If he is correct, then terrorism can be seen as a method of fighting. Tactics change in terrorism just as they change in war. Groups change structures and goals, and terrorists learn from the past and from their previous successes and mistakes. Terrorists change tactics continually. This means security forces must be willing to change the way they respond to terrorists.

Victor Davis Hanson (2002) argues that the Western way of war is based on the ancient Greek method of fighting a battle. This involved one city state placing its men in a block formation called a phalanx and charging an opposing army arranged in the same formation. The phalanx was a simple formation, but its power could be enhanced by innovative methods. For example, at the Battle of Marathon the Athenian commander put two large blocks of soldiers on each side of his phalanx, allowing him to surround an opposing army. Alexander the Great changed the phalanx and increased the role of supporting troops from the cavalry and light infantry. The Romans eventually added a flexible checkerboard formation to the phalanx as they deployed their legions in three ranks. The tactic was simple, but innovation brought complexity. The same process can be observed in modern terrorism.

six tactics of terrorism: As defined by Brian Jenkins: (1) bombing, (2) hijacking, (3) arson, (4) assault, (5) kidnapping, and (6) hostage taking.

force multiplier: A method of increasing striking power without increasing the number of combat troops in a military unit. Terrorists have four force multipliers: (1) technology to enhance weapons or attacks on technological facilities, (2) transnational support, (3) media coverage, and (4) religious fanaticism.

Brian Jenkins (1984, 2004a, 2004b) says that there are **six tactics of terrorism**: bombing, hijacking, arson, assault, kidnapping, and hostage taking. Recently, the arsenal of terrorism has grown to include threats from weapons of mass destruction (WMD), but the public does not clearly understand these threats. Technology has also modified bombing to include virtual attacks through computer systems (B. Jenkins, 1987; Brackett, 1996, p. 45; J. White, 1986, 2000; Parachini, 2003).

Jenkins says that the six tactics can be enhanced by **force multipliers**. In military terms, a force multiplier increases striking power without increasing the strength of a unit. Terrorists routinely use force multipliers because they add to their aura. All political terrorists want to give the illusion that they can fight on a higher, more powerful level.

⁘ ANOTHER PERSPECTIVE

Force Multipliers

Transnational support increases the ability of terrorist groups to move and hide across a nation.

Technology allows a small group to launch a deadly attack.

Media coverage can make a minor group appear to be politically important.

Religion transcends normative political and social boundaries, increasing violence and decreasing opportunities for negotiation.

Four force multipliers give terrorists more striking power (see *Another Perspective: Force Multipliers*). Researchers have known for many years that technology can enhance a terrorist group's ability to strike (see Ketcham and McGeorge, 1986, pp. 25–33; Bunker, 1998; Linstone, 2003; Brookbank, 2006; Wright, 2008). Cyberterrorism and potential WMD attacks are examples of technological force multipliers. Daniel Benjamin and Steven Simon (2002, pp. 365–382) demonstrate that media coverage and interpretation of terrorist events often serve as force multipliers. One incident can be converted into a "campaign" as electronic media scramble to break the latest news. Jeffrey Goldberg's (2002) research on the **Triborder region** in South America demonstrates that transnational support networks multiply the striking power of terrorists. A frightening new force multiplier has been the introduction of religious fanaticism in terrorist activities (B. Hoffman 1995; Laqueur, 1999; Juergensmeyer, 1988, 2000; von Hippel, 2002; Stern, 2003b). The introduction of religion has introduced suicide attacks into the arsenals of terrorism.

Triborder region: The area where Brazil, Paraguay, and Argentina join. The major city in the area is Cuidad del Este.

Although terrorist tactics change over time, the most common weapon of terrorism has been and is still the bomb. In 1848, anarchists talked about the **philosophy of the bomb**, meaning that the only way to communicate with the social order was to destroy it. In the late 1800s, militants used bombs to attack governments and businesses, culminating in a bombing campaign in 1919. The Irish Republican Army (IRA) found the bomb to be its most important weapon after 1969, and by 1985 the organization was deploying extremely sophisticated ones (Garrison, 2004). Groups in the Middle East, Sri Lanka, and eventually throughout the world found that bombs could be delivered by suicide attackers (Pape, 2003). Hijackers first used bombs to take over planes, and then, on September 11, 2001, terrorists turned civilian airliners into bombs. In the campaign against the U.S. military in Iraq after 2003, suicide bombings and roadside bombs became the weapons of choice (Ricks, 2006, p. 118).

philosophy of the bomb: A phrase used by anarchists around 1848. It means that social order can be changed only through violent upheaval. Bombs were the first technological force multiplier.

Terrorists tend to increase their effectiveness in bombing by applying improved explosive technology to their weapons just as conventional military forces constantly improve the killing power of their munitions. In 2004, *New Scientist* reported that Middle Eastern terrorist groups were working on a two-stage military-style weapon called a mininuke. This type of explosive is designed to spread fuel in the air and then ignite it. Known as a **thermobaric bomb**, it actually explodes the air in the blast area. One analyst speculated that an attack on a Tunisian synagogue in 2002 used this technology (Hambling, 2004).

thermobaric bomb: A two-stage bomb. The first stage spreads either a fuel cloud or finely ground powder through the air. The explosive material mixes with the oxygen present in the atmosphere. The second stage detonates the explosive material, which explodes in all directions in a series of shock waves. The cloud can penetrate a number of barriers. A person breathing the material explodes from the inside out when the material is ignited.

EXPANDING THE CONCEPT

The Most Common Tactic of Terrorism

Although terrorist tactics change over time, the most common weapon of terrorism has been and is still the bomb. In 1848, anarchists talked about the "philosophy of the bomb," meaning that the only way to communicate with the social order was to destroy it. In the late 1800s, militants used bombs to attack governments and businesses. The Irish Republican Army (IRA) found the bomb to be their most important weapon after 1969, and by 1985, the organization was deploying extremely sophisticated ones. Groups in the Middle East, Sri Lanka, and eventually throughout the world found that bombs could be delivered by suicide attackers. Hijackers first used bombs to take over planes, and then, on September 11, 2001, terrorists turned civilian airliners into bombs.

Although the tactics are simple, they always represent a variation on a theme. Force multipliers enhance destructive power, whereas innovation is used to achieve shock and surprise. Again, this is nothing more than the tactics used by conventional military forces, but here they are used outside the rules of a war with front lines and a beginning and an end. This explains why terrorism is different from war, even though terrorists and military forces sometimes use the same tactics. Donald Black (2004) points out that terrorism lacks the gaming quality of war. Terrorist tactics, though simple, create terror because they are designed to attack civilians and symbolic targets exclusively. The only purpose of a terrorist attack is to send a message of chaos and destruction to a larger audience. In fact, the victims most often do not constitute the real target; they are killed merely to send a message.

✓ Self-Check

> Describe the basic tactics of terrorism.
> Define and describe force multipliers.
> How do force multipliers affect the tactics of terrorism?

Gender and Terrorism

Criminologists frequently complain that females are often ignored in the study of crime, unless the study focuses on victimization. Researchers have said the same thing about the study of gender and terrorism (Oliverio and Lauderdale, 2005; Sjoberg, 2009). The main reason for this is a cultural stereotype that brackets women in traditional roles. Many researchers and the general public tend to envision women performing the "male" tasks involved in terrorism (Neuberger and Valentini, 1996, pp. 28–36). These attitudes ignore reality. Women have been and remain active in terrorist causes, and their role is increasing. They increase the tactical effectiveness of terrorist groups and the complexity of counterterrorism.

Women Active through the Evolution of Terrorism

Female terrorists are not new to the history of terrorism. It is safe to say that when the term terrorism emerged in late-eighteenth-century France, women were in the forefront. Although they were gradually excluded from full participation in the revolutionary government, they were victims of, witnesses to, and participants in French terrorism (see Proctor, 1990). They were also active in Russia in the nineteenth century (Verhoeven, 2009, pp. 30–37), and they were involved in attempts to repress the African American population in the United States through the early twentieth century (Blee, 2005). Women took part in rebellions in Ireland (Burleigh, 2009, pp. 20–21). More than 10,000 women joined the ranks of the National Liberation Front in the Algerian War from 1954 to 1962 (Kutchera, 1996, 2012). Women played leading roles in the revolutionary terrorism of the 1960s and 1970s, and their representation surged in Western revolutionary groups after 1968 (Neuberger and Valentini, 1996, pp. 22–28; Ness, 2005). They are actively recruited by religious terrorists today (Sofer and Addison, 2012). They have been active in historical and contemporary terrorism, but their role has often been overlooked.

Kathleen Blee (2005) researched the role of women in racial terrorism in the United States. **Racial terrorism**, according to Blee, is repressive in nature. It involves organized groups from a dominant race violently intimidating racial minorities to keep them from achieving higher social standing and political power. Blee says this has been a common form of terrorism in the United States since the end of the Civil War.

Women played an indirect role when racial terrorism emerged in the South after the Civil War. At first, they served as a symbol to inspire male violence. The idealized version of Southern femininity, as socially defined by Southern white males, was threatened by the emancipation of black slaves. White males would not accept the

racial terrorism: A dominant group using violence to intimidate a racial minority. Tactics would include lynching, murder, beatings, and other forms of violence against a minority group. For example, the Ku Klux Klan historically has practiced racial terrorism.

possibility of interracial social or sexual relations. White women were not part of the violence, according to Blee. The stereotypical image inspired male violence. This role changed in the early twentieth century as women became prominent in lynchings and other forms of racial violence. Photographs and documents indicate that women participated in such brutality as observers. It is not clear, Blee concludes, whether they were active in the bloodshed or if they led racist groups, but they were present during racial murders and other forms of violence. The role of women changed again in the late twentieth century as the white supremacy movement began relegating women to a support role. The future of women in American racial terrorism, Blee concludes, depends on the direction of white supremacists in the twenty-first century.

Organizational Impact on Gender Roles

Margaret Gonzalez-Perez (2008) found that the role of women in terrorist groups is more closely related to the political orientation of an organization than to its tactics. She examined 26 terrorist organizations that emerged in the decades after World War II. She separated these groups into those with an **international focus** and those that embraced **domestic issues**. Her findings indicate that political and social ideology is closely related to the roles women play in terrorist groups. She says that paternalism, religious traditions, and political orientation are the dominant influences in the process.

Gonzalez-Perez says that women are more attracted to domestic terrorist organizations than to international groups. The reason, she believes, deals with the purposes of the respective groups. Domestic organizations are focused on revolution and social change. Women are attracted to such groups because they have a chance to redefine their roles, and males and females welcome them since they want the same change. Some groups even have a feminist agenda. Women also have opportunities for leadership in revolutionary groups. International terrorists resist outside forces such as capitalism and imperialism. They try to defend a traditional culture that limits the role of women. Yet women also emerge in traditional organizations when there is a need to recruit personnel and when terrorism becomes a popular means of social expression.

Gathering data from a variety of geographical areas, Gonzalez-Perez offers a strong argument. After examining domestic and international terrorism in the Americas, Africa, the Middle East, Asia, and Europe, her data show that women in domestic groups gravitate toward combat and leadership. The same findings reveal that women in international groups are given more limited roles. International terrorists tend to employ women as supporters, sympathizers, and spies. They seldom receive combat or leadership positions. This pattern remains constant even in social systems that emphasize male dominance. For example, she says that one would think that the *machismo* influence in Central and South America would blunt female leadership and combat roles, but the opposite is true. Most Central and South American groups have a left-wing revolutionary focus. Women move into active roles because the groups are seeking to restructure their culture and political structure. Every geographical area produced a common trend: Domestic groups emphasized the role of women even when they had no stated feminist agenda.

Cindy Ness (2005) offers a similar argument after examining the behavior of women in secular and religious terrorist groups. Using the Liberation Tigers of Tamil Elaam (LTTE), Hamas, and Islamic Jihad, Ness argues that modern terrorism began around 1968. Females played an immediate role. Women were relegated to support and service in religious terrorist groups, but they developed combat and leadership positions in secular organizations. Ness argues that this has been fairly constant since the spread of ideological terrorism after 1968. She points to **Ulricke Meinhof** and **Leila Khalid** as examples of female participation in revolutionary terrorism. Both women not only served as combatants, they were also leaders and served as inspiration for supporters. Unfortunately, Ness believes, most terrorism analysts have ignored the role of women in revolutionary groups.

international focus: Gonzalez-Perez uses international focus to refer to terrorist groups operating in multiple countries.

domestic issues: Gonzalez-Perez uses domestic issues to refer to groups within a country fighting to change the social or political structure of that nation.

Ulricke Meinhof (1934–1976): Co-created the Red Army Faction with Andreas Baader in 1970. She was the co-leader of the group. Arrested in 1972, she committed suicide in prison.

Leila Khalid (b. 1944): was a member of the Popular Front for the Liberation of Palestine. In 1969, she was part of a team that hijacked four aircraft that were destroyed after the passengers and crews disembarked. Arrested in 1970 after another attempted hijacking, she was released as part of a prisoner exchange.

Religious terrorist groups began to emerge in the 1980s, and nationalistic and ethnic groups continued to operate. Ness says the roles of women followed a similar path in each of these movements. Conservative male-dominated religious terrorists relegated females to secondary status. Ethnic and nationalistic groups also limited the role of women. Given the fact that revolutionary groups offered more opportunities for women, one would expect that females would not be as active in religious and nationalistic movements. The opposite was true. The reason, Ness explains, is that these movements appeal to a wider audience. Revolutionary groups attracted women, but the groups were small and so were the number of supporters. Religious and ethnic nationalists recruited from a larger pool of supporters than the earlier left-wing groups. Even though the role of women is more limited in the traditional groups, there are more women available to work in them. Therefore, Ness explains, more women are involved in traditional movements.

The number of women attracted to religious terrorist organizations also suggests that their roles will be expanded. Ness believes that they will increasingly receive combat assignments because they are so numerous. Aside from all of the traditional restrictions of male-dominated religious hierarchies, terrorist groups need personnel. When women are available, they are given combat assignments as the need arises. Ness does not know if this practice will extend to leadership. There is no reason to believe automatically that religious groups will continue to limit the opportunity for female leadership. Women may begin organizing and taking leadership roles, or they may take charge out of necessity when male leaders are captured or killed.

Gender and Tactics

Chapter 3 explained the manners in which terrorist groups are organized, but it is also important to consider the social aspects of the organized groups. Groups with diverse missions tend to recruit and operate in different ways. Ideology draws certain types of recruits to a movement, and it influences the tactics terrorist groups employ. For example, a revolutionary group trying to overthrow a government and win popular support is not likely to attack with a nuclear weapon. The reason is clear: If political terrorists were to use a nuclear weapon, the public would unite against them, placing the terrorists at a disadvantage. Small groups cannot achieve their objectives against a united mass of people. Religious terrorists, on the other hand, might be tempted to detonate a nuclear device. They have no concern about popular support, and if they lose, they believe a deity will call new followers to carry the struggle forward. Ideology and mission affect operations.

Gender also impacts tactics and, in turn, is often related to ideology. Groups with different philosophies draw recruits from different age groups and sexes, and they rarely violate these barriers unless forced to do so by circumstances. Consider suicide bombing, for instance. When suicide terrorism reappeared in the 1980s, audiences were appalled. They wondered why a grown man would strap on a bomb and kill himself. Terrorists took advantage of this, and suicide bombings increased. As such attacks became more routine, audiences grew accustomed to seeing suicide bombers. Some terrorist groups, seeking increased psychological impact from suicide attacks, sought new types of bombers. They began using women. This shocked people, especially in the West, more than the original suicide attacks because many people could not think of women as terrorists. Eventually, this led some groups to employ children in suicide bombings.

Impact of Terrorism on Men and Women

Women and men view terrorism differently. A study of perception in more than 500 people in New York City and Washington, D.C., revealed that women are more fearful of terrorism than men. As a result they engage in behaviors to avoid being victimized, and they are more likely to seek information about terrorist events than men. Researchers concluded that women have a greater sense of vulnerability to crime, and these feelings seem to transfer to terrorism (Nellis, 2009).

A group of researchers looking at fear of terrorism in Turkey came to similar conclusions. Researchers used survey data from high school seniors in Turkey. They measured both the fear of crime and of terrorism in young men and women. They also accounted for vicarious exposure through television and other media. They found that young women were more fearful of crime than men. This seemed to be due to the fear of sexual crimes and violence. They concluded that the fear of crime transferred into a fear of terrorism (Wilcox et al., 2009).

A study in Israel focused on cities that have been hit hard by terrorism. Researchers interviewed 326 Israeli citizens in this study, 198 women and 128 men. The researchers found that women were less exposed to terrorism than were the men, but they felt greater vulnerability. This seemed to be because women experienced terrorism more vicariously. They had more subjective interpretations of events, often formulated with secondary roles such as helping victims. They were more likely to suffer from posttraumatic stress and were more willing to seek assistance in overcoming anxiety. Unlike the men in the study, the women also approached the fear of terrorism with problem-solving strategies (Server et al., 2008).

Overlooking Female Terrorists

If women have been terrorists throughout history, one wonders why their role has been overlooked. Alisa Stack-O'Conner (2007) says female terrorism has been ignored for the same reason that female criminality has been underplayed. Researchers do not tend to think of women as terrorists or criminals, and when they do look at females, researchers usually see them as victims. In addition, law enforcement officers do not tend to arrest females. Historically, male terrorist leaders reinforce this bias because they have been reluctant to use females. This is changing, Stack-O'Conner says, because female terrorists, especially suicide bombers, have unique propaganda value. Women also give terrorists tactical advantages because police and military forces are not as quick to confront women.

Other scholars argue that women have been overlooked because it is generally assumed that terrorism is a violent male occupation. Americans like to think of female terrorists as an aberration, according to Cindy Ness (2005), and American popular culture does not accept the idea that females are terrorists. When females are used as attackers or suicide bombers, Katharina von Knop (2007) believes, they are following a male model instead of assuming roles they would define on their own. Von Knop believes that women have a greater role to play in leadership and maintaining organizations. They do not need to imitate males, von Knop argues. Female warriors differ from their male counterparts. Research from the International Crisis Group (2009) in Kyrgyzstan suggests that this is correct. The ISG found that when women move into radical religious groups on their own, they seem to create organizations that provide social organization and sustainability.

Another perspective takes the argument further. Laura Sjoberg (2009) is extremely critical of the scholarly literature on women and terrorism. For the most part, her research shows, studies of women in terrorism are generally ignored, and when females are discussed it is in gendered terms. They are not "terrorists," they are "women involved in terrorism," she says. There are exceptions, such as the work of Bruce Hoffman, but most scholars and analysts conclude that women play some type of nebulous role in terrorism. They cannot define the role, and they do not seem to care to do so. Media presentations follow the same tack. Women are neither significant nor worthy of analysis.

Sjoberg vehemently disagrees with such characterizations. Women, she writes, do have a special place in terrorism; women are terrorists in the same way that men are terrorists. There are terrorists who happen to be women, and they have been around for quite some time. There is also no feminist perspective on terrorism; there are feminists who study terrorism in a variety of ways. Sjoberg says that scholars and other researchers are reluctant to study political and criminal violence among women because it violates idealized notions of womanhood. Their behavior should be studied from a variety of feminist perspectives, Sjoberg concludes. Such studies would enrich the field.

Sjoberg has a point. Women are playing an increasing role in terrorist operations in all types of organizations. Groups with revolutionary or feminist objectives give them leadership and combat roles. More traditional groups relegate women to support roles, but they are being employed more frequently in tactical operations. Even the most traditional terrorist groups find that there are tactical advantages to using women. In central Asia women have even developed their own path to terrorism and the organization to sustain it. Finally, while gender-specific roles exist, Sjoberg is correct. There are men and women who happen to be terrorists. Each gender can be deployed with certain tactical benefits.

✓ Self-Check

> Where have women been active over the course of modern terrorism?
> What roles do women tend to play in differing types of terrorist groups?
> Why do Americans ignore female terrorists?
> Why have researchers failed to study the roles of women in terrorist groups?

Technology

Terrorism is influenced by technology. Some analysts believe that when the technological impact is so great that it turns a tactic or weapon into a strategy, it is possible to look at the resulting activity as a specific type of terrorism (see Pape, 2003, 2005). Others believe that this technique confuses the issue and that types of terrorism refer only to tools any terrorist group could use (see Dyson, 2004). Striking a balance between these two positions, this section will examine four types of terrorism that are potentially powerful enough to transform the nature of terrorism. As stated earlier, these types may be different only in terms of the weapons used in terrorist attacks, but special types of terrorism have become so individualized they deserve a separate review.

Cyberterrorism

cyberterrorism: Using computers to attack other networks or to conduct physical attacks on computer-controlled targets. The most frightening scenario involves an attack designed to create catastrophic failure in the economy or infrastructure.

Cyberterrorism refers to the use of computers to attack technological targets or physical attacks on computer networks. The National Conference of State Legislatures (2003) defines *cyberterrorism* as "the use of information technology by terrorists to promote a political agenda." Barry Collin (2004), who coined the term in the early 1990s, believes it involves disrupting points where the virtual, electronic realm of computer networks and programs intersect with the physical world. Miami attorney Mark Grossman (1999) argues that the threat of cyberterrorism is real and international legal systems are not prepared to deal with it. Cyberterrorism is computer hacking with a body count, according to Grossman. The Council on Foreign Relations (2004) defines cyberterrorism by the ways terrorists might use computers and information networks. The targets for cyberterrorism include computers, computer networks, and information storage and retrieval systems. Terrorists differ from hackers, the council argues, because their purpose is to launch a systematic attack for political purposes. The most common tactic to date has been the defacement of websites.

There are many potential targets for cyberterrorists. Yael Shahar (1997) envisions scenarios in which a computer virus—a program that typically copies itself and moves through a computer system to disrupt a computer or computer network—is implanted in an enemy's computer. He predicts the use of "logic bombs," or snippets of program code that lie dormant for years until they are instructed to overwhelm a computer system. Shahar also believes that bogus computer chips can be sold to sabotage an enemy's computer network. Trojan horses, or malicious programs that seem to be harmless, can contain a malevolent code that can destroy a system, and "back doors" in computer systems can allow terrorists to enter systems thought to be secure. Furthermore, Shahar believes that conventional attacks, such as overloading an electrical system, threaten computer security.

Cyberterrorism is an attractive, low-risk strategy. Michael Whine (1999) agrees with Shahar's conclusions, claiming that computer technology is attractive to terrorists for several reasons. Computers allow terrorist groups to remain connected, providing a means for covert discussions and anonymity. Computer networks are also much less expensive and work-intensive than the secretive infrastructures necessary to maintain terrorist groups. Bowers and Keys (1998) believe cyberterrorism appears to be a threat because of the nature of modern society. More and more, Western society needs information and the flow of information to function, and cyberterrorists threaten to interrupt or confuse that flow of information. This leads Tiffany Danitz and Warren Strobel (1999) to remind policy makers that violent political activists also use the Internet as a command-and-control mechanism. They say there is no doubt that computers are vulnerable to crime, and terrorists do use and will continue to use them.

Some research points to attacks that have already occurred rather than focusing on potential targets. A group from the Center for Strategic and International Studies (2004) examined attacks on America's cybersystems. Chaired by a former director of the FBI and Central Intelligence Agency (CIA), William Webster, the group states that there has been a sharp rise in such attacks, with the Internet providing the vehicle for launching most of the strikes. His group was especially concerned with documented attacks on the National Security Agency, the Pentagon, and a nuclear weapons laboratory. Operations were disrupted in all of these cases.

The greatest fear around cyberterrorism is of catastrophic or multiple failures. Both the public and private sectors are experiencing attacks on websites and computer systems. Some attackers simply wait outside the targeted system, gathering enough data to infiltrate and steal corporate or government secrets. Other attacks are more nefarious. The main fear is that a worm, virus, or some other type of weaponized computer signal will suddenly strike a target. Due to the automation and computerized control of large segments of the infrastructure, a massive failure at one point could cause a series of failures, closing an entire support structure (Matusitz, 2010; Helms, Constanza, and John, 2012).

There are frightening scenarios for catastrophic failure. For example, if a terrorist organization could infiltrate the banking or investment sector of the economy, a program could conceivably start draining accounts. This would create an economic crisis. In another scenario, imagine a major switching station on the power grid of a large metropolis. If the computer program running the station were attacked, the station could be the source of a catastrophic failure. As other portions of the grid pick up the slack from the down station, they would find circuits overloading and could begin shutting down. It is conceivable that a large segment of the country could be without power for days. Finally, suppose that a malicious program were to enter the nuclear power plant. It is possible that the offending virus could cause a meltdown and explosion. Technological societies are vulnerable to such cyberattacks (see Mallish and Wright, 2011).

WMD: Biological Agents

Terrorism by WMD presents a potential strategic scenario and even served as the United States' excuse for invading Iraq in 2003. WMD include biological agents, or biological weapons, which have been used for centuries. Modern arsenals contain **bacterial weapons** and **viral weapons**, with microbes cultured and refined, or weaponized, to increase their ability to kill. When people are victims of a bacterial attack, antibiotics may be an effective treatment. Antibiotics are not usually effective against viruses, although some vaccines issued before the use of viral weapons could be effective (see Hinton, 1999; Young and Collier, 2002). Because bacterial agents are susceptible to antibiotics, nations with bacterial weapons programs have created strains of bacterial microbes resistant to such drugs. Viral agents are produced in the same manner, and they are usually more powerful than bacterial agents. Biological agents are difficult to control but relatively easy to produce. Terrorists may find them to be effective weapons.

There are four types of biological agents: (1) natural poisons, or toxins that occur without human modification, (2) viruses, (3) bacteria, and (4) plagues. The Centers for Disease Control and Prevention (CDC) lists the most threatening agents as smallpox, anthrax, plague, botulism, tularemia, and hemorrhagic fever. Michael Osterholm and John Schwartz (2000, pp. 14–23) summarize the effect of each of these. Smallpox is a deadly, contagious virus. Many people were vaccinated against smallpox in their childhood, but these old vaccinations are no longer effective against the disease. Anthrax is a noncontagious bacterial infection, and plague is transmitted by insects. Botulism is a kind of foodborne illness, and other bacteria can be modified to serve as weapons. Hemorrhagic fevers are caused by viruses. One of the most widely known hemorrhagic fevers is the Ebola virus.

America has experienced two notable biological attacks since 1980. The first modern use of biological terrorism in the United States was engineered in 1984 by followers of a religious group in Oregon. The group spread bacteria in area salad bars in an attempt to sicken voters during a local election. Their intent was to elect their religious followers to local office (Miller, Engelberg, and Broad, 2001). Hundreds of people suffered food poisoning as a result.

The second attack involved anthrax and came in the wake of 9/11. It began in Florida when two workers from a news tabloid were infected by anthrax received through the mail. One of the victims died. In the following days, anthrax appeared again as NBC *Nightly News* received spores in its mail.

The situation grew worse in October. The office of former Senate Majority Leader Thomas Daschle received its regular mail delivery after lunch on Friday, October 12. Fortunately, staff members were in a class that afternoon, learning how to recognize suspicious packages. When staffers returned to work on Monday, they opened Friday's mail and someone noticed a white powdery substance in a letter. Alerted by information from Friday's class, the staffer took immediate action, perhaps saving many lives. The powder contained anthrax spores, and although there were no fatalities, legislative offices were closed in Washington, D.C., for several weeks. Mysteriously, other people died on the East Coast with no explanation of how the anthrax was spreading (Parker, 2002; Schoof and Fields, 2002). By the end of November 2001 the anthrax outbreak had claimed five lives. Cases were reported in Florida, Washington, D.C., New York, New Jersey, and Connecticut. Two conclusions remain: (1) The public health response was poor and disorganized, and (2) the case is still under investigation (O'Neill et al., 2007).

The United States planned to take massive steps to prevent biological terrorism after the anthrax attacks. Congress created a bipartisan commission to deal with the issue, but the effectiveness of all these efforts has been questionable (Commission on

bacterial weapons:
Enhanced forms of bacteria that may be countered by antibiotics.

viral weapons: Enhanced forms of viruses. The virus is "hardened" so that it can live for long periods and enhanced for deadlier effects.

the Prevention of Weapons of Mass Destruction Proliferation and Terrorism, 2010). *Security* (2010) magazine reported that the commission conducted a review of the systems to prevent and respond to WMD attacks and found that preparations were lacking. Most important, in terms of bioterrorism, the commission concluded that the United States had no structure in place to respond to a biological attack. The commission also criticized Congress for failing to properly clarify and oversee the missions of the Department of Homeland Security and for failing to create the education and training systems needed to prepare the next generation of national security experts.

Bioterrorism Report Card
Capability to Respond to Biological Attacks F
Controlling Containment Labs D+
Review Program to Secure Pathogens A
Strengthen Disease Surveillance C
Plan International Biological Weapons Convention B+
Develop Bio-Forensic Strategy A

Source: Commission on the Prevention of Weapons of Mass Destruction Proliferation and Terrorism, 2010, http://www.preventwmd.gov/1_26_101/.

Two former senators voiced harsh criticism and a warning. According to the commission's now inactive government website (http://www.preventwmd.gov/1_26_101/), former Senator Daniel Robert Graham (D-FL) said that the United States had failed to address several urgent threats, especially bioterrorism. Although three presidential administrations had been in place since the anthrax attacks, the federal government had been slow to recognize and respond to the biothreats, he said. He also stated that Americans no longer have the luxury of a slow learning curve; terrorists want to use bioweapons. Former Senator James Talent (R-MO) expressed frustration about the failure of Congress to reform homeland security oversight. The lack of coordination and duplicative oversight leaves the United States open to biological attacks.

WMD: Chemical and Radiological Weapons

The massive power and heat from atomic bombs place nuclear weapons in a class of their own, but chemical and radiological attacks are basically similar. Radiological poisoning and "dirty" radioactive devices are forms of chemical attack. Chemicals are usually easier to deliver than biological weapons, and they are fast acting. Radiological devices act more slowly than most chemicals, but their poison lasts longer and they can be spread like chemicals. Radioactive materials are also more resistant to heat than chemicals, so bombs or other heat-producing devices can be used to scatter them.

There are four types of chemical agents: nerve agents, blood agents, choking agents, and blistering agents (Table 5.1). Nerve agents enter the body through ingestion, respiration, or contact. Blood and choking agents are usually absorbed through the respiratory system, and blistering agents burn skin and internal tissue upon contact (Organization for the Prohibition of Chemical Weapons, 2000; for a summary, see Federation of American Scientists, 2010).

Chemicals present an attractive weapon for terrorists because they are easy to control and, unlike biological weapons, the users can avoid the area they attack. Nonetheless, chemical weapons present four problems. First, terrorists must have a delivery mechanism; that is, they need some way to spread the chemical. The second

TABLE **5.1**
Chemical and Radiological Agents and Their Effects

Agent	Common Entry	Effect
Nerve	Food, water, air, skin contact	Convulsions, flood of body fluids
Blistering	Skin contact, air	Burns, choking, respiratory failure
Blood/Choking	Breathing, skin contact	Failure of body functions
Radiological	Food, air, water	Burns, long-term skin contact illness

Sources: Organization for the Prohibition of Chemical Weapons, 2000; U.S. Congress, Office of Technology Assessment, 1995.

highly enriched uranium (HEU): A process that increases the proportion of a radioactive isotope in uranium (U-235), making it suitable for industrial use. It can also be used to make nuclear weapons. Nuclear weapons are made from either HEU or plutonium.

radiation sickness: Caused by exposure to high doses of radiation over a short period of time. It is characterized by nausea, diarrhea, headaches, and fever. High doses produce dizziness, weakness, and internal bleeding. It is possible to treat patients who have been exposed to doses of radiation, but higher doses are usually fatal. Other than the two nuclear bombs used in World War II, most radiation sickness has been caused by industrial accidents.

problem is related to the first. Bombing is a popular tactic, but the heat of most explosives incinerates the chemical agents. It takes a lot of chemicals to present a threat. Finally, weather patterns, air, and water can neutralize a chemical threat. Chemical weapons are most effective when used in a confined space, and they are difficult to use effectively in large outdoor areas.

Radiological weapons are closely related to chemical weapons. Exposure to radiation can produce short-term burns and long-term contamination and health problems. Radiological poisoning takes place when a contaminated material comes in contact with any source that conducts radiation. The contacted material, such as food, water, or metal, becomes a contaminated object that could poison humans. Small contaminated pieces of matter can also become a means of spreading radiation through the air.

Some experts believe that terrorists will use radioactive material in a dirty bomb. This means that a conventional explosive would be used to spread a radioactive agent around a large area. Unlike the incineration that takes place when chemicals are placed in a bomb, radiation is not affected by the heat of an explosion. It is only affected by the type of radiological agent that is used in the device and the dispersal pattern created by the explosion. Most dirty-bomb scenarios are based on the premise that a radiological agent will be used with a conventional explosive.

Countdown to Zero, a film by Lucy Walker, is a documentary about the dangers of nuclear war. She interviews experts and powerful heads of state in the movie, but one of her most frightening interviews, according to the *Times* of London (Goodwin, 2010), came in a jail cell in Tbilisi, Georgia. Her interviewee was a man sentenced to eight years in prison for trying to sell **highly enriched uranium (HEU)** to an undercover officer posing as a member of al Qaeda. In the film, he tells Walker that there is plenty of HEU available and that it is easy to obtain. HEU is so potent that not only could it be used in a dirty bomb, it could also be used to construct a nuclear device. The most frightening aspect of the scenario is that the culprit was a bumbling amateur. If he was able to obtain the material, certainly, determined terrorists would be able to do the same.

Other analysts believe that the dirty-bomb scenario is misunderstood. Under most circumstances, P. Andrew Karam (2005) writes, the impact of the radiation from a dirty bomb would not be as disruptive as most people think. Terrorists can spread radioactive material through a bomb, but lethality depends on the type of material used in the device. Spreading material through a conventional explosion is not the optimal means for distributing radiation. Most bombs would not cause **radiation sickness** or an upsurge of cancer rates. Karam believes that the primary danger of such a bomb is the psychological effects. The public, in turn, would be prone to panic if they heard about the detonation of a dirty bomb, and public safety officials might refuse to work in the blast area because they would not understand the nature of radioactivity. Many health experts are not trained to recognize symptoms of radiation poisoning, and they might refuse to respond to victims or treat patients.

Sources of Highly Enriched Uranium

Although the construction of a nuclear bomb is a sophisticated process, terrorists could build a device with HEU without the assistance of a nuclear state. The United States Research Council has suggested that stocks of HEU be secured. Civilian industries around the globe have created more than 50 tons of HEU. It takes about 40 to 60 kilograms to make a crude nuclear bomb. Terrorists could obtain HEU from nuclear reactors used for:

Power plants

Production of medical isotopes

Propulsion engines in ice breakers

Power source for space vehicles and satellites

Research facilities

Source: Nuclear Threat Initiative, 2009.

Karam believes that it is possible to expose thousands of people to intense radiation, but that it will probably not be the result of a dirty bomb. He suggests that prevention should focus on preparing for a response rather than trying to detect low amounts of radiation. This involves training public service and medical personnel. Response personnel should understand the low risks of poisoning in the areas affected by a dirty bomb. It is also important, he says, to remind emergency medical personnel and hospital staffs that patients suffering from radioactive poisoning are not contagious.

James David Ballard (2003) looks at the problem of nuclear terrorism another way. Congress has designated a site in Nevada as the repository for all the radioactive waste from America's nuclear power plants, and all this material must be shipped across the country. Ballard wonders what would happen if terrorists seized some of this material. He points out that nuclear waste is a ready-made dirty bomb.

The power plants themselves, as well as other nuclear facilities, present another scenario. Since dirty bombs are less effective than popularly believed, an attack on a nuclear facility with conventional weapons presents a more tempting target. For example, a nuclear power plant could be attacked with a hijacked airplane or a strong explosive device. It could also be overrun in a terrorist attack. A meltdown of its core reactor would lead to the dispersal of concentrated radioactive material over a relatively large area surrounding the plant (Hagby et al., 2009).

 Self-Check

> How does technology impact terrorism?

> Describe the ways cyberterrorists might operate.

> Describe the effectiveness of differing types of WMD.

Nuclear Terrorism

The most fearful scenario around WMD involves a nuclear explosion. A stolen atomic weapon conjures the worst images of mass destruction, and it is no secret that several terrorist groups would love to have a nuclear bomb. Nonetheless, it is much easier for terrorists to use a conventional weapon than it is to build a nuclear weapon. Nuclear weapons are also difficult to obtain and detonate. Difficulty has not hampered desire. One of Osama bin Laden's former bodyguards told an Arab newspaper that al Qaeda wants to build or purchase a nuclear bomb. A top counterterrorism official in the United States confirmed the story (AFP, 2010). Fearing the worst, many governments have installed nuclear detection devices in ports of entry and cities that are attractive targets for terrorists (*Daily News and Analysis*, 2010).

There are two methods for constructing a nuclear device. The simplest method is to use HEU. Rarely used in military weapons today, it was the type of bomb used at Hiroshima, and it can be built without the assistance of a nuclear state. It involves placing two pieces of material in a tube and forcing them to collide to cause a nuclear reaction. The second method involves plutonium, and it is much more complicated. The principle behind a plutonium bomb involves compressing the metal until its density produces a nuclear reaction. Although HEU seems to represent the greatest danger in the hands of terrorists, security experts are not sure whether HEU or plutonium represents the worse threat. An HEU device is easier to make, but far less effective than plutonium. Simen Ellingsen (2008) of the Department of War Studies at King's College London suggests that terrorists will prefer the HEU method even though an HEU homemade device might produce fewer casualties than a conventional attack. He believes that the fear generated by a nuclear explosion would cause public hysteria, achieving the goal of terrorism.

The United States has been aware of the possibility of a clandestine nuclear attack long before al Qaeda appeared. Micah Zenko (2006) says the American intelligence community has studied the issue for the last 50 years, not caring whether the attack is from Russia, China, or some other source. The possibility of an attack is frighteningly real because nuclear weapons or bomb-grade material can be stolen with relative ease. American intelligence agencies believe that it would be rather simple to smuggle a bomb into the United States without it being detected. Although the United States is woefully unprepared for a nuclear attack from terrorists, it is an ominous possibility made more threatening, Zenko concludes, by fanatics who believe it is their religious duty to obtain a nuclear bomb.

A group of Russian scholars agree with Zenko and expand on his thesis. While Zenko examined the threat to America, the Russian researchers believe that nuclear terrorism is a threat to every major country. International terrorists, they argue, want to disrupt their enemies by destroying a large portion of London, Paris, Moscow, or any other international metropolis. Two factors inhibit their ability to do so: the cost of obtaining a weapon and the technological skills needed to use it. Regardless, the ability of international terrorists to operate globally increases the chances that nuclear weapons will be added to their arsenals (Arbatov, Pikaev, and Dvorkin, 2008).

Scholars from Tel Aviv University suggest that the probability of nuclear terrorism is low (Schachter, Guzansky, and Schweitzer, 2010). The nuclear threat is based on the crime causation model: victim, opportunity to commit a crime, and the desire on the part of the criminal to commit the crime. Al Qaeda—the only group that has made an effort to obtain a nuclear device—has the desire to make any one of their enemies victims, but it has consistently lacked the opportunity to strike. Further, there is no evidence to suggest that al Qaeda has the ability to obtain a nuclear weapon or to construct one. No state has ever supplied a terrorist group with a nuclear weapon; even if Iran builds a nuclear arsenal, its religious differences with al Qaeda would negate the possibility of sharing one of its weapons with them. Nuclear terrorism, these scholars conclude, is equivalent to "crying wolf." It diverts attention from actual threats increasing the probability of their success.

Michael Levi (2007) steers a middle course in a comprehensive work entitled *On Nuclear Terrorism*. The book gives a balanced, straightforward analysis of the issue and the probability in nontechnical terms. Levi explores the possibility of an attack on the United States, concluding that the country is not ready to deal with it. Careful to avoid writing a "how-to" guide for terrorists, he discusses scenarios for attacks, methods for creating a defensive system, and policy changes needed to prepare for

Overcoming Popular Misconceptions about Nuclear Terrorism

Michael Levi says that it is necessary to debunk the myths about nuclear terrorism and to understand the following:

1. Security is never 100 percent effective.
2. The nuclear black market does not exist.
3. Building a nuclear bomb is not a simple process.
4. Nuclear defense should be based on realistic, comprehensive scenarios.
5. We should create total intelligence pictures of terrorist groups beyond nuclear terrorism.
6. Total protection is not possible, but we can tip the scales in our favor.

Source: Levi, 2007, pp. 140–141.

nuclear terrorism. Military experts, such as Martin van Creveld (2008), conclude that this is one of the definitive works on nuclear terrorism.

As stated by others, Levi (2007, pp. 124–127) reiterates that the easiest method for utilizing a nuclear bomb is to build it. The theoretical homemade bomb would surely strike terror, but it has another major drawback. It is not as lethal as a military weapon. Yet, if terrorists were to obtain a military-grade weapon, it would also comes with disadvantages. Nuclear devices have sophisticated security mechanisms that terrorists might not be able to overcome. Nations provide physical security for their arsenals, and they have the technology to detect military weapons. Sheer weight is also an issue. If terrorists were to obtain one of Pakistan's devices, for example, the warhead is designed to fit on a missile. It weighs more than a ton. Despite these limitations, Levi says, the possibility of nuclear terrorism is real, and the approach to deal with the problem should be equally realistic.

Levi (2007, pp. 140–142) suggests that the United States should approach nuclear terrorism in two ways. The first involves debunking popular myths about the subject. Policy makers and the public need to understand the basic aspects of nuclear security and must realize that it is never 100 percent effective. Irrational fears should be dealt with. For example, building a homemade bomb is complicated. A terrorist cannot go to the Internet, download the instructions, and build it in the backyard. Another irrational fear is the **nuclear black market**. It does not exist, Levi says. American officials currently base their possible scenarios on the worst case. Levi believes it is more logical to look at several realistic scenarios and aim preventive measures at high-probability targets. Finally, it is not enough to limit the focus to nuclear terrorism. Levi argues for a comprehensive approach to a terrorist group and all its activities. This would provide a better threat analysis than limited attention to nuclear terrorism.

The second response to nuclear terrorism is to revamp defense systems. Protection against any form of terrorism does not involve a single agency working against a single group. Defense involves a multitude of agencies and organizations at all levels of government and liaison with private organizations. Levi argues that the current bureaucracy does not provide protection because agencies protect their own turf; that is, they do not share information, and administrations are confused and competitive. Oversight of defense systems needs to be clarified and streamlined, and agency managers should be routinely evaluated on their ability to work with other agencies and to share information.

Reforming popular misconceptions and defensive systems will not prevent nuclear terrorism. Levi, quite correctly, concludes that no security network is always

nuclear black market: When the Soviet Union collapsed, it was difficult to account for all the nuclear weapons that were in the control of military officials and the newly independent states. People feared that these weapons would be sold to terrorists. Similar fears exist for Pakistan's nuclear bombs and nuclear development programs in North Korea and Iran.

Levi's Five Goals for Policy Makers

1. Support international efforts to stop the proliferation of nuclear weapons.
2. Address nuclear terrorism in conjunction with all other terrorist threats.
3. Mandate nuclear threat analysis based on the most probable dangers.
4. Create a cooperative multiagency defense system.
5. Audit the defense system and reward cooperation.

Source: Levi, 2007, p. 142.

---

effective. America can only tip the scales in its favor, he concludes. This means that the United States needs to be able to recover from a nuclear explosion, and Levi adds that the country also needs a little luck.

✓ Self-Check

> What two elements are used in the construction of nuclear bombs?
> Explain two positions on the debate about the possibility of nuclear terrorism.
> What must the country do to prepare for nuclear terrorism?

The Media as a Force Multiplier

Governments benefit when media sources portray the savage cruelty of terrorist groups. As images of carnage and distraught victims are beamed into their homes, viewers are frequently sickened by the suffering and destruction. Security forces—symbols of sanity in a world turned upside down—assume the role of heroes, whether the report is favorable or not. They are trying to restore order. Terrorists, however, also benefit from the coverage. Constant reporting makes small terrorist groups seem important, and, when attacks are shown over and over again, the striking power of a group is magnified. Both governments and terrorists see the media as a force multiplier.

Every group involved in a terrorist conflict tries to manipulate images, seeking to use the media as a force multiplier. Paul Wilkinson (1997) says that terrorists try to multiply force through communication. This gives terrorists and the media an interdependent relationship. Terrorists use their own underground systems, but they seek to send messages through mainstream media because it serves as a better psychological weapon. Their goal is to trap the media into spreading their message in the hope that blame for an incident shifts from terrorists to victims or governments. If the process is successful, terrorism is no longer criminal; it becomes legitimate violence for a respectable political position.

According to Brigitte Nacos (2000), most terrorist groups have objectives beyond publicity, and public attention is not the only goal of terrorism. Groups want recognition of their causes, grievances, and demands. She concludes that the media is an important tool and that new forms of communication enhance the spread of information. Terrorists will try to portray respectability in all media. Nacos's analysis leads to another conclusion: If terrorists are seeking legitimacy and they use the media as one of their tools, then projection of an image is crucial. For terrorists, as well as their opponents, the crucial image is victory. Whether the image is conveyed by print, television, radio, or the Internet, respect comes with success. To paraphrase Sun Tzu, the worst way to defeat a city is to surround and attack it. The best measure of victory is to make the city believe it is defeated. This gives all media a special role in terrorism. When it portrays victory, it multiplies the enemy's force.

Gadt Wolfsfeld (2001) says that media victories are crucial for terrorism. In the al Aqsa Intifada, both sides tried to use the media, and Wolfsfeld believes there are lessons to be learned from this experience. He says that struggles for the way a battle is reported are as important as the combat on the battlefield. Neither side wants to be portrayed as the aggressor. The Palestinians know that sensational television coverage presents one of their best chances to receive outside intervention, leaving Israel to practice damage control. Both sides have structures in place to capture media attention and to present their respective views.

Wolfsfeld also believes that the media is the primary tool for demonizing the enemy, and the most powerful tool is the way television reports casualties. Both sides use the same pattern. Each side compassionately presents its own casualties and describes in horrific terms how they got their injuries, whereas the other side's killed and wounded are described as statistics. Although radio and print media are important, television takes center stage because it can show bloody images. The worst images are shown many times over on the 24-hour networks.

The media makes conflict worse in a subtle way, Wolfsfeld believes, because drama dwindles when news organizations report peace efforts. Most reports about peace efforts focus on the breakdowns. When an explosion threatens peace talks or terrorists behead a hostage after fighting has ended, television, radio, and newspaper reporters flood the world with gruesome stories. Negotiations during civil unrest are not dramatic, Wolfsfeld notes, but explosions and machine-gun fire are riveting. The only time peace becomes dramatic is when major treaties are signed by heads of state. Unfortunately, violence is more frequent.

All forms of media can be used to multiply force, and the Internet is one of the most important force multipliers easily available to terrorists. Natalya Krasnoboka (2002) says that research shows that the electorate in most countries is gravitating to online reporting and discussion. Many people think that the Internet will make countries more democratic, but other media analysts believe that it will have the same impact as traditional news sources. Krasnoboka says that empirical evidence presents a different conclusion. The Internet does not have an overwhelming impact in democratic countries, but it is a powerful tool for opposition forces in authoritarian regimes.

Krasnoboka says that the Internet is gaining the attention of security forces. When the media is heavily controlled, online communication brings the only measure of freedom, and it is emerging as a major source of information. By extending Krasnoboka's logic, it would seem that when two sides engage each other, they would see the Internet as a tool for propaganda. Indeed, Krasnoboka concludes, this is exactly what happens under authoritarian regimes. Governments try to control the Internet for their own purposes. They see its potential as a weapon for opposition and revolution.

Cinema presents another venue for both assisting terrorism and distorting issues. Medhi Semati (2002) says that movies create popular images of propaganda. The American image of a terrorist is generally a cinematic picture, but terrorists use the same medium in other parts of the world to project their own image. Fouzi Slisli (2000) says that any such image is grounded in simplicity and cultural stereotypes. In the final analysis, movies are responsible for strong emotional projections. Unlike the news, they can be completely grounded in fiction. Mock documentaries even give the illusion that a propaganda film is an objective news analysis (see *Expanding the Concept: Fighting for the Media*).

No matter what the means of communication, the mass media is part of terrorism. Gadt Wolfsfeld (2001) concludes that it is necessary to accept that both the media and security forces will fight to control media images and that bias in the media is totally misunderstood. When searching for political bias, Wolfsfeld says, slanted news is taken for granted given the orientation of the station, press, or theater. The actual bias comes from the media's endless quest for sensational violence. The mass media compete for the most dramatic, bloody imagery. He does not hold the media responsible for terrorism but concludes that it is part of the story. Wolfsfeld wryly says that gladiators keep one eye on the opponent and one eye on the crowd.

EXPANDING THE CONCEPT

Fighting for the Media

Terrorists and security forces battle for media control by

- Creating organizations to place stories in a good light
- Demonizing their enemies
- Creating the best images for the media
- Appearing to support peace proposals

Source: Wolfsfeld, 2001.

 Self-Check

> How do the media enhance terrorism?

> What are the ways to responsibly cover terrorism?

> Why do terrorists and governments want to be portrayed favorably?

Economic Targeting and Transnational Attacks

Terrorists may use transnational support or transnational operations as a force multiplier. As the world moves closer to a global economy, terrorists have found that striking transnational economic targets increases the effectiveness of operations. If governments run counterterrorist operations against underground networks and sources, terrorists turn the tables by striking the economic system. Some systems are tied closely to the international economy, and they present tempting targets to terrorists. Three types of transnational attacks can be used to illustrate the issue: tourism, energy, and shipping.

Tourism

On the evening of October 12, 2002, several hundred people were gathered in a resort area of Bali in Indonesia. Many of the people were tourists in a nightclub, and most of the tourists were Australians. According to one of the investigators from the Australian Federal Police, who asked to remain anonymous, Indonesians were quietly advised to leave the area around the bar in the late evening. Shortly before midnight, a firebomb went off inside the bar, trapping the patrons. A second bomb ignited the exterior. Within minutes more than 200 people had been killed. The perpetrators called themselves Jamaat Islamiyya, and they vowed to strike Indonesia's tourist industry again. They would target hotels and resort areas. Leaders of Jamaat Islamiyya had multiple motives for targeting tourists. They wanted to create fear among foreigners and resented the presence of outsiders in Muslim lands. They also felt that it was a method of directly striking the West. One of the leaders claimed that as long as Western troops were in Afghanistan and Iraq, his group would continue killing Westerners in Indonesia. The leaders also felt that they were targeting economic interests (Abuza, 2006b).

There is a relationship between terrorism and tourism, but it is not simple. Terrorism does not seem to have an impact on domestic travel. Terrorism most frequently affects international travelers. If a host country has had widespread media attention to a terrorist event, tourism may drop in selected areas (Sonmez and Graefe, 1998). The impact of terrorism on tourism is not always clear. Some researchers have found that low-level terrorism gradually reduces tourism over a period of time; sudden, vicious attacks have an immediate negative impact (Drakos and Kutan, 2003). Other researchers believe that the frequency of violence is more important than the severity of terrorist attacks (Pizam and Fleischer, 2002). Regardless of mixed findings, one aspect is clear. Terrorism against tourists has a negative economic impact. Attacks on tourists have economic consequences.

Energy

The economic relationship between energy and terrorism is clearer than the impact on tourism, and terrorists have a vested interest in disrupting oil and gas production. Fossil fuels present tempting targets for two reasons: They represent the power and strength of the industrialized world, and strikes against oil refineries or transfer facilities have an economic impact on the West. Iraq serves as an example. U.S. forces invaded Iraq in the spring of 2003. An insurgency grew during the summer, and it was in full swing by November. The primary economic target of the insurgents was oil production. From June 2003 to February 2006, there were 298 attacks against oil-production facilities. The economic impact from the 26 percent reduction in oil production was devastating. The attacks resulted in $6.25 billion in lost revenue for 2005 (Daly, 2006a).

Al Qaeda noticed the impact of the oil attacks in Iraq. In January 2006, Osama bin Laden broke a 14-month silence to announce that the war against the United States would not be limited to Iraq. Saudi Arabia was a tempting target. Bin Laden considers Saudi Arabia as nothing more than an American colony. Oil production represents 40 percent of the country's gross domestic product (Daly, 2006a). Al Qaeda in the Arabian Peninsula, an offshoot of the original al Qaeda, began targeting Saudi oil facilities in 2003 with a varied strategy. It sought to destroy production facilities; destroy transfer systems, such as pipelines, storage facilities, and shipping; and target individual oil workers, especially foreigners. In an Internet posting, a spokesperson for al Qaeda said the Saudi attacks were designed to destroy the Saudi economy and create an energy crisis in the West. He also mentioned that attacking energy sources brought a good deal of press coverage (Bakier, 2006b). The lessons of Iraq have not been lost on al Qaeda.

The International Crisis Group (2006b) reports that Pakistan is experiencing a similar problem in the Balochistan province, which produces 45 percent of the country's natural gas. At issue are the tribal divisions inside Pakistan and the energy produced in Balochistan. The Pashtun tribe controls the central government in Islamabad, and it exploits the natural gas resources in Balochistan to support ethnic Pashtuns. But Balochistan's major fields lie in the Bugti tribal area, and the Bugtis resent and resist Pashtun incursion into their native land. This has led to sharp fighting and a guerrilla war. John Daly (2006b) points out that the situation has become more complicated because of the resurgence of the Taliban along the Afghan–Pakistan border. Some Bugtis, who previously had few ethnic or political links with the Taliban, have allied with the exiled Afghan Taliban as well as al Qaeda members who fled Afghanistan in the wake of the October 2001 American offensive. Daly says that the Taliban believes that the most effective way to destroy the Pakistan government is to attack economic targets. Attacks on gas facilities, which cripple gas production and are force multipliers, started in 2003. J. Bowyer Bell (1975) refers to **endemic terrorism** as a form of violence that occurs in Africa where arbitrary national boundaries have been drawn without regard to ethnic and tribal divisions. These areas breed all forms of tribal and ethnic conflicts, including terrorism. The Niger Delta is one of the largest oil-producing areas outside the Middle East, and it is beset with endemic terrorism (Cilliers, 2003). Oil plays crucial roles in violence that has killed hundreds of thousands in the past decade. First, it is used to fund endemic terrorism and corrupt governments. Second, it becomes a target of those who cannot control production. Finally, oil companies investing in the area have a greater incentive to focus on security than on the debilitating poverty engulfing the region (International Crisis Group, 2006a).

Oil in the Niger Delta represents a different opportunity for economic attack. It simultaneously funds terrorists and other violent groups while serving as a target for terrorism. In addition, dilapidated storage facilities and pipelines have become an ecological disaster for the impoverished local residents. The result is an environment

endemic terrorism: Terrorism that exists inside a political entity. For example, European colonialists created the nation of Rwanda by combining the lands of two tribes that literally hate each other. The two tribes fight to eliminate each other. This is endemic to political violence in Rwanda. The term was coined by J. Bowyer Bell.

that encourages subnational violence and that might serve as a base for international terrorism. Jakkie Cilliers (2003) notes that the energy environment in Africa represents an interesting paradox. According to Cilliers, if poverty, endemic terrorism, and criminalized politics are not addressed by the industrial world, areas like the Niger Delta will evolve in two directions. They will become the base for the emergence of new international terrorist groups, providing excellent resources for training and eluding detection. At the same time, the energy resources in the delta will provide a target-rich environment for terrorists.

Transportation

Transportation systems also present a tempting economic target because they produce mass casualties with minimal effort. Another benefit for terrorists trying to strike economic targets is that the costs of protecting transportation are staggering. Transportation is a major concern of homeland security, and it will be discussed in the last section of the text. We restrict our discussion here to examination of an economic attack on transportation as a force multiplier. Such attacks are quite effective.

After the September 11 attacks, the federal government immediately budgeted $4.8 billion to protect the aviation industry. In addition, it created a new federal agency, the Transportation Security Administration, with 30,000 employees (Hobijn, 2002). The shipping industry is also affected by security costs. Indonesia, Malaysia, and Singapore have joined to protest insurance premiums on ships traveling through the Strait of Malacca. Rates have soared because insurance companies believe terrorist groups might start cooperating with pirates (Raymond, 2006). Critics of homeland security policies, such as Stephen Flynn (2002, 2004a, 2004b), argue that ports remain unsecured because of the costs associated with increased protection. Although all of these examples represent policy issues, the economic impact is clear. Attacks on aviation, shipping, and transportation facilities increase the cost of security. If terrorists wish to increase the economic impact of an attack, the transportation industry presents a tempting target.

 Self-Check

> What is economic targeting?
> Describe the targets and methods of economic targeting.
> Why are attacks on energy and transportation targets force multipliers?

Suicide Attacks—Conflicting Opinions

altruistic suicide: The willingness of individuals to sacrifice their lives to benefit their primary reference group such as a family, military unit, ethnic group, or country. It may involve going on suicide missions in combat, self-sacrifice without killing others, or self-sacrifice and killing others.

Sacrifice in times of conflict is nothing new, and sometimes warriors are sent on missions where they know their lives will be lost. At other times in history, people intentionally sacrifice their lives for a greater cause. Diego Gambetta (2005) tracks incidents of suicide tactics and attacks since World War II. His edited volume develops three types of suicide attacks: (1) suicide in warfare, (2) suicide for a principle without killing others, and (3) suicidal terrorism. Several scholars note that a suicide attack is not a method chosen simply to end one's life. The social and psychological appeal is the idea of sacrificing one's self for the betterment of the community; it is a freely given sacrifice in the form of **altruistic suicide**. Suicide terrorists may be fatalistic, they may be psychologically duped, or they may be wealthy with a bright future. One thing they have in common, however, is that they frequently believe that they are sacrificing their lives for a greater good (Padahzur and Perlier, 2003; Pape, 2003, 2005, pp. 171–195).

Although common logic sometimes dismisses suicide terrorists as psychologically unstable and early studies suggested that suicide bombers were young, frustrated males, data suggest that neither is true (Howard, 2004). Robert Pape (2003,

2005) presents an extensive empirical analysis of suicide terrorist attacks from 1980 to 2001, concluding that the attackers are so diverse it may not be possible to find a single profile.

A Theory of Suicide Terrorism

Instead of searching for social or psychological factors, Robert Pape (2005) suggests that suicide terrorism be considered as a strategic tool. It is popular because it works, and although suicide attacks began as a form of religious violence, secular groups use the strategy because it is so effective. Suicide terrorism, Pape argues, gives a small group the power to coerce large governments. Suicide terrorists tend to be more lethal than those carrying out other types of attacks, they strike greater fear in the target audience, and each attack hints at future horrific violence. It is a strategy designed to multiply expectations of political victory.

theory of suicide terrorism: A theory developed by Robert Pape that states that a group of people occupied by a democratic power are likely to engage in suicide attacks when there are differences between the religions of the group and the democratic power and when the occupied religious community supports altruistic suicide.

Pape (2005) takes his empirical study of suicide bombing beyond a simple description of how it happens and offers a **theory of suicide terrorism**. He believes three factors must be in place before a suicide terror campaign can take place. First, a nationalistic or ethnic group must be resisting the occupation of a foreign power. Second, the foreign power must have a democratic government whose voters will not routinely allow the indiscriminate slaughter and total repression of the people in the occupied area. Finally, there must be a difference in the religions of the occupying power and the people living under occupation. This is a key point in the theory. Such terrorism does not happen when the occupied and occupier share a single religion; it is caused by differences between the two religions.

Pape (2005, pp. 127–128) says that it is difficult to test this theory because there are so many different factors, but he argues that it might be possible to test it by focusing on the evidence from case studies. He does so by looking at the Israeli occupation of the Shiite areas of Lebanon, the Sinhalese (Buddhist) control of the Tamil (Hindu) region of Sri Lanka, the fighting between Sunni Kurds and Sunni Turks in eastern Turkey, and the Indian (Hindu) struggle with the occupied Sikhs.

The popular conception in Lebanon is that suicide operations are grounded in Islamic extremism; that is, militant Islamic theology causes suicide terrorism. Pape's examination of bombings casts doubt on this conclusion. Of the 41 suicide attacks Pape studied, only eight involved the suicide of Islamic militants. Twenty-seven were conducted by communists who followed no religion, and the remaining three were carried out by Christians. Although Iran supports Hezbollah, the group that first employed suicide attacks, terrorism is homegrown in Lebanon. Bombers come from local communities where self-sacrifice is glorified by religious leaders (Pape, 2005, pp. 128–139).

Sri Lanka presents an interesting scenario because the Hindu Tamil area has been occupied by two powers—native Buddhist Sinhalese and primarily Hindu Indian soldiers. Again, the popular theory of suicide terrorism in Sri Lanka is that the Black Tigers, the suicide organization within the LTTE, brainwashes its bombers. The LTTE Black Tigers have conducted more suicide bombings than any other group, and they have assassinated two political leaders—an Indian prime minister and a president of Sri Lanka. Yet, when the Hindu Indian soldiers were stationed in Sri Lanka from 1987 to 1990, suicide bombings stopped (Pape, 2005, pp. 139–154).

Pape attributes the cessation of suicide bombings during the Indian occupation to the differences between the Sinhalese Buddhists and the Tamil Hindus. The Tamils believe their existence is threatened by the dominant Sinhalese government, and many of their religious leaders have demonized the Buddhists. Extremist Buddhists respond by dismissing Hinduism. This difference, Pape believes, is the primary cause of suicide terrorism in Sri Lanka. He does note that there are exceptions. The Hindu prime minister of India was assassinated by the Black Tigers in 1991 when it appeared that Indian forces might return to Sri Lanka. Pape says that he is not proposing a rule that cannot be broken; rather, he is pointing to a trend.

This logic may also apply to Pape's ideas about democracy. For example, the Russians (Orthodox Christians) occupy Chechnya, which is populated by Sunnis with a strong Sufi influence. The Russians believe Chechnya is a Russian state, but Chechens believe they are an independent country. Although Russia has experienced the birth of some forms of democracy, the central Russian government has revoked many of the resulting democratic reforms. The Chechens have used suicide operations, including massive suicide attacks. Again, Pape is probably not insisting that the occupying power must be a full democracy; rather, he is pointing to a trend, and his evidence suggests that trends exist.

The Kurdistan Workers' Party (PKK) in eastern Turkey conducted 14 suicide attacks from 1996 to 1999, and they were unique. They were the least deadly attacks in the course of modern suicide bombing, killing an average of two people per incident. They started when the popular leader of the PKK called for them, and they stopped at his command. More interestingly, they were conducted by long-term members of the group, and they were not followed by more attacks. Pape believes that the reason the attacks never became popular is that the Sunni Kurd community identified with the Sunni Turks. Pape (2005, pp. 162–167) found the same trend in the Indian province of Punjab.

Other Research on Suicide Bombing

Studies by many scholars and terrorism analysts confirm Pape's findings. Journalist B. Raman (2003, 2004) says that terrorists favor suicide attacks because they are so intimidating. He points out that suicide bombers can penetrate secure targets with a good chance of success. Audrey Cronin (2003, pp. 9–11) gives several reasons for the popularity of suicide attacks. They generate high casualties as well as publicity for the attacking group. The nature of the attack strikes fear into an enemy, and the attacks are effective against superior forces and weapons. Suicide bombers give terrorist groups maximal control over the attack.

Other studies bring Pape's finding into question. Domenico Tosini (2009) notes the alarming increase of suicide attacks by terrorist groups over the last 25 years, and he examines the explanations presented in scholarly studies. Most examinations of suicide bombings are based on the idea of strategic logic; that is, studies assume that both the bomber and the supporting organization are rational actors seeking to accomplish goals. In fact, Tosini finds that almost all the literature focuses on rational choice. He argues that rational choice is not the only explanation for suicide bombing.

Tosini believes the link between suicide and religion has been disproved, given that secular terrorist groups have employed the tactic. To be sure, religion remains a strong factor for many groups. Not only can it be used to justify attacks; it can also serve as a tool to recruit and retain terrorists. Yet Tosini believes that rational choice and religion are secondary factors in suicide attacks. The major factor is the social structure and culture of the group engaged in suicide terrorism.

Tosini says that groups take actions inside social structures based on their understanding of reality. This can create the group dynamics that lead to suicide terrorism. The dynamic agents involved in a suicide bombing are the armed terrorist group, the group's supporters, and the bombers. These three entities operate in social networks where decisions are made based on the interpretations of situations. The decision to engage in suicide bombing is based on the interactions of terrorists, supporters, and attackers within a surrounding social network.

Moving beyond rational choice, Tosini argues that the social climate must readily accept suicide bombings. Supporters of a terrorist group have to embrace the idea and create social rewards for bombers and their relatives. Beyond this, the entire community must accept violence as a normative response to social grievances and believe that suicide bombing is an acceptable expression of violence. Supporting groups need material and symbolic rewards, and attackers must have a deep attachment to idealized representations of their communities. When altruism enters the equation, Tosini says that it produces a culture of martyrdom. This, in turn, combines with two common military approaches to war—dehumanization and depersonalization of enemies.

Tosini's research indicates that suicide bombing is not simply a strategic model based on rational choice. It also calls into question the relationship of religion and democracy to suicide attacks. He argues that suicide terrorism develops when a culture accepts it as an expression of altruistic martyrdom and when terrorist groups within the culture embrace the tactic. A bomber consumed with dreams of becoming a martyr can be launched against innocent people or military targets because enemies have been defined as something less than human. For Tosini, suicide bombing takes place through a social process that endorses self-sacrifice as a legitimate expression of normal behavior.

Sara Jackson Wade and Daniel Reiter (2007) examined suicide bombings from 1980 to 2003, and their findings differ from Pape's. Wade and Reiter argue that the form of government is not an important factor. In other words, suicide bombings are not used mainly against democracies. Their data show that differing forms of governments with strong religious minorities experience attacks more frequently than democracies, and they think that Robert Pape missed this point because he used different variables in his research model.

In contrast to Pape, Wade and Reiter believe that Islam is an important factor in suicide bombings, but it is not simply an attack developed to use against the West. They found that Muslim states suffer more suicide attacks than Western states, and more Muslims are targeted in suicide attacks than any other group. A democracy occupying a foreign land with a different religion has little to do with these attacks, they argue. The presence of Islam is more important, and past experience with suicide bombing makes the tactic more acceptable and more likely.

Models for Suicide Bombing

There is a debate about modeling attacks. Rohan Gunaratna (2000) suggests that it may be possible to model some precursors of suicide bombings. After examining suicide attacks between 1983 and 2000, Gunaratna sees three things that all attacks have in common: secrecy, reconnaissance, and rehearsal. He believes that local groups operate in secret to prepare the bomber and the target area. Because locals can blend in with the surroundings, they provide supplies and information. They also conduct the initial scouting or reconnaissance of the target. A support group far away from the target can rehearse the attack in secrecy; the better the rehearsal, the greater the chance of success. The bomber usually conducts the final reconnaissance during the operation, but he or she can detonate the bomb in case of discovery. These factors could serve as the basis for a model.

Another school of thought suggests that models may exist, but there are so many factors that a single set of precursors cannot exist. Audrey Cronin (2003, pp. 6–8) believes that different styles of bombings emerge from different places. The Hamas model, patterned after the actions of Hezbollah, uses a professional group to plan and execute the attack and a support group to prepare the attacker. For many years, researchers believed that this was the only model for suicide bombing (Institute for Counter-Terrorism, 2001).

Cronin finds, however, that different models have emerged over time. The LTTE trained suicide bombers from an early age. The PKK leadership coerced victims to take part in suicide bombings. The September 11 suicide attacks defied the previous models, and bombings in Chechnya represent a different combination of social and psychological factors. There is no single model for suicide bombing.

> Why is suicide used as a weapon?
> What do empirical studies suggest about suicide terrorism?
> How might suicide terrorism be stopped?

CHAPTER TAKE AWAYS

The tactics of terrorism are straightforward and simple, but they are employed in innovative ways. The study of terrorism is complex as a result of tactical innovation. Force multipliers—technology, transnational support, religion, and the media—enhance the power of terrorist groups. It is important to understand the tactical impact of gender on terrorism, but research on the roles of women has been neglected. Technological attacks can be made more effective by using WMD, cyberattacks, or economic targeting. Suicide bombing has become a particularly terrorizing tactic, but there is no single explanation for either understanding or preventing it.

OBJECTIVE SUMMARY

- The six basic tactics of terrorism are bombing, arson, hijacking, assault, kidnapping, and taking hostages. Terrorists employ these tactics in a variety of ways.
- Terrorists use force multipliers to increase their attacking power. Force multipliers include technology, transnational support, media coverage, and religious fanaticism.
- Women have been involved in terrorist groups throughout the history of modern terrorism, but their role has been ignored. Many researchers and the general public have found it difficult to believe that women could become terrorists. More inclusive studies of gender in terrorist activities will increase the understanding of terrorism.
- Female terrorists impact tactics, and security forces often overlook the threats they pose. Different types of groups tend to use females in different manners. Nationalistic and ethnic groups tend to use them in supporting roles, but women emerge as warriors and leaders in revolutionary groups. The importance of women in terrorism is growing. Some male-dominated traditional groups are openly recruiting females for suicide bombings and other operations.
- Technology can enhance striking power when it is employed as a weapon or it becomes the target of an attack. Any form of technology may be used. Cyberterrorism is a growing threat. Computer systems can be infected or data can be stolen. Terrorists or other enemies might attack cybernetic control system to cause a catastrophic failure in the economic sector or infrastructure.
- Technology also increases the lethality of potential weapons, giving them the potential for mass destruction. Biological agents include bacterial and viral weapons. There are four types of biological agents: (1) natural poisons, or toxins that occur without human modification, (2) viruses, (3) bacteria, and (4) plagues. There are four types of chemical agents: nerve agents, blood agents, choking agents, and blistering agents. Radiological weapons are closely related to chemical weapons, and they could be used by dispersing high doses of radiation in a conventional manner.
- Nuclear terrorism involves the potential employment of a nuclear bomb. There are two methods for constructing a nuclear device. The simplest method is to use HEU in a homemade bomb. The other method would be to gain control of

an existing device. Some scholars and analysts believe that this will not happen, and others think that it will. Regardless, America is not prepared for nuclear terrorism. The country needs to develop a cooperative climate among security bureaucracies and create a multifaceted defense in depth.

- Terrorists use the media as a weapon for enhancing the power of attacks by using it to broadcast a political message, gaining publicity for a violent political movement, and providing respectability for their cause.
- The force of terrorism can be multiplied by the selection of transnational economic targets. Tourism, energy, and transportation present excellent opportunities for increasing the economic impact of an attack.
- Pape's theory of suicide terrorism is based on examining religious differences when a democracy occupies a foreign country or the enclave of an ethnic group. Local religious leaders must create a climate where martyrdom is supported. Other research suggests that religion has no link to suicide bombings. It is difficult to model suicide terrorism because there is no single group or individual profile of suicide attackers. Different groups use different methods, and suicide bombers come from a variety of backgrounds.

Critical Engagement: Gender and Security

The 1965 film *The Battle of Algiers* focused on the actions of Yocef Saadi and the National Liberation Front (FLN) during the Algerian War, 1954–1962. The film is a classic study of anticolonial terrorism, and it also features a tactical shift in the war. Nearly 11,000 women joined the FLN, with a few hundred accepting combat roles. Even though many of the men were reluctant to work with women, Saadi took full advantage of their abilities.

The movie highlights the tactical role of women. The French police were reluctant to search women, and the public did not expect women to engage in violence. As a result, women could go into areas where men were denied access. They could smuggle weapons. Saadi had women dress in Western clothes and smuggle bombs into areas dominated by French colonists. In a particularly gruesome scene, Saadi, who played himself in the movie, arms a young woman with a handbag bomb. She goes to a French sector, enters a club, and places the bomb by the bar. She casually walks away, leaving the purse. The ensuing explosion decimates the patrons.

French journal Chris Kutchera (1996, 2012) interviewed several former FLN women 30 years after the war. The majority of them were socialists, and they fought to create an Algeria where women would have equality with men. They tended to come from conservative families, and most of their relatives could not believe their daughters, nieces, and sisters were engaged in terrorism. Kutchera concludes that the women made up only a small percentage of the fighting force, and most of them engaged in noncombat operations in support of the FLN. Still, she says, the tactical impact on the Battle of Algiers was far greater than the numbers.

The experience in Algeria is directly applicable to terrorism today. As stated in the introduction to this chapter, the Center for American Progress (Sofer and Addison, 2012) reports that the official U.S. counterterrorism plan ignores the increasing participation and impact of women in terrorism. The study almost looks as if it is based on the experiences in Algeria. Women are able to infiltrate areas where men cannot go. Police officers are reluctant to search them. Politicians and the public trust women, accepting the incorrect stereotype of nurturing females who would not engage in violence. As a result women terrorists are responsible for 65 percent of all political assassinations. Although they account for only 15 percent of suicide bombings, the media give more coverage to female bombers than to their male counterparts. They are joining the ranks of terrorist groups in record numbers, according to the report. It is dangerous to ignore these trends.

Consider these issues in terms of future developments:

- What measures should be taken to counter security lapses created by gender bias?
- Women have completed the same hazardous duty assignments as men in law enforcement for four decades. Given the nature of guerrilla war in both Iraq and Afghanistan, women assigned to combat support are targeted just as men. Should these experiences serve as a platform to utilize women in all combat roles in the military?
- Criminological research in general has suffered from a gender bias when examining female criminality. What steps could be taken to correct this weakness?

KEY TERMS

Six tactics of terrorism, p. 5-110

Force multipliers, p. 5-110

Triborder region, p. 5-111

Philosophy of the bomb, p. 5-111

Thermobaric bomb, p. 5-111

Racial terrorism, p. 5-112

International focus, p. 5-113

Domestic issues, p. 5-113

Ulricke Meinhof, p. 5-113

Leila Khalid, p. 5-113

Cyberterrorism, p. 5-116

Bacterial weapons, p. 5-118

Viral weapons, p. 5-118

Highly enriched uranium, p. 5-120

Radiation sickness, p. 5-120

Nuclear black market, p. 5-123

Endemic terrorism, p. 5-127

Altruistic suicide, p. 5-128

Theory of suicide terrorism, p. 5-129

PART **2**

International Terrorism: National and Ethnic Movements

CHAPTER 6

Long-Term Separatist Terrorism

Mirrorpix/Newscom

LEARNING OBJECTIVES

After reading this chapter, you should be able to:

> Explain the nature and characteristics of nationalistic and ethnic separatist terrorism.

> Describe the emergence of the modern IRA and terrorism in Northern Ireland.

> Outline the basis for negotiating peace in Northern Ireland.

> Summarize the nature of Basque culture and its separateness within Spain.

> Explain the impact of the Spanish Civil War on the Basque region.

> Summarize the birth and evolution of the ETA.

> Explain the rise of the GAL.

> Outline the Spanish government's approach to Basque separatism.

> Describe the rise of the LTTE and the role of the Tamil diaspora.

> Summarize the unique aspect of LTTE suicide bombings.

> Describe the end of the LTTE and the danger of possible reconstitution.

The Basque Nation and Liberty (ETA), an organization that waged a campaign of terrorism against Spain for nearly a half century, released a declaration in October 2011. According to an article in the *New York Times* (Burns, 2011), the ETA stated that it was ending its campaign of violence. It had accepted a ceasefire a few years earlier, and except for a few flare-ups, the fragile peace remained intact. This new declaration went further. It was not a simple agreement to stop fighting. It was a call for a complete cessation of all violence. The long war appeared to be finally over.

The statement was important both for the items it addressed and for the things it did not say. Acknowledging the suffering and the nature of terrorism, the ETA recognized the need to abandon violence. It was not working. In addition, Spanish security forces had become increasingly effective. They had also formed close working relationships with French law enforcement in the Basque region of France, denying an important refuge for the separatists. Finally, the Spanish government had been making political progress in the Basque homeland in Spain. Authorities recognized that separatist issues could not be handled by force alone. As expressed in counterinsurgency doctrine, the government recognized that it had to win a political consensus with the Basque people. The Spanish government was dedicated to this effort and its actions were paying off.

There were also unspoken issues in the statement. The ETA did not say that it was surrendering, and there was no indication that the group was forever disbanded. The statement also gave no hint that it had dropped its demands for Basque independence or that it would agree to any of Spain's long-term demands. It simply called for direct talks with the Spanish government. The political issues surrounding the decades-long conflict had not been settled.

The first decade of the twenty-first century brought seemingly peaceful political solutions to three violent separatist movements: the renewed troubles in Ireland resulting from civil disturbances in 1969, the ETA's campaign for Basque autonomy, and a long campaign of savage guerrilla warfare and terrorism among two ethnic groups on the island nation of Sri Lanka. All of the conflicts appeared to end. Yet terrorism involves extremist positions, and extremists are seldom satisfied with compromise. The central question for the next two decades is: Will the political solutions in Ireland, Spain, and Sri Lanka mollify the extremists who call for no compromise? The answer will be determined by the actions of governments as separatists are reintegrated into mainstream politics. Not all of the signs are promising.

Ethnic and Nationalist Separatist Movements

The focus on international terrorism has diverted attention from some of the world's separatist movements; yet these struggles have shaped modern terrorism. Such wars are asymmetrical, pitting small groups of separatists against larger government forces. This usually leads to the most common tactic in asymmetrical warfare, terrorism (Hanzich, 2003). Since ethnic separatists use the same tactics as ideological terrorists, most analysts and policy makers have approached the two forms of terrorism in the same manner. By the end of the twentieth century, some American diplomats began to question this approach, saying that because the structure of ethnic violence had changed, the old models were no longer applicable. The earlier approach obscured the nature of separatist violence (Trundle, 1996; Porath, 2010).

Characteristics of Ethnic and Nationalist Terrorism

Peter Neuman (2007), director of the Center for Defense Studies at King's College London, applauds this shift because it presents an opportunity for understanding and approaching separatists. Unlike religious terrorists, separatists usually have a clear-cut, achievable goal, and they are usually not imbued with the nihilism of ideological groups with pure "absolute" goals. This point presents an opportunity for political pragmatism and negotiation, Neuman argues. Indeed, much of the violence described in this chapter might have been settled much earlier had the governments opposing the separatists moved to the negotiating table. Political accommodation is the most effective method for ending a terrorist campaign, according to a recent study by the RAND Corporation (Jones and Libicki, 2008).

In an earlier RAND study, Daniel Byman (1998) concludes that ethnic terrorism differs from terrorism carried out in the name of ideology, religion, or economic gain. He acknowledges the growing influence of religion on terrorism, but he believes ethnic terrorism is a unique entity, though the line between ethnic and religious violence is blurred. Ethnic terrorists are usually more nationalistic than their religious counterparts. He uses evidence from the LTTE, the Kurdistan Workers' Party (PKK), the Provisional Irish Republican Army (PIRA), and the ETA as evidence for his thesis.

Ethnic terrorists try to forge a national identity. Their primary purpose is to mobilize a community, and they do so by appealing to the nationalistic background of a particular ethnic group. Byman says that terrorist activity is used to make a statement about the group's identity. When the inevitable governmental persecution follows terrorist actions, it draws attention to the group and allows the terrorists to present themselves as victims. This process may increase public awareness of ethnic or nationalistic grievances, and it may lead to new sources of support. Terrorism also polarizes other ethnic groups and forces them to either ally with the terrorists or oppose them.

In the past decade, jihadist networks have come to play a significant role in European terrorism. North African groups operate in Spain and Italy. Middle Eastern networks are active in Germany, Belgium, the Netherlands, France, and the United Kingdom. France also has ties with groups from Algeria (Kohlman, 2004). Yet a recent analysis of European law enforcement data suggests that separatist violence is the most dangerous threat to Europe. Measured by the sheer number of attacks, separatists present more of a threat to Europe than any other form of terrorism (Renard, 2009). Separatist violence differs from ideological and religious terrorism, and it needs to be examined to unveil its unique qualities.

Violence plays a special role in ethnic terrorism. Whereas political terrorists use violence in a symbolic manner and religious extremists use it to make a theological statement, violence is the *raison d'être* of ethnic terrorism. It keeps an idea alive. Some data even suggest that separatist terrorism is the most violent form of terrorism in the modern world (Masters, 2008). As long as a bomb goes off or a police officer is murdered, the identity and existence of ethnic differences cannot be denied. Violence sustains the conflict, even when political objectives are far out of reach. The fear created by violence serves ethnic interests. Violence also serves to undermine moderates who seek peaceful solutions; yet peaceful negotiated settlements have proved to be the most effective method for ending ethnic and nationalistic terrorism.

Three Cases of Ethnic and Nationalist Separatism

Nationalistic and ethnic separatist groups studied the tactics of the People's Will and began to copy them in the early part of the twentieth century. Three of these campaigns lasted for many years, and one in Spain still remains active. The longest campaign took place in a series of waves in Ireland beginning in 1916 and slowly diminishing in the early twenty-first century. Modern terrorism is associated with the 1916 Easter Rising, the Black and Tan War of 1919 to 1921, and the resurgent Irish Republican Army of 1956 and 1969. Irish nationalists, long angered by the colonial rule of England, incorporated terrorist techniques into their revolt against British rule, and their experiences evolved as weapons technology improved. The Irish Republican Army set the stage for modern separatist terrorism, and terrorism in Ireland is the product of a long, long story.

Another lengthy struggle grew in the Basque region of Spain. During a savage civil war in the 1930s, two ethnic Basque provinces sided against the fascist forces. When the fascists were successful, the government introduced repressive measures, angering the Basques and causing them to create a government in exile. In the midst of a turbulent series of ideological struggles in the late 1960s, a group of Basque students and workers decided the time was ripe for independence. The Euskadi Ta Askatasuna (ETA) was born, and it is Europe's longest surviving ethnic conflict. It also produced death squads, at times devolving into a dirty war pitting terrorists against self-appointed guardians of the government who operated outside the rule of law.

The island of Sri Lanka has two primary ethnic groups—Sinhalese who dominate the population and minority Tamils. Tensions between the two groups grew after independence in 1948, resulting in sporadic outbursts of violence. Many Tamils left the island, and some of them became economically successful. Their money flowed back to the island as ethnic tensions increased. Fearing repression from the Sinhalese and a deteriorating political situation, a militant group of Tamils, the Liberation Tigers of Tamil Elam (LTTE), used the money to buy weapons. The Sri Lankan government and the LTTE fought each other savagely from 1983 to 2009, and the LTTE pioneered many methods of terrorist attacks, including the secular use of suicide bombings.

Ethnic terrorism in separatist movements ranges through many parts of the world. Ireland appears to have degenerated into low-level criminal activity by small groups of former terrorists. It also continues to have lingering political hate crimes, including the murder of people of another religious tradition. The LTTE was defeated in 2009, but it may rise again. Despite negotiated peace settlements, the ETA continues to conduct operations. These three examples constitute the longest ethnic–nationalist conflicts since the advent of modern terrorism.

Self-Check

> What separates ethnic and nationalist terrorism from other forms of terror?
> How do separatist movements impact the level of violence?
> Why might separatist movements be amenable to negotiated solutions?

Modern Terrorism in Northern Ireland

Eamon de Valera was elected prime minister of the Republic of Ireland in 1927. Although he passed several anti-British measures, he was soon at odds with the IRA. Two important trends emerged. Bell (1974) records the first by pointing to the split in IRA ranks. By the 1930s, some members of the IRA wanted to follow the lead of their political party, Sinn Fein. They felt that the IRA should express itself through peaceful political idealism. They believed that they should begin working for a united socialist Ireland in the spirit of James Connolly.

Another group of IRA members rejected this philosophy. They believed that the purpose of the IRA was to fight for independence. They would never be at peace with the British or the Unionists until Northern Ireland was united with the south. They vowed to carry on the fight. They broke with the de Valera government and formed a breakaway wing of the IRA in the 1930s. The Provisional IRA vowed to keep up the fight, and de Valera turned on them. Robert White (1993, p. 26) says that the IRA was active from 1939 to 1944 in England. They launched an ineffective terrorist campaign in Northern Ireland from 1956 to 1962, when they fell out of favor with Irish Republicans.

Provisionals: The nickname for members of the Provisional Irish Republican Army. They are also known as Provos. The name applies to several different Republican paramilitary terrorist groups.

J. Bowyer Bell believes that the reason for IRA impotence can be found in the second generation of **Provisionals**. Wanting to follow in the footsteps of their forebears, the Provisionals began to wage a campaign against the RUC in Northern Ireland in the late 1950s. They established support bases in the republic and slipped across the border for terrorist activities. Although the Provisionals initially enjoyed support among Republican enclaves in the North, most Irish people, Unionists and Republicans alike, were appalled by IRA violence. Even the Official IRA—the segment embracing a socialist ideology—criticized the military attacks of the Provisionals. Faced with a lack of public support, the Provisional IRA called off its offensive in the north. By 1962 almost all of its activities had ceased. Some Provisionals joined the civil rights movement; others rejoined former colleagues in the Official wing. Most members, however, remained in a secret infrastructure, hoping events would restore their ranks and prestige.

Just when it seemed that the Provisional IRA was defunct, a Catholic civil rights campaign engulfed Northern Ireland in 1969. The failure of the civil rights movement in Northern Ireland can be directly linked to modern Irish terrorism and the rebirth of the IRA. Alfred McClung Lee (1983, pp. 59–97) notes that the economic situation in Northern Ireland favored the Protestant Unionists. From 1922 to 1969, the government in Northern Ireland systematically reduced the civil rights of Catholics living in the North. During the same period, the economic power of the Unionists increased. When Catholics demanded the same rights as Protestants in 1969, demonstrations grew violent. The British army was called in to support the RUC.

The IRA and the Modern "Troubles"

According to Lee (1983, pp. 59–97), the political and economic conditions in Northern Ireland provided the rationale for a major civil rights movement among the Catholics. Although the movement had Republican overtones, it was primarily aimed at achieving adequate housing and education among Ulster's Catholic population in an attempt to improve economic growth. The civil rights movement was supported by both Protestants and Catholics, but the actions of the Northern Ireland government began to polarize the issue. Increasingly the confrontation became recognized as a Unionist–Republican one, and the old battle lines between Protestants and Catholics were redrawn. By 1969, the civil rights movement and the reaction to it had become violent.

The IRA had not been dormant throughout the civil rights movement, but it had failed to play a major role. For the most part, the leaders of the civil rights movement were peaceful Republicans. The IRA could not entice the civil rights leaders to join it in a guerrilla war, and it had virtually destroyed itself in an earlier campaign against

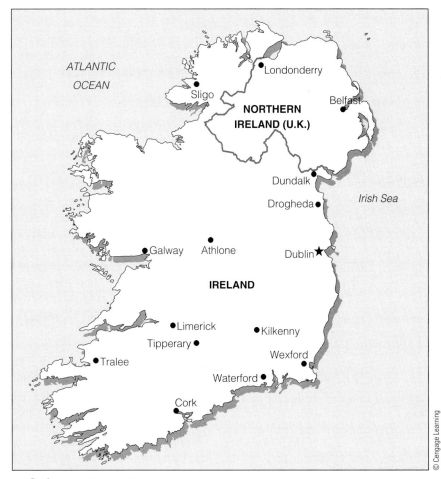

FIGURE **6.1** Map of Ireland

the government of Northern Ireland. In 1969, the Provisional IRA was popular in song and legend, but it held little sway in day-to-day Irish politics. Some type of miracle would be needed to rejuvenate the IRA.

Repression on the part of the Northern government was the answer to IRA prayers. The government in Northern Ireland reacted with a heavy hand against the civil rights workers and demonstrators. Max Hastings (1970, pp. 40–56) writes that peaceful attempts to work for equal rights were stymied by Northern Irish militancy. Catholics were not allowed to demonstrate for better housing and education; if they attempted to do so, they were attacked by the RUC and its reserve force, known as B-Specials. At the same time, no attempts were made to stop Protestant demonstrations. The Catholics believed the RUC and B-Specials were in league with the other anti-Catholic Unionists in the north.

Issues intensified in the summer of 1969. Civil rights demonstrators planned a long, peaceful march from Londonderry to Belfast, but they were gassed and beaten by the RUC and B-Specials. On August 15, 1969, the Protestants assembled for their traditional Apprentice Boys celebration. Just a few days before, the RUC had enthusiastically attacked Catholic demonstrators, but on August 15, 1969, it welcomed the Protestant Apprentice Boys with open arms. The Catholics were not surprised: Many B-Specials had taken off their reservist uniforms to don orange sashes and march with the Protestants.

Protestant marchers in Londonderry and Belfast armed themselves with gasoline bombs, rocks, and sticks. They not only wished to celebrate the seventeenth-century victory in Derry, but they were also thrilled by the recent dispersal of the civil rights marchers and hoped to reinforce their political status by bombarding Catholic neighborhoods as they marched by. When the Protestants began taunting Catholics, violence broke out. By nightfall, Belfast and Londonderry were in flames. Three days later, Britain sent the British army in as a peacekeeping force. The British army became the miracle the IRA so desperately needed.

The Army and Overreaction

According to most analysts and observers, the early policies and tactics of the British army played an important role in the rebirth of the IRA. In an article on military policy, J. Bowyer Bell (1976, pp. 65–88) criticizes the British army for its initial response. He says that the British army came to Ulster with little or no appreciation of the historical circumstances behind the conflict. According to Bell, when the army arrived in 1969, its commanders believed they were in the midst of a colonial war. They evaluated the situation and concluded that there were two "tribes." One tribe flew the Irish tricolor and spoke with deep-seated hatred of the British. The other tribe flew the Union Jack and claimed to be ultrapatriotic subjects of the British Empire. It seemed logical to ally with friends who identified themselves as subjects.

Bell believes that this analysis was a fatal flaw. Far from being a conflict to preserve British influence in a colony, the struggle in Northern Ireland was a fight between two groups of Irish citizens. Neither side was "British," no matter what their slogans and banners claimed. The British army should have become a peaceful, neutral force, but it mistakenly allied itself with one of the extremist positions in the conflict.

Bell argues that the reaction of Republican Catholics fully demonstrates the mistake that the British army made. The Unionists greeted the army with open arms, but this was to be expected. Historically, the British army had rallied to the Unionist cause. Surprisingly, however, the Republicans also welcomed the British army. They believed that the RUC and B-Specials were the instruments of their repression and that the British army would not continue those restrictive measures. It was not the British army of the past. In Republican eyes, it was a peacekeeping force. The Republicans believed that the British army would protect them from the Unionists and the police.

Such beliefs were short-lived. As the British army made its presence felt in Ulster, Republicans and Catholics were subjected to the increasing oppression of British army measures. Catholic neighborhoods were surrounded and gassed by military forces searching for subversives, and the soldiers began working as a direct extension of the RUC. Londonderry and Belfast were military targets, and rebels fighting against the government were to be subdued. As confrontations became more deadly, Republican support for the British army vanished.

Feeling oppressed by all sides, Catholics and Republicans looked for help. They found it, partly, in the form of the IRA. The Officials and Provisionals were still split during the 1969 riots, and the IRA was generally an impotent organization; but the IRA pushed its internal squabbles aside, and the Officials and Provisionals focused on their new common enemy—the British army. The new IRA policy emphasized the elimination of British soldiers from Irish soil and brushed aside internal political differences (see Hamilton, 1971; R. White, 1989, 1993, pp. 74–88).

The British army found itself in the middle of a conflict that it had hoped to forestall. Alienated nationalists offered support for the growing ranks of the IRA. Each time the British army overreacted, as it tended to do when faced with civil disobedience, the Republican cause was strengthened. IRA ranks grew from a few dozen to nearly 2,000, and members adopted an elaborate justification of violence. As IRA ranks grew, Unionists watched with horror. When crackdowns by British army patrols and incidents of alleged torture by intelligence services increased the ranks of the IRA, Unionist paramilitary organizations grew in response. The British army also began taking action against Unionist organizations and then truly found itself in the midst of a terrorist conflict (see Moss, 1972, pp. 16–18; Winchester, 1974, pp. 171–180; Munck, 1992; R. White, 1993, pp. 26–28, 64–99, 130–133; Kuusisto, 2001; Alonso, 2001).

In 1972, the British government issued a report on the violence in Northern Ireland. Headed by Leslie Scarman (1972), the investigation concluded that tensions inside the community were so great once they had been unleashed that little could be done to alleviate them. The policies of the police and the British army had done much to set those hostile forces in motion. The report concluded that normative democracy could not return until the people in Northern Ireland had faith in all governmental institutions, including the security forces. The report indicated that a legal method was needed to resolve the violence.

Robert White (1989, 1993) explains violence in Northern Ireland as a group process. Socially constructed meanings evolved in three ways: (1) small-group interpretation within the IRA, (2) general interpretation of activities by the Catholic population, and (3) meanings assigned from the interaction between the small and large groups. IRA operatives were recruited according to different patterns; each recruiting style affected tactics, such as bombings, shootings, or hunger strikes. When the people of Northern Ireland, at least the Catholic minority, felt repressed by the British, this legitimized IRA violence. The IRA could not move without popular support. In addition, popular support came when peaceful actions appeared to produce no results. Finally, as the IRA in the republic and in Ulster grew closer together, they also identified with the Republicans of Ulster. The British were, and remain, outsiders to Republicans.

Unionist Terrorism

Although most Irish terrorism is associated with the IRA and its radical splinter groups, it is not proper to conclude that all Irish terrorism is the result of Republican violence. Unionist organizations also have a long history of terrorism. They represent the Unionist and Loyalist side of terrorism. Historically, it has appeared in three forms: (1) state repression, (2) vengeance, and (3) revolutionary violence for political change. Repression developed because the Unionists held power throughout most of modern Irish history. Vengeance came as Loyalist organizations struck back at Republicans. Finally, some Unionist activity has been directed at the British or other authorities. This happens when extreme Unionists feel that the government is abandoning the Unionist cause (see Elbe, 2000; Wright and Bryett, 2000, pp. 63–66; Bruce, 2001).

Ulster Volunteer Force: One of a number of militant Unionist organizations. Such groups wage terrorist campaigns against Catholics and militant Republican organizations.

Before the 1916 Easter Rising, Unionists feared Irish independence. If home rule were granted, they planned to go to war with the south to gain the independence of the north. They created the **Ulster Volunteer Force** (UVF) as a result. As long as the British remained, however, Unionists had little need of subversive groups. They controlled events in Ireland through the police and military. For example, the Irish Republican Brotherhood (IRB) began importing arms before World War I. Unionists, fearful of Catholic Republican power, decided to arm themselves as well. Although the British government had forbidden importing arms, police officers turned a blind eye as thousands of illegal arms were smuggled one night into the Orange Lodges. The British army also condoned the smuggling by confining soldiers to their barracks while the arms were distributed.

The Unionist position also enjoyed the backing of the military in other ways. Before World War I, it appeared home rule would be passed by the British parliament. To influence the vote, British officers began to resign their commissions en masse, forcing a crisis in government. Since the United Kingdom was on the verge of war with Germany, it could hardly fight without the leadership of its officer corps. Home rule was withdrawn, and Ireland remained under British control.

Things changed after the Tan War and the creation of the Republic of Ireland. Although de Valera waged war against his old colleagues, the IRA still brought terrorism to the North. Some Unionist groups formed terrorist enclaves of their own to terrorize the Republicans.

At this point, Unionist terrorism focused on retribution. When Republicans struck, the Unionists hit back. After the IRA was reborn in the 1969 violence, Orange organizations watched in fear. When IRA bombings and assassinations began, the Unionist terrorists targeted Republican leaders, especially outspoken civil rights advocates. Unionist terrorism has never matched Republican terrorism, simply because Unionists were able to use official organizations to repress Catholics in Northern Ireland.

✓ **Self-Check**

> What impact did the civil rights movement have on political order in Northern Ireland?
> How did the actions of the British Army contribute to the rebirth of the IRA?
> Identify the differences between Unionist terrorism and Republican terrorism.

Negotiating a Peace Settlement in Ireland

Anglo-Irish Peace Accord: An agreement signed in 1985 that was the beginning of a long-term attempt to stop terrorist violence in Northern Ireland by devising a system of political autonomy and by protecting the rights of all citizens. Extremist Republicans rejected the accord because it did not unite Northern Ireland and the South. Unionists rejected it because it compromised with moderate Republicans.

In 1985, the United Kingdom and the Republic of Ireland signed a peace accord regarding the governance of Northern Ireland, but the violence continued. While the **Anglo-Irish Peace Accord** sought to bring an end to terrorism by establishing a joint Irish-British system of government for the troubled area, many Protestant groups felt betrayed and the Republicans continued to view Britain as a colonial power benefiting from the occupation of Northern Ireland (Dunn and Morgan, 1995). Republican and Unionist narratives had lasted hundreds of years, and their mystical hold on both sets of extremists was hard to break. This discord forced the British government to take a radical step.

Negotiating with Terrorists

Although the United Kingdom and the Republic of Ireland were in direct negotiations and had agreed to share power, Unionist and Republican terrorists continued to fight the settlement and the government. In 1990, the British decided to take another step. Realizing that they had no economic or political interest in controlling

Northern Ireland, British intelligence contacted Sinn Fein and began negotiations with the political leadership of the IRA. Something remarkable happened. The IRA signed a ceasefire, the first in 15 years, in December 1990.

Dean Pruitt (2007) argues this effort turned the peace process in a positive direction. British intelligence units and the IRA kept talking after the ceasefire, and in 1992 Sinn Fein produced a paper calling for peace in Northern Ireland and recognizing that both Unionists and Republicans had to be included in any future agreement. It seemed as if peace would finally develop, but negotiations began to break down. Terrorists took up their arms again, but a new British prime minister, **Tony Blair**, was determined to end the violence. He formally invited Sinn Fein to the negotiating table. Despite emphatic rhetorical statements to the contrary, counterterrorists and terrorists sat down together. Pruitt says that what had once been a spiral of escalating violence turned into a process of conciliation.

On Good Friday 1998, Britain and Ireland signed the **Belfast Agreement**, which called for independent human rights investigations, compensation for the victims of violence, and decommissioning of paramilitary groups (Northern Ireland Office, 2007). More radical Republicans and Unionists tried to break away. These groups renewed a campaign of violence in 1998, hoping to destroy the Anglo-Irish peace initiatives (Bell, 1998); however, the peace talks gained momentum, and radicals on both sides found that they were losing public support. In addition, people who were jailed for terrorism and violent political activity seemed to be more concerned with reintegrating into their families and communities after their incarceration than with carrying on the struggle (Monaghan, 2004; Hughes and Donnelly, 2004; Carmichael and Knox, 2004). The few remaining violent radicals resorted to criminal activities, and the leadership of the major terrorist groups began suppressing violent activities within their ranks (McGinn, 2006).

The peace process resulted in two important new bureaucratic structures, the **Independent Monitoring Commission (IMC)** and the **Police Service of Northern Ireland (PSIN)**. The IMC investigated claims of both terrorist and governmental abuses, and its actions have resulted in the arrests of Republican and Loyalist terrorists, as well as members of the security forces who acted beyond the law (Henderson, 2006). In 2005, the IRA officially disbanded and handed over its weapons. Its leader disavowed terrorism and urged his followers to cooperate with the police (BBC News, 2005a). The government followed suit by creating the PSNI to replace the RUC.

Rational Political Goals and Negotiated Settlements

Experiences in Ireland exemplify the nature of ethnic and nationalist separatist movements. The long, long story shows the emotional power of narrative, a tale used to justify centuries of revolutionary violence and suppression. It also demonstrates an ironic pattern. When Republican organizations began to engage in violence in the nineteenth century, the British responded with increased violence to put an end to Republican activities. It did not work. When the government sat down to negotiate with terrorists, however, the campaign wound down. Dean Pruitt (2007) contends that this is due to four factors: (1) Military victory was unattainable for either side; (2) allied governments and other organizations lobbied both sides for peace; (3) as negotiations began, both sides grew increasingly optimistic; and (4) the final peace included a broad coalition of diverse groups.

Terrorism in Northern Ireland no longer grabs attention as it did in the past. The major campaigns are over and the groups have disbanded. Still, the situation remains volatile. Unionist and Republican activists carried out 124 attacks against each other in 2009, and two British soldiers were killed during the same year (Pantucci, 2010). In January 1972, British paratroopers opened fire on Catholic protestors in Londonderry on a day that became known as Bloody Sunday. The British government investigated the incident and absolved the paratroopers, but it later reopened

---

Tony Blair: (b. 1953) The Labour Party prime minister of the United Kingdom from 1994 to 2007.

Belfast Agreement: Also known as the Good Friday Agreement, an agreement signed in April 1998 that revamped criminal justice services, established shared government in Northern Ireland, called for the early release of prisoners involved in paramilitary organizations, and created a Commission on Human Rights and Equity. Its provisions led to the decommissioning of paramilitary organizations.

Independent Monitoring Commission (IMC): A commission created in 2004 to investigate paramilitary actions and alleged governmental abuses during the Irish peace process.

Police Service of Northern Ireland (PSNI): The police force created in November 2001 to replace the Royal Ulster Constabulary.

the investigation. The new investigation, one of the most lengthy and costly inquiries in British Parliamentary history, condemned the action. David Cameron, the British prime minister, reviewed the report in June 2010. He publicly apologized to the demonstrators for the army's actions, according to the *New York Times* (Burns, 2010). Such an apology would not have been given over the previous two centuries.

Self-Check

> Why did the Anglo-Irish peace accord promise success?
> What steps did the British take to create successful negotiations?
> What bureaucratic reforms helped to ensure success to the Belfast Agreement?
> Why were the negotiations successful?

The Basque Nation and Liberty

In March 2004, a series of bombs exploded in the central train station of Madrid, Spain, killing nearly 200 people. Although the plot was eventually tied to jihadists, the first response from Spain and the international media pointed to the group ETA, or Basque Nation and Liberty). The ETA has waged a campaign of violence since 1959 that has killed more than 800 people. It has specialized in car bombings and assassinations, and ETA terrorists have targeted Spain's number-one industry—tourism. The ETA's goal is to establish an autonomous homeland in northern Spain and southern France (Foreign Policy Association, 2004; Council on Foreign Relations, 2002; Goodman, 2003).

Background

The Basque region of France and Spain has been a source of separatist terrorism for more than 50 years. Primarily located in Spain, the Basque region extends over the Pyrenees into France. Basque separatists believe that they should be allowed to either develop a homeland in Spain or maintain a separate culture and language, and this has made Basque separatism an important issue in Spanish politics. Many Americans are not aware of the Basque lands because they are unacquainted with the evolutionary nature of European nations. Modern European nation-states only appeared in recent centuries. While many Americans use a word like *British* to describe anyone from the United Kingdom, citizens of the islands frequently describe themselves using such words as *Welsh*, *Cornish*, *Scottish*, *Irish*, or *English*. Modern Spain also developed from separate ethnic groups, and the Basque region of Spain has always had its own language and culture. At times, it was an independent kingdom, and, even though it has not enjoyed full autonomy for almost 1,000 years, Basques hold to their ethnic identity (R. Clark, 1979).

The origins of the Basques, like the Irish, are shrouded in lore and legend, and these stories are ingrained in ethnic narratives supporting separateness. Emerging as a linguistic group between 4,000 and 3,000 years ago, the Basque region challenges popular notions of Spanish nationalistic history. It has been shaped by Spain, but there are more Basques outside Spain than in the country. In fact, more Basques live in Latin America than in Europe. Residents of the region fought the Romans with Hannibal and emerged through the milieu of Iberian history. They have a proud male-dominated history of militarism and independence embedded in the fabric of ethnic identity (Linstroth, 2002). The Basques have been a key factor in Spanish history, but they have had and maintain distinct literary, cultural, and linguistic separateness (Zulaika, 2003). These factors have produced a tradition centered in pride, ethnocentrism, and independence.

Modern Spain emerged from the unification of several Hispanic kingdoms in 1479 and was solidified at the end of the **War of the Spanish Succession (1702–1714)**.

War of the Spanish Succession (1702–1714): The first global war exported from Europe, pitting the French and Austrians against each other for familial control of the Spanish throne. Although it involved myriad political factors, it set the stage for the evolution of modern Spain. There are several dates given for the end of the war due to the many peace treaties that ended military operations in Europe and around the world.

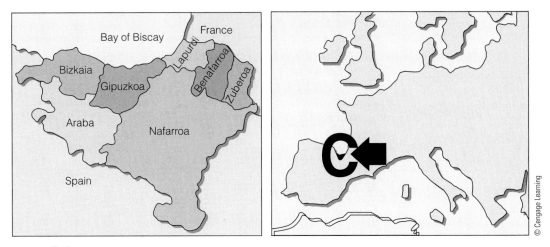

FIGURE **6.2** Existing Map of Spain

The new monarchy joined the independent kingdoms together in 1716, but it granted the Basque region semiautonomy within the realm. The Basques developed commerce and a middle class, but their autonomy and national identity began to wane in the nineteenth century (Payne, 1971). Although the Basques considered themselves "un-Spanish," Spanish power gradually enfolded the region in the twentieth century. The cultural incursion sharpened ethnic and ideological divisions. The Basque region in France was unaffected by the spread of Spanish culture and contributed to the feeling of ethnic autonomy in Spain.

The Spanish Civil War

Spanish Civil War (1936–1939): A war that pitted pro-communist Republicans against pro-fascist Nationalists. The war ended with a Nationalist victory and a fascist dictatorship under Franco.

Francisco Franco: (1892–1975) Leader of the nationalist forces during the Spanish Civil War and the fascist dictator of Spain from 1939 to 1975.

Spain's search for national identity and a philosophy of government came to a head in the **Spanish Civil War (1936–1939)**. Republican forces battled fascists, and some Basques sided against the fascists, using the civil war as an excuse to fight for autonomy. As fascist forces grew increasingly powerful, many Basque soldiers lost interest in both politics and the war. They were more concerned with ethnic identity than the governing power of Spain (Seixas, 2005). The same philosophy did not hold true, though, for **Francisco Franco**, the leader of fascist forces. After achieving victory in 1939, Franco forcibly campaigned against Basque national identity. Franco completely incorporated the Basque region into Spain, banning its language and expressions of national culture. Regaining them became the focus of the modern struggle (Moxon-Browne, 1987).

The importance of the civil war is difficult to overemphasize. Franco's repression made the Basque region seem as though it was occupied by a foreign colonial power. Priests were forbidden to make references to the Basque region in religious services, and parents were forced to give their children Spanish first names. The Basque language was banned. Franco applied these rules to the entire Basque region, even though only two of the four provinces opposed his forces in the civil war. After World War II, many Basques believed the Allies would assist their bid for independence or greater autonomy because Franco had supported Hitler; but the United States courted Franco's fascist government in return for American air bases in Spain (Woodworth, 2001, pp. 34–35). This resulted in a resurgence of Basque nationalism during the 1950s and the formation of a government in exile in Paris. The exiled Basques became an idealized expression of nationalism and ethnic identity; while it was virtually powerless, it attracted a following in the Basque provinces (Muro, 2009). A group of disgruntled middle- and working-class students traveled from Spain to Paris to meet the exiled government in 1959. This would prove to be an incubator for violence.

Twentieth-Century Basque Nationalism

The students were irritated by the rhetoric of the exiles and their willingness to accommodate Spanish authority through lofty speeches and gatherings in Paris. The students wanted action in the Basque homeland. Leaving the exiles, they formed a new group, the ETA, to serve as a stronger expression of national and cultural identity inside Spain. Composed of young, frustrated nationalists who wanted regional autonomy, the ETA advocated neither violence nor terrorism. Its central themes promoted Basque separateness and culture. Like most Basque nationalists, the ETA sought to preserve their cultural and linguistic identity. Although the language of ethnic minorities is frequently banned or discouraged by the dominant political power, the Basque tongue evolved into an important entity in resisting Spain. The language became the basis of ethnic identity, and many social scientists believe that the early nationalist campaign focused on preserving the Basque language to preserve identity and culture (Spencer and Croucher, 2008). Others think this point is overemphasized (Beck and Markkuse, 2008). Irrespective of the debate, the ETA employed the Basque tongue as a nonviolent weapon to separate their homeland from Spain. The words, they believed, should be spoken in the homeland and not in Paris.

EXPANDING THE CONCEPT

The Basque Conflict

The Issue. Basque separatists want a homeland completely independent of Spain. The nationalists control a semiautonomous Basque parliament, but they are divided in their desire for autonomy. A substantial minority of Basques want to remain united with Spain.

The Group. Although the Basque region has never been independent, it has its own language and culture. Francisco Franco, the Spanish dictator, tried to crush Basque culture and force the Basques to become Spanish.

*The Campai*gn. The Basque Nation and Liberty (ETA) began a campaign against Spain in 1959. The group was responsible for assassinating Franco's probable successor and many other officials. They agreed to a ceasefire in 1998, but they broke the treaty a year later. The Spanish government gave the Basques regional governing authority, and the Basques use their own language and run their own schools. The majority of Spaniards believe the ETA to be the most important issue in Spain, and both Basques and Spaniards are tired of ETA violence. Spain also has a strong jihadist movement, but there is no connection between the jihadists and the ETA.

The Situation. The ETA agreed to a second ceasefire, but they resumed violence after the 2006 ceasefire. Spanish and French police forces increased their intelligence operations, resulting in a number of arrests in late 2009 and early 2010. By most estimates, the ETA has gone into decline. The ETA declared an end to hostilities in October 2011.

Sources: Goodman, 2003; Agence France Presse, 2004; *The Economist*, 2009; Burns, 2011.

The original members of the ETA reflected the composition of the local population, except that most of the members were male. The ETA was primarily a working-class movement, as are many nationalistic terrorist groups, with pockets of students and intellectuals. Its members were raised in Basque enclaves and felt a strong ethnic attachment to their homeland. The overwhelming majority felt that they represented all the members of their community. They began by engaging in public advocacy within the Basque region of Spain, and this tactic eventually gave way to peaceful activism. By 1960 it also created fractures with the ranks. Some members of the ETA wanted to move from activism to confrontation (R. Clark, 1980).

The ETA Turns to Terrorism

After much internal bickering, some members of the ETA decided that the time had come to actively strike Spain. Their ideas were symbolic, and the ETA's first "attacks" involved spraying walls with nationalistic graffiti. In 1961, members attempted to derail a train carrying fascist Civil War veterans to a memorial ceremony, but they failed because they could not figure out how to conduct the operation without injury or death. Franco responded with brutal suppression, and this caused the ETA to examine its methods. The world was engulfed in a variety of revolutionary movements in the 1960s, and the ETA decided to follow the example of the third world. It would take the path of armed revolution. Paddy Woodworth (2001, p. 36) cites this period as the beginning of a "dirty war," a cycle of violence causing violent repression, leading to more violence against the repression, and so on. Terrorism and counterterrorism spiraled upward.

In 1968, the group started a true terrorist campaign. Like many terrorist groups composed of strongly opinionated people, the radicals of the ETA were not prone to compromise and agree with one another. Although the group decided to strike violently, members could not agree on a single strategy. This led to a series of splits in the ETA. A more militant group, the ETA-M, broke away from the ETA in 1974. ETA-M described itself as the military wing of the ETA. Other factions also began to appear.

After embracing violence, one of the most interesting characteristics of the ETA was that its members did not view terrorism as a full-time activity. According to Edward Moxon-Browne's (1987) research, the early recruits maintained some type of employment while serving in the ETA. In addition, most members engaged in terrorism for only about three years. After this, they returned to their full-time occupations. Another interesting aspect is that as ETA violence expanded, women grew more active in the movement. They would eventually move into positions of authority and leadership by the twenty-first century (see Hamilton, 2007).

The development of the early ETA is ironic by some measures. Franco died in 1975, and the Spanish political system began to reform. Spain adopted a new constitution in 1978, and while it did not give the Basque region autonomy, it restored the Basque language and turned the educational system over to local governments. In spite of these reforms, tensions increased and the ETA amplified its campaign of violence (Gil-Alana and Barros, 2010). On the other hand, as avenues for regional cultural and political expressions opened, ETA violence slowly began to wane. Unfortunately, this did not happen before the emergence of Spanish death squads.

ETA Tactics and Spanish Death Squads

The ETA evolved and so did its tactics. As Spanish repression increased in the 1970s, the ETA escalated its attacks. It began a Marighella-style campaign of assassination, robbery, and banditry. It targeted government officials, academic advisors to the government, and members of the police and military. The government responded with martial law, and the ETA responded with more violence. Highly visible shootouts with police forces glamorized the revolutionary image of the ETA among Basque youth. More women joined, at first as supporters, but a few emerged as leaders at the beginning. In 1980, the ETA's most violent year, terrorists killed 92 people. As more and more Spanish officials and police officers were killed, some members of the government became angry enough to take action on their own. If martial law was not strong enough to stop the ETA, they would engage in counterterrorism outside the law. Death squads, such as Warriors of Christ the King and the Basque Spanish Battalion, began to torture and murder suspected terrorists and their supporters (Woodworth, 2001, pp. 39–44).

The death squads evolved into the Anti-Terrorist Liberation Groups (GAL). Composed of Spanish police officers and illegally supported through some governmental agencies, GAL death squads had one common goal: ETA terrorists could strike from the Basque region of France and return beyond the reach of Spanish law. The French government was not willing to cooperate in the suppression of the ETA, so death squads began to slip into France to search for and kill the ETA. The GAL murdered 28 people between 1983 and 1987, sometimes mistakenly killing the wrong people. In 1984, a GAL terrorist entered a French bar frequented by the ETA. Thinking she was executing ETA members or Basque supporters, the GAL terrorist shot a group of gypsies sitting at a table where the Basques usually sat. Both the ETA and the government denounced the death squads, but violence continued (BBC, 1998; Woodworth, 2001, p. 139).

While death squad activity peaked in the mid-1980s, ETA terrorism reached its zenith between 1977 and 1980, declining steadily throughout the following decades (*The Economist*, 2009). This was not the result of death squad activity but of Spanish attempts to reframe the conflict and end the suppression of Basque culture. The ETA slowly began losing support in the Basque region. The ETA conducted a sporadic campaign during the 1990s, agreeing to a short ceasefire in 1998. Returning to terrorism in 1999 with a bombing campaign, the ETA decided to attack one of Spain's major industries—tourism. ETA terrorists murdered a total of 30 foreign tourists in 2001 as it continued a bombing campaign against symbols of Spanish power.

Reframing the Conflict

By the late 1980s, the Spanish government had had enough. Unwilling to support GAL, it began investigating law enforcement agencies and related bureaucracies in the Spanish government. It tried to delegitimize the ETA by fostering democracy in the Basque region. Rather than trying to suppress ethnic identity, the government sought to give nationalists a peaceful outlet for their views. One of the biggest changes was the creation of a Basque national police force. This not only served to quash death squad terrorism, it created the opportunity for self-policing (Greer, 1995). By opening peaceful avenues, such as self-policing, both the Spanish and the Basques found it easier to denounce violence. The ETA found it harder to operate.

The Spanish government also made comprehensive social moves in the Basque region by opening political opportunities and allowing cultural expression. The Basques were given total control of the educational system, something Spain was unwilling to do in 1978, and greater political autonomy. Language was accepted as an expression of culture. As the political system opened, the desire for ethnic cultural identity was not strong enough to support violence, especially when the means of suppression were removed. Repressive policies created tension; when they were removed, much of the support for fighting eroded (Wieviorka, 1993).

As Spanish authorities opened opportunities for democracy and national expression, the ETA transformed itself into a social movement. Only hard-core militants were left to preach violence. Faced with decreasing support in Spain, they began seeking sanctuary in France. The French government, however, began taking actions of its own; although the government traditionally had been sympathetic to Basque nationalism, French prosecutors reversed their position (Mata and Irvin, 1993).

By the end of the twentieth century, hard-core militants began embracing ideas of class revolution. The ETA and its political wing became more entrenched in working-class ideology. Although the militants never abandoned ethnic separatism, they began to speak of revolution in economic terms. This changed the social structure and gender composition of the ETA, but it further weakened the movement by strengthening Spanish connections to the Basque community. Most Basques were interested in cultural identity, not class revolution. Spain found an effective weapon against the ETA as it opened doors to political participation and cultural expression (Khatami, 1997).

Yet violence did not stop. Despite greater opportunities for political and cultural expression, as well as the cooperation of French law enforcement, the ETA continued to operate. Spain took another aggressive step, offering the possibility of a negotiated settlement. When jihadist terrorists struck Madrid on March 11, 2004, it drew attention to the ETA. Although some reporters immediately blamed the ETA for the Madrid train explosions, the ETA was quick to deny it and denounce the bombings. Terrorism analysts in Spain pointed out that indiscriminate murder did not follow the ETA's tactical philosophy. Many people hoped it would lead to a political solution between the Spanish government and the Basque region. The ETA declared a ceasefire in March 2006, and at first it appeared that the ETA and Spain might negotiate a settlement. Some analysts concluded that ethnic terrorism no longer seemed to have a place in a Europe that was seeking greater unification (Rabasa et al., 2006, pp. 115–117). Unfortunately, though violence had waned, sporadic ETA bombings began again in 2007.

The ETA is Europe's oldest active terrorist group, and its future is by no means clear. It operated with terrorists in Colombia in 2008, and authorities feared that they would join forces to become a transnational terrorist group. This never materialized (Berti, 2009). The ETA never embraced the negotiation strategy of the IRA, even though the Spanish government opened the door and it would be an effective method for ending violence (Shepard, 2002; Neuman, 2007). *The Economist* (2010) says that the ETA has lost much of its original strength. Following a united French and Spanish law enforcement campaign, most of the major leadership was in custody by 2010. Some analysts believe that this type of action will bring an end to the ETA, but others note that it still has the capacity for murder and violent action (Steward, 2009). Other analysts believe that proactive political policies are more effective (Gil-Alana and Barros, 2010).

The story took another turn in the autumn of 2011. The ETA announced that it was abandoning its military campaign, and a communiqué stated that the ETA was offering to end one of the longest ethnic wars in Europe (Burns, 2011). The future remains unclear because the ETA has not renounced its goal of total Basque autonomy. This may not be the defining point, because Spanish policies within the Basque areas have been politically popular. Spanish and French security efforts have also become more effective. The ETA may have renounced violence because it became politically and militarily impotent. If this is the case, Spain's counterinsurgency policy was successful.

Self-Check

> What is the source of ethnic identity for the Basques?
> How did the Spanish Civil War influence Basque separatism?
> Why did the ETA inspire Spanish death squads?
> Describe possible future paths for ETA terrorism.

The Liberation Tigers of Tamil Eelam

Tamils: An ethnic minority in southern India and Sri Lanka. The Tamils in Sri Lanka are primarily Hindu, and the Sinhalese majority, mostly Buddhist. Ethnicity, however, not religion, defines most of the conflict between the two groups.

The LTTE (or Tamil Tigers) fought for an independent homeland for nearly 3 million **Tamils** in northern and eastern Sri Lanka. Formed by **Velupillai Pirapaharan** in 1976, the Tamil Tigers used terrorism both as a prelude to guerrilla warfare and as a way to support uniformed guerrillas in the field. The LTTE pioneered the use of secular suicide bombings, beginning in 1987, and it created a special suicide squad known as the Black Tigers. The Black Tigers killed thousands, assassinated prominent political figures, such as Indian Prime Minister **Rajiv Gandhi** and President **Ranasinghe Premadasa** of Sri Lanka, and murdered moderate Tamils who opposed their cause. The Sri Lankan Army began a series of massive strikes against the LTTE in 2008, and by 2009 the LTTE was in full retreat. The government completely displaced the Tamil population, and it actively sought all Tamil Tigers suspected of being guerrillas or terrorists. After killing the leader of the LTTE, the government declared victory in May 2009. The struggle for Sri Lanka produced a long, dirty, and terrible war.

EXPANDING THE CONCEPT

The Sri Lankan Conflict

Velupillai Pirapaharan:
(1954–2009) Founder
and leader of the LTTE.
Pirapaharan's terrorists
conducted more successful
suicide bombings than any
other terrorist group in the
world.

Rajiv Gandhi:
(1944–1991) Prime
minister of India from
1984 until 1991, when
he was assassinated by an
LTTE suicide bomber.

Ranasinghe Premadasa:
(1924–1993) President
of Sri Lanka from 1989
until 1993, when he was
killed by an LTTE suicide
bomber.

The Issue. In 1948, the British granted Sri Lanka independence. The island was inhabited by the dominant Sinhalese and the Tamils. Although the constitution granted Tamils representation in the government and civil service, by 1955 they felt that they were being systematically excluded from Sri Lanka's economic life.

The Group. As ethnic tensions increased, some Tamils turned to violence. The Liberation Tigers of Tamil Eelam (LTTE, or Tamil Tigers) were formed in 1976 to fight for the Tamil minority.

The Campaign. The Tigers began a campaign against the Sri Lankan army, and they targeted India when the Indian prime minister tried to bring peace by deploying security forces. The LTTE is known for kidnapping young children and indoctrinating them in LTTE camps. The Tigers also became masters of assassination and suicide bombings. The LTTE was the first modern secular group to use suicide bombers. Many members lived in a virtual death cult, and the Black Tigers, the suicide wing of the LTTE, were known for carrying cyanide capsules around their necks when they attack.

The Cease-Fire. The LTTE agreed to a ceasefire in December 2001 and began peace negotiations in 2002. Although occasional outbreaks of violence occurred, many experts believe the LTTE was suffering from a lack of resources.

Renewed Fighting. Hostilities renewed in late 2006. After four years of relative peace, the Sinhalese refused to recognize a Tamil homeland. Both sides began sporadic fighting, and terrorism returned to Sri Lanka.

Conflict Ends. The Sri Lankan military and police forces launched a major offensive against the LTTE in 2008. Segregating the Tamil community, Sri Lankans forced them to either stay in a war zone or go to refugee camps. The next step involved systematically attacking and destroying all LTTE members and their supporters in the geographical region. Sri Lankan forces reduced the LTTE. Pirapaharan committed suicide rather than surrender. Fighting ended in May 2009, bringing one of Asia's longest violent separatist conflicts to an end.

Sources: Council on Foreign Relations, 2004; ICG, 2006f, 2010.

The Origins of Tamil Dissatisfaction

Manoj Joshi (1996) traces the struggle's origins to the autonomy India gained at the end of World War II. As India sought to bring internal peace to Hindus and Muslims, the island of Sri Lanka (formerly known as Ceylon) faced a similar problem. In addition to religious differences, the Tamil minority in Sri Lanka was concerned about maintaining its ethnic identity among the Sinhalese majority. Tamils along the southeastern coast of India supported the Sri Lankan Tamils in this quest. As the Sri Lankan government was formed, some Tamils found themselves in positions of authority. Although they accounted for only 17 percent of Sri Lanka's population, the Tamils were well represented in the bureaucracy. This changed in 1955.

Claiming that Tamils dominated the Sri Lankan government, the Sinhalese majority forced the government to adopt a Sinhalese-only policy. Tamils began to grumble, and some spoke of violence. A Tamil assassin killed the Sinhalese leader in 1959, setting the stage for further violence. Seeking sanctuary in the Tamil region of India, militant Tamils sailed across the short expanse of ocean from Sri Lanka to India to wage a low-level terrorist campaign through 1975. Spurred by their successes, they began larger operations.

The Tamil experience was similar to the situation in Ireland. Buoyed by religious differences and ethnic support, Tamil separatists could begin a guerrilla campaign

TIMELINE 6.1   *The Sri Lankan Civil War*

1972	New constitution favors Buddhist Sinhalese.
1976	Pirapaharan forms the LTTE.
1983	Anti-Tamil riots; Tamils hunted and killed.
1987	First LTTE suicide bombing.
1991	Indian Prime Minister Rajiv Gandhi killed by a suicide bomber.
1996	Suicide bomber kills 91 people at Colombo Central Bank.
2002	Government and Tamil Tigers sign a ceasefire.
2004	Ceasefire threatened when a tsunami kills thousands.
2006	Fighting renews.
2008	Military begins large-scale offensive.
2009	Pirapaharan commits suicide. Hostilities come to an end.

Sources: Wall Street Journal Research Staff, January 2005; ICG, 2006f, 2010.

by waging terrorist war. Their ethnic support base gave them the opportunity to do so. In 1976, Velupillai Pirapaharan, a young Tamil militant, took advantage of the situation and formed the LTTE (The Liberation Tigers of Tamil Eelam; *Eelam* means "homeland"). Pirapaharan faced problems similar to those of other terrorists. He had to raise money, which he did through bank robberies and assassinations, and he needed to eliminate rival terrorists to claim leadership of the movement.

Sri Lanka and the Tamil Tigers

The LTTE eventually emerged as the leading revolutionary group and launched Sri Lanka into a full-blown terrorist campaign. The Tamil Tigers wanted to move beyond terrorism and build a guerrilla force that could eventually evolve into a conventional army. The Sinhalese majority reacted violently in 1983, and Sinhalese protesters flocked to the streets of **Colombo**, Sri Lanka's traditional and economic capital, in a series of anti-Tamil riots. Many Tamils fled to India, and the LTTE returned to terrorism.

Colombo: The traditional capital of Sri Lanka and the country's largest city, with a population of 5,648,000. The Sri Lankan government moved the capital to Sri Jayawardenapura Kotte, five miles away, in 1982. Colombo remains the economic center of Sri Lanka.

Reactions to the riots were a turning point for the LTTE. Unable to foment the revolution from above, the group established contacts with the Popular Front for the Liberation of Palestine. After that time, the Tamil Tigers mounted three on-again, off-again terrorist campaigns. At first, India responded by forming a joint peacekeeping force with Sri Lanka. India's primary purpose was to keep violence from spilling over onto the mainland. India reevaluated its policy after several assassinations and violent encounters, and the government vowed never to send troops to Sri Lanka again.

LTTE Tactics

The LTTE incorporated a variety of tactics after 1984. Their ability to operate was directly correlated to the amount of popular support they enjoyed during any particular period. In 1988 and 1992, they sought to control geographic areas, and they moved using standard guerrilla tactics, forming uniformed units. They even created an ad hoc navy. In times of weakness, they relied on bank robberies, bombings, and murder. In the weakest times, they employed suicide bombers. They used suicide attacks in 1995 on land and at sea.

Joshi estimates that before 1983 the LTTE had only 40 followers. The anti-Tamil riots were a catalyst to growth, as links were formed in the Middle East. Terrorist training camps appeared in the Tamil region of India in 1984 and 1985, and the

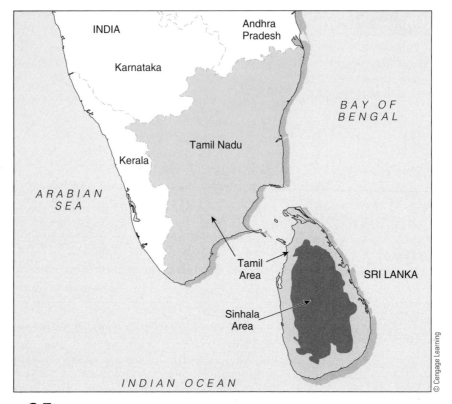

FIGURE **6.3** Existing Map of Sinhalese and Tamil Areas in Sri Lanka; Tamil Areas in India

training cadre included foreign terrorists. India responded by signing a joint peace agreement with Sri Lanka and soon found itself under attack from a highly organized terrorist group of between 10,000 and 16,000.

When not attacking India, the Tamil Tigers launched operations in Sri Lanka. Although they had once struggled to be recognized as the leaders of the independence movement, the Tigers now ruthlessly wiped out their opponents and terrorized their own ethnic group into providing support. Yet security forces enjoyed several successes, and by 1987 the Tamil Tigers were in retreat.

According to Joshi, this was a very dangerous period for the group. In fact, it was almost wiped out. Driven into the jungle, the Tamil Tigers practiced terrorism from jungle hideaways. They increased contact with Tamil bases in India, using India for logistical support. Politically adept, the LTTE asked for a ceasefire in 1989, giving India a chance to withdraw from the joint security force. No sooner had the Indian army left than the LTTE renewed its attack on the Sri Lankans.

In 1990, the LTTE expanded its operations by converting a fishing fleet into a makeshift navy. Suicide boats and other seaborne operations threatened shipping between Sri Lanka and India. By 1991, India was once again targeted by Tamil terrorists, and the Indian navy was forced to respond to the growing threat. Not only did the LTTE fight small-scale sea battles with the Indians; its terrorists also succeeded in assassinating Prime Minister Rajiv Gandhi on May 21, 1991. When Indian authorities cracked down on Tamil bases, the Tamil Tigers increased their terrorist attacks against India.

From 1994 to 1995, the Tamil Tigers waged another bombing and assassination campaign, and they did what no other terrorist group has been able to do. Although their bases in India were limited, they had strongholds on Sri Lanka. Supported by guerrilla strongholds, Tamil Tigers appeared in uniforms in 1994 and fought pitched battles with the Sri Lankan security forces. Suicide bombings increased during the same period. Faced with open revolution, the Sri Lankan government signed a peace agreement in January 1995.

Fighting Renewed

The peace accord broke down, and the Sri Lankan army went on the offensive. The LTTE suffered several setbacks, but the group made headlines in 1996 with suicide bombings in Colombo. In the spring of 1996, Sri Lankan security forces launched an all-out assault on Tamil strongholds in the northern portion of the island. Some commentators (de Silva, 1996; Berthelsen, 1996) believed this would be the end of the LTTE. They were wrong.

Rohan Gunaratna (1998) argues that the LTTE was in a unique position because it had such a large guerrilla base. The guerrillas were perfectly capable of fighting a protracted war against security forces, and if weakened in the field, the LTTE reverted to terrorism. Indeed, this was the LTTE's standard tactic. In the wake of new fighting, the LTTE followed the path of suicide bombing. Although the guerrilla campaign subsided a bit in 1999, suicide bombings increased in 2000, and the LTTE became the secular masters of suicide attacks.

In December 2001, the LTTE agreed to a ceasefire with the government of Sri Lanka. Although the Tigers still threatened violence, their resources may have been depleting. The Council on Foreign Relations (Zissis, 2006) believes that the international community's efforts to thwart terrorism after September 11 were responsible for this situation. Arms shipments were virtually eliminated, and expatriate Tamil communities in Australia, Canada, and the United States were forbidden to gather and ship resources to Sri Lanka. Draining economic resources accomplished what Sri Lankan security forces could not do. The Tamil Tigers lost their striking power.

Facing a weakened LTTE, Sri Lankan security forces developed a new strategy for a final offensive. They created "no-fire zones" and moved into Tamil areas. People in the area could stay and fight; stay and hope that they would not be killed or injured; flee, risking injury or death; or move into the no-fire zone. Police and military forces established order in the no-fire zones, interrogating and arresting suspects at will. The Manchester *Guardian* (Chamberlain and Tran, 2009) reported that human rights groups were concerned about conditions in the zones. They resembled unsanitary concentration camps where hundreds of homeless people were interred.

The strategy worked. Every person who remained in the area was considered to be an enemy, and the army unleashed a conventional offensive. The LTTE had remained the aggressor through most of the campaign, and it had forced security forces onto the defensive. The role was now reversed, and the Tamil Tigers fought on the military's terms. Unable to use guerrilla or terrorist tactics, the Tamil Tigers fought a defensive battle against conventional assaults. With limited communications and no ability to resupply or use the airport, the LTTE lost ground in every encounter. Many of the commanders began blowing themselves up rather than surrender. Pirapaharan died in this manner. Fighting ended in May, with the remaining Tamil Tigers surrendering (Chamberlain and Tran, 2009).

Government Repression after Victory

The International Crisis Group (2011, 2012a, 2012b) has issued a series of reports outlining government actions in the wake of the LTTE's defeat. The ICG states that the Sinhalese majority government has reverted to policies similar to the ones that caused earlier Tamil unrest. The northern part of the island has always been a Tamil stronghold, and it was the scene of the most ferocious fighting at the end of the war. Rather than repatriating the Tamil population and rebuilding the area, the government has kept the area under virtual military occupation. Tamils are not free to move, and many remained in internment camps.

The government is also encouraging a "Sinhalesation" of the north. Although the area has been almost exclusively Tamil, the north is now dotted with Sinhalese signs along roads and on buildings. New Sinhalese farms have been established all along the borders of former Tamil enclaves, and Sinhalese contractors and business firms are favored over those of the Tamils. Massive numbers of troops keep the Tamils at bay. The ICG also reports that Tamils lack funds and housing. Many have been forced to live in poverty. All of this takes place under the watchful eyes of a victorious military force that rules the area with little Tamil input.

Sinhalese military policies have had a tremendous impact on the role of Tamil women. Unable to fully function in a repressive economic and political climate, Tamil families are fragile and in disarray. The ICG says that women in the north are facing a desperate lack of security. They are constantly victimized, but they have neither the means of protecting themselves nor redressing their grievances. The Sinhalese security forces that govern their lives have expressed no interest in their plight, publicly denying that there is any type of problem. Sexual assault is rising, but governmental forces overlook the problem. The ICG concludes that the Tamils are in political and economic trouble.

This could be a prescription for renewed violence. The Tamil diaspora extends to wealthy nations in the West, especially Canada. Many of these Tamils actively supported the LTTE during the long civil war. News of government repression is circulating in the diaspora. Tamils in the north are at risk, families are in disarray, and women are being victimized. The area is stricken with politically imposed poverty and ruled with military force. Unlike negotiated settlements in Ireland and Spain, the Tamils accepted peace because they were defeated. The LTTE was resilient because it had a large base of support throughout the world. That base is listening. Perhaps the best chance of peace is to negotiate a new settlement and to find common political goals among the Sinhalese and Tamils. If the situation remains dominated by repression and victimization, the LTTE or its clone may rise again in the diaspora.

✓ **Self-Check**

> What are the root causes of Tamil–Sinhalese animosities?
> What role did the diaspora play in the formation of the LTTE?
> What guerrilla and terrorist tactics did the LTTE employ?
> How might the LTTE be reconstituted?

CHAPTER TAKE AWAYS

Ethnic and separatist movements involve attempts to gain full or partial independence. When such groups employ terrorism, it may be possible for each side to negotiate an end to violence because each position is based on a logical, attainable political solution. Despite the promise of negotiated peace, these movements seem to be more violent than ideological and religious terrorism. Modern terrorism in Ireland grew from dissatisfaction with Catholic emancipation in the north. Basque separatism became violent when the ETA launched a terrorist campaign in support of Basque independence. Both of these cases have resulted in a peace settlement through negotiations, although radical extremists would like to disrupt the agreements. Sri Lankan violent ended with the military elimination of the LTTE. Rather than negotiate with the defeated Tamil minority, the government has continued to routinely suppress them. This may lead to renewed violence and the rebirth of the LTTE or similar organization in the Tamil diaspora.

OBJECTIVE SUMMARY

- Many scholars and terrorism analysts believed that the purpose of terrorism had little impact on the tactical and political aspects of violence. Studies over the past 20 years have questioned such conventional wisdom. Newer research suggests that nationalist and ethnic separatist terrorism differs from other forms of terrorist violence. Separatists usually have well-defined goals that can lead to political negotiation, and they are more violent than other types of terrorists. Unlike people who practice indiscriminate terror for an unattainable ideal, the clear objectives of separatist terrorists often seem to offer the possibility of a negotiated political settlement.

- The IRA fought to bring Ulster under Irish control from 1939 to 1944 and from 1956 to 1962, but these attempts were ineffective. The IRA split into factions and the Irish government worked against it. Fighting renewed in 1969, and the IRA rose from the ashes. Its position solidified when the British army overreacted to civil disorders. Unionists responded with their own brands of terrorism. Unionist terror came in three forms: (1) repression, (2) vengeance, and (3) revolutionary violence.

- Both the United Kingdom and the Republic of Ireland began to support a serious peace process for Northern Ireland in 1995. Law enforcement policies had weakened the IRA, and the public was tired of violence. Prime Minister Blair also recognized that Sinn Fein was seeking rational political goals. This provided the basis for a long-term political settlement. Extremists in the IRA attempted to derail this process, but they were unsuccessful.

- Modern Spain was formed through the unification of several ethnic areas. The Basque region has existed for at least 3,000 years, and ethnic Basques have never totally embraced Spanish culture. Basques have their own national mythology, literary tradition, culture, and language.

- The Spanish Civil War brought Franco to power, and he violently sought to eradicate Basque culture. This caused a surge of nationalism and resulted in the formation of a Basque shadow government in Paris in the 1950s.

- A group of working-class students formed the ETA in 1959 to express nationalism in the Basque homeland. It began with a campaign of advocacy, transforming into activism. This led to a splintering of the ETA and the formation of a terrorist group. It reached its zenith in 1980, but it remains Europe's oldest violent separatist group.

- Disgruntled Spanish police officers and government officials formed death squads to counter the ETA. These squads eventually merged into the GAL. The Spanish government began taking actions against the GAL in 1987.

- Sri Lanka gained its independence in 1948, giving the Sinhalese majority most of the political power in the country. As Tamils felt discrimination from the Sinhalese, they resorted to violence when peaceful methods failed to address their grievances.

- The LTTE was formed in 1976, obtaining arms and logistical support from the Tamil diaspora. They developed several effective terrorist and guerrilla tactics and assassinated prominent political leaders. The secular Tamil Tigers mastered the art of suicide bombing, even creating a suicide unit.

- The LTTE was defeated when funds and supplies from the diaspora were cut off. The Sri Lankan government still needs to negotiate an equitable political settlement with the Tamils lest the LTTE be reconstituted in the diaspora.

Critical Engagement: Separatist Negotiations

This chapter discussed three ethnic–nationalist separatist movements culminating in the IRA, ETA, and LTTE. The ETA continues and the LTTE has been defeated, although it may have the logistical ability to rekindle. The IRA disbanded with a negotiated settlement, and former Sinn Fein leaders were freed to participate in the political process. Peter Neuman (2007) says nationalistic separatists present a unique opportunity for negotiated settlements because they have recognizable goals.

Separatists are no more rational than other types of terrorists, and their goals are certainly no less absolute. Regardless, Neuman argues that they are easier to bring to the negotiating table than groups like al Qaeda. He also includes Hezbollah, Hamas, and offshoots of the Palestine Liberation Movement as nationalist organizations. Despite their claims to operate under the mantle of religion, they have secular political goals and constituencies to satisfy. They operate like nationalists, and they could become open to political negotiations and settlements.

Neuman understands that negotiations do not develop in a vacuum. The first step is for policy makers to shift their focus of analysis. Instead of focusing on a group's ideology and political objectives, a government should examine a group's attitude about the utility of violence. Many terrorist groups did not begin activities with a violent agenda; they turned to it when they came to see violence as the most efficacious means of achieving their objectives. He points to the IRA as an example. It accepted overtures from British intelligence when its leaders came to realize that total military victory was impossible and marginal objectives could not be achieved with violence. If a group reaches a point where it questions the utility of violence, it might be open to political compromise. Negotiations are always a matter of timing.

Neuman points out that in order to negotiate, a group must have some type of effective command and control structure. A government must weigh a group's ability to control its members if it seeks a political settlement. If a terrorist group splinters as a result of negotiations, any settlement is jeopardized. When a terrorist group is sponsored by a state, new difficulties arise. Neuman says that a government must assess a group's relationship with its national sponsor and evaluate the need to include the supporting state in discussions.

Neuman's guidelines for negotiating are pragmatic. First, a government cannot be too eager to negotiate or the offer could backfire. Terrorists might simply use the reprieve to refit and rest. Second, formal negotiations should begin only after a group agrees to a ceasefire. Democracies should clearly indicate that a small group of violent people cannot replace the will of its citizens. Third, negotiations should proceed down two paths—one toward a political settlement and the other toward the welfare of terrorists. It may be necessary to grant amnesty for previous crimes. Although distasteful, it takes momentum away from hard-core terrorists who use punishment as justification for continuing violence. Finally, negotiations must be broad-based. The purpose is to get all parties to participate in a political process, and this can happen only when representatives of the major parties sit at the table.

Terrorists should be given a stake in the democratic process, Neuman concludes, only when they agree to become a part of that process. If negotiations begin, a government must buttress a group's moderates and avoid anything that would strengthen hardliners. For their part, terrorists must abandon violence and participate in politics according to democratic principles. It is the price, says Neuman, terrorists must pay.

Consider these issues in terms of future developments:

- Neuman's arguments are directed toward democracies. How might democracies deal with the types of absolutist goals typified by violent extremism? How can extreme unattainable positions be subject to compromise? What if the electorate or legislature rejects compromises?
- The British government condemned the actions of the paratroopers on Bloody Sunday, January 1972. Some officials called for criminal prosecution. Is it fair to

prosecute security forces if terrorists have been given amnesty? Are there crimes so heinous that perpetrators cannot be given amnesty? If so, how might this empower hardliners?

- The LTTE has been defeated, and if reconstituted, it will be developed in the diaspora. Negotiated settlements are effective, but how does the concept apply to Sri Lanka? How might the Sri Lankan government negotiate a permanent settlement? What types of groups should be invited to negotiations?

KEY TERMS

Provisionals, p. 6-140

Ulster Volunteer Force, p. 6-144

Anglo-Irish Peace Accord, p. 6-144

Tony Blair, p. 6-145

Belfast Agreement, p. 6-145

Independent Monitoring Commission (IMC), p. 6-145

Police Service of Northern Ireland (PSIN), p. 6-145

War of the Spanish Succession (1702– 1714), p. 6-146

Spanish Civil War (1936–1939), p. 6-147

Francisco Franco, p. 6-147

Tamils, p. 6-151

Velupillai Pirapaharan, p. 6-152

Rajiv Gandhi, p. 6-152

Ranasinghe Premadasa, p. 6-152

Colombo, p. 6-153

CHAPTER 7

Nationalistic and Endemic Terrorism

LEARNING OBJECTIVES

After reading this chapter, you should be able to:

> Summarize the revolt of EOKA on Cyprus, FLN in Algeria, and Mau Mau in Kenya.

> Explain the danger posed by Russia's breakaway states.

> Describe the political and security issues surrounding violence in Chechnya.

> Summarize the terrorist issues facing Turkey.

> Describe ethnic tensions in China's Xinjiang province.

> Explain the rationale behind China's policy toward Uighar separatism.

> Briefly summarize Sikh separatism in India.

> Define the term *endemic terrorism*.

> Explain the relative importance of terrorism in light of Africa's other issues.

> Summarize political conditions in western and central Africa.

Sunday March 11, 2012, began like most other Sundays during the Christian season of Lent at St. Finbarr's Catholic Church in Jos, Nigeria. The priests celebrated the first Mass and the congregation was dismissed. Congregants for the next Mass were filtering into the church through a gate in the fence that surrounded the church. A small group of Boy Scouts guarded a gate, the only entrance to the church, screening people before they entered. Some security was necessary because northern Nigeria had been the scene of recent religious violence.

Five months earlier, in November 2011, a shadowy group called Boko Haram attacked several targets north of the city of Jos. The group's primary victims were Christians. Loosely translated as "Western learning is a sin," Boko Haram had been founded in 2002. The Muslim group became increasingly radicalized over the next few years in a country already torn asunder by religious extremism. Both Christian and Muslim militants had attacked one another, but the November attacks were the worst in recent history. When the violence ended 150 people were dead (Duku, 2011).

Nigeria is plagued by poverty, political corruption, police brutality, and violent religious fanaticism. As the worshippers at St. Finbarr's filed through the gate on Sunday morning, they were aware that religious services held the potential for violence. They did not resent the group of Boy Scouts who checked each vehicle before it passed through the gate. After all, the Boy Scouts provided an illusion of security.

According to press reports (Agbese, 2012), the boys refused to let one car pass through the gate. The driver became irritated and an argument ensued. Heads turned toward the confrontation to search for the cause of increasingly heated voices. Suddenly, the car exploded in a flash of light. The driver and four of the boys were dead. Another boy lay in the parking lot gasping for life, and three parishioners, including a pregnant woman, were found dead in the debris. A few minutes later Boko Haram released a statement claiming credit for the attack. Christians went on a rampage. Angry young people stormed away from the church in search of anyone thought to be Muslim. At least ten people were beaten to death in reprisal attacks. Such is the nature of Africa's endemic terrorism.

Post–World War II Anticolonial Terrorism

Bruce Hoffman (1998, pp. 48–69; 2006, pp. 43–63) of Georgetown University, one of the world's leading experts on terrorism, sees the politics and strategy of anticolonial revolution in the twentieth century as the basis for modern terrorism. This developed as former colonies rejected European dominance of their cultures. Terrorist campaigns were aimed at the security forces, and they also targeted audiences in the imperial homelands. Wise terrorist leaders sought out opportunities to gain sympathy from the international community and anti-imperialist voters in the home country. The British were exposed to two differing forms of terrorism in Cyprus and Kenya. The French suffered a revolt more akin to the British experience in Cyprus during a struggle in Algeria. Both powers responded to these revolts with brutal repression.

Cyprus 1955–1959

The United Kingdom retreated from its empire throughout the 1950s, sometimes negotiating peaceful withdrawals and, at other times, fighting small uprisings. Having claimed Cyprus (Figure 7.1) as a crown colony after World War I, the United Kingdom established its Middle East military headquarters there at the end of World War II. As more British troops arrived on the island, departing from the Suez Canal by an agreement with Egypt, Cypriots of Greek descent deeply resented British control. They sought unification with Greece, but Turkish Cypriots, formerly governed by the Ottoman Empire, looked to Turkey. Tensions seethed below the surface while the British remained in control (Paul and Spirit, 2008).

Georgios Grivas (1898–1974) had been an officer in the Greek army. He fought the Turks in a war from 1919 to 1922, and he later served in a resistance organization against the Nazis. He viewed the British occupation of Cyprus the same way he saw German annexation of Greek territory in World War II. Hoffman says that he began planning a resistance campaign as early as 1953. When British military units began arriving from the Suez Canal Zone in 1954, increasing British presence on the island, Grivas had had enough. Disregarding the Turkish Cypriot desire to partition the island into Greek and Turk sectors, he created an organization to overthrow the British, the Ethniki Organosis Kyprion Agoniston (National Organization of Cypriot Fighters, EOKA).

Grivas did not seek a direct military victory, given that the relative strength of the British Empire was much greater than any Greek Cypriot force he could raise. Therefore, Gravis developed a twofold strategy. First, he wanted to draw international attention to the occupied island. He believed that international sympathy, especially in the West, would favor Cypriot independence. Such attention could be drawn through a clandestine campaign of violence similar to resistance movements in World

162 PART 2 · International Terrorism: National and Ethnic Movements

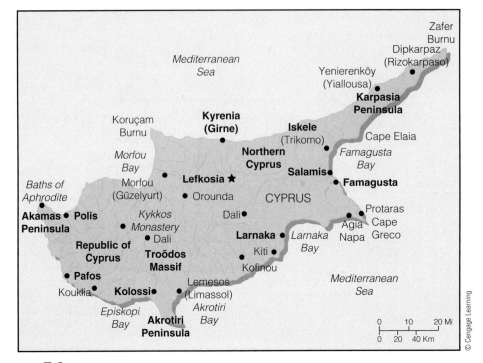

FIGURE **7.1** Cyprus

War II. Second, because the British army had powerful resources, he wanted to tie large numbers of troops up in an urban environment (Coyle, 1983, pp. 151–187).

Grivas reasoned that small groups of EOKA terrorists could strike in Cypriot cities, thwarting any potential military offensive against rebel forces. In the end, his strategy worked. Although he only commanded about 400 personnel, the British responded with more than 40,000 troops. The EOKA kept them busy. Bombing began with a series of attacks in April 1955. Another series of explosions came two months later, including an attack on a police station. The Cypriots rioted at times during the summer, and the local population began to feel that the colonial government was vulnerable.

The United Kingdom responded with force, appointing a field marshal as military governor and flooding the island with troops. The new governor imposed harsh penalties, including capital punishment for crimes less than murder. He used the military in police operations and attempted to crush the EOKA. This produced the effect that Grivas had been seeking. It brought press coverage and a political crisis. As Greek Cypriots sought union with Greece, Turkish Cypriots appealed to Istanbul for assistance. This resulted in an uncomfortable conflict of interests with the NATO partners of the United Kingdom and Turkey, and it threatened the stability of the alliance. The United States suddenly became interested in Cyprus, and it pressed Britain for a successful political conclusion (Fairfield, 1959).

The crisis was resolved in February 1959. Responding to international pressure from their allies and from British citizens who opposed colonial repression, the United Kingdom negotiated a deal with the EOKA. While Cyprus did not achieve unification with Greece, it did receive independence, and its first president was a Greek Orthodox archbishop. Britain retained the right to maintain two military bases, but it surrendered its authority to govern the island. Although Cyprus would continue to suffer tension and eventual forced partition between the Greek and Turk communities, the EOKA achieved its objective. As Bruce Hoffman (1998, p. 60) points out, terrorism worked. The EOKA won a political victory without achieving a military one.

The Battle for Algiers 1954–1962

France invaded and occupied parts of North Africa in the mid-nineteenth century, including Algeria (Figure 7.2). Brutally using military force to subdue the population in the vast interior of Algeria, France established control of the urban Mediterranean centers and encouraged immigration. Europeans flocked to the area, creating a large community that grew wealthy from the resources it developed. Moving beyond imperial occupation, France directly incorporated the northern part of Algeria and administered it as if it were a French state. Some Algerians benefited from the move, but the majority deeply resented the loss of ethnic autonomy. They began forming political associations to advocate independence in the 1930s, and the groups increased activity with the fall of the French government during World War II. Most Algerians thought that they could negotiate a peaceful separation from France (Branche, 2008).

By 1953, France, like the United Kingdom, was retreating from its colonial empire. Already involved in a long guerrilla war in **Indochina**, France faced revolts in Tunisia and Morocco. The French public wanted the Indochina war to end, and they had no stomach for more campaigns in Tunisia and Morocco. The government sought to end its colonial occupation of these regions and brought French troops home. Algeria was another matter. The northern coast was not an imperial holding, most French people reasoned; it was part of France. When Algerian nationalists made overtures for independence, the French government thought that their request was out of the question. The Algerian National Liberation Front (FLN) was formed in this atmosphere. Its purpose was violent revolution.

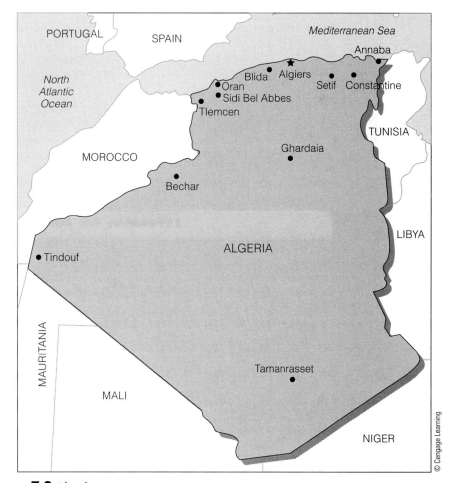

FIGURE **7.2** Algeria

David Galula
(1919– 1967): French captain who fought in Algeria in 1956–1958. He returned to Paris to analyze the Algerian campaign, producing a critique of the strategy followed in the war. His work inspired the development of counter-insurgency doctrine in the U.S. military.

blind terrorism: Tactic used by the FLN. It included indiscriminant attacks against French outposts, which involved bombing, sabotage, and random assassination.

David Galula was a French Army officer who possessed an astute understanding of the situation in Algeria. The FLN developed a twofold strategy, according to Galula (1963, pp. 9–25). Too impatient to launch a guerrilla campaign from the interior regions of Algeria, the FLN decided to strike directly in areas dominated by French colonials. The first part of its strategy was to terrify the European population through violence. Terrorism, the more horrific the better, was designed to communicate insecurity and fear. The other side of the strategy also involved communication. Like the revolt in Cyprus, the FLN sought international publicity and sympathy. The FLN did not do much planning beyond the first strategy, and it improvised as violence increased. They began with **blind terrorism**, violence designed to show that the French system could not control the social environment. They planned to gradually move to selective terrorism, targeting only Europeans and their Algerian supporters.

Despite its claim to conduct a revolution by organized phases of terrorism, Galula found that the FLN never really moved beyond the first stage of blind terrorism. The FLN mainly improved the lethality of its operations by improvising tactical innovations. It also increased the quantity of attacks. These actions struck fear in the hearts of French settlers and their Algerian allies, and they brought worldwide attention to the FLN. At first the French were determined not to leave Algeria, as they had left Indochina, due to the special relationship with French Algerians. The FLN responded with more violence.

The FLN began its campaign on November 1, 1954, launching 70 clandestine attacks against an unsuspecting enemy. Raphaëlle Branche (2008) says that a most dreadful attack came almost a year later in August 1955, when groups from the FLN slipped into Algerian suburbs and outlying French towns to massacre entire groups of colonial families. Their primary tactic was to slit the throats of their victims, making sure their bodies would be on display the next morning. The goals were to create fear and gain publicity through the horrific nature of multiple murders. It should be noted that Algerian jihadist rebels would use the same tactic against Algerian Muslims during a civil war three decades later.

The FLN was innovative and fully utilized women in their campaign. FLN leaders noted that French police officers and soldiers were more likely to confront men than women, so they used females to carry weapons and communiqués. As the fighting grew more intense, the role of women increased. Women were able to infiltrate the French areas of Algiers, so the FLN stuffed their handbags with explosives. The

EXPANDING THE CONCEPT

Hoffman Compares Algeria to Iraq

Bruce Hoffman describes several interesting parallels between the French experience in Algeria and the initial American response to the Iraq insurgency. These include:

- The absence of a clear doctrine to thwart an insurgency
- Failure to recognize warning signs of an impending insurgency
- Insurgent focus on urban areas
- Failure to separate the population from the insurgents
- The necessity to avoid alienating the indigenous population
- Promoting women's rights to counteract support for the insurgency
- The need to emphasize law enforcement over military tactics
- Failure to realize the limited effect of neutralizing insurgent leaders
- The critical importance of intelligence
- The importance of sealing borders
- The critical impact of the humane treatment of captured insurgents

Source: Hoffman, 2006.

women roamed through French urban environments in European dress, depositing their time bombs in highly populated areas. They frequently targeted gathering places known to attract large numbers of French youth (Branche, 2008).

Hoffman (1998, pp. 62–65) and Branche (2008) point out that French forces played into the hands of the FLN. The police and military, not knowing their enemy, responded with crackdowns on the Algerian population. As the terrorist campaign continued, the French increasingly used mass arrests and torture in an effort to gain information. Military and law enforcement officials justified torture by stating that FLN terrorists were not like other enemies. They could not be treated as normal criminals because they would use French law to expand their terrorist campaign. One paratrooper unit received instructions saying that the methods they needed to employ might appear uncivilized, but FLN terrorists had made themselves something less than human through their horrific tactics. Torture and even summary execution were the only tactics terrorists could understand, and French military and police units subtly endorsed these harsh measures. Hoffman points out that such an approach is rarely effective. Interestingly, the same debate arose in the United States in the wake of 9/11.

Algeria received independence in 1962 as counterterrorist tactics drove Algerian sympathy toward the FLN and French citizens lost their taste for a dirty war. Galula (1963, p. 5) was one of the few observers to grasp the meaning of the French campaign. The tactics alienated the very people the security forces needed to attract. Counterinsurgency, he concluded, required a subtler form of strategy. A political settlement trumps a military victory.

The Mau Mau in Kenya 1950–1960

The United Kingdom and Germany began vying for imperial control of East Africa in the late nineteenth century, with Britain gradually pushing the Germans out and solidifying control after World War I. After establishing British rule in Kenya, the colonial government gave Kenya's agricultural areas to European farmers, displacing tribes from their ancestral lands. One tribe, the Kikuyu, was forced to resettle deep in western Kenya in an area that threatened its ability to support all of the families in the tribe. British commissions recommended the expansion of Kikuyu land in the 1930s and 1940s, but the expansion was far less than the land given to white settlers. Around 1950, rumors reached the government in Nairobi indicating that there was some type of violent movement taking place in the Kikuyu tribal area. The movement, according to the rumors, was called Mau Mau (Throup, 1988, pp. 224–233).

The Mau Mau movement represents several factors that bear no resemblance to the anticolonial urban revolts in Cyprus and Algeria. First, it was based in rural areas. Although there was some Mau Mau violence in Kenya's cities, most violence took place in agrarian areas. Second, Mau Mau was based on tribal rites and ceremonies where symbols were used to solidify the group. Becoming a Mau Mau warrior involved taking an oath in a mystical tribal ceremony. Third, violence was frequently typified by massacres. Fourth, it brought an overwhelming British military and police response with massive detainment and torture. Fifth, Mau Mau insurgents suffered the brunt of the casualties, losing 10,000 men, while Kenyan loyalists lost 1,700 and European losses could be counted in the dozens. Finally, repression destroyed Mau Mau, but it brought many of the political reforms that Mau Mau had been seeking (Kariuki, 1963, pp. 12–24; Percox, 2003: Lonsdale, 2003; Anderson, 2005, pp. 224–327). Mau Mau lost militarily but won the political settlement.

The rebel Kikuyus began assembling in the forests of western Kenya around 1950. Fueled by anger over the loss of land, they began burning fields of European farmers. These activities emboldened some of the Kikuyu, and groups became more daring. Although they were wary of direct attacks on colonial farmers, they were willing to strike economic targets. They began to move into barns at night, hamstringing cattle. This tactic irritated farmers more than it frightened them, and they complained to Nairobi. It had another effect on the Kikuyu. These small victories seemed to indicate that they had power from the land and their ancestors. The rebel Kikuyu began to include magical ceremonies in preparation for their resistance, and Mau Mau was born. By January 1952, Mau Mau revolutionaries moved beyond economic attacks. They began killing Kenyans loyal to the colonial government.

Although highly selective in their targets, Mau Mau warriors began moving back toward the Kikuyu homeland, eventually entering the homesteads where European farmers had displaced them. The Mau Mau grew more daring, targeting farm houses when they thought they were unoccupied. This dramatically changed in January 1953 when Mau Mau insurgents entered the farm house of a politically popular local farmer and police reservist. Hearing a disturbance outside his house early one evening, he took a pistol to investigate. He was ambushed and slashed to death by a group of men swinging **pangas**. Alarmed by his screams, his wife ran outside only to meet the same fate. The men entered the house and broke down the locked bedroom door of the couple's 6-year-old son. They slashed him to death in his bed. This event outraged European farmers, and their anger grew when pictures of the young boy's blood-soaked bed were circulated through the white community (Anderson, 2005, pp. 92–95). The British responded with force and what they believed to be unbridled moral authority in the face of savagery. The colonial government declared a state of emergency.

panga: A heavy-bladed machete used in agricultural work. It was the weapon favored by people who took the Mau Mau oath.

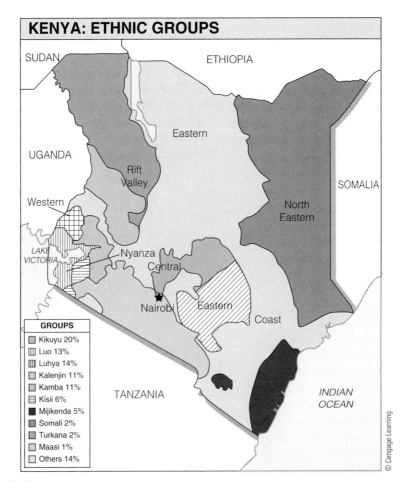

FIGURE **7.3** Kenya

Noam Chomsky (2002) states that counterterrorism often produces more violence and suffering than the actions of the terrorists themselves. The Mau Mau rebellion in Kenya illustrates his point. After the state of emergency went into effect, thousands of British soldiers arrived in Kenya. They were charged with ending the rebellion, and they made military plans to do so. The government recruited and trained a large local force to assist the army. The ensuing campaign was ruthless and violent. In addition, 90,000 suspected rebels were detained in special internment camps. The level of rebel violence dropped as government violence increased.

The magic/religious ritual of the Mau Mau movement gave it a mystical aura that inspired rebels and frightened whites. Josiah Kariuki (1963, pp. 52–54), a recruit interned for years by the government, describes the night he went through the ritual. He had been invited by one of his friends to go for a walk one evening after dark, and they came upon an arch made of banana stalks. After being told to join two other men, a leader came forward and told Kariuki that he would be bound in unity to his homeland. At this point, the three young initiates walked around the arch seven times and stooped, then stood before seated Mau Mau men and women. The head of the ceremony sacrificed a goat and ritually forced the young men to eat the lungs while taking an oath to defend the land and be loyal to the group. The leader then cut each initiate's wrist three times, poured goat's blood over the wounds, and pronounced that they were sealed together. Such practices frightened settlers and united Mau Mau initiates.

Unlike urban terrorist campaigns in Cyprus and Algeria, the Mau Mau movement failed in the field. David Anderson (2005, p. 244) explains the outcome by breaking the movement into three phases. From October 1952 through June 1953, Mau Mau units gathered in camps in the lower forests of western Kenya. Morale was high, the mood was optimistic, and they successfully attacked carefully selected targets. Ranks grew to about 12,000. From July 1953 through April 1954, Mau Mau units were forced to retreat deeper into the forest in the wake of British military offensives. They devolved into forest gangs. The third phase lasted from May 1954 until the summer of 1955. Military and police units laid siege to the forest. Recruitment dropped and the gangs were isolated from one another. After the summer of 1955, the Mau Mau movement became a paper tiger: It existed in the minds of the government and European settlers. The state of emergency would not end until 1960, and various gangs interned in Kenyan prisons tried to organize under the Mau Mau banner. The forests, however, presented a different picture. The Kikuyu struggled to survive. This situation continued until the end of fighting in 1960.

Governmental policy was ruthless. Over 90,000 Mau Mau suspects were interned during the state of emergency, and the conditions of custody were appalling. Thousands of suspects were tortured, and a few were executed outside the justice system. Beatings were routine until suspects confessed that they had taken the oath and renounced it. As groups of Mau Mau detainees began to band together in prison, the government began to break up prison gangs by increasing individual torture. The military began employing two additional tactics in the forest. Separating rebels from food sources, they began starving the Kikuyu. In addition, they systematically singled out women after entering villages for rape and torture (Elkins, 2003).

Ironically, as Mau Mau units and their families were driven to total defeat, the British public grew increasingly disgusted with the colonial government's repressive violence. Labour Party members of Parliament, who frequently spoke against imperial policies, began clamoring for an end to emergency powers in 1956. The issue came to a head in 1959 when prison guards murdered 11 Mau Mau detainees in an internment camp. This event, David Anderson (2005, pp. 326–327) concludes, signaled the end of the British empire in Kenya. Reaction was symbolized by a young Conservative MP who supported security measures in Kenya and rose in Parliament to state that the United Kingdom had no moral authority to claim an empire.

Kenya would gain its independence, and a former suspected Mau Mau exile would become its president.

**Self-
Check**

> What factors led to Grivas's success in Cyprus?
> Identity the parallel issues in Cyprus and Algeria.
> Why did the Mau Mau movement fail to achieve a military victory?
> Why did repression ultimately fail in Kenya?

The Russian Federation

Since the collapse of the Soviet Union, the Russian Federation has been seeking its place among the world's powers. Weakened by the growth of its former eastern European holdings, Russia faces internal economic and political problems. Its leadership is becoming increasingly centralized, and relations with the United States and the West are less than stable. Two issues dealing with terrorism surface in the federation. The first deals with the problem of breakaway states. The second problem is nearly two centuries old—the status of Chechnya and the spread of violence to the entire North Caucasus region.

The breakaway states present a problem within the newly independent nations that emerged from the collapse of the former Soviet Union. Three nations—Moldova, Georgia, and Azerbaijan—have internal separatist movements, creating areas where neither the government nor the separatists are in control. This has resulted in virtual shell states, where crime flourishes and corruption rules. The breakaway regions are ripe for illegal arms trading, and they present a tempting location to headquarter internal criminal and terrorist groups (Lynch, 2004). Ethnic tensions in these regions also add to the problem. For example, the Russian Federation launched a brief invasion of Georgia in 2008 to protect Russian nationals in South Ossetia.

The separatist movement in Chechnya threatens regional stability, and it has resulted in two internal wars in the Russian Federation—one from 1994 to 1996 and the other from 1999 to 2009. It has also created a campaign of internal terrorism involving the deaths of hundreds of people. Fighting has spread throughout the North Caucasus region to Dagestan, Ingushetia, and Kabardino-Balkaria. Attacks in Moscow and other areas outside the region have accelerated Russia's drift away from democracy. Russia has responded by installing local regional political bosses, but they have introduced a culture of political corruption and repression (King and Menon, 2010).

Breakaway States and Crime

After the collapse of the Soviet Union, Russia experienced widespread economic dislocation and a drop of close to 50 percent in gross domestic product (GDP). Stuart Goldman (2007), reporting for the Congressional Resource Service, says that the economy was worse than the American economy during the Great Depression. Economic conditions have improved, but Russia still suffers from environmental troubles, a poor health system, and sharp declines in life expectancy. It also suffers from organized crime and corruption. All of these factors serve to destabilize the country. Another problem that plagues the country is the rise of de facto states. These are parts of the Russian Federation that simply refuse to accept Russian government and control from Moscow.

Dov Lynch (2004, pp. 22–39) explains the situation. The former Soviet Union broke into 15 new nations in the early 1990s. Each nation had its own problems, and each one had to establish new relations with Moscow and the rest of the world's

FIGURE **7.4** States in the Russian Federation That Have Declared Independence from Russia

governments. The issue for the Russian Federation, however, was that five other states declared their independence from Russia and some of the former Soviet republics. Four are Nargorno-Karabakh in Azerbaijan, South Ossetia and Abkhazia in Georgia, and Transnistria in Moldova (Figure 7.4). The fifth, Chechnya, is the only one whose claim to independence Russia has been successful in countering, but fighting continues to rage there.

Lynch says the inability to pull these states back into their respective countries creates a haven for organized crime and terrorism. Because they lie outside the authority of the central government but remain unrecognized by the community of nations, they have become failed states where arms trade, organized crime, and narcotics trafficking flourish. These regions are a hotbed for terrorism. Lynch concludes that if this situation is to be addressed, the international community must adopt methods for dealing with the regions so that some type of legal order can be introduced. The rebellion in Chechnya is another issue.

Chechnya

The Caucasus region of the Russian Federation has been problematic since the fall of the Soviet Union. Guerrillas and terrorists in the Russian-controlled province of Chechnya called on nationalism in a struggle for autonomy, and the struggle has spread to surrounding states. Russia has tried to label unrest in the Caucasus as part of the global jihad. Although jihadists have come to the area, the actual problem is one of nationalism. If Moscow cannot deal with political corruption and poverty, the people of the region will continue to seek autonomy. The Chechen nationalists and ethnic groups in the region have many followers because of their appeal to patriotism. This has not stopped either the Russians or international jihadists from claiming that Chechnya is a microcosm representing the West's struggle with al Qaeda. Although Russia has been able to assert more control in Chechnya than is the case in the other breakaway states, it has experienced savage fighting in the region and terrorism in the Russian homeland itself. In Daniel Byman's words, the tried-and-true methods of counterterrorism do not work against ethnic violence. Chechnya serves as an example (*Timeline 7.1: Chechnya as a Nationalistic Revolt*).

TIMELINE 7.1   *Chechnya as a Nationalistic Revolt*

Many jihadists have flocked to the Transcaucasia region, thinking of it as another Afghanistan. However, if the history of the area is examined, Chechnya can be explained as a revolt based in nationalism or ethnicity.

1830	Imperial Russia expands into the Caucasia region.
1859	Russia annexes Caucasia, including Dagestan and Chechnya.
1917–1923	Dagestan and Chechnya declare independence.
1923	The communists conquer Caucasia, adding Dagestan and Checheno-Ingush to the USSR.
1944	Stalin purges the Caucasia area, fearing Chechens and others were influenced by Germany.
1991	The USSR falls; Chechens declare independence, but Russia rejects the claim.
1994–1996	Russia invades Chechnya; agrees to a ceasefire after severe casualties.
1997	Chechens launch bombing campaign in Russia; rebels enter Dagestan.
1999	Russia renews the war, takes Dagestan and launches devastating strikes on Chechnya.
2002	The Moscow theater takeover.
2003–2004	Suicide bombing campaign. Suicide bombers destroy two airliners in flight.
2004	The Beslan school takeover.
2009	April: Kremlin announces the end of the second Chechen War.
2009	November: High-speed train between Moscow and St. Petersburg derailed, killing 30 passengers.
2010	Two female suicide bombers kill 40 on Moscow Metro during morning rush hour.

Source: Walker, 2001; D. Lynch, 2004; Johnson and Brunner, 2004; King and Menon, 2010.

Groups in Asia have made their presence felt in the ethnic struggle between the Russian Federation and the would-be breakaway state of Chechnya. The Chechens seek legitimacy in the nationalistic struggle, but the conflict started long ago. Imperial Russia sought to impose Russian power in Chechnya in the early nineteenth century. Felix Corley (2004) says that the current dispute can be traced directly to the communist era, when Joseph Stalin (ruled from 1922 to 1953) imposed Soviet power in the region. Since the fall of the Soviet Union, the Russians and Chechens have fought two conventional wars for control of the area. The first war lasted from 1991 to 1996. The current round of fighting began in 1999. Faced with overpowering Russian military force, some Chechens decided to strike inside Russia using the tools of terrorism. International jihadists came and sought to expand the war to the entire Caucasus region. They felt that this could become the base for a large Islamic state.

Despite the presence of international jihadists, the U.S. Department of State (2004c) says that Chechen rebels should not be lumped with other jihadist movements. According to the U.S. ambassador to Russia, Chechens are engaged in a legitimate war of independence and are not like other jihadist terrorists (Turks.US, 2004). Al Qaeda has tried to claim the Chechen–Russian conflict, the ambassador said, but Chechnya has been seeking independence for many years, and the struggle predates the jihadist movement by 200 years. Others believe jihadists influence the violent

FIGURE **7.5** Chechnya and Dagestan

Shamil Basayev:
(1965–2006) A jihadist leader in Chechnya, Basayev engineered several operations resulting in mass civilian casualties.

Moscow theatre:
(Theatrical Center, Dubrovka, Moscow, 2002) The site of a Chechen attack where approximately 40 terrorists took 850 hostages. Russian forces stormed the theater on the third day of the siege, killing 39 terrorists and at least 129 hostages.

Beslan school: A Chechen terrorist attack on the first day of school in September 2004 in North Ossetia. The scene was chaotic and Russian forces were never able to establish a security perimeter. Although details remain unclear, the incident resulted in the murder of nearly 400 people, including more than 100 children.

ibn al Khattab:
(1969–2002) Also known as Emir Khattab or the Black Wahhabi, a Saudi international jihadist who went to fight in Chechnya. He tried to move the Chechen revolt from a nationalistic platform to the philosophy of religious militancy. He was killed by the Russian secret service in 2002.

nature of the independence movement. Chechnya thrives on support from jihadist groups and imports jihadist tactics. Ayman al Zawahiri went to Chechnya to recruit and fight with new mujahedeen groups after the Soviet–Afghan War. The Russians even jailed him, but released him through an oversight (Sud, 2004).

Stuart Goldman (2007) says the current wave of fighting began when international jihadists moved from Chechnya to Dagestan in 1999 in an attempt to broaden the conflict (Figure 7.5). An irregular militia, claiming to be members of the international jihadist struggle, occupied several villages in Dagestan. The group's leaders, two ruthless men known for hostage taking and murder, proclaimed an Islamic republic and the beginning of a new caliphate. At the same time, a series of explosions in a Moscow apartment complex killed more than 300 people. Vladimir Putin, the newly elected Russian prime minister, blamed the Chechens for both attacks and sent overwhelming military force into the breakaway state.

Paul Murphy (2004) believes that there were three primary characters in the 1999 rebellion. The first was **Shamil Basayev**, a man who had gained fame by taking an entire hospital hostage in 1995 during the first Chechen war and whose 1999 actions in Dagestan started the second. Murphy describes Basayev as a Che Guevara–type figure who led by charisma and example. Basayev would increase his reputation by planning the takeover of a **Moscow theater** in 2002. An estimated 200 people—130 hostages and the remainder terrorists and security forces—were killed. Two years later, on the opening day of the **Beslan school**, Basayev masterminded another takeover. Using children as hostages, his terrorists killed an estimated 300 to 400 people, mostly children. Basayev was killed in the summer of 2006.

Murphy identifies two other jihadists. The second international jihadist leader, a mysterious leader known by the nom de guerre **ibn al Khattab**, was a Saudi. Basayev brought Khattab to Chechnya in 1995. Described as the "Black Wahhabi," he became known for his ruthlessness. He was assassinated by Russian agents in 2002. The third leader, Salman Raduyev, took more hostages than any other terrorist. Before he went mad, Raduyev threatened to attack Russian nuclear facilities, Murphy says. Khattab and Basayev were responsible for the Dagestan invasion.

Although the Russian army took Grozny, the capital of Chechnya, after heavy fighting in 2000, conflict continued. Murphy (2004) describes the pattern of both wars. At times the Chechens would stand and fight. This would result in conventional battles, in which the Russians were generally successful, but at a heavy cost. At other times, the Chechens used the hit-and-run tactics of guerrilla warfare. These were more effective, but they brought reprisals from the Russians. The Russian army used massive bombardments, summary execution, rape, and torture to counter guerrilla tactics. The Chechens responded in kind. Although this was a savage war, it was not entirely linked to the jihadist movement. Most Chechens fought for state autonomy.

Murphy points out that Basayev and Khattab approached the situation differently. They called for international jihadists to flock to Chechnya to begin an Islamic revolution. With this in mind, their tactics went far beyond guerrilla warfare. They introduced the tactics of terrorism and suicide bombings. Given the Russian tendency to ravage areas where they were attacked, the jihadists sought a new weapon, female suicide bombers called the **Black Widows**. The Black Widows were women who had suffered at the hands of the Russians and who gained a reputation for effectiveness (*Timeline 7.2: Chechen Suicide Attacks: The Black Widows*).

In October 2002, about 50 Chechen rebels took over the Theatrical Center in Moscow during an evening performance. They took about 700 hostages. The group contained men and self-described Black Widows, and they demanded that Russian troops leave Chechnya. In the early morning on the third day of the siege, Russian special forces assaulted the theater, thinking hostages were being killed. The plan called for the introduction of sleeping gas, then the actual assault. It was a disaster. Aware that something was happening, the male terrorists engaged in a prolonged gun fight with the rescuers. The Black Widows, who may have been armed with explosives, were to set off their suicide explosives in an effort to kill as many hostages as possible. Fortunately, they hesitated while awaiting instructions from the men. Before Russian forces had restored order, about 200 people were dead, many killed by the sleeping gas (CNN, 2002).

Black Widows: Chechen female suicide bombers. They are known as Islamic martyrs in the Chechen language.

| **TIMELINE 7.2** | *Chechen Suicide Attacks: The Black Widows* |

In the twenty-first century, the Chechen Black Widows have become a terrorist force in Russia. They get their name from the fact that many of them are widows of Chechen fighters.

June 2000	Suicide car bomb against Russian troops.
November 2001	A single attacker kills herself and a Russian officer with a hand grenade.
June 2002	A single bomber kills herself on a bus loaded with Russian pilots.
October 10–26, 2002	Forty-one rebels with female suicide bombers take hostages in a Moscow theater. One hundred twenty-nine people die when Russian forces attack.
May 12, 2003	Two females explode a truck at a Russian checkpoint.
May 14, 2003	Two females explode body bombs at a religious service.
July 5, 2003	Two females attack a rock festival in Moscow.
July 10, 2003	A bomb carried by a single bomber accidentally explodes as the bomber is en route to a Moscow target.
July 27, 2003	A single bomber kills herself and a security guard when she is stopped for an inspection.
December 5, 2003	Three females kill 44 people on a commuter train. More than 150 are injured.
December 9, 2003	A single bomber attacks the National Hotel in Moscow.
August 24, 2004	Two females bring down two passenger planes.
August 31, 2004	A lone female bomber kills nine in a Moscow subway station.
2009	Bombing campaign renewed.
March 29, 2010	Two female suicide bombers kill 40 on the Moscow Metro.

Source: Saradzhyan, 2004; National Post, 2010; *Guardian*, 2010

In March 2003, Russia agreed to a new Chechen constitution, giving the region limited autonomy within the federation. Although Russia hoped that this would help resolve the fighting, hopes were in vain. The Russian-appointed leader was assassinated in May 2004. Russia quickly introduced a new pro-constitution candidate, who was elected in August of the same year. It appeared that an end to the fighting might be negotiated. Unfortunately, another Basayev-engineered disaster was on the horizon.

Jihadists staged the deadliest raid of all in September 2004, crossing from Chechnya into Beslan, a village in North Ossetia. This time, the terrorists herded the hostages into the school's gymnasium and wired it with explosives. Outside, the situation was a mess. Russian security forces responded, but so did parents. There were soldiers, police officers, and civilians running around with weapons. One of the

---

EXPANDING THE CONCEPT

Learning to Be Ruthless in Chechnya

Of the many suicide operations carried out by Chechens, two gained the most attention in the United States: the October 2002 attack on a Moscow theater and the September 2004 attack on a school in Beslan. Both attacks were suicide missions designed to produce massive casualties. A comparison of the two attacks demonstrates the way jihadists learned from and corrected previous mistakes.

MOSCOW Dubrovka Theatrical Center: October 2002

What went as planned:

1. Terrorists took over a theater and isolated it.
2. Terrorists segregated hostages into small groups.
3. Terrorists planted enough bombs to kill most of the people in the theater.
4. Terrorists drew international attention to their cause.

What went wrong:

1. Terrorists formed partial bonds and relationships with some hostages.
2. Female terrorists took orders from the males. When Russian special forces attacked, the females waited for instructions to detonate the bombs, but the males were busy fighting and could not give the orders.
3. Some hostages kept and used cell phones.

What the terrorists learned:

1. Ruthlessness, including random executions, keeps human bonds from forming.
2. Bombers should be prepared to detonate explosives readily at the first sign of an assault.
3. Cell phones must be destroyed.

The Beslan Middle School Number 1 Attack: September 2004

Jihadists learned lessons from the theater attack. To eliminate bonding and maintain control they did the following:

1. Publicly executed hostages at the beginning of the incident.
2. Destroyed cell phones.
3. Executed a terrorist who stated he had never intended to attack a school.
4. Humiliated and intimidated the children taken hostage.
5. Played psychological games to keep parents in fear.
6. Denied food and water to hostages.
7. Bayoneted a young boy when he cried for a drink of water.
8. Gave selected females leading roles.
9. Placed bombs to detonate upon any counterattack without orders.

Source: Ostovsky, Beliakov, and Franchetti, 2004; Spechard et al., 2004.

Russians observing the situation told this author that there was no chance to establish a perimeter. A bomb went off in the building and people started to flee. Gunfights broke out, parents ran to get their children, and children fled the building as terrorists were shooting them. There were at least 330 people killed, including 156 children (*Time Europe*, 2004).

By 2005, Moscow had been able to suppress large-scale military action, but it faced the prospect of prolonged fighting. The Russians managed to kill Basayev in 2006. Many foreign governments criticized Russia's heavy hand, but it seemed to produce results. Separatist suicide attacks dwindled. Violence continued spreading to other areas, but the separatist violence slowed. Goldman estimates that Russia lost more than 15,000 troops in Chechnya from 1999 to 2006. He says that this is comparable to total Soviet losses in Afghanistan (1979–1989). He also writes, "Russian authorities deny there is a 'humanitarian catastrophe' in the North Caucasus and strongly reject foreign 'interference' in Chechnya. . . . Russian forces regularly conduct sweeps and 'cleansing operations' that reportedly result in civilian deaths, injuries, and abductions" (Goldman, 2007, p. 7). Even so, Russia sought a "Chechenization" of the war. As violence dropped, Moscow began relying more on local power in all the Caucasus states, declaring an end to the second Chechen war in April 2009. The declaration was premature.

Russia faces two major problems in trying to pacify Chechnya and the surrounding states. First, by moving toward "Chechenization," Moscow faces the problem common to all imperial powers. Local officials may be loyal to Moscow, but they remain loyal to their local constituencies as well. Second, many of the local insurgents have targeted officials who seem to be little more than Russian surrogates. This has resulted in increased assaults and assassinations of local political and law enforcement officials. Separatists began strikes against Russia shortly after it declared the end of antiterror operations (King and Menon, 2010).

Moscow has tried to paint Chechnya and the entire Caucasus region with a jihadist brush, claiming that radical Islamic extremists are behind the violence. Writing for *Foreign Affairs*, Charles King and Rajan Menon (2010) offer a different perspective. Former Russian Federation President Dmitry Medvedev, they say, knows full well that jihadists are not behind the unrest. Violence is caused by corruption, unemployment, and poverty. Violence will subside if Russia solves these problems. If not, separatists will continue to seek their own solution by parting from Moscow.

Self-Check
> How are breakaway states related to terrorism?
> How do jihadists describe the two wars in Chechnya?
> How do Chechen nationalists view the conflict?
> How does Chechen unrest impact the Caucasus region?

Turkey

Turkey is an enigma in its standing with Europe. The country is 99 percent Muslim and was the home of the last caliphate. Long ago, it was the seat of the Eastern, or Byzantine, Roman Empire, but when its capital Constantinople fell to Mahmet II in 1453, it became the center of Islam. Ironically, Mustafa Kemal, better known as Kemal Atatürk, dissolved the Islamic government in 1923 and established Turkey as a secular republic. Although most of the country is in Asia, Turkey was accepted as a partner in NATO, and it sought close trade ties with Europe and the United States after World War II. It was the first Muslim-majority country to recognize the state of Israel.

Esther Pan (2005b) says that Turkey looks to Europe for both cultural and economic reasons. Many Europeans and Americans encourage it, hoping that Turkey will join the European Union (EU). Other Europeans have been reluctant to accept Turkey, citing demographic, cultural, and religious differences. They fear that if Turkey joins the EU, Europe will be flooded with poorly educated workers and radical jihadists will strengthen their foothold in Europe. They also worry about Turkey's human rights record.

For its part, Turkey has many people who like the idea of blending religion and government. Other Turks are not enamored of this idea. In May 2007, nearly 500,000 people demonstrated to protest the influence of Islam in Turkey's internal affairs. The Turkish army has declared that it will not accept a religious government (Associated Press, 2007). In the midst of this dilemma, Turkey has attempted to modernize its law enforcement agencies and military within the norms of Western democracies. It has opened its doors to Western police agencies, and the Turkish National Police has one of the most highly educated police command staffs in the world. Turkey has also experienced several different types of terrorist campaigns over the past three decades.

Turkey's Struggle with Terrorism

Turkey has suffered 40,000 deaths from terrorism since 1980. In Istanbul, a police commander in Turkey's counterterrorism unit said to the author, "You Americans came to see terrorism as a problem after the World Trade Center. We've suffered thousands of casualties for three decades." Although the largest issue is with the Kurdistan Workers' Party (see the next section), other groups operate in Turkey. In the mid-1980s, a group known as Turkish Hezbollah appeared in eastern Turkey. It has no connection with the Lebanese Shi'ite group Hezbollah. Formed from a Sunni Kurd–Turk Islamic base, Hezbollah sought to counter the activities of the Kurdistan Workers' Party. Critics claim that it received some forms of clandestine support from the government in the 1990s, but Turkish security forces might disagree. Hezbollah expanded its targets in the 1990s to businesses and other establishments that it deemed to be non-Islamic. Following the path of other terrorist groups, Hezbollah began to kidnap and torture Muslim business persons who refused to support its activities. Hezbollah's goal is to establish an Islamic state by force of arms (BBC News, 2000).

Brian Williams and Fezya Altindag (2004) point out that Turkey developed an internal jihadist problem after 1994. They believe that Hezbollah is part of this problem, and they state that that is the blowback, or unwanted effects, from the government's attempt to create Hezbollah as a counterterrorist movement against the Kurdistan Workers' Party. Yet the real problem started in 1994 when several thousand Turkish young people began to attend militant madrassas, or private religious schools, in Pakistan. They returned to Turkey with an Islamic agenda. Atatürk's secular Turkey was anathema to them.

Williams and Altindag believe that the Pakistani-trained young people eventually resulted in a jihadist movement in Turkey, including an al Qaeda splinter group, El Kaide Turka, or al Qaeda in Turkey. By 2001, a group of madrassa-trained young men placed themselves under the leadership of **Habib Akdas**, who had undertaken a task from Osama bin Laden. Bin Laden wanted to punish Turkey for its partnerships with the United States and Israel, and he believed that Akdas was the man to lead the charge. With bin Laden's encouragement, Akdas sought to strike American and Israeli interests in Turkey. Al Qaeda in Turkey would eventually expand its attacks to other Westerners.

Habib Akdas and his followers returned to Turkey after the American-led coalition attacked al Qaeda strongholds in Afghanistan in October 2001. Williams and Altindag say that coalition forces found training manuals translated into Turkish, and this prompted the United States to send a warning to Turkey's police and military forces. Akdas bided his time. Not wanting to rush his attacks, he planned for the

Habib Akdas: (birth date unknown) Also known as Abu Anas al Turki, the founder of al Qaeda in Turkey. Akdas left Turkey to fight in Iraq after the American invasion. He was killed in a U.S. air strike in 2004.

next two years. Bin Laden wanted Akdas to attack an American air base in Turkey, but Akdas believed it was guarded too well. He searched for softer targets. The U.S. embassy in Ankara and the U.S. consulate in Istanbul also proved to be too well fortified. Akdas decided to turn to British and Israeli targets. He launched suicide attacks against two synagogues in Istanbul on November 15, 2003. He struck the British consulate and a British bank with suicide bombers less than one week later.

The double bombings backfired. Infuriated by the attacks, Turkish citizens demanded that the government take action because the majority of people killed in the al Qaeda bombings had been Muslims. The Turkish National Police unleashed their full power against al Qaeda in Turkey. Williams and Altindag say that dozens of al Qaeda operatives and supporters were arrested, and Akdas removed himself to Iraq to fight the Americans. The militants fanned out across Turkey and began a low-level bombing campaign. Akdas is believed to have been killed in fighting around Fallujah in November 2004 (NewsMax.com, 2006). BBC News (2006) reported that Turkish police were able to arrest several important al Qaeda leaders in Turkey in December 2006, including Akdas's replacement.

The Kurdistan Workers' Party and Its Alter Egos

Turkey is currently facing a wave of religious terrorism, but for the past three decades its major problem came from Kurds, an ethnic group inhabiting parts of southern Turkey, northern Iraq, and northern Iran (see *Expanding the Concept: The Kurdish Conflict*). The Kurdistan Workers' Party (PKK) is a Marxist-Leninist terrorist organization composed of Turkish Kurds. Officially changing its name to Kurdistan Freedom and Democracy (KADEK) in 2002 (see *Another Perspective: The PKK by Any Other Name*), it operates in Turkey and Europe, targeting Europeans, Turks, rival Kurds, and supporters of the Turkish government. It represents the same ruthless brand of Maoism as the Peruvian guerrilla organization Shining Path, murdering entire villages whose residents fail to follow its dictates. The PKK/KADEK has developed chameleon-like characteristics, and although it is a revolutionary Marxist group, it has since 1990 employed the language of nationalism. Even more startling, since 1995, it has also used the language of religion.

The PKK was founded in 1974 to fight for an independent Kurdistan (Criss, 1995). Unlike other Kurdish groups, the PKK wanted to establish a Marxist-Leninist state. Although the PKK targeted Turkey, the Kurds claim a highland region spanning southeast Turkey, northeast Iraq, and northwest Iran (see Figure 7.6, on page 178). Taking advantage of Kurdish nationalism, the PKK began operations in 1978, hoping to launch a guerrilla war.

The plans for revolution, however, proved too grandiose. There was sentiment for fighting the Iraqis, Iranians, and Turks, but not enough support for the communists. Most Kurds wanted autonomy, not communism. The PKK was not strong enough to wage a guerrilla war without some type of support, and its political orientation prevented it from allying with other Kurdish groups. The PKK had two choices: It could either wage a propaganda campaign or throw itself into terrorism. Its leadership chose the path of terrorism.

PKK leaders increased their efforts to build a terrorist organization by moving into Lebanon's Bekaa Valley in September 1980. While training there, they met some of the most accomplished terrorists in the world, and after the 1982 Israeli invasion of Lebanon, they quickly found allies in the Syrian camp. For the next two years, the group trained and purged its internal leadership. In the meantime, some PKK members cultivated sympathy among several villages in southern Turkey. By 1984, the PKK was ready for a campaign against Turkey.

Support turned out to be the key factor. Moving from base to base in Turkey, the PKK also received money and weapons from Syria. The relatively weak group of 1978 emerged as a guerrilla force in 1984, and it ruthlessly used terrorism against the Turks and their allies. Civilians bore the brunt of PKK atrocities, and within a few years the PKK had murdered more than 10,000 people. The majority of these murders came as a result of village massacres (Criss, 1995). Turkey responded by isolating the PKK from their support bases and counterattacking PKK groups. Turkish security forces operated with a heavy hand.

The tactics had a negative effect on the Kurds. Although they were ready to fight for independence, they were not willing to condone massacres and terrorist attacks. The PKK responded in 1990 by redirecting offensive operations. Rather than focusing on the civilian population, the PKK began limiting its attacks to security forces and economic targets. Having expanded into western Europe a few years earlier, PKK leaders stated that they would strike only "legitimate" Turkish targets. The PKK also modified its Marxist-Leninist rhetoric and began to speak of nationalism.

Abdullah Ocalan:
(b. 1948) The leader of the PKK. Ocalan was captured in 1999 and sentenced to death, but his sentence was commuted. He ordered the end of a suicide bombing campaign while in Turkish custody and called for peace between Turkey and the Kurds in 2006.

In a 1995 interview (Korn, 1995), PKK leader **Abdullah Ocalan** reiterated the new PKK position. When asked whether he was a Marxist, Ocalan stated that he believed in "scientific socialism." Ocalan said that this would become a new path because the Muslim population in general, and the Kurds in particular, had suffered at the hands of Marxist-Leninists. He cast his statements in anti-imperialist terms, stating that Kurdistan was only resisting imperialist powers.

In October 1995, Ocalan asked the United States to mediate between the PKK and Turkey, saying that the PKK was willing to settle for a federation instead of complete autonomy. U.S. officials immediately rejected the terrorist's rhetoric, which was nothing new. The PKK had started speaking of federal status in 1990 (Criss, 1995). Irrespective of the form of government, Ocalan wanted semiautonomy. In the October 1995 letter to the United States, Ocalan asked for federal status "like the United

EXPANDING THE CONCEPT

The Kurdish Conflict

The Issue. The Kurds are an ethnic group inhabiting northern Iraq, southern Turkey, and northern Iran. When other groups received national sovereignty at the end of World War I, the Kurds remained divided among the three nations. The Treaty of Sèvres (1920) created an independent Kurdistan, but it was never implemented. About 12 million Kurds live in Turkey.

The Group. The Kurdistan Workers' Party (PKK) was formed in 1978 as a Marxist-Leninist group. Its goal was to create an independent socialist Kurdistan.

The Campaign. After training in Syria, the PKK launched a guerrilla campaign in Turkey. By the early 1990s, the PKK turned to urban terrorism, targeting Turks throughout Europe and Turkey. After its leader Abdullah Ocalan was captured in 1999, the PKK pledged to work for a peaceful solution; however, it maintained various militant organizations operating under a variety of names. The PKK maintains links with other revolutionary groups in Turkey and with some international terrorist groups.

The Campaign Renewed. Turkey is being considered for admission to the European Union. The EU, NATO, and the United States list the various entities of the PKK as terrorist organizations. In October 2003, the United States agreed to crack down on the PKK in northern Iraq, but the group remained. Turkey began clandestine incursions into the Kurdish area of Iraq around 2006. (Turkey officially denies this.) Open confrontation began in 2008, and by 2010 PKK units were crossing into Turkey, attacking military outposts.

The Future. After years of challenges, the U.S. Supreme Court ruled that the PKK is a foreign terrorist group. Turkey conducts intelligence, military, and law enforcement operations against the PKK, and it is gradually moving further from Europe, seeking closer ties with the Middle East.

Source: Council on Foreign Relations, 2004; Dymond, 2004; U.S. Department of State, 2004b; *Economist* 2008; Liptak, 2010.

States." Earlier that year, he had asked for the same thing, but "like the Russian Federation" (Korn, 1995). The most dramatic announcement came later. By December, the PKK was using the rhetoric of Islam, citing religious texts instead of Marxist-Leninist ideology. Ocalan appealed to Muslim Kurds, in the name of God, to revolt against the so-called secular Turkish government.

ANOTHER PERSPECTIVE

The PKK by Any Other Name

The PKK operates under a variety of names. According to the U.S. Department of State, these include

- Freedom and Democracy Congress of Kurdistan
- Kurdistan People's Congress (KHK)
- People's Congress of Kurdistan
- Liberation Units of Kurdistan (HRK)

Source: U.S. Department of State, 2004.

- Kurdish People's Liberation Army (ARGK)
- National Liberation Front of Kurdistan (ERNK)
- Kurdistan Freedom and Democracy Congress (KADEK)
- Kongra-Gel (KGK)

The PKK officially changed its name to KADEK in April 2002 and to Kongra-Gel in 2003.

At first it might sound surprising to hear the Marxists of the PKK using religious language, but it is politically understandable. The PKK shifted its position to achieve the greatest amount of support. Ocalan had been moving in an anti-Western direction for many years. His terrorists attacked a NATO base in 1986, and they kidnapped 19 Western tourists in 1993. As jihadist rhetoric grew against the West, Ocalan simply copied the language. But there was something more. In June 1996, an Islamic religious government came to power in secular Turkey. Ocalan wanted to prove that he was not an ogre who massacred civilians in their villages, but simply a good Muslim.

Ocalan's shift to religion gave the PKK new life. Leftist movements in Turkey followed the path of their European counterparts: They went into hibernation. When Ocalan proclaimed a doctrine of Marxist Islam, the PKK managed to survive. A unilateral ceasefire on the part of the PKK in December 1995 placed Turkey in an awkward position. According to Nur Bilge Criss (1995), Ocalan's religious rhetoric played well not only among Kurds but also throughout the Middle East. Writing before the

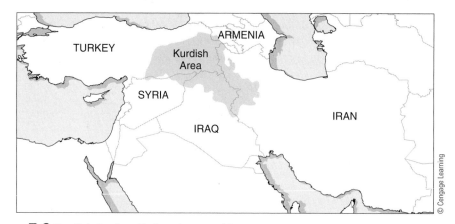

FIGURE **7.6** Kurdish Region: Turkey, Iraq, and Iran

1996 election, Criss predicted that Turkey would move closer to the Islamic world to counter this threat. He also said that the supreme irony is that Turkey may be drawn away from NATO to an alliance with Iraq or Iran in an effort to counterbalance the Kurds and the Syrians. His predictions turned out to be incorrect.

The PKK represents the pejorative nature of terrorism. When the terrorist label is applied to a group like the PKK, the whole movement is questioned. Kurds have long suffered at the hands of their neighbors. The Iranians have slaughtered them, Saddam Hussein used rockets and poison gas to destroy entire Kurdish villages, and the Turks have repressed them. The PKK is a terrorist organization, but expressing Kurdish nationalism is not a terrorist act. Many thousands of Kurds were victimized by state terrorism long before the PKK unsheathed its sword.

Turkish authorities captured Abdullah Ocalan in Kenya in February 1999, and a security court sentenced him to death in June. Ocalan offered to chart a new course for the PKK a few weeks later. Because Turkey was lobbying to join the EU, it delayed and eventually reversed the death sentence. (Members of the EU may not invoke capital punishment.) It appeared as if there might be a window for peace.

The situation deteriorated after the U.S.-led invasion of Iraq. Kurds in northern Iraq were empowered when free from Baghdad's oppression, and the area began to thrive. As economic power grew, so did the threat to Turkey. PKK operatives and other Kurdish nationalists saw an opportunity to renew their struggle. Although Turkey denied any activity, troops may have crossed the Iraqi border as early as 2006. By 2008, there was no longer a question of secrecy as Turkey launched punitive strikes against the PKK, sometimes by air and at other times with ground troops (*The Economist*, 2008). The PKK responded. During the summer of 2010, it was sufficiently strong to hit isolated army outposts inside Turkey. During the same time period, the Kurds lost a political battle to legitimize the PKK. The U.S. Supreme Court declared that it was a terrorist organization, upholding the State Department's designation, and ruled that it was a federal crime to support it (Liptak, 2010).

✓ Self-Check

> How is Turkey's struggle against terrorism similar to issues in Europe?
> How is it dissimilar from those issues?
> Cite the types of groups that practice terrorism in Turkey.
> What are the principal goals of the PKK?
> What role did the Iraq War have in reviving the PKK?

China's Problems in Xinjiang

Uighar nationalists: China's ethnic Turkmen. Some Uighar nationalists organized to revive an eighteenth-century Islamic state in China's Xinjiang province. Using Kyrgyzstan and Kazakhstan as a base, they operate in China.

After September 11, China was eager to join America's "war on terror." Beijing claims that international jihadists, trained in Afghanistan and Pakistan, are attempting to overthrow Chinese rule in the Xinjiang (New Frontier) province and establish an Islamic state. In 2003, China asked for international assistance in clamping down on what the government claims to be its own "jihadist terrorists," **Uighar nationalists** who believe Xinjiang is their homeland. Although the Chinese communists link the Uighars to al Qaeda and the 9/11 attacks, the movement predates al Qaeda by 245 years (Lufti, 2004).

The Uighars are ethnic Turkmen, mostly Sufi Muslims, and they have lived in and governed parts of the Xinjiang province for 200 years (Figure 7.7). Many of them are fighting to become independent from China. Chienpeng Chung (2002) says that the ethnic Uighars are mostly Islamic mystics who are inspired by the collapse of the Soviet Union, not by Osama bin Laden. As the former central Asian Soviet republics gained autonomy after 1991, the Uighars saw it as an opportunity to reassert their

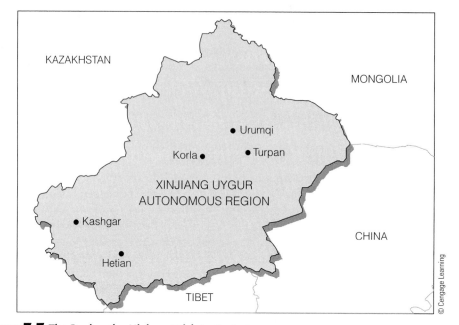

FIGURE **7.7** The Region the Uighars Wish to Be Autonomous

independence. Separatists launched a terrorist campaign in the Xinjiang province aimed at throwing the Chinese out. Despite their best efforts, Chung says, the Chinese have not been able to eradicate the rebellion.

China annexed the area in 1759, and the first uprising came in 1865, lasting 12 years. Chung says that the revolt set the stage for Muslim independence from China, which the Uighars achieved twice, 1931–1934 and 1944–1949, calling their land East Turkestan (see Figure 7.7). The communist Chinese brutally repressed the Uighars and reasserted control in 1949. The Chinese have settled the area with ethnic Chinese, displacing the Uighars, in an effort to assimilate the area. In 1949, the area was 90 percent Uighar, but it may be less than 50 percent today. Displaced Uighars throughout the world support the separatists. Beijing has asked Washington to list militant Uighar organizations as terrorist groups, and the United States has been sympathetic to Chinese demands. Washington needs Beijing as an ally.

Although one of the militant groups fighting for independence trained in Afghanistan, the majority of militants are not jihadists. To be sure, some separatists are terrorists. Bombings and assassinations have cost almost 200 lives and 600 casualties. Ahmed Lufti (2004) says that it is important to remember that China is experiencing a terrorist campaign. Aside from religious differences causing strife, China fights for Xinjiang because it has China's largest oil and gas reserves. The growing Chinese economy needs its resources, but the Uighars feel that it is their country. Fighting continues. Groups based in Kyrgyzstan and Kazakhstan leave those countries to raid across the Chinese border, and internal groups run their own campaigns.

Chung says that, although this is terrorism, there are two problems with that classification. Most Uighar terrorism is not part of the jihadist movement. Uighars are not fighting an international jihad for a caliphate; they want independence. The greater problem, however, is that many of the separatists are not violent, and they do not endorse terrorism. Chung says that they only want independence. Through the process of labeling, the Chinese have deemed all expressions of Uighar separatism as terrorism based in the jihadist movement. The United States, disinclined to lose China's support against central Asian terrorism, is reluctant to criticize China when it justifies repression in the name of counterterrorism.

Self-Check
> How did China interpret the "war on terror"?
> What is the goal of Uighar nationalists?
> Why do some Uighars want independence?

Sikh Separatism in India

India has a variety of terrorist problems stemming from political, religious, and ethnic strife . The country has a diverse population, including a religious group known as the Sikhs. *Sikh* is a Punjabi word meaning "disciple." Founded over 500 years ago, Sikhism emphasizes an inner journey to seek spiritual enlightenment, followed by external behavior to live in peace with the world. The religion has enshrined ten great teachers, or gurus, and it embodies elements of Islam and Hinduism (Singh, 1999; Brar, 2003). After India was partitioned in 1947, some Sikhs sought independence in Punjab, a state where they represented the majority of the population. This gave birth to a small, violent independence movement in 1977.

Golden Temple: The most sacred shrine of Sikhism. Its official name is the Temple of God.

India responded to the revolt by strengthening central authority in Punjab. This move divided the Sikhs into a majority orthodox group that wanted to peacefully resolve the situation and a small radicalized group that wanted to fight India. Issues came to a head in 1984 when Indian military forces entered the Sikhs' most sacred site, the **Golden Temple**, and engaged in a bloody battle with armed militants. Thousands of people were killed (Singh, 1999, pp. 214–215). Small groups of Sikhs formed terror cells, targeting Indian security forces, unsympathetic journalists, and the majority community of Sikhs who called for the restoration of peace (GlobalSecurity.org, n.d.). A few months after the Golden Temple raid, the Sikh bodyguards of the prime minister of India assassinated her.

Sikh extremists planned assassinations all over the world, including the United States. Several cells were active in North America. Extremists compiled a hit list of moderate Sikhs in Canada, and radical members preached violence. One radical pleaded guilty in 2003 to making the bomb that brought down Air India Flight 182, an explosion that killed 329 people in 1985 (Commission of Inquiry, 2007). By 1988, more than a hundred people per month lost their lives. Fighting took place as militant Sikhs attacked police and nonmilitant Sikhs, while the police struck back. Violence continued in India through 1994 and then decreased. When one Sikh was asked to explain why the violence had tapered off, he responded that the government killed all the militants (Juergensmeyer, 2000, pp. 86–101).

Self-Check
> Who are the Sikhs?
> What is the Golden Temple?
> Describe the course of terrorism, as applied to the Sikhs.

Endemic Ethnic Terror in Sub-Saharan Africa

Many years ago, J. Bowyer Bell (1975, pp. 10–18) used the term "endemic terrorism" to describe the state of terrorist violence in Africa. He defined this as a form of terrorism created by artificial divisions of tribes, families, and ethnic groups. South of the Sahara, it is possible to see the extent of endemic terrorism, but problems in sub-Saharan Africa extend beyond terrorism. War, famine, and disease are more pressing. Both children and women are exploited, and totalitarian governments control some countries. Africa is the poorest region on earth.

Lord's Resistance Army:
Ugandan guerrilla force opposing the government since 1987. The LRA has conscripted thousands of children, forcing them into its ranks or mutilating and killing them. Dropping all pretense of political activity, it roams through Uganda, southern Sudan, the Democratic Republic of the Congo, and the Central Africa Republic. Its primary tactics are mass murder, mass rape, theft, and enslavement of children. Uganda has referred the LRA to the International Criminal Court.

Joseph Kony: (b. 1961) The leader of the Lord's Resistance Army in Uganda. His group has branched out to several other nations in central Africa. He is wanted by the International Criminal Court for crimes against humanity.

AIDS pandemic: Great numbers of people with HIV/AIDS (human immunodeficiency virus/acquired immuno-deficiency syndrome). In 2005, Africa had 25.8 million HIV-positive adults and children. Africa has 11.5 percent of the world's population but 64 percent of its AIDS cases. From 1982 to 2005, AIDS claimed 27.5 million African lives (Cook, 2006).

sweet crude: A type of oil with less than 0.5 percent sulfur content. Nigeria sits on a large sweet crude field, giving the country potential wealth. The people who live above the oil, however, are poverty-stricken, and oil production has been harmful to the environment.

It is easier to understand terrorism in Africa by using the logic in Bowyer's definition. Africa was colonized by European nations in the nineteenth and early twentieth centuries, and they divided the continent based on European spheres of influence. The Europeans paid no attention to traditional regions or tribal boundaries in sub-Saharan Africa, placing various ethnic groups in the newly formed European-ruled colonies, which later became independent countries. This was problematic. Many times, competing tribes or groups of deadly rivals were joined in the new countries. Postcolonial revolts and political pressure slowly forced European countries out of the area after World War II, leaving many countries seething with internal hostilities. In addition, some countries were dominated by white colonists who refused to yield power to black majorities after the European rulers departed. Feelings of social animosity were exacerbated by extreme disparities in the distribution of Africa's limited wealth and fierce economic exploitation of the continent's mineral and energy resources.

Ethnic cleansing, child armies, wars by self-appointed militias such as the **Lord's Resistance Army (LRA)**, crime and corruption, and internal strife have evolved into sub-Saharan Africa's unique brand of nationalist terrorism. This became better known in the West after a YouTube video on **Joseph Kony**, the LRA's leader, went viral in 2012. It is endemic indeed. In western and central Africa, terrorism represents a potential problem. The Horn of Africa has active groups, including a jihadist movement, but even there ethnic cleansing, revolts, slavery, and starvation outweigh the problems presented by terrorism. Africa is suffering from a colonial past, poverty, and a modern epidemic. Some policy makers believe that these issues must be addressed but that they are separate from terrorism. Others argue that a comprehensive approach to Africa's massive social problems is a more effective method of controlling terrorism.

Sources of African Terrorism

It is difficult to single out terrorism in Africa because Africa is the locus of conventional and guerrilla wars, several revolutions, and criminal violence. One of the primary reasons for this is Africa's position in the world. It is the most poverty-stricken region on earth, and the sub-Saharan portion of the continent has negative economic growth. In other words, the countries in the south produce less income year by year. Health conditions in Africa are also the worst on the planet, and the **AIDS pandemic** is creating havoc. There are hundreds of thousands of homeless orphans (Sachs et al., 2004). Tribal violence has led to genocide and countless deaths (see Berkeley, 2001). Child armies, slavery, and starvation are part of the social problems plaguing the region (Singer, 2001; Polack, 2004). Terrorism is only one problem among many in Africa.

Thomas P. M. Barnett (2004, p. 351) points out that certain regions have specialized problems. The center of the continent is plagued by tribal strife, and the Horn—the eastern section bordered by the Red Sea and the Indian Ocean—witnesses religious and ethnic conflicts. The southwestern coastal countries along the Atlantic Ocean are involved in struggles for resources. There was a recent deadly political racial struggle in South Africa, and there is political turmoil in Zimbabwe. Despite this, Barnett points out that there are large portions of Africa where people are getting along. The continent is not completely awash in violence, and Barnett believes that the long-term solution to most African violence, including terrorism, is to bring about economic development and stabilization.

Oil Regions

In sub-Saharan Africa, most of the oil resources are located in the west (Figure 7.8). These fields are attractive to the United States for several reasons: First, the oil is **sweet crude**; that is, it has a lower concentration of sulfur, and it is easier and cheaper to refine into gasoline. Second, the oil fields are closer to the east coast of the United

FIGURE **7.8** West Africa

States than the Middle East is, thus reducing transportation costs. Third, Africa is increasing its oil production. It is estimated that by 2020 the United States will purchase one-quarter of its oil imports from western Africa (Donnelly, 2005).

Although violence, crime, and warfare threaten oil production, terrorism has not been a major issue. It should be viewed as a potential problem. Princeton Lyman, the former U.S. ambassador to Nigeria, and Stephen Morrison, a specialist in AIDS policy for the Center for Strategic and International Studies (2004), are concerned about the potential for terrorism and America's approach to Africa in general. They are critical of America's naïve foreign policy approach to western and central Africa, and they feel humanitarian assistance in the entire region will increase political stability.

Lyman and Morrison argue that U.S. foreign policy has focused on jihadists and the areas where jihadists are most prevalent. Although this is important, they say, it misses the areas where jihadists have tremendous potential and other areas where they can move without scrutiny. This occurs in western and central Africa, areas where criminal networks are in league with corrupt leaders and where governments and rebels struggle for power. These situations are exploited by jihadists, but the United States has not sufficiently reacted to the situation because the United States is so closely focused on other areas. The United States does not have a holistic approach to Africa.

Stated more bluntly, Lyman and Morrison do not believe that countries like Nigeria and Liberia appear on the strategic foreign policy radar screen. Nigeria has a population of 133 million, with 67 million Muslims, making it the second largest Islamic country, behind Egypt, in Africa. Its economy is crucial to the United States, as America currently gets 7 percent of its oil imports from Nigeria. Yet America has not paid attention to the violence in Nigeria or in the rest of western Africa.

From 1999 to 2003, fighting in Nigeria between the Muslim north and the Christian south claimed 10,000 lives. The conflict did not involve established terrorist cells, but the conflict's source is so deeply rooted in the community that terrorism could easily result from the tensions between north and south. Lyman and Morrison say that this is due to the factors behind regional conflict. There are tribal differences in Nigeria and the surrounding regions, and tribes have created their own armies. Many of these armies have children as recruits. Tribal rivalries and religious

Liberian Civil War: Two episodes of conflict involving rebel armies and militias as well as neighboring countries. The First War, 1989–1996, ended when a rebel army brought Charles Taylor to Monrovia, the capital. The Second War, 1999–2003, toppled Charles Taylor from power. Both wars were characterized by village massacres and conscription of child soldiers.

Charles Taylor: (b. 1948) A warlord in the First War of the Liberian Civil War and president of Liberia from 1997 to 2003.

Liberians United for Reconciliation and Democracy (LURD): A revolutionary movement founded in 1999 in western Africa. LURD was instrumental in driving Charles Taylor from power in 2003.

Big Man: An anthropological term to describe an important person in a tribe or clan. *Big Man* is sometimes used by political scientists to describe a dictator in a totalitarian government.

differences intermingle, and those religious differences have become sharper since 1970. In the past, Christians and Muslims tolerated one another, and western African Islam, strongly influenced by local mystical, or Sufi, traditions, was especially tolerant. After 1970, however, Wahhabi missionaries came to the area, and they were extremely critical of the religious practices of western African Muslims. In Nigeria, this resulted in an internal struggle among the country's Muslims over the purity of Islam.

The internal situation became more critical after 2009 when a local Muslim group, Boko Haram, began attacking Christians. Violence increased, and by 2011 the murder of Christians in the north was common. The year culminated in several attacks in November resulting in the deaths of 150 people. Christians responded with attacks on Muslims, although they have yet to organize a group as effective as Boko Haram. The U.S. State Department believes Boko Haram is associated with the international jihadist movement and with al Qaeda in the Maghreb (Johnson, 2011).

Lyman and Morrison argue that Liberia, another country in the region, presents a second example of misguided U.S. policy. The **Liberian Civil War**, from which Liberia is only now emerging, fostered criminal networks, corrupt leaders, and local military adventurers. The country's former leader, **Charles Taylor**, was known for corruption. In 2003, it looked as though the United States was going to intervene in Liberia's problems, and leaders of all independent armies and militias stated that they would accept a U.S.-enforced peace. Instead of intervening, though, President George W. Bush, under pressure from the military and from his vice president, stated that American efforts would be limited to humanitarian aid. Marines landed but departed in three months. Taylor eventually fell to the **Liberians United for Reconciliation and Democracy (LURD)**. Although not supporting Taylor, Lyman and Morrison believe that such actions are shortsighted. When a state fails, they argue, it creates a haven for terrorist groups.

The International Crisis Group (ICG, 2006c) agrees with Lyman and Morrison's approach. In Nigeria, an insurgent group emerged in January 2006 to eliminate governmental control of the oil industry. One of its primary tactics has been kidnapping foreign oil workers. Oil production has suffered. Failure to support democracies in other countries leads to further disruptions (see ICG, 2006e). The International Crisis Group (2005b) sees western Africa as a region that is delicately balanced between moderate Islam and an undercurrent of jihadism. If the United States in particular, and the West in general, would approach the area's problems in a way to ensure economic stability, fair and democratic elections, and an end to corruption, a political crisis could be averted. The threat of terrorism can be eliminated with supportive foreign policies. Africa has much to offer the West. Active diplomacy supporting democracy would prevent terrorism, they argue.

Lyman and Morrison (2004) apply the same logic in other areas of Africa. In the central region of Africa, tribal conflicts and lack of governmental control have created large lawless areas. Jihadists have exploited this. They have created criminal enterprises and links with criminal organizations to expand their financial structures. In addition to the human tragedies of ethnic cleansings, child exploitation, and slavery, failing states encourage the emergence of a jihadist solution.

Another potential problem in central and western Africa is the **Big Man**. An autocratic ruler—a Big Man—may ally himself with other countries at crucial times. A Big Man might be a tempting ally, but he may present a short-term payoff. After a revolution topples the Big Man, as did the 1978– 1979 revolution in Iran, the new government may be openly hostile to any country that supported the Big Man. Thomas P. M. Barnett (2004, p. 133) points out another problem. Big Men are often followed by Little Men. In other words, autocrats tend to put their children in power. A distasteful alliance can be carried into the next generation.

A good example is Kenya. Joel Barkan (2004) points out that Kenya is vital to the U.S. struggle against terrorism. It houses several U.S. governmental entities and allows the U.S. military to use its ports. The United States gained its foothold there by courting Kenyan Big Men, who tended to favor their own tribes. In addition, prosperity was based on tribal relations. In 2002, Kenya achieved a hard-won, fragile democracy that terrorism, if allowed to establish itself, could destroy. Barkan concludes that the best way for the United States to fight terrorism in the region is to help Kenya consolidate its democracy. A strong autocratic ruler may be the best ally in the world, but when the ruler falls—they all fall sometime—there is no guarantee that the next government will maintain the old alliances. When Western governments support a Big Man, they frequently incur the wrath of common people.

Ted Dagne (2002) has another perspective on American foreign policy in sub-Saharan Africa. Reporting for the Congressional Research Service in 2002, Dagne says that the government is aware that Africa represents potential bases for terrorism. He argues that dozens of African governments have voiced their support for the war on terrorism. They have cooperated with investigations and intelligence-gathering efforts, provided bases and staging areas for military forces, and shared intelligence. Because they are aware that Africa might be a haven for terrorist groups, they monitor activities in their own countries. He says that the Bush Administration was pleased with the support it received from sub-Saharan African governments.

By the same token, Dagne acknowledges concerns among African governments. Some of them feel that they are not full partners with the United States. Others feel that although they have given support, the United States has refused to assist them economically. Other leaders express concerns that regions in their own lands might become targets for American military action. Some governments would prefer that international antiterrorist efforts be led by the United Nations, not the United States. The greatest fear is the Big Man. Many Africans believe that the United States will ally with governments that support antiterrorist efforts even if they have poor human rights records.

Rita Abrahamsen (2004) offers an alternative view, focusing on the post-9/11 African policy of the United Kingdom. She states that, unlike the United States, Britain has maintained a moral and humanitarian approach to Africa. Its primary foreign policy efforts have been aimed at expanding economic development and increasing human rights. She is worried that the new U.S. approach in the antiterrorist environment favors security. She admits that this is a subtle policy shift, but she sees it taking shape in Africa. Abrahamsen believes that the long-term security policy would be better served by emphasizing development and human rights. In the long run, such an approach is more successful than seeking short-term security objectives. She also believes that Britain's approach emphasizing economic development has been far more productive than America's preoccupation with security.

Over the past few decades, France has maintained an African policy that sharply differs from either the United States' or the United Kingdom's (Gauthier-Villars, 2007). Faced with anticolonial revolts after World War II, France created a special military unit known as the **African Cell**. Its purpose was to extend French influence in the oil- and mineral-rich areas of Africa. It has been used to support Big Men, overthrow governments, and protect tribes loyal to France in times of war. The African Cell operates outside the normal channels of French government and is responsible to neither the legislature nor the courts. It reports directly to the president. Supporters view it as a means to deal with terrorism. Critics think that its tactics border on terrorism. When Nicolas Sarkozy was elected president of France in 2007, he promised to review the activities of the African Cell.

Terrorism is a threat in western and central Africa. Although Thomas Barnett is correct in saying that the area is not awash in violence, it has been the scene of countless tragedies, mass murders, genocides, and epidemics. Terrorism is not the overriding issue. Hunger, disease, violence, and human rights abuses are. Abrahamsen is probably correct. If the developed nations would aggressively intervene for humanitarian

African Cell: A French military unit stationed in Africa and France. It retains between 10,000 and 15,000 troops in various African countries and answers directly to the president of France.

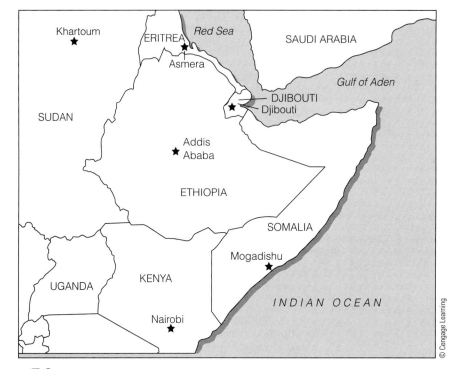

FIGURE **7.9** Horn of Africa

purposes, it would do much to prevent state failures that would provide an environment supporting terrorism. The same argument could be made for the Horn of Africa.

Self-Check

> Why does endemic terror thrive in Africa?
> What types of social problems plague Africa?
> What are the primary governmental problems in sub-Saharan Africa?

CHAPTER TAKE AWAYS

Quite a bit of nationalistic terrorism came in the wake of World War II as European colonial empires began to break apart. Cyprus and Algeria became the forerunners of urban ideological terrorism. Kenya served as the stage for a quasi-religious uprising, and although Kenya would eventually win independence, its people were brutally repressed during the Mau Mau rebellion. Terrorism continued to evolve in nationalistic, ethnic, and religious movements in Russia and in breakaway semiautonomous states in the former Soviet Union, Turkey, China, and India. Africa has experienced endemic terrorism due to artificial national boundaries imposed by Europeans. While terrorism is a horrendous problem, poverty and the AIDs crisis have been the cause of most of Africa's suffering.

OBJECTIVE SUMMARY

• The EOKA followed an urban strategy using a small number of terrorists to fight 40,000 British soldiers. Their efforts brought international attention to Cyprus and aroused international support for independence. The struggle ended with a negotiated settlement. Like the EOKA, the FLN focused on urban areas and used terrorism to attract international publicity. Unlike the situation in Cyprus, most French people believed northern Algeria to be a part of France, and they saw the separatist movement as an internal rebellion instead of a revolt against a colonial power. As a result, both the FLN and French security forces employed terrorism against each other. The Mau Mau movement in Kenya represents another postwar colonial revolt, but it differed from urban terrorism in Cyprus and Algeria. It was a rural resistance movement by a tribe displaced by colonial agricultural policies. Mau Mau fighters were defeated by repression, but Kenya achieved independence when the British public rejected inhumane measures.

- Breakaway states present a number of problems caused by political instability. In the former Soviet states, the breakaway states represent criminal shell states where terrorism, black market arms deals, and continued ethnic violence can grow. The political instability even caused a brief war between Georgia and Russia in 2008. Violence in the Caucasus region threatens regional stability, and, at times, it has attracted foreign terrorists.

- Chechnya has resisted Russian rule since the nineteenth century. After the failure of bids for independence, violence spread throughout the North Caucasus. Russia has responded by empowering local ethnic political bosses, but these are among the most corrupt political leaders in the federation. Violence spread to Dagestan, Ingushetia, and Kabardino-Balkaria.

- Turkey has experienced several forms of terrorism in the past three decades. Some forms are based on religion, others are political. In addition, Turkey has a major ethnic separatist movement. Turkey has lost 40,000 people to terrorism since 1980. The PKK is Turkey's largest terrorist threat. A Marxist group growing from Kurdish separatism, the PKK seeks a Marxist Kurdistan. After the capture of its leader and the end of a brief secular suicide bombing campaign, it appeared that a peace settlement might be negotiated. The creation of a strong economic Kurdish region in northern Iraq, however, has reenergized the PKK.

- Ethnic tensions are prominent in China's Xinjiang province because the native Uighar population aspires for autonomy. The Uighars are ethnic Turkmen. China annexed the area in 1759, and the Uighars have resisted this move throughout history. They won independence twice only to be subjugated by China again.

- China has introduced many ethnic Chinese to the Xinjiang province in an attempt to exert political control. Uighars operating from Central Asia have resisted this policy. After 9/11, China eagerly endorsed the United States' "War on Terrorism," claiming that the Uighar nationalists were part of an international jihadist movement.

- Some Sikhs embraced terrorism after a deadly clash with Indian forces. The most damaging attack was on an Indian airliner. They planned an international terror campaign, but it fizzled by the mid-1990s.

- *Endemic terrorism* is a term used by J. Bowyer Bell to describe violence in sub-Saharan Africa. It results from European imperialism and the creation of artificial national boundaries that link unrelated tribal and ethnic groups.

- Sub-Saharan Africa's main problem is poverty. It also suffers from internal wars, child armies, slavery, crime, and tribal violence. Terrorism is a potential problem, but millions of Africans die from these other issues.

- Western Africa is beset by political divisions and struggles over the control of wealth generated by oil. Several militia-style armies battle one another, often employing children as soldiers. Central Africa is plagued by tribal and political violence, exacerbated by roving bands of private armies. Rape, kidnapping, and mass murder are among the common tactics of these groups.

Critical Engagement: Preemptive Strikes and Future Policies

After the terrorist attacks of September 11, the Bush Administration began an active campaign of counterterrorism with the goal of thwarting jihadist terrorism. Several of its steps were controversial, and many of them were continued in the Obama Administration. One of the most controversial aspects of American policy has been the decision to engage in preemptive strikes. The United States has assumed that it has the right to launch military actions in any region of the world, if it feels that terrorists are planning to attack American targets. This policy has been used partially to justify the invasion of Iraq, military operations in Afghanistan, and the elimination of suspected terrorists through military actions in foreign countries.

Other countries that might have been critical of the American policy quietly support it. The reason is that they cite the policy when taking actions against their own ethno-nationalist separatists. For example, the Russian Federation fought two wars in Chechnya, and it has placed military units in the Caucasus region to prevent potential ethnic separatism. In 2008, the Russian army launched an attack on Georgia to support a Russian separatist movement in the newly independent state. The United States often complains or cautions Russia about such actions, and the Russian government frequently responds with American rhetoric: It claims to be following the United States in preempting terrorism.

The People's Republic of China has been seeking to force ethnic Turkmen in the Xinjiang region to accept Chinese immigration and domination, fueling Uighar hostility. This has resulted in increased ethnic tension, violence, and major rioting in 2010. It has also produced a separatist movement operating from central Asia and supported by the Uighar diaspora in the West. The United States has aggressively supported ethnic Uighars and has diplomatically resisted Chinese attempts to label the Uighars as jihadists. Regardless, China has conducted military and other types of operations against the Uighars. When criticized by the United States, China frequently cites its right to launch preemptive strikes.

Consider these issues in terms of future developments:

- When might a nation take military action outside its borders to prevent a terrorist strike? If it does so, how is it justified on moral grounds? Does justification have more to do with the power to strike or the right to self-defense?
- How could a policy of preemptive strikes be used to subdue and suppress ethnic groups?
- In what ways are the Russian Federation's and the People's Republic of China's policies similar to the United States' policy? In what ways are they different?

KEY TERMS

Background
to the Middle East

LEARNING OBJECTIVES

After reading this chapter you should be able to:

> Define the Middle East as a historical, geographical, and cultural metaphor.

> Briefly sketch the origins of Islam.

> Describe the difference between Shi'ites and Sunnis.

> Explain the emergence of militant theology.

> Discuss the historical significance in the decline of the Ottoman Empire and the birth of Zionism.

> Summarize the impact of World War I on the Middle East.

> Describe the formation of Israel and the Arab–Israeli wars.

> Explain the emergence of terrorism after the 1967 Six Days' War.

> Briefly sketch the history of modern Iran.

The first decade of the twentieth century brought a new twist to what seemed to be a perpetual crisis in the Middle East. It started shortly after the beginning of the century when the Iranian leader Mahmoud Ahmadinejad announced that Iran would be pursuing a nuclear program. Ostensibly, the goal of Iran's nuclear quest was to develop energy, but the rub was that the same process used to enrich uranium for the peaceful production of power is closely related to the methods for constructing nuclear devices. The issue was exacerbated by several public proclamations of Ahmadinejad. He claimed, for example, that Israel had no right to exist and that nuclear weapons could be used to eradicate the country. He made further statements repeatedly indicating his desire to see Israel disappear from history. Ahmadinejad's words were backed by several decades of Hezbollah activities.

Although the government publicly denied it, Israel had had a nuclear arsenal for quite some time. They also had medium-range rockets and aircraft that could be used to deliver a nuclear strike. The Israelis had a track record of stopping the production of nuclear facilities in the Middle East. Using conventional weapons they had destroyed a suspected Syrian nuclear site in 2007 following a similar attack in Iraq in 1981. The Israelis did not intend to let the Iranians develop a nuclear bomb, and their allies in the West knew it.

United States military forces in the Middle East conducted a war game in the spring of 2012 based on the assumption that Israel had launched a conventional strike on Iranian industrial centers involved in its nuclear program. Much to the dismay of American commanders, a likely scenario in the war game suggested that the entire Middle Eastern region would erupt in a major war resulting in massive casualties and hundreds of American deaths.

Problems in the Middle East can be associated with multiple factors over the past two centuries. The origins of the problems can be found in imperialism, poverty, government corruption, political repression, and religious fanaticism. Terrorism, sometimes seemingly synonymous with the Middle East, interacts with all of these problems and further complicates virtually every issue. Fear of a regional war over the potential development of a nuclear arsenal or even a nuclear exchange is one of the latest new wrinkles in a politically unstable region.

Defining the Middle East

Bernard Lewis (1995, pp. 64–67) implies that the Middle East is not a geographical region; it is a concept. It is based on a Western orientation to the world. Historically, the term *Middle East* was used by Captain Alfred Thayer Mahan, the most important naval theorist in American history, to describe a section of the world that encompasses part of North Africa and southwest Asia directly south of Turkey, including the Arabian Peninsula, Iran, and Afghanistan. Geographically, Middle East is a term of convenience with a European bias. If Europe and America are the West, and China and Japan are the Far East, then there is an east "near" Europe, one "far" away, and one in the "middle." Albert Hourani (1997), in a comprehensive history, says the area is dominated by two major concerns: the religion of Islam and the history of the Arab people. Yet many people who live in the Middle East are not Arabs. Culturally, the Middle East is an area dominated by a religion, Islam, but John Esposito (1999, pp. 214–222) demonstrates that there are many differing cultures within Islam as well as myriad interpretations of the religion.

Bernard Lewis (1995, p. 65) also says that the term Middle East is used out of convenience. In a broader sense, people are really speaking about the sociogeographical relationship between Islam and Christianity. Yet distinctive social meanings attach to the term Middle East. It is a region that witnessed the birth of three great monotheistic religions: Judaism, Christianity, and Islam. The Middle East is an area dominated by Islam, but most Muslims live outside the region. The social mores of the Middle East—family and tribal loyalty, male dominance, honor, and resentment of Western imperialism—extend across northern Africa and into central Asia. The traditional Middle East includes Arabs, but many other people live there.

The Middle East is a historical, social, and geographical concept. It seems to be dominated by questions about Palestine and Israel, but Lewis (2004, pp. 196–204) demonstrates that many other problems beset the region. Lewis (1995, pp. 45–55) also points out that it is the historical tinderbox that ignited several centuries of conflict between Muslims and Christians. The area is the home of Islamic conquests and Arab empires. It also witnessed the Crusades and Western and Mongol invasions, which were followed by Turkish and then European domination. It gave birth to modern nations in the twentieth century, including Lebanon, Syria, Jordan, Yemen, the independent **Gulf States**, Iraq, Saudi Arabia, Iran, and Israel. It is the home of multiple ethnic groups, and violence in the region has influenced international terrorism. Three issues help illustrate the importance of the region: (1) the birth and spread of Islam, (2) historical confrontations between Christianity and Islam, and (3) the expansion of conflict beyond the traditional geographical realm of the Middle East.

Gulf States: Small Arab kingdoms bordering the Persian Gulf. They include Bahrain, Qatar, the United Arab Emirates, and Oman.

> Why is the Middle East a geographical concept?
> What do most be mean by "Middle East"?
> How do culture and values shape the Middle East?

A Brief Introduction to Islam

Many aspects of Middle Eastern and, by extension, international terrorism are embodied in rhetorical religious sloganeering. If terrorism is to be understood in this context, it is necessary to become familiar with the basic aspects of Islam. For those readers of this book who are unfamiliar with the basics of Islam, this section is necessary; others may wish to skip it. It is not possible to capture the theological richness of any major religion in a short section in a college text, and the following description is a simple overview to provide background information essential to understanding terrorists who misuse religious imagery.

The description here is taken primarily from Western scholars and Islamic sources in English. It is based on the work of Karen Armstrong (2000a, 2000b), Abdullah Saeed and Hassan Saeed (2004), Thomas W. Lippman (1995), Caesar Farah (2000), John Esposito (1999, 2002), Haneef Oliver (2002), Bernard Lewis (1966, 1995, 2004), Heinz Halm (1999), Malise Ruthven (2000), Moojan Momen (1985), Robin Wright (2000), Edward Said and C. Hitchens (1989), Charles Kurzman (2004), Rudolph Peters (1996), and Rueven Firestone (1999).

The Centrality of Mohammed's Revelation

Mohammed was born about 570 by the Western calendar in the Arabian city of Mecca. He was orphaned at an early age and taken in by his uncle, Abu Talib. He was extremely spiritual, by most accounts, and exposed to three great monotheistic religions, Judaism, Christianity, and Zoroastrianism. As he grew older, Mohammed became a trader under the tutelage and protection of his uncle. He also became close to his cousin **Ali ibn Talib**, who looked upon Mohammed as an older brother. While on a caravan he met an older widow, Khadijah. They were married and had a daughter, Fatima. Khadijah was impressed with Mohammed's character and by his spiritual nature. She encouraged him to continue a religious quest, but Mohammed was confused. He had been exposed to several religions, but he did not know which aspect of spirituality was correct. That changed when he was meditating at age 40.

Mohammed had a vision of the angel Gabriel (Jabril), who told him that God had chosen Mohammed to be a prophet to the Arabs. (*Allah* is Arabic for "the God." Muslims believe that Jews, Christians, and Zoroastrians worship the same deity.) Mohammed was overwhelmed by the voice of Gabriel, and he begged for silence. Gabriel did not comply. He told Mohammed that Moses had been sent to tell the Jews of the one true God, and Jesus had been sent to the world with the same message. Mohammed, the angelic voice said, had been chosen as the final Prophet to complete the message. The first vision stopped after 40 days, and Mohammed came to accept that he had been chosen. Visions would continue periodically until 632, the year of his death.

Mohammed's role as a prophet, as *the* Prophet, is crucial in Islam. He stands in a long line of Jewish prophets—the visionaries later adopted by Christians—and Jesus of Nazareth. Muslims believe that Mohammed was given the direct revelation of God through Gabriel. In Muslim theology, God is vast, all-encompassing, and without form. The pronoun *he* is used, but God is gender neutral. The little that can be known about God comes through revelations from the four major Prophets—Abraham, Moses, Jesus, and Mohammed—and the law that God has given them. The Hebrew and Christian Bibles contain those revelations, but humans corrupted the message when writing the stories, according to Islamic theology. One of the greatest mistakes, according to Muslims, was the deification of Jesus. All the Prophets are human, and they will be judged by God according to their deeds with an overwhelming, loving

Ali ibn Talib: (circa 599–661) Also known as Ali ibn Abi Talib, the son of Mohammed's uncle Abu Talib and married to Mohammed's oldest daughter Fatima. Ali was Mohammed's male heir because he had no surviving sons. The followers of Ali are known as Shiites. Most Shiites believe that Mohammed gave a sermon while perched on a saddle, naming Ali the heir to Islam. Differing types of Shiites accept authority from diverse lines of Ali's heirs. Sunni Muslims believe Ali is the fourth and last Rightly Guided caliph. Both Sunnis and Shiites believe Ali tried to return Islam to the purity of Mohammed's leadership in Medina.

mercy that comes from God's benevolence. God has given divine law through the Prophets. Mohammed was chosen to correct the errors of the past.

Creating the Muslim Community at Medina

Mohammed won early converts in Mecca, including his cousin Ali, his wife Khadijah, and three influential friends: **Abu Bakr, Umar**, and **Uthman**. Many of the wealthy merchants of Mecca were not impressed. Messages of God's love were acceptable, but Mohammed's emphasis on social egalitarianism called on them to share their wealth. They resented that and asked Abu Talib to remove familial protection from the young Prophet, a request Abu Talib refused. After Abu Talib's death, Mohammed's life was in jeopardy. At the same time, representatives from warring Jewish and polytheistic tribes in Yathrib, later Medina, asked Mohammed to serve as their leader and make peace. Mohammed agreed, provided that they would acknowledge the one God and the legitimacy of Mohammed's calling. They agreed, with the Jews reserving the right to judge Mohammed's calling as a Prophet. Legend says that he left for Medina in 622 with 72 families. Most Western historians believe that the families left in waves and that Mohammed escaped to Medina even as Meccans were plotting his death.

Muslims believe Mohammed created the perfect Islamic community at Medina, combining a just government with religion. Mohammed stressed the importance of community over tribal relations and the governance of God's law in every aspect of life. Because there were not enough resources to live in Mecca, Mohammed's followers chose a traditional Bedouin path for survival: raiding passing caravans. In 624 this led to a confrontation with an army from Medina at Badr. It was a small battle, but politically important. As a result of their victory at **Badr**, Muslims increasingly came to believe that God was on their side and that their cause would be championed in heaven. Mohammed eventually conquered Mecca, and the new religion spread along trade routes. Suddenly, in 632, Mohammed died, leaving the community of believers to chart the path for the new religion.

The Shi'ite–Sunni Split

The Muslims who followed Mohammed agreed on many aspects of the new faith. God's revelation to Mohammed was critical. The poetic utterances of Gabriel were eventually codified in a single book, the Quran. The things Mohammed had said and done were recorded, and his actions became the basis for interpreting the Quran. All Muslims came to believe that it was necessary to confess the existence of one God and to acknowledge Mohammed as God's Prophet. They were also expected to pray as a community, to give to the poor, to fast during holy times, and to make a pilgrimage to Mecca if they were able to do so. Problems arose, however, over the question of leadership. According to Arabic tradition, Mohammed's male heir should lead the community, but Mohammed claimed to have revealed a new law that said the importance of the community would take precedence over tribal rules of inheritance. Questions over leadership spawned a debate and eventually a civil war. These questions still affect the practice of Islam today.

The question of leadership focused on the community. One group of people believed the community should select its own leaders, but another group believed that Mohammed had designated Ali, his cousin and son-in-law, as the Muslim leader. The proponents of community selection carried the day, but Ali's followers came to believe that God had given a special inspiration to Mohammed's family. The community selected a political and religious leader, a caliph, but Ali's followers encouraged him to exercise the authority they believed God had bestowed. When Ali's sons, Hasan and Hussein, were born, his followers believed that they also carried special gifts based on their relationship with their grandfather Mohammed.

The Muslim community eventually split over this question. Mohammed's friend Abu Bakr became the first caliph in 632 (see Table 8.1). After his death in 634, Umar became caliph. The Arabs expanded under his leadership, handing defeats to the Romans, or Byzantines, and the Persians. Umar was assassinated in 644 by a Persian captive, and

---

Abu Bakr: (circa 573–634) Also known as Saddiq, the first caliph selected by the Islamic community (*umma*) after Mohammed's death in 632. Sunnis believe Abu Bakr is the rightful heir to Mohammed's leadership, and they regard him as the first of the *Rishidun*, or Rightly Guided caliphs. He led military expeditions expanding Muslim influence to the north of Mecca.

Umar: (circa 580–644) Also known as Umar ibn al Khattab, the second Rightly Guided caliph, according to Sunnis. Under his leadership, the Arab empire expanded into Persia, the southern part of the Byzantine empire, and Egypt. His army conquered Jerusalem in 637.

Uthman: (circa 580–656) Also known as Uthman ibn Affan, the third Rightly Guided caliph, according to Sunnis. He conquered most of the remaining parts of North Africa, Iran, Cyprus, and the Caucasia region. He was assassinated by his own soldiers for alleged nepotism.

Badr: The site of a battle between the Muslims of Medina and the merchants of Mecca in 624. Mohammed was unsure whether he should resist the attacking Meccans, but decided God would allow Muslims to defend their community. After victory, Mohammed said that Badr was the Lesser Jihad. Greater Jihad, he said, was seeking internal spiritual purity.

TABLE **8.1**
The Four Rightly Guided Caliphs

Caliph	Period of Caliphate
Abu Bakr	632–634
Umar	634–644
Uthman	644–656
Ali	656–661

another of Mohammed's friends, Uthman, was selected as caliph. The Arabs continued to expand, and they soon held a vast empire. All was not well, however. As Uthman consolidated wealth, groups of Arab soldiers came to feel that he favored his own family over the community. They broke into his house in 656 and assassinated him. The followers of Ali came forward and proposed that he become caliph. Ali believed that Uthman's family in particular, and Muslims in general, were forgetting the straight path that had been revealed to Mohammed. He led an army against Uthman's family but sought a negotiated peace between the factions. His hopes were in vain, and he was assassinated. The family of Uthman assumed control of the Islamic movement and ruled the first Arab empire.

Sunnis believe that Four Rightly Guided Caliphs (Rushadin) served as the true successors to Mohammed. Shi'ites recognize only Ali.

Umayyads: The first Arab and Muslim dynasty ruling from Damascus from 661 to 750. The Umayyads were Uthman's family.

The followers of Ali were not satisfied. They felt that the **Umayyads**, Uthman's family, had abandoned the principles of Islam in favor of worldly goods. This split came to dominate the Muslim community. The Umayyads believed that they represented Islam, even as they fought other Muslims to maintain control of the new Arab empire. Some of the followers of Ali invited **Hussein (Hussain ibn Ali)**, Ali's oldest living son, to meet with them in what is present-day Iraq. They wanted him to lead a purified Islamic movement, returning to the simple principles of his grandfather, Mohammed. The Umayyad governor was alarmed and sent an army to intercept Hussein. He was killed with a small band of followers at Karbala in 680. His martyrdom cemented the schism between the Umayyad dynasty and the followers of Ali, and Karbala became one of the most important events in Shi'ite history. Its importance is similar to the meaning of the Day of Atonement for Jews and the Easter story for Christians.

Hussein ibn Ali: (626–680) Also known as Hussein ibn Ali, Mohammed's grandson and Ali's second son. He was martyred at Karbala in 680. The majority of Shiites believe that Hussein is the Third Imam, after Imam Ali and Imam Hasan, Ali's oldest son.

Mainstream Muslims following the caliph were conventionally called Sunnis, and the followers of Ali became known as Shi'ites. In actuality, though, several differing types of Shi'ism developed in the formative years of Islam. Zaidi Shi'ites recognize a line of succession differing from Hussein's. Many Zaidi Shi'ites live in Yemen today. Ismalis believe that there were seven Imams who followed Mohammed. They sponsored a cult known as the Assassins in the Middle Ages, but they live quite peacefully on the Indian subcontinent today (see Lewis, 2003a). Ithna Ashari, or Twelver, Shi'ites comprise the majority of Shi'ite Muslims, dominating Iran, southern Iraq, and southern Lebanon.

Initially, there were few theological differences between Sunnis, who comprise an estimated 85 to 90 percent of all Muslims today, and Shi'ites. The main difference focused on the line of succession from Mohammed. Over the years, however, differences did emerge. Ithna Ashari Shi'ites believe that the Twelfth Imam went into hiding in 934. Some of them believe that he divinely transcended life with a promise to return. Another group of Shi'ites believe that he died but was resurrected, and a final group believes that God hid the Twelfth Imam, but left part of the imam's spirit on earth. Sunnis claim that all three beliefs are more reminiscent of Christianity than Islam. The split between Sunnis and Shi'ites remains today.

The Golden Age of Arabs

Mohammed's followers spread Islam and Arabic culture through the Middle East in the years after his death. Two dynasties, the Umayyads (661–750) and the **Abbasids**

Twelver Shi'ites and the Imamate

Ithna Ashari Shi'ites believe that twelve divinely inspired Imams followed Mohammed. Although theological divisions with Sunnis would eventually arise and the Shi'ites themselves would split into competing sects, the first division within Islam was political. It focused on leadership of the Islamic community.

Ali's followers, known as the Partisans of Ali, believed that he should lead the community. They refused to recognize Abu Bakr, Umar, and Uthman. The Twelvers came to believe that twelve divinely inspired men were sent by God to lead the community. These men were:

> Predicted by the Quran

> God's Representatives on Earth

> Infallible

> Existing without Sin (like Mohammed and Fatima)

> Inspired by the Spirit of God

> Able to Recognize Their Successors

> The Best of All Men

> Divinely Charged to Lead with Special Knowledge of God

The first Imams openly opposed the emerging Sunni consensus and met violent deaths. The Sixth Imam ordered that Shi'ites should appear as Sunnis in public, maintaining their religious practices and beliefs only among their fellow believers. This increased Sunni fears that the Shi'ites were subversive.

Martyrdom and voluntary sacrifice became the trademark of the Twelve Imams, and this deeply influenced Shi'ite tradition. A review of the Imams and the Shi'ite traditions surrounding their martyrdom reveals the importance of sacrifice.

Imam	Shi'ite Tradition of Death
1. Ali (died 661)	Assassinated
2. Hasan (died 669)	Poisoned
3. Hussein (died 680)	Martyred at Karbala

Karbala is commemorated during the month of Ashura. A traditional Twelver verse says: "Every day is Ashura, every place is Karbala."

4. Ali zain al Abid (died 714)	Poisoned
5. Mohammed al Baqir (died 731)	Poisoned or martyred in battle
6. Jafar al Sadiq (died 765)	Poisoned
7. Musa al Kazim (died 799)	Imprisoned and poisoned
8. Ali al Rida (died 818)	Poisoned
9. Mohammed al Jawad (died 835)	Poisoned
10. Ali al Hadi (died 868)	Traditions disagree
11. Hasan al Askari (died 874)	Poisoned
12. Mohammed al Muntazar	Taken into divine hiding and will be revealed as the Mahdi before the Day of Judgment.

The Mahdi will restore peace and justice after a final battle with evil. This will herald the return of Jesus, the Imam Hussein, the remaining Imams, and all the prophets and saints.

Sources: Momen (1985, pp. 23–45); Ruthven (2000, pp. 174–191, 434).

(750–1258), ruled the area in the years following Mohammed. Hourani (1997, pp. 25–37) points out that these caliphs theologically divided the world into the Realm of Islam and the Realm of War. The purpose of Islam was to subject the world to God's will. Indeed, Islam means "submission to the will of God," and a *Muslim* is "one who submits."

About 1000, the Turks began to take the domains of the Abbasids. Struggles continued for the next hundred years, until a Mongol advance from East Asia brought the Abbasid dynasty to an end. The Mongols were eventually stopped by an Egyptian army of slaves, giving rise to a new group of Turks, known as Ottomans. The Ottomans were aggressive, conquering most of the Middle East and large parts of Europe. The Ottomans fought the Iranians on one border and central Europeans on the other border for many years.

European relations with Islamic empires were not characterized by harmony. The West began its first violent encounters by launching the Crusades, attempts to conquer the Middle East, lasting from 1095 to about 1250. These affairs were bloody and initiated centuries of hatred and distrust between Muslims and Christians. European struggles with the Ottoman Empire reinforced years of military tension between the two civilizations. Modern tensions in the area can be traced to the decline of Ottoman influence and the collapse of Iranian power in the eighteenth century. When these Islamic powers receded, Western Christian powers were quick to fill the void.

Bernard Lewis (1995) points to the Age of Discovery as the origin of modern confrontation between the West and Islam. Americans might think of 1492 as the beginning of European discovery, starting with Christopher Columbus, but Lewis points out that it is also the year that the final Islamic stronghold in Spain was destroyed. In addition, although Ottoman Turks conquered Constantinople in 1453, renaming it Istanbul, 1492 represented a reversal of fortune for expanding Islamic armies. Western Christian military forces gradually gained the upper hand in world affairs through their superior navies and military technology. When the Turks were driven back from the gates of Vienna, nearly 200 years later, it symbolized the ascendancy and domination of the West.

Additional Reading

Most Americans know about Islam from skewed media images. However, several good books introduce English-speaking audiences to the religion. Here are some suggestions for further reading:

Start with Karen Armstrong's (2000a) *Islam: A Short History*. It is thorough yet easy to read. Armstrong outlines the major figures and theological issues that have developed over the past 1,400 years. If theology is an interest, Thomas W. Lippman's *Understanding Islam* is a good place to begin. His review of most of the major theological developments in Islam is written crisply and with a news reporter's passion for the facts. Caesar Farah (2000) presents a more detailed view in *Islam*, and Malise Ruthven (2000) offers an extremely comprehensive view with *Islam in the World*. Start with Armstrong, then read Lippman. If you want more detail, Farah and Ruthven will take you deeper into the ideas.

For works on Shi'ites, Heinz Halm's *Shi'a Islam* is an easy place to start. Halm gives an overview of the birth and growth of Shi'ism to the modern period. A definitive English-language work is Moojan Momen's *An Introduction to Shi'a Islam*. It is detailed, comprehensive, and informative.

To read about the misunderstandings between Western Jews and Christians and the Islamic world, two authors have several illustrative books. Bernard Lewis and John Esposito are two scholars with differing views, but they are internationally recognized as leading scholars in Islamic and Middle Eastern studies. Their works provide rich theological and historical explanations of Islam and the Muslim world.

✓ Self-Check

> How is Mohammed's revelation central to both Islam and the Golden Age?

> What is the difference between Sunnis and Shi'ites?

> Explain Armstrong's theory of the rise and fall of agrarian empires.

Militant Philosophy

Mohammed ibn Abdul Wahhab: (1703– 1792) Also known as Abdul Wahhab; a religious reformer who wanted to purge Islam of anything beyond the traditions accepted by Mohammed and the four Rightly Guided caliphs. He conducted campaigns against Sufis, Shi'ites, and Muslims who made pilgrimages or who invoked the names of saints.

Sayyid Qutb: (1906–1966) An Egyptian educator who called for the overthrow of governments and the imposition of purified Islamic law, based on the principles of previous puritanical reformers. Qutb formed a militant wing of the Muslim Brotherhood.

Taqi al Din ibn Taymiyyah: (c. 1269–1328) Also known as ibn Taymiyya; a Muslim religious reformer in the time of the Crusades and a massive Mongol invasion.

As religions develop, various interpretations arise, and this is especially true in times of crisis. As Armstrong suggests, reformers emerged in Islam, calling believers to an idealized past when crisis erupted. Many people argue that this gave rise to militancy, but others argue that militants misused the theology of the reformers (see Oliver, 2002; Esposito, 2002; Saeed and Saeed, 2004). Taqi al Din ibn Taymiyya introduced new ideas about militancy and the faith after Arab setbacks by the Mongols and the Crusaders. **Mohammed ibn Abdul Wahhab** "rediscovered" ibn Taymiyya when preaching puritanical reform of Islam 500 years later. **Sayyid Qutb**, who lacked theological training, militarized the ideas of ibn Taymiyya and Wahhab in the twentieth century. Although apologists defend these men as peaceful thinkers seeking a pure Islam, critics maintain that their theological writings gave rise to militancy.

Ibn Taymiyyah

Western Crusaders began waging war against the Muslims in the eleventh century, and Mongol invaders struck the Arab lands a hundred years later. Hundreds of thousands of Muslims were killed in each invasion. **Taqi al Din ibn Taymiyyah** (c. 1269–1328), an Islamic scholar, was appalled by the slaughter and sought to find an answer in his faith. He believed that Muslims had fallen away from the truth and needed to internally purify themselves. He called for jihad (struggle or effort), the destruction of heretics and invaders, calling it the sixth pillar of Islam.

Ibn Taymiyyah fled Baghdad to escape the invading Mongols. He believed that the Crusaders and the Mongols defeated Islamic armies because Muslims had fallen away from the true practice of Islam. Emphasizing *tawhid*, the oneness of God, ibn Taymiyyah attacked anything that threatened to come between humanity and God. He forbade prayers at gravesites, belief in saints, and other practices that had worked their way into Islam. He was especially harsh on the mystical Sufis, who believed that deep prayer revealed the will of God beyond the prophecy of Mohammed and the Quran. Individual Sufis pledged allegiance to various masters and followed their masters even when their actions violated Islamic law. According to ibn Taymiyyah, any belief that went beyond Mohammed's revelation was to be subjected to a purifying jihad. He preached that holy war should be waged against all people who threatened the faith. His targets included Muslims and non-Muslims alike.

Ibn Taymiyyah's teaching is important. Islam is frequently described as a monotheistic religion based on five tenets, or pillars: (1) a confession of faith in God and acceptance of Mohammed as God's last and greatest Prophet, (2) ritual prayers with the community, (3) giving alms, (4) fasting, especially during holy periods, and (5) making a pilgrimage to Mohammed's birthplace, Mecca (Farah, 2000, pp. 132–148). Jihad has a place in this system, and different Islamic scholars (*ulema*) interpret jihad in various ways. There are many meanings, but most Muslims defined *jihad* as defending a community and waging an internal struggle against one's own tendency toward evil (Firestone, 1999, pp. 5, 65–91; Peters, 1996, pp. 1–8, 115–119).

Ibn Taymiyyah expanded the meaning of jihad by advocating attacks on nonbelievers and impure Muslims; however, he preached toleration for Muslims who accepted one of the more rigid versions of Sunni Islam. He claimed that this was another pillar of Islam (Hourani, 1997, pp. 179–181; Esposito, 2002, pp. 45–46; see Gerges, 2006, p. 209).

Abdul Wahhab

John Esposito (1999, pp. 6–10) says that reform movements are common throughout the history of Islam. Two recent movements became important to the jihadists. In the late eighteenth century, a purification movement started by Mohammed ibn Abdul Wahhab (1703–1792), who was influenced by ibn Taymiyya, took root in Arabia.

Wahhab preached a puritanical strain of Islam that sought to rid the religion of practices added after the first few decades following Mohammed's death. This doctrine deeply influenced the Saud family as they fought to gain control of Arabia, and it dominates the theology of Saudi Arabia and the Gulf States today. Militant application of Wahhab's puritanical principles spread to India and other parts of Asia. Strict Muslims who follow the practices of Wahhab argue that they are trying to rid the religion of superstition and return it to the state envisioned by Mohammed and his first followers (Oliver, 2002, pp. 10–11). Critics maintain that his militant followers force their puritanical views on those who disagree with them (Farah, 2000, p. 230).

ANOTHER PERSPECTIVE

Wahhab as a Mainstream Reformer

Many American security experts use the Taymiyya–Wahhab–Qutb theological link to explain militant jihadist religion. Natana DeLong-Bas throws this assumption aside. In a study of Wahhab's original works, she concludes that he was a mainstream reformer who was trying to bring Islam back to its roots. She conducts a detailed examination of Wahhab's extensive writings and historical accounts of his life, combining these with an in-depth analysis of Wahhab's interpretation of the Quran, Mohammed's life and actions, and Islamic law. DeLong-Bas believes that Wahhab favored academic argument and logic over the use of force and that he subtly divorced himself from military conquests in the name of Islam. Wahhab opposed any action that detracted from faith in and prayer to the oneness and total unity (*tawhid*) of God. By

the eighteenth century, many Muslims were praying at the tombs of the departed, asking for their intercession. They wore charms, and some of them accepted older superstitions. These activities defied the sovereignty of God, Wahhab believed, and he challenged Islamic scholars (*ulema*) to justify them. He sought to restore the rights of women as established by the Prophet, and he wanted Muslims to guide their lives by practical interpretations of the Quran. This upset the established rulers because it challenged their authority and the general social order. Wahhab's actions provoked strong negative reactions, DeLong-Bas says. Current militants like bin Laden and Zawahiri do not understand Wahhab's theological writings, and his interpretation of religion has little to do with jihadists who murder in God's name.

Source: DeLong, 2004.

Muslim Brotherhood: An organization founded by Hassan al Banna, designed to recapture the spirit and religious purity of the period of Mohammed and the four Rightly Guided caliphs. The Brotherhood seeks to create a single Muslim nation through education and religious reform. A militant wing founded by Sayyid Qutb sought the same objective through violence. Hamas, a group that defines itself as the Palestinian branch of the Muslim Brotherhood, has rejected the multinational approach in favor of creating a Muslim Palestine.

Sayyid Qutb

Sayyid Qutb (1906–1966) was an Egyptian teacher and journalist who was initially employed by the Ministry of Education. He traveled to the United States and lived as an exchange professor in Greeley, Colorado, from 1948 to 1950. Qutb's experience in America soured his opinion of Western civilization. He returned to Egypt and became an active member of the **Muslim Brotherhood**, an organization that sought to create a single Muslim nation through education and religious reform. Qutb was arrested in 1954 after the Brotherhood tried to overthrow the Egyptian government, but he was released in 1964 because of health problems. He published his most famous work, *Milestones*, in 1965. The book outlines the theology and ideology of jihadist revolution, and its militant tone led to Qutb's second arrest and subsequent hanging by the Egyptian government in 1966 (see Bozek, 2009).

Qutb's books and articles popularized many militant ideas, and they continue to influence jihadists today. He believed that the Islamic world descended into darkness (*jahaliyya*) shortly after the death of Mohammed (A.D. 632). The so-called Islamic governments of the Arab empires were really corrupt nonreligious regimes. Pure Islam had been lost, but a few people, such as ibn Taymiyyah, Mohammed ibn Abdul

Wahhab, and Mawlana Mawdudi (1903–1979), kept the faith alive. Qutb rejected the West and called on Muslims to overthrow their corrupt governments. He argued that rulers should impose Islamic law on their subjects, and when pure Islamic states are created, they should confront the world (Esposito, 2002, pp. 56–64).

In *Milestones*, Qutb (1965, pp. 112–134) argued that Muslims were in a cosmic battle with the forces of darkness. Whereas Mohammed mandated tolerance of those who would not embrace Islam, Qutb called for the destruction of all enemies. The forces of darkness could not be tolerated, he wrote, and although God was ultimately responsible for the destruction of darkness, Muslims were called to fight it. Qutb's writings were banned in many Islamic countries, and they infuriated the Egyptian government under Gamal Nasser. Qutb was arrested and sent to prison after he returned from the United States. The *al Qaeda Manual* (White, 2004a) cites Qutb as a source of inspiration.

Hassan al Banna: (1906–1949) Founder of the Muslim Brotherhood in 1928. He was murdered by agents of the Egyptian government.

Jihadists cite ibn Taymiyya, Wahhab, and Qutb to justify violence (see Esposito, 2002, pp. 40–64). Esposito adds **Hassan al Banna**, founder of the Muslim Brotherhood. Two other factors play into the rise of extremism: the birth of modern Israel and the collapse of Western imperialism. Both of these factors interact with the jihadist movement at points, but they have their own distinct aspects. In addition, the collapse of imperialism has influenced diverse forms of terrorism, from the 1979 **Iranian Revolution** to ethnic fighting in Africa and to Maoist rebellions in Nepal. Modern Middle Eastern terrorism extends far beyond the traditional concept of the Middle East and involves far more than jihadist philosophy.

Iranian Revolution: The 1979 religious revolution that toppled Mohammed Pahlavi, the shah of Iran, and transformed Iran into an Islamic republic ruled by Shi'ite religious scholars.

ANOTHER PERSPECTIVE

A Critique of Western Interpretations

The strict Hanbali rite of Sunni Islam emphasizes the importance of the elders (*salafiyya* or *salafi*). Most of them revere Taqi al Din ibn Taymiyya and Mohammed ibn Abdul Wahhab, and they become incensed when the two Islamic scholars are linked to violence. Haneef James Oliver reflects this position in The *"Wahhabi" Myth* (2002). He points out the following:

- There is no such thing as a Wahhabi, or follower of Wahhab. Orthodox Muslims in Saudi Arabia and other areas emphasize the oneness of God and the importance of Mohammed and the Rightly Guided caliphs, the salafiyya. To call them Wahhabis suggests that there is more than one correct interpretation of Islam, Oliver says.
- Mohammed ibn Abdul Wahhab was not a radical Muslim. His call for reform was based on the Quran.

- Osama bin Laden, Ayman al Zawahiri, and other members of al Qaeda do not follow the teachings of Wahhab, the Quran, or Islam. They are mystics who believe their personal experiences and theologies are superior to those of Mohammed. Oliver believes, as did Wahhab, that mystical Sufis corrupted Islam by emphasizing their own encounters with the holy and that al Qaeda follows this tradition. Mohammed provided the last revelation. There are no more Prophets despite Sufism and mystics in other religions.
- When terrorists are called Salafis, Wahhabis, or Salafi-Wahhabis, it completely miscasts and misinterprets Islam. Terrorists follow the teachings of Sayyid Qutb, who was neither an Islamic scholar nor a good Muslim.

Self-Check

> Explain the relationship among the philosophies of Taymiyya, Wahhab, and Qutb.
> Does Qutb's theology represent orthodox Islam?
> How might Wahhab's and Qutb's ideas reflect the theory of agrarian empires suggested in the previous section?

Synopsis of Traditional Middle Eastern Issues

To understand terrorism in the Middle East, it is necessary to appreciate certain aspects of the region's recent history. To best understand the Middle East, keep the following in mind:

> The current structure of Middle Eastern geography and political rule is a direct result of nineteenth-century European imperial influence in the region and the outcomes of World War I.

> Many of the Arab countries in the Middle East place more emphasis on the power of the family than on contemporary notions of government. However, Israel rules itself as a parliamentary democracy.

> Most Western government officials and scholars do not believe the modern state of Israel is the biblical Kingdom of David mentioned in the Hebrew and Christian Bibles or the Islamic Quran. They tend to see it as a secular power dominated by people of European descent. Many religious Israelis and their Jewish and Christian supporters disagree with this assessment.

> Arabs in general, and Palestinians in particular, do not hold a monopoly on terrorism.

> Religious differences in the region have developed over centuries, and fanaticism in any religion can spawn violence. Fanatical Jews, Christians, and Muslims in the Middle East practice terrorism in the name of religion.

> Although the Middle East has been volatile since 1948—the year in which Israel was recognized as a nation-state—modern terrorism grew after 1967. It increased after 1973 and became a standard method of military operations in the following two decades.

> In 1993 the Palestine Liberation Organization (PLO) renounced terrorism; however, instead of decreasing tension, the move has created tremendous tension. On the Arab side, some groups have denounced the PLO's actions, whereas others have embraced it. The same reaction has occurred in Israel, where one set of political parties endorses peace plans and another prepares for war. Middle Eastern peace is a very fragile process, and terrorism is a wild card. It can upset delicate negotiations at any time, even after a peace treaty has been signed and implemented (for an example, see Hoffman, 1995).

> All of these issues are complicated by shortages of water and vast differences in social structure. The area contains some of the world's richest and some of the world's poorest people. Most of them are far from water sources.

One can best begin to understand the Middle East by focusing on the world of the late 1800s. During that time period, three critical events took place that helped to shape the modern Middle East.

Ottoman Empire: A Turkish empire that lasted for 600 years, until 1924. The empire spanned southeastern Europe, North Africa, and southwest Asia, and reached its zenith in the fourteenth and fifteenth centuries.

First, the **Ottoman Empire**, the Turk-based government that ruled much of the Middle East, was falling apart in the nineteenth century. The Ottoman Turks encountered domestic challenges across their empire as various nationalistic, tribal, and familial groups revolted. In addition, they faced foreign threats. The Persian Empire had collapsed earlier, but Great Britain, France, Germany, and Russia intervened in the area with military force. Each European country was willing to promise potential rebels some type of autonomy if they revolted against the Turks. Turkey was reluctantly drawn into World War I, and the victorious Allies partitioned the empire after victory in 1918. A group of military officers took control of Turkey, banned religious government, and in 1924 brought an end to the caliphate (Fromkin, 2001, pp. 406–426).

The second critical event involved a political movement called Zionism. From 1896 to 1906, European Jews, separated from their ancient homeland for nearly

2,000 years, wanted to create their own nation. Some of them favored Palestine, whereas others wanted to move to South America or Africa. In 1906 those who backed Palestine won the argument, and European Jews increasingly moved to the area (Armstrong, 2000a, pp. 146–151). The sultan of the Ottoman Turks allowed them to settle, but refused to grant them permission to form their own government. Palestinian Arabs, the people who lived in Palestine, were wary of the Jewish settlers and tensions rose (Nasr, 1997, pp. 5–8).

Finally, European armies occupied the Middle East between 1914 and 1918, as they fought World War I. European governments continued to make contradictory promises about Arab autonomy as they sought to establish spheres of influence in the region. When the war ended, the victorious nations felt that they had won the area from the Turks. They divided the Middle East, not with any regard for the area's political realities, but to share the spoils of victory. This created long-term political problems. Historian David Fromkin calls this "the peace to end all peace," satirizing the Western depiction of World War I as the "war to end all wars" (Fromkin, 2002, pp. 15–20).

Three Sources of Violence in Mahan's Middle East

The situation at the end of World War I set the stage for developments over the next century, and it is the basis for terrorism in the traditional Middle East, defined by the U.S. Navy's Captain Mahan as Israel, Lebanon, Jordan, Egypt, Syria, Iraq, and the Arabian Peninsula. As events unfolded, three factors became prominent in Middle Eastern violence: (1) questions about the political control of Israel and Palestine, (2) questions of who would rule the Arab world, and (3) questions concerning the relations between the two main branches of Islam—Sunnis and Shi'ites. Stated another way, these problems are the following:

1. The Palestinian question (control of Palestine)
2. Intra-Arab rivalries and struggles
3. The future of revolutionary Islam

These problems are all separate, but they are also all interrelated. The sources of terrorism in the Middle East are symbiotic. That is, they are independent arenas of violence with a dynamic force of their own, but they are also related to and dependent on each other (Figure 8.1).

All forms of Middle Eastern terrorism share certain traits. First, many Arab groups express dissatisfaction over the existence of Israel. They are not necessarily pro-Palestinian, but they find the notion of a European-created, non-Arab state in their lands offensive. Most Middle Eastern terrorist groups are anti-imperialist. The intensity of their passion varies according to the type of group, but terrorism has largely been dominated by anti-Western feelings. Another related factor is the pan-Arabic or pan-Islamic orientation of terrorist groups. Although they fight for local control, most wish to revive a united Arab Islamic realm. Finally, Middle Eastern terrorism is united by kinship bonds. In terrorist groups, as in Middle Eastern politics in general, familial links are often more important than national identification.

When the Israelis practice terrorism, they usually claim their activities are conventional military actions. At times, however, the Israelis have used the same tactics the PLO used in the 1960s and 1970s. It is perhaps more accurate to argue that all Middle Eastern violence, Arabic and non-Arabic, is locked in symbiosis—its various sides are interdependent (see Nasr, 1997; Said and Hutchinson, 1990). It can best be understood by looking at political affairs in the Middle East during the build-up to the First World War.

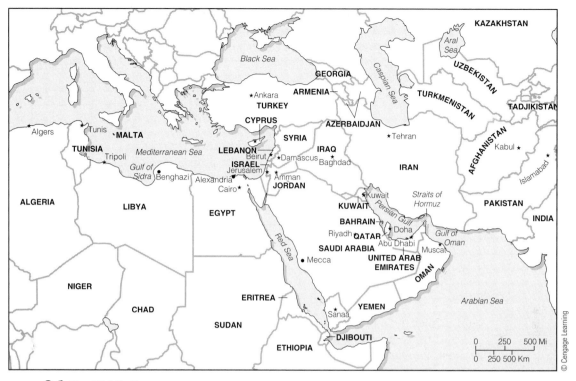

FIGURE **8.1** The Middle East

The Early Zionist Movement in Palestine

The Zionist movement took place at the same time the Ottoman Empire was breaking up, which created opportunities for several groups interested in the region. For Arabs in general it signaled the possible recreation of the Arab empire as it was shortly after the death of Mohammed. Palestinian Arabs, much more modest in their political views, sought to join with Syria to form a new country. Many Palestinians welcomed the Zionists, thinking that Jews would assist them in the formation of this new country. The Zionists held no such belief: The Jews had no intention of becoming part of Syria. Nasr (1997, pp. 6–7) argues that the Palestinian Arabs represented a cohesive mixture of Muslims and Christians and that they were leery of Jewish settlements. Regardless, Palestinians sold land to the Zionists, who linked their holdings with the ultimate purpose of creating a Jewish state.

Nasr (1997, pp. 9–16) points out that sporadic violence accompanied these new settlements. Tensions became apparent in confrontations between the ethnic groups and conflicts between individuals. Violence was seldom organized, and it did not reflect the forms of terrorism that would engulf the region within two decades. That situation changed during World War I.

In the years preceding the war, Zionism caused confusion in Palestine. Even though most of the Jewish immigrants were European, the Arabs thought of them as Semitic people, and both groups identified with Palestine. Furthermore, the Zionists originally stated they had no desire to displace the Palestinians; they wanted to coexist with them. As Jewish settlers bought land, however, they purchased large parcels next to each other. They established governing councils for their farmland and refused to sell land back to Arabs. They were acting in defiance of the sultan's refusal to allow Jewish self-government (see Hourani, 1997, pp. 323–324).

World War I and Contradictory Promises

Jewish immigration into Palestine played into the political issues of World War I. Because the Turks were allied with the Germans, the British encouraged the Arabs to revolt against the Turks. If the Arabs would fight for the British, the British promised to move the caliphate from Istanbul to Mecca and to name an Arab as caliph. The military commander in Cairo, who promised to restore the caliphate, thought he was promising the Islamic equivalent of a pope and that secular, individual Arab states would continue to exist. He did not understand the nature of the caliphate. On October 24, 1915, the British made an unclear promise to the Arabs. In return for a general Arab revolt against the Turks, the British agreed to support the creation of a united, independent Arab state at the close of the war. The British believed this to be sound foreign policy. They believed that the nebulous understanding was not a promise of support to the Arabs. However, the Arabs felt that they had received a promise for the ancient Arab realm of Islam. Although the British had gained an ally at little expense, the circumstances were ripe for resentments (Fromkin, 2001, p. 179).

Balfour Declaration: A policy statement by the British government in November 1917 that promised a homeland for Jews in the geographical area of biblical Israel. Sir Arthur Balfour was the British foreign secretary.

The British made other promises. Partly in response to the Zionist movement and partly to maintain the goodwill of American Jews, the British promised the Zionists a Jewish homeland in Palestine. The **Balfour Declaration** of November 1917 promised to create the state of Israel. It was backed by Protestant Christians who understood neither the nature of the caliphate nor the importance of Jerusalem, or al Quds to Muslims, in Islam. Supporters of the Balfour Declaration were unaware that their promise directly contradicted the British commander's promise in Cairo, the promise to reestablish an Arab-dominated caliphate. All Arab Muslims would expect the caliphate to include the three most important cities in Sunni Islam: Mecca, Medina, and Jerusalem. The Balfour Declaration threatened to transfer Jerusalem to the new state of Israel (Fromkin, 2001, pp. 274–300).

Mark Sykes: (1879–1919) A British diplomat who signed a secret agreement with Francois Georges-Picot in May 1916. The Sykes-Picot Agreement divided the Middle East into spheres of French, British, and Russian influence.

The British also made promises to their allies. Sir **Mark Sykes,** a British foreign service officer, negotiated a treaty with the French to extend spheres of British and French influence in the states of the old Ottoman empire. On the other side of the region, in ancient Persia (modern Iran), the British approached the Russians with another deal. Iran would be divided into three parts, a northern area controlled by Russia, a southern zone under British rule, and a neutral area in between. When the war ended in 1918, the entire Middle East was controlled by the British, French, and Russians, but it was a powder keg (Fromkin, 2001, pp. 189–196, 291–293).

Explicable in a time when national survival was threatened, these contradictory promises were nothing more than an extension of prewar British imperial policies. They did not alleviate the tensions between the Palestinian Arabs and the newly arrived Palestinian Jews. At the end of the war, the British created a series of Arab countries dominated by strong, traditional family groups. Far from representing a united Arab realm of Islam, the British-led division was challenged internally by rival families and externally by other Arab states. Each family and each of the Arab leaders wished to unite Islam under their own banner. Major states eventually emerged from this scenario: Syria, Iraq, Saudi Arabia, Jordan, and the Gulf States. Some of the new nations dreamed of a pan-Islamic region, but none was willing to let another run it. Other ethnic groups, like the Kurds, wanted autonomy. Christian Assyrians and Jewish settlers in Palestine also wanted independence (Hourani, 1997, pp. 315–332; Fromkin, 2001, pp. 558–561).

Mandate of Palestine: The British Mandate of Palestine was in effect from 1920 to 1948. Created by the League of Nations, the mandate gave the United Kingdom the right to extend its influence in an area roughly equivalent to modern Jordan, Israel, and the Palestinian Authority.

The Arabs also could not counter the continuing British influence, and neither a pan-Arabic realm nor a Jewish national state could develop under the watchful eyes of the British. In 1922 Great Britain received permission from the League of Nations to create the **Mandate of Palestine.** The mandate gave Britain control of Palestine and placed the British in the center of Middle Eastern affairs, but it came with a cost. It left neither Arab nor Jew satisfied. The Arabs believed that they had received a false promise, and the Jews demanded their right to a homeland (Fromkin, 2001, pp. 562–565).

The Birth of Israel

While the British established the protectorate, in Palestine feelings of nationalism and anger increased. Both Jews and Arabs resented the British, but neither side was willing to submit to the other if the British were expelled. Sporadic violence against the Jews began in 1921, and the Jews formed a defense force known as the Haganah. They did not see themselves as ordinary settlers, but as fellow colonialists alongside the British. They had come to establish a Zionist state (Burleigh, 2009, p. 90).

Tensions increased throughout the decade, culminating in a riot in 1929 when the Islamic mufti of Jerusalem inspired an attack against Jewish worshippers. More than 60 Jews were killed and another 60 would be killed in sporadic violence during the remainder of the year. This prompted a debate and a split in the Haganah. Some members wanted to take action against the Arabs and the British, and they saw terrorist violence as the only means to create a Jewish state in Palestine. They called the new group the Irgun Zvai Leumi (Burleigh, p. 91). Bruce Hoffman (1998, pp. 48–53) states that the Irgun would become the prototype of the anticolonial urban terrorist group. He is not sure whether the EOKA in Cyprus or the FLN in Algeria deliberately based their campaigns on Irgun tactics, but each movement followed the Irgun model.

An Arab revolt in Palestine began in 1936 and lasted until 1939. It was primarily aimed at the British, but the brewing hatred and distrust between the Arab and Jewish communities also came to the surface. Both Jews and Arabs fought the British, but they fought each other at the same time. Animosity was overshadowed by the events of the early 1940s but resurfaced after the war. Both Jews and Arabs firmly believed that the only possible solution to the problems in Palestine was to expel the British and eliminate the political participation of the other (Nasr, 1997, pp. 17–25).

Michael Burleigh (2009, pp. 95–111) says the British responded to violence with the same ruthless tactics they had applied elsewhere but that the Irgun took matters further. Seeing threats from both the Arabs and the British, the Irgun's leaders—who later became prominent Israeli leaders—plotted a campaign against both sides. At first the Irgun sought to avoid British casualties. That would change after World War II.

In late 1945 and into 1946, thousands of Jews displaced by the Holocaust flocked to Palestine. Palestinian Arabs, sensing danger from this massive influx of Jews, began to arm themselves. They had little assistance. The British Empire was collapsing, and other Arabs were too concerned with their own political objectives to care about the Palestinians. Officially, the British had banned Jewish immigration, but there was little that could be done about the influx of immigrants. Jews continued to arrive, demanding an independent state (Lewis, 2004, pp. 181–187).

In 1945, the Irgun began a campaign of all-out terrorism. Burleigh says that the Irgun adopted a twofold strategy: (1) It would attack in the urban centers of Palestine to tie up massive numbers of British soldiers and to terrorize the Arabs into flight or submission. (2) It would wage an international campaign to win sympathy. Many Jews in America and Europe applauded the Irgun's efforts, and its activities grew in ferocity. Individual British soldiers were assassinated, and the Irgun launched a bombing campaign. When three Irgun terrorists were tried and executed for murder, the Irgun kidnapped two British sergeants and hanged them. They bombed prominent places, such as the King David Hotel, killing British and Americans.

If the Irgun's trail of murder and mayhem predated the EOKA and the FLN, it was modeled on a previous campaign of selective terrorism, the Irish Republican Army in the Black and Tan War. In a four-part series on terrorism, the History Channel (2000) pointed to one of the threads running through Jewish terrorism. Leaders of the Irgun studied the tactics of the Irish Republican Army's Michael Collins. They incorporated Collins's methods in the Jewish campaign, and the Irgun's leader took the Irishman's name as his *nom de guerre*. The Irgun knew that it could not hope to defeat the British in a conventional war, but terrorism gave hope for political victory. Within 20 years, Palestinian Arabs would make the same discovery.

In 1947, the situation was beyond British control. Exhausted by World War II, the British sought a UN solution to their quandary in Palestine. The United Nations suggested that one part of Palestine be given to the Arabs and another part be given to the Jews. The Zionists were elated; the Arabs were not. Caught in the middle, the British came to favor the UN solution, and they had reason to support it: The Jews were in revolt.

On May 15, 1948, the United Nations recognized the partition of Palestine and the modern nation-state of Israel. The Arabs attacked the new Jewish state immediately, and the Irgun's terrorism fell by the wayside. Both Arabs and Jews shifted to conventional warfare and would fight that way until 1967.

Arab Power Struggles and Arab–Israeli Wars

Modern Middle Eastern terrorism is the result of continuing conflicts in the twentieth century. This section reviews the formation of some of the most important Arab states in North Africa and southwest Asia. Instead of considering each story separately, the narrative blends Israel's development with the symbiotic nature of the conflict. This approach explains the relationship between intra-Arab rivalries and terrorism.

Although the control of Palestine is always mentioned when dealing with contemporary Middle Eastern violence, since as far back as after World War I, the situation has not been conducive to peace. Britain and France divided the ancient realm of Islam, known as dar al-Islam, and left the area ripe for confusion and bitterness. Aside from the Palestinian issue, other Arabs felt slighted by various peace settlements, and their dissatisfaction continued through the end of World War II. The French and British created states that did not realistically reflect the divisions in the Middle East.

North Africa was completely dominated by Britain and France. Libya was divided into British and French sections, and it did not become independent until 1951. In 1969, Colonel Muammar Gadhafi seized power in a military coup, claiming Libya as an anti-Western socialist state. Egypt achieved its independence before World War II but did not fully break with Britain until Gamal Nasser took power in 1954. Gadhafi sought to follow Nasser's footsteps but broke with Egypt after Nasser's death in 1970 (Halliday, 2005, pp. 167–175).

Syria was under French rule from 1922 to 1946. After several military coups and a failed attempt to form a united republic with Egypt, a group of pan-Arabic socialists, the Baath Party, seized power in 1963. They were purged by an internal Baath revolution in 1966, and Baathist president Hafez Assad came to power in 1970, ruling until his death in 2000. Aside from internal problems (especially problems involving a minority group of Alawites who practiced Muslim, Christian, and pagan rituals), Assad believed that Lebanon and Palestine were rightly part of Greater Syria (Dawisha, 2003, pp. 160–213).

Lebanon has become one of the most violent regions in the area. Ruled by France until 1943, the government of Lebanon managed a delicate balance of people with many different national and religious loyalties. In 1948, when Palestinians displaced by Israel began flocking to the country, the delicate balance was destroyed. Lebanon has suffered internal conflict ever since. Violence has included civil wars in 1958 and 1975–1976, continued fighting up to 1978, an Israeli invasion in 1978, another Israeli invasion in 1982, an Iranian revolutionary intervention following the 1982 Israeli invasion, a fragile peace in 1990, and the growth of a terrorist militia from 1983 to 1996. Several large militias still roam the countryside, despite their agreement to disarm under the terms of the 1990 peace plan. Israel began abandoning Lebanon in the spring and summer of 2000. Militant Lebanese forces moved into the former occupied zones, seeking vengeance on the **South Lebanese Army**, whose members supported Israel (Friedman, 2000, pp. 126–137).

South Lebanese Army: A Christian militia closely allied with and supported by Israel. It operated with Israeli support from 1982 to 2000.

The Persian Gulf region has a different history. In an effort to secure the land route to India, the British established several states from the Mediterranean Sea to the Persian Gulf in the nineteenth and early twentieth centuries. One branch of the Hashemite family received Jordan as a reward for assisting the British; another branch received Iraq. Jordan became a constitutional monarchy ruled by King Hussein from 1952 to 1999 and by his son, King Abdullah, from 1999 to the present. Iraq's path was more turbulent. A 1958 coup eliminated the Iraqi Hashemites from power, and another coup in 1968 brought **Baathist** rule. Saddam Hussein, a Baathist, came to power in 1979 (Dawisha, 2003, pp. 169–171, 276–277).

Baathist: A member of the pan-national Arab Baath Party. Baathists were secular socialists seeking to unite Arabs in a single socialist state.

Saudi Arabia and the Persian Gulf States fared somewhat better because of their immense wealth and independence from Europe. In 1902, the Saud family began expanding its control of Arabia, which included Mecca, the most sacred shrine in Islam, and it unified the kingdom in 1932. The Gulf States remained independent from the Saud family. The social situation changed in 1938 when oil was discovered on the Arabian peninsula. As operations intensified, explorers found that the entire region was rich with oil. Poorer states, such as Iraq and Jordan, looked at the Persian Gulf with envy, believing the oil wealth should benefit all of dar al-Islam. Not all has been peaceful in the Persian Gulf or Saudi Arabia.

From 1947 to 1967, the Middle East was dominated by a series of short conventional wars. Arab states failed to achieve unity, often seeming as willing to oppose each other as they were to oppose Israel. Rhetorically, all the Arab states maintained an anti-Israeli stance, but Jordan and Saudi Arabia began to move closer to the West, enthusiastically led by the shah of Iran (B. Rubin, 2003).

In the meantime, Israeli armed forces grew. Composed of highly mobile combined combat units, the Israeli Defense Forces became capable of launching swift, deadly strikes at the Arabs. In 1967, the Israelis demonstrated their superiority over all their Arab neighbors. Although the combined Arab armies were equipped with excellent Soviet arms and outnumbered the Israeli forces, in six days Israel soundly defeated its opponents and doubled its territory (Armstrong, 2000b, p. 171; Dawisha, 2003, 250–258).

Six Day War: A war between Israel and its Arab neighbors fought in June 1967. Israel launched the preemptive war in the face of an Arab military buildup, and it overwhelmed all opposition. At the end of the war, Israel occupied the Sinai Peninsula, the Golan Heights, and the West Bank of the Jordan River. It also occupied the city of Jerusalem, or al Quds to Muslims.

After the 1967 **Six Day War**, the Palestine Liberation Organization (PLO) began a series of terrorist attacks against civilian Israeli positions. Its military approach mimicked the old terrorist tactics of the Irgun and its violent offshoot, the Stern Gang. These attacks embittered most Israelis and served to define Israeli relations with Arab neighbors. The PLO soon split between moderates and radicals, but terrorism against Israel increased. Israel struck back against the PLO wherever they its operatives were located (Nasr, 1997, pp. 40–47).

In the meantime, the Arab states also split into several camps. One group, represented by King Hussein of Jordan, was anxious to find a way to coexist with Israel. A few nations, like Egypt, simply wanted to avenge the embarrassment of the Six Day War. Egypt would negotiate with Israel, but as an equal, not as a defeated nation. Other Arab views were more militant. Represented by the Baath Party, groups of Arab socialists called for both Arab unity and the destruction of Israel. They formed the Rejectionist Front, a coalition that included several terrorist groups rejecting peace with Israel. Finally, a group of wealthy oil states hoped for stability in the region. They publicly supported the struggle against Israel, while privately working for peace. Peace would ensure sound economic relations with their customers in the West.

Despite the myriad positions, the embarrassment of the Six Day War proved to be the strongest catalyst to action. The Egyptians and the Israelis kept sniping at one another along the Suez Canal. Gamal Nasser, Egypt's president, vowed to drive the Israelis back and asked for Soviet help to do it. Breaking relations with the United States, Nasser moved closer to the Soviet camp. When he died in September 1970, Anwar Sadat, his successor, questioned the policy of moving closer to the Soviets. By 1972, he had thrown the Soviets out, claiming that they were not willing to support another war with Israel. Coordinating activities with Syria, Sadat launched his own war on October 6, 1973 (Esposito, 1999, pp. 72–73, 93–96).

Yom Kippur War: A war between Israel and its Arab neighbors fought in October 1973. Also known as the Ramadan War, hostilities began with a surprise attack on Israel. After initial setbacks, Israel counterattacked and regained its positions.

The **Yom Kippur War,** named after the Hebrew festival celebrating God's atonement for all sin and reconciliation with humanity, psychologically reversed the defeat of the Six Day War for many of Israel's Arab neighbors. Catching the Israelis by surprise in 1973, the Egyptians drove Israeli forces back into the Sinai, while the Syrians drove onto the Golan Heights. The Syrians were attempting to launch a tank offensive into central Israel before the Israeli Defense Forces managed to stabilize the front. Israel counterattacked, driving their enemies back, but the Egyptians celebrated their initial victory. Peace came three weeks later, and the Egyptians felt that their honor had been restored.

Satisfied with this sense of victory, Sadat took a series of bold initiatives. Responding to an overture from the United States, Sadat renewed relations with Washington and stopped the minor skirmishes with Israeli troops by 1975. He visited Jerusalem in 1977 and publicly talked of peace (Esposito, 1999, pp. 96–98).

Former Irgun leader Menachim Begin became prime minister of Israel in September 1977. Begin was committed to maintaining control of the occupied territories, including Jerusalem, that Israel had won in the Six Day War. Begin's position precluded peace with the Arab states because the Arabs demanded the return of the occupied territories. Despite the obvious differences, Anwar Sadat maintained a dialogue with Washington. Under the mediation of U.S. President Jimmy Carter, Sadat agreed to a separate peace with Israel, provided that Israel would withdraw from the Sinai Peninsula. Begin agreed, and on May 26, 1979, Egypt and Israel signed the **Camp David Peace Accord** under Carter's watchful eye. The decision cost Sadat his life. He was assassinated by Muslim fundamentalists in 1981 for agreeing to peace.

Camp David Peace Accord: A peace treaty between Egypt and Israel brokered by the United States in 1979.

The Return of Terrorism

The Arabs rejecting peace with Israel fell into two camps. The radicals rejected any peace with or recognition of Israel. The more moderate group was concerned about the fate of the Palestinians. Egypt's peace with Israel did not account for the Palestinian refugees in Israel or the occupied territories. At the same time, much of the West failed to pay attention to legitimate claims of the Palestinians because radical Palestinians were involved in dozens of terrorist attacks.

In the symbiotic world of Middle Eastern terrorism, Palestine was frequently used as a cover for the intra-Arab struggle for power. In 1978, Israel launched a minor invasion of Lebanon, followed by a full-scale attack in 1982. During this same period, Middle Eastern governments were consolidating internal power and looking at potential regional rivals. The Iranian government fell to revolutionary Shi'ites, and the American embassy and its occupants were seized by Iran's revolutionary government. As the United States eventually achieved the return of its embassy hostages, Saddam Hussein's Iraq and revolutionary Iran went to war. Terrorism increased as a horrible sideshow, and thousands died each month on conventional battlefields (Wright, 2000, pp. 15–19).

In the melee of the 1980s, Middle Eastern terrorism fell into several broad categories. These included: (1) suicide bombings and other attacks on Israeli and Western positions in Lebanon; (2) various militias fighting other militias in Lebanon; (3) state-sponsored terrorism from Libya, Syria, and Iran; (4) freelance terrorism by high-profile groups; (5) terrorism in support of Arab Palestinians; (6) attacks in Europe against Western targets; and (7) Israeli assassinations of alleged terrorists. Terrorists mounted dozens of operations for supporting governments, and several nations used terrorists as commandos. Airplanes were hijacked; airports were attacked; the United States responded with naval action, once accidentally shooting down an Iranian civilian airplane and killing hundreds; and Europe became a low-intensity battleground (Pluchinsky, 1982, 1986).

Iran–Iraq War: A war fought after Iraq invaded Iran over a border dispute in 1980. Many experts predicted an Iraqi victory, but the Iranians stopped the Iraqi army. The war produced an eight-year stalemate and more than a million casualties. The countries signed an armistice in 1988.

Despite the appearance of terrorism, conventional war continued to dominate the Middle East, and Arabs struggled against Arabs. As the **Iran–Iraq War** neared its end, Saddam Hussein turned his attention to Kuwait. Feeling that the British had unfairly separated Kuwait from Iraq before World War I, Saddam Hussein invaded the small country to gain control of its oil production. The result was disastrous for Iraq. Leading a coalition of Western forces and the Persian Gulf States, the United States struck with massive force. Saddam Hussein's army suffered greatly, and terrorism reemerged as a weapon with which to strike an overwhelming military power. As Iraq retreated in the Persian Gulf, terrorists began plotting new methods for striking the United States.

✓ Self-Check

> How did misunderstandings between Arabs and Jews develop?
> Why did terrorism become a part of these misunderstandings?
> What role did terrorism play in the creation of Israel?
> Why did conventional warfare lead to renewed terrorism?

Iran

Americans found it convenient in the 1980s to speak of Iranian terrorism. After all, the Iranians had violated international law in the early stages of their revolution by taking the American embassy in Tehran. They were alleged to have staged several bombings in Lebanon as well as attacks on other American interests in the Middle East. They had planted mines in the Persian Gulf and were responsible for the deaths of U.S. troops. Finally, intelligence sources reported that the Iranians were allied with other terrorist states and supported a shadowy group known as Islamic Jihad—which turned out to be a cover name for an operational group of Hezbollah. The media attributed this rise in terrorism to the rise of Islamic fundamentalism in Iran.

In some ways this popular conception is correct, but in other ways it is completely wrong. The 1979 revolution in Iran represented the flames from friction that started centuries earlier. Far from being a rebirth of fundamentalism, it was more indicative of the religious split within Islam.

Uniquely Persian

Iranians are not Arabs; they are Persians, and they have strong ethno-national ties to the ancient Persian Empire. They have struggled with Arabs for centuries, and these struggles are indicative of Iran's place in Islam. After the martyrdom of Hussein ibn Ali, Mohammed's grandson, at Karbala, Shi'ite Islam moved east. It came to dominate Persia, further separating Persians from many Arab Sunnis. When conquering Arab and Mongol armies rode through Persia over the next centuries, the Persians maintained their historical cultural identity. It came into full flourish when Iran re-established its own agrarian empire under Shi'ite domination. Iranians resisted the Turks and later European imperialists. Bernard Lewis (2004, pp. 43–45) says that Iran never adopted the habits of nations that conquered them; they remained uniquely Persian.

majilis council: The Islamic name given to a religious council that advises a government or a leader. Some Islamic countries refer to their legislative body as a majilis.

Negative reaction to European imperialism cannot be overemphasized when considering the politics of modern Iran. There is a healthy Iranian distrust of the West. Karen Armstrong (2000a) shows the religious side of the struggle. During the nineteenth century, Persians developed a hierarchy of Shi'ite Islamic scholars, including local prayer leaders, masters of Islam, ayatollahs, and grand ayatollahs. Armstrong says that the leading scholars formed a theological advisory board to the government called the **majilis council**. In the early twentieth century, the majilis resisted British exploitation by taking political leadership. The scholars' activities helped bring about a constitution in 1906, and they virtually shut the country down in a general strike against British policies a few years later.

British Influence and Control

British imperialism came to Iran in the 1800s. After 1850, the British began to view Iran as the northern gateway to India. At the same time, they were also very concerned about German imperialism and possible Russian expansion. For their part, the Russians saw a potential opportunity to gain a warm-water port and expand their empire. They moved into northern Iran and prepared to move south. The British countered by occupying southern Iran. Both countries used the occupation for their own economic and military interests (Nima, 1983, pp. 3–27; see also Esposito, 1999, pp. 41–52).

Oil production had a tremendous impact on the way the British used Iran. The British established the Anglo-Persian Oil Company in 1909 and started taking oil profits out of Iran. Although direct economic imperialism has ended in Iran, Iranians still regard Western oil companies as an extension of the old British arrangement. They believe that the shah stayed in power by allowing Western corporations to exploit Iranian oil.

To some extent, this attitude reflects the history of Iran. The British became very concerned about Iran in the 1920s after the communist revolution in Russia, believing Iran might be the next country that the communists would target. No longer in direct control of the south, the British searched for a leader to stem the potential Soviet threat, a leader whose Iranian nationalism would make him an enemy of Russia. They did not believe that such a man would be difficult to find because working-class Iranians hated the Russians as much as they hated the British. The British found their hero in **Reza Shah Pahlavi**. In 1925, with British support, he became shah of Iran (Wright, 2000, pp. 44–46).

Reza Shah Pahlavi: (1878–1944) Shah of Iran from 1925 to 1941. He was forced from power by a British and Soviet invasion.

Robin Wright says that Reza Shah was under no illusions about his dependency on British power. For Iran to gain full independence, he needed to develop an economic base that would support the country and consolidate his strength among the ethnic populations in Iran. Dilip Hiro (1987, pp. 22–30) says that Reza Shah chose two methods for doing so: First, he encouraged Western investment, primarily British and American, in the oil and banking industries. Second, he courted various power groups inside Iran, including the Shi'ite fundamentalists. At first, these policies seemed successful, but they created long-term problems.

Reza Shah's long-term failure was a result of his foreign policy. In the 1930s, Reza Shah had befriended Hitler, and he saw German relations as a way to balance British influence. He guessed that Iran would profit from having a powerful British rival as an ally, but his plan backfired. When World War II erupted, the British and Russians believed Reza Shah's friendship with the Nazis could result in German troops in Iran and Iranian oil in Germany. In 1941, the British overran southern Iran, while the Russians reentered the north (Wright, 2000, pp. 45–46).

Prelude to the 1979 Revolution

Mohammed Reza Pahlavi: (1919–1980) Shah of Iran from 1941 to 1979. The shah led a rigorous program of modernization that turned Iran into a regional power. He left the throne and accepted exile as a result of the 1979 Iranian Revolution.

Reza Shah's reign was over. He fled the country, leaving his son, **Mohammed Reza Pahlavi,** nominally in charge of the country. Mohammed Pahlavi became the modern shah of Iran, but his ascent was traumatic. An Allied puppet in the beginning, the shah had to fight for the same goals that his father had failed to achieve. When he was on the verge of achieving power in the early 1950s, he found himself displaced by democratic and leftist forces. Like his father, the shah fled the country (Kurzman, 2004, pp. 103–124).

In August 1953, Pahlavi returned to the office that had been denied him during Iran's brief fling with democracy. The Iranians had attempted to create a constitutional assembly, but the British believed that they were moving too far to the left and would be swept into a communist revolution. Playing on their fear of communism, the British convinced the American CIA that the only hope for stability in Iran was to empower the shah, Mohammed Pahlavi. The CIA conducted propaganda operations, but the new government was so ineffective that it would have fallen without the help of the United States. In the popular Iranian version of the story—the story that most Iranians believe today—the CIA launched a well-orchestrated coup against the government (B. Rubin, 2003). America looked on the shah as a friend, not realizing Iranians viewed America's actions as part of a long tradition of imperialism.

In an extensive account using primary sources, Dilip Hiro (1987, pp. 30–100) provides details of the shah's attempt to build his base and of his eventual failure. Once back in power in 1953, the shah formulated a plan to stay in power. Like his father, he believed that only modernization would lead to Iranian autonomy. Yet he also feared his own people. He created a secret military police force, **SAVAK**, to locate and destroy his enemies. SAVAK was aggressive.

SAVAK: Mohammed Pahlavi's secret police, established after the 1953 downfall of the democratic government.

The shah used a fairly effective strategy with SAVAK. Rather than taking on all his enemies at once, he became selective. He allied with one group to attack another group. SAVAK's enthusiasm for the torture and murder of political opponents complemented the policy. After 1953, the shah found it convenient to ally with the Shi'ite holy men, who welcomed the shah's support and turned a blind eye to SAVAK's activities. Charles Kurzman (2004, p. 126) points out that SAVAK's ruthless tactics, effective at first, would eventually fail.

The Western reforms of Iranian society were popular with the middle class—the members of which profited from modernization. The Shi'ite clergy, however, felt the increasing power of the state as Shi'ite influences and traditions were questioned or banned. From their seminary in the holy city of Qom, the clergy began to organize against the shah, but it was too late. The shah no longer needed the fundamentalists.

According to Hiro, by 1960, the shah's tenuous relationship with the fundamentalist clergy began to waver. This caused the clergy to organize demonstrations among theology students in Qom and marches of the faithful in Tehran. SAVAK infiltrated Shi'ite opposition groups in Tehran, and the army attacked Qom. There were thousands of arrests; demonstrators were ruthlessly beaten or, in some cases, shot in the streets. By 1963, many potential opponents were murdered, and the shah had many others in custody. One of his prisoners was the *hojatalislam* (master of Islam) **Ruhollah Khomeini**. In a gesture of mercy, the shah ordered Khomeini deported to Iraq instead of executing him. That proved to be a mistake.

Ruhollah Khomeini: (1900–1989) The Shi'ite grand ayatollah who was the leading figure in the 1979 Iranian Revolution. Khomeini toppled the shah's government and consolidated power by destroying or silencing his enemies, including other Shi'ite Islamic scholars. Iran was transformed into a theocracy under his influence.

The Revolution

Khomeini's rise to power was a key to the revolution. He was intolerant, not only of the shah's American infatuation, but of other Shi'ites who refused to accept his narrow interpretation of Islam. The shah and his father had been very successful in limiting the power of the clergy because of the popularity of Western-style reforms. The Shi'ite scholars wisely sidestepped the reforms and attacked the shah where he was most vulnerable, the apparent link to imperialism through America. Khomeini had spoken several times about the shah's love affair with America, and this raised the ire of common Iranians, to whom America seemed no different than their former Russian and British colonial masters (Esposito, 1999, pp. 60–66).

Khomeini's influence increased after he was arrested and deported in 1963. He was promoted to the rank of ayatollah and ran a campaign against the shah from Iraq. Under his leadership, the mosque came to be perceived as the only opposition to the shah and the hated SAVAK. Khomeini headed a network of 180,000 Islamic revolutionaries in addition to 90,000 mullahs (low-ranking prayer leaders), 5,000 hojatalislams (middle-ranking scholars), and 50 ayatollahs (recognized scholars with authoritative writings). The Shi'ite scholars were able to paint the shah in satanic terms, owing to his relations with the United States; they called for a holy revolution and the restoration of Islam. Khomeini led the way while in Iraqi exile (Wright, 2000, pp. 46–48; Kurzman, 2004, pp. 44–45).

Revolutionaries gained momentum after the election of Jimmy Carter as president of the United States in 1976. Carter pressured the shah to end SAVAK's human rights abuses. Fearful of losing American aid, the shah ordered SAVAK to ease off the opposition, increasing the ability of revolutionaries to operate inside Iran. There were many different groups: Secular socialists sought to topple the shah and remove Iran from the cold war. Communists wanted to shift allegiance to the Soviet Union. Many democrats wanted to create an Iranian democracy, and Shi'ite scholars sought to reintroduce religious values within a secular government. Khomeini, who viewed Carter as a manifestation of satanic power, felt no gratitude toward the United States. He wanted to create an Iranian theocracy with the majilis in charge of spiritual and temporal life. Increasing revolutionary activities from Iraq, Khomeini moved against the shah and other Iranian groups (Rasler, 1996) (Figure 8.2).

The shah pressured Saddam Hussein, then president of Iraq, to remove Khomeini, who was forced to flee Iraq in fear for his life. He received asylum in Paris, where, ironically, he was better able to control the revolution because Paris had a modern telephone system from which he could directly dial Tehran.

By 1977, Khomeini's revolutionary headquarters in Paris maintained an open telephone line to Tehran. Khomeini sent hundreds of revolutionary sermons to a

FIGURE **8.2** Iran

multiple-audiotape machine in Tehran, and his words were duplicated and delivered throughout the Iranian countryside. Khomeini's power increased dramatically (Wright, 2000, pp. 46–49).

Khomeini returned to Tehran in 1978. There was little the shah could do. Although he had unleashed SAVAK and ordered his troops to fire on street demonstrators, the public had risen against him. Several groups were vying for power, but Khomeini seemed to be on top. In February 1979, the shah fled Iran. Khomeini, riding victoriously through the streets of Tehran, was still faced with problems. It was necessary to eliminate all opposition if the Islamic revolution was to succeed. The starting point was to attack all things Western. In his first victory addresses, Khomeini was unrestrained as he called for world revolution. He said it was time to launch a holy war against the West and the traitors to Islam.

The Iranian Revolution of 1979 caused another form of terrorism to spread from the Middle East. Khomeini, filled with hatred for Saddam Hussein after having been driven from Iraq, was at first content to wage a conventional war with his neighbor. However, such direct tactics would not work against a superpower. The United States and the Soviet Union, if they dared to intervene, would be subjected to a lower-level form of warfare. Because the superpowers would win any war fought out in the open, the Ayatollah Khomeini chose to fight in the shadows (Esposito, 1999, pp. 17–20).

In 1982 Israel invaded Lebanon, moving through the Shi'ite areas of the south. Revolutionaries left Iran and traveled through Syria, brokering deals with the Syrians to assist them in resisting the Israelis. The Iranian Revolutionary Guard arrived in the Bekaa Valley and established the nucleus of a new type of revolutionary force, Hezbollah. It subsequently became a multifaceted organization with elements representing terrorism, social services, Lebanese politics, and a military wing of Iranian foreign policy (Esposito, 1999, 154–157).

The Call to Karbala

Khomeini used a mixture of repressive tactics and political strategies to consolidate his power in Iran, and he is best understood within the Shi'ite tradition of Islam. Although many Western observers believe the fanaticism of the revolution was due to a resurgence of fundamentalism, in reality it gained its intensity from the repressed lower classes of Iran emerging to practice their traditional religion.

As imperialism made its way into nineteenth-century Iran, public plays about Hussein ibn Ali's martyrdom at Karbala gained popularity. The emotional displays of Hussein's death at the hands of the Umayyads and his heroic acceptance of martyrdom became a Shi'ite equivalent of the Christian passion play. Such plays reinforced the distinction of the Shi'ites from all other religions, the uniquely Persian character of Iran, and the nobility of sacrifice for the sake of God (Armstrong, 2000b, pp. 299–319; see Rasler, 1996; Kurzman, 2001).

The Ayatollah Khomeini was guided by the message of Karbala, and he removed Islamic scholars and political leaders who disagreed with his message. He believed that the Iranian Revolution was the first step in purifying the world. Israel needed to be eliminated and returned to Islamic rule. The West was the handmaiden of the Jews, but the West remained the source of imperialism. Its influence was satanic and needed to be destroyed. Holy warriors were called to battle. After Khomeini's death in 1989, several competing schools of thought emerged in Iran. Although opposed by some Islamic scholars and almost all political moderates, a Khomeini-influenced majilis council came to dominate Iranian politics. It was guided by a belief that suggests the martyrdom of Karbala should be experienced every day. Many Islamic scholars rejected this notion, and a number of political analysts believed that most Iranians, although proudly and uniquely Persian, do not wish to usher in a new age of martyrdom (Kurzman, 2001).

Self-Check

> What social and political factors separate Iran from the Arab-dominated Middle East?
> How did British imperial policy help to shape modern Iran?
> How did reactions to Western policies influence the 1979 Iranian Revolution?

CHAPTER TAKE AWAYS

Terrorism in the Middle East is the result of historical processes, and the area is a cultural concept, not an actual place. Since extremists couch violence in religious terms, there is a brief summary of Islam for those who need it. Militants cite ibn Tayymiyya, Abdul Wahhab, and Qutb when justifying violence. Terrorism is the result of cultural and religious factors interacting with the birth of modern Israel, competition for power within and among Arab states, and the rise of militant religious fervor. Iran presents a set of separate issues, but its problems can also be linked to European imperialism.

OBJECTIVE SUMMARY

- The Middle East is a cultural concept. It can refer to a geographical area, but the boundaries are not distinct. The Middle East means different things to different people.
- Islam is one of the world's great monotheistic religions. Believers contend that God is revealed through prophets and that Mohammed was the last and greatest Prophet. God's holy law is revealed in the Quran, and Islamic law can be interpreted by the sayings and actions of Mohammed.
- Islam has many different branches. The two main branches—the Shi'ites and the Sunnis—initially split over the leadership of the Muslim community. Today, there are theological and structural differences.
- Militant interpretations of Islam developed as the Islamic world faced military, political, and economic crises. Some researchers believe that the disciples of ibn Taymiyyah and Abdul Wahhab were violent, but that these Islamic scholars were nonviolent reformers. Most Islamic scholars blame violent interpretations of the religion on Qutb.
- The collapse of the Ottoman Empire led to the dissolution of the caliphate. British and French forces divided the Middle East into spheres of influence after World War I. Zionist activists had purchased land in Palestine, and they sought to create a Jewish state. European actions led to the creation of modern Israel within the British sphere of influence, and the first modern terrorists were Zionist separatists in Palestine.
- The Arabs and Israelis engaged in a series of conventional wars from 1948 to 1973, and the Israelis demonstrated their military superiority in each one. After the devastating defeat of June 1967, some Palestinians turned to terrorism as a method of confronting Israeli military superiority.
- Modern Iran formed within the context of European imperialism. The British were instrumental in placing Iranian leaders on the throne, and the United States took their place after World War II. Iran disavowed the United States after the 1979 Iranian Revolution.

Critical Engagement: Nuclear Terrorism and the Future Middle East

Both Republican and Democratic administrations have vowed to keep Iran from developing nuclear weapons, and many policy makers feel that Israel will launch a military strike against Iran if it comes close to producing weapons-grade material, the material needed to create a nuclear bomb. Fareed Zakaria (2009) addresses the issue in several opinion pieces in *Newsweek* and other media outlets. Zakaria writes that it is not clear that Iranian leaders actually want a nuclear weapon. Over the past few years several leaders have plainly stated that it would not be in Iran's interest to build nuclear weapons, and the Ayatollah Khomeini declared that such weapons were un-Islamic. In 2004, the supreme religious leader of Iran issued a religious opinion stating that nuclear weapons were immoral. Zakaria believes that Iran wants nuclear power, but this does not automatically translate to a desire for nuclear weapons.

Zakaria (2010a, 2010b) also writes that even if this argument is incorrect, the United States can do little to stop Iran from building nuclear weapons. By the same token, Iran can be contained. He believes that there are signs of an emerging military dictatorship in Iran. While it is difficult to assess whether this will be better than rule by the mullahs, one thing is clear. Zakaria argues that military dictatorships make rational choices, and they choose survival over annihilation. Therefore, he concludes, Iran can be contained.

In the same article, he makes the point that many Americans stereotype Iranians. They are different, Americans believe. They embrace death, live for religious mysticism, and they will not engage the rest of the world. Experience in the early twenty-first century suggests otherwise. Iranian officials cooperated with the United States in a coalition against the Taliban; they helped form the Afghan government; and, when Israel warned Hezbollah not to fire missiles as it fought a 2008 war with Hamas, Iran kept Hezbollah under control. Despite American misconceptions, Iran can follow a rational foreign policy.

A nuclear Iran will not automatically lead to a nuclear weapons race in the Middle East, Zakaria believes, and it will not lead to nuclear-armed terrorists. American and Western policy should be based on containment and engagement. That is far more potent, he concludes, than bellicose rhetoric and the threat of war.

Consider these issues in terms of future developments:

- If Iran develops a nuclear weapon, what motivation would it have to supply a terrorist group with a nuclear weapon? If it did give a group a weapon and that group used it against Europe or the United States, what might happen to Iran?
- The Iranian president has stated that the Holocaust is a myth and that Israel has no right to exist. Israel has nuclear weapons and delivery systems. Iran does not. How does this reduce or increase the potential threat of nuclear terrorism?
- The Iranians tried to approach the United States during the first phases of America's war in Iraq. They were rebuffed. How effective is such a policy of rejection in reducing Middle Eastern terrorism and the possibility of a nuclear Iran? How do Zakaria's arguments apply to the situation?

KEY TERMS

Gulf States, p. 8-190
Mohammed ibn Abdul Wahhab, p. 8-196
Sayyid Qutb, p. 8-196
Taqi al Din ibn Taymiyyah, p. 8-196
Muslim Brotherhood, p. 8-197

Hassan al Banna, p. 8-198
Iranian Revolution, p. 8-198
Ottoman Empire, p. 8-199
Balfour Declaration, p. 8-202

Mandate of Palestine, p. 8-202
Baathist, p. 8-205
Six Day War, p. 8-205
Yom Kippur War, p. 8-206
Camp David Peace Accord, p. 8-206
Iran–Iraq War, p. 8-207

Reza Shah Pahlavi, p. 8-208
Mohammed Reza Pahlavi, p. 8-208
SAVAK, p. 8-209
Ruhollah Khomeini, p. 8-209

CHAPTER 9

Terrorism in Israel and Palestine

MAZEN MAHDI/EPA/Newscom

LEARNING OBJECTIVES

After reading this chapter, you should be able to:

> Describe the rise of Fatah and the Palestine Liberation Organization (PLO).

> Identify factional groups that emerged from squabbles among the Palestinians.

> Discuss the origins and growth of Hezbollah after the 1982 Israeli invasion of Lebanon.

> Explain the current political and military aspects of Hezbollah.

> Outline the impact of the first Intifada and the birth of Hamas.

> Describe the current operational capabilities of Hamas.

> Summarize the tactics of the al Aqsa Martyrs Brigades.

> Summarize controversial Israeli counterterrorist policies.

*N*ew York Times columnist Thomas Friedman (2012) made an astute observation about the Palestinian–Israeli conflict in the wake of the 2011 Arab spring. Israel is facing an unprecedented problem, Friedman writes, due to a series of populist uprisings that occurred in Tunisia, Egypt, Libya, and Syria in 2011. Islamist organizations are moving to replace ousted dictators, and the new political actors may not be willing to accept a peaceful standoff with Israel. This is especially true in Egypt. If violence were to escalate on the West Bank or other Palestinian-controlled area, other nations might become involved. This is a strong incentive, Friedman concludes, for Israel to seek a peaceful settlement of the conflict with the Palestinians. He believes it is time to create a Palestinian state.

The lessons of the Arab spring have not been lost on the Palestinians. Two of the revolutions in the Arab spring had been based on nonviolent confrontation with repressive forces. A dictatorship in Tunisia collapsed in the wake of massive protests and demonstrations. Egypt followed a similar pattern. To be sure, the political shifts in Tunisia and Egypt were accompanied by violence, but it was minimal compared to events in Libya and Syria. Peaceful confrontation against repressive forces worked.

By 2012 some Palestinian leaders were calling for nonviolent action. Friedman says that this is a crucial tipping point favoring the Palestinians. If the Palestinians were to follow the path of nonviolent confrontation, Israel would be placed in a bind. Should the country overreact to demonstrations, the new Islamist governments might be tempted to intervene. The time for peace, a negotiated settlement, and a Palestinian state has arrived, Friedman writes. These themes have been heard before, but political terrorism has been the dominant factor in Israel and Palestine for decades.

PLO from the Six Day War to the al Aqsa Intifada

Yasser Arafat:
(1929– 2004) The name assumed by Mohammed al Husseini. Born in Cairo, he was a founding member of Fatah and the PLO. He merged the PLO and Fatah in 1964 and ran a terrorist campaign against Israel. After renouncing terrorism and recognizing Israel's right to exist, Arafat was president of the Palestinian National Authority from 1993 to 2004.

In 1968 Cuba hosted revolutionary groups in a training session outside Havana (History Channel, 2000). Several leftist and nationalistic groups and individuals from around the world attended the event, including **Yasser Arafat** (1929–2004), the leader of the Palestine Liberation Organization (PLO). Arafat stated that revolution united all revolutionaries from the past to the present. He embraced other terrorists in the Cuban training camps and promised to join them in international revolution. It seemed to some that Arafat's organization could be part of an international conspiracy.

In reality, however, the PLO was a secular organization attempting to establish a government for displaced Palestinians. Some PLO members lived in Israel, some in Palestinian areas controlled by Israel, and some had simply moved to other countries, including a good number to Jordan. In 1957, Arafat gathered groups of disgruntled Palestinians in Jordan, forming the PLO in 1964. His purpose was to create a political organization to help form a multinational alliance against Israel. He hoped that Arab governments would jointly launch a war against the European-created state.

Fatah and the Six Day War

In 1959, Arafat formed Fatah, a guerrilla organization, to wage a campaign against the Israelis. He advocated the use of small-unit tactics and terrorist actions, patterned after the Irgun Zvai Leumi. Fatah's attacks were annoyances to Israel, but they did not represent a serious threat. Israel was more concerned about the large armies of its Arab neighbors. Frustrated, Arafat merged Fatah into the PLO in 1964.

Arafat's frustrations multiplied after the Six Day War in June 1967. After the Arab armies' sound defeat, Arafat's Fatah moved to center stage. An engineer educated in Cairo, the self-made leader of the PLO proposed terrorizing unfortified civilian targets (Wallach and Wallach, 1992). Using a group of Fatah warriors known as **fedayeen**, Arafat began to attack Israel. The initial media coverage of Fatah's attacks caused the PLO's status to rise throughout the Arab world, and Arafat's fortunes rose along with it. All the conventional Arab armies were in disarray. Only the PLO had the courage and will to strike, despite being outnumbered, outgunned, and without a country. They had only the fedayeen (Dawisha, 2003, pp. 256–257).

fedayeen: Warriors who sacrifice themselves. The term was used differently in Arab history; the modern term is used to describe the secular warriors of Fatah.

King Hussein:
(1935–1999) King of Jordan. King Hussein drove the PLO from Jordan in September 1970. After his death his son Abdullah assumed the throne.

Arafat conducted Fatah operations from Jordan, despite protests from Jordan's **King Hussein**. Fatah had only a few hundred fedayeen, but their numbers slowly increased, allowing Arafat to launch more raids against Israel. With the Arabs in complete military disarray, Fatah's reputation rose. Rival groups tried to outdo Arafat, but it was Fatah's attacks that drew Israel's attention, making Arafat a hero in Palestinian eyes and moving Fatah into the leading role (Nasr, 1997, pp. 44–45).

Fatah after Karamah

The hit-and-run strikes from Palestinian bases in Jordan drew protests from Israel. They demanded that King Hussein put a stop to Fatah's operations. King Hussein sympathized with Israel; in addition, he grew increasingly concerned over the growing militancy of Fatah. Still, he was afraid to act, fearing a rebellion among his own people if he moved against Fatah. Many Jordanians were of Palestinian origin, and they identified with the PLO. Israel, angered by a lack of action, decided to take matters into its own hands. On March 21, 1968, Israel sent a combined tank and mechanized infantry unit into Jordan to raid the Palestinians, backing the attack with helicopters and artillery.

Important Terms, Dates, Concepts, and People in the Middle East

Arab-Israeli Wars: A generic term for several wars

1948–1949: Israel's War of Independence

1956 Suez Crisis: Britain, France, and Israel attack Egypt to keep the Suez Canal open; Israel takes the Gaza Strip

1967 Six Day War: Pits Israel against its Arab neighbors; Israel takes Jerusalem, the West Bank, and other areas

1973 Yom Kippur War: Egypt and Syria strike Israel to regain occupied territories; Egypt is initially successful, but its major army is surrounded in a counterattack (Muslims frequently call it the Ramadan War)

Arafat, Yasser: Leader of the Palestine Liberation Organization (PLO), later the Palestine National Authority (PNA), and later still the Palestine National Council (PNC); widely recognized secular leader of the Palestinian movement

Baalbek: Lebanese city in the Bekaa Valley; original headquarters of Hezbollah

Camp David Peace Accords: 1978 peace agreement between Egypt and Israel

Dome of the Rock: The place where Muslims believe Abraham (Ibrahim) had a vision of God

Eretz Israel: The land of Israel under King David; many Jewish fundamentalists feel that God has called them to retake this land and expel the Arabs

Fedayeen: Warriors who sacrifice themselves and others

Gaza Strip: Palestinian strip of land along the Mediterranean

Golan Heights: Region in Syria overlooking Israel

Gush Emunim: Literally, "Bloc of the Faithful"; Jewish group formed in 1974 that believes that God literally promised Jews the Kingdom of David

Habash, George: Christian founder of the Popular Front for the Liberation of Palestine

Hawatmeh, Naiaf: One of the founders of the Popular Front for the Liberation of Palestine; later led the Democratic Front for the Liberation of Palestine

Interim Agreement: Follow-up to 1993 Oslo Accords in 1995 to allow elections in Palestinian territory

Intifada: 1987–1993 uprising in Palestinian areas; al Aqsa Intifada began in 2000

Jabril, Ahmed: Leader of the Popular Front for the Liberation of Palestine; later leader of the Popular Front for the Liberation of Palestine, General Command

Jewish settlements: Legal and illegal settlements in Palestinians lands; in 2004 Israeli Prime Minister Ariel Sharon proposed withdrawing from the Jewish settlements

Knesset: The Israeli parliament

Labor Party: The liberal Israeli political party

Likud Party: The conservative Israeli political party

Mossad: The Israeli intelligence service

Mujahedeen: Holy warriors

Muslim Brotherhood: An Islamic revivalist organization founded by Hassan al Banna in Cairo in 1928

Occupied territories: Initially, Palestinian territories under the post–World War I British division of Palestine; later occupied by Israel after the 1967 Six Day War

Palestinian diaspora: The displacement in 1948 of Palestinians living in Israel

Palestine Authority (PA): Semiautonomous body established after the Oslo Accords

Palestine National Council (PNC): Representative body from the occupied territories, the Gaza Strip, and the Palestinian diaspora

Peace process: Generic term used to describe efforts to create a lasting peace between Palestine and Israel as well as general peace in the region

Rabin, Yitzak: Israeli Labor Party leader, politician, and prime minister; assassinated in 1995 by a Jewish extremist for brokering a peace plan

(Continues)

Rejectionist Front: A group of individuals, political parties, and states that reject Israel's right to exist

Road Map for Peace: The term used by President George W. Bush while trying to bring peace to the Middle East, starting in 2002

Sharon, Ariel: Israeli military officer, defense minister, and prime minister; maintained a hard line against Palestinians

South Lebanon Army: The security force established by Israel to control south Lebanon after the withdrawal of the Israeli Defense Force in 1985

Sykes–Picot Agreement: A 1916 agreement between Britain and France for control of the Middle East

Tanzim: Fatah's militia

Temple Mount: The site of the ancient Jewish Temple, a former Christian church, and the al Aqsa mosque

Wailing Wall: The remaining western wall of the ancient Jewish Temple in Jerusalem

West Bank: The West Bank of the Jordan River, formerly controlled by Jordan; seized by Israel in the 1967 war

Wye Accords: 1998 Israeli–Palestinian agreement to abide by previous commitments

Zion: The hill on which Jerusalem stands

Zionist: In contemporary usage, a Jew wishing to reestablish the Jewish homeland; Arabs and many Muslims frequently use the term to refer to all Jews

---

The target of the Israeli action was fedayeen in the village of Karamah, a tiny refugee center. They had no intention of holding the town or maintaining operations in Jordan. Their plan was to conduct a fairly heavy hit-and-run operation of their own. As Israeli forces crossed Jordan's border, King Hussein ordered Jordanian tanks to counterattack. A tank battle ensued as the leading Israeli forces were hitting Karamah (Kometer, 2004, pp. 38–42).

Fedayeen grabbed their assault rifles and fought back. It seemed that they were going to be overrun when the Israelis pulled back. The Israelis had no intention of provoking a war with Jordan, and their tanks disengaged from the Jordanian counterattack. Infantry units in Karamah also pulled back, having lost their tank support. It was a small engagement, but the Israelis were retreating. Arafat became an overnight hero to the Arabs. That the Israelis had chosen to retreat and not be driven off was immaterial. The legend of the battle told of Fatah's fedayeen standing at Karamah and defeating the Israeli Defense Forces (IDF). No other Arab forces had been able to do that. Always one to strive for media attention, Arafat welcomed the role of the heroic commander of the fedayeen. Millions of donated dollars flowed into his coffers, making the PLO the most powerful Palestinian group—and corrupting the PLO leadership. Ironically, the Israeli raid on Karamah did not eliminate fedayeen; instead, it gave the PLO an aura of power. It would not be the last time an Israeli attack would backfire (Nasr, 1997, pp. 46–47; Dawisha, 2003, pp. 256–259).

The PLO Expelled

King Hussein of Jordan viewed the increasing strength of the PLO in his land with growing concern. He had entered the Six Day War against Israel with some reluctance and preferred to take a moderate stance in the pan-Arab struggle. Closely identified with British culture and friendly with the West, Jordan did not endorse the radicalism of Syria and other militant Arab states. King Hussein was especially wary of Syrian and Iraqi expansionist dreams and was more concerned with the protection of Jordan than with a united Arab realm (see Shlaim, 2001, pp. 298–299).

As the PLO grew, it drew closer to militant Arab states, giving them a potential base in Jordan. Concerned with the growing influence of foreign nationals in his own land, King Hussein ordered the PLO to stop attacking Israel. He was not trying to protect Israel; he was trying to stop the spread of rival influences in Jordan.

The PLO, though, was at an all-time high and not about to quit. Radical elements in Iraq and Syria encouraged Arafat to defy Hussein's order. Members of the Baath Party, the pan-Arab socialist movement with branches in Syria and Iraq, saw the PLO as a tool that could be used against the Israelis. More importantly, they came to view the organization as a weapon to help the cause of revolution and socialism among all the Arabs. Arafat defied Hussein's order and stepped up operations against Israel.

Arafat continued training in Jordanian PLO camps and invited revolutionaries throughout the Middle East to participate. His exiled Palestinian government took no orders from its Jordanian host. Raids against Israel were conducted by a variety of PLO and foreign terrorist groups, and Arafat's reputation as a revolutionary hero spread beyond the Middle East. This became too much for King Hussein. After Palestinian terrorists hijacked three airplanes and destroyed them in Jordan, the king decided to act. In September 1970, Hussein attacked the PLO.

Arafat and the PLO were taken completely by surprise. The PLO terrorist offensive against Israel had worked because the terrorists operated in base camps that, although subject to Israeli attack, were relatively immune from annihilation. This was not the case when King Hussein's Jordanian army struck; the PLO had nowhere to run. As Jordanian regulars bombarded PLO camps and launched an all-out assault, Arafat had no alternative. Too weak to stand and fight, he fled to southern Lebanon. It was his only option.

Black September and Munich

Arafat blamed the Israelis for King Hussein's actions, and he wanted to strike back. He could not control terrorists in the many PLO splinter groups, so he created a new group after King Hussein's September attack. He called the group Black September. Using German leftist allies, Black September began planning a strike against the Israelis. It came, with German terrorist help, in Munich at the 1972 Olympic Games. Black September struck the Olympic Village and took most of the Israeli Olympic team hostage, killing those who tried to escape. German police moved in, and the world watched a drawn-out siege.

Black September terrorists negotiated transportation to Libya, but while they were on the way to the aircraft designated to fly them from Germany, the German police launched a rescue operation. Plans immediately went awry. Reacting quickly, terrorists machine-gunned their hostages before the German police could take control. The Israeli hostages and a German police officer were killed. It was a terrorist victory, and European leftists and nationalists saw it as partly their triumph (Shalev, 2006).

The 1982 Invasion of Lebanon

In southern Lebanon the mainstream PLO under Arafat became a fairly autonomous and potent force. Farther to the north, nationalistic Lebanese Christian and Islamic militias opposed each other as well as the Palestinians and foreign interests. Syria backed its own militia in the hope of increasing its influence in Lebanon, and Iran joined the fighting after the revolution of 1979, establishing a new terrorist organization called Islamic Jihad. Endemic civil war raged in Lebanon as dozens of terrorists slipped across the border to attack Israel (see Nasr, 1997, pp. 125–135; Creed, 2002).

By 1982, the Israelis had had enough. On June 6, a massive three-pronged IDF force invaded Lebanon. The PLO and other militias moved forward to take a stand, but they were no match for the coordinated efforts of IDF tanks, aircraft, and infantry. The Israelis rolled through Lebanon. Soon they were knocking on the doors of Beirut, and Lebanon's civil war seemed to be over.

Surrounded and bombarded by the Israelis in Beirut, even as the Syrian-backed forces fought the IDF, Arafat knew that the Syrians had no love for him. If the Israelis won, Arafat would be doomed. If the Syrians won, they intended to install their own surrogates in place of the PLO. In August 1982, Arafat left Beirut for Tripoli with 14,000 fedayeen. More than 10,000 guerrillas stayed, but they joined the Syrians.

Self-Check

> Explain the emergence of Fatah from the Six Day War.
> How did Karamah and the Jordanian offensive change Fatah?
> What impact did the 1982 invasion of Lebanon have on Palestinians?

Factionalism in Palestinian Terrorism

Sabri al Banna: (1937–2002) The real name of Abu Nidal. Al Banna was a founding member of Fatah but split with Arafat in 1974. He founded militias in southern Lebanon, and he attacked Western and Israeli targets in Europe during the 1980s. In the 1990s, he became a mercenary. He was murdered in Iraq, probably by the Iraqi government.

Intifada: The first spontaneous uprising against Israel, lasting from 1987 to 1993. It began with youths throwing rocks and creating civil disorder. Some of the violence became more organized. Many people sided with religious organizations, abandoning the secular PLO during the Intifada.

Black June: The rebel organization created by Abu Nidal in 1976. He changed the name to the Fatah Revolutionary Council after a rapprochement with Syria in 1981. Most analysts refer to this group simply as the Abu Nidal Organization.

From 1967 to 1982, the PLO was characterized by internal splintering. Arafat found that he could not retain control of the military wing, and several groups split from it. These groups included the Democratic Front for the Liberation of Palestine; the Popular Front for the Liberation of Palestine; and the Popular Front for the Liberation of Palestine, General Command. Another notable defector, **Sabri al Banna,** created the Abu Nidal Organization, a group that evolved into a global mercenary organization (see Seale, 1992; Gordon, 1999). Kameel Nasr (1997, p. 46) concludes that all of these groups were at their best when they fought each other.

New groups formed after the 1982 invasion of Lebanon. Unable to tolerate Israel's presence in the area, the Syrians rallied all local militias, and accepted help from Iran. A new group, Hezbollah, began forming in Lebanon. A popular uprising in 1987, the **Intifada,** gave rise to a new group, Hamas. As Hamas challenged the PLO for power, Arafat disavowed terrorism in 1988 and called for peace. A second Intifada in 2000 created even more groups. The conflict between the Israelis and Palestinians has spawned a multitude of differing organizations.

In order to place the many divisions in context, the next section lists the dominant groups within the context of the Israeli–Palestinian struggle. You may wish to use this as a quick reference when examining terrorism in Israel and Palestine. Succeeding sections will focus on the current activities of the three dominant groups: Hezbollah, Hamas, and the al Aqsa Martyrs Brigades.

Listing Major Groups

Abu Nidal Organization (Black June): Sabri al Banna (whose code name was Abu Nidal) and Yasser Arafat were once comrades in arms in the struggle for Palestine, but as others broke from Arafat, so too did Abu Nidal's rebel organization, called **Black June.** In the end, Abu Nidal and his organization became a mercenary group, not only abandoning Arafat but also completely forsaking the Palestinian cause. The group's international exploits drew more attention than did those of its rival terrorist organizations as Nidal conducted ruthless operations in the 1980s, including:

• The murder of Jordanian ambassadors in Spain, Italy, and India
• Raids on Jewish schools in Antwerp, Istanbul, and Paris
• Attacks on airports in Rome and Vienna
• Assassinations of PLO leaders in Tunis
• The attempted assassination of the Israeli ambassador to the United Kingdom
• An attack on a synagogue in Istanbul

The Abu Nidal Organization evolved into an international group operating in more than 20 countries. It faded from significance by the 1990s, and Abu Nidal was murdered in Iraq in 2003.

al Aqsa Intifada: An uprising sparked by Ariel Sharon's visit to the Temple Mount with a group of armed escorts in September 2000. The area is considered sacred to Jews, Christians, and Muslims. Muslims were incensed by the militant aspect of Sharon's visit because they felt he was invading their space with an armed group. Unlike the 1987 Intifada, the al Aqsa Intifada has been characterized by suicide bombings.

Al Aqsa Martyrs Brigades: The al Aqsa Martyrs Brigades are based in West Bank refugee camps. Formed after the beginning of the **al Aqsa Intifada**, the Brigades appear to be Fatah's answer to the jihadists. Some members are motivated by Hezbollah, suggesting to some analysts that the Brigades have Shi'ite elements. Other analysts think that the Brigades are Fatah's attempt to take the Intifada's leadership away from Hamas and the Palestinian Islamic Jihad (PIJ). The Brigades were organized along military lines and became one of the first secular groups in the Middle East to use suicide bombers. Many experts believe that Arafat either directly controlled the Brigades or that they operated with his approval. A command council is responsible for leadership, and terrorist operations are divided into six geographical areas. If Yasser Arafat controlled the Brigades, members directly violated his orders on several occasions. The division commanders control the rank-and-file members, not the command council.

Black September: Named after the September 1970 Jordanian offensive against Palestinian refugees in western Jordan, Black September was the infamous group that attacked the Israeli athletic team at the 1972 Munich Olympics. Israel spent years hunting down and killing the members of Black September. The 1972 attack also prompted the Germans to create a new elite counterterrorist group, Federal Border Guard Group 9 (GSG-9), headed by Ulrich Wegener.

Democratic Front for the Liberation of Palestine (DFLP): A Christian, Naiaf Hawatmeh, created the DFLP in 1969 when he broke away from the Popular Front for the Liberation of Palestine. This Marxist-Leninist group seeks a socialist Palestine and was closely associated with the former Soviet Union. In 2000, the group joined Arafat in Washington, D.C., to negotiate with Israeli Prime Minister Ehud Barak. As a reward, the U.S. Department of State took the DFLP off its list of terrorist groups. The DFLP currently limits its attacks to the IDF.

Fatah: Fatah began as the military wing of the former PLO and was Yasser Arafat's strongest military muscle. Formed in the early stages of the PLO, Fatah was part of an underground organization formed in 1959. It emerged in the open in 1965 after making terrorist attacks against Israel in 1964. Fatah rose to prominence after the 1967 Six Day War because it became the only means of attacking Israel. Fatah fought the Jordanians for ten days in September 1970 and regrouped in Lebanon. It joined in the Lebanese Civil War (1975–1990) and was eventually expelled to Tunisia. In the first Intifada (1987–1993), Fatah Hawks, political militants in the PLO, organized street demonstrations and disturbances, but emerging religious groups threatened Fatah's leadership among the militant Palestinian groups. Fatah went to the bargaining table in Oslo in 1993 and joined the peace process. It currently holds the majority of seats in the Palestinian government. Although it is now a political party, many analysts associate it with the al Aqsa Martyrs Brigades. The Tanzim Brigade and Force 17 come from the ranks of Fatah, and it has traditionally championed Palestinian nationalism over ideology or religion.

Force 17: Officially known as Presidential Security, Force 17 is an arm of Fatah. It operated as Yasser Arafat's security unit.

Hamas: In December 1987, a few days after the first Intifada began, the Islamic Resistance Movement (Harakat al Muqawama al Islamiyya, or Hamas) was formed. It was composed of the Palestinian wing of the Muslim Brotherhood. The Brothers advocated an international Islamic movement, and most of them did not support violence. Hamas differs from the Brothers' position in that it has localized the Islamic struggle and accepts violence as a norm. Hamas is organized as a large political union, and its primary mission is to oppose the PLO; today, it represents an alternative to the Palestine National Council. Its military wing is called the Izz el Din al Qassam Brigades, named for a martyr in the 1935 Arab Revolt against the British in Palestine. In 2004, Israel assassinated Hamas's spiritual leader, Sheik Ahmed Yassin. As soon as Hamas appointed a new leader, the Israelis killed him, too. Hamas is a large organization, but its terrorist wing is rather small. Frequently allied with the PIJ, Hamas competes with other Fatah organizations.

Hezbollah: Hezbollah is the Iranian-backed Party of God, operating from southern Lebanon. The local branch of the group forms alliances of convenience with other organizations participating in the al Aqsa Intifada. The international branch is believed to run the most effective terrorist network in the world.

Palestinian Islamic Jihad (PIJ): A small group emerging from the Muslim Brotherhood in Egypt in 1979, forming in the Gaza Strip in 1981. Whereas the Brothers spoke of an international Islamic awakening, the PIJ felt that the struggle could be nationalized and had to become violent. The PIJ leaders were enamored with the 1979 Iranian Revolution, and even though they were Sunnis, they sought contact with Iran's revolutionary Shi'ites. The PIJ operates out of the Gaza Strip and forms alliances of convenience with other organizations. It has grown closer to Hamas since the al Aqsa Intifada. The PIJ seeks to destroy Israel and establish an Islamic state in Palestine.

The group has strong links to the United States. In 2003, the U.S. Department of Justice (2003) took actions against the PIJ in Florida. The Justice Department argued that the group had an organized network of financial supporters around the world, including in the United States, and it brought charges against a professor at the University of South Florida for supporting the PIJ as part of that network. Another government report (U.S. Navy, 2008) cites multiple financial structures as another source of strength. Its presence in a multitude of countries leads to a number of funding sources. These funds have allowed the PIJ to remain in the field and to join Hamas in intermittent rocket attacks against Israel. Many analysts believe that the majority of funding comes from Iran, and that the group is still shielded by Syria. They also believe that Hezbollah provides most of the training (Non-State Armed Groups, 2008).

Palestine Liberation Front (PLF): Three different groups call themselves the Palestine Liberation Front: The Abu Abbas faction, based in Iran, follows the old-style leadership used by Arafat; the Abdal Fatah Ghanem faction received support from Libya; and the Talat Yaqub faction sought favor with Syria. The name used by all three groups comes from Ahmed Jabril, a former Syrian army captain, who formed the first PLF in 1961. After the Six Day War in June 1967, the PLF merged with two small radical groups to form the Popular Front for the Liberation of Palestine, but Jabril broke away and formed the Popular Front for the Liberation of Palestine, General Command . The PFLP-GC split in 1977 after Syria backed Lebanese Christians in the Lebanese Civil War (1975–1990), and the anti-Syrians formed a new group, reviving the PLF name.

The PLF had yet another internal war in 1984, and Abu Abbas, a militant leader who rebelled against Syria, returned one faction to Arafat, expelling all Syrian influence. Abdal Fatah Ghanem broke from Abbas and sided with Syria. His group remained active in Lebanon. Talat Yaqub tried to remain neutral. After Abdal Fatah Ghanem died of a heart attack, his faction gravitated toward Libyan support. All three factions of the PLF seek to destroy Israel. The PLF's most notorious action was the hijacking of an Italian luxury liner, the *Achille Lauro*, in 1985. American forces captured the hijackers, but Abu Abbas was released. He went to the Gaza Strip and eventually to Iraq. He was captured during the U.S. invasion of Iraq in 2003 and died in captivity.

Popular Democratic Front for the Liberation of Palestine (PDFLP): The PDFLP is the military wing of the DFLP.

Popular Front for the Liberation of Palestine (PFLP): The PFLP is a Marxist-Leninist Arab nationalist group that emerged after the June 1967 Six Day War. Egypt initially supported the PFLP but withdrew financing in 1968 when PFLP leaders criticized the Egyptian president. Operating in Lebanon under the command of Wadi Hadad, the PFLP began attacking Israeli airliners in 1968. In 1970, the group staged four hijackings in a six-day period; three of the planes were destroyed in the Jordanian desert in front of international media. Because the PFLP was closely linked to Arafat's Fatah, the Jordanians drove Arafat from their territory in September 1970. In 1975, it allied with Carlos the Jackal, a Latin American terrorist, and the Red Army Faction, a left-wing terrorist group in Germany, to attack an oil ministers' conference in Vienna. Although the PFLP has been successful at times, it has been riddled with factionalism. The first splits came in 1968 and 1969 when Ahmed Jabril and George Habash broke from the PFLP. Wadi Hadad left the organization in 1976 when the Palestine National Council disavowed the use of terrorism outside the vicinity of Israel and the territories it occupied. He formed the Popular Front for the Liberation of Palestine, General Command, but died in 1978. Habash returned to the PFLP in 1976 and directed the campaign against Israel. He eventually reconciled with Fatah and handed leadership over to Abu Ali Mustafa in 2000. Mustafa was assassinated by the Israelis in August 2001. Ahmed Sadat, his successor, retaliated by killing an Israeli official. The PFLP has grown in stature since the al Aqsa Intifada.

Popular Front for the Liberation of Palestine, General Command (PFLP-GC): The PFLP was formed in 1967 when George Habash agreed to ally his group with Ahmed Jabril's PLF. Habash, a Christian, assumed leadership of the group, but he soon clashed with the Syrian-oriented Jabril. Syria continued to court Jabril, and he broke from Habash in 1968 to form the PFLP-GC. The PFLP-GC advocates armed struggle with Israel; it became one of the most technically sophisticated organizations in the region. It originally operated from southern Lebanon with support from Syria. By the late 1980s, the PFLP-GC was following the lead of the Abu Nidal Organization and renting its services to various governments. Some analysts believe the group was behind various international airline bombings. The PFLP-GC has been eclipsed by suicide bombers since 2000, but Jabril is increasingly emphasizing religion. This places the PFLP-GC closer to jihadist groups, but it still remains one of the most technically sophisticated terrorist organizations in the area. Jabril has always favored military action over sensationalized terrorist events.

Tanzim Brigade: Claiming not to be directly involved in terrorism, the Tanzim Brigade is the militia wing of Fatah.

Self-Check
> What factors led to the breakup of the Palestinian movement?
> How did Hezbollah become involved in the conflict?
> When did Hamas form?

Hezbollah: Local and International

Hezbollah is one of the more enigmatic organizations in the Middle East due to the manner in which it was formed, its historical metamorphosis, and its desire to play a leading role in Lebanon's politics. It grew out of the Iranian Revolution (1978–1979) and maintains close links with Iran. Some analysts argue that it is an instrument of Iranian foreign power, but others insist that Tehran does not and cannot control the organization (Perry, 2010, p. 143). A former deputy secretary of state referred to Hezbollah as the deadliest terrorist group in the world and some officials link it to al Qaeda (Byman, 2003 and Kaplan, 2006). Others note that Hezbollah suicide attacks peaked in the period 1985–1986, and al Qaeda has denounced the group (Perlinger, 2006). Although it is most frequently associated with violence in Lebanon and Israel, Hezbollah has an international wing believed to be based in Damascus. It has also created the organizational style that jihadist groups such as the Egyptian Islamic Group, the Egyptian Islamic Jihad, the Armed Islamic Group in Algeria, and al Qaeda would use.

The Origins of Hezbollah

Hezbollah is a configuration of political actors from the 1979 Iranian Revolution and the Shi'ite community of southern Lebanon. Its roots can be traced to a desire to export revolutionary ideals from Iran and Shi'ite emancipation in Lebanon. The linkage of the two came through Syria's desire to build both a relationship with Iran and to control politics in Lebanon. This configuration is complex but logical. The story begins in southern Lebanon after Israel's 1982 invasion.

Shi'ites dominated southern Lebanon. They thought the Israelis would free them from Christian and Sunni domination, but this did not happen. Augustus Norton (2009, p. 33) believes that young Lebanese Shi'ites would eventually have attempted to copy the Iranian Revolution without the Israeli invasion, but the attack made it inevitable.

Revolutionary Guards:
The militarized quasi-police force of the revolutionary government during the Iranian Revolution.

The Israeli invasion of Lebanon created an unlikely alliance among Iran's **Revolutionary Guards,** secular Syrian Baathists, and southern Lebanese Shi'ites. Iran's foreign policy under the Ayatollah Khomeini's Revolutionary Guards was designed to spread religious revolutionary thought throughout the Muslim world. On the surface, the fervently religious Khomeini had little in common with the secular socialists in Syria, but the Syrians were supporting Shi'ites in southern Lebanon. When Israeli tanks rolled through southern Lebanon, they passed through Shi'ite villages, and the Revolutionary Guards begged the Ayatollah Khomeini for a chance to protect their fellow believers in Lebanon. Secular Syria and religious Iran now had a common enemy.

Both nations needed a surrogate to fight the Israelis. If Iran openly intervened in the Lebanese Civil War (1975–1990), Israel or the United States might attack Iran. Syria also needed a proxy because its troops were no match for the IDF and, like Iran, it feared the United States. As Shi'ite militias resisted the Israeli invasion, religious leaders thought resistance should be based on faith and not on secular politics.

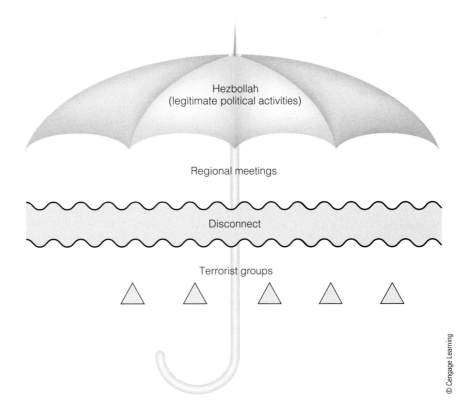

© Cengage Learning

FIGURE **9.1** Hezbollah Umbrella, circa 1985

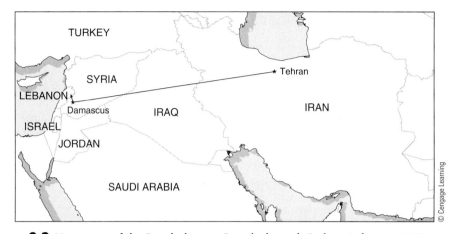

FIGURE **9.2** Movement of the Revolutionary Guards through Syria to Lebanon, 1982

The Revolutionary Guards joined with local Shi'ites to form confederated militia groups. The movement gradually became known as Hezbollah, or the Party of God (Harik, 2004, pp. 39–49).

They were not well organized at first (see Figure 9.1). Hezbollah began as a social movement gravitating around young Shi'ites ready to resist the Israelis. Initially, it was little more than an idea, but small unorganized groups began to fight. Their attacks were characterized by extreme violence and heated rhetoric. It was the beginning of a metamorphosis (Azani, 2009, pp. 2–3, 47–48).

Iranian officials made contact with the Syrians in 1982. Promising reduced oil prices to Syria, the Iranians asked for permission to move 1,000 Revolutionary Guards from Syrian territory across its borders and into the Bekaa Valley in eastern Lebanon. The Revolutionary Guards made connections with the emerging Hezbollah and provided the Lebanese Shi'ite group with money, weapons, and training. Both Syria and Iran wanted to maintain their distance, and the religious leaders of Hezbollah wanted to deny any affiliation with military action. As a result, Hezbollah became a terrorist organization like one no one had ever seen before (see Hiro, 1987, pp. 113–181, 240–243; Taheri, 1987; Kurz, 1994; Wege, 1994; Ranstorp, 1994, 1996).

Hezbollah grew from a council of Shi'ite scholars who claimed to be part of a spiritual movement. Its structure—really, lack of structure—simply developed because no one was in charge. In essence, the council became a large umbrella for semi-autonomous groups that were buoyed by the council's charisma and sheltered by its protection. Syrian and Iranian money and supplies poured into the council, and Hezbollah denied any direct connection with the network gathering under its umbrella. Below the umbrella, several Shi'ite cells operated autonomously and received money, weapons, and ideas through hidden channels linked with the spiritual leaders. The leadership also formed alliances with two Lebanese Shi'ite groups, claiming to be a religious movement designed to support Lebanon's Shi'ite community (Gambill and Abdelnour, 2002).

During the first few years of its existence, Hezbollah acted more or less like a terrorist clearinghouse (Reuters, 1996; Azani, 2009, p. 47). Influenced by Iran, Hezbollah met as an independent organization, always willing to deny its Iranian connections. Hezbollah developed under the leadership of three central figures: **Sheik Mohammed Hassan Fadlallah, Abbas Musawi,** and **Hassan Nasrallah** (Norton, 2009, pp. 33–35; see Israeli Foreign Ministry, 1996). Fadlallah, the target of an attempted U.S.-sponsored assassination, was a charismatic spiritual leader. Musawi provided the loose connections to Iran. Nasrallah was a practical militarist, organizing Hezbollah into a regional force.

Sheik Mohammed Hassan Fadlallah: (1935–2010) A grand ayatollah and leader of Shi'ites in Lebanon. The spiritual leader of Hezbollah. He was the target of a 1985 U.S.-sponsored assassination plot that killed 75 people.

Abbas Musawi: (1952–1992) A leader of Hezbollah, who was killed with his family in an Israeli attack in 1992.

Hassan Nasrallah: (b. 1960) The secretary-general of Hezbollah. He took over the leadership of Hezbollah after Musawi's death in 1992. Nasrallah is a lively speaker and charismatic leader.

TIMELINE 9.1	*Phases of Hezbollah*

1982–1985, Organizing	Different groups carry out attacks under a variety of names.
1985–1990, Kidnapping and bombing	A terrorist organization is created.
1990–2000, Legitimacy	The group organizes social services, a political party, and a military wing.
2000–2004, Coalition	Hezbollah forms temporary alliances with others in the September 2000 Palestinian uprising against Israel (the al Aqsa Intifada).
July 2006	Israel launches offensive in Lebanon.
August 2006	Israel withdraws, Hezbollah claims victory.
September 2006	Iran begins to rebuild Lebanese infrastructure.

In phase one of the development of Hezbollah, from 1982 to 1985 (see Timeline 9.1, "Phases of Hezbollah"), the Hezbollah umbrella covered many terrorist groups, including a shadowy organization known as Islamic Jihad. According to Amir Taheri (1987), Hezbollah leaders met in the city of Baalbek in Lebanon's Bekaa Valley and issued vague "suggestions" to Islamic Jihad. They also provided financial and logistical support for terrorist operations but kept themselves out of the day-to-day affairs of the terrorist group. By keeping their distance, Hezbollah's leaders were able to claim that they had no direct knowledge of Islamic Jihad. More important, though, they were able to keep Iran from being directly linked to Islamic Jihad's terrorist campaign against Israel and the West. The tactic was successful, and other groups formed under the umbrella.

After 1985, Hezbollah began to change. As part of an organization designed to spread the Shi'ite revolution, Hezbollah was not content to act only as an umbrella group to support terrorism (Enteshami, 1995; Reuters, 1996). Its leaders wanted to develop a revolutionary movement similar to the one that gripped Iran in 1978 and 1979. Lebanon was inundated with several militias fighting for control of the government, and Nasrallah saw an opportunity. Following the pattern of the Amal militia, he began changing the structure of Hezbollah. In 1985, he established regional centers, transforming them into operational bases between 1987 and 1989.

After introducing suicide bombers in its initial phase, Hezbollah struck U.S. Marines and the French army in October 1983, forcing the withdrawal of a multinational peacekeeping force. The Marine-barracks bombing resulted in the deaths of 200 Marines, and a second suicide bomber killed 50 French soldiers. In its second phase, Hezbollah's leadership launched a kidnapping campaign in Beirut. Westerners, especially Americans, were taken hostage, but Hezbollah, as always, denied any affiliation with the group conducting the operation.

Tactics were extremely effective in the first two phases. Suicide actions and other bombings disrupted Lebanon. The U.S. embassy was targeted for a bomb attack, and Hezbollah managed to kill the top six CIA operatives in the Middle East. Two of Hezbollah's kidnappings were simply designed to murder the victims. Hezbollah kidnapped, tortured, and murdered the CIA station chief in Beirut, as well as a marine colonel working for the United Nations. Judith Harik (2004, p. 37) points out that no evidence directly linked Hezbollah to these actions, and the group denied links to terrorism, denouncing terrorism as a tactic. This strategy made the group extremely effective.

The third phase of Hezbollah's metamorphosis came in 1990. Taking over the organization after the death of Musawi, Nasrallah created a regional militia by 1990. In 1991, many of Lebanon's roving paramilitary groups signed a peace treaty, but Hezbollah retained its weapons and revolutionary philosophy and became the primary paramilitary force in southern Lebanon. It claimed to be a legitimate guerrilla force, resisting the Israeli occupation of the area. Hezbollah's militia, however, soon found itself in trouble. Squabbling broke out among various groups, and Hezbollah was forced to fight Syria and Islamic Amal. Diplomatic pressure increased for the release of hostages. Nasrallah took bold steps in response. He sought peace with the Syrians, and with Syrian approval, Western hostages were gradually released. Far from claiming responsibility for the hostages, both Hezbollah and Syria claimed credit for gaining their freedom. Hezbollah's militia began to operate in the open, and it stepped up its campaign against the Israelis in Lebanon. This made the organization popular among Lebanese citizens and gave the group the appearance of a guerrilla unit (see Azani, 2009, pp. 105–135).

ANOTHER PERSPECTIVE

Nasrallah's Management of Image

What is Hezbollah? Judith Harik (2004) says the answer to this question depends on the audience. For the four audiences below, Hassan Nasrallah has four different answers.

1. *Jihadists:* He uses militant language and speaks of holy war.
2. *Nationalists:* He avoids jihad analogies and calls on Sunnis, Shi'ites, Christians, and secularists to fight for Lebanon.

3. *Pan-Arabic:* He points to Israel as a colony of the West and denounces Europe's imperial past.
4. *International:* He cites UN resolutions and claims that Israel violates international law.

Harik concludes that this is not the pattern of an intolerant religious fanatic. Instead, this ability to compromise for various purposes demonstrates Nasrallah's political skills.

Source: Harik, 2004.

Nasrallah had one more trump card. With the blessing of fellow council members, Hezbollah joined the Lebanese political process. Hezbollah's fourth phase brought the organization out of the shadows. Its militia, operating as a guerrilla force, repeatedly struck the Israelis in Lebanon. The success of this action brought political payoffs, and by 1995 Hezbollah developed strong political bases of support in parts of Beirut, the Bekaa Valley, and its stronghold in southern Lebanon. It created a vast organization of social services, including schools, hospitals, and public works. This final change worked. In 1998, Hezbollah won a number of seats in Beirut while maintaining control of the south. When Palestinians rose up against the Israelis in 2000, Hezbollah embraced their cause, and its transformation was complete (see *Another Perspective: Nasrallah's Management of Image*). It was a nationalistic group with a military wing, and its stated goals were to eliminate Israel and to establish an Islamic government in Lebanon.

Mark Perry (2010, pp. 141–162) questions conventional approaches to Hezbollah. He argues that the United States bases its view of Hezbollah on stereotypes. Its political leaders do not deny that they manage an armed group, but they claim no responsibility for kidnappings and bombings in the 1980s. Leaders also admit that they are allied with Iran, yet Hezbollah is distinctively Lebanese. After Hezbollah forced Israel to retreat from Lebanon in 2006, its popularity soared. Its goal is to become a force in Lebanese politics.

Hezbollah's Operational Capabilities

By the end of the twentieth century, Hezbollah became one of the strongest nonstate groups in the Middle East (Ranstorp, 1994). It became the most technologically sophisticated nonstate actor in the first decade of the twenty-first century (Perry, 2010, p. 162). Its leaders are associated with the Shi'ite seminary in Najaf, Iraq. It is organized in three directorates: a political wing, a social services wing, and a security wing (see Figure 9.3). A separate international group, Hezbollah International, operates outside the domestic structure (J. Goldberg, 2002). Its former leader, master terrorist **Imad Mugniyah**, was killed in Damascus in 2008. A weak Lebanese government allows Hezbollah to maintain strongholds in southern Lebanon, the Bekaa Valley, and central pockets in Beirut. Each directorate is subservient to the Supreme Council, currently headed by Hassan Nasrallah.

Most of Hezbollah's activities deal with the politics of Lebanon and the vast social service network it maintains in the south. The security wing is based in Lebanon and is responsible for training guerrillas and terrorists. (Supporters of Hezbollah do not make a distinction between *guerrilla* and *terrorist*.) Guerrillas are assigned to militias that operate along Israel's northern border, especially in the **Shaba farm region**. These paramilitary fighters frequently conduct operations in the open, and they engage in conventional military confrontations with the IDF. Hezbollah can maintain all of these operations because it receives funding from Iran.

Terrorists also operate along the border with and sometimes inside Israel, engaging in murder and kidnapping. Although Israel is their acknowledged enemy, Hezbollah terrorists have targeted Lebanese Christians and other Arabs unsympathetic to their cause. The primary terrorist tactic is bombing, and Hezbollah has mastered two forms: suicide bombing and radio-controlled bombs for ambushes. Gilles Kepel (2004, p. 34), a specialist in French and Middle Eastern terrorism, believes Hezbollah suicide bombings are directly related to the Shi'ite emphasis on martyrdom.

Hezbollah's international branch appears to have three major functions:(1) In Europe and in the United States, Hezbollah raises money to support operations (*United States of America v. Mohamad Youseff Hammoud et al.*, 2002). (2) Iran uses Hezbollah as an extension of its own power. Hezbollah protects Iranian interests in Lebanon and projects an Iranian-influenced military presence in other parts of the Middle East. Hezbollah also acts as a buffer between Iran and Israel (Byman, 2003).

Imad Mugniyah: (1962–2008) The leader of the international branch of Hezbollah. He has been implicated in many attacks, including the 1983 U.S. Marine and French paratrooper bombings. He is also believed to have been behind bombings of the U.S. embassy in Beirut and two bombings of Israeli targets in Argentina. He was assassinated in Damascus in February 2008.

Shaba farm region: A small farming region in southwest Lebanon annexed by Israel in 1981. When Israel withdrew from southern Lebanon in 2000, it remained in the Shaba farm region, creating a dispute with Lebanon, Hezbollah, and Syria.

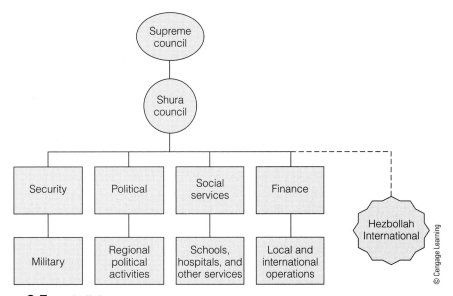

FIGURE **9.3** Hezbollah

(3) Hezbollah has established a strong presence in South America. It uses this base to raise funds through legitimate and illegitimate methods, conduct propaganda, and launch terrorist operations. Should the United States and Iran enter a war, South American members of Hezbollah plan to attack the United States (Gato and Windrem, 2007).

According to Jeffery Goldberg (2002), then writing for the *New Yorker*, Hezbollah International is a shadowy group, and the Supreme Council denies its existence. The international section has cells in several different countries, including the United States, and maintains an extensive international finance ring partially based on smuggling, drugs, and other criminal activity. Imad Mugniyah kept close ties with operatives in the Triborder region and Ciudad del Este and also ran a terrorist training camp off the coast of Venezuela. Mugniyah met with al Qaeda, possibly Osama bin Laden, in the mid-1990s and allegedly taught al Qaeda terrorists methods for attacking buildings.

Scott Macleod (2008) of *Time* has no doubt that Mugniyah was a deadly terrorist. According to one former CIA agent, he was one of the worst the United States has ever faced. The links to Hezbollah are not as clear. Mugniyah certainly had some type of contact with Hezbollah, though the extent of it is unknown. Hezbollah's leaders deny any involvement in Mugniyah's activities. Perhaps he was one of the autonomous operators working independently from the leadership council in Hezbollah's early days. Most analysts do not accept this. They believe that he headed Hezbollah's international wing.

In 2006, Israel launched a month-long attack against Hezbollah in Lebanon and was surprised by the results. Far from operating as a small terrorist organization, Hezbollah fielded thousands of fighters and recruited more. Regardless of its international wing, Hezbollah has transmogrified into a militia capable of fighting one of the strongest military powers in the region. By most estimates, Hezbollah emerged with a strategic and political victory (Cordesman, 2006; Matthews, 2008; Lindeman, 2010).

Anthony Cordesman (2006) conducted an analysis of the fighting and says the Israelis entered Lebanon with several specific goals. These included:

- Neutralizing Hezbollah's effectiveness before Iran could develop nuclear weapons
- Countering the IDF's image after the 2000 Lebanon and 2005 Gaza withdrawals
- Forcing Lebanon to control Hezbollah
- Rescuing two Israeli soldiers without a prisoner exchange

Writing soon after the war ended, Cordesman cautions that immediate conclusions are often inaccurate. Given that reservation, Israel appeared to achieve only modest objectives, although many Israeli officers thought that the operation had been successful.

The IDF made several mistakes. Matt Mathews (2008), in a review for the U.S. Army, believes that Israel prepared for the war incorrectly. It followed an American doctrine of destroying the enemy's ability to fight with precision weapons and air power, but it did not adequately plan for a ground offensive after the initial strikes. Cordesman (2006) adds that the Israelis had prepared for a strike against terrorists only to find that they had been fighting a more conventional war. They also lost much sympathy by multiple strikes on civilian targets. In *Infantry* magazine, Yousef Aboul-Enein (2008), of the U.S. Navy, notes that Hezbollah spent years studying the tactics of superior military forces. When the IDF attacked, Hezbollah was able to disperse and hold its ground.

The most important aspect of the 2006 war was the political perception of the results. After years of countering Hezbollah and other groups, the Israelis came to believe that terrorists were weak against a military onslaught. Hezbollah was the aggressor, having fired rockets into Israel in the months prior to the attack, and Israel sought to end this. That did not turn out to happen, as Israel lost sympathy because much of the international community believed that its actions were far out of proportion compared to the damage it received. In the end, Israel's military forces were not defeated, but the operation was a failure (Harel and Issacharoff, 2008). Hezbollah managed the media's images of the war, and set back Israel's strategy to normalize relations with its neighbors (Lamloum, 2009).

A Sympathetic View of Hezbollah

Many voices in Lebanon and elsewhere claim that Hezbollah is a legitimate self-defense force. Hala Jaber (1997, pp. 38–39) summarizes this view in a journalistic examination of Hezbollah. Although Western analysts date the origin of Hezbollah to 1982, the organization claims that it was formed in 1985. Members say that they had nothing to do with the suicide bombings of U.S. Marines and the French army in 1983, and they deny that they were behind the kidnappings of Westerners in Beirut from 1983 to 1990. Instead, they claim that Hezbollah grew from the Lebanese Civil War.

According to Jaber's research, supporters claim that Hezbollah had no intention of spreading the Iranian Revolution; it merely wanted to defend its community. Although it began to fight against the Israeli invaders in 1985, it also fought the Syrians and the Amal militia in 1988. Supporters claim that it is a religious and political organization supporting a guerrilla army, and the purpose of the army is to defeat Israel.

According to Jaber (1997, pp. 207–212), Hezbollah members maintain that it is not a crime to resist the Israelis. In fact, many Hezbollah guerrillas simply refer to themselves as the "Islamic resistance." The military wing is a small part of the organization. The main focus is social service in the form of education, health services, and social security. Jessica Stern (2003b, p. 47) says that Hezbollah knows that it cannot confront the IDF in a conventional war, so it uses guerrilla tactics, and Hezbollah guerrillas believe that fighting the Israelis is not an act of terrorism.

Research by the Council on Foreign Relations (2004) concludes that most Arabs find Hezbollah to be a source of inspiration. Although no Arab nation has ever beaten the Israelis or the West, Hezbollah has a track record of success. If one dates the origin of the group to 1982 and credits Hezbollah with the October 1983 suicide bombings, Arabs believe that Hezbollah forced the French and Americans to withdraw from Lebanon. In 1985, the IDF fled from Hezbollah in central Lebanon, and Israel abandoned the south in 1990. Far from being viewed as a terrorist organization, Hezbollah has achieved heroic status in the eyes of many Arabs.

Gary Gambill and Ziad Abdelnour (2002) say that Hezbollah's entry into politics further legitimized its activities. **Mohammed Fneish**, a Hezbollah representative in the Lebanese Parliament, told journalist Tim Cavanaugh (2004) that Hezbollah has the right to resist Israeli aggression after Israel's invasion of Lebanon. Even after the Israelis left, Fneish claims, the Israelis continued to strike targets in Lebanon and to occupy Palestinian lands. Fneish says Hezbollah is a political and social service organization, but it will resist Israel. He says that there is no relation with Iraqi Shi'ites but that the Iraqis are inspired by Hezbollah's example.

Alasdair Soussi (2004) writes that most Hezbollah members share Fneish's feelings, pointing to Hezbollah's large-scale health care and education systems as evidence that their emphasis is primarily humanitarian. They also claim that the group's goal is to assist the 400,000 Palestinians living in Lebanon. Hezbollah supporters believe that the organization is nothing more than a resistance movement against Israel and that its soldiers are the guerrillas and commandos stationed along the border. Supporters point to the condemnation by Hassan Fadlallah, Hezbollah's spiritual

Mohammed Fneish: (age unknown) A Hezbollah politician and minister of energy in the Lebanese prime minister's cabinet.

leader, of the September 11 attacks as un-Islamic, refusing to call the hijackers "martyrs" and maintaining that they committed suicide while murdering innocent people (Council on Foreign Relations, 2004).

After the 2006 war, support for Hezbollah grew to an all-time high. Far from seeking to topple the Lebanese government, supporters maintain that Hezbollah's objective is to become a dominant political force in a coalition of Lebanese political parties (Perry, 2010, pp. 143–145). The Shi'ites inside Lebanon strongly support Hezbollah. They see it as a defensive force, but believe its religious base embeds the group in the community. One survey reported that Lebanon's Shi'ites stood with Hezbollah against Israel. It also found that they would resist the Lebanese government if it tried to disarm Hezbollah's military wing (Haddad, 2006).

A Critical View of Hezbollah

Despite the above arguments, many people in the world consider Hezbollah to be a terrorist organization. The U.S. Department of State (2004b) summarizes this point of view in its 2004 revised report on terrorism: Hezbollah is a deadly international terrorist organization that has developed international links and uses international crime to finance its operations. Its primary sponsor is Iran, and it receives secondary support from Syria—nations that are listed as state sponsors of terrorism. In addition to its murders of Israelis, Hezbollah has killed U.S. citizens and kidnapped and tortured Americans. The State Department sees Hezbollah as a group of international murderers.

The Council on Foreign Relations (2004) echoes the State Department's view. Hezbollah is a terrorist organization because of the suicide attacks it carried out against civilian and peacekeeping forces and because of its kidnapping rampage between 1983 and 1990. It was also involved in the **1985 hijacking of a TWA flight**, during which an American was murdered, and two bombings in **Argentina in 1992 and 1994**. It has been responsible for a campaign of suicide bombings, the murders of Lebanese Christians, international arms smuggling, and a host of international criminal activities, including crimes in the United States.

Critics also point to Hezbollah's uncompromising political stand, saying that it exists for only two reasons: to impose a Shi'ite government on Lebanon and to destroy the state of Israel. Hezbollah parliamentary representative Mohammed Fneish says that Hezbollah will not force Lebanon to become an Islamic republic like Iran, but his party will campaign for it. After Hezbollah is elected, it can take the necessary steps to consolidate power. As far as the elimination of Israel is concerned, Fneish says Israel was created illegally by Europeans and Americans who felt guilty about the Nazi death camps. They created Israel, he says, as a way of apologizing. Hezbollah does not recognize Israel's right to exist, and it must be eliminated (Cavanaugh, 2004).

Other researchers also condemn Hezbollah. Alasdair Soussi (2004) says that Hezbollah exports its revolutionary ideals, claiming that contacts exist between Hezbollah and the Iraqi resistance movement. Muqtada al Sadr, the Shi'ite leader of the Mahdi Army in Iraq, is linked to Hezbollah's Hassan Nasrallah. Daniel Byman (2003), a professor in security studies at Georgetown University, says that there is no question about the terrorist agenda of Hezbollah. It might have credibility in the Islamic world, but its record of bloodshed and hostility speaks for itself. It is not a question of whether the United States should stop Hezbollah, Byman writes, but of how.

Jessica Stern (2003b) points out that Hezbollah interacts with other terrorist groups around the world. Rather than standing alone as a terrorist group, it is part of a network of groups that range from jihadists to traffickers in narcotics. Jeffery Goldberg (2002) says that Imad Mugniyah, the director of Hezbollah International, is the primary culprit behind these links. Both Stern and Goldberg believe the network blends Hezbollah with al Qaeda. The existence of the international aspect of

1985 hijacking of a TWA flight: The hijacking of TWA Flight 847 by a group believed to have links to Hezbollah while it was en route from Athens to Rome. The plane went to Beirut and then to Algeria, where terrorists tortured and murdered U.S. Navy diver Robert Dean Stethem, a passenger on the flight. The plane returned to Beirut, and passengers were dispersed throughout the city. Terrorists released began releasing hostages as the incident continued. After Israel agreed to release 700 Shiite prisoners, the terrorists released the remaining hostages and escaped.

Argentina in 1992 and 1994: Two bombings in Buenos Aires. Terrorists struck the Israeli embassy in 1992, killing twenty-nine people, and the Jewish Community Center in 1994, killing eighty-five people. Imad Mugniya his suspected to have been behind the attacks.

Hezbollah, according to such research, proves that the organization is part of an international jihadist struggle that uses crime and state support to wage a campaign of terrorism.

Hezbollah provided a model for the formation of an international umbrella of terrorist organizations. The international section remains a conglomeration of like-minded semiautonomous groups. The model inspired the formation of other networks, and none was as important as the groups related to al Qaeda. As Osama bin Laden and Ayman al Zawahiri modified the Hezbollah model within al Qaeda, a plethora of terrorist groups exploded from the Afghan jihad. The allied and semiautonomous groups add to the al Qaeda mystique, and the jihadist network strengthens al Qaeda's striking power.

 Self-Check

> What circumstances gave rise to Hezbollah, and how did the group change over time?
> What are Hezbollah's current operational abilities?
> What caused the 2006 war, and what were the results?
> Is Hezbollah a terrorist group? Why or why not?

Hamas and the Rise of Sunni Religious Organizations

Arab nationalism: The idea that the Arabs could create a European-style nation, based on a common language and culture. The idea faded after the 1967 Six Day War.

Arab nationalism grew through the early part of the twentieth century and flourished until the June 1967 Six Day War. Groups spawned from Fatah and independent organizations like the PIJ began their activities by embracing some form of nationalism. Before Abu Nidal degenerated into mercenary activities, he favored Arab socialism as a form of nationalism. In the 1970s and 1980s, Baathist nationalists in Syria and Iraq also believed in socialism. Adeed Dawisha (2003, pp. 253–280) points out that nationalism ultimately failed. It did not unite the Arabs, nor did it raise their standard of living. As nationalism waned, religious fervor took its place. The PIJ began using religious imagery, and other groups were born from religious fervor.

An Overview of Hamas

Ahmed Yassin: (1937–2004) One of the founders and leaders of Hamas. Yassin originally started the Palestinian Wing of the Muslim Brotherhood but merged it into Hamas during the Intifada. He was killed in an Israeli-targeted assassination.

The story of Hamas is tied to the late Sheik **Ahmed Yassin**. Born in 1938, Yassin grew up in Gaza under the influence of the Muslim Brotherhood. He believed that Islam was the only path that could restore Palestine, and he preached reform and social welfare. Many Palestinians in Gaza began to follow Yassin's powerful call. When he told followers to secretly gather weapons in 1984, they obeyed, but it cost him his freedom. The Israelis discovered Yassin's plans and jailed him. He was released in 1986, and decided that in the future his organization would have a military wing. The Palestinian Muslim Brothers would become the nucleus of Hamas (Institute for Counter-Terrorism, 2004).

Hamas was formed in December 1987 at the beginning of the first Intifada (Isseroff, 2004). Yassin was disappointed with the secular direction of the PLO and wanted to steer the resistance movement along a religious course. Several technically trained university graduates—engineers, teachers, and Islamic scholars—joined the movement. They published the Hamas Charter in 1988, declaring that Palestine was a God-given land, from the Jordan River to the Mediterranean. There could be no compromise with the Israelis, and Israel could not be allowed to exist. Unlike Arafat's PLO, Hamas would fight Israel with religious zeal. Unlike the PIJ, Hamas would be much more than a military organization. It would be a Muslim government, the forerunner of a Palestinian Muslim state (Levit, 2006, pp. 17–18, 30–32).

Hamas's organization reflects this original charter (Hamas, 1988), maintaining a political wing to oversee internal and foreign relations. Its largest unit, especially in

Gaza, is its social wing. According to the third pillar of Islam, *Zakat*, Muslims are to give alms and share with the poor. Hamas runs charities, schools, hospitals, and other social service organizations in Gaza, where unemployment is sometimes as high as 85 percent. These social services have made Hamas popular among the Palestinians. Hamas's military wing, the **Izz el Din al Qassam Brigades**, is named after a martyr from the time of the British occupation of Palestine.

Hamas's relationship with the PLO and the PA has been shaky (Westcott, 2000). The reason can be traced to its religious orientation. Although Yassin and his followers vowed never to use violence against fellow Palestinians, they have always opposed Arafat.

Izz el Din al Qassam Brigades: The military wing of Hamas, named after the Arab revolutionary leader Sheik Izz el Din al Qassam (1882–1935), who led a revolt against British rule.

Struggles for Leadership

After the first Intifada, Hamas faced an internal power struggle. Yassin was jailed from 1989 to 1997, and during that time, the American-educated **Musa Abu Marzuq** took over Hamas. His strategy was much more violent than Yassin's had been. He also sought financial backing from Syria and Iran in an attempt to assert greater power in the organization. He assembled a new leadership core and based it in Jordan, leading others to call it the "outside" leadership, in contrast to the "inside" leadership group of Yassin, which believed the struggle should remain inside Palestine (Levitt, 2002, pp. 34–37).

Musa Abu Marzuq: (b. 1951) The "outside" leader of Hamas, who is thought to be in Damascus, Syria. He is believed to have controlled the Holy Land Foundation.

Marzuq's leadership also caused a struggle with the Palestinian Authority (PA) (Institute for Counter-Terrorism, 2004). In 1996, Marzuq authorized a campaign of suicide bombing inside Israel. The PIJ launched one at the same time, and both campaigns continued into 1997. They were especially savage, targeting civilians and public places. Bombs were designed to kill, cripple, and maim. Some bombs were even laced with rat poison to cause wounds to continue bleeding after treatment. Israel gave Arafat an ultimatum: Crack down on Hamas or Israel would. The PA arrested a number of Hamas's leaders, and Marzuq's offensive waned.

After Yassin was released from prison in 1997, he gradually reasserted control over Hamas, even though he remained under house arrest. He moved operations back to the Gaza Strip. Violence continued up until 2000 but was slowly decreasing. Leaders of the al Qassam Brigades were incensed at the decrease, claiming that both the inside and outside leadership were placing too much attention on political solutions (see Levitt, 2002, pp. 33–51). In the meantime, Jordanian officials closed Hamas operations in Amman, and the outsiders who could avoid arrest fled to Syria. By 2000, some observers believed a lasting peace might be at hand. They were disappointed (Karman, 2000; Wikas, 2002). The al Aqsa Intifada started in September.

The al Aqsa Intifada

It is hard to overstate the effect of the al Aqsa Intifada on Hamas. Quarreling between the al Qassam leaders and the political wing came to a standstill. Moderates and hard-liners drew closer together. As the IDF swarmed into Palestinian areas, Arafat's makeshift government, the PNA, lost much of its power. Hamas, therefore, had the opportunity to assert its muscle. The distinction among the various Palestinian forces began to blur, and Hamas grew stronger by forming alliances with Hezbollah and the PIJ. It then joined the largest suicide-bombing campaign the Middle East had ever seen.

In the summer of 2003, PA Prime Minister **Mahmud Abbas** brokered a limited ceasefire, asking Hamas, the PIJ, and related groups to end their campaigns. However, the peace effort ended in August after a suicide bombing on a bus in Jerusalem. The Israelis responded by renewing a policy of selective assassination; that is, they identified leaders of Hamas and systematically murdered them (see *Expanding the Concept: Israeli Selective Assassination*). Hamas passed another milestone in the

Mahmud Abbas: (b. 1935) The president of the Palestinian Authority since 2005, founding member of Fatah, and an executive in the PLO.

campaign against Israel: It used a female suicide bomber in a joint operation with a newer group, the al Aqsa Martyrs Brigades (J. Stern, 2003a). Hamas had followed the lead of the Liberation Tigers of Tamil Eelam (LTTE), the Kurdistan Workers' Party, and the Chechen rebels, who also had used female suicide bombers.

Seeking Election

In March 2004, Yassin was leaving a mosque in Gaza when Israeli helicopters appeared and fired three missiles at him. He met the fate of other Hamas leaders before him and was killed instantly. Hamas announced his replacement, **Abdel Aziz Rantisi**, an old member of the inside faction. However, the Israelis assassinated Rantisi in the same manner, shortly after he took office. A new leader was appointed, but Hamas kept his identity secret (Oliver, 2004; Keinon, 2004).

Some analysts believed the new leader was **Khalid Meshal**, an outsider operating from Damascus. At first, this suggested that Hamas would change its focus from Israel to the global jihad because the outside leadership had a larger perspective (Lake, 2004). Analysts looked at two Hamas communiqués issued in August 2004 as U.S. and Iraqi forces battled the Shi'ite militia of **Muqtada al Sadr** in Najaf, Iraq. In the midst of the battle, Hamas's first communiqué condemned the United States for fighting around Najaf, the site of a Shi'ite holy shrine, and it called on all Iraqi people to band together to defeat America. The second statement was different; it called on all Iraqis to support the militia of Muqtada al Sadr. This was stunning as Sunnis from the Muslim Brotherhood would be unwilling to support a Shi'ite militia in defense of a Shi'a shrine. Evidence indicated that Hamas had undergone some type of internal transformation (Paz, 2004).

Hamas had indeed undergone a transformation, and Khaled Meshal was its new leader, but few were prepared for the impact that this would have on the PA. The transformation began after the 1993 Oslo Accords and the growing disillusionment with Fatah. Despite Arafat's domination of Palestinian politics, Fatah was a corrupt organization. Arafat received millions of dollars from supporters and through international aid, and he doled out funds like a big-city political boss. The majority of the money went to local political leaders instead of to needy Palestinians. Even when the PA seemed to be on the verge of achieving independence, Fatah functioned by its familiar corrupt rules, and it continued to do so after Arafat's death (McGreal, 2006). When elections were slated for 2006, Palestinians were given the opportunity to select a new parliament. They voted Fatah out of power in January, and Hamas won the election.

Hamas versus Fatah

Hamas controlled the majority of seats in the Palestinian Parliament, while Mahmud Abbas retained the presidency. This set the stage for a confrontation between Hamas and Fatah. Tension festered between the rival groups after the election, and Meshal continued to lead Hamas in exile. In Syria, he was free for international travel and fund-raising, something that he could not have accomplished from Gaza, where Israeli restrictions would have limited his movements. This benefited Hamas, ironically, because Meshal's new government needed money. The United States and the European Union refused to recognize Hamas's victory, stating that they would neither support nor discuss settlements with a terrorist organization. They cut off all aid to the PA, increasing bitter feelings between Hamas and Fatah.

Disheartened by the split in Palestinian leadership, Saudi Arabia brokered a power-sharing arrangement between Hamas and Fatah. It was a tenuous agreement, and the United States and the European Union still refused to restore foreign aid to the PA. That brought matters further along. Hamas and Fatah never really considered themselves full partners, and violent skirmishes between the two groups broke out in November 2006. According to news reports, several Arab nations restored peace,

Abdel Aziz Rantisi: (1947–2004) One of the founders of Hamas along with Ahmed Yassin. He took over Hamas after Israeli gunships assassinated Yassin. He, in turn, was assassinated by the Israelis a month after taking charge.

Khalid Meshal: (b. 1956) One of the "outside" leaders of Hamas, in Damascus, Syria, Meshal became the political leader of Hamas in 2004. After the 2006 election he continued to lead in exile.

Muqtada al Sadr: (b. 1974) An Iraqi ayatollah. Al Sadr leads the Shi'ite militia known as the Mahdi Army.

but intermittent assaults and counter assaults continued into the summer of 2007. All pretense of power sharing broke down in June when Hamas openly attacked Fatah's strong points in Gaza. Fatah responded by forcibly closing all Hamas offices on the West Bank, but Hamas grew stronger in Gaza. By June 15, Hamas had driven Fatah from Gaza, and Abbas had dissolved the government. He formed a new parliament and cabinet, excluding Hamas. The United States and the European Union restored foreign aid to the West Bank, but Hamas controlled Gaza despite Abbas's actions. Over 200 Palestinians were killed in the fighting (Fisher, 2007).

Rockets and Operation Cast Lead

Meshal wasted no time taking advantage of the new base in Gaza. According to the Council on Foreign Relations (2009b), Meshal wanted to attack Israel. In the past, Hamas had relied on suicide bombers—Meshal called them the F-16s of the Palestinians—but control of Gaza gave them a geographical base. They began launching homemade rockets across the border into Israel.

On December 27, 2008, Israel kicked off Operation Cast Lead, a devastating air and artillery assault on Gaza, followed by a ground invasion on January 3. According to news reports, several nations condemned the Israeli incursion, and the United States urged Israel to show restraint (Partriquin, 2009). Supporters of Israel were infuriated, stating that Israel had a right to defend itself. They asked why had there been no international outcry against Hamas's rocket attacks. Critics only emerged, the supporters argued, when Israel took steps to defend its borders (R. Freedman, 2009). Israel maintained the attack for 22 days, destroying munitions and supplies. It also targeted underground tunnels that Hamas used to bring in military stores. The fighting caused hundreds of casualties.

Controversy over the invasion centered on proportionality. Anthony Cordesman (2009) said that the strategic results might eventually be questionable but that the tactical results were clear. Faced with rocket attacks, Israel responded with overwhelming military force. This temporarily eradicated Hamas's military capability while ensuring that Israeli troops suffered only minimal casualties during the fighting. This exacts a high humanitarian toll, Cordesman argues, but it reflects legitimate military action. In addition, it was a tactical success.

George Bisharat (Bisharat et al., 2009), writing for an American law journal, argues that the Israeli response was illegal under international law. Two primary factors weigh against Israel. Even though the military response was designed to be overwhelming, the massive response produced hundreds of civilian casualties. In addition, Israel effectively occupied the Gaza Strip. It withdrew from the region in 2005, but it controlled the entry and exit of people and provisions. Such control, Bisharat says, made Israel legally responsible for protecting all the residents of Gaza. The response to Hamas's attacks should have been measured.

✅ **Self-Check**

> Why did religion merge with the Palestinian movement? How did Hamas obtain power in Gaza?

> Was Operation Cast Lead justified?

> Can there be any hope for peace with Hamas?

Fatah Restructured—The al Aqsa Martyrs Brigades

Suicide bombing became the most important tactic of all the Palestinian terrorist groups at the beginning of the al Aqsa Intifada in September 2000. Hezbollah, Hamas, and the PIJ were in the forefront, giving leadership to local religious groups. Fatah also became involved, but it continued in its secular orientation. Its two main forces were the politically oriented Force 17 and the Tanzim Brigade. Other Fatah splinter groups joined the Intifada, and although they resisted Arafat's control, they also steered clear of religion. This became a problem because local jihadists and religious terrorists dominated the al Aqsa Intifada (Shahar, 2002). If Fatah wanted to play a leading role, it had to move from the secular to the religious realm.

BBC News (2003) reports that Fatah has shown a newfound religious streak that comes from the grass roots of Palestinian society. The al Aqsa Brigades were formed to put Fatah at the center of the new Intifada. The Brigades began as a secular group, but they increasingly used jihadist rhetoric. They were also the first secular Palestinian group to use suicide tactics. Hezbollah, Hamas, and the PIJ do not recognize Israel's right to exist. This is not so with the Brigades. They claim their purpose is limited: Their goal is to stop Israeli incursions and attacks in Palestinian areas, and they intend to punish Israel for each attack. Whether this explanation is accepted or not, one thing is clear: The Brigades have become the most potent Palestinian force in the al Aqsa Intifada.

Effective Tactics

The Council on Foreign Relations (2004) believes that the tactics of the al Aqsa Martyrs Brigades have made the group particularly deadly to the Israelis. At first, shadowy spokespeople said that they would strike Israeli military targets only inside Palestinian territory. This practice was soon abandoned, however, and attacks moved into Israel proper. The Brigades' primary tactics have been drive-by shootings, sniper shootings, ambushes, and kidnap-murders. Yet, as with so many other terrorist groups, their most devastating tactic has been the use of suicide bombers.

Yael Shahar (2002) says that the al Aqsa Martyrs Brigades suicide bombers were frightening for two reasons: They were secular, and they sought out targets crowded with civilians. They delivered human bombs filled with anti-personnel material, designed to inflict the maximum number of casualties. Their purpose was to kill and maim as many victims as possible in the most public way possible. Furthermore, as mentioned earlier, they used the first female suicide bomber in the Middle East on January 27, 2002, in conjunction with Hamas. They expanded their targets, and their casualties increased; after initially allowing the PIJ and Hamas to play the leading role in the rebellion, the Brigades moved to the forefront of the rebellion.

Leadership in the Martyrs Brigades

Leadership of the Brigades is a controversial topic. They seem to be directly associated with their parent group, Fatah, but it is unclear how their operations are directed and from where. One school of thought maintains that Arafat led and paid for the Brigades. Israeli intelligence claims that they have proof of Arafat's involvement. Shahar (2002) says that the IDF raided Arafat's headquarters in Ramallah in 2002 and captured PNA documents that show payments to various factions inside the Brigades, payments personally approved by Arafat. The Israelis say that Arafat may not have determined targeting and timing but that he paid the expenses and set the agenda.

Marwan Barghouti: (b. 1969) A leader of Fatah and alleged leader of the al Aqsa Martyrs Brigades. A Brigades statement in 2002 claimed that Barghouti was their leader. He rose to prominence during the al Aqsa Intifada, but he is currently held in an Israeli prison.

Other investigations point to another conclusion. The Council on Foreign Relations (2004) believes that Arafat may have run the Brigades but admits that there may be another source of leadership. A BBC News (2003) investigation points to **Marwan Barghouti** (currently in Israeli custody) as the commander. A Palestinian spokesman, Hassan Abdel Rahman, says that the documents Israel seized in 2002 are false and claims that the Israelis planted them (Rothem, 2002). Arafat claimed that he knew nothing about the Brigades.

PBS's *Frontline* (2002) conducted an interview with a Palestinian leader code-named Jihad Ja'Aire at the height of the first bombing campaign. Ja'Aire claimed that he and all of the other Brigades commanders were under Arafat's control. Arafat provided the direction, Ja'Aire said, and all the members obeyed him. This does not condemn Arafat, Ja'Aire pointed out, because the group operates with a different philosophy. The al Aqsa Martyrs Brigades will accept a negotiated peace. If Israel had accepted the 1967 borders, that is, the borders before Israel added the West Bank and Gaza Strip after the Six Day War, and stopped incursions into Palestinian areas, Arafat could have called off the attacks.

Whether Arafat had direct control of the Brigades remains a subject of debate, partly because of the way the Brigades are organized. Taking a cue from the international jihadist groups, the al Aqsa Martyrs Brigades have little centralized structure. Their administration has been pushed down to the lowest operational level so that they may function almost autonomously. Cells exist in several Palestinian communities, and leaders are empowered to take action on their own without approval from a hierarchy. In addition, Israel has targeted the Brigades' leadership for selective assassination; nevertheless, the organization continues.

Beginning a Network

No matter where the leadership authority lies, the managerial relations within the Brigades remain a mystery, even to the Palestinians. In June 2004 some of the leading figures in the Palestinian territories formed the Fatah General Council to investigate the al Aqsa Martyrs Brigades and Arafat's relation to them. This enraged some in the Brigades because they believed that Arafat was manipulating the entire investigation. Claiming that Arafat had abandoned them, disgruntled members of the Brigades surrounded his house and threatened him. If Arafat controlled the Brigades, his hold may not have been very tight (Algazy, 2004).

The structure of the Brigades is testimony to Michael Scheuer's (2006) comments about the nature of modern terrorism, and it hearkens back to points made by Marc Sageman (2004). Although the leaders of the group are unknown, the Brigades have been effective even without centralized leadership. Their strength comes from the ability of small cells to operate without a strong leader. The Brigades have been effective because they operate within a network (MIPT, n.d.).

The Arab spring has brought new thinking, however. Marawan Barghouti, who is currently serving five life sentences for terrorism in Israel, made a pronouncement from his cell in 2012. He called for mass demonstrations and nonviolent resistance. If it worked in Tunisia and Egypt, Barghouti believed it could work in Israel.

Self-Check

> What started the al Aqsa Intifada?
> What tactics did terrorists use in the al Aqsa Intifada?
> Do the al Aqsa Martyrs Brigades unite the Palestinians in a common effort? Explain.

ANOTHER PERSPECTIVE

David's Kingdom and Israeli Settlements

Many supporters of Israel and a good number of Israeli peace activists do not favor expansion into Palestinian areas. Moshe Amon (2004) writes that although Israel is a secular democracy, it is being influenced by religious extremists. Ultraorthodox rabbis, he maintains, seek to conquer the biblical Kingdom of David. Jewish extremists, with the support of the state, have moved into Palestinian areas to establish permanent settlements. Many militants believe that when David's Kingdom is restored every person on earth will follow the teachings of the God of Israel. Amon says some of the militants fight Israeli soldiers, and some of their leaders call for the murder of non-Jews. Amon believes this behavior threatens not only Israel's moral character but its very survival.

Controversial Counterterrorist Policies

Mossad: The Israeli intelligence agency, formed in 1951. It is responsible for gathering foreign intelligence. Shin Beth is responsible for internal security.

Many Israeli police and military units have established excellent reputations in counterterrorist operations. **Mossad**, the Israeli intelligence service, is known for its expertise. Shin Beth, the domestic Israeli security service, is one of the most effective secret police forces in the world. The IDF is an excellent fighting machine. The Israeli police know how to handle bombs, snipers, kidnappings, and everyday crime. The tactical operations of these units are second to none.

Tactical operations, however, differ from policies. Governments decide the broad philosophy and practice of a policy, and tactical operations take place within the guidelines of long-term political goals. Policy involves a strategic view of a problem and the means to settle it. Unlike Israel's excellent tactical record, its counterterrorist policies have stirred international controversy (see *Another Perspective: Controversial Tactics*).

Bulldozing

When Israel first faced suicide bombings, the government implemented a controversial policy called *bulldozing*, whose purpose was to destroy the family homes of suicide bombers. If militant charities and governments were going to compensate families of martyrs, the Israelis reasoned, bulldozing homes would be more painful than the pleasure of economic reward. Soon, the homes of not only families but of suspected leaders in militant groups and others were targeted for bulldozing. In 2004, farms and other areas were bulldozed. The policy expanded to include clearing ground for military reasons and clearing space to build a security fence, that is, a wall separating Israel from Palestinian areas (*Palestine Monitor*, 2004; *New York Times*, International, 2004). Critics maintain that bulldozing is done to further Israel's self-interests.

Invading Lebanon

Judith Harik (2004, pp. 117–124) describes another controversial policy: punishing Lebanon for the sins of Hezbollah. As discussed earlier in the chapter, Israel launched its first invasion of Lebanon to rid the south of the PLO. That ended after an 18-year occupation and the creation of a new enemy, Hezbollah. In 1996, Israel launched a limited offensive in Lebanon to disrupt Hezbollah operations, and dozens of innocent Lebanese were killed in the process.

The Israelis responded with force again in July 2006. Israel was surprised when Hezbollah launched rockets into Israel while Hezbollah ground forces ambushed

---

❉ ANOTHER PERSPECTIVE

Controversial Tactics

Israel has engaged in tactics that have enraged the Palestinians and many others. Critics call these tactics Israeli terrorism. Defenders say that Israel has a right to protect itself. The United States almost always supports Israel, frequently using its veto power in the UN Security Council to keep the United Nations from condemning Israeli actions. Controversial tactics include

- Destroying the homes of suicide bombers' families

- Selective assassination of Palestinian leaders
- Killing innocents when striking militants
- Excessive use of force
- Commando raids in neighboring countries
- June 2006 invasion of Lebanon
- December 2008 invasion of Gaza
- Blockade of Gaza
- May 2010 violent interception of ships during Gaza blockade

a military unit inside the borders of Israel. Israel launched an immediate attack, and then announced that it planned to destroy Hezbollah (al Jazeera, 2006). The IDF launched a massive series of strikes for nearly a month. Critics maintained that the operation was overkill. In a war that lasted nearly a month, hundreds of Lebanese civilians were killed, nearly a million Lebanese were displaced, and Lebanon's infrastructure was destroyed (*Daily Mail*, 2007; Chomsky, 2006; Salem, 2006).

The Wall

In an effort to stop Palestinian attacks, the government of Ariel Sharon proposed an idea that dates back to Hadrian of the Roman Empire. The Israelis began constructing a massive wall. On the surface, this might seem to be an uncontroversial issue, but the path of the wall grabbed the attention of the world. The concrete and barbed-wire barrier snaked through Palestinian areas, often putting water and other resources in the hands of the Israelis. It also separated people from services, jobs, and their families. Much of the international community condemned the wall (I. Black, 2003).

Selective Assassination

The most controversial aspect of Israel's counterterrorist policy is selective assassination. Israel has maintained a consistent policy against terrorism. When it is struck, it hits back hard. Israeli commandos and the IDF units have allegedly killed opposition leaders in the past, including Abu Jihad of the PLO and Fathi Shekaki of the PIJ, but the policy expanded during the al Aqsa Intifada when Israel began the wholesale assassination of Hamas leadership.

Reuven Paz (2004) questions the effectiveness of this policy, suggesting that it might internationalize the conflict. Left-wing political leaders in Israel deplore the policy, calling such assassinations "gangster murders" (Kafala, 2001). Human rights groups have condemned the policy and challenged it in Israeli courts (BBC News, 2002). Nations all over the world have condemned Israel for these targeted assassinations as well.

Daniel Byman (2006) defends the controversial policy, arguing that Israel's selective assassinations are publicly transparent. Each proposed attack must go through several stages, excluding legal review. The public is aware of the moral dilemma and various tradeoffs. Byman admits that the policy remains controversial, and says it would be stronger if the judiciary were involved in the process. It is important to note that Israeli deaths from terrorism have dropped since it began employing its controversial policy.

EXPANDING THE CONCEPT

Israeli Selective Assassination

Israel has targeted Hama's leaders throughout the al Aqsa Intifada.

Person	Position	Israeli Action
Riyad Abu Zayd	Military commander	Ambush, February 2003
Ibrahim Maqadah	Military commander	Helicopter attack, May 2003
Abdullah Qawasmah	Suicide bomb commander	Ambush, June 2003
Ismail Shanab	Political leader	Bomb strike, August 2003
Sheik Ahmed Yassin	Head of Hamas	Helicopter attack, March 2004
Abdel Aziz Rantisi	Replaced Yassin	Helicopter attack, April 2004
Mahmud al Mabbuh	Political/military leader	Murdered in Dubai hotel, February 2010

Charles Krauthammer (2004) reflects the feelings of those who support these controversial policies. Israel is under attack, he writes. Though the United Nations, for instance, condemned the security fence, Krauthammer maintains that its construction reduced suicide attacks. Many Israelis feel that harsh policies must be implemented to deter terrorism (Kafala, 2001). Furthermore, the United States has repeatedly taken the position that Israel cannot be condemned for harsh measures until the international community also denounces Palestinian terrorism.

Although supporters claim that Israel should be allowed to take the steps necessary for self-defense, the policies remain controversial. The important question to try to answer is, do harsh policies reduce terrorism or increase the cycle of violence? Thus far, the question remains unanswered, and violence continues from both sides of the fence.

Self-Check

> Why might Israeli policies toward Lebanon be described as a failure?
> Is collective punishment for terrorist violence effective?
> Do retribution and intensive security measures stop terrorism? Explain.

CHAPTER TAKE AWAYS

The modern conflict between Israel and Palestine is based in terrorism. Fatah imitated the Irgun by using terrorist tactics, but the movement was not united. Palestinian militancy is characterized by factionalism. Terrorism moved to the international arena in the 1980s, but it has remained localized for the last three decades. The current major operational groups are Hezbollah, Hamas, and the al Aqsa Martyrs Brigades. Israeli policies are controversial. Critics claim the Israelis overreact. Defenders maintain strong tactics are necessary to counter terror.

OBJECTIVE SUMMARY

- The PLO emerged in 1964 and took center stage after the June 1967 Six Day War. Fatah was its main military wing, but groups kept splitting off. After the 1982 invasion of Lebanon, the PLO retreated to North Africa and the occupied territories. Though it still sponsored terrorism, Fatah's activities were eclipsed by other groups.
- A number of groups emerged from the PLO, and other organizations emerged from the Israeli–Palestinian conflict. Fatah sponsored its own internal groups, including the al Aqsa Martyrs Brigades, Black September, Force 17, and the Tanzim Brigade. Other splinter groups included the Abu Nidal Organization, the Democratic Front for the Liberation of Palestine, the Palestine Liberation Front, the Popular Democratic Front for the Liberation of Palestine, and the Popular Front for the Liberation of Palestine, General Command. Related groups such as the PIJ, Hezbollah, and Hamas developed independently and assumed leading roles in the conflict between Israel and the Palestinians.
- The PIJ emerged from Egypt in the 1970s. It evolved into a religious organization with the philosophy that while religious law would be implemented after victory, the more immediate objective was the destruction of Israel. By 1995, most of its founding leaders had been killed. New leaders purposely maintain a small group of operatives in a rigid hierarchy. Several groups use *Islamic Jihad* in their names. There are even factions in the PIJ.
- Hezbollah grew when Revolutionary Guards joined Shiites in Lebanon after the 1982 Israeli invasion. Beginning as a social movement, it evolved into an

umbrella group covering independent operators and its own military wing. It employed suicide bombings and other attacks against Israeli targets.

- Hezbollah has gone through distinct phases, moving from small terrorist operations in Beirut to political and social action. It also created a defense force and successfully fought Israel in the 2006 war. The status of Hezbollah is hotly debated. Supporters see it as a legitimate militia defending Lebanese Shi'ites from Israelis and other threats. Critics maintain that it is an international terrorist organization representing Iranian foreign policy.

- Hamas emerged from the first Intifada. It embraced the principles of religious law and expressed disgust for the secular policies and corruption of the PLO. It formed a large organization and mastered the art of suicide attacks. It opposes any peace with Israel, and its charter calls for the destruction of Israel.

- Hamas won control of the Palestinian government in 2006. Although the United States has refused to negotiate with Hamas, many people believe that Hamas will target neither the United States nor other Western countries.

- The al Aqsa Martyrs Brigades formed from Fatah, embracing religion and suicide attacks. There are many questions about its leadership. Currently, it operates within a network of independent cells having no central command structure.

- Several militant Jewish groups have called for the elimination of non-Jewish people in traditional Jewish lands. They believe that the biblical kingdom of Israel is a literal and geographical gift to them from God.

- Israel has responded to terrorism with controversial policies. These include bulldozing, invasions of Lebanon, constructing a wall to separate Palestinians from Israelis, and targeted assassinations.

Critical Engagement: Elections and Security

In January 2006, Hamas stunned the world by winning the majority of seats in the Palestinian Parliament. It did not control the presidency, but it gained the parliament and the cabinet. The United States and the European Union refused to endorse the election, labeling Hamas a terrorist group. Hamas's charter called for the destruction of Israel, and Hamas's leader Khaled Meshal supported this aim. He has said he might be willing to talk if Israel would withdraw to its pre–Six Day War boundaries, but he was in Damascus, far from local leaders in Gaza. Having been the target of an Israeli assassination attempt in the 1990s, he could not return to any area that Israel could enter at will.

Regardless, Hamas could not hold legitimate power even though it had won the elections. Mahmud Abbas refused to transfer control of the Palestinian security forces from Fatah to Hamas, and he appointed a strong Fatah leader to govern Gaza, the major source of Hamas's power. Tensions continued, but Hamas and Fatah finally formed a government in March 2007, with the help of a truce brokered by Saudi Arabia. Within months, however, Hamas and Fatah gunmen routinely fought battles, and Hamas took direct control of Gaza in the summer of 2007. President Mahmud Abbas dissolved the Palestinian government and created a new parliament and cabinet based in the West Bank. Abbas refused to let Hamas participate; nevertheless, Hamas maintained de facto power in Gaza. Hamas also started shooting missiles into Israel.

The United States, the European Union, and Israel renewed negotiations with the PA under Abbas, and foreign aid was restored to the PA on the West Bank. Israel continued to build settlements in Palestinian areas, and it planned on attacking Gaza to silence Hamas's Katyusha rockets. Israel struck Gaza, starting in December 2008 and continuing into January 2009. Hundreds of Palestinians were killed. Abbas criticized the Israeli incursion, but Palestinian sympathies turned to Gaza and subsequently Hamas.

Violence, terrorism, and counterterrorism create a climate conducive to moral outrage. Any person seeking to justify violence only needs to point to one of the many victims. This leads to a self-perpetuating cycle of violence, moral outrage, and returned violence from each side. The United States launched an effort to begin indirect peace talks in 2010, something it has tried to do for decades. Even if the two sides were to talk, questions remain about the hard-liners on every side. They tend to sabotage hopes for peace.

Consider these issues in terms of future developments:

- Victimization is constantly used to justify further violence. Since all sides have been victimized by violence, how might the stories of victims be used to create an atmosphere conducive to negotiation?
- Assuming that such an arrangement could be made, extremists in Israel and Palestine have assassinated leaders and launched terrorist strikes to sabotage peace talks in the past. What types of steps would be needed to thwart extremists from all parties? Why is it difficult to create a secure environment among a multitude of groups unwilling to compromise?
- What role should the United States play in this region? If the United States values democracy, how can it deny the validity of election results?

KEY TERMS

Yasser Arafat, p. 9-215
Fedayeen, p. 9-215
Sabri al Banna, p. 9-219
Intifada, p. 9-219
Black June, p. 9-219
al Aqsa Intifada,
    p. 9-220
Revolutionary Guards,
    p. 9-223

Sheik Mohammed Hassan
    Fadlallah, p. 9-224
Abbas Musawi, p. 9-224
Hassan Nasrallah,
    p. 9-224
Imad Mugniyah,
    p. 9-227
Shaba farm region,
    p. 9-227

Arab nationalism,
    p. 9-231
Ahmed Yassin, p. 9-231
Izz el Din al Qassam
    Brigades, p. 9-232
Musa Abu Marzuq,
    p. 9-232
Mahmud Abbas,
    p. 9-232

Abdel Aziz Rantisi,
    p. 9-233
Khalid Meshal,
    p. 9-233
Muqtada al Sadr,
    p. 9-233
Marwan Barghouti,
    p. 9-235
Mossad, p. 9-237

PART3

International Terrorism: Ideological and Religious Movements

CHAPTER 10

Revolutionary and Counter Revolutionary Terrorism

REUTERS/Anibal Solimano PO

LEARNING OBJECTIVES

After reading this chapter, you should be able to:

> Define revolutionary and counter revolutionary terrorism.

> Outline the history, philosophy, and influence of the Tupamaros.

> Summarize the emergence and current status of FARC and the ELN.

> Describe the function and purpose of the MeK.

> Describe the rise, fall, and resurgence of the Shining Path.

> Explain the Maoist rebellion in Nepal.

> Outline the issues surrounding Naxalite terrorism.

> Explain the operations and tactics of the New People's Army.

> Describe the rise, fall, and transformation of revolutionary terrorism in Europe.

> Explain the rise of death squads as a reaction to revolutionary terrorism.

It is an old story in southern Peru. A group of Maoist revolutionaries from the Shining Path captured a group of hostages to use as leverage against the Peruvian government. According to the CNN (2012), terrorists from the Shining Path entered the town of Kepashiato and seized at least three dozen prisoners from oil and gas production companies. They demanded $10 million in ransom as well as weapons and explosives. Instead of negotiating, the government responded by launching a search operation, surrounding the entire town with 1,500 police officers and military personnel. After a week of fighting, the Shining Path released 36 prisoners. The context of the operation was quite ironic because security forces captured one of the leading figures of the Shining Path in February 2012. The president of Peru stated that the Shining Path's campaign was over and that group had been defeated. The new attack came within weeks of the president's pronouncement.

This is not the first time the government had announced the demise of the Shining Path. After years of bitter fighting, Peruvian security forces captured Abimael Guzmán, the group's ideological leader and founder, in 1992. Guzman was tried, convicted, and sentenced to life in prison. The Shining Path was dead, the president announced, but it resurged. Guzmán's successor was taken into custody in 1999. Police captured three of its leaders in 2000, and the military destroyed the Shining Paths training camps a few years later. This ended the campaign of terrorism, the government claimed. Yet within a few years new leaders emerged. When they were defeated in 2012, the president reiterated the now-familiar claim. The attack at Kepashiato followed.

Revolutionary Terrorism

Modern revolutionary terrorism reached its zenith in the 1960s and 1970s. It was a global movement expressing dissatisfaction in the wake of anticolonialism. Western policy and the United States' international economic system fell under intense scrutiny, and tensions caused by the Vietnam War fanned the flames of heated political behavior. Small ideological groups appeared in Central and South America, and revolutionary groups emerged in Europe. Guerrilla movements spawned ideological spin-offs. The East–West confrontation came into play as the former Soviet Union supported its own revolutionary groups while Maoist rebellions gave a new twist to old Leninist ideologies. Japan experienced unique forms of violence that combined ideology and religious elements.

Revolutionary and Counter Revolutionary Terrorism Defined

A common misconception is that the American Revolution was based on terrorism. If this were true, rebels would have indiscriminately murdered British citizens and clandestinely destroyed symbolic targets. General George Washington would not have fought to destroy the British Army; he would have waged a campaign of symbolic murder in the hope that the horror of it all would change British political behavior. Instead, although many Americans operated as guerrillas, the majority joined a conventional army and fought within the accepted norms of conventional warfare. Revolutions cannot be equated with terrorism, although terrorism is sometimes used during the course of revolutions.

When examining ideological terrorism, it is possible to broadly categorize a revolutionary style. Martha Crenshaw (1972), a pioneer in the field, summarized the aspects of revolutionary terrorism early in her career. She says that revolutionary terrorism can be defined as an insurgent strategy in the context of internal warfare or revolution. It is an attempt to seize power from a legitimate state for the purpose of creating political and social change. It involves the systematic use of terrorism to achieve this goal. Violence is neither isolated nor a series of random acts, and it is far from guerrilla warfare or conventional warfare. Revolutionary terrorism differs from other forms of violence because it occurs outside the normal realm of violent political action. It involves acts of violence that are particularly abominable, and it usually occurs within a civilian population. The violence is symbolic, and it is designed to have a devastating psychological impact on established power.

Revolutionary terrorism refers to movements designed to overthrow and replace a political system. After World War II, it involved mainly left-wing and Marxist movements; right-wing groups copied these models. Some revolutionary groups are sponsored by nation-states.

Revolutionary terrorism involves violent activity for the purpose of changing the political structure of government or the social orientation of a country or region. Maoist terrorism is a form of revolutionary terrorism. Its goal is to establish a communist society similar to that of revolutionary China. Counterterrorism involves the legitimate legal activities of security forces, but some unofficial groups operate outside the law. When these groups engage in violence, it can be described as counter revolutionary terrorism.

Modeling Revolutionary Terrorism: Uruguay's Tupamaros

In the early 1960s, a group of revolutionaries called the Tupamaros surfaced in Uruguay (Figure 10.2). Unlike their predecessors in the Cuban Revolution, the Tupamaros spurned the countryside, favoring an urban environment. City sidewalks and asphalt became their battleground. A decade later, their tactics would inspire revolutionaries around the world, and terrorist groups would imitate the methods of the Uruguayan revolutionaries. The Tupamaros epitomized urban terrorism.

In the years immediately after World War II, Uruguay appeared to be a model Latin American government. Democratic principles and freedoms were the accepted basis of Uruguay's political structures. Democratic rule was complemented by a sound economy and an exemplary educational system. Although it could not be described as a land of wealth, by the early 1950s Uruguay could be called a land of promise. All factors seemed to point to peace and prosperity.

Unfortunately, Uruguay's promise started to fade in 1954. The export economy that had proved so prosperous for the country began to crumble. Falling prices for

FIGURE **10.1** Central and South America

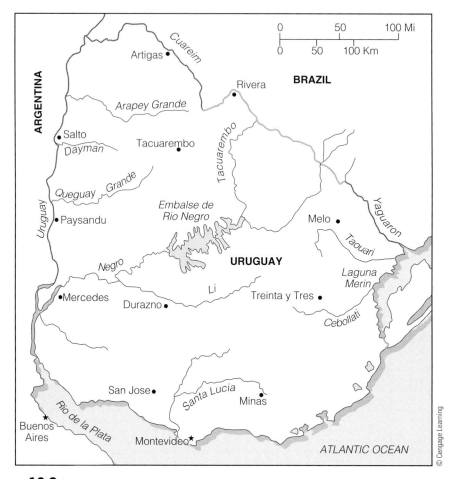

FIGURE **10.2** Uruguay

exported goods brought inflation and unemployment, and economic dissatisfaction grew. By 1959, many workers and members of the middle class faced a bleak future. Uruguay had undergone a devastating economic reversal, and workers were restless.

In the northern section of Uruguay, sugar workers were hit particularly hard. Sugar exports had decreased in the 1950s, and sugar workers suffered all of Uruguay's economic woes. As a result, the workers took steps to form a national union. Several militant radicals injected themselves into the union movement. When the sugar workers organized in 1959, the militants dominated the union and called for confrontation with the government.

By 1962, the union organizers believed that they should move their organization from the rural north to Montevideo, the capital, to make its presence felt. Moderates joined militants in a united front and headed south. Though their rhetoric was violent, union members felt an appearance in Montevideo would not only draw attention to their cause but also help legitimize it.

Their logic seemed sound. Uruguay's population center is Montevideo, a metropolis of 1.25 million people. Demographically, the capital offered the promise of recognition. Unfortunately for the union, though, they did not achieve the type of recognition that they were seeking. Far from viewing the marchers as a legitimate labor movement, the government considered them potential revolutionaries.

The sugar workers clashed with police, and several union members were arrested. One of those taken to jail was a young law student named **Raúl Sendic** (1926–1989).

Raúl Sendic: (1926–1989) A Uruguayan revolutionary leader. Sendic founded the National Liberation Movement (MLN), popularly known as the Tupamaros. Following governmental repression in 1973, he fled the country. Sendic died in Paris in 1989.

Disillusioned with law school and his prospects for the future, Sendic had joined the sugar workers. Sendic remained in jail until 1963. When he emerged, he had a plan for a revolution.

Sendic had not seen the brighter side of Uruguayan life in prison. The stark realities of Uruguay's now-shaky political system were evident, as torture and mistreatment of prisoners were common. If the population could not be kept content by a sound economy, it had to be subdued by fear. Democracy and freedoms faded as Uruguay's economic woes increased. Sendic described the repression he saw in *Waiting for the Guerrilla*, in which he called for revolt in Montevideo.

After Sendic was released from jail, several young radicals gravitated toward him. María Gilio (1972) paints a sympathetic picture of Sendic's early followers. According to Gilio, these young people were primarily interested in reforming the government and creating economic opportunities. Although they had once believed they could attain these goals through democratic action, the ongoing repression in Uruguay ruled out any response except violence. Gilio believed that the group of people who surrounded Sendic were humanist idealists who wanted to bring Uruguay under direct control of the people.

Others did not hold this opinion of Sendic and his compatriots. Arturo Porzecanski (1973) provides a more objective view of the group's next move. Sendic's group felt excluded from participation in the political system, and Sendic believed that violence was the only appropriate tool to change the political order. In 1963, Sendic and his followers raided the Swiss Hunting Club outside Montevideo. The raid was the first step in arming the group, and the first step toward a revolution.

The Urban Philosophy

According to Porzecanski, the group was not willing to move outside Montevideo to begin a guerrilla war for several reasons. First, the group was not large enough to begin a guerrilla campaign because it represented radical middle-class students. Mainstream workers and labor activists had moved away from the militants' position before the march on Montevideo. Second, the countryside of Uruguay did not readily lend itself to a guerrilla war because unrest grew from the urban center of Uruguay. Third, the peasants were unwilling to provide popular support for guerrilla forces. Finally, Montevideo was the nerve center of Uruguay. All of these factors caused the small group to believe that it could better fight within the city.

National Liberation Movement: The Tupamaros' official name.

In 1963, the group adopted its official name, the **National Liberation Movement** (MLN). As they began to develop a revolutionary ideology and a structure for violent revolt, the group searched for a name that would identify them with the people, one with more popular appeal than MLN. According to Christopher Dobson and Ronald Payne (1982, p. 206), the MLN adapted the name of the heroic Inca chieftain Tupac Amaru, killed in a revolt against the Spaniards 200 years earlier. Porzecanski notes this story but also suggests the group may have taken its name from a South American bird. In any case, Sendic's followers called themselves the Tupamaros.

By 1965, their ranks had grown to 50 followers, and they were building a network of sympathizers in the city. Instead of following the prescribed method of Latin American revolution based on a rural guerrilla operation, the Tupamaros organized to do battle inside the city, following the recent guidelines of Carlos Marighella. Terrorism would become the prime strategy for assaulting the enemy. The Tupamaros, unlike Castro, were not interested in building a conventional military force to strike at the government.

Ross Butler (1976, pp. 53–59) describes the growth of the terrorist group by tracking their tactics. He says that they engaged in inconsequential activities in the early stages of their development. From 1964 to 1968, they concentrated on gathering arms and financial backing. After 1968, however, their tactics changed, and according to Butler, the government found it necessary to take them seriously.

In 1968, the Tupamaros launched a massive campaign of decentralized terrorism. They were able to challenge governmental authority because their movement was growing. A series of bank robberies had financed their operations, and now, armed with the power to strike, the Tupamaros sought to paralyze the government in Montevideo. They believed, as had Carlos Marighella in Brazil, that the government would increasingly turn to repression as a means of defense and that the people would be forced to join the revolution.

The government was quick to respond but found there was very little it could do. The Tupamaros struck when and where they wanted and generally made the government's security forces look foolish. They kidnapped high-ranking officials from the Uruguayan government, and the police could do little to find the victims.

Counter Revolutionary Terrorism

Kidnapping became so successful that the Tupamaros took to kidnapping foreign diplomats. They seemed able to choose their victims and strike their targets at will. Frustrated, the police turned to an old Latin American tactic: They began torturing suspected Tupamaros.

Torturing prisoners served several purposes. First, it provided a ready source of information. In fact, the Tupamaros were destroyed primarily through massive arrests, based on information gleaned from interrogations. Second, torture was believed to serve as a deterrent to other would-be revolutionaries. Although this torture was always unofficial, most potential governmental opponents knew what lay in store for them if they were caught.

The methods of torture were brutal. Gilio (1972, pp. 141–172) describes in detail the police and military torture of suspected Tupamaros. Even when prisoners finally provided information, they continued to be tortured routinely until they were either killed or released. Torture became a standard police tactic. A. J. Langguth (1978) devotes most of his work to the torture commonplace in Uruguay and Brazil. The torturers viewed themselves as professionals who were simply carrying out a job for the government. Rapes, beatings, and murders by torturers were common, and the police refined the art of torture to keep victims in pain as long as possible. According to Langguth, some suspects were tortured over a period of months or even years.

Early Successes

In the midst of revolution and torture, the Tupamaros accused the United States of supporting the brutal Uruguayan government. Their internal revolt thus adopted the rhetoric of an anti-imperialist revolution, which increased their popular support. The Tupamaros established several combat and support columns in Montevideo, and by 1970 they began to reach the zenith of their power. Porzecanski says that they almost achieved a duality of power; that is, the Tupamaros were so strong that they seemed to share power equally with the government.

Their success was short-lived, however. Although they waged an effective campaign of terrorism, they were never able to capture the hearts of the working class. Most of Montevideo's workers viewed the Tupamaros as privileged students with no real interest in the working class. In addition, the level of their violence was truly appalling.

During terrorist operations, numerous people were routinely murdered. The eventual murder of a kidnapped American police official disgusted the workers, even though they had no great love for the United States. Tupamaro tactics alienated their potential supporters. In the end, violence spelled doom for the Tupamaros.

By bringing chaos to the capital, they succeeded in unleashing the full wrath of the government. In addition, the Tupamaros had overestimated their strength. In 1971, they joined a left-wing coalition of parties and ran for office. According to Ronald MacDonald (1972, pp. 24–45), this was a fatal mistake. The Tupamaros had alienated potential electoral support through their terrorist campaign, and the left-wing coalition was soundly defeated in national elections.

The electoral defeat was not the only bad news for the Tupamaros. The election brought a right-wing government to power, and the new military government openly advocated and approved of repression. A brutal counterterrorist campaign followed. Far from being alienated by this, the workers of Montevideo applauded the new government's actions, even when it declared martial law in 1972. Armed with expanded powers, the government began to round up all leftists in 1972. For all practical purposes, the Tupamaros were finished. Their violence helped bring about a revolution, but not the type that they had intended.

Tupamaro Organization

The Tupamaros were one of the most highly organized yet least structured terrorist groups in modern history. In some ways, the Tupamaros seemed to anticipate the growth of networked organizations. By the same token, the Tupamaros maintained a hierarchy. Only groups like the Palestine Liberation Organization (PLO) and the Irish Republican Army (IRA) rivaled the hierarchical organization of the Tupamaros. But, while both the PLO and the IRA enjoy a tremendous amount of external support, the Tupamaros existed almost entirely within the borders of Uruguay. Because they were virtually self-sufficient, the growth, operations, and organization of the Tupamaros were amazing. If they failed to achieve success in the long run, their organizational structure at least kept them in the field as long as possible. The Tupamaros were nominally guided by a National Convention, which had authority in all matters of policy and operations. In reality, the National Convention seldom met more than once per year and was disbanded in the 1970s. Christopher Hewitt (1984, p. 8) notes that the National Convention did not meet at all after September 1970. John Wolf (1981, p. 31) believes that an executive committee controlled all activities in Montevideo. Arturo Porzecanski (1973), probably the most noted authority on the Tupamaros, makes several references to this same executive committee. For all practical purposes, it seems to have controlled the Tupamaros (see *Memorial Institute for the Prevention of Terrorism*, n.d.).

The executive committee was responsible for two major functions. It ran the columns that supervised the terrorist operations, and it also administered a special Committee for Revolutionary Justice. The power of the executive committee derived from internal enforcement. The job of the committee was to terrorize the terrorists into obedience. If an operative refused to obey an order or tried to leave the organization, a delegation from the committee would usually deal with the matter. It was not uncommon to murder the family of the offending party, along with the errant member. The Tupamaros believed in strong internal discipline.

In day-to-day operations, however, the executive committee exercised very little authority. Robert Moss (1972, p. 222) states that the Tupamaros lacked a unified command structure for routine functions. The reason can be found in the nature of the organization. Because secrecy dominated every facet of its operations, it could not afford open communications. Therefore, each subunit evolved into a highly autonomous operation. There was little the executive committee could do about this situation, and the command structure became highly decentralized. The Tupamaros existed as a confederacy.

Operational power in the Tupamaros was vested in the lower-echelon units. Columns were organized for both combatant (operational) and staff (logistical) functions. Wolf (1981, p. 35) writes that most of the full-time terrorists belonged to cells in the combatant columns. They lived a precarious day-to-day existence and were constantly in conflict with the authorities. According to Wolf, they were supported by larger noncombatant columns that served to keep the terrorists in the field.

The importance of the noncombatant columns cannot be overemphasized—the strength of the Tupamaros came from its logistical columns. Without the elaborate support network of sympathizers and part-time helpers, the Tupamaros could not have remained in the field. Other groups that have copied their organizational model have not had the ability to launch a campaign because they lacked the same level of support.

Wolf's analysis of the support network includes peripheral support that was not directly linked to the Tupamaro organization. With Porzecanski, Wolf classifies supporters into two categories. One group operated in the open and provided intelligence and background information to the noncombatant sections. The other type of supporters worked on getting supplies to the operational sections. These sympathizers provided arms, ammunition, and legal aid. Both groups tried to generate popular support for the Tupamaros. When the government attacked the terrorists in 1972, its primary target was the support network. Police officials reasoned that if they destroyed the logistical network they would destroy the Tupamaros.

In looking at the organizational chart of the Tupamaros (Figure 10.3), it is easy to envisage the entire operation. The Executive Committee was in charge, but it ran a highly decentralized operation. Its main power came from the internal rule enforcement provided by the Committee for Revolutionary Justice. Columns were the major units, but they tended to be tactical formations. The real operational power came from the cells, which united for column-style operations on rare occasions. The combat striking power of the Tupamaros came from the four- to six-person groups in the cells. This organization epitomized Marighella's concept of the firing unit. Peter Waldmann (1986, p. 259) sums up the Tupamaros best by stating that they became the masters of urban terrorism. He believes that in terms of striking power, organization, and the ability to control a city, no group has ever surpassed the Tupamaros. They epitomized the terrorist role.

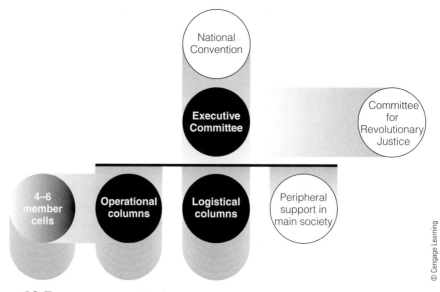

FIGURE **10.3** Tupamaro Organization

Tupamaro Tactics

- Assassination
- Bank robbery
- Kidnapping
- Propaganda
- Bombing
- Internal discipline
- Infiltration of security forces
- Temporary control of urban areas
- Redistribution of expropriated goods to the poor

Influencing Modern Terrorism

As the champions of revolutionary terrorism, the Tupamaros were copied around the world, especially by groups in the United States and in western Europe. Many American left-wing groups from 1967 to 1990 modeled themselves after the Tupamaros. In western Europe, the Tupamaro structure and tactics were mimicked by such groups as the Red Army Faction and Direct Action. The **Red Brigades** split their activities among different cities, but they essentially copied the model of the Tupamaros.

William Dyson (2004) argues that, although some terrorist structures change and suicide bombing has become more common, the strategic and tactical practices of terrorists remain constant. Several groups still follow the model of the Tupamaros. The fact that the Tupamaros created an urban movement is important in terms of the group's impact on violence in Latin America, but it also has a bearing on the way terrorist methods have developed in Europe and in the United States. Historically, Latin American terrorism had been a product of rural peasant revolt. The Tupamaros offered an alternative to this tradition by making the city a battleground. They demonstrated to Western groups the impact that a few violent true believers could have on the rational routines of urban life. The urban setting provided the Tupamaros with endless opportunities.

Red Brigades: An Italian Marxist terrorist group that had its most effective operations from 1975 to 1990. It amended the centralized Tupamaro model by creating semiautonomous cells.

FIGURE **10.4** Tupamaro Symbol

The tactics and organization of the Tupamaros have also been copied by right-wing groups. In the United States, right-wing extremist organizations have advocated the use of Tupamaro-style tactics. Many revolutionary manuals and proposed terrorist organizations are based on Tupamaro experiences.

In the right-wing novel *The Turner Diaries* (MacDonald, 1980), Earl Turner joins a terrorist group similar to the Tupamaros in Washington, D.C. The author describes the mythical right-wing revolution in terms of Carlos Marighella and the Tupamaros. The right does not give credit to the left, but it does follow its example.

Self-Check

> What are revolutionary and counter revolutionary terrorism?

> How did the Tupamaros envision urban revolution?

> In what ways did Tupamaro tactics impact terrorism, in general?

Would-Be Revolutionaries: FARC, the ELN, and the MeK

Illegal drugs are part of Colombia's problem with terrorism. Originally liberated by Simón Bolívar in 1812, Colombia became part of a large nation known as Grand Colombia. By 1830, regional interests in Colombia and Panama began to surface, and Panama gained independence during a U.S. sponsored revolution in 1903. While Panama developed relative stability, Colombia's history was marked by internal violence and political instability. During the last half century, the country has been in the midst of a dirty war in which terrorists and governmental forces fight a shadow war that is interconnected with drug production (see Figure 10.5).

The Revolutionary Armed Forces of Colombia (FARC) is Latin America's oldest and largest terrorist group. Formed as a military wing of the Colombian Communist Party in 1964, it is probably the most capable terrorist group in South America.

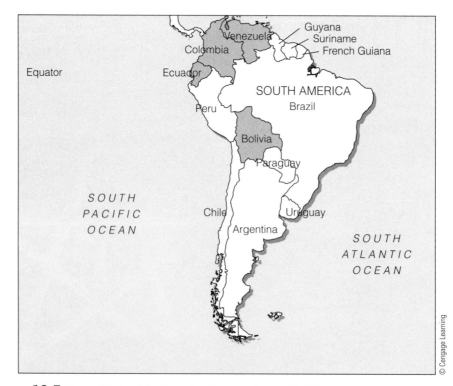

FIGURE **10.5** Map of Colombia, Ecuador, Venezuela, and Bolivia

Although it operates against the Colombian government, its activities have spread to surrounding countries. It has engaged in a full range of terrorist activities, including attacks on Colombian military forces. FARC also found that it could profit from the drug trade. At first, it made alliances with Colombian cartels; then it graduated to production after the cartels were destroyed (National Counterterrorism Center, 2010).

The United States had long been involved in Colombian affairs, and it stepped up measures in 1999 with a new project "**Plan Colombia.**" The purpose was to move against three different groups: FARC, the National Liberation Army (ELN), and the United Self-Defense Forces of Colombia (AUC). Like FARC, the ELN is a revolutionary group that extends into surrounding countries; the AUC is composed of underground government officials who terrorize in the name of security. The goal of Plan Colombia was to disarm all the groups and to deal with an endemic cocaine trade.

Modern Colombian violence cannot be separated from the production of cocaine. Although criminal syndicates in Mexico assumed control of the drug routes to the United States after 2000, Colombia still accounts for the lion's share of cocaine production. Opinions about the success of antidrug efforts are mixed. Officially, the U.S. Department of State (2008) claims that Plan Colombia has been a success. Not only have groups been disarmed, but drug production has decreased. Other assessments are not so optimistic. Two researchers from the Council on Foreign Relations, Michael Bustamante and Sebastian Chaskel (2008), argue that Plan Colombia has been a dismal failure. Violence has been reduced, but the drug problem remains. It has more to do with demand for cocaine in the United States than with internal issues in Colombia.

To understand recent shifts of violence in Colombia and the surrounding region, it is necessary to look at the 2002 presidential election. **Alvaro Uribe** won both the election and widespread popular support by augmenting Plan Colombia. He promised that he would bring FARC and the ELN to the negotiating table while dismantling the underground governmental counterterrorists of the AUC. He was quick to seize on the United States' reaction to September 11, claiming that Colombia's contribution to the war on terror would be the elimination of these three groups. The illegal drug problem remains, although Uribe has managed to reduce violence (Bustamante and Chaskel, 2008).

The National Counterterrorism Center (2010) suggests that FARC has been weakened by several setbacks. In 2008, Uribe's aggressive counterterrorism policy struck deeply into FARC, and some of its key leaders were killed in military operations. Its structures were disrupted by aggressive military action, and a rescue mission freed 15 hostages who had been held in captivity for many years. One of the co-founders of FARC died the same year, and in 2009 security forces turned a FARC offensive back. At that time, government forces also captured Swedish military hardware that had been sold to Venezuela in 1980. Bustamante and Chaskel (2008) argue that Uribe's most successful military actions came between his first election and 2005. FARC has broken into smaller units operating over a wider geographical base, they believe.

There are mixed opinions on the AUC. Officially, Uribe has forced the counterterrorists to disband, but they remain active. Bustamante and Chaskel note that death squad violence dropped after 2005, yet human rights workers and union organizers still disappear even when they have nothing to do with terrorism. The AUC has been particularly aggressive against the general population. Melissa Herman (2008) says that this has involved the usual tactics, such as intimidation, murder, and rape, but it also appears more subtly. FARC operates in peasant communities, and much of Plan Colombia has disrupted entire regions, leading to the dislocation of many families. This has in turn resulted in the emergence of women as strong voices for Colombian democracy.

The ELN is smaller than FARC and less active. Founded during the same time period, it emerged as the more effective organization by the 1980s, only to be dwarfed

---

Plan Colombia: A joint effort by the United States and Colombia to reduce violence and illegal drugs. It began in 1999.

Alvaro Uribe: (b. 1952) President of Colombia, 2002–2010. He was known for his tough stance against FARC and other revolutionary movements.

by FARC. The BBC (2009) reported that the ELN began staging a comeback in 2009 with a raid to free its jailed leader. Uribe's hard-nosed policies have inflicted losses, but the ELN is composed of determined Marxists who are funded through the drug trade. Cuba sponsored unsuccessful peace talks in 2005 and again in 2007, only to have the ELN leaders balk at any ceasefire that fails to establish a communist government. In another twist, the ELN began intermittent fighting with FARC for control of drug routes leading into Colombia in 2008. The groups are linked by a radical socialist ideology but are torn over control of drug profits.

The Council on Foreign Relations (Hanson, 2009) writes that FARC had about 9,000 guerrillas at its strongest point. After Uribe's offensives, FARC lost its ability to operate in Colombia's rural jungles, and local populations turned against it. ELN, on the other hand, has abandoned the rural orientation, shifting to urban centers. Both groups are suffering. According to the Council on Foreign Relations, FARC is in a state of crisis and ELN's move to an urban environment is a sign of weakness. Noting these changes, the International Crisis Group (ICG, 2010) writes that Uribe's offensive was extremely effective. A new government came to power after Uribe's term expired in August 2010, and an emerging threat has become more complex. New types of local hybrid criminal and ideological groups are appearing. The ICG believes that Colombia needs to develop better law enforcement tools to handle the new form of terrorism.

The Mujahedin-e Kahlq

The Mujahedin-e Kahlq (MeK) was founded in 1965, 14 years before the Iranian Revolution, for the purpose of overthrowing the Iranian government. It has been designated as a foreign terrorist organization by the United States, primarily due to the assassinations of six Americans in Tehran during the 1970s and its anti-American activities during the 1979 Iranian Revolution. It is estimated to have about 3,800 members, and Saddam Hussein used its services during the Iran–Iraq War. During the United States' invasion of Iraq, the group was officially designated as a hostile force, but the MeK negotiated a ceasefire with American forces in April 2003. The new Iraqi government decided to exile MeK members to Iran in 2003 (Goulka et al., 2009).

The Council on Foreign Relations (Fletcher, 2008) states that the MeK was responsible for attacking a number of Western targets in the 1970s and for supporting the 1979 **American embassy takeover** in Tehran. It is the largest and most militant group opposed to the Islamic Republic of Iran. The group espouses a mixture of Marxism and Islam, and its original purpose was to overthrow the governments of the Shah and to replace it with a socialist government. It supported the 1979 revolution, but its philosophy of socialism and women's liberation contrasted sharply with the conservative views of Iran's mullahs.

American embassy takeover: During the Iranian hostage crisis, revolutionary students stormed the U.S. embassy in Tehran with the support of the Iranian government. They held 54 American hostages from November 1979 to January 1981.

Mujahedin-e Khalq presents a conundrum for the United States. Officially listed as a terrorist group since 1997, the MeK had settled in a camp about 40 miles north of Baghdad in 2003. As soon as the invading U.S. military forces negotiated a peace settlement with the MeK, they found that they could not fit its members into a neat package. American military planners had not prepared for MeK prisoners. At first, American forces sought to treat the group's members as prisoners of war; but, according to the Geneva Convention, each member was entitled to a separate hearing to determine their status. In addition, a significant portion of the membership had been duped into joining during the Iran–Iraq war. Secretary of Defense Donald Rumsfeld changed the members' status in 2004 without a legal review, stating that all members were civilian "protected persons." According to a RAND study (Goulka et al., 2009), this was the result of improper planning. It also placed the United States in the hypocritical position of having a relationship with a designated terrorist group.

The *Times* of London points out that the relationship became even more uncomfortable. In 2007, President George Bush received a budget of $400,000,000 from Congress to support groups violently opposed to Iran's Islamic regime. One of the groups included on the list was the MeK (Philp and Evans, 2009). According to *Vanity Fair* (Unger, 2007), prominent advisors to the Bush administration were advocating that the United States form a link with the MeK. It was the best hope for destabilizing Iran, the advisors argued.

According to the Council on Foreign Relations (Fletcher, 2009), the MeK conducted a number of attacks between the 1970s and 2001. These include hit-and-run military attacks against Iran, assassinations of Iranian officials, attacks on Iranians and foreign countries, and large bombings. The group's leader is Maryam Rajavi, and she hopes to be president of Iran after the current regime is deposed. The group has been trying to remove itself from the State Department's terrorist list.

An in-depth Canadian press report (Petrou, 2009) suggests that MeK's strategy is trying to demonstrate that it has amended its terrorist past. The MeK held a large rally in Paris in the summer of 2008, and it paid the expenses for several Western politicians who attended the event. The group has been removed from the British and the European Union list of terrorist organizations, and it has shared information with clustered intelligence agencies. The group is not popular in Iran because of its alliance with Saddam Hussein and the Iran–Iraq War. Though the group has been fairly inactive since 2001, numerous critics have pointed to its human rights abuses. Others suggest that the MeK is little more than a personality cult built around Maryam Rajavi.

Self-Check

> How did FARC, the ELN, and the MeK originate and operate?

> What are their connections to the drug trade?

> Why does the West have an ambivalent relationship with the MeK?

Maoist Revolutionary Terrorism

While the Tupamaros exerted tremendous influences on the development of urban terrorism, rural revolutionary models also flourished. Guerrillas in Malaysia, Vietnam, and South Africa used terrorism as a tactic to support a larger strategy. The guerrilla movement failed in Malaysia, but it was at least partially successful in Vietnam and South Africa. Other guerrillas saw a few chances for success, and some of these experiences gave way to campaigns of rural terror. Some were influenced by Marxism and others by a more extreme form of Maoism.

Maoist terrorism is a form of revolutionary terrorism, and it can be understood within the same framework Martha Crenshaw originally used to define the term. In practice, Maoist groups tend to be more violent than other revolutionary groups. Critical scholars debate the differences among various Marxist schools of thought, but, in terms of terrorism, Maoist groups exhibit three striking differences from most other revolutionary terrorists. First, they practice ruthless domination in the areas they control, and they rule by terrorism. Second, Maoist groups have a reputation for maintaining internal discipline. They purge and control their own members. Finally, and most important, Maoist groups follow the revolutionary philosophy of Chinese communist leader Mao Zedong. Maoist groups are based in rural peasant movements.

Peru's Shining Path

A Maoist group, the Shining Path (*Sendero Luminoso*), launched a campaign in rural Peru that began in 1980 and lasted for the following two decades (Fraser, 2007; and see Taylor, 2006). The Tupac Amaru Revolutionary Movement (MRTA)

Tupac Amaru: (?–1572) An Inca chieftain who led a revolt against Spain in the sixteenth century. His story has inspired many liberation and democratic movements in South America.

Abimael Guzmán: (b. 1934) A philosophy professor who led the Shining Path from 1980 until his arrest in 1992. Guzmán is serving a life sentence in Peru.

Cultural Revolution: A violent movement in China from 1966 to 1976. Its main purpose was to rid China of its middle class and growing capitalist interests. The Cultural Revolution ended with the death of Mao Zedong.

joined the Shining Path in 1984, although it was much less violent. Peru's revolutionary past was grounded in anticolonialism as the indigenous people sought to free themselves from European rule. **Tupac Amaru** (d. 1572) led a revolt against Spain from 1571 to 1572. Although the country did not gain its independence until 1824, he came to symbolize Peruvian independence. As military coups took control of the government throughout the nineteenth and twentieth centuries, his name was used to invoke a democratic spirit. After a civilian-elected president took power in Lima in 1980, Tupac Amaru came to symbolize another type of revolution. The Shining Path would wage a Maoist campaign of terrorism for the next 20 years using his name.

Scholars have debated the political orientation of the Shining Path almost from its inception. Led by a philosophy professor, **Abimael Guzmán,** the group was deeply influenced by China and its **Cultural Revolution.** Guzmán believed that the leftist politics of Peru's Communist Party were too tame, and he embraced the radical violence espoused by Maoist revolutionaries (Gorritti, 2006). In addition, the Maoist approach matched Peru's economic structure. Most of its economic and political strength came from the countryside (Zarazadich, 2006). Guzmán moved to build a rural power base, and most scholars view the organization as a violent Maoist movement.

Other scholars do not accept the view that the Shining Path was based in Maoism. Paul Navarro (2010) believes that the entire Peruvian left was influenced by Mao but that the influence was rhetorical. Most Peruvian leftists were mainstream Marxists. While they called for violent revolution, the starting point was thought to be decades away. Peru's communists were not inherently violent. Ronald Osborn (2007) argues that the Shining Path was hyper-Marxist/Maoist group, unique among all groups in Latin America because of its proclivity for violence. He says that the Shining Path became the first insurgent force on the left to surpass the military in waging a systematic campaign of violence against civilians.

Guzmán led the Shining Path in a twofold strategy. First, the guerrillas operated in rural areas, trying to create regional military forces. Second, Guzmán attempted to combine Mao Zedong's ruthless revolutionary zeal with the guerrilla philosophy of Che Guevara. The result was a ruthless campaign of violence designed to force peasants into a new egalitarian society. For most guerrillas, terrorism is minimized because it alienates potential supporters. Guzmán's philosophy was different. Anyone who refused to support the Shining Path was considered an enemy. Not only did Guzmán's followers target individuals with terrorism, they also engaged in indiscriminate violence against anyone not supporting their call. Some victims suffered from car bombings and drive-by shootings; in other areas, guerrillas wiped out entire villages. The Shining Path's lethal methods demanded the deaths of all people who resisted or even gave the impression that they did not support the revolution (Theidon, 2006).

The government responded with its own campaign of counterterrorism. Security forces attacked the Shining Path with reckless abandon. Throughout the 1980s, they struck suspected areas of guerrilla support, and they grew more ruthless after the election of **Alberto Fujimori** in 1990 (Fraser, 2007). Fujimori created a system of secret courts and political repression. He dissolved Congress and ran Peru as a virtual police state. The rural peasants were caught in the middle. Soldiers and guerrillas following a scorched earth policy, embracing the moral necessity of eradicating all enemies, while peasants suffered from the actions of both sides. The struggle degenerated into a series of massacres and individual murders (Theidon, 2006).

Security forces seemed to gain the upper hand in September 1992 when police surveillance teams took Guzmán into custody. Fujimori began a campaign of economic reform despite his draconian measures against Peruvian democracy. The Shining Path, however, responded with a new campaign of terrorism, and the MRTA

Alberto Fujimori: (b. 1938) President of Peru from 1990 to 2000. He fled to Japan in 2000 but was extradited to Peru in 2007. He was convicted of human rights violations and sentenced to prison.

gained headlines with sensational operations. The government responded with even more repression and police death squads. The fighting ended in 2000 with all guerrillas abandoning terrorism and the with fall of Fujimori. The new Peruvian government created a Truth and Reconciliation Commission, which released a final report in 2003 after a two-year investigation. Two decades of violence had resulted in the deaths of nearly 70,000 people. The Shining Path was responsible for about 54 percent of the total death count (Theidon, 2006).

Despite its tactics of individual masked murders and the elimination of anyone suspected of not supporting the revolution, the Shining Path was committed to social egalitarianism, at least rhetorically. The structure of the organization reveals two interesting social patterns. The role of families was prominent in day-to-day operations, and the Shining Path was committed to feminism. It actively recruited and engaged the services of revolutionary females, and Guzman's second-in-command was a woman from 1980 until she was killed in 1988 (Heilman, 2010).

The fighting supposedly came to an end in 2000; however, the *New York Times* (2009) reports that the Shining Path reemerged around 2007, reinventing itself as a drug trafficking organization. According to the newspaper, the Shining Path moved into Peru's cocaine-producing areas and abandoned Maoist practices for the lucrative profits of the drug trade. In 2008, the Shining Path was responsible for more than two dozen murders, making it the deadliest year since the fall of Fujimori.

Lack of leadership remains a problem. According to the Jamestown Foundation (2012), the Shining Path has partially taken over the drug trade in southern Peru. It is attempting to resurrect the organization in the mode of the ELN and FARC. This has caused the group to split. The Communist Party of Peru is lobbying for an end to bickering, but it has been unsuccessful. No longer as strong as it was under Guzmán, the Shining Path may resume its Maoist revolution in Peru when it is reconstituted with drug money.

The Maoist Rebellion in Nepal

The small Himalayan nation of Nepal experienced a ruthless Maoist rebellion from 1995 to 2005. A small group of Maoist rebels began a series of local attacks with homemade weapons in 1995. At first, most of the people and the government treated the rebellion as a joke. The rebels were hardly effective, they had no support, and they appeared to have no future. Still, the revolution grew (see Figure 10.6).

The Maoist rebels were unique. They had international connections through their leftist positions, yet their specific objectives were aimed only at the national level. They sought to dismantle autocratic, futile social structures and to create a democratically inclusive government. They also sought to end Nepal's monarchy (Upreti, 2004; see also Hutt, 2004; BBC, 2010).

In order to understand the Maoist rebellion, it is necessary to place it in the context of recent history. Nepal appeared to be on its way to becoming a constitutional monarchy in the 1950s. A new king ascended the throne in 1955, and the country created a multiparty parliament in 1959. Unfortunately, the experience with democracy was short-lived. The king suspended parliament in 1960 and ended party politics in 1962. Nepal was a feudal society with a landed aristocracy and a strong monarchy. The king saw democracy as a threat and moved to stop it. These actions frustrated many people, especially a small communist party.

A large democratic party, the Nepali Congress Party (NCP), began agitating for a greater role in government and for the restoration of parliament. The NCP began a campaign of civil disobedience in 1985. After five years, a new king found that he could not operate in a perpetual state of political confusion. In 1990, the king agreed to a new constitution, and the NCP won elections in 1991. This changed three years later when the 1994 elections brought a communist government, something that the king would not tolerate. He dissolved the parliament in 1995, and the Communist Party began a rural rebellion (BBC, 2010).

After an inauspicious beginning, the rebellion began to take shape. The Maoists were ruthless, and their goal was to create a psychological climate of fear among government supporters by a campaign of brutality. As they grew stronger, they began attacking police and military outposts. The Maoists executed prisoners, kidnapped prominent citizens, conducted high-profile assassinations, and launched hit-and-run attacks. They detained government officials, bringing them to their own courts for a "people's trial." After each trial, the officials would be executed. They evicted peasants from their land and set up local governments to redistribute their holdings. The Maoists' goal was to create a core group of peasant supporters and to terrorize the remaining population into subservience (Upreti, 2004).

King Gyanendra: (b. 1947) King of Nepal from 2001 to 2008. After the attack and murder of several members of the royal family, Gyanendra became king of Nepal in 2001. He took complete power in 2005 to fight the Maoist rebellion. In the spring of 2006, he was forced to return power to parliament, and he was removed from power in 2008.

Over the next ten years, 12,000 people would be killed, and 100,000 peasants would be displaced. The army responded with its own campaign of counterterrorism, and, as in Peru, the peasants were caught in the middle. Both sides engaged in horrific human abuses. The government, in the person of the authoritarian **King Gyanendra**, who took control of Nepal's government in 2001, he ordered the military to wage a brutal campaign of counterterrorism. The army conducted summary executions, torture, and abductions. The Communist Party of Nepal responded with more "arrests" and "people's trials." If peasants sided with the government, rebels labeled them as "class enemies," and they were frequently murdered. If they gave in to rebel demands for food and shelter, governmental forces punished them (Adams, 2005).

Nepal's rebellion did not follow the path of other forms of terrorism in Asia. One interesting difference was the role of women in the Maoist movement. As the rebellion grew, the role of women expanded. Their numbers increased along with the narratives of their struggles and their roles in the rebellion. It opened the possibility of more women participating in the government, but it came at a contradictory cost. The Maoists were known for authoritarianism, violence, and human rights abuses. Although 30 percent of the Maoists were female, many did not want to support such

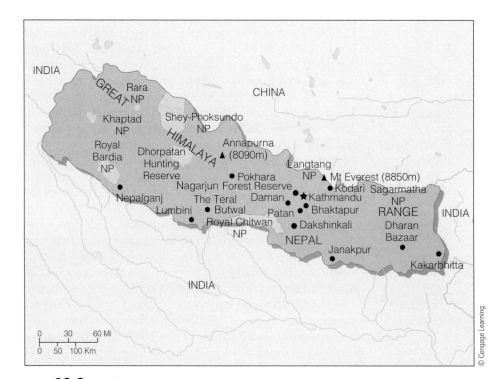

FIGURE **10.6** Nepal

actions. Nevertheless, they had little incentive to return to the old patriarchy, where they would be relegated to the most subservient roles. They had come to the ranks because they had been the most downtrodden segment of the population. Many believed that the women were more committed than the men because men returned home to a hero's welcome but women returned home to serve (Manchanda, 2004).

After September 11, 2001, the democratic aspects of the rebellion were hidden by international rhetoric. In an analysis of press releases during the course of the war, one research study summarized the changes in attitude. When the rebellion first began, the Maoists were called terrorists. As their effectiveness grew, news reports began calling them rebels, guerrillas, and insurgents. This changed after September 11, when the Maoists were universally lumped in with international terrorists and when they became targets of the war on terrorism. The simplification missed the point of many villagers and the nationalistic nature of the rebellion. Though peasants who refused to support the Maoists suffered greatly, many of the lowest peasants felt empowered by local Maoist governments (Shneidermann and Turin, 2004).

The government and the Maoists signed a peace agreement in late 2006, with both sides promising to agree to a power-sharing arrangement and to write a new constitution. The International Crisis Group (2007b) believed that the only way the process would work was if the Maoists controlled the extremists in their own ranks. Things seemed to be heading in that direction when the 2008 election brought the Maoists to power and allowed them to bring the monarchy to an end. The Maoist coalition, however, fell apart, and a new government excluded the Nepalese Communist Party. The constitution remained in limbo.

Some members of the Maoist movements began to resent the lack of activity by 2010, but the peace process and negotiations over the constitution continued. The Maoist officially handed over their weapons in September 2011. The Maoists officially left their enclaves and rejoined their country in February 2012, although some threatened violence if the government reneged on its promises (Singh and Popeski, 2012).

Naxalites of India

India has a variety of terrorist problems arising from political, religious, and ethnic strife (see *Timeline 10.1: A Sample of Terrorist Events in India*). It is also in the throes of a Maoist rebellion. In order to understand the Maoist problem, it is necessary to remember that Indian society was governed by a rigid caste system for centuries. Even though the system has been formally abandoned, many lower-class peasants still suffer from its effects. India's agrarian system is based on large, wealthy landholders and unlanded peasants, formerly of the lower caste, who are alienated from the current economic structure. Great economic disparities have led to the growth of left-wing movements that demand a more equal distribution of resources. One of these movements has turned violent (Zissis, 2007) (Figure 11.7).

The Naxalites emerged in a 1967 uprising in West Bengal. Peasants demanding the right to land ownership and better wages staged mass demonstrations with the support of the communist party. Police confronted the demonstrators with deadly force, and protests turned into rebellion. The confrontation occurred in the Indian village of Naxalbari, and the unorganized groups of rebels that gathered in the countryside were known collectively as Naxalites. When tensions between the Soviet Union and China led to a breakup of the Sino-Soviet alliance, the Naxalites chose a Maoist path. Their rebellion was short-lived after Indian security forces targeted the group, and it virtually disappeared by 1975 (Banerjee, 2009).

Some members of the Indian government began to lobby for real reform as a result of the unrest. They saw social injustice at the base of the agrarian rebellion. Although they attempted to pass reform legislation, they were thwarted by

| TIMELINE 10.1 | *A Sample of Terrorist Events in India* |

1948	Mahatma Gandhi assassinated by Hindu extremist.
1967–1975	First Naxalite rebellion.
1984	Prime Minister Indira Gandhi assassinated by Sikh bodyguards.
1985	Air India Flight 182 bombed, 329 killed.
1990	Muslim separatists launch campaign in Kashmir.
1991	Prime Minister Rajiv Gandhi assassinated by LTTE.
	Mid-1990s–2004 Naxalites begin organizing, forming the Red Corridor.
1995	Sikh bomb kills Beant Singh, the chief minister of Punjab.
2001	Jihadists attack legislative assembly in Srinagar.
2001	Jihadist suicide attack on Indian parliament building.
2003	Jihadists execute 24 Hindu civilians in Kashmir.
2003	Jihadist terrorist bombs kill 46 in Bombay.
2004	Present Naxalite rebellion. India employs Special Police reservists.
2006	Seven explosions kill 185 on train in Mumbai.
2008	LeT launches simultaneous attacks in Mumbai.
2008	CoBRA units created to fight Naxalites.
2009	Naxalites routinely inflict dozens of casualties in police ambushes.
2010	Train derailment kills 148, injures over 200. Naxalites suspected.

Sources: BBC News, December 2001; Scaruffi, 2007; *Wall Street Journal* 2010.

several aspects of India's bureaucratic and political systems. The social separation between landlords and tenants was deeply ingrained in Indian society. The civil service agencies assigned to agricultural areas were inefficient, and there was little cooperation among different units of government. Complete land records did not exist. Many peasants were illiterate, with no economic future other than working as tenant laborers for absentee landlords. When the government finally passed modest reform legislation, it did not allocate enough money to implement the program. In the end, India decided to handle any agricultural unrest as a police problem (Tharu, 2007).

The Naxalites began to emerge again in the 1990s in a variety of smaller movements. Anthropologist George Kunnath (2006) spent a year living with and observing a former member of the Naxalites. He believes that this grass-roots movement gained strength because the landlord system had created a virtual feudal state. The Naxalites saw the landlords as unproductive external proprietors who exploited cheap labor. The Naxalites' goal evolved into a movement with three promises: land to the tiller, higher wages for agricultural work, and ending the de facto caste system.

Red Corridor: The area of Naxalite violence in India. The corridor runs from Nepal through southern India, and from India's east coast to the central regions.

As the group began to solidify, it formed a **Red Corridor,** stretching from the northern Nepal border to south-central India. This became a strong geographical base of power. When two movements—the People's Guerrilla Army of the People's War Group and the People's Liberation Army of the Maoist Center of India—joined together in 2004, the Naxalites reemerged with power. A pan-Naxalite rebellion burst onto the scene, and by 2005 the Naxalites were challenging India's police with attacks on police stations and jungle ambushes, producing law enforcement casualties in the hundreds (Turiville, 2005; Ganguly, 2009).

The Jamestown Foundation (2010) reports that the Indian government believes that the Naxalite rebellion has become its number-one internal security problem. In the summer of 2010, the prime minister was considering calling on the military to deal with the problem. Other research suggests that the violence has grown because of an ineffective response (Oetken, 2009). The police launched a campaign of brutality, and they have suffered hundreds of casualties themselves. There is some speculation that they have authorized death squads. One of the more controversial moves has been the establishment of a Special Police force composed of local peasants. With no training and little regard for human rights, the Special Police frequently operate outside the law. The Naxalites have responded in kind, and more than half the states in India are involved in the dirty war (Guha, 2007; Banerjee, 2009).

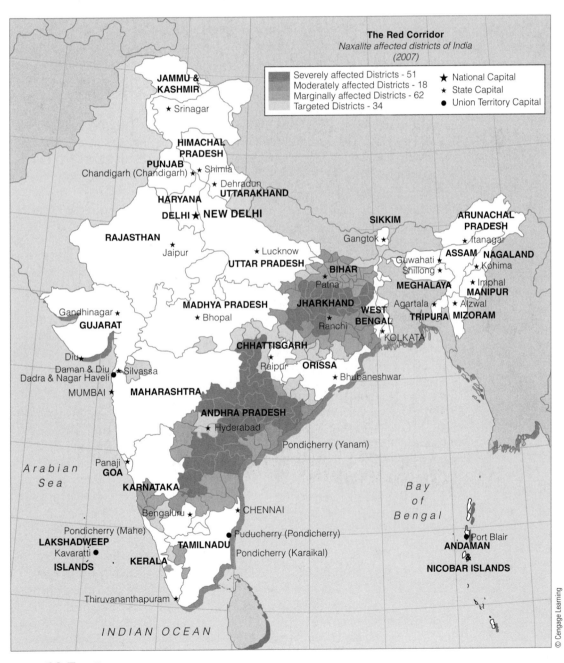

FIGURE **10.7** India

There is an interesting aspect to gender roles in the Naxalite movement. When it first began in 1967, females began protest movements, sometimes resulting in violence. Eventually, many joined the militants in the jungles. Many women regarded their activities as a "magic moment," a time that defined their lives. Although they did not achieve emancipation, they created a new self-identity, apart from their role as peasants, and a women's movement began to emerge (Sinha Roy, 2009). Paradoxically, they also found that they were defined by their participation in the Naxalite movement. Imprisonment, shared dangers, and a spirit of brotherhood created lifelong bonds among many groups of men (Donner, 2009).

Shameul Tharu (2007) argues that the rebellion cannot be stopped by either police or military power. It is simplistic, he says, to classify the Naxalite rebellion as a criminal problem. The Indian government needs to address several structural issues, including land reform, political reform, and ending bureaucratic corruption. Sumanta Banerjee (2009) adds that the government reform would rectify the peasants' alienation from the land. On the other hand, Naxalite violence and human rights violations against peasants have alienated their potential supporters.

No-go areas: An informal term to describe geographical areas that the duly empowered government cannot control. Security forces cannot routinely patrol these places.

The Aspen Foundation (Van Dongen, 2012) believes that the rebellion is far from over for three reasons. First, India is one of the most underpoliced countries of the world. It does not have enough personnel to confront the Naxalites effectively. Second, reversing their previous public posture, the Naxalites have begun providing social services to the poor inside the Red Corridor. These are effective **no-go areas**, and the Indian government cannot respond in kind. Even if the Indians could, they have demonstrated no interest in doing so. Finally, the most important reason the rebellion continues is that the fundamental issues which caused the unrest have not been addressed.

The New People's Army

While many Americans conceive of the Philippine Islands as a monolithic modern state, the reality is different. The Philippines has differing cultures, radical gaps in income, different religious traditions, and divisive politics. In addition to foreign occupation by three different countries in the nineteenth and twentieth centuries, Philippine politics has been characterized as a struggle for democracy in the midst of local revolts. In 1986, a grand **"People Power Revolution"** toppled a long-term repressive leader and promised to bring real democracy. The promise failed. Many local revolts continue, including a campaign by the military wing of the Philippine Communist Party, the New People's Army (NPA).

People Power Revolution: A mass Philippine protest movement that toppled Ferdinand Marcos in 1986. Marcos ruled as a dictator after being elected as president in 1965 and declaring martial law in 1972. When Gloria Macapagal-Arroyo (president, 2001–2010) assumed the presidency in January 2001, her government proclaimed a second People Power Revolution.

The NPA is the longest-running communist insurgency in the world. It is a rural movement that began in 1969 as a response to a Philippine dictatorship. It had as many as 25,000 members in the 1980s, though its membership dwindled after the return of democracy in 1986. By the mid-1990s, NPA ranks had slimmed to a cadre of less than 10,000. Today, its estimated strength is less than 7,000 (Montlake, 2007). The group eventually adopted a Maoist revolutionary philosophy, targeting security forces, politicians, judges, and U.S. military personnel assigned to the Philippines. It also gained a reputation for self-purges, killing many of its own members.

The NPA represents one aspect of Philippine violence and terrorism, and other movements are discussed under the analysis of jihadist networks. The NPA is unique due to its ideological orientation (Coronel, 2007). Most of its power base is in rural Luzon, but it has made inroads in Manila and Mindanao. It sustains operations by levying a "revolutionary tax," extorting money from local residents and merchants. The NPA's income averages about $30 million per year (Montlake, 2007). There are many female members who operate as full-fledged guerrillas in the jungle, though the NPA is hardly a bastion of feminism. While girls are recruited at a young age, all aspects of their lives are controlled. Dubbed "Amazonas" for the mythic race of Greek female warriors, they are not allowed to engage in any activity, including romantic liaisons, without permission of the male leaders (Marshall, 2008).

The rural NPA campaign also symbolizes the paradox of counterterrorism; that is, when faced with terrorism, governments frequently resort to terrorism. In 2006, the Philippine government announced an all-out offensive against communism, including the NPA. One of the goals was to reduce NPA membership, and the military took this as a signal to move against all leftists (Coronel, 2007). Professors Patricio Abinales and Donna Amoroso (2006) say that the offensive started with extrajudicial murders. Hundreds of people were killed outside the law. When U.S. military personnel began assistance, the public often welcomed the presence of the American troops. They felt that death squad activities would be curtailed when Americans were present. The professors also note that more soldiers than insurgents were killed in the first year of the crackdown.

Many Philippine counterterrorist activities have taken place outside the law since 2000. Over 1,700 people have been murdered in extrajudicial executions, and the United Nations has placed the Philippine government on an international watch list for human rights violations (Lywe, 2010). Underground death squads began eliminating suspected enemies in Mafia-style executions in 2001, and murders increased with the campaign against terrorism in 2006 (Abinales, 2008). The Philippine government used the war on terrorism as an excuse to move against church workers, union organizers, lawyers, and human rights workers. The Armed Forces of the Philippines (AFP) have dehumanized the NPA, virtually creating a blood feud that can only be ended through complete annihilation (Montlake, 2007).

The Philippines have been plagued by terrorism since the mid-1970s. Two of the issues that keep the NPA in the field are the structure of political power and the distribution of wealth. The Philippines have democratic roots dating back to 1898, when the United States seized the islands from Spain. Americans quickly established democratic institutions, and they were unique. Instead of giving power to all Filipinos, the new democracy favored prosperous, landed elites. When the United States granted the Philippines independence in 1946, the elites continued to run the government. This resulted in a political structure in which most of the people are excluded from active participation (Hutchcroft, 2008).

Poverty does not cause terrorism, but social inequities can draw people to revolutionary causes. Patricio Abinales (2008) says that the political system is somewhat stable because power is not centralized in Manila. It is maintained through relations with local power structures, and the majority of the people are apathetic about the elitist government. Poverty is another issue, and there is no apathy there. Large gaps in the distribution of wealth provide a pool for revolutionaries. These potential actors are not drawn to terrorism. They are motivated by economic disparity (Coronel, 2007).

Self-Check

> What is Maoist terrorism?
> How is it manifested in the Philippines? in Nepal? in India?
> What social factors caused Maoists to gain popularity in these three countries?

The Transformation of European Revolutionary Terrorism

Europe's problems with revolutionary terrorism have changed in recent years. A brief overview explains the reasons. Researchers in the 1980s were noting the left's declining role in European terrorism. The ideological terrorists of the 1960s, on both the left and the right, were expressing their frustration with the social structures imposed by a modern industrial society (Corrado and Evans, 1988, pp. 373–444).

The Decline of Revolutionary Terrorism

By 1988, Corrado and Evans conclude, the popularity of nationalistic and left-wing terrorism was declining. They suggest that the pluralism of Western democracies opened the door to peaceful participation in the political system and offered opportunities for change. Violence no longer seemed an attractive method for groups to express their grievances. As pluralistic governments worked to relieve frustration, the attractiveness of terrorism waned, and terrorists lost their support base. Corrado and Evans predicted that terrorist violence would fade away, reappearing in only a few sporadic incidents. Had the political structure of Europe remained constant after their writing, they would have been correct: Left-wing terrorism was out of vogue, and nationalistic terrorism was on the decline.

Few analysts of terrorism—indeed, few scholars, politicians, soothsayers, or prophets—predicted three key events that changed the political landscape of Europe and the world. In 1989, the Berlin Wall came down, leading to the reunification of Germany. To the south, new nations emerging from the former Yugoslavia took up arms and resumed a centuries-old struggle. The greatest change, though, of all came in the East. The Soviet Union dissolved, along with the authoritarian rule of the Communist Parties in the republics of the former Soviet Union and eastern Europe. These three changes occurred at a time when western Europeans were taking bold steps toward economic and political unity.

A State Department terrorism specialist, Dennis Pluchinsky (1982, pp. 40–78), saw potential changes a decade before they occurred. The left might decline, but he feared that Europe would become a terrorist battleground. Pluchinsky also believed that international and state-sponsored terrorism would grow in Europe and that a greater threat was posed by what he called supraindigenous terrorism. By this, Pluchinsky meant that local terrorist activities would extend beyond local boundaries. Each time a government checks one variety of terrorism, Pluchinsky argued, a new strain appears. Unfortunately, no analyst of terrorism was more correct. Middle Eastern religious terrorism spilled into Europe, and murderous ethnic cleansing (killing or driving out ethnic or religious groups inhabiting an area) dominated the Balkan Peninsula.

As the structure of Europe and the world changed between 1989 and 1992, European terrorism also changed, just as Pluchinsky had predicted. Ideological terrorism swung from left to right, changing its structure as it moved. Nationalistic terrorism remained, but conflict arose in the form of ethnic violence. Ethnic violence grew into open warfare in the Balkans. New criminal organizations appeared, and old ones were revitalized. The threat of jihadist terrorism replaced threats from the left, and Europe experienced new strains of terrorism.

Red Army Faction: a West German Marxist group modeled as Marighella-style urban guerrillas. They were the most violent and active revolutionary group during the heyday of left-wing European terrorism. After German reunification, the records of the former East German secret police led to the demise of the RAF. It was also known as the Baader-Meinhof Gang when it first formed.

Modern European terrorism emerged in the 1960s as an extreme reflection of left-wing activism. Fueled by the Vietnam War, European leftists were influenced by events in Latin America, as well as by revolutionary leaders such as Carlos Marighella. The **Red Army Faction** (RAF)—known as the Baader-Meinhof Gang in its early days—began a campaign in Germany, followed by copycat groups and more long-term terrorist organizations in other countries. By 1970, most left-wing groups and the resurgent nationalistic groups modeled themselves after the Marighella model. Seagaller said that although European terrorists longed for a Marighella-style revolution, they never achieved it because they were too weak. In 1985, they faced their weakness and tried to form a confederation to gain momentum. The left-wing coalition was an effort to pool dwindling resources and support (Seagaller, 1987, pp. 36–40).

On May 28, 1998, the RAF issued a communiqué stating that it was ceasing operations. Christoph Rojahn (1998) says that the RAF mirrored the demise of the European leftists but that they were responsible for Germany's massive security apparatus. In addition, mainstream left-wing politicians had limited effectiveness while the RAF was in the streets. The RAF ceased operations because it was a miserable failure. Although it had maintained a campaign of violence for decades, it was never able to link with a mainstream issue. The group could not attract the support of the radical left, with the exception of the following in its own narrow circle. Rojahn concludes that the 1998 declaration of peace was the group's recognition of its failure.

Southern Europe has experienced a similar decline in left-wing terrorism, and Xavier Raufer (1993) looks at Italy's Red Brigades as another example of the weaknesses of the left. When the Red Brigades approached Direct Action in 1985, they were already rapidly fading from their glory days of headline-grabbing murders. Raufer believed that the Red Brigades would soon follow the unilateral peace declaration of the RAF.

Renato Curcio: (b. 1941) The founder and leader of the Red Brigades in Italy.

Margherita Cagol: (1945–1975) Also known as Mara Cagol, the wife of Renato Curcio and a member of the Red Brigades. She was killed in a shoot-out with Italian police a few weeks after freeing her husband from prison.

There were nearly 300 left-wing groups in Italy that appeared between 1967 and 1985, and most of them had a Marxist-Leninist orientation. The best-known group was the Red Brigades, which formed in Milan after **Renato Curcio** broke away from a left-wing working-class political organization. Leaders gathered more militant followers and announced plans for a terrorist campaign in 1970. **Margherita Cagol** joined Curcio and later became his wife. The future militants called their organization the Red Brigades, and Curcio's 1970 group of militants became known as the Historical Nucleus.

The organization of the Red Brigades was unique in European terrorism. They came closer to matching the Marighella model than did any other group in Europe. They were bound in a loose confederation, with a central committee meeting periodically to devise a grand strategy. A key difference, however, was that whereas the Tupamaros operated only in Montevideo, the Red Brigades existed in a variety of urban centers. Each unit, therefore, became a fairly autonomous organization within its own area. The Red Brigades managed to establish independent headquarters in several major Italian cities (see Pisano, 1987). Regardless, the Red Brigades followed the same path as other left-wing groups.

Immigration, the Economy, and a Return of Reaction and Revolution

Anonymous left-wing groups set off or attempted to detonate bombs sporadically in the first decade of the twenty-first century, but they failed to establish any pattern or mount a campaign. Albena Azmanova (2004), a sociologist at the University of Kent in the United Kingdom, may have the explanation. Mainstream left-wing political groups have failed to offer any sort of positive agenda in the face of changing economic patterns. As globalization takes control of the international economy, Azmanova argues, the former split between labor and capitalism, the traditional strength of the left, no longer has an agenda. The only thing that the left can offer is an anti-globalization stance. It has nothing positive to offer. If an analogy can be made with the decades before the new century, it is that violent left-wing extremists claimed the political agenda of the mainstream left. They wanted to impose reforms violently. The left and the right peacefully instituted reforms. Pluchinsky argues that the mainstream stole the extremist agenda.

Revolutionary Struggle

Greece was ruled by a military junta from 1967 to 1974, and the roots of Greek revolutionary terrorism can be traced to this time. Two terrorist groups appeared shortly after democracy returned to Greece: the Revolutionary People's Struggle (ELA) and November 17 (N17). Between 1975 and 2000, no fewer than 250 revolutionary terrorist groups operated in Greece, of which N17 was the most notorious. During the same period, the Greek police were fairly inactive in the face of revolutionary terrorism, and no member of N17 was taken into custody. This finally changed in 2002 after an aborted bombing, when police arrested a member of the group. More arrests followed, bringing an end to N17, at least on the surface (Karyotis, 2007).

According to the Council on Foreign Relations (2007), N17 was a tiny group, numbering no more than 25 members. The group hated America, the West, and capitalism. The small membership protected the group, as did the inefficiency of the Greek police. When Greece was awarded the 2004 Olympic Games, international pressure forced the Greek police to take action. After the 2002 arrests, Greek police dealt a crippling blow to N17 by taking most of the remaining members into custody in 2003. Several members of the group and its leader were given multiple life prison sentences.

Georgios Karyotis (2007) argues that it took the Greeks so long to respond to terrorism because the political system did not view it as a security threat. He explains Greek counterterrorism policy by examining three phases of recent history. In the first phase, Greek security forces simply did not consider terrorism to be a problem. When revolutionary terrorism appeared in 1974, the Greeks did not understand either its roots or the manner in which violence was manifested. This continued until 1989. At that point, the Greek political system deemed terrorism to be a problem, but instead of developing a strong security policy, Greek politicians debated the issue of terrorism until 1999. Karyotis says that the third phase of the Greek response came in 1999, when authorities accepted the reality of the threat and developed security mechanisms to deal with it. These factors led to the arrests of 2002 and 2003. Despite these efforts, a new group emerged in 2003—Revolutionary Struggle (EA). Its campaign began with the bombing of an Athens courthouse. This was followed by bombing attacks that began in 2008 and continue today. This may signal the return of left-wing terrorism.

Economic Crisis and Political Dissatisfaction

Reuters news service (Doyle, 2010) reports that a number of bombs have been detonated during the financial crisis. New groups claimed responsibility for these attacks, and Revolutionary Struggle may emerge to lead a movement. While revolutionary terrorism faded in Europe from its heyday in the 1970s to its demise in the 1990s, the concept remains alive in Greece.

The so-called Great Recession was a worldwide phenomenon. Far beyond its impact on the United States, the economic crisis destabilized an already fragile European economic situation. By 2009 the Greek economy took a turn for the worse during the recession. In 2010, Greece was in an economic meltdown. The European Union came to the rescue with a massive loan, and the Greek government implemented a severe austerity program. This brought demonstrators to the street and renewed threats of revolutionary terrorism.

The Huffington Post (Gongloff, 2012) reports that economic crisis has been passed around Europe since the recession began. It started with Greece, but then Ireland faced economic collapse. Italy came next, followed by Spain. Street violence has accompanied every meltdown, and the European Central Bank has not taken the tough economic measures needed to end the problem. This may be an indicator of future problems.

The other side of the political spectrum has also been impacted by the economic downturn, which has strengthened right-wing and xenophobic political movements in many European countries. On July 22, 2011, **Anders Breivik** placed a time bomb in Oslo, Norway. It exploded, killing eight people and wounding more than 200, but it was only a diversion. Breivik went to a small island where a number of teenagers active in Norway's liberal Labor Party were attending a summer camp. Dressed as a police officer, he called the children together. Then, to the world's horror, he began methodically shooting them. He calmly described in actions in court a year later (Blair, 2012).

Right-wing terrorism is often a response to left-wing violence. In Breivik's case, he opposed open European immigration policies and challenges to the Christian church. Sixty-nine people died on the island, 33 under the age of 18. Political terrorism may be on Europe's horizon. While most European law enforcement agencies believe it will arise from ethnic enclaves, it may well develop on the fringes of both the left and right. Europe has a long tradition of such violence.

Anders Breivik: (b. 1979) A violent right-wing extremist who went on a one-day killing spree in Norway in July 2011. He detonated a bomb in Oslo and went on a shooting spree at a Labor Party youth camp for political reasons.

Self-Check

> When did modern revolutionary groups appear in Europe?
> Why did European revolutionary groups fade from popularity?
> How does ideological terrorism seem to be manifested in Europe today?

Death Squads and Counter Revolutionaries

Although a body of theoretical literature addresses revolutionary terrorism, very little has been written on death squads. By some estimates, the subject has been understudied. Death squads have one common base—they protect the established order. Their purpose is to stop social change, and they terrorize those who threaten their position. Forms of extrajudicial death squads have existed throughout history, and they have resurfaced with modern terrorism. They were prominent in Latin America when revolutionary movements swept through Central and South America.

Death squads come into being when people who hold economic and political power believe that their position is being threatened and that the threat is beyond the control of law and order. The purpose of a death squad is to eliminate opposition when a government is either unable or unwilling to do so. The tactics of death squads vary. They range from semiofficial raids on government opponents to torture and secret murder. In a common scenario, uniformed members of a death squad will "arrest" a victim. The victim is carried away and there are no records. The arresting officers frighten lucky victims and torture and murder the unlucky ones. In other cases, people simply disappear.

Death squads have been associated primarily with right-wing activities, but they are used across the political spectrum. For example, after the 1979 Sandinista revolution in Nicaragua, unofficial groups began to crack down on the press and on potential opposition parties. People who opposed the communist regime began to disappear. More recently, death squads appeared in Iraq after the fall of Saddam Hussein. Many parties in Iraq used death squads to intimidate their opponents.

Julie Mazzei (2009, pp. 1–24) posits a theory about the emergence of death squads in a work on counter revolution in Latin America. Mazzei states that paramilitary groups develop based on the perceptions of power elites in the face of economic and political threats. She believes, first and foremost, that death squads must be understood as a method for resisting structural shifts. They are opposed to reform. Prior to mass electronic information networks, this task was delegated to military and law enforcement forces, but modern international pressure, resulting from global communications, frequently prevents power elites from using institutional power structures in this manner. Therefore, power elites have begun creating their own extra-institutional forces to achieve their desired goals.

Perception is the key to Mazzei's theory. Paramilitary death squads come into play only when power elites feel that social changes are undermining their societies and that nothing can be done to stop it. This does not refer to political movements that displace parties within a legitimate and socially accepted system; it applies to movements that shift the basic structure of a social organization. In Mazzei's study, the hard-liners in every country that created death squads viewed reform efforts as an illegitimate method for redistributing wealth and power, and each government in question was either unwilling or unable to stop reform. Mazzei says that both the power elites and members of the paramilitary units justify their actions because they feel that their methods are the only legitimate defense of the social and political order.

Mazzei argues that the conditions giving rise to death squads develop when several factors coalesce to form a favorable environment. First, political elites must be entrenched in a society and have a vested interest in maintaining societal structures, and these elites have a history of employing armed force to protect their positions. This combines with a second factor—a reform movement that threatens to break up elite power structures and redistribute wealth and power. Third, the government must be either unwilling or unable to stop the reform movement. Finally, hard-liners among the political elites break away from their mainstream counterparts, based on the belief that moderate political elites are too soft and unable to stop the reform movement. The only action that will maintain social order, the hard-liners believe, is physically eliminating opponents and destroying the mentality seeking reform.

Augmenting Mazzei's theory is a case study by Brenda Breuil and Ralph Rozema. They looked at the operation of death squads in Davao City, in the Philippines, and in Medellín, Colombia, and found that perception of social change is indeed the key factor behind death squad activity. Breuil and Rozema explain death squads by social imagination. Their study suggests that entire groups of people in a geographical location within the same socioeconomic structure create and sustain an imaginary perception of the world. These perceptions are shared and accepted within the group, but they are not shared among other groups.

Social acceptance is a critical part of an imagined world. It involves an "in group" and a group that does not belong. The in group behaves the "right" way and lives life "as it should be lived." When an outside group threatens this perception, it also becomes part of a social imagination. The in group comes to believe that members of the outside group are less than human and that they are so deviant that their existence is illegitimate. A group creating a death squad believes that its place in society is natural and legitimate. Any group threatening that place is illegitimate and is usurping the rightful order. The threatening group is thus dehumanized and deemed unworthy of existence. This justifies the death squad.

Self-Check

> What is the common factor among death squads?
> What factors are present when death squads are created?
> How is social imagination used to justify death squads?

CHAPTER TAKE AWAYS

Revolutionary terrorists call for radical change in either the structure of government or the underlying political philosophy of governance. Its current origins can be traced to twentieth-century movements in Latin America, especially the urban orientation of Uruguay's Tupamaros. Groups such as the FARC and ELN were originally inspired by the Tupamaros, but they drifted into drug trafficking to survive. Other terrorists, including the MeK of Iran, fight for political dominance. Maoist revolutionaries mirror the revolutionary theories of the communist takeover in China. Peru's Shining Path was a pioneer Maoist group, and it inspired communists in Nepal, India, and the Philippines. Counter revolutionary terrorism is frequently based on the formation of illegal military and police units who torture and kill suspected terrorists and their supporters. They are known as death squads.

OBJECTIVE SUMMARY

- Revolutionary terrorism involves violent activity for the purpose of changing the political structure of government or the social orientation of a country or region. Maoist terrorism is a form of revolutionary terrorism. Its goal is to establish a communist society similar to revolutionary China. Counterterrorism involves the legitimate legal activities of security forces, but some unofficial groups operate outside the law. When these groups engage in violence, it can be described as counter revolutionary terrorism.

- The Tupamaros established an urban organization. The active cadre conducted terrorism (robbery, kidnapping, attacking symbolic targets) while waiting on sympathizers to create a revolutionary climate. The organizational structure included firing teams, small units described in Marighella's *Minimanual*, separated from one another in secretive cells, a command structure, and logistical support. The Tupamaros thwarted efforts by Montevideo police and security forces and gained limited support from the urban poor. Modern network and cellular concepts are rooted in the Tupamaro structure.

- The FARC and ELN emerged as revolutionary groups in Colombia. They formed alliances with drug cartels, and their influence spread beyond Colombia. They remain operational, but their effectiveness is believed to have been reduced.

- The MeK fought against the revolutionary government of Iran. Its operations and finances were influenced, and at times controlled, by Iraq.

- The Shining Path launched a 20-year terrorist campaign in Peru in 1980. It was a Marxist/Maoist movement that prompted a harsh governmental response. Peru's population was caught in the middle as the Shining Path systematically waged a campaign of terrorism against them. It reemerged around 2007, but its major goal was control of the drug trade. The Shining Path broke into two major factions centered on drug trafficking, and it gained a strong foothold in the coca-producing regions in southern Peru by 2012.

- The Naxalite rebellion began in 1967 in west Bengal. It started as several communist movements agitating for agrarian reform and peasants rights. The first rebellion was repressed with military and police power. In the second phase, Naxalites began to spread and organize in central India, creating a Red Corridor. The third phase began in 2004 when two major groups united and launched an open rebellion. Its most deadly year was 2010, but the group suffered setbacks in 2011 after one of its main leaders was killed. It remains active, although the level of violence dropped in early 2012.

- The Maoist rebellion in Nepal began in 1995 and grew into a major insurrection. A peace treaty in 1995 temporarily brought the Nepalese Communist Party into the government and resulted in limitations on the power of the monarchy. However, Maoist rebels launched attacks in 1996, resulting in a civil war that last until a ceasefire in 2006 and UN monitoring from 2007. The Maoists threatened to renew violence in 2012.

- Europe experienced revolutionary terrorism from about 1965 to 1990. Most groups waned after the demise of the former Soviet Union. Ethnic terrorism has emerged as the most likely threat, although single-issue groups may emerge to replace the former left-wing terrorists. N17 followed the path of most revolutionary groups in Europe, except that it lasted until the twenty-first century. The Revolutionary Struggle emerged after the demise of N17 and remains operational in Greece. Anarchist violence has increased recently as a result of the economic crisis in Europe.

- Death squads developed as a reaction to revolutionary terrorism. The premise behind extrajudicial arrest, torture, and murder is that normative law cannot cope with terrorist violence. People supporting death squads believe that their existence is threatened; therefore, it is necessary to operate outside the law and terrorize the terrorists.

Critical Engagement: The Future of Public Policy and Actual Practice

According to journalist Julie Kosterlitz (2008), the Mujahedeen-e Khalq (MeK) seems like an organization the United States would like to befriend. It is a group of well-organized Iranian dissidents whose intention is to topple the theocratic government of Iran. It has established a shadow government in exile, called the National Council of Resistance in Iran, and its stated goal is to bring a secular government, a democracy, and women's rights to Iran. On paper, it seems like a perfect ally. There have even been those in Washington who have suggested that MeK's past should be forgiven and the group should be embraced as an ally. This is where the problem begins, she concludes.

The MeK has been designated a foreign terrorist organization. It has engaged in terrorist bombings, costing hundreds of lives. It has also assassinated officials and murdered American citizens. During the Iranian Revolution, the MeK assisted in the takeover of the United States embassy. It fought for Saddam Hussein in the Iran–Iraq War; and, in 2003, during Operation Iraqi Freedom, it engaged in combat against American Special Forces. It has a long record of terrorism, dating back to the 1970s.

The most problematic aspect of the MeK is the position that the United States has taken on international terrorism. The United States has openly condemned countries that support or have relations with terrorist organizations. In addition, when a group like Hamas comes to power through a democratic election, the United States refuses to deal with it. At times, the United States has approached international terrorism in a very simplistic manner. For example, after the September 11 attacks, President George W. Bush told the world that nations were either for us or against us. There was no ambiguity, no middle of the road, no nuance. The U.S. government cannot embrace MeK and remain true to its stated policy.

Despite the obvious contradiction of public policy, a study by the RAND Corporation (Goulka et al., 2009) concludes that the MeK has not been treated as a foreign terrorist organization. After the United States took control of the MeK's main facility in Iraq, it did not exert control over the organization, and it did not disarm it. The RAND study says that the group was treated as an ally for intelligence-gathering purposes. The study concludes by stating that this has exposed the United States to charges of hypocrisy and that there has been no attempt to counter this accusation through policy changes.

Consider these issues in terms of future developments:

- Is it possible to have a public policy concerning terrorism and then violate that policy in practice? For example, the United States says that it does not negotiate with terrorists. In reality, the government often negotiates with terrorists. In what ways is the United States' relationship with the MeK similar?
- If the United States establishes either a formal—or informal—relationship with the MeK, how can the Department of State maintain a listing condemning state sponsors of terrorism?
- What is the moral responsibility of democratic governments in maintaining standards about international terrorism? Is it morally acceptable to engage in a relationship with any organization that practices terrorism? The United States has done so in the past. What implications does this have on the moral force of public policy?

KEY TERMS

Raúl Sendic, p. 10-248

National Liberation Movement, p. 10-249

Red Brigades, p. 10-253

Plan Colombia, p. 10-255

Alvaro Uribe, p. 10-255

American embassy takeover, p. 10-256

Tupac Amaru, p. 10-258

Abimael Guzmán, p. 10-258

Cultural Revolution, p. 10-258

Alberto Fujimori, p. 10-258

King Gyanendra, p. 10-260

Red Corridor, p. 10-262

No-go areas, p. 10-264

People Power Revolution, p. 10-264

Red Army Faction, p. 10-266

Renato Curcio, p. 10-267

Margherita Cagol, p. 10-267

Anders Breivik, p. 10-269

CHAPTER 11

Al Qaeda and Jihadist Networks

-/AFP/Getty Images/Newscom

LEARNING OBJECTIVES

After reading this chapter you should be able to:

> Describe the rise of religious terrorism and its relationship to the Soviet–Afghan War.

> Summarize the important roles of Osama bin Laden and Ayman al Zawahiri.

> Outline the early history of al Qaeda.

> Explain the structure and operations of al Qaeda up to September 11, 2001.

> Describe al Qaeda's current franchise-style structure and current operational capabilities.

> Outline the operations of franchises including AQAP, AQIM, and al Shabaab.

> Summarize al Qaeda's political theology.

> Describe other forms of terrorism in Pakistan.

> Summarize operations in other parts of Asia and the Pacific.

Mohammed Merah was a 23-year-old French citizen of Algerian origin. French intelligence had been concerned about his activities, and agents maintained a file on him. Merah had a history of petty crimes, some of them involving violence, and he was known to have jihadist sympathies. He spent time in Afghanistan and Pakistan, and he was also on a "no-fly" list in the United States. While he was a person of interest, French authorities could not link him to a terrorist group. They kept an eye on him in case he decided to take action. For the time being, they believed he was not a risk. They were not prepared for the actions he eventually took.

On March 11, 2012, he approached three off-duty French paratroopers on his motorbike. Suddenly, without warning, he opened fire and killed them. A few days later he entered the Ozar Hatorah School in Toulouse, France. Once again he was seeking targets. This time the victims were three Jewish children and a Jewish teacher. The murders were particularly brutal. French police responded, searching the region for a suspect. They found him barricaded in an apartment, and Merah was killed after a 32-hour siege.

French authorities stated that Merah was a unique case. He became self-radicalized in prison while reading the Quran. Although he exhibited none of the standard indicators of suspicious behavior, he wanted to join al Qaeda. Yet Merah was not part of the group. He did not belong to an underground network. He had no terrorist contacts inside France. He was, however, inspired. Operating alone he sought to wage a one-man terror campaign in the name of his religion. French security forces and intelligence agents had successfully disrupted jihadist terrorist cells for a number of years, but they were not prepared for the loner operating outside of a group or network (Siegal, 2012).

The Rise of Religious Terrorism and the Soviet–Afghan War

In May 2004 the ABC news service reported that the terrorist organization al Qaeda, operated by Osama bin Laden, had 18,000 fighters poised throughout the world and that the group was ready to strike Western interests (ABC News, 2004). The report's source was the United Kingdom's Institute for Strategic Studies, as originally reported by the Reuters news service. Various news agencies around the world ran their own versions of the Reuters story without doing their own research. If they had, they would have found that many people had passed through al Qaeda training camps, but the actual number of terrorists was much lower. The real problem was the secret nature of al Qaeda's structure. It seemed that al Qaeda was capable of running an organized international operation even though it had been surrounded and pounded by U.S. military forces in Afghanistan. Before 2001, al Qaeda maintained a command hierarchy. After 2001, its leaders ran virtual networks and inspired autonomous jihadists around the globe (see Scheuer, 2006).

Cold War Origins

Al Qaeda's origins can be traced to the cold war. From 1945 until the collapse of the former Soviet Union in 1991, the United States confronted the Soviet Union in the cold war. The world was divided into two camps—the communist and noncommunist nations—and each side formed alliances with any government willing to offer its assistance. The form of an ally's government was immaterial. Today, the United States claims to support the emergence of democracies throughout the world, but during the cold war there was little concern with the type of government of an allied nation. The central focus was a country's stance against the Soviet Union. Saudi Arabia, deemed to be an important ally, was a monarchy bolstered by lucrative oil profits and maintained by authoritarian autocratic rule. The last thing the United States wanted to do was to introduce democracy and thereby destabilize ally (Bowman, 2005).

This relationship was not unusual. The United States formed alliances not only with the democracies of western Europe but with some of the most brutal dictatorships in the late twentieth century, all in the name of anticommunism. Saudi Arabia was one of many countries that stood for a form of government that violated expressed American ideals. American foreign policy makers also embraced the conservative religious views of the Saudi upper classes. The zealous enthusiasm expressed by conservative Muslims against atheistic socialism served American purposes. The United States supported any form of Islam as a stand against communism.

Rachel Bronson (2005) says the religious nature of Saudi Arabia was an asset during the cold war. For nearly a half century the kingdom's antisocial stance kept the country in the U.S. political orbit. The Soviet Union, on the other hand, supported the emergence of revolutionary socialism in the Islamic world. This drove the Saudis deeper into the U.S. camp. When the Soviet Union invaded Afghanistan in 1979, both the Saudis and the United States saw an opportunity to strike back. They would support Muslim resistance to the atheist invader.

John Cooley (2002, pp. 64–104) believes that the foundation of modern jihadist power grew from the cold war, and he blames the West for incubating the network. The idea of using militant reformers against the Soviet Union was born in France. The French intelligence community knew that Islamic militants hated the communists for several reasons and, therefore, suggested to intelligence counterparts in Washington and London that militant Islamic reformers might be used against communist regimes. America, Great Britain, and France soon began to seek alliances with militant Islamic radicals. Using ties with oil-rich Muslim states, especially Saudi Arabia and Kuwait, the Western allies channeled support to both militant and nonviolent purification movements within Islam.

The Soviet–Afghan War, 1979–1989

Western efforts to support Islamic reformers came to fruition in 1979. In December of that year, the Soviet Union invaded Afghanistan to bolster a failing communist regime. According to Cooley, this was the chance the West had been waiting for. President Jimmy Carter's State Department encouraged Arab and other Islamic allies to send money and religious puritans to fight the Soviets in a guerrilla war. The puritans were called *mujahedeen*, or "holy warriors." The United States formed an alliance with Pakistan, and the Pakistani **Interservice Intelligence Agency (ISI)** began to train and equip the mujahedeen. When Ronald Reagan became president in 1980, American efforts against the Soviets increased.

Interservice Intelligence Agency (ISI): The Pakistani domestic and foreign intelligence service, created by the British in 1948. Supporters claim that it centralizes Pakistan's intelligence. Critics maintain that it operates like an independent state and supports terrorist groups.

Several researchers have looked at the relationship between the United States and the mujahedeen during the Soviet–Afghan War (see, for example, Benjamin and Simon, 2002, pp. 98–102; Cooley, 2002, pp. 64–75; Gunaratna, 2002, p. 18; Kepel, 2002, pp. 136–150; Ruthven, 2000, p. 365). Their research points to several important conclusions. First, the United States helped Saudi Arabia develop a funding mechanism and underground arms network to supply the mujahedeen. Second, the United States agreed to give most of the weapons and supplies to the ISI, which built mujahedeen groups with little American participation. Third, Islamic charities flourished in the United States, and their donations supported the mujahedeen. Finally, when the Soviets left Afghanistan in 1989, the United States rejoiced and abandoned war-torn Afghanistan.

The mujahedeen were not united at the end of the Soviet–Afghan War. Up to 31 different groups fought the Soviets, with six major mujahedeen guerrilla armies controlling most operations. The power that held the many groups together was a mutual hatred of the Soviets (Shay, 2002, pp. 108–109). When the Soviets finally retreated, the Afghan mujahedeen believed that the power of God had prevailed over Satan. The major leaders wanted to turn their efforts against the other enemies of God: apostate Islamic governments, Israel, and the West. Some mujahedeen returned to their homes to spread holy war, but others had grander schemes. Virtually ignored by the United States, the jihadist movement grew, and terrorism grew with it.

✓ Self-Check

> How did the United States select allies during the cold war?
> Why did the United States favor religious zealotry against the Soviet Union?
> What was the impact of the Soviet–Afghan War on the mujahedeen?

Bin Laden, Zawahiri, and al Qaeda

As the Soviets began leaving Afghanistan in April 1988, the United States celebrated a vicarious victory. The Soviets were on the run, in full retreat from the battlefields of the cold war. The defeat was another blow to a crumbling empire; and, by 1991 the Soviet Union had dissolved. The cold war was over, and it appeared that a new world of peace was at hand. As the world stepped back from the brink of nuclear annihilation, America's leaders and people paid very little attention to events in far-off Afghanistan (see Crile, 2003, pp. 470–484).

The fighting, however, was not over in Afghanistan. Shaul Shay (2002, pp. 76–81) writes that the mujahedeen groups continued to fight for control of the country. Al Qaeda was one of many paramilitary organizations to join the fray, and the United States failed to recognize the problem on two levels. Cooley (2002, p. 122) and Napoleoni (2003, pp. 189–191) say that American oil companies sought alliances with some groups in hopes of building an oil pipeline from central Asia to the Indian Ocean. This oil would run through Afghanistan. Americans paid more attention to potential profits than to the political problems brewing in Afghanistan. On another level, the United States simply ignored issues. As the Afghan groups continued to build and strengthen, Americans celebrated the ending of the cold war and the beginning of the **peace dividend**—the money that the United States diverted from military spending.

The Rise of Osama Bin Laden

Osama bin Laden was a large part of America's blissful ignorance. The report of the **9/11 Commission** (2004, pp. 53–54) notes that bin Laden's reputation began to grow as the mujahedeen searched for a continuing jihad. When international terrorist violence increased in Africa and Asia during the 1990s, bin Laden emerged as a symbol of Islamic discontent. Oil-rich Muslim countries were faced with a growing population of young men who had technical educations but no broad understanding of humanities, social sciences, or the larger world. They also faced unemployment due to the uneven distribution of wealth. Bin Laden emerged as a spokesman for the discontented, and his own movement began to take form.

Rohan Gunaratna (2002) documents the origins of al Qaeda and its actions from the end of the Soviet–Afghan War until the attacks of September 11, 2001. Yoseff Bodansky (1999) offers a biography of bin Laden that predates the September 11 attacks. The 9/11 Commission Report (2004, pp. 47–70) also documents the growth of al Qaeda. All three works point to the importance of the personality of Osama bin Laden.

Osama bin Laden was the son of Mohammed bin Laden, a wealthy construction executive who worked closely with the Saudi royal family. The elder bin Laden divorced Osama's mother, but he continued to provide for the family. Osama decided that he wanted to become a good Muslim at an early age. Because of his father's connections, bin Laden was raised in the Saudi royal court, and his tutor, Mohammed Qutb, was the brother of the Egyptian radical Sayyid Qutb. Bin Laden was influenced by Sayyid Qutb's thought. While attending university, bin Laden left the nonviolent Wahhabism of the Saudi royal family and turned to Qutb's philosophy (see H. Oliver, 2002, pp. 10–38). Inspired by the mujahedeen of Afghanistan, bin Laden dropped out of college to join the Soviet–Afghan War. At first, he lent his support to the mujahedeen, but later he formed his own guerrilla unit (L. Wright, 2006, pp. 60–83).

Bin Laden and Abdullah Azzam

While in Afghanistan, bin Laden fell under the influence of **Abdullah Azzam**, a doctor of Islamic law. Azzam was a Palestinian scholar who was influenced by Qutb's writings. He came to believe that a purified form of Islam was the answer to questions of poverty and the loss of political power. He had been working for the Palestinians in the mid-1970s, but he became disillusioned with their nationalism and emphasis on politics over religion. Azzam believed that Islam should be the guiding force for war, and he would not abandon religious principles for the sake of a political victory. He left the Palestinians for a Saudi university to teach Islamic law, later joining the Afghan jihad (L. Wright, 2006, pp. 99–106).

peace dividend: A term used during President William Clinton's administration (1992—2000) to describe reducing defense spending at the end of the Cold War.

9/11 Commission: The bipartisan National Commission on Terrorist Attacks upon the United States, created after September 11, 2001, in order to investigate the attacks.

Abdullah Azzam: (1941–1989) The Palestinian leader of Hizb ul Tahrir and the spiritual mentor of bin Laden.

According to Azzam, the realm of Islam had been dominated by foreign powers for too long. It was time for all Muslims to rise up and strike Satan. He saw the Soviet–Afghan War as just the beginning of a holy war against all things foreign to Islam. At first, bin Laden found the theology of Azzam to his liking and the answer to his prayers for a path to holy war.

According to the 9/11 Commission Report (2004, p. 58), bin Laden and Azzam "established what they called a base or foundation (al Qaeda) as a potential general headquarters for future jihad" toward the end of the Soviet–Afghan War. Bin Laden was its leader, and the organization included an intelligence component, a military committee, a financial committee, a political committee, and a committee in charge of media affairs and propaganda.

Training in Pakistan and Afghanistan under Azzam's spiritual mentoring, bin Laden financed mujahedeen operations and taught the guerrillas how to build field fortifications. By 1986, he had left the training field for the battlefield. Enraged with the Soviets over their wholesale slaughter of Afghan villagers and their use of poison gas, bin Laden joined the front ranks of the mujahedeen. Allied with hundreds of radical militants throughout the world, Osama bin Laden became a battlefield hero. (When interviewed by John Miller for ABC News [1998], bin Laden would not discuss these exploits. He simply stated that all Muslims are required to fight in the jihad.) After taking part in the war, bin Laden returned to Pakistan and joined Azzam in a new venture: registering all the foreign jihadists in a single computer database.

Ayman al Zawahiri and the Path from Egypt

Dr. Ayman al Zawahiri was born into a prominent Egyptian family in 1951. An intelligent, high-achieving student, he fell under the influence of violent religious philosophy in high school after being exposed to militant interpretations of Islam. His passion and intolerance grew in college as he studied at Cairo's al Azhar University. One of his mentors was **Sayyid Imam al Sharif**, also known as Dr. Fadl. Sharif would eventually be jailed for his views, but he converted back to Islam and denounced violent radicalism (see Brachman, 2009). During their time together at al Azhar's medical school, however, Sharif validated Zawahiri's growing radical theology.

Zawahiri was arrested in 1967 and charged with being a member of the Muslim Brotherhood. After his release from jail, he continued his studies to become a physician. Still active in underground politics, he opposed the government of Anwar Sadat. When Sadat signed a peace treaty with Israel, Zawahiri threw himself into the resistance. Egyptian police arrested dissidents from all over Egypt after Sadat's assassination in 1981. Zawahiri was arrested and charged with weapons violations, although he was not officially charged in the assassination. Zawahari was sentenced to three years in prison; after serving his term, Zawahiri left for Afghanistan to join the mujahedeen.

Lawrence Wright (2002) says that bin Laden and Zawahiri were bound to meet each other. Both men were highly educated, members of an elite class, and extremely pious. Bin Laden was a charismatic idealist who needed someone to frame his positions with pragmatism. Zawahiri became that person. He not only had practical abilities, Zawahiri was surrounded by an entourage of doctors, engineers, and soldiers. Bin Laden had the charisma, Zawahiri had the brains.

The Early History of al Qaeda

Abdullah Azzam, bin Laden's spiritual mentor, had big plans after the Soviets retreated. The mujahedeen had defeated the Soviet atheists, and Azzam felt that they could turn their attention to the apostate regimes in other Muslim countries. Things did not go well for Azzam, however. When the Soviets prepared to withdraw from Afghanistan in 1988, the ISI created its own Afghan guerrilla force and used it to

Sayyid Imam al Sharif: (b. 1951) Also known as Dr. Fadl, one of Egypt's leading militants in the 1970s. While jailed, he embraced Islam and renounced the violence of al Qaeda–style militancy. He is viewed as a traitor by violent jihadists. He has provided much of the information about religious militancy, and he continues to publish works denouncing it. Still maintaining anti-Western and anti-government views, he sees jihad as a necessary part of Islam. Al Qaeda's version, he claims, violates the morality of Islamic law.

take control of major areas of the country. Azzam believed that the United States was behind this action, and he broke with the ISI. According to a U.S. federal agent who spent many months in Pakistan and Afghanistan apprehending and interrogating jihadists (private discussion with author, 2005), Azzam called together five mujahedeen leaders in 1989, including bin Laden and Ayman al Zawahiri, a leader of the Egyptian Islamic Jihad (described below), in an attempt to unite the jihadist movement. The meeting ended in shambles, however, with each leader declaring the other four heretics. Bin Laden and Zawahiri left, disillusioned and angry with Azzam. At this point, Zawahiri began sketching out a grand model for al Qaeda, proposing an umbrella structure with multiple independent groups gathered under the loosely guiding hand of al Qaeda.

According to Gunaratna (2002, p. 25), Zawahiri became the brains behind a new operation. Using bin Laden's notoriety and charisma among the Afghan mujahedeen, he transformed the organization. Zawahiri knew from experience that an umbrella-style organization was difficult to penetrate. He persuaded bin Laden that this was the type of organization to take control of Afghanistan and spread the new Islamic empire.

Using Zawahiri's ideas, Osama bin Laden took advantage of America's inattention and Azzam's waning power. He began to recruit the mujahedeen registered in his computer database for al Qaeda, while Zawahiri organized training camps and cells. Bin Laden also expressed a willingness to work with the Shi'ite terrorist organization Hezbollah (Waxman, 1998a; J. Goldberg, 2002). Yael Shahar (1998) says that bin Laden saw the Soviet collapse in Afghanistan as a sign of God's victory. Islamic law was to be imposed on the world, and bin Laden believed that al Qaeda was the organization to do it.

The only problem was Azzam, who resisted bin Laden and Zawahiri's takeover. Then in November 1989, Azzam was killed by a remote-controlled car bomb. Whether the assassination was by Egyptian radicals or perhaps by bin Laden himself, the result was that bin Laden and Zawahiri became the undisputed leaders of al Qaeda. Following the philosophy of Sayyid Qutb, their enemies were defined as the United States, the West, Israel, and Muslims who refused to accept jihadist theology.

Bin Laden's first target was the Saudi government and its "corrupt" royal family. As bin Laden's mujahedeen fighters, or "Afghans," as he called them, either went home to their native lands to wage jihad or stayed in Afghanistan to train and fight, bin Laden returned to Saudi Arabia, enjoying warm relations with the ISI. But the Saudi government, which does not tolerate diverse opinions or dissent, was not happy to see him return. When bin Laden brought several of his Afghans into his Arabian construction business, the Saudis watched carefully. While they looked on, bin Laden became independently wealthy, and his agents began making real estate purchases in Sudan (see L. Wright, 2006, pp. 140–156).

Desert Shield: The name of the defensive phase of the international coalition, created by President George H. W. Bush after Iraq invaded Kuwait on August, 2, 1990, to stop further Iraqi attacks and to liberate Kuwait. It lasted until coalition forces could begin an offensive against Iraq in January 1991.

Desert Storm: The military code name for the January–February offensive in the 1991 Gulf War.

The situation changed in 1990 when Iraq invaded Kuwait. The United States joined Saudi Arabia in a large international coalition opposing the invasion, and bin Laden was infuriated. As thousands of non-Muslim troops arrived in Saudi Arabia, radical Muslims were appalled to find Muslims fighting Muslims under U.S. leadership. The U.S.-led coalition called this military buildup **Desert Shield**, and it became **Desert Storm** in February 1991 when American, British, and other allied forces poured into Iraq and Kuwait. For bin Laden, however, it was a desert apostasy.

After Desert Storm, the Saudi government allowed U.S. troops to be stationed in Saudi Arabia. While non-Muslim troops never entered the cities of Mecca and Medina, two of the most holy shrines in Islam, their presence in Saudi Arabia was controversial. Millions of Muslims believe that these sacred sites must be protected. Having foreigners so near was too much for bin Laden, who now thought of declaring his own war on the Saudi royal family and the United States. By April he was training and financing terrorist groups and calling for the overthrow of unsympathetic Muslim governments.

Self-Check

> How did bin Laden emerge at the end of the Soviet–Afghan War?
> What was Zawahiri's role?
> After Azzam's death, how was the new organization structured?

The Evolution of al Qaeda

Taliban: The Islamicist group that governed Afghanistan from 1996 to 2001.

Mullah Omar: (b, 1959) The leader of the Taliban. After the collapse of the Taliban government in 2001, Omar went into hiding.

Al Qaeda was born in the last stages of the Soviet–Afghan War, and it grew until the U.S. offensive in Afghanistan in October 2001, when U.S. forces struck the al Qaeda and **Taliban** forces there. Led by **Mullah Omar**, the latter group was composed of Islamic students who wanted to bring order to Afghanistan through the forced imposition of Islamic law (Matinuddin, 1999, pp. 21–22, 41). As Peter Bergen (2001, pp. 195–235) says, al Qaeda transformed after 2001. It became what he calls al Qaeda 2.0, a group that, he believes, became a decentralized alliance of al Qaeda terrorists spread throughout the world. The movement never had mass appeal, however, because its theology was unsound despite its constant references to Islam.

In the 1990s, press reports tended to present the jihadist movements in North Africa as an expansion of al Qaeda, but this interpretation is incorrect. In some cases, jihadist groups shared training and members with al Qaeda; in other cases, they established new groups after returning from the Soviet–Afghan War. Emerging groups are using "al Qaeda" in their names, but these tend to be fully autonomous networks with no direct connection to the al Qaeda structure that exists in Pakistan today. Egypt differed, however. After Azzam's assassination and the breakup of the muja-hedeen confederation in Afghanistan, Zawahiri returned to Egypt with the hope of creating an Islamic state. He formed a new movement based on the umbrella-style structure of the mujahedeen groups in Afghanistan. Some of the structures had existed prior to his return, and some jihadists were new to the movement. Zawahiri thought that the conditions in Egypt were conducive to revolution.

The Egyptian Islamic Group

1993 World Trade Center bombing: A carbomb attack by a cell led by Ramzi Youseff. The cell had links to the Egyptian IG.

Sheik Omar Abdel Rahman: (b. 1938) A Sunni Islamic scholar linked to the Egyptian IG. He came to the United States in 1990 even though his name was on a State Department watch list. He was arrested and convicted of conspiracy after the 1993 World Trade Center bombing. He is currently serving a life sentence in the American federal prison system.

One of the organizations operating in Egypt was known as the Islamic Group (al Gamaat al Islamiyya, or IG). Three interrelated factors were prevalent in the rise of IG: the 1981 assassination of Anwar Sadat by religious extremists, the failure of Arab nationalism, and the decline of Arab socialism. When the nationalistic movement collapsed after the 1967 Six Day War, dreams of an Arab socialist state followed suit. Religious extremism took the place of socialism and nationalism. The religious fanatics dismissed nationalism because they believed Muslims should not be divided by European-style borders, and they feared that socialism would displace God. Sadat's assassination electrified the Egyptian militants.

According to the U.S. Department of State (2007), IG formed in the early 1970s. It came to the forefront after mujahedeen returned from the Soviet–Afghan War, and it embraced a new style of organization. Instead of a centralized hierarchy, it operated in a loosely structured network spanning several Egyptian cities. It also established foreign wings, and IG was even active in the United States. It was connected with the **1993 World Trade Center bombing** and with plans for further attacks in New York City.

A prominent member of IG, known to many Americans, is **Sheik Omar Abdel Rahman**. He has been convicted of complicity in the World Trade Center bombing. Less well-known to many Americans are IG members in Egypt, though they have caused more death and destruction. IG has been responsible for attacks on Egyptian security forces, Christians, and tourists. An attack on a group of tourists in Luxor drew international attention to the IG (Figure 11.1)

FIGURE **11.1** Egypt and Luxor

At the time, it seemed like an isolated event. On November 17, 1997, four Egyptian jihadists dressed in police uniforms approached a group of 58 tourists visiting the Pyramids, Most of whom were Swiss. As the tourists disembarked from a bus, the jihadists attacked. They shot more than 50 tourists. In a gruesome act, they pulled out small knives and worked their way through the dead and wounded. Victims were mutilated and decapitated to increase the drama of the attack. The jihadists were later killed by Egyptian security forces (Plet, 1999), and the IG declared a ceasefire in 1997.

Egyptian Islamic Jihad

Ayman al Zawahiri was the driving force behind another terrorist group in Egypt, the Egyptian Islamic Jihad (EIJ). Zawahiri and EIJ demonstrate both the power of an ideology to hold a group together and the evolutionary path of terrorist networks. Like IG, EIJ was loosely bound, with autonomous cells taking action on their own. Unlike IG, EIJ specifically targeted the Egyptian government (Keats, 2002).

near enemy: A jihadist term referring to forms of Muslim governments and Islamic law (*sharia*) that do not embrace the narrow-minded philosophy of Sayyid Qutb.

Zawahiri did not get along with either IG's leaders or its philosophy. He felt that targeting Christians and tourists would turn Egyptians against the jihadist movement. The government repressed the people; therefore, the government should be the sole target of the terrorist campaign (L. Wright, 2006, pp. 53–55). Zawahiri believed that the government represented the **near enemy**. It was the so-called Muslim government that should be overthrown, as Sayyid Qutb had argued. Zawahiri believed local groups could defeat their own governments and then unite the entire Islamic community. When this was achieved, the united jihadists could focus on the **far enemy**: Israel, the United States, and the West (see Gerges, 2005).

far enemy: A jihadist term referring to non-Islamic powers or countries outside the realm of Islam.

After returning from the Afghan jihad, Zawahiri threw himself into the Egyptian Islamicist revolt. Using Egyptians trained in camps in Afghanistan, EIJ focused on governmental targets. Terrorists tried to assassinate Egypt's interior minister. After that failed, they pulled off a bombing attack on the Egyptian embassy in Islamabad, Pakistan. Although Zawahiri believed that the true Muslims of Egypt would arise when EIJ began its religious revolt, the opposite happened. The government cracked down, and few people stepped forward to take up EIJ's version of jihad. Zawahiri left for Afghanistan, and several members of EIJ followed in 1996 (Gunaratna, 2002, p. 45).

Bin Laden Returns to Afghanistan

Bin Laden had returned to Afghanistan by a separate path. The PBS television show *Frontline* (2002) noted that bin Laden's protests against Desert Storm brought a Saudi crackdown on his operations, and he was forced to flee the country. Bin Laden

Hassan al Turabi:
(b. 1932) A Sudanese intellectual and Islamic scholar. He served in the Sudanese government during the time bin Laden was in exile in Sudan.

found friends in Sudan's radical government, formed under the influence of **Hassan al Turabi.** Turabi was the intellectual leader of the jihadist cause and was connected to radical and mainstream Muslims throughout the world. He could provide respectability to jihadist philosophy, and bin Laden and Turabi formed a mutually helpful alliance. Turabi served as the philosopher, and bin Laden provided organizational skills. Bin Laden brought 500 Afghan veterans to Sudan and built a network of businesses and other enterprises. By the end of 1992, bin Laden employed Afghan-hardened mujahedeen in Sudan. He also began to internationalize, creating multinational corporations, false charities, and front companies. Al Qaeda became stronger with each economic expansion (Bergen, 2001, pp. 76–91; for further discussion, see Reeve, 1999, pp. 45–134; Gunaratna, 2002, pp. 1–15; 9/11 Commission Report, 2004, pp. 63–70, 108–143; Randal, 2004, pp. 115– 162, 201–221; Palmer and Palmer, 2004, pp. 100–105).

Mogadishu: The capital of Somalia. This note is a reference to "Black Hawk Down." U.S. troops moved into Mogadishu during Operation Restore Hope from December 9, 1992, until May 4, 1993, when the United Nations took over the operations. American forces were involved in a major battle in October 1993 involving a downed U.S. Army helicopter.

While bin Laden's fortunes increased in Sudan, Americans were on the move in Somalia. President George H. W. Bush sent U.S. forces to **Mogadishu** to end a humanitarian crisis there, and they were joined by other armies, including Muslim forces. The people of Somalia were threatened with mass starvation due to continual struggles among several rival warlords. President Bush hoped peacekeeping efforts could open the area for food distribution. When the Democrats came to power in 1992, President Clinton continued the effort. Most of the world saw the multinational peacekeeping force as a method for feeding the starving Somalis, but not bin Laden. He believed that it was another U.S.-led assault on a Muslim nation.

In December 1992, a bomb exploded in a hotel in Yemen that had been housing American troops. According to *Frontline* (1999), U.S. intelligence linked the attack to bin Laden. It was the opening shot in bin Laden's war against the United States and an international campaign of terrorism. In the 1980s, terrorism was frequently associated with a particular state. Bin Laden, however, transcended the state and operated on his own, with the wealth of his construction empire providing financial backing. Yael Shahar (1998) argues that bin Laden's entrepreneurial efforts gave him the freedom to finance and command the al Qaeda terrorist network. His connections with the Afghan mujahedeen and his reputation as a warrior gave him legitimacy. Bin Laden did not need a government to support his operations. He had the money, personnel, material, and infrastructure necessary to maintain a campaign of terrorism. The 9/11 Commission Report (2004, pp. 185–186), however, disagrees with Shahar. The commission believes that bin Laden was and remains funded by wealthy sympathizers. Financial operations in Sudan covered only day-to-day expenses, and many of the companies were not profitable. Regardless of its source, bin Laden had financing and did not need the support of a rogue nation. He needed only a place to hide.

According to *Frontline*, bin Laden went on the offensive in 1993. Using his contacts in Sudan, he began searching for weapons of mass destruction. His Afghans sought to purchase nuclear weapons from underground sources in the Russian Federation, and he began work on a chemical munitions plant in Sudan. Bodansky (1999) says that he also sent terrorists to fight in other parts of the world, including Algeria, Egypt, Bosnia, Pakistan, Somalia, Kashmir, and Chechnya. U.S. intelligence sources believe that bin Laden's Afghans also came to the United States.

Bin Laden was active in Somalia when U.S. troops joined the forces trying to get food to the area. In October 1993, a U.S. Army Black Hawk helicopter was downed while on patrol in Mogadishu. U.S. Army Rangers went to the rescue, and a two-day battle ensued in which 18 Americans died. In an interview with John Miller of ABC News (1998), bin Laden claimed that he trained and supported the troops that struck the Americans.

Bin Laden was also involved in assassination attempts. In 1993, his Afghans tried to murder Prince Abdullah (now King Abdullah) of Jordan. U.S. intelligence sources believe that he was behind the attempted assassination of Egyptian president Hosni

Mubarak in 1995. According to *Frontline*, bin Laden called for a guerrilla campaign against Americans in Saudi Arabia, also in 1995.

Declaring War on the United States

Bin Laden was forced from Sudan in 1996 by international pressure, and Zawahiri fled Egypt when security forces began cracking down on the jihadists. Both men went to Afghanistan, where many displaced jihadists joined them. Bin Laden consolidated power and absorbed the new jihadists in his ranks. Then he made a most unusual declaration. Seated in front of a camera with Zawahiri and al Qaeda's security director, Mohammed Atef, bin Laden declared war on the United States in 1996. He followed this by having his religious council issue two religious rulings, called fatwas, in 1998, though few Muslims recognized the authority of the council's religious scholars and bin Laden had no theological credentials.

World Islamic Front against Jews and Crusaders: An organization created in 1998 by Osama bin Laden and Ayman al Zawahiri. It represents a variety of jihadist groups that issued a united front against Jews and the West. It is commonly called al Qaeda.

In 1998, the Egyptian Islamic Jihad (EIJ) was absorbed into al Qaeda when Osama bin Laden announced that he was forming the **World Islamic Front against Jews and Crusaders**. The story of EIJ is taken over by al Qaeda at this point; however, the experience of EIJ dominated al Qaeda's new alliance as al Qaeda evolved into a sophisticated international network. Interestingly, Zawahiri announced that IG joined the network in 2006. This might have been simply propaganda by Zawahiri because the past animosity between EIJ and IG would seem to prohibit their joining forces. Regardless, bin Laden and Zawahiri brought a new style of organization to the world of international terrorism.

Magnus Ranstorp (1998) argues that the two declarations reveal much about the nature of al Qaeda and bin Laden. First, bin Laden represented a new phase in Middle Eastern terrorism. He was intent on spreading the realm of Islam with a transnational group. Second, he used Islam to call for religious violence. Bin Laden was a self-trained religious fanatic ready to kill in the name of God. Finally, bin Laden wanted to cause death. Whether with conventional weapons or weapons of mass destruction, bin Laden's purpose was to kill. In his fatwas of February 1998, he called for the killing of any American anywhere in the world.

In August 1998, bin Laden's terrorists bombed the U.S. embassies in Nairobi, Kenya, and Dar es Salaam, Tanzania. The Nairobi bomb killed 213 people and injured 4,500; the Dar es Salaam explosion killed 12 people and wounded 85. These attacks signaled a new phase in al Qaeda terrorism. The Nairobi and Dar es Salaam bombs demonstrated how al Qaeda had matured. For the first time, the group could operate a cell planted in a country hundreds of miles away from al Qaeda training camps. It used sophisticated bombs and demonstrated complex planning. Then came the attack on the USS *Cole* in 2000, a failed millennium plot, followed by the attacks of September 11, 2001 (see L. Wright, 2006). After the United States and allied forces struck al Qaeda bases in Afghanistan in October 2001, structured operations gave way to a loose network.

Despite al Qaeda's reputation as an international organization, bin Laden and Zawahiri failed to emerge as the masterminds of a worldwide terror organization. They served mainly as symbols. The 9/11 plot can be traced to another operative, Khalid Sheik Mohammed, who planned the attack and put the people in place to carry it out. After the U.S.-led offensive in Afghanistan, bin Laden and Zawahiri saw their control diminish even further. They were able to indirectly influence bombings in Madrid on March 11, 2004, and an operational commander had direct contact with bombers on the London subway on July 7, 2005. They almost produced mass casualties in the summer of 2006 with a number of simultaneous airline suicide attacks, but good intelligence and police work stopped the attacks in the planning stage. However, their ability to control activity waned. They became symbols of religious violence, and this also had an adverse effect. Their theology was so poor that Muslims vehemently began to reject it.

✓	Self- Check	> Why was the Egyptian experience important to al Qaeda? > How did bin Laden and Zawahiri create a new organization in Afghanistan? > What resulted from the declaration of war and the alliance against Jews and crusaders?

Al Qaeda's Operational Capabilities

Al Qaeda's ability to attack changed after September 11, 2001. It still inspired attacks, and it helped plot different attacks, including a devastating subway bombing in London in 2005. The United Kingdom and the United States were able to stop an attack against seven Atlantic passenger planes in 2006. Had they not done so, casualties would have numbered over 1,000 (Bergen, 2009). By the end of the decade, however, al Qaeda's offensive capabilities were changing.

The operational capabilities of al Qaeda have stirred debate in the counterterrorism community. Marc Sageman (2009) believes that al Qaeda has been diminished. No longer capable of launching massive strikes, it is limited to supporting small operations, and these attacks lack the command and control system so evident between 1998 and 2001. Sageman argues that networks give al Qaeda's loose association a de facto command structure. Bruce Hoffman (2008) disagrees. He argues that al Qaeda commanders remain active and ready to strike.

The Sageman–Hoffman Debate

Marc Sageman and Bruce Hoffman are two of the most notable analysts of modern terrorism. A former CIA analyst, Sageman developed two of the most widely used public resources about jihadist operations, *Understanding Terror Networks* (2004) and *Leaderless Jihad* (2008a). Hoffman, the author of several noted studies on terrorism, including *Inside Terrorism* (revised 2006), directed counterterrorism research at the RAND Corporation for many years before joining the faculty at Georgetown University. Both researchers have made significant contributions to scholarly and professional literature, but they disagree about the operational capabilities of al Qaeda.

The debate started in the summer of 2008 when Hoffman (2008a) published a book review of *Leaderless Jihad* in *Foreign Affairs*. Hoffman applauds Sageman's counterterrorist credentials. He has a PhD in sociology and an MD in psychiatry, and he served as a U.S. Navy flight surgeon before joining the CIA. Sageman complemented his impressive academic résumé with experience in Iraq and Afghanistan. All of this, Hoffman says, does not overcome Sageman's fundamental flaw in understanding al Qaeda: Sageman believes that al Qaeda is no longer the main threat to the West. The more immediate threat comes from marginalized Western Muslim immigrants and citizens who feel disenfranchised.

Hoffman states that this thesis flies in the face of the evidence about al Qaeda. It is not a dismembered force sitting on the Afghanistan–Pakistan border; it remains a primary threat. This is demonstrated, Hoffman argues, by intelligence assessments in Europe and the United States. Hoffman goes on to argue that Sageman misunderstands the current threat because he improperly applies historical parallels out of context. He claims that Sageman's theory of how terrorist networks behave stands in contradistinction to most of the literature on terrorism, and he criticizes Sageman for ignoring most of the social science data on terrorism in favor of his own methodology. He also believes that homegrown terrorists have yet to emerge as a major threat. Finally, Hoffman states that Sageman's work is a psychological study written from an individual standpoint.

Hoffman concludes by stating that al Qaeda has regrouped in the border area between Afghanistan and Pakistan and that it has reemerged as a central threat to the United States. It will not be destroyed by focusing on networks. Al Qaeda must be defeated by eliminating its leadership and delegitimizing its ideology.

In summary, Hoffman says:

- Leadership connections are intact and dangerous.
- Al Qaeda remains a threat to the West.
- Organizations are structured.
- Sageman's theory of terrorist networks does not match the scholarly and applied literature about the subject.
- Sageman has ignored important data.
- Sageman focused on individual behavior instead of the way terrorist groups behave.

Sageman (2008b) responded in the next issue of *Foreign Affairs*. He says that Hoffman fundamentally misrepresented his argument and that Hoffman cited information that did not appear in his book. Al Qaeda, Sageman writes, remains a substantial threat, and it will reemerge unless the West maintains constant vigilance and action against the core leadership. Al Qaeda's central command, the men with blood on their hands, are still plotting against the United States. He says that Hoffman missed this point by portraying *Leaderless Jihad* as a simple-minded polemic. The truth is, Sageman concludes, that al Qaeda has evolved over time.

According to Sageman, the al Qaeda aura has also spawned the radicalization of homegrown terrorists. Pointing to evidence in several Western countries, Sageman defends his methodology, and maintains that he reviews several differing research methodologies in the literature on terrorism in *Leaderless Jihad*. Sageman says that he specifically rejects an individualized view and focuses on groups. He sees group behavior as an essential element of analysis.

In summary, Sageman counters:

- Hoffman misrepresented information in *Leaderless Jihad*.
- Al Qaeda remains a threat to the West.
- It has an active command structure.
- The threat of terrorism is evolving.
- He reviews the literature on terrorism and his methodology is correct.
- *Leaderless Jihad* focuses on groups, not individuals.

Foreign Affairs allowed Bruce Hoffman (2008b) to comment on Sageman's response in the same issue. He says that Sageman's theory that terrorist groups emerged from friendship networks seemed compelling at first, but the 2005 London subway attacks and the thwarted 2006 airliner attacks disprove the theory. Both groups had contact with Pakistan. Their plans developed within a hierarchy, and they were launched from an organized base. Hoffman concludes that the disagreement is not personal. Terrorism remains a threat and proper research is necessary to understand it.

Retired U.S. Marine Corps Lieutenant Colonel F. G. Hoffman (2008) analyzed both arguments for the United States Naval Institute. He says that Sageman's approach concerning decentralized networks makes sense. The Internet has become the prime source of radicalization, and it is spreading the al Qaeda ideology to a growing network. Yet Lt. Colonel Hoffman argues that Bruce Hoffman is also correct. Al Qaeda is still a threat and it has retained the ability to command and control operations. Lt. Colonel Hoffman concludes that the disagreement centers on methodology, and that both Bruce Hoffman and Marc Sageman make important points.

Reid Sawyer and Michael Foster (2008) posit an argument to reinforce Lt. Colonel Hoffman's point. Al Qaeda has survived and it is waging a battle of ideas. They argue that American policy has not taken this into account and that it is based on eliminating a hierarchy. This is the wrong approach. U.S. policy should be aimed at striking at a network. They suggest a four-fold strategy: (1) Understand the nature of the network threat, (2) disrupt al Qaeda communications, (3) neutralize sanctuaries for leadership, and (4) deny opportunities to link networks. These procedures need to be accomplished within a framework that counters al Qaeda's central message.

Degraded Leadership and the al Qaeda Franchise

The Sageman–Hoffman debate is important because it represents the fundamental thrust of counterterrorism policy. Former CIA executive Paul Pillar (2004) illustrates the point. Al Qaeda's central control structure was disrupted after the 2001 offensive in Afghanistan. This resulted in the creation of a loose international network. If the leadership has been reconstituted, networks still remain, and networks call for a new counterterrorism strategy. Bin Laden has been killed, al Qaeda is fractured, and the West faces a new network with new challenges.

Al Qaeda has become a franchise—that is, a brand name. Central leadership operates in the tribal areas of Pakistan. It has power because of an alliance with other groups in the area. These include Lashkar-e-Taiba and the Pakistani version of the Taliban. It is also based on a large family that looks more like a criminal group rather than a terror network. The **Haqqani network** runs its own militias, shadow governments, protection rackets, legitimate businesses, and terrorist groups. Dating back to the Soviet–Afghan War, leaders of the Haqqani clan are the major players in Pakistan's tribal region. They can plan and administer highly complex terrorist attacks at a great distance.

Haqqani network:
A family in the tribal area of Pakistan that has relations with several militant groups and the ISI. The Haqqani family is involved in organized crime, legitimate businesses, the ISI, and terrorism groups. It is the major power broker in the tribal region.

Peter Bergen (2009) believes al Qaeda central has been significantly degraded due to U.S. drone attacks in Pakistan. He points to the following significant number of al Qaeda operatives killed by the drones:

- Abu Laith al Libi—led al Qaeda behind bin Laden and Zawahiri
- Abu Sulyman al Jazairi—member of Algerian jihad
- Abu Khabab al Masri—weapons of mass destruction expert
- Abdul Rehman—Taliban commander, South Waziristan
- Abu Haris—al Qaeda chief in Pakistan
- Khalid Habib—senior al Qaeda leader
- Abu Zubair al Masri—senior al Qaeda leader
- Abdullah Azzam al Saudi—senior al Qaeda leader
- Abu Jihad al Masri—al Qaeda propaganda chief
- Tahir Yulashev—commander, Islamic Movement of Uzbekistan
- Baitullah Mehsud—leader, Pakistani Taliban

Of course, the symbolic nature of the change came on May 1, 2011, when President Barak Obama announced that U.S. Navy SEALs had attacked Osama bin Laden's compound in Pakistan. The nemesis from 9/11 was dead. Although the leadership has been degraded, the threat continues due to the franchised approach to terrorism. Al Qaeda in the Arabian Peninsula (AQAP) has emerged as both a major tactical threat and a propaganda machine. Al Qaeda in the Islamic Maghreb (AQIM) began as an offshoot of the Algerian Civil War. It raises money by kidnapping, and according to the congressional intelligence sources, it has become al Qaeda's most important financial resource (Rogers, 2012). Al Qaeda in Iraq remains a local threat. Bin Laden was an important symbol, and his compound proved to be a treasure trove of intelligence. Threats live on through the franchise.

The Role of Women

Katharina von Knop (2007) notes that the role of women in terrorism is frequently overlooked and that this has been true of studies of al Qaeda. Suicide bombers capture the public imagination, but females in al Qaeda tend to follow traditional gender roles within the radical ideology. The female jihad involves supporting male relatives,

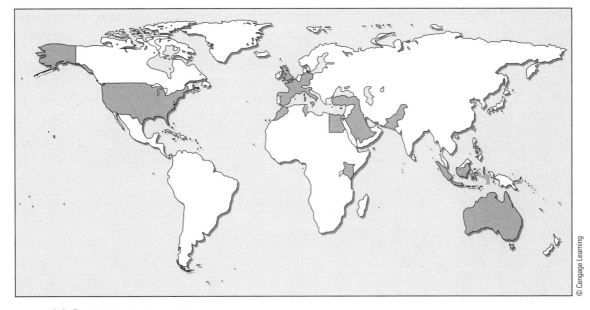

FIGURE **11.2** Global Jihadi Attacks

educating children in the ideology, providing support for operations, and assisting with financing. The female role is transformed when women assume the male role of suicide bomber, rendering women less effective in their supporting roles.

Al Qaeda's women tend to be better educated than its men, and they are more interested in fulfilling traditional roles rather than assuming an operative position. They have a strong influence on family cohesion and provide the familial network to support operatives. Bin Laden stated in his 1996 declaration of war that the role of al Qaeda women was to motivate their sons, brothers, and husbands. They are to encourage jihad. In the 1998 declaration against Jews and crusaders, bin Laden portrayed women as the victims of Western imperialism.

Women are typically recruited in sisterhoods, an offshoot of Hasan al Banna's Muslim Brotherhood, and radical sisterhoods are prevalent in Europe. Von Knop states that they have three central functions in Germany. They hold breakfast meetings simply designed for the sisters, and they also have general receptions open to everyone. They also hold fund-raising receptions.

Al Qaeda members prior to 9/11 would have been offended if one of their female relatives had been recruited as an operative. Von Knop believes that this attitude is changing. Bin Laden's latest documents called for women to actively join the jihad. Their operative role is in the formative stage and growing. Von Knop notes that between 1985 and 2006, 225 women were involved in suicide bombings, and she expects that this will have an impact on al Qaeda. Al Qaeda created a women's suicide division in 2003.

Virtual War

One last aspect of al Qaeda, besides its physical presence in Pakistan, is its orientation toward the electronic media. In 2005, Ayman al Zawahiri stated that over half the battle is being waged in the media. Communications are central to the al Qaeda strategy. Even before September 11, Zawahiri and bin Laden used satellite television, the Internet, and their video and audio tape distribution system. The media are used to recruit followers, for propaganda, and to get Muslims to accept the idea of a clash of civilizations. The Internet has also become a forum for spreading tactical advice, bomb-making instructions, and theological debates (Lynch, 2006).

Al Qaeda casts its central message as a war of ideas. It projects the virtuous Qutb-style purity of Islam over the infidels. Many people believe that the group's video releases are associated with an increased threat, but a review of the release dates and al Qaeda attacks reveal no such pattern (Gips, 2006). Al Qaeda runs a global marketing campaign in an attempt to capture the imagination and support of Muslims. Carl Ciovacco (2010) collected a sample of 64 al Qaeda media releases from 2001 to 2008 from the holdings of the Combating Terrorism Center at West Point. He found that al Qaeda is quick to exploit local issues and surround them with its own theology. Anniversaries are used as propaganda platforms, and most releases use carefully redacted passages of the Quran and a selective history to tailor the message.

Ciovacco says that the following seven themes are present in most media releases:

- A call to jihad
- The clash of civilizations
- Apostate (*takfiri*) Muslim regimes
- U.S.–Israeli friendship
- Muslim unity
- American strategic weaknesses
- American exploitation of Muslim oil

Al Qaeda runs its own media outlet, As Sahab (the Cloud), to support its media campaign. As Sahab continually streams video to the Internet from its production studio in Pakistan, and al Qaeda augments As Sahab by releasing selected television footage to mainstream Arab media outlets, according to Marc Lynch (2006).

Sometimes al Qaeda's external media strategy backfires. Lynch says new Arab media outlets are fragmented and faced with increasing competition. In addition, many stations have been known to represent the vast diversity of Muslim opinion. For example, the 2005 London bombing attacks drew quite a bit of criticism in the Arab world, and many of the media outlets aired this dissatisfaction. One station even accused al Qaeda of murdering innocent people. The American-managed al Hurra has not been an effective participant in the debate. It is generally ignored throughout the world.

Peter Bergen (2009) believes that the increasing criticism of al Qaeda in the Arab media will result in increasing unpopularity for its intolerant dogma. By glorifying violence and sticking to an inflexible message, al Qaeda's attacks—especially those that kill innocent Muslims—continue to alienate the group from mainstream Muslims. In 2009 and 2010 As Sahab responded to criticism with a media blitz. Bergen believes that the media onslaught was the result of al Qaeda's tarnished image.

Self-Check

> How does the Sageman–Hoffman debate impact the way al Qaeda's operational capabilities are viewed?
> What roles do women play in al Qaeda?
> How does al Qaeda attempt to use the media?

Al Qaeda's Franchises

While Bruce Hoffman and Marc Sageman debate the nature of jihadist networks, groups have moved beyond the original structure of al Qaeda. Diverse movements have appeared in different parts of the world, and their effectiveness is growing. They have demonstrated an ability to develop and support terrorist attacks beyond their immediate geographical location. Such groups are emerging as threats to regional stability; others threaten Western security.

AQAP

One of the newest jihadist groups grew from the tangled political situation in Yemen, and it maintains cross-border ties with radicals in Saudi Arabia. Andrew McGregor (2010) says that al Qaeda in the Arabian Peninsula (AQAP) is the most active group in the jihadist network outside Pakistan. Yemen suffers from three differing conflicts: a struggle for control of the central government, a rebellious southern region, and a growing presence of AQAP in the Marib. Tribal power and rivalries dominate the region and limit the government's power. Although American drone strikes have eliminated known and suspected terrorists, they increasingly alienate local tribal chiefs (Figure 11.3).

Yemen did not become a unified country until 1990, and its internal divisions have created an environment where AQAP can grow. Its spiritual leader is **Nasir al Wuhayshi.** He has expressed a desire to wage an international jihad and has called on all members of AQAP to kill Americans wherever they are found. According to a report from CBS News (Raghavan, 2010), government attempts to centralize its power and American activities against AQAP are backfiring. Yemeni military officers think that both are strengthening AQAP. This is complicated by unrest in the south and AQAP strongholds in the north. The government's military commander in the southern tribal region even abandoned his position and joined local tribal chieftains. Each time the government moves against the south, it brings the southern tribes closer to Wuhayshi, according to the news report.

According to the National Counterterrorism Center (2010), AQAP evolved from earlier organizations in the Arabian Peninsula. Al Qaeda was active in Yemen in October 2000 when it launched a suicide attack on the **USS Cole.** Another movement began in Saudi Arabia shortly after 9/11, but it was eventually wiped out by Saudi security forces. In February 2006, a group of 23 al Qaeda prisoners escaped from prison in Sanaa, the capital of Yemen, and they created al Qaeda in Yemen (AQY) later that year. The group launched a series of suicide attacks against Yemen's oil facilities in September and posted an Internet statement about the attacks in November. Ayman al Zawahiri responded by embracing AQY and encouraging the group to make further attacks that same year.

The NCTC says that attacks continued through 2007 and 2008 and that they became more intense. AQY began targeting embassies, the presidential compound in Sanaa, and Yemeni military bases. In January 2009, AQY became AQAP, embracing

Nasir al Wuhayshi: (age unkown) The spiritual leader of AQAP and a former aide to Osama bin Laden. Wuhayshi escaped from a Yemeni prison in 2006 to form AQY. In 2009, he joined his group with dissidents in Saudi Arabia to form AQAP.

USS Cole: A U.S. Navy destroyer attacked by two suicide bombers in the port of Aden, Yemen, on October 12, 2000. Seventeen American sailors were killed in the attack.

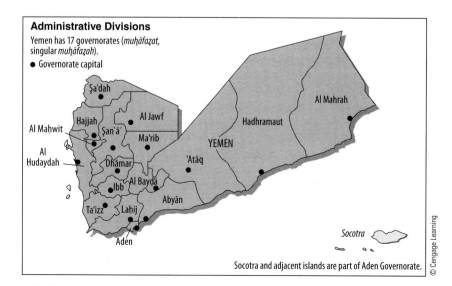

FIGURE **11.3** Yemen

rebellion in both Yemen and Saudi Arabia. The group announced that it would attack all foreigners. Its stated purpose is to unite Saudi Arabia and Yemen in one religious government under AQAP's narrow interpretation of Islamic law. AQAP claimed responsibility for the attempted downing of a Northwest airliner outside Detroit on Christmas Day, 2009. It also sheltered the American violent preacher, **Anwar al Awlaki**, the man who inspired homegrown terrorism and other AQAP attacks on the United States. He was killed in September 2011 by a strike from a predator drone.

Anwar al Awlaki: (1971–2011) An American-born Muslim cleric who worked to build U.S.-Muslim relations after 9/11. He became increasingly militant and called for attacks on America. He was arrested in Yemen in 2006 and released in 2007. In 2009, he swore allegiance to AQAP.

AQIM

Algeria's jihadist civil war in the 1990s spawned the Salafi Group for Preaching and Combat (GSPC) in 1998; the GSPC gave rise to a new group, al Qaeda in the Maghreb (AQIM) in 2006. The Congressional Research Service (CRS) (Rollins, 2010) says that the GPSC split from the Algerian Islamic Group (GIA) in order to oppose the GIA's indiscriminate targeting of civilians. In 2006, the GSPC announced its unity with al Qaeda and changed its name to the AQIM. At first, it was difficult to distinguish AQIM from any other organized crime group. It was able to raise funds from cells in Europe, but its primary income was derived from criminal activities. It raised funds through kidnapping, trafficking drugs and contraband, and human trafficking (Figure 11.4).

The NCTC (2010) says that the group began changing its targets in late 2006 and early 2007. Using roadside bombs, it began to attack the energy industry. Throughout 2007, it stepped up activity in Algiers, the capital of Algeria, and it launched an attack against the Israeli embassy in neighboring Mauritania. The group also introduced suicide bombing, and by year's end, more than 30 people in Algiers had lost their lives to AQIM attacks. This prompted a crackdown by the Algerian government, and AQIM was forced from the capital. It operates primarily along the coastal region outside of Algiers and in the Sahel desert area bordering Mali and Algeria. While it employs terror tactics, it has also launched guerrilla-style ambushes and light artillery attacks. The desert provides a vast area to recruit and train potential operatives.

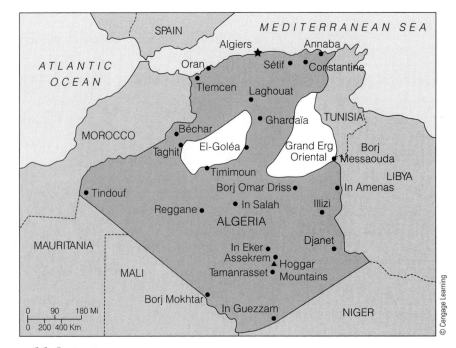

FIGURE **11.4** Algeria

The CRS adds that Morocco and Tunisia have managed to keep AQIM from crossing their borders, but they fear the outbreak of al Qaeda–style violence.

AQIM's allegiance to al Qaeda is ambiguous. It claims loyalty and unity, but in practice it does not take direction from Afghanistan or Pakistan. It is possible that the al Qaeda brand was adopted to enhance its legitimacy among extremists and to attract recruits. It has called for jihad against the United States, France, and Spain, and Americans and Europeans have been targeted for kidnappings and attacks (Rollins, 2010). AQIM has executed two European kidnap victims as part of its jihad. When a French hostage was murdered in July 2010, Nicolas Sarkozy vowed revenge. According to Reuters (Felix, 2010), a 78-year-old French engineer was taken hostage in Mali. After AQIM threatened to kill the victim, French commandos made an unsuccessful rescue attempt. This prompted AQIM to murder their hostage, and a spokesman released the news on al Jazeera. Sarkozy stated that he would dispatch French military units to deal with AQIM.

Dario Cristiani (2010) believes that AQIM has been hobbled by the arrest of many of its leaders. A three-way debate about the true nature of AQIM has unfolded among counterterrorism experts. One set of analysts believes that AQIM is emerging as a regional force in West Africa. A second opinion is that it is nothing more than an Algerian group and that its effectiveness is questionable. A third group classifies AQIM in the same way that they look at the Abu Sayuff Group in the Philippines—it is little more than a criminal organization hiding under the rhetoric of al Qaeda.

The Horn of Africa and al Shabaab

Combined Joint Task Force, Horn of Africa (CJTF-HOA): An American-led counterterrorist unit combining military, intelligence, and law enforcement assets of several nations in the Horn.

Terrorists are currently active in the Horn of Africa (Figure 11.5). After 9/11, the United States worked with governments in the region to create the **Combined Joint Task Force, Horn of Africa (CJTF-HOA)**. Its purpose was similar to the domestic Joint Terrorism Task Forces (JTTFs) in the United States. The CJTF-HOA detects and

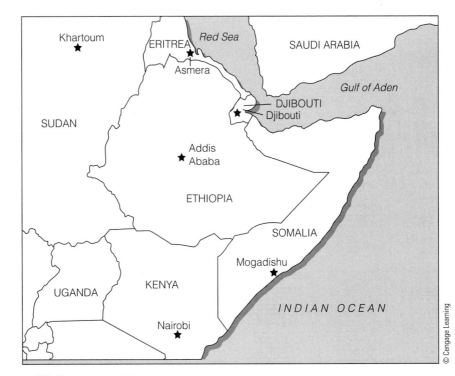

FIGURE **11.5** Horn of Africa

disrupts terrorist activities before the terrorists can commit violence. But unlike a JTTF, CJTF-HOA relies heavily on military force and national security intelligence; it is not limited to law enforcement activities. Francis Miko (2004) states that although the CJTF-HOA has been effective, terrorism in the Horn will remain a problem because of porous borders, lax security, and political instability.

United States activities in the Horn have ranged from targeted killings to intelligence gathering. As in the cold war, U.S. foreign policy has favored repressive governments when it benefits American interests. Miko (2004) says that America justifies its actions by the regional presence of al Qaeda and other jihadist groups. Kenya is the only sub-Saharan country with known al Qaeda cells, but there are many other known jihadist organizations in the Horn. Jihadist activities bleed across Kenya's borders into Somalia. The **Islamic Courts Union** (ICU), for example, represented a coalition of groups wanting to rule Somalia under Islamic law. An Ethiopian offensive in 2006 displaced the ICU, but left militants in its wake. Opponents contentiously debate the relationship of these groups to the jihadist network, and they dispute Miko's claim about the presence of al Qaeda, believing that it has had cells in Somalia since 1998 (Bruton, 2009; Rothmyer, 2009).

Debra West (2005) says that the United States faces differing terrorist threats in the Horn of Africa, and each threat requires a different policy response. The most obvious threat comes from the ability of terrorist groups to take immediate action. From bases in the Horn, they attack American interests and stage operations. Another threat is the ability of terrorist groups, especially jihadists, to organize in the region. They are able to do this because of two other factors: (1) unstable political environments and (2) a population that supports terrorism against the United States and its allies. The CJTF-HOA is an answer for the immediate threats, West believes. Diplomatic relations, foreign aid, and governmental assistance are required to deal with threats from the political environment.

West points to the success of the CJTF-HOA as a measure of tactical effectiveness. When the CJTF-HOA first began to operate in 2002, it sought three terrorist organizations and 25 supporters. By 2004, it had killed or captured 65 terrorists and had identified 550 probable supporters. Working with other military forces, the CJTF-HOA has successfully struck numerous targets. Yet, West concludes, the biggest challenge for American foreign policy is promoting political stability.

Andrew Feickert (2005) says that the CJTF-HOA has been so successful that some observers believe it should be used as a model for the war on terrorism. The struggle against terrorism cannot be measured in conventional military terms, according to this logic; success comes when American military and intelligence units are able to work hand in hand with local military and police forces. The CJTF-HOA's close relationship with indigenous forces will build a long-term partnership with governments in the Horn. Security forces from local governments can operate in places where American troops cannot go. In a report for Congress, Feickert says that champions of this policy point to the number of terrorists the CJTF-HOA's approach has identified, captured, or killed, but he acknowledges that not everyone agrees with this assessment.

Two people who disagree are John Prendergast and Colin Thomas-Jensen (2007). They argue that the Horn represents the hottest war zone in the world, and it is a region of massive humanitarian crises and ethnic conflicts. Two clusters of conflicts lay at the heart of the matter. The first involves rebellions in Sudan, particularly in Darfur. These conflicts have spilled into Uganda, Chad, and the Central African Republic. The second cluster of conflicts involves a dispute between Ethiopia and Eritrea over complicated fighting in Somalia. This includes a new secular faction trying to take power in Mogadishu, Islamic militias, anti-Islamic militias, private armies of united tribes, individual warlords, and terrorist groups. The problems go far beyond simply eradicating terrorism, but American policy has been shortsighted.

Islamic Courts Union (ICU): A confederation of tribes and clans seeking to end violence and bring Islamic law to Somalia. It is opposed by several neighboring countries and internal warlords. Some people feel that it is a jihadist organization, but others see it as a grouping of clans with several different interpretations of Islamic law.

Prendergast and Thomas-Jensen believe that political stability will make the situation better and solve terrorism in the long run, but stability involves more than calling out the CJTF-HOA. In fact, by approaching the Horn as a military problem, the United States has actually made the situation worse. The United States has supported authoritarian governments that encourage repression. In addition, foreign policy favors covert military action over long-term diplomacy. This has been a disaster, the authors argue. Nearly 9 million people have been displaced, and the 16 million people who do not have access to aid could become a humanitarian crisis. People are murdered, entire populations are "cleansed," and children are taken into slavery or used as soldiers. Prendergast and Thomas-Jensen believe that a long-term policy to stabilize the region would be the most effective counterterrorist policy, but they feel that the United States has acted without an overall strategy.

The International Crisis Group (2005b, 2005d) summarizes the foreign policy problem from this perspective. The ICG (2005b, 2005d, 2010) maintains that the United States stereotypes as jihadists Muslims who want to live under Islamic law. The situation is much more complicated than that. For example, the ICU briefly took power in Somalia in mid-2006 (and lost power in December of the same year). Some analysts immediately feared that Somalia would follow the path of Afghanistan under the Taliban (see Nzwili, 2006). The International Crisis Group says that the ICU is simply a tribal confederation of leaders who are tired of constant warfare and criminal activity in Somalia.

To understand this, it is necessary to briefly consider the overall political situation in Somalia. During the cold war, the United States used Somalia as a base against communism in Africa. This resulted in a fragmented system in which a central government tried to control policy from Mogadishu, but political power was exercised by local tribes and clans. This situation gave rise to several humanitarian crises, American intervention under President George H. W. Bush, and the "Black Hawk Down" incident during the Clinton administration. Somalia degenerated into virtual anarchy, with local warlords controlling sections of the country (Bruton, 2009).

The country served as a base for some of the al Qaeda operatives who attacked the United States' embassies in Dar es Salaam and Nairobi in 1998, and known al Qaeda suspects were present after the 9/11 attacks. The Bush Administration responded by joining with the United Nations to establish a **Transitional Federal Government (TFG)**, but the TFG could never gain control from competing clans and tribes. Fed up with violence, a group of clans formed the ICU to impose Islamic law and bring order to the country in early 2006. The United States, alarmed that this move represented a takeover by the jihadists, supported an Ethiopian invasion of Somalia in December 2006. This lasted until 2009, but its results were disastrous. Somalia became a quagmire of violent political chaos (see Bruton, 2009; Rothmyer, 2009; International Crisis Group, 2010).

The Harakat Shabaab al-Mujahedeen, better known as al Shabaab, or the Youth, emerged after the retreat of the ICU. The U.S. government maintains that al Shabaab is the military wing of the ICU, but other analysts see it as one of many offshoots of the ICU confederacy (see NCTC, 2010). Regardless, al Shabaab began an offensive in central and southern Somalia for the purpose of imposing its narrow brand of Islamic law on Somalia. Al Shabaab emerged as one of the most vicious and merciless groups in the region, and the U.S. Department of State officially dubbed it a foreign terrorist organization in 2008.

Al Shabaab has influenced America in two ways. First, it has spawned a policy debate. Some American policy makers believe that it is affiliated with al Qaeda and that it serves as a wing of the global jihad. Al Shabaab has claimed to represent al Qaeda, and some of its leaders have sworn an oath of loyalty to Osama bin Laden. Other analysts believe al Shabaab is a regional movement and that the Islamic members of Somali society are hardly united. They seek political order far removed from

Transitional Federal Government (TFG): A group established to govern Somalia in 2004 until a permanent government could be established. It was backed by the United Nations, with American support, and the African Union.

al Qaeda's jihad. This is evidenced by the formation of Sufi militias to counter al Shabaab (LeMelle, 2009).

The second policy concern deals with the Somali diaspora in the United States. Over the past few decades, over a million Somalis have been displaced from their homeland, and many of them are in the United States, especially in the Minneapolis area. Most Somali families send money and goods back to their relatives, and stories of the homeland abound in the lives of the second and third generations. Even though many second- and third-generation young people are quite successful in the United States, they feel drawn to the struggle in their ancestral home. Some of them have seen al Shabaab and jihad as the method to serve. They have joined al Shabaab's ranks, causing law enforcement officials to believe that they will later return to the United States as domestic terrorists (Elliot, 2010). This is discussed further in the next chapter.

At this point al Qaeda rhetoric embraces the youth of al Shabaab, and it has encouraged them to strike in Yemen and surrounding countries. Al Shabaab claimed responsibility for setting off a bomb in Uganda in 2010 during the World Cup football championships, but it has exhibited little ability to wage an international campaign. Still, al Qaeda has not fully embraced al Shabaab, and it is not popular among Somali Muslims. In fact, several of them have joined to fight it. Bronwyn Bruton (2009) of the Council on Foreign Relations believes that the United States has fundamentally misunderstood the situation in Somalia. Al Shabaab and issues surrounding the TFG are centered in regional rivalries. Many believe it should not have been seen as part of an international conflict. They think that the failure to understand this situation will drive groups like al Shabaab closer to the jihadist camp.

Daveed Gartenstein-Ross (2009) argues from a different perspective. He says that al Shabaab has demonstrated that it is part of the global jihad. Because it swears allegiance to al Qaeda and embraces objectives beyond the immediate area, al Shabaab represents a strategic threat to the United States. In addition, he is concerned with the number of Americans who travel to Somalia for military training. He believes that the numbers of young men who have traveled to Somalia for al Shabaab training render the group among America's most strategic threats for domestic terrorism. Gartenstein-Ross uses al Shabaab's ability to control vast amounts of Somali territory as proof of the group's threat. Critics argue that America's very presence gives al Shabaab power. If the United States withdraws, they counter, other Muslims will strike al Shabaab. Al Shabaab officially joined al Qaeda in 2012.

Self-Check

> What types of threats are posed by AQAP?
> How did the GIA transform into AQIM?
> How did violence emerge in Somalia?

Al Qaeda's Political Theology

Because jihadists make religious claims, many Muslims become upset when their faith is portrayed in terms of violent terrorism. Many Christians feel similarly, for instance, when the fighting in Ireland is described as a "religious war." They believe that even though militants invoke either Protestantism or Catholicism, Irish violence is a violation of Christian principles. Mainstream Muslims feel the same way. In fact, Magnus Ranstorp (1998) says that the jihadists are doomed to failure within their own culture because their theology of violence does not convey the meaning of Islam.

Many Muslims agree with Ranstorp's conclusion. Feisal Rauf (2004, pp. 41–77) responds with a popular theological treatise explaining the strengths of Islam. Islam is a religion, Rauf says, that values peace and toleration. There are violent passages in the Quran, but there are violent passages in the writings of all major religions, including Judaism and Christianity. Islam teaches universal human love, submission to God's will, and a life of morality preparing for the final judgment of God. He calls Muslims to embrace the roots of their faith and the commonalities among Muslims, Jews, and Christians.

Former Congressman Paul Findlay (2001), who is Christian, is enraged by attacks on stereotyped Muslims. Findlay recounts stories and actions of friends who have embraced the Islamic faith. He tells of personal travels to Islamic lands to demonstrate his belief in a simple fact: people are people everywhere. The religion of Islam, he concludes, does not foster militancy.

Others point to violent sects in Islam. Steven Emerson (2002, pp. 221–233) says that Islam has always been associated with political expansion and that militancy is a product of the twentieth century. His research shows that many seemingly legitimate Islamic organizations support the jihadists and directly or indirectly fund radical Muslim terrorist groups. Missionaries from intolerant sects within Islam travel to the West by the hundreds, Emerson says, and millions of dollars from such sects build mosques in Europe and in the United States.

madrassas: Islamic religious schools.

Confusion about mainstream Islam complicates attempts to understand jihadists. Misunderstandings increase when jihadists use religious rhetoric. For example, Catholic IRA terrorists did not justify their operations in the name of God. Jihadists do. In addition, some **madrassas** (Islamic schools) in many areas of the world glamorize violence and inspire young people to join terrorist organizations (J. Stern, 2003b, pp. 258–259). Samuel Huntington (1996, p. 176) points out that Christians, Hindus, and Buddhists do not create international associations of nation-states that are based on religion. Muslims do. Such religious and cultural issues are factors that complicate attempts to understand the nature of jihadist networks.

Revolutionary Vanguard versus Religion

Theologians from many traditions try to understand other religious beliefs through study and dialogue, but militants seldom have such concerns. Al Qaeda continued to operate in Pakistan, and its hardcore leadership never questioned its interpretation of religion (see Ibrahim, 2007, pp. 17–62). It inspired bombings around the world, and bin Laden and Zawahiri remained the symbols of violent religion. Despite this, they have lost most of their religious appeal (Palmer and Palmer, 2004, pp. 9–34). The primary reason is that al Qaeda is not a religious movement. It is a violent political organization that attempts to hide under the mantle of religious rhetoric. Martin Hart (2008) explains this rationale.

Hart argues that al Qaeda has lost its appeal in the Muslim world because of its basic mission. Far from being a religious movement, it pictures itself as the vanguard of a popular uprising that will destroy Western influence and reestablish the caliphate. This resembles Lenin more than Mohammed. Many Muslims viewed al Qaeda's early attacks as the heroic resistance to unjust colonialism, but al Qaeda's central message failed to evoke a resurgence of religion. This is primarily due to its emphasis on violence over the message of Islam.

Hart believes that the overreliance on violence ultimately isolates al Qaeda from Islam. Its weakness is exacerbated because it has no organizational structure. Its most effective tactic is inspiration, and this does not move it beyond its small cell structures. Al Qaeda cannot expand, and it has weak support from any potential sponsor as well as insufficient areas to regroup in safe havens. Theologically, al Qaeda cannot correct this because it emphasizes violence over religion and exhibits no flexibility. The majority of Muslims who do not support the movement are deemed heretics, and the few people who do lend their voices are only given the rhetoric of preordained victory. There is no practical strategy and no solid theological foundation.

> How does Islamic theology pose a threat to al Qaeda?
> How do many mainstream Muslims view terrorism in the name of their faith?
> Why does al Qaeda's theology place politics before religion?

Pakistan

Mohammed Ali Jinnah:
(1876–1948) The leader of the Muslim League and the founder of modern Pakistan. He served as Governor-General until his death in 1948.

Pakistan became a country in 1947 as part of the political settlement when the British departed India. Officially, it was to be a Muslim country, but unofficially, its first leader, **Mohammed Ali Jinnah**, was quite happy to have an independent democracy of landed elites, according to Tariq Ali (2008, pp. 29–49). The country was composed of East and West Pakistan, separated by 1,000 miles of mainland India. The name was derived from a conglomeration of tribes and ethnic groups. P stood for Punjab, A for Afghan, K for Kashmir, and S for Sind. Unfortunately, Ali adds, there was no B for Bengal (East Pakistan) or for the massive group of Baluchs in the large state of Baluchistan. The country began as a fusion of tribes with the army providing the only common element in the diverse ethnic mix. The army became a staunch ally of the United States during the cold war, and it maintains a close relationship with Washington, although this influence is resented by many Pakistanis (Figure 11.6).

Ali says that both the democracy and the myth of a unified country were short-lived. The ethnic Bengals left Pakistan in 1971 to form the country of Bangladesh.

FIGURE **11.6** Pakistan

Ayub Khan: (1907–1974) The second president of Pakistan, from 1958 to 1974. Khan seized control of the government in 1958 and then staged elections. He was the first of Pakistan's many military leaders.

Asif Ali Zardari: (b. 1955) The husband of Benazir Bhutto, Zardari, inherited control of the Pakistan People's Party after Bhutto's assassination in December 2007. He was elected president in 2008.

Pervez Musharraf: (1943–) The president of Pakistan (2001–2008). A career army officer, Musharraf took power in a 1999 military coup and declared himself president in 2001. After 9/11 he sought closer relations with the United States, while trying to mollify sources of domestic religious strife.

North-West Frontier Province (NWFP): One of four Pakistani states, inhabited primarily by ethnic Pashtuns. Several areas of the NWFP are controlled by tribes, and jihadists operate in the area. Peshawar, NWFP's capital, served as a base for organizing several mujahedeen groups in the Soviet-Afghan War.

Waziristan: Literally, the land of the Waziris, a tribal region between the North-West Frontier Province and Baluchistan. Waziri tribes clashed with the Pakistan Army from 2004 to 2006, and they support several jihadist operations in Afghanistan and Pakistan. Al Qaeda and Taliban forces operate in Waziristan.

Before the Bangladeshi secession, Pakistan's democracy fell to General **Ayub Khan** when the Pakistani Army seized control of the government in 1958. Although Pakistan has restored democracy on occasion, including the election of its current President **Asif Ali Zardari**, the army stands as the power behind the government. The country is composed of five major states (four provinces and one territory) divided primarily along ethnic lines. Control of Jammu and Kashmir is disputed with India.

Two international issues dominate Pakistan: nuclear weapons and relations with the United States, and both of these issues are ultimately tied to terrorism. Pakistan is the only Islamic country with nuclear capabilities, and it has shared the technology with other nations. While the West lives in fear of a radical regime gaining control of atomic weapons, Pakistan already has them. Officially, Pakistan has been a long-standing ally of the United States. After 9/11, the former Pakistani President **Pervez Musharraf** reaffirmed this relationship, though relations had been strained due to the ISI's support of the Taliban. Musharraf reasoned that Pakistan could either accept America as an ally or confront it as an invader. The United States was fighting against Islamic extremism, and one of the paths was through Pakistan. The safest bet was to seek an understanding with America (Hadar, 2002).

Pakistan's efforts to curb terrorism are complicated by dissenting views. Some Pakistani leaders support terrorism, some want to establish the caliphate while rejecting terrorism, and some want to fight the jihadists. The Council on Foreign Relations (2005) summarizes the issues well. Musharraf allowed Coalition forces fighting in Afghanistan to enter Pakistani airspace, allowed American personnel to operate within its borders, and had its military forces conduct counterterrorist operations, especially in the northwest, where al Qaeda, Taliban, and other jihadist forces are housed. Musharraf did not have the support of his people for allowing these measures. He walked a fine line every time he took actions against terrorism.

The International Crisis Group (2006e, 2006g, 2007a) points to another internal problem. Pakistan is not so much a modern country as it is a series of tribal confederations. Pakistan was formed in 1947 when British rule in India and in the region ended. Pakistan was divided into East and West; East Pakistan revolted in 1971 and formed the new country of Bangladesh. The Pakistan Army—probably the most respected and, certainly, the most powerful institution in the country—is the power behind the president's office. The jihadist movement is strong in the **North-West Frontier Province (NWFP)** and strongest in the province's tribal area, **Waziristan**. Baluchs are staging a revolt in **Baluchistan**, and two major religious parties resent Pakistan's relationship with the United States. Bombings, kidnappings, and terrorist assaults by multiple groups are commonplace.

There is also tension between Pakistan and India all along their border, especially in the area of **Jammu and Kashmir**, where both countries claim sovereignty (Figure 11.7). Kashmir is a flashpoint because Pakistan and Muslim residents want the area under Islamic control, whereas India sees Kashmir as part of a secular multiethnic state. The ISI has supported some of the Islamic groups operating in Kashmir, and Pakistan accuses India of attacks on Muslims. The Council on Foreign Relations (2006) says that Kashmir has its own homegrown Muslim terrorists, and international jihadists have also come to the area.

The Lashkar-e-Taiba

Pakistan has two groups associated with jihadist networks. Lashkar-e-Taiba (LeT) was created in 1993 under the watchful eye of the ISI to strike at Indian targets in Jammu and Kashmir. Its philosophy and operational base have expanded. Peter Chalk (2010) says that many of the homegrown terrorist threats in Europe, North America, and Australia have LeT connections. The group seems to be emerging as

Baluchistan: The largest of four states in Pakistan dominated by the Baloch tribe. Many Balochs are fighting a guerrilla war against the Pakistan Army in a dispute over profits from natural resources. The central government is creating a deepwater port and international trade center in Gwadar, Pakistan's principal sea-port, and displacing many Baluchs.

Jammu and Kashmir: A mountainous region in northern India claimed by India and Pakistan. It has been the site of heavy fighting during three wars between India and Pakistan in 1947–1948, 1971, and 1999. Kashmir is artificially divided by a line of control (LOC), with Pakistani forces to the north and India's to the south. India and Pakistan made strides toward peace after 2003, but many observers believe that the ISI supports jihadist operations in the area.

Red Mosque: *Lal masjid,* located in Islamabad, with a madrassa and a school for women. It taught militant theology. The government ordered the mosque closed in 2007. This resulted in a shootout and a standoff. Government forces stormed the mosque on July 2007, killing more than 100 students. One of the leaders, Abdul Rashid Ghazi, was killed. His brother Maulana Abdul Aziz, the mosque's other leader, was captured while trying to escape in women's clothing.

a new global jihadist organization working in conjunction with al Qaeda. It is best known for its attacks in India, including a deadly series of attacks in Mumbai in November 2008, and it rejects all forms of Islam except its own interpretation.

According to Chalk, Pakistan officially banned the LeT in 2002, so it operates under a series of different names. The LeT traditionally defined its operations around the Jammu and Kashmir conflict. Its major terrorist operations include:

- 2009 swarm attack on the Sri Lankan cricket team in Lahore
- 2008 multiple attacks in Mumbai
- 2006 attack in Varanasi
- 2005 series of bombs in Delhi
- 2002 massacre in Kaluchak
- 2001 attack on Indian national parliament
- 2000 attack on Red Fort in Delhi
- 1993 Mumbai bombings, resulting in 300 deaths

The LeT has also launched numerous attacks in Jammu and Kashmir. Chalk believes that the LeT began to expand operations in Asia and the West in 2003. The LeT may be operating with al Qaeda, and the two groups share many ideological concepts. In addition, the LeT was involved with the 2005 subway bombings in London. It has been especially effective because of its relationship to the ISI. This relationship protects the LeT from crackdowns when the Pakistani government moves against terrorist groups, and it allows LeT planners to have access to intelligence data. The ISI denies any connection but works informally with the LeT.

Ryan Clarke (2010) believes that the LeT is well entrenched and in a position to launch further attacks. He argues that the LeT was a part of Pakistan's original regional strategy and an arm of the ISI. The growth of militancy in the tribal regions, however, has spawned growth in the LeT. It has moved far beyond the ISI's ability to control the organization. Clarke fears that the LeT will not only continue to execute Mumbai-style attacks; it will continue to evolve as part of the international jihadist network.

The Pakistani Taliban

Although the Taliban is most closely associated with Afghanistan, its core emerged from Pakistan after the Soviet–Afghan War. The Taliban seized control of Kandahar in 1994 and controlled 95 percent of the country by 1997. After the American offensive in Afghanistan in October 2001, many members of the Taliban retreated into the Federal Administered Tribal Area (FATA) of Pakistan. They used this area for two primary purposes: (1) as a base for launching anti-NATO attacks into Afghanistan and (2) to form a new Pakistani movement, the Tehrik-e-Taliban or Pakistani Taliban (Afsar, Samples, and Wood, 2008).

There are several bases of political power in Pakistan, and the Pakistani Taliban has grown in importance in the FATA. Tariq Ali (2008, p. 24) believes that the movement does not represent the greatest power base but that it has emerged because of the war in Afghanistan and the complex political situation in Pakistan. Tribal sympathies remain with the Taliban in Afghanistan, and ISI activities have kept the Taliban strong. This has caused the militant religious movement to expand in Pakistani society, something the ISI did not necessarily want to happen. The militants moved into a moral vacuum in Pakistani society, giving them a greater power base.

The United States urged Musharraf to move against the Pakistani Taliban as its influence grew. When militants began to get a stronger voice in Islamabad, Musharraf was more inclined to accept American pressure. Issues came to a head in July 2007. The **Red Mosque** in Islamabad contained a madrassa full of militant students. They not only fanned the fires of rebellion, they also openly called for Musharraf's assassination. Musharraf was inclined to take this threat seriously because he had survived two previous attempts on his life at the hands of religious militants. As a result, he ordered troops to close the Red Mosque in July. It ended with more 100 militants dead (Shaikh, 2008).

The deputy leader of the Red Mosque, Abdul Rashid Ghazi, was also killed, and a group of students vowed to take revenge in his name. This spawned the Ghazi Brigades and a series of suicide attacks in several areas of Pakistan, beginning in 2009. The Ghazi Brigades are more closely allied with the Pakistani Taliban than any of Pakistan's other terrorist groups. As a result, they do not enjoy the protection of the intelligence community. They have been targeted by the ISI, the army, and Pakistan's law enforcement agencies (Roul, 2010).

Although the ISI was heavily involved in the formation and maintenance of jihadist groups, such as the LeT and the Taliban, its efforts began to misfire after the Red Mosque. The Pakistani Taliban openly challenged the government, and more radical groups emerged. One such group, the Asian Tigers, is actively fighting the Pakistani government and anyone who would ally with it, including fellow jihadists. In April 2010, the Asian Tigers captured and executed an ISI officer, and they publically displayed his body with a note claiming that he worked for the CIA. By summer, the ISI joined the army in South Waziristan to attack the Asian Tigers. The ISI's goal was to rid the Pakistani Taliban of its rogue organizations (Jamal, 2010).

Bruce Riedel (2008) notes that as the Pakistani Taliban expanded, the influence of the United States waned. No democratic government in Pakistan can support American interests because the United States is only anchored in the military elite. The struggle to limit jihadist networks in Pakistan, the critical battleground according to Riedel, has shifted from American military and intelligence efforts to diplomacy. Riedel argues that American aid can be directed toward the Pakistani military but that it should be conditional. The army needs to remove itself from politics as a precondition to continued aid, and its main focus should shift from confronting India to maintaining internal and regional stability. More important than military aid, though, is the need to assist average Pakistanis and to build an infrastructure. Military aid will not solve the problem of terrorism.

Riedel also states that diplomacy should be based on regional politics. The United States should focus on repairing relations between the two regional nuclear powers—Pakistan and India. Another diplomatic effort should be aimed at stabilizing relations with Afghanistan. Part of this focus should be the border region between Afghanistan and Pakistan to increase Pakistani security and decrease fears of Indian influence in Afghanistan . It runs through tribal areas, dividing ethnic groups. A realistic agreement about tribal rights within the border region would help to smooth hostilities. Finally, in addition to finding common ground between India and Pakistan, it is necessary to move the relationship forward enough to solve the problem of Jammu and Kashmir.

Religious militancy is the result of several issues that make the region a ticking time bomb. If the underlying problems are ignored, Riedel concludes, terrorism will continue and sooner or later India and Pakistan will be on the brink of nuclear war. If Pakistan will not agree to address these issues in a constructive manner, groups like the Tehrik-e-Taliban will continue to emerge. Riedel believes that this will consume the region in a wave of terrorism. The potential expansion of terrorism, he concludes, is far more important than al Qaeda.

 Self-Check

> How did Pakistan become a mixture of tribes and ethnic groups?
> What was the original purpose of the LeT, and how has it changed?
> Why did elements of the Pakistani Taliban grow beyond ISI control?

Other Networks in Asia

There are other groups in the Islamic world that give lip service to religion, but they are not as closely associated with the al Qaeda franchise. They are mainly driven by local issues, and some of the groups are little more than criminal gangs.

Bangladesh

The ports of Bangladesh have become centers for international crime, including drug trafficking and illegal weapons trade, and the country has a strong internal jihadist movement. Wilson John (2005) concludes that this makes Bangladesh an ideal place for militant religion to emerge. Radical religious parties have grown over the past decade, fueled by an increase in madrassas funded by Saudi Arabia and other Gulf States.

John believes that the growth of militant fundamentalism threatens Bangladeshi political stability and promotes terrorism. The militant religious climate has spawned the birth of ul-Jihad ul-Islami (Islamic Jihad), a local group that John believes is the Southeast Asian wing of al Qaeda. Of more concern, he says, is the creation of the Harkat ul-Jihad (HJ; Jihad Organization), a clone of ul-Jihad ul-Islami. In addition to terrorist violence, these groups threaten to bring a larger revolution to Bangladesh. He also fears the strong presence of HJ because its infrastructure tends to intersect with local radical groups. If crime and corruption problems overwhelm Bangladesh's weak government, the religious militants have their standard answer. It is the same answer that the Taliban offered Afghanistan (see ICG, 2006b).

Thailand

Thailand is experiencing a rebellion in its southern provinces. Although the country is dominated by Buddhism, Islam is the primary religion of the three southernmost states—states that border Islamic Malaysia. Zachary Abuza (2006) says that Muslims failed in a revolt about 40 years ago because they were ideologically divided. Another revolt today is smaller but more united. Abuza identifies the main groups involved in the fighting.

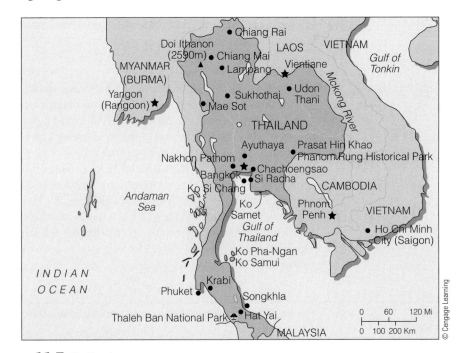

FIGURE **11.7** Thailand

The Pattani United Liberation Organization (PULO) was formed in India in 1968 to create a Muslim state through armed struggle. Its leadership is aging, but it maintains a propaganda campaign through the Internet. It held a reunification meeting in Damascus in 2005, hoping to support the insurgency in the south. PULO controls no insurgents, but some of its leaders have made public threats. It claims to be secular, but Abuza says that it has Salafi undertones. New PULO, which was formed in 1995, is much more effective. Its leaders trained in Syria and Libya and have considerable bomb-making skills.

The Barisan Revolusi Nasional, Coordinate (BRN-C), is leading the insurgency and carries a jihadist agenda. One of three BRN groups involved in the insurgency, BRN-C is active in southern Thailand's mosques. Running a network of madrassas, the BRN-C has become the training ground for militants and fundamentalists. More than 2,500 madrassa graduates went for further training in the Middle East before returning to Thailand. BRN-C membership is estimated at 1,000, and it controls 18 schools and a number of teachers. Thai security forces estimate that 70 percent of southern villages have at least one cell.

Complementing the BRN-C is the Gerakan Mujahedeen Islami Pattani (GMIP), with 40 active cells. Afghan veterans reassembled the group in 1995, but it deteriorated into a criminal gang. Abuza says that it began to embrace the insurgency by 2003 and that GMIP has contacts with Jamaat Islamiyya in Indonesia and the Moro Islamic Liberation Front (MILF) in the Philippines. The GMIP staged raids on police and army outposts in 2002.

Ian Storey (2007) notes that the southern insurgency is becoming an international affair. Militant groups in Malaysia have embraced the Muslim rebellion in Thailand, though the Malaysian government does not. Radicals in the Philippines and Indonesia see the revolt as part of the international jihad.

Indonesia

Jihad also grew in Southeast Asia. Zachary Abuza (2003b, pp. 121–187), in an analysis of terrorism in that region, says that jihadist groups began forming in Indonesia in the early 1990s. The International Crisis Group (2004, 2005a) says that these movements had their origins after World War II when Indonesia gained its independence from the Netherlands. Islamic associations became part of the political process, but they were suppressed by the government and the army in the name of nationalism. Abuza notes that new leadership gained power in 1998, and Islamic groups blossomed, asserting their independence. In 1999, fighting broke out between Christians and Muslims in the eastern islands, and militant Islamic groups grew (Figure 11.8).

FIGURE **11.8** Indonesia

The political situation in Indonesia provided a climate for the growth of jihadist groups. According to Abuza, many of the members of jihadist movements had been trained in the mujahedeen camps of Afghanistan. Lashkar Jihad was formed to fight Christians in the east. A more sinister group, Jamaat Islamiyya, was formed with the purpose of bringing Indonesia under strict Islamic law. Both groups had contacts with al Qaeda (Gunaratna, 2002, pp. 174–203; Abuza, 2003b, pp. 138–142), although leaders of both groups claimed to be independent of Osama bin Laden (J. Stern, 2003b, pp. 75–76).

The Philippines

The Philippines have also experienced jihadist violence. Historically, the relationship between the Christian islands in the north and a few Muslim islands in the south has been marked by strife (Figure 11.9). The U.S. Army fought Muslim rebels after the Spanish-American War (1898), and the Philippine government faced both Muslim and communist rebellions in the 1950s. Religious and ideological rebellions were repeated themes in the Philippines during the twentieth century.

Abuza (2003b, pp. 89–120) outlines the formation of three recent terrorist groups in the Philippines. The Moro National Liberation Front (MNLF) is a continuation of the old religious struggle. Having proposed negotiations with the Philippine government, the MNLF seeks an independent Islamic state. Breaking away from the

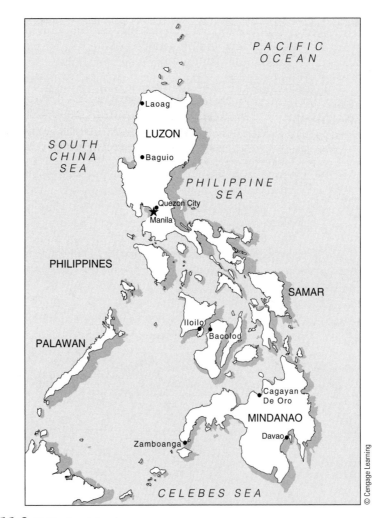

FIGURE **11.9** Philippine Islands

MNLF is the more radical Moro Islamic Liberation Front (MILF). It has ties with jihadist movements and seeks to create an Islamic state under strict interpretations of Islamic law. A third group, Abu Sayyuf, claims to be part of the jihadist movement, but it is most closely associated with criminal activity and seems more interested in money than religion.

Islam in Southeast Asia

Senator Christopher Bond (R-Missouri) and award-winning journalist Lewis Simmons (2009) believe that Southeast Asia is critical to the war on terrorism. They do not see Thailand, Indonesia, and the southern Philippines as a hotbed for jihadist networks. Rather, they believe these nations represent the future direction of Islam. Southeast Asia has a long tradition of toleration and respect for other religions, they argue in *Foreign Affairs*. They suggest that American foreign policy should be aimed at religious and cultural engagement in these areas, and it should reduce the projection of military force. Southeast Asia is not part of a global jihadist network, they argue. It presents an opportunity to engage the majority of the world's peaceful Muslims.

Self-Check

> What is the potential for religious terrorism in Bangladesh?
> Where and why has Thailand experienced religious terrorism?
> How did religious extremism evolve in Indonesia and the Philippines?

CHAPTER TAKE AWAYS

The jihadist terror network known as al Qaeda was spawned in the late stages of the Soviet–Afghan War. Osama bin Laden, the founder of the group, joined Egyptian Ayman al Zawahiri to expand the group in Taliban-controlled Afghanistan in 1996. Al Qaeda quickly evolved into an international umbrella group, conducting large-scale attacks throughout the world. A Western military offensive in the wake of 9/11 changed the nature of al Qaeda's structure, resulting in differing leadership hubs and a more decentralized organization. Although some operations were tightly structured and controlled, the nature of al Qaeda changed. Different regional groups formed in various parts of the world under the al Qaeda franchise. Many of al Qaeda's leaders, including bin Laden, have been killed by American attacks in Pakistan. The group remains active mainly due to its franchised network and an alliance among Pakistani and Afghan allies.

OBJECTIVE SUMMARY

- During the cold war, the United States formed an alliance with any government that opposed communism, including conservative Muslims who detested Soviet atheism. Militant Islam found its greatest expression in Afghanistan, and it took root there after the Soviet–Afghan War.
- Osama bin Laden was born into a wealthy Saudi construction family. He was strongly influenced by the ideas of Sayyid Qutb. Bin Laden left Saudi Arabia to fight in the Soviet–Afghan War and he organized a base to service mujahedeen. Ayman al Zawahiri accepted Qutb's theory of religious revolution and led a terrorist group in Egypt, only to flee after its defeat. He joined bin Laden in 1996 in Afghanistan, leading his Egyptians into an alliance with the Saudis. The new group became al Qaeda.
- Zawahiri and bin Laden expanded al Qaeda and focused on the far enemy. By 1998, the year of a second declaration of war, al Qaeda had become a loose conglomeration of ideological cells with a hierarchy in Afghanistan.

- The group launched large-scale attacks against American targets in Southwest Asia and Africa, culminating in the 9/11 attacks in the United States. Although reorganized after a Western offensive in October 2001, the group and its offshoots have been able to conduct organized attacks as well as smaller-scale operations conducted in its name.

- Al Qaeda's organizational effectiveness is hotly debated. Some analysts believe it is structured and tightly controlled. Others think it gains power through its network. Regardless, the group has franchised hierarchies in Yemen, Iraq, Somalia, and the Maghreb. Its central leadership in Pakistan is backed by local Pakistani groups and a crime network controlled by the Haqqani family. This loosely bound network inspires individuals to take action on their own, but some operations, such as subway attacks in London in 2005 and a 2011 attack on American targets in Kabul, are tightly controlled.

- Franchise operations under the al Qaeda brand name allowed the group to expand operations. AQAP is one of the more important groups. Taking advantage of an unstable political environment in Yemen, AQAP has planned international attacks while maintaining a sophisticated propaganda campaign. Many of its leaders have been killed, but it is seeking to build permanent bases inside of Yemen.

- AQIM formed from disaffected jihadists after a long civil war in Algeria. It began in the Maghreb region of West Africa, looking more like a criminal gang been a terrorist group. Gathering profits through kidnappings, AQIM slowly became financially solvent. Some analysts believe that it is a major source of funding for al Qaeda operations.

- Somalia's weak government and political corruption have created a haven for terrorist groups. Jihadist groups are present in the Horn of Africa. Al Shabaab claims that it represents al Qaeda's ideology, but it was so violent leaders in Pakistan were reluctant to make it part of the franchise. This changed in early 2012 as al Qaeda central and al Shabaab declared they were in an alliance.

- Al Qaeda's theology is based on a militarized version of Islam, an interpretation rejected by the vast majority of Muslims and Islamic scholars. The theology derives from the political-religious writings of Sayyid Qutb.

- Tribal areas in Pakistan harbor militants and international jihadists. There are several groups that operate either in loose association with the al Qaeda franchise or independent of it. Many analysts believe that some groups operate closely with the ISI. This creates problems for all of central Asia. Religious militants spread throughout the region from Bangladesh to Kazakhstan. The ISI has supported jihadist groups in Jammu and Kashmir, further fanning the flames of religious violence.

- Southeast Asia has a variety of jihadist movements, but groups generally operate within nationalistic contexts. Thailand has a rebellion in its southern provinces, and Indonesia's groups can be tied to madrassas. The Philippines has three active groups, but one of them behaves more like a criminal gang.

Critical Engagement: Afghanistan and the Future

Counterinsurgency operations seem to have been successful in Iraq. Whether the invasion was a realistic response to terrorism or not involves another set of issues. The same concept serves as a strategic guide to Afghanistan, but there are several major differences. First, Afghanistan does not have a history of operating as a single political entity. It has local tribal and warlord power bases, and the country has experienced war and internal violence since the 1979 Soviet invasion. Second, the diffuse power bases are exacerbated by public corruption and crime. Third, despite their ferocity, the Taliban have support in some areas. Finally, Afghanistan has been closely linked to the drug trade. Geologists have recently discovered a treasure trove of precious minerals, but it will take years to develop production capacity. It does not seem likely that Afghanistan will develop a stable economy in the near future.

From 1996 to 2001, al Qaeda maintained a strong foothold in Afghanistan. It effectively ran operations in several countries and was responsible for many attacks, including the attacks of September 11. Its leaders were driven into Pakistan in 2001, and the U.S. invasion created an alliance among the Taliban, the Pakistani Taliban, other Pakistani militants, and al Qaeda. Yet al Qaeda is not an automatic ally of these other groups. They are separated by ethnicity and theology. For most of the Afghan war, however, the militants have been portrayed as a united entity.

The United States and members of the International Security Force (ISFA) are attempting to create a stable environment in Afghanistan. This implies that the tribal and ethnic concerns of regional populations within the country must be addressed. Terrorism cannot be controlled until the social environment is stabilized. In addition, al Qaeda has moved to the tribal areas of Pakistan, and new militant groups are emerging from the same region. The Pakistani military have generally supported the ISFA, but the ISI has a long relationship with many of the militant groups. It is doubtful that large-scale Western military forces will enter Pakistan, even though it is the seat of the jihadist movement, and this has caused Americans and other Western allies to question the Afghan mission. They are not convinced that operations in Afghanistan are focused on terrorism.

Consider these issues in terms of future developments:

- Will counterinsurgency in Afghanistan help protect the West from al Qaeda–style terrorism? If yes, can the ISFA leave Afghanistan in the near future? If no, how can the ISFA disengage?
- How does fighting in Afghanistan impact al Qaeda? How does Western impatience with ISFA operations in Afghanistan affect al Qaeda?
- The Taliban has many factions and there are splintered jihadist groups apart from al Qaeda. Each group has its own goals. What would happen if the ISFA began separate negotiations with each group? How would corruption in the Afghan government impact such negotiations?

KEY TERMS

Interservice Intelligence Agency (ISI), p. 11-276

peace dividend, p. 11-277

9/11 Commission, p. 11-277

Abdullah Azzam, p. 11-277

Sayyid Imam al Sharif, p. 11-278

Desert Shield, p. 11-279

Desert Storm, p. 11-279

Taliban, p. 11-280

Mullah Omar, p. 11-280

1993 World Trade Center bombing, p. 11-280

Sheik Omar Abdel Rahman, p. 11-280

near enemy, p. 11-281

far enemy, p. 11-281

Hassan al Turabi, p. 11-282

Mogadishu, p. 11-282

World Islamic Front against Jews and Crusaders, p. 11-283

Haqqani network, p. 11-286

Nasir al Wuhayshi, p. 11-289

USS *Cole*, p. 11-289

Anwar al Awlaki, p. 11-290

Combined Joint Task Force, Horn of Africa (CJTF-HOA), p. 11-291

Islamic Courts Union (ICU), p. 11-292

Transitional Federal Government (TFG), p. 11-293

madrassas, p. 11-295

Mohammed Ali Jinnah, p. 11-296

Ayub Khan, p. 11-297

Asif Ali Zardari, p. 11-297

Pervez Musharraf, p. 11-297

North-West Frontier Province (NWFP), p. 11-297

Waziristan, p. 11-297

Baluchistan, p. 11-297

Jammu and Kashmir, p. 11-297

Red Mosque, p. 11-299

Domestic Terrorism and Homeland Security

CHAPTER 12

Domestic Terrorism

Mario Tama/Getty Images

LEARNING OBJECTIVES

After reading this chapter you should be able to:

> List the factors that improve and inhibit our understanding of domestic terrorism.

> Use a typology of criminal extremism to classify domestic terrorism.

> Distinguish anti-government criminal extremism from right-wing activities.

> Explain the fluctuations in left-wing criminal extremism.

> Summarize extremist crimes motivated by racism.

> Describe threats from homegrown radicalization.

> Define single-issue terrorism.

> Summarize criminal activities supporting ecological extremism.

> Describe the criminal activities involving Puerto Rican nationalism.

> Summarize criminal activities conducted against abortion providers.

Robert Paudert, the retired chief of the West Memphis Police Department, tells the story with deep emotion. On May 20, 2010, two of Chief Paudert's officers made a routine vehicle stop of a car traveling on the local interstate highway. They were confronted by a driver who produced various forms of official-looking identification and vehicle registration papers. The officers were confused. They had never seen these types of documents before.

As one officer examined the papers with the driver, the passenger exited the vehicle with an assault rifle. Both officers were killed in the ensuing shoot-out. The suspects were killed while attempting to escape the next day. They were a father and son team who claimed that they were completely independent of the United States. They were not subject to its taxes, regulations, or laws. They were sovereign citizens.

Chief Paudert tours the country teaching police officers about the sovereign citizen movement. He asks officers to be aware of the warning signs and tells them to take protective actions. Police officers who lose a comrade frequently mourn for life. Chief Paudert certainly does. One of the officers killed that day was his son. Audiences pay particular attention when Chief Paudert tells them about domestic terrorism.

Understanding Domestic Terrorism

The United States has a long history of political violence, but until recently few scholars characterized it as "terrorism." Three exceptions were H. H. A. Cooper (1976), J. Bowyer Bell (Bell and Gurr, 1979), and Ted Robert Gurr (1988a), all three of whom initiated work in this area before it was popular to speak of domestic terrorism. Cooper and his coauthors produced a presidential report on the political context of domestic terrorism. Bell and Gurr looked at the long history of domestic political violence in the United States, and Gurr later developed a typology of domestic terrorism. It included *vigilante terrorism* from the extremist right, *insurgent terrorism* of various revolutionaries, and *transnational terrorism* from foreigners fighting on American soil.

The Problem of Understanding Terrorism in Law Enforcement

Some American police agencies have gone to great lengths to prepare for terrorism; others have not. American law enforcement is a localized affair, with chiefs of police and sheriffs reporting to local boards. At the same time various state and federal agencies also exercise law enforcement power. This leads to confusion in preparing for terrorism.

For example, one senior Utah law enforcement officer, charged with coordinating security in preparation for the 2002 Winter Olympics in Salt Lake City, related the following story to this author. After the initial security meeting, the director of France's security detail approached him to ask which agency was in charge. When the officer explained that the federal, state, local, and tribal law enforcement systems in the United States were in charge, the French officer replied that he understood those divisions, but he wanted to know which agency was in charge. The officer responded that each agency had its own leaders, and the leaders coordinated the response. The Frenchman shook his head, saying that he would never understand American policing. Law enforcement is a local affair in the United States, complicated by layers of competing state and federal bureaucracies. Agencies approach terrorism with their own interpretations.

Improved Understanding

One of the reasons law enforcement has difficulty understanding terrorism is that when U.S. law enforcement officers deal with terrorism, they call it something else. Even the FBI labels the majority of domestic terrorist activities using common crime designations in the Uniform Crime Report, an annual standard measure of criminal activity in the United States.

Another reason for the difficulty is that recent terrorism developed slowly in America. Terrorism grew among radical groups beginning about 1965, and although there were some sensational activities, terrorists did not routinely target the United States until 1982. According to Daniel Levitas (2002, pp. 341–342), domestic terrorism includes violent right-wing extremists, the Ku Klux Klan, paramilitary organizations (or militias), abortion clinic bombers, violent anti-immigrant groups, and others who use violence in the name of race or ethnicity. Many police officers would agree with this analysis, but they call it hate crime. The definition of domestic terrorism has a confusing history.

Christopher Hewitt's (2002) analysis of domestic terrorism helps to illustrate why American law enforcement has grown increasingly aware of the problem. Terrorism has occurred in recent American history, but it has been approached as typical criminal behavior. Community policing helps solve the problem, Hewitt says, because it is the most effective method of preventing terrorism. In other words, the nature of policing provides a de facto definition.

Law enforcement agencies have made great strides in understanding domestic terrorism over the past decade. This is partially due to the nature of politically motivated crime and violence. As Donald Black (2004) states, the three main ingredients of modern terrorism are: an angry group of people, or sometimes even a single enraged individual, with the ability to travel and with access to technology that can cause massive casualties. All three ingredients are available to people who wish to take criminal action based on various political positions. Stated simply, state, local, and tribal law enforcement agencies have had quite a bit of experience with such criminal activity and they are getting better at handling it.

In the past 20 years, law enforcement agencies have participated in antiterrorist training, especially after a massive bombing in Oklahoma City in 1995. Many law enforcement executives came to see that terrorism was no longer an exotic problem that only happened overseas, but that it was a real criminal problem in the United States. Large urban agencies established units to deal with terrorism, and they frequently operated in conjunction with the federal government. The reaction to Oklahoma City expanded such units. Chicago, New York, Washington, D.C., Miami, and Los Angeles had experienced various forms of terrorism for years. Oklahoma City was different—if it could happen there, it could happen anywhere. American law enforcement began to respond. Of course, the process was accelerated in the wake of 9/11.

Another factor that has improved the understanding of domestic terrorism is the growth of law enforcement's improved criminal intelligence collecting techniques and the way criminal intelligence is examined. Supporting this is new academic research in the field of domestic terrorism and several databases that summarize domestic terrorist activity. This will be more fully discussed in Chapter 14. At this stage, it is important to know that improving criminal intelligence has enhanced law enforcement capabilities.

Inhibiting the Understanding of Domestic Terrorism

Unfortunately, there are still factors that serve to inhibit our understanding of domestic terrorism. One of the main factors is the continually shifting political environment. Domestic terrorism was addressed during the Clinton administration (1994–2000) by enacting federal legislation to combat it and by introducing federally supported training for state, local, and tribal law enforcement. Although the problem was not immediately emphasized in the Bush administration (2000–2008), it became a top priority after the focus shifted to international terrorism in the wake of 9/11. In fact, antiterrorist activities at home became part of the Global War on Terrorism. This changed again in 2008 after the election of President Barack Obama. Phrases like the "War on Terrorism" were abandoned, and the federal government engaged in multilevel reviews of antiterrorist activities to ensure that individual interest groups would not be offended by government actions (Department of Justice, 2012).

The definition of domestic terrorism is also confused by political interest groups that lobby for various positions. Some groups are quick to label extremist right-wing political activism as terrorism. Other groups extend the definition to all abortion providers. Examinations of Islam have produced heated emotional debates in which extreme positions dominate public discourse. Quite a bit of information is distorted in this atmosphere, further confusing rational inquiries and understandings of domestic terrorism.

Finally, the definition is also confused by the government. Many times large federal organizations such as the Department of Justice and the Department of Homeland Security attempt to micromanage the dissemination of information about terrorism. At other times, agencies like the FBI simply refuse to share information. This is more fully discussed in the next chapter, but these actions inhibit our ability to understand domestic terrorism.

Classifying Terrorism in Criminal Justice

There is a great deal of tension between theoretical criminologists and practical analysts who look for an immediate solution to a specific problem. Classical, or theoretical, criminologists look for an explanation of social phenomena, and they search for theories to explain crime or behavior in general. This crucial work produces theories that guide policies. From a tactical, or practical, perspective, however, an immediate response to crime does not depend on general explanations. It is more important to understand the nature of the immediate problem and the possible practical solutions. The same is true for terrorism: A label appropriate for theoretical criminology will not always lead to a response that solves an immediate problem. U.S. police officers routinely handle terrorism even though they call it by a variety of names. It would be helpful if law enforcement officers had a practical framework that explained their counterterrorist role.

Tactically, police and security forces should keep two issues in mind: First, a beat police officer is usually the first responder to domestic terrorism. Second, the investigation techniques used in large, sensational terrorist incidents are the same techniques a local agency would use to investigate a stink bomb placed in the locker room of a high school football team. From a practical perspective, counterterrorism depends on the fundamentals. Good investigative skills, such as the collection and preservation of evidence and good interviewing techniques, are important; it is also important for law enforcement officers to understand the context of the crimes that they are investigating. Nevertheless, terrorism investigations differ from routine crime scenes because terrorists behave differently. This calls for increased intelligence, long-term surveillance, and informant development. Therefore, it is important for officers to recognize terrorism when they encounter it.

The FBI categorizes activities on the basis of origin. It is based on the gathering and sharing of information; but, as discussed earlier in the chapter, information sharing still remains difficult in police work. According to publicly released information (FBI, 2004), the classification system has two basic categories: domestic terrorism (DT) and international terrorism (IT). DT involves violent political extremism, single-issue terrorism, and lone-wolf activities. IT is defined as threats that originate outside the United States. In 2002, the FBI's JTTF arrested six suspects near Buffalo, New York, for supporting jihadists. The JTTF called this DT because the activities originated in the United States. The attacks of September 11 are called IT because they originated outside U.S. borders (see FBI, 2002).

Brent Smith (1994; Smith and Roberts, 2005) places terrorist groups into three broad categories: (1) right-wing extremists, (2) left-wing and single-issue terrorists, and (3) international terrorists. This approach can be used to develop a general typology to approach domestic terrorism, keeping in mind the FBI's separation between IT and DT. Some overlap cannot be avoided, but Smith's typology can be expanded to focus on the types of criminal activity that fall under the rubric of domestic terrorism.

Rather than using the pejorative and somewhat ambiguous term "domestic terrorism," it may be more fruitful to approach the topic in terms of the activities of law enforcement. Troopers, officers, deputies, and agents focus on the crimes associated with extremism. It is not a crime to hold extremist views, but taking criminal action in the name of those views is illegal. The police already handle violent and nonviolent criminal activity by politically motivated extremists. The types of activities include: anti-government crimes from both the left and right, crimes associated with racism, homegrown threats, and single issues.

Self-Check

> Why is domestic terrorism difficult to define?

> How has law enforcement's approach to the problem enhanced the understanding of domestic terrorism?

> How does a typology of criminal extremism help simplify an approach to domestic terrorism?

A Typology of Criminal Extremism
- Anti-Government Crimes (both right and left)
- Race- and Ethnicity-Motivated Crimes
- Homegrown Radicalization
- Single-Issue Crimes

© Cengage Learning 2014

FIGURE **12.1**   Criminal Extremism

Anti-Government Criminal Extremism

Throughout much of American history, anti-government activity associated with the extreme right has been based in ethnic and racial violence, but it has expanded to include extreme religious views and declarations of autonomy such as the sovereign citizen movement. It can also be associated with revolution and criminal activity on the left. At times, it is even difficult to distinguish between left-wing and right-wing crimes because their rhetoric is so similar.

On the morning of April 19, 1995, special news reports on television and radio indicated that some type of explosion had occurred in Oklahoma City in or near the federal building. These reports were quickly amended, and reports of the size and extent of damage increased with each moment. By noon, it was apparent that the United States had suffered a devastating terrorist attack. As scenes of the injured and dead, including children, and smoldering wreckage dominated the nation's television screens, attention turned toward the Middle East. Conventional wisdom placed blame for the incident on some militant Islamic sect. Many Arab Americans were harassed, and some were openly attacked. The country was shocked when a young white man with a crew cut was arrested for the bombing. It was hard to believe that the United States had produced terrorists from its own heartland.

The Development of Right-Wing Violence

Although many people were surprised, even a cursory look at the history of right-wing extremism in the United States reveals that extremist ideologies and violent political behavior are nothing new (J. White, 2001). The first incident of antifederal behavior came shortly after the American Revolutionary War (1775–1783) in 1791: The federal government levied an excise tax on the production of whiskey, and farmers in western Pennsylvania, a major whiskey-producing area, were incensed. The unpopular tax provoked riots and created general disorder. In October 1794, President George Washington mobilized the National Guard of several states and sent the troops to Pennsylvania. The **Whiskey Rebellion** quickly ended, but not the resentment against the federal government (Phillips, 1999, pp. 332–334).

Antifederal attitudes were common in some circles in the early 1800s. The so-called **Know-Nothings** operated in the eastern United States before the Civil War (1861–1865). Organizing under such names as the Order of the Sons of America and the Sons of the Star Spangled Banner, these groups were anti-Catholic, anti-Irish, and anti-immigration. They felt that Catholic immigrants were destroying American democracy. When confronted by authority, party members would claim to "know nothing," hence their name (McPherson, 1988, pp. 135–143).

Although the Civil War had many causes—slavery, farming versus industry, and sectionalism—one of the greatest causes was disagreement over the power of the federal government. Southerners questioned the legitimacy of the federal government, and they believed that Congress was taking powers reserved for the states. Most Southerners were not fighting to preserve slavery; they were fighting to keep

Whiskey Rebellion: The uprising that took place in 1791 when a group of Pennsylvania farmers refused to pay a federal tax on corn used to make alcohol. The rebellion ended when President George Washington sent troops to stop the rebellion.

Know-Nothings: Different groups of American nationalists in the early nineteenth century who championed native-born whites over immigrants.

the power of local governments. When the Confederacy was defeated in 1865, the issue did not die (McPherson, 1988, pp. 858–859; Foote, 1986a, pp. 35–40; 1986b, p. 1042).

Agrarian failures and depressions gave life to radical economic theories during the 1870s and 1880s. These rural movements were complemented by labor violence and the introduction of anarchism from the left. Businesses and local and state governments frequently repressed both left-wing and right-wing versions of extremism. After the turn of the century, though, mainstream Americans came to believe that the left posed a greater threat to democracy. This attitude increased after 1919, when a wave of left-wing terrorism swept the country. As a result, right-wing extremist organizations grew. They popularized extremist views and claimed judges, elected officials, and police officers in their ranks. Right-wing extremists also turned to an organization that had been created in the wake of the Civil War, the Ku Klux Klan.

The KKK had been the brainchild of Confederate cavalry genius General **Nathan Bedford Forrest** (Berlet and Lyons, 2000, pp. 58–62). Forrest had intended to create an antiunionist organization that would preserve Southern culture and traditions. When the newly formed KKK began terrorizing freed slaves, Forrest became disillusioned with the movement and he tried to disband the organization. It was too late, however, and the KKK began a campaign of hate. By the early twentieth century, the organization had nearly died, but it was revived in the extremist atmosphere after World War I (1914–1918).

The KKK has operated in three distinct phases over its history (Berlet and Lyons, 2000, pp. 58, 85–103, 265–286). Shortly after the Civil War, hooded **Knight Riders**, as they were called, terrorized African Americans to frighten them into political and social submission. This aspect of the Klan faded by the end of the century. The second phase of the Klan came in the 1920s as it sought political legitimacy. During this period, the KKK became popular, political, and respectable. It collapsed, however, in the wake of a criminal scandal. The modern KKK grew after World War II (1939–1945), becoming, up to the present day, fragmented, decentralized, and dominated by hate-filled rhetoric.

Sovereign Citizens

The sovereign citizen movement is not new, and it is not limited to any racial group or political orientation. The movement is traditionally linked to white supremacists. It was also related to the militia movement of the 1980s, though issues have changed since then. African American groups like the **Moorish Nation** can be classified as part of the sovereign citizen movement, as can some Hispanic groups. One American Indian group has claimed autonomy. An economic downturn in 2008 caused a number of people to begin declaring themselves sovereign citizens. Crimes like mortgage fraud and other swindles began to grow. Violent encounters with law enforcement officers also increased (BJA, 2010).

Although there is no centralized structure or organization, sovereign citizens tend to hold some common beliefs. First, they believe that they can declare themselves free of American citizenship as well as laws and taxes. This can develop in a variety of manners. For example, some people believe that using an odd signature declares that they are free citizens. Some other people write letters to government officials declaring that they are no longer citizens of the United States. One popular belief is that the United States did not have citizens after the American Revolution, but constitutional amendments added after the Civil War tricked free citizens into accepting American citizenship. If you are aware of that fact, you can simply opt out of the government. Still another group believes there is a missing 14th Amendment to the Constitution, an amendment allowing them to declare themselves free of citizenship.

The Anti-Defamation League (2010) says that sovereign citizens also tend to believe that there are two governments. One is legitimate and devoid of governmental

Nathan Bedford Forrest: (1821–1877) A famed and gifted Confederate cavalry commander who founded the Ku Klux Klan in Pulaski, Tennessee. Forrest tried to disband the KKK when he saw the violent path that it was taking.

Knight Riders: The first terrorists of the Ku Klux Klan. Donning hoods and riding at night, they sought to keep newly freed slaves from participating in government and society.

Moorish Nation: An African American group that does not recognize the validity of the United States government.

regulation except for English common law. The illegitimate government includes all federal and state governments. Like most right-wing groups, they believe taxes, traffic fines, and other government actions result from a conspiracy of evil.

Paper terrorism: Using false documents to clog legal, financial, or bureaucratic processes.

Sovereign citizens have had several violent confrontations with police officers and other government officials, but their most common activity is **paper terrorism**. They file false liens, tying up the property of people who have irritated them. They also write bogus checks or sight drafts against nonexistent accounts. Some sovereigns, like the two murderers of the West Memphis police officers, defraud people by conducting seminars to tell participants how they can fill out special forms and renounce their American citizenship. They charge hefty fees to attend their seminars. Others carry so-called constitutional driver's licenses and vehicle registrations (ADL, 2010; BJA, 2010).

This is not to suggest that they are a docile group. According to the Southern Poverty Law Center (2011), more than 30 police officers have been killed in confrontations with sovereign citizens. In addition, they have staged well-publicized armed standoffs against law enforcement officers. They have also made violent threats against government officials.

Sovereign citizens represent one other aspect of anti-government criminal extremism. They tend to merge into other forms of extremism. For example, some sovereigns belong to racist organizations. Others follow a particular religion. Some may be survivalists, while others live in urban environments. There are sovereign citizen compounds where armed militias patrol in fear of government invasion, and there are seemingly normal citizens who hold jobs and refuse to pay their taxes. There is no single sovereign citizen ideology.

Contemporary Right-Wing Behavior, Beliefs, and Tactics

Modern right-wing extremism came to fruition around 1984 and has remained active since that time. According to this author's research (J. White, 1997, 2000, 2002), several issues hold the movement together. First, the right wing tends to follow one of the forms of extremist religion. The name of God is universally invoked, even by leaders who disavow theism (a belief in God). Second, the movement is dominated by a belief in international conspiracy and other conspiracy theories. Followers feel that sinister forces are conspiring to take away their economic status and swindle them out of the American dream. The primary conspiratorial force was communism, but after the fall of the Soviet Union, it became the United Nations. The extremist right believes that a conspiracy of Jewish bankers works with the United Nations to create a New World Order in which Jews control the international monetary system. Finally, right-wing extremists continue to embrace patriotism and guns. They want to arm themselves for a holy war (see Barkun, 1997; Berlet and Lyons, 2000, pp. 345–352).

In his popular historical work *Dreadnought: Britain, Germany and the Coming of the Great War*, Robert K. Massie (1991) points to the hysteria in Great Britain and Germany during the naval race before World War I. Both the British and the Germans demonized one another, and their national rivalries often gave way to irrational fears. In one of the more notable British reactions, the fear of German naval power gave rise to a particular genre of popular literature. These stories had a similar theme. Secret German agents would land in the United Kingdom and destroy the British Empire through some type of subversive plot. Whether they were poisoning the water supply, destroying the schools, or infiltrating the economic system, the fictional Germans never attacked directly. They were mysterious, secretive, and everywhere.

The actions of right-wing extremists fit Massie's description of the hysterical fears in Britain. Extremists believe that alien forces are conspiring to destroy the United States. Bill Stanton (1991, pp. 78–82) says that in 1978 the KKK led the way into the modern era when it emerged in Georgia and North Carolina as a paramilitary organization. Within a decade, many members of the extremist right had followed suit.

They were not only willing to accept conspiracy theories but also ready to fight the hordes that they believed were bent on destroying the American way of life.

Brent Smith (1994) paints a realistic picture of right-wing extremism, arguing that terrorism from the right wing is fairly limited. Groups are rural and tend to emerge from farm-based compounds. For example, Posse Comitatus formed as a tax-protest group and engaged in violent resistance to local law enforcement. The most well-known case of Posse Comitatus resistance involved Gordon Kahl, who killed three law enforcement officers in North Dakota and Arkansas before being killed in a shoot-out. Another group, The Order, was a militant offshoot of the **white supremacy movement**. By 1987, however, The Order was defunct, and the right wing was fading.

Even while this was happening, however, most right-wing criminal activities were not labeled as terrorism. But, though the notorious cases of violent right-wing extremism faded from public awareness in 1987, the ideology that fueled them did not. So-called hate crimes increased, creating concern among criminal justice researchers (Hamm, 1994). Membership in extremist groups grew after their apparent collapse in 1987, and by 1994, the extremists were back in business. The late Richard Butler, former leader of the Aryan Nations, interacted with the leaders of several white supremacy movements and held an Aryan Congress each year to draw the white supremacists together.

Three issues rejuvenated the extremist right (K. Stern, 1996). First, the **Brady Bill** (named for President Reagan's press secretary, who was disabled by a gunshot wound to his brain in an assassination attempt on Reagan) caused many conservatives to fear federal gun-control legislation. The extremist right played on these fears, toning down issues like white supremacy and Christian Identity and claiming that the intrusive federal government was out to eliminate gun ownership. Extremists felt that they had an issue that appealed to mainstream conservatives. By stressing the fear of gun control, right-wing extremists hoped to appear to be in the mainstream.

The second issue dealt with a botched U.S. Marshal's office attempt to arrest Randy Weaver on a bench warrant at Ruby Ridge in the mountains of Idaho. A white supremacist and adherent of Christian Identity, Weaver was charged with selling illegal firearms to undercover agents from the Bureau of Alcohol, Tobacco, and Firearms (ATF). Weaver was arrested and released on bail. When he refused to appear for his assigned court date, U.S. marshals tried to bring him in. Tragically, U.S. Marshal William Degan and Weaver's young son, Sammy, were killed in the ensuing shoot-out. The FBI responded by laying siege to Weaver's mountain cabin. In the following days, an FBI sniper shot and killed Weaver's pregnant wife before Weaver surrendered (Walter, 1995).

The **Ruby Ridge** incident had a strong symbolic impact on the extremist right. According to K. Stern (1996), Bo Gritz, a leading extremist figure, drew national attention to the siege when he came to negotiate surrender. Gritz is an articulate, charismatic individual who retired as a colonel from the U.S. Army Special Forces, and his voice and opinions carry far beyond the extremist right. He left Ruby Ridge saluting Skinhead demonstrators and calling for the formation of SPIKE groups (special resistance forces) to prevent further standoffs (Walter, 1995).

Closely related to Ruby Ridge, in the minds of the extremist right, was a third event: the federal siege of the **Branch Davidian** compound near Waco, Texas. In 1993, ATF agents attempted to serve a search warrant on the compound, but they were met with a hail of gunfire. Four agents were killed, and several were wounded. After a three-month siege, FBI agents moved in with tear gas. Unknown to the agents, the compound was laced with gasoline. When the FBI moved in, the Branch Davidians burned their fortress, killing 82 people, including several young children, inside the compound.

Stern says that the **Waco siege** also became a symbol for the extremist right even though it had very little to do with the right-wing movement. An ATF report (1995)

White Supremacy: A political philosophy claiming that white people are superior to all other ethnic groups.

Brady Bill: A law that limits gun ownership, named for President Ronald Reagan's press secretary after he was disabled by a gunshot in a 1981 assassination attempt on Reagan.

Ruby Ridge: The location of a 1992 standoff between survivalists and U.S. federal law enforcement officers in Idaho during which a U.S. marshal and survivalist Randy Weaver's wife and son were killed.

Branch Davidians: Followers of Vernon Wayne Howell, also known as David Koresh. They lived in a compound outside Waco, Texas.

Waco Siege: The 1993 standoff between members of the Branch Davidian cult and federal law enforcement officers. The standoff ended when FBI agents tried to bring the siege to an end, but Branch Davidian leaders set fire to their compound killing eighty-two of the followers.

Vernon Wayne Howell:
(or David Koresh, 1959–
1993) The charismatic
leader of the Branch
Davidian cult.

Survivalist: A person
who adopts a form of
right-wing extremism
advocating militant re-
jection of society. The
members advocate a
withdrawl from society in
preparation for a coming
internal war. Secluded in
armed compounds, they
hope to survive the coming
collapse of society.

said that, in reality, the Waco siege involved a group of people led by a dismissed Seventh Day Adventist, **Vernon Wayne Howell**, who had changed his name to David Koresh. Taking advantage of the weak and distraught, Koresh established the Branch Davidian compound outside Waco. According to the ATF, Koresh gathered illegal weapons and engaged in a variety of unlawful activities. He ruled his flock in accordance with his messianic illusions, claiming that the end was near and that he would save the world. In the end, he simply murdered his followers rather than admit his messianic failings; however, he set the stage to be embraced by the extremist right. Though Koresh had nothing to do with right-wing extremists *per se*, he had the right formula: guns, a **survivalist** compound, and a belief in a warrior God.

If Stern is correct, the Brady Bill, Ruby Ridge, and Waco gave new life to the fading right-wing movement, and a shift in the religious orientation of the extremist right helped to rejuvenate their ranks. Although many American Protestants would agree that the United States was the new chosen land—perhaps even a new Israel— few could stomach the blasphemy and hatred of Christian Identity. In the 1990s, however, the religious message changed. Patriotism and anti-Semitism proved to be as strong as the Christian Identity message.

Today, the situation has shifted again. After being revitalized in the 1990s, the movement mutated after September 11, 2001. Violent members of the right-wing movement melted away from large organizations and began to congregate in small groups. Following the pattern of international terrorist groups, they organized chains or hubs, small groups operating autonomously. The days of large meetings seemed to fade as well. One Montana criminal intelligence commander told this author he believed that the current leaders of the movement do not know how to arrange large rallies. As a result, he said, the movement in the Pacific Northwest, for instance, looks more like a conglomeration of terrorist cells. By 2010 new groups were emerging under a variety of anti-government banners.

More, smaller groups led to more individual violence (see *Another Perspective: Criminal Behavior among Right-Wing Extremists*). Additionally, these groups began to form links with single-issue groups, including anarchists and left-wingers. The trend is currently unclear. The groups may be fading as the left wing did in the 1980s, or they may be repositioning themselves. Militias tended to turn to patriotism and more normative behavior after September 11. The path of the violent offshoot groups remains undetermined.

The wild card is the vacuum in leadership. Richard Butler, the leader of the defunct Aryan Nations, died in September 2004. No one had been able to unite the

ANOTHER PERSPECTIVE

Criminal Behavior among Right-Wing Extremists

Right-wing extremists fall into three categories:

Nonviolent offenders. Tend to be high school dropouts, engage in rhetoric or publication, disrupt public meetings, use "constitutional" driver's licenses and permits, use "common law" court documents that they print on their own. Such documents are not valid. Common criminal behavior: fraud schemes.

Violent defenders. Stockpile survivalist materials and weapons, wait for the U.S. government to attack. Violent defenders call the government the Zionist Occupation Government (ZOG) or the Jewish Occupation Government (JOG) because they believe that it is controlled by an international conspiracy of Jewish financial interests. Common criminal behavior: violent standoffs.

Violent attackers. Use standard terrorist tactics such as weapons violations, assaults, bombings, arsons, ambushes, and murders. Common criminal behavior: shooting sprees.

Source: Pitcavage, 1999a, 1999b, 1999c, 2000.

Anglo-Israelism: The belief that the lost tribes of Israel settled in western Europe. God's ancient promises to the Hebrews became promises to the United Kingdom, according to this belief. Anglo-Israelism predated Christian Identity and is the basis for most Christian Identity beliefs.

William Potter Gale: (1917–1988) An American military leader who coordinated guerrilla activities in the Philippines during World War II. Gale became a radio preacher and leader of the Christian Identity movement after returning home.

Richard Butler: (1917–2004) A self-made millionaire and white supremacist. Butler founded the Aryan Nations in Hayden Lake, Idaho.

Aryan Nations: An American antigovernment, antiSemitic, white supremacist group founded by Richard Butler. Until it was closed by a suit from the Southern Poverty Law Center, the group sponsored a Christian Identity Church called the Church of Jesus Christ, Christian.

Christian Identity: An American extremist religion proclaiming white supremacy. Adherents believe that white Protestants of western European origin are the true descendants of the ancient Israelites. Believers contend that Jews were spawned by Satan and that nonwhites evolved from animals. According to this belief, white men and women are the only people created in the image of God.

Nordic Christianity: A religion that incorporates the ancient Norse gods in a hierarchy under the Christian triune deity. It is similar to Odinism, but it does not completely abandon Christianity.

extremist right the way Butler did. Leaders are jockeying for power, but no single leader with Butler's charisma and organizational skills has moved to the forefront. A number of potential leaders are due for release from prison, so a leader may emerge. In the meantime, small groups dominated by Christian Identity theology and Christian patriotism engage in localized violence.

Conspiracies and a Call to Arms

The development of the modern Klan parallels the growth of right-wing extremism from the 1930s to the present. Michael Barkun (1997) describes the growth of extremism from a religious point of view. Barkun says that a new religion, Christian Identity, grew from the extremist perspective. Starting with a concept called **Anglo-Israelism**, or British Israelism, American right-wing extremists saw white Americans as the representatives of the lost tribes of Israel. Wesley Swift preached this message in a radio ministry from California beginning in the late 1940s. Two of his disciples were **William Potter Gale** and **Richard Butler**. Gale went on to form several right-wing associations, including Posse Comitatus. Butler retired from an engineering career, moved to Idaho, and formed the **Aryan Nations**. Gale and Butler preached Swift's message of Christian Identity.

Christian Identity is a strange blend of Jewish and Christian biblical passages and is based on the premise that God was the white male Deity (J. White, 1997, 2001). It is a religion of racial supremacy, and its theology is based on a story of conflict and hate. According to this theology, Jews have gained control of the United States by conspiring to create the Federal Reserve System. The struggle between whites and Jews will continue until whites ultimately achieve victory with God's help. At that point, the purpose of creation will be fulfilled. Such theological perversions are necessary when converting a religion of love into a doctrine of hate.

Barkun points out that Christian Identity helped to provide the basis for violence among the extremists. Before the Christian Identity movement, American extremism was characterized by ethnocentrism and localized violence. Christian Identity gave a new twist to the extremist movement: It was used to demonize Jews. Christian Identity provided a theological base for stating that white people originated with God and Jews came from the devil. Such eschatological presumptions are deadly (see Stanton, 1991, p. 36).

Christianity has undergone some strange transformations within the violent circles of right-wing extremism, sometimes known as the hate movement (J. White, 1997, 2001). For example, some extremists have adopted Norse mythology. Following Erich Ludendorff, a member of the German High Command in World War I, extremists began preaching **Nordic Christianity** in northern Germany in the early 1920s. This belief system migrated to the United States and took root in Michigan, Wisconsin, Montana, and Idaho in the 1990s. Using ancient Norse rites, they claimed to worship the Triune Christian Deity, but they added Odin (Wotan) and Thor. Odin, the supreme Norse god, called Nordic warriors to racial purification from Valhalla, the Viking heaven. Thor, the god of thunder, sounded the call with a hammer that shook the heavens.

In another religious derivation, **Creativity** rejects Judaism and Christianity altogether (see *Creativity Movement*, n.d.). Formerly called the World Church of the Creator, the movement changed its name to the Creativity Movement after being challenged by a Christian church with a similar name. Founded by **Ben Klassen** in 1973, Creatorists claim that the Creator left humanity on its own, and each race must fend for itself. Embracing the urban **skinheads**, Creatorists call for a racial holy war, or RAHOWA. They produce racially oriented comic books designed to appeal to alienated white youth. They also publish *The White Man's Bible*, which emphasizes racial purity. Creatorists argue that an intervening, loving God is nothing more than an idle lie. White people have been left on their own by a deistic Creator, and they are

Creativity: The deistic religion of the Creativity movement. It claims that white people must struggle to defeat Jews and non-white races.

Ben Klassen: (1918–1993) The founder of the Creativity Movement.

Skinheads: Young people or groups who embrace racial hatred and white supremacy.

New World Order: A phrase used by President George H. W. Bush to describe the world after the fall of the Soviet Union. Conspiracy theorists use the phrase to describe what they believe to be Jewish attempts to gain control of the international monetary system and, subsequently, to take over the U.S. government.

free-wheeling fundamentalists: White supremacists or Christian patriots who either selectively use Bible passages or create their own religion to further the patriot agenda.

Militia Movement: A political movement started in the early 1980s, possibly spawned from survivalism. Militias maintain that the Second Amendment gives them the right to arm themselves and form paramilitary organiztions apart from governmental control and military authority.

Protocols of Zion: A forged document written in czarist Russia allegedly explaining a Jewish plot to control the world. It was popularized in the United States by Henry Ford. It is frequently cited by the patriot and white supremacy movements. Jihadists also use it as evidence against Jews.

expected to fight for their survival. Essentially, Creatorism is a deistic religion with more violent tendencies than Christian Identity.

If extremists were trying to achieve mainstream political acceptance through issues like gun control, taxation, and the **New World Order**, however, they could not merely appeal to Odin. The majority of right-wing extremists retreated to more conservative churches and relied on individual interpretations of scripture to justify anti-government actions. This group can loosely be described as **free-wheeling fundamentalists**.

Unlike the hate religions, the free-wheeling fundamentalists do not believe that the American government is part of a conspiracy involving the ultimate forces of evil. They do believe, however, that the federal government and local governments are their enemies and that God will assist them in their confrontation with any form of governmental power. Using antifederalist rhetoric, they boost their call to revolution with appeals to the Christian theology of lay preachers. They call on a personal God—a self-defined concept of divinity usually not recognizable in the Hebrew, Muslim, or Christian scriptures. By 1995, this movement became popular in the rural West and Midwest, and it has set the stage for right-wing extremism in this century (see O'Conner, 2004).

Free-wheeling fundamentalism has affected the Christian patriot movement. Although many Christian patriots believe that the United States is God's promised land, many of them are not willing to demonize other races or religions. Many Christian patriots believe that the government no longer serves average Americans; they believe that bankers and businesspersons work together against farmers and other rural Americans. They believe in God, America, and freedom, but they do not accept the hate-filled tenets of Identity theology and they reject Nordic Christianity as a collection of heretical myths. They feel that the government will not defend the country against foreign enemies and that it favors the United Nations over the United States. As survivalist ideology grew in the 1980s, the free-wheeling fundamentalists turned to a new idea—the **militia movement**.

Paramilitary organizations, unauthorized armed civilian militias that organize themselves in a military manner, thrive on conspiracy theories. They believe that the U.S. government is leading the country into a single world government controlled by the United Nations and that the New World Order is a continuation of a conspiracy outlined in the **Protocols of Zion**, a document that appeared in this country after World War I, claiming that Jews are out to control the world (Stern, 1996). The militias play on conspiracy fears, fear of government, racism, antiabortion rhetoric, and anti-Semitism. In Stern's analysis, militia leaders and white supremacy leaders are one and the same. Stern links the militia movement to Christian Identity (see Maise and Burgess, n.d.).

ATF analysts believe that militias tend to be issue-oriented. Groups unite around taxes, abortion, gun control, or Christian Identity. Other research supports the ATF findings (J. White, 1997, 2001). Militias are almost always religious, but few embrace Christian Identity, Nordic Christianity, or Creativity. For justification, they rely on free-wheeling fundamentalism and violent passages of Christian scripture quoted out of context. These passages reinforce their issue-oriented positions. Most simply interlace their antitax, anti–gun control rhetoric with such biblical passages.

There is one more thing to say about the militia movement. Simply joining a militia group does not make a person a terrorist. Observations have indicated that a number of people join the militias out of a sense of powerlessness. As a reporter from the *Toledo Blade* expressed to this author, these are folks who never quite made it. The reporter said that the militia makes them feel important, and he is probably correct. Many militia members are frustrated, feel overwhelmed, and are socially unable to cope with the rapid pace of change in the modern world. They may be extremists, but they are not terrorists.

Paramilitary groups operate on different levels. For example, the Arizona Vipers allegedly planned to blow up federal installations in 1996, and many of them eventually pleaded guilty to possessing illegal explosives. Interviews with several prominent members of other militias indicate, however, that they had never heard of the Arizona Vipers. The Freemen of Montana represent another variation. They allegedly terrorized a small town—Jordan, Montana—by flouting laws as though they were an urban gang. When the federal government took action in 1996, initiating another siege, militia members across the country expressed support but took steps to increase their ideological distance from the Freemen. Paramilitary groups come in a variety of shapes and sizes, and most of their actions are rhetorical. The Arizona Vipers and the Freemen of Montana are exceptions. Rhetoric turns to violence when small, detached groups emerge from larger extremist groups.

A new trend emerged after the sieges of Ruby Ridge in 1992 and Waco in 1993, and after the Freemen standoff in 1996 in Jordan, Montana. Old left-wing extremists and new right-wing extremists began to search for common ground. One philosophy, the **Third Position**, tried to unite both extremes. Radicals (left wing) and reactionaries (right wing) found that they had some things in common. They hate the government, they have no use for large corporations, and they distrust the media. The Third Position serves to blur the line between left and right by uniting former enemies around common themes. This becomes more apparent when examining the newest form of domestic terrorism—ecological violence.

Third Position: A movement started after the Branch Davidian standoff at Waco. It attempts to unite left-wing, right-wing, and single-issue extremists in a single movement.

After September 11, small violent groups began taking action without a centralized structure. In several areas, two or three people began to operate without contacting other groups or meeting at large convocations. They planned bombings and chemical attacks. In addition, they spoke of a spontaneous revolution (CNN, 2004b; CBS News, 2004). These unrelated groups felt that any act of violence would help to create the mayhem necessary to topple the government (Damphousse and Smith, 2004). The organization style was new, but the ideology that drove the groups had been transplanted earlier from the hills of West Virginia. It was contained in the philosophy of William Pierce.

The Turner Diaries and Hunter: Blueprints for Revolution

William Pierce was a white supremacist with headquarters in rural West Virginia. He led an organization called the **National Alliance** and purchased Resistance Records, a recording label for skinhead hate music. Pierce held a doctoral degree and worked as a college professor. Until his death in 2003, he drew the attention of watchdog groups, scholars, and law enforcement officers (Pitcavage, 1999a). Pierce wrote two novels that summarized his thought and provided a blueprint for revolution.

National Alliance: The white supremacist organization founded by the late William Pierce and headquartered in Hillsboro, West Virginia.

Pierce's most noted novel, *The Turner Diaries*, was written under the pseudonym Andrew MacDonald (1985); it is a fictionalized account of an international white revolution. The work begins as a scholarly flashback from "New Baltimore" in the "year 100," and it purports to introduce the diary that the protagonist, Earl Turner, kept during the "Great Revolution," a mythical race war set in the 1990s.

For the most part, *The Turner Diaries* is a diatribe against minorities and Jews. It is well written and easy to read. The danger of the work is that from a technical standpoint, it is a how-to manual for low-level terrorism. Using a narrative, or storytelling, format, Pierce describes the proper methods for making bombs, constructing mortars, attacking targets, and launching other acts of terrorism. Most readers of *The Turner Diaries* will come away with an elementary idea of how to become a terrorist.

The second potential danger of *The Turner Diaries* is more subtle. The book could serve as a psychological inspiration for violence; that is, it could inspire copycat crimes. The frequent diatribes in the book and the philosophy behind it justify murder and mayhem. Pierce presents the destruction of nonwhite races, minorities, and Jews as the only logical solution to social problems. Although Pierce himself was not religious, he used a general cosmic theology, presented in a "holy" work called The Book, to place Earl Turner on the side of an unknown deity.

Some extremists who have read this book have taken action. **Robert Matthews**, for example, founded a terrorist group called the **Brüder Schweigen** (the Silent Brotherhood), or The Order, based on Turner's fictional terrorist group. When arrested, the Oklahoma City bomber Timothy McVeigh was carrying a worn copy of *The Turner Diaries*.

Written in 1989, *Hunter* is another novel by Pierce under his pseudonym, Andrew MacDonald. Although not as popular as *The Turner Diaries*, *Hunter* tells the story of a lone wolf named Hunter who decides to launch a one-person revolution. He stalks the streets to kill African Americans, interracial couples, and Jews. The book is dedicated to a real-life killer, and like *The Turner Diaries*, it could inspire copycat crimes. In 1999, two right-wing extremists went on killing sprees in Chicago and Los Angeles in a style reminiscent of the violence in *Hunter*.

Extremist literature is full of hate, instructions, and suggestions. Pierce introduced nothing new in the literature of intolerance. However, he popularized terrorism in two well-written novels. Unfortunately, they could also serve as a blueprint for violence.

Resurgent Violent Right-Wing Extremism

The election of President Barack Obama had an impact on right-wing and anti-government extremism, although the government has been reluctant to release the evidence of increased activity (see Marshal, 2009). According to a restricted report now available on the Internet, the Department of Homeland Security (2009) warned that while no specific right-wing terrorist threat had emerged, several issues drew potential recruits to violent extremist organizations. The report notes that extremists capitalized on the 2008 national election and fears of gun control. The economic downturn and new political climate also made violent extremist groups more attractive. The report says that right-wing extremists exploited these issues in the 1990s and that they were in a position to do so again in 2008. Frustration over illegal immigration and threats from emerging foreign powers would increase their potential appeal. The report also says that right-wing extremists would be anxious to recruit military veterans returning from Iraq and Afghanistan.

The report met a storm of controversy and the Department of Homeland Security recalled it. However, in the summer of 2009, a neo-Nazi entered the Holocaust Museum in Washington, D.C., and began to shoot the patrons. He killed a security guard before he was subdued. In 2010, nine members of a paramilitary group were taken into custody in Michigan for allegedly plotting attacks. In another 2010 incident, a person angered by the Internal Revenue Service committed suicide by flying an airplane into a government facility in Austin, Texas. He left a 36-paragraph suicide note, expressing rage at the federal government. Later in the year, two Arkansas law enforcement officers were killed by anti-government activists. The report had warned of this type of violence.

The issue remains controversial. The Southern Poverty Law Center (Beirich, 2010) warns that hate groups are on the rise and that violent militias may move to the forefront of domestic threats. Professor Philip Jenkins (2009) agrees that actual right-wing threats should be investigated, but he believes that the government will overreact. This was the result, he says, of the militia scare of the 1990s. No matter which position is correct, one fact is clear. If the terrorist attacks of 9/11 are removed from the equation, violent right-wing groups have killed more law enforcement officers than any other domestic movement in the last 20 years (Harris, 2010).

✓ **Self-Check**

> How do modern right-wing groups reflect a long history of extremism?

> How do ideologies tend to blend into one another?

> What types of threats arise from right-wing criminal extremism?

Change on the Left

Left-wing terrorist groups dominated terrorism in the United States from about 1967 to 1985. Fueled by dissatisfaction with the Vietnam War, violent radicals broke away from student protest movements. Soon, various groups emerged, separating from the student movement to join ranks with nationalist terrorists. Their favorite tactic was bombing, but unlike right-wing groups, they tried to avoid causing casualties. Various groups made headlines, but their influence faded. By the late 1980s, several leftist groups had formed coalitions such as the Armed Resistance Unit, but they were forced to do so out of weakness rather than strength (Wolf, 1981, pp. 40–43).

Several things contributed to the demise of left-wing terrorism in the United States. One major problem was that the intellectual elites controlled the movement (Serafino, 2002). During a time of student activism, leftist elites developed followings and sympathy across a broad spectrum of collegiate and highly educated people. Kevin J. Riley and Bruce Hoffman (1995) note that this gave the left a broad constituency. Nevertheless, the movement lost its base when student activism began to disappear from American academic life. As the mood of the country shifted toward more conservative patterns of behavior, the left-wing terrorists had little sympathetic ideological support.

Riley and Hoffman surveyed several U.S. law enforcement agencies in the mid-1990s to determine their concern with domestic terrorism. Police departments were worried about terrorism, but left-wing groups were not at the top of their agenda. Only 25 percent of the urban agencies surveyed reported any left-wing activity; the responding departments reported much more activity from other types of groups. Riley and Hoffman say that the left-wing groups had engaged in symbolic violence. Some identified with Marxist-Leninist ideology, whereas others worked against specific political issues, such as U.S. military involvement in Central and South America. The collapse of the Soviet Union did not help left-wing popularity. In 1995, police perceived right-wing and Puerto Rican groups to be the greatest threats. The greatest concentration of left-wing groups was on the West Coast, but they posed a comparatively minor threat.

Loretta Napoleoni (2003, xix–xxiii) finds that guilt was a factor as left-wing terror faded in Europe. People who may have been sympathetic to the ideology of left-wing terrorists could not tolerate their violent activities as terrorism increased. This may have been a factor in American terrorism as well. Furthermore, left-wing violence waned with the fall of the Soviet Union, and police tactics improved with time, putting many terrorist groups on the defensive (Peacetalk, 2003).

The decline of American left-wing terrorism may reflect a similar trend in Europe. Xavier Raufer (1993) says that German leftists failed when the government stole their agenda. The conservatives of the Reagan era certainly did not adopt the left-wing agenda, but they did capture the country's heart. American mainstream interests turned from the extremist left. Donatella della Porta (1995) points a parallel process in Italy. The Red Brigades were able to attract a broad and sympathetic audience, but the government and authorities came to understand this and turned the tables, winning the support of the public. Unfortunately, as their power base waned, the Red Brigades increased violence in an effort to gain new recruits. American groups were too weak to do this, though they grabbed headlines.

 Self-Check

> When did left-wing extremism dominate political violence?
> Why did it go into decline?
> Are there parallels between the left in the United States and in Europe?

Homegrown Violent Extremists

While Christian and quasi-Christian religious extremists on the right have engaged in violence, the United States has also experienced homegrown Islamic criminal violence. These homegrown extremists are Americans or American residents who adopt the jihadist philosophy. Many law enforcement officials fear that a new style of jihadist group is appearing, a hybrid of foreign and homegrown terrorists. Such groups were involved in many foiled attacks, ranging on a plan to go on a shooting spree at Fort Dix, New Jersey, in 2007 to an attempt to detonate a car bomb in New York City's Times Square in 2010.

Homegrown terrorists are produced a number of ways (Holden and White, 2010). The United States has experienced two styles of homegrown attacks or attempted attacks. The first involves individuals who become radicalized by personal experiences. This could be caused by any number of things, from listening to radical sermons to being encouraged to commit suicide bombings by family members. The second might involve a similar path to radicalization, but it also involves some type of foreign connection. For example, Nidal Hasan went on a shooting spree in Fort Hood, Texas, killing several U.S. service personnel and wounding others. He appears to have been influenced by radical preaching and literature on the Internet. Faisal Shazad attempted to detonate a bomb in Times Square. He apparently received training in Pakistan.

Some homegrown terrorists choose not to strike in the United States. For example, **John Walker Lindh** and **Adam Gadahn** left the United States to join the jihad overseas. This always leaves the possibility of returning home. If that happens, a new third type of threat could come in a hybrid form: a returning homegrown jihadist experienced and trained in terrorism. Authorities fear that American citizens may join experienced international sleeper cells hiding in America (see Thachuk, Bowman, and Richardson, 2008).

The country has had some experience with hybrid terrorists. One instance includes Black Muslims who were recruited away from their faith to a traditional form of Islam. Afterward, they experience further conversion into militancy. Still another model involves normative American Muslims radicalized in their mosques. Finally, some Muslims are radicalized while in foreign countries and then return to the United States. Mark Hamm (2007 and 2009) says that prison recruiting creates

John Walker Lindh: (b. 1981) An American captured while fighting for the Taliban in 2001 and sentenced to 20 years in prison.

Adam Gadahn: (b. 1958) The American spokesperson for al Qaeda. His nom de guerre is Azzam the American.

ANOTHER PERSPECTIVE

Hamas in the United States

- In the summer of 2004, the Department of Justice charged several people with terrorist activities, including money laundering, threatening violence, possessing weapons, and a series of other related crimes. The indictment charges the suspects with being members of Hamas.
- In October 2003, law enforcement officers found small Cincinnati grocery stores raising millions of dollars for Hamas through price fraud.
- In September 2003, agents seized two men in the Virgin Islands after they left the mainland to launder money for Hamas.
- In Dearborn, Michigan, law enforcement officials charged two men with bank fraud. The alleged purpose was to raise money for Hamas.

Source: United States of America v. Mousa Mohammed Abu Marzook et al., 2003.

EXPANDING THE CONCEPT

The Charlotte Hezbollah Cell

A deputy sheriff moonlighting as a security guard in Charlotte, North Carolina, noticed a group of people buying cigarettes at a discount tobacco store. He noticed them because they were buying hundreds of cigarette cartons and loading them into vans. The deputy assumed it was a cigarette smuggling operation and called the Bureau of Alcohol, Tobacco, and Firearms (ATF). Buying cigarettes in one state and then selling them in another can be criminally profitable because of varying state tobacco laws and tax systems. When the ATF agents started investigating, they were surprised at what they found. The FBI, CIA, and many other agencies were also interested in the case.

Hezbollah was operating in Charlotte.

In this case the suspects purchased cigarettes in North Carolina and ran them to Michigan. North Carolina had a tax of five cents per pack on the cigarettes (50 cents per carton). Michigan, however, taxed cigarettes at 75 cents per pack and $7.50 per carton. North Carolina did not require a tax stamp, but Michigan did. Smugglers transported the cigarettes from North Carolina to Michigan, stamped them with Michigan tax stamps, and then sold them at regular prices without paying the taxes.

The U.S. attorney for western North Carolina, Robert Conrad, assumed the suspects were smuggling North Carolina cigarettes to Michigan and profiting by not paying tax. This turned out to be the base of the investigation, as the smugglers kept some of the money, but other illegal profits took a strange path. Conrad followed some of the money to Vancouver, Canada; other profits went overseas. Conrad's office traced the money to Lebanon. Far from a simple cigarette scheme, the smuggling operation turned out to be an operation to support Hezbollah. The Charlotte Hezbollah cell, as it came to be known, was broken because investigators and prosecutors looked beyond the surface.

Source: United States v. Mohamad Hammoud et al., 2002.

a problem because it is much easier to radicalize people in jail. For example, a group of convicted armed robbers in Southern California formed a jihadist cell in this manner.

In 2006, after British authorities uncovered a homegrown jihadist plot, FBI director Robert Mueller stated that the United States had to be vigilant against similar plots. International jihadists are a threat, Mueller said, but like the United Kingdom, the United States could be threatened by its own citizens. One of the incubators for homegrown jihadists is the American prison system. America's prisons are already awash with many variations of Islam, and Wahhabi missionaries covertly preach religious militancy in the prisons. Aware of this danger, some institutions have established special units to gather information about religious militancy and to intercept violent missionaries (Moore, 2006).

Although prisons and jails are recruiting grounds, homegrown jihadists appear in different areas. In June 2006, JTTF officers in Miami and Atlanta arrested a group of jihadists who were not involved in any network but who, authorities claimed, were plotting to blow up the Sears Tower in Chicago. The group did not even follow Islam. Its leader made up a religion combining Islam and other beliefs. According to media reports, the suspects were amateurs who had no real understanding of explosives, Islam, or the jihadist movement. Mueller said that such groups might become the greatest domestic threat. They are self-recruited, self-motivated, and self-trained. Their only direct contact with the jihadists is via the Internet (Josson, 2006). The jihadists who pulled off the March 11, 2004, Madrid attacks were amateurs, too.

Homegrown terrorism is not an American problem alone, nor is it limited to radical Islam. It is a "bottom-up event," in which a person hears a radical message and decides to pursue the radical goal. Lorenzo Vidino (2009) argues that this is hardly new, citing several cases to illustrate the point. For example, in 1977 a group of ten homegrown religious radicals stormed three sites in Washington, D.C., taking more than 150 hostages. This is just one of many homegrown instances in the second half of the twentieth century. While it may differ in scope from modern suicide bombing, Vidino concludes that it represents an extension of a problem. Homegrown terrorism is not something new.

Homegrown jihadist terrorism began drawing attention after 9/11. In May 2007 a group in New Jersey planned to enter Fort Dix and murder American soldiers. They were indicted after police were informed of their videotaped training exercises (Hauser and O'Connor, 2007). A month later, the New York City Police Department and the New York JTTF completed an 18-month investigation of an attack planned for JFK Airport (MSNBC, 2007). In 2009, FBI agents arrested an Afghan-born permanent legal resident of the United States and two friends for planning suicide attacks in New York City. They were tied to groups in Pakistan and had possible links to al Qaeda, according to *The New York Times* (Rashbaum, 2010). The plot was followed by an attempted bombing in Times Square by a Pakistani-trained homegrown terrorist in 2010, according to ABC News (Katersky, 2010).

Brian Jenkins (2010) found that 46 publicly recorded attacks or attempted attacks came from homegrown jihadist terrorists between September 11, 2001, and December 2009. Far from having been recruited by a nefarious network of hidden operatives, most of the people involved in the cases were self-radicalized, seeking to join the jihad on their own. Jenkins believes that the attacks were thwarted because American law enforcement changed its focus from apprehension after the fact to prevention. This is effective when criminal intelligence is gathered and analyzed on a local level, he argues. He also warns about overreacting. Although a single event can produce massive casualties, the United States experienced more domestic terrorism in the 1970s than it has in the first decade of the twenty-first century. Intelligence gathering is necessary, Jenkins concludes, but it must take place within the norms of democracy.

Self-Check
> How are homegrown terrorists involved in the jihadist movement?
> How are homegrown terrorists supported?
> What are the characteristics of homegrown terrorists?

Single-Issue Criminal Extremists

Left-wing terrorism did not disappear, however; it was transformed. Leftist movements became more specific, focusing not only on certain political behaviors, but on particular causes. When the left faded, single-issue groups emerged to take their place. These new groups grew and began a campaign of individual harassment and property destruction.

Ecoterrorism, Animal Rights, and Genetic Engineering

According to the FBI (Jarboe, 2002), supporters of ecoterrorism and animal rights and opponents of genetic engineering came together in the United Kingdom in 1992. The new group called itself the Earth Liberation Front (ELF). Composed of radicals from Earth First!, the Animal Liberation Front (ALF), and other disaffected environmentalists, the group migrated from Europe to the United States. The alliance has been responsible for more than 600 criminal acts since 1996. Its tactics include sabotage, tree spiking, property damage, intimidation, and arson, resulting in tens of millions of dollars of damage. One ELF member recently called for violent action, though both ELF and ALF deny this.

The formation of ELF was prefigured when radical ecologists began to sabotage road-working and construction machinery in the late 1970s. As was the case with the right wing, a novel inspired the ecoterrorists. *The Monkey Wrench Gang*, a 1975 novel by Edward Abbey, told the story of a group of ecologists who were fed up with industrial development in the West. "Monkey wrenching" referred to small acts of sabotage against companies undertaking projects in undeveloped areas. Abbey, however, was an environmental activist rather than a hate-filled ideologue like William Pierce. His novel is a fictional account that inspired others. In *The Monkey Wrench Gang*, the heroes drive through western states sabotaging bulldozers, burning billboards, and damaging the property of people they deem to be destroying the environment. (This is the same type of low-level terrorism German leftists used in the mid-1990s.) Such monkey wrenching has become a key tactic of ecoterrorists.

Bryan Denson and James Long (1999) conducted a detailed study of ecological violence for the Portland *Oregonian*. They found a shadowy conglomeration of violent ecologists who were unwilling to watch developers move into undeveloped areas. ELF had no hierarchy and was not tied to any particular location. They used a terrorist tactic long associated with the past, however: ELF targeted its victims with arson.

Denson and Long found that damage from ecoterrorism reached into the millions of dollars. They conducted a ten-month review that considered only crimes that caused more than $50,000 worth of damage. Cases that could not be linked to environmental groups were eliminated. They found 100 cases, with very few successful law enforcement investigations. ELF mastered firebombs and would not strike their targets when people were present. Their goal was to destroy property. Their firebombs grew increasingly sophisticated, and they placed bomb-making instructions on the Internet.

According to Denson and Long, most violence associated with ecoterrorism has taken place in the American West. From 1995 to 1999, damages totaled $28.8 million. Crimes included raids on farms, destruction of animal research laboratories at the University of California at Davis and Michigan State University, threats to individuals, sabotage of industrial equipment, and arson. ELF activities have increased each year since 1999 and have expanded throughout the country (Schabner, 2004). At least some members want to take their actions in a new direction. In September 2002, an ELF communiqué stated that it would "no longer hesitate to pick up the gun" (Center for Consumer Freedom, 2004).

In the past decade, ecological and animal-rights extremists have united and are known by a variety of names with a number of extremist causes. For instance, ELF, Earth First!, and a group satirically calling itself the Justice Department are interested in preserving the planet. The ALF, Animal Rights Militia, Band of Mercy, and Paint Panthers champion animal rights. Like their right-wing counterparts, many of these groups merely engage in rhetoric or disruptive behavior. The violent groups, such as ELF and ALF, advocate and engage in economic damage. They want to economically harm land developers, ski lodges, farms, and research labs, forcing them out of business.

Ecoterrorists are uncompromising, illogical extremists, just like their right-wing counterparts. A review of their ideological literature shows that they use ecology as a surrogate religion; that is, they are attached to their ideology in the same way many religious people are attached to their faith (J. White, 2000). Like all extremists, their positions are full of contradictions, but they brush these aside because they feel their cause is more important than being consistent.

Puerto Rican Nationalism

Ronald Fernandez (1987, 1996) offers two insightful views of Puerto Rico. In *Los Macheteros*, he explores the reasons for terrorism carried out by Puerto Rican nationalists in the United States; in *The Disenchanted Island*, he explains the island's relationship with the United States from the Puerto Rican point of view. Puerto Rico was colonized by the Spanish shortly after the European discovery of America, and the Spanish ruled the island for nearly three centuries. This changed in 1898, when the United States captured Puerto Rico in the Spanish-American War.

At first, the Puerto Ricans welcomed the United States as liberators, believing that they were going to be granted independence; they were disappointed. Instead of freeing the island, the United States granted Puerto Rico commonwealth status. Its special relationship to the United States grew with the increasing military importance of the island. Currently, the population is divided among three opinions. Some desire Puerto Rican statehood. Others want to create an independent country, and some of these people favor a Marxist government. A third constituency wants to maintain commonwealth status. This leaves the United States with a paradox: No matter which group it satisfies, two other groups will be disappointed.

Violent revolutionaries in Puerto Rico appeared more than 50 years ago. Puerto Rican nationalists tried to assassinate President Harry S. Truman in 1950; they also entered the chambers of the House of Representatives in 1954, shooting at members of Congress on the floor. Holes from the bullets remain in some of the desks in the House chamber today. Like their nationalist counterparts in Europe, revolutionary groups merged with left-wing organizations from around 1970 through roughly 1980. Puerto Rican groups were able to continue operating despite the decline in left-wing terrorism (Smith, 1994).

A number of revolutionary organizations embraced the nationalistic terrorist campaign. The Armed Forces of National Liberation (FALN) began operating in the United States after 1945, and they were joined by other Puerto Rican terrorists in the following decades. One of the most notorious groups was the Macheteros. Other groups included the Volunteers for the Puerto Rican Revolution (OVRP), the Armed Forces of Liberation (FARP), the Guerrilla Forces of Liberation (GEL), and the Pedro Albizu Campos Revolutionary Forces (PACRF). Before the decline of the left, Puerto Rican terrorists routinely joined left-wing operations.

Smith (1994) notes that the Puerto Rican groups were the only domestic terrorists with strong international links during the 1980s. He believes that Puerto Rican revolutionary support comes primarily from Cuba, and many members are in hiding there. Besides carrying out the largest armored car robbery in the history of the United States in 1983, Puerto Rican groups have conducted several bombings, assassinations, and even a rocket attack against FBI headquarters in San Juan. They have selectively murdered U.S. citizens, especially targeting U.S. military personnel stationed in Puerto Rico.

Since the fall of the Soviet Union, Puerto Rican terrorists have been less active, but their infrastructure remains intact. According to Fernandez (1987), terrorism has become one means of revolution. Smith believes that the problem of Puerto Rican violence will not simply evaporate. Law enforcement officers must continue to respond to Puerto Rican terrorism, but at some point, American policy makers need to resolve the status of Puerto Rico to the satisfaction of its people. Currently, as Fernandez (1996) argues, Puerto Rico is economically dependent on the United States. In 1998, the House of Representatives asked for a binding vote to determine Puerto Rico's status, but the vote failed to alter the future. Only 3 percent of Puerto Rican voters wanted independence; 46 percent wanted statehood. Fifty percent said they did not want statehood, commonwealth status, or independence; these voters did not say what they did want (Rivera, n.d.). The future of Puerto Rico remains uncertain, although terrorist violence decreased in the first decade of the twenty-first century.

Antiabortion Violence

For the past three decades, violence against abortion clinics and personnel has risen. Violent antiabortionists began with bombing and arson attacks more than 20 years ago, and they have expanded their tactics since then. Doctors and nurses have been assaulted when entering clinics. A gunman murdered Dr. David Gunn as he entered a clinic in Pensacola, Florida, in 1993. A year later, the Reverend Paul Hill killed another doctor and his bodyguard when he entered the same clinic (Risen and Thomas, 1998). Hill was convicted of murder and executed in 2003. Dr. Barnett Slepian was killed at home in 1998 when a sniper shot him through a window. **Eric Rudolph** evaded federal authorities for years after bombings at the 1996 Olympics, a gay night club, and an abortion clinic in Birmingham, Alabama.

Eric Rudolph: (b. 1966) A right-wing extremist known for bombing the Atlanta Olympics, a gay night club, and an abortion clinic. Rudolph hid from authorities and became a survivalist hero. He was arrested in 2003 and received five life sentences in 2005.

Abortion is a heated topic pitting pro-life and pro-choice advocates against one another. Most pro-life advocates abhor and denounce antiabortion violence because it is a contradiction of what they represent. Violent antiabortion advocates, however, justify their actions in the same manner as other political extremists. They feel they have the right to define morality in absolute terms. According to Risen and Thomas (1998), both murderers in Pensacola felt a specific holy duty to kill the doctors they confronted. Paul Hill, for example, shot his victims five times, laid his gun down, and walked away. Michael Griffin, Gunn's murderer, felt that God gave him instructions to give Gunn one final warning. When Gunn ignored him, Griffin waited for five hours and then shot him three times in the back as he left the clinic. To these people, accepting the status quo is more evil than using violence to change behavior. This is the standard justification for terrorism (see *Alternative Perspective: Tactics in Violent Antiabortion Attacks*).

Violence is not the only illegal action among those who break the law. The manual of the Army of God (n.d.) includes "99 Ways to Stop an Abortionist." It discusses low-level tactics such as gluing locks, shutting off water, and slashing tires. These are the tactics of radical ecologists in Germany (Horchem, 1986), but the manual does not credit a source of inspiration for the suggested tactics. The manual also describes methods for confronting workers and those seeking an abortion.

ANOTHER PERSPECTIVE

Tactics in Violent Antiabortion Attacks

- Suspected anthrax sent through the mail
- Malicious destruction of property
- Threatening letters and phone calls to workers
- False bomb threats
- Individual harassment
- Bombing and arson
- Bombing with secondary devices (designed to kill the people who respond to the first bombing)
- Assaults
- Intentional murder on the premises
- Assassination-style murders

David Nice (1988) attempts to build a theory of violence by examining trends in abortion clinic bombings. Though done in 1988, Nice's research remains applicable today. He found that abortion clinic bombings were positively correlated with every theory of violence except the theory of economic deprivation. There was no relation between abortion clinic bombings and economic conditions. Nice concludes that antiabortion violence appears in areas of rapid population growth where the abortion rate is high.

When informal social norms fail to control public behavior, some people want to replace norms with law. If the norm involves an important moral aspect of behavior and laws do not replace the former norms, some people are called to violence. They feel their opposition to a grossly immoral act, such as abortion, justifies their actions. This thought process represents the logic of terrorism. As social controls decrease and the desire to substitute political controls increases, bombings develop into a form of political action. Nice notes that the literature reveals several explanations for violent political behavior. One theory suggests that social controls break down under stress and urbanization. Another theory says that violence increases when people are not satisfied with political outcomes. Violence can also be reinforced by social and cultural values. Finally, violence can stem from a group's strength or weakness, its lack of faith in the political system, or its frustration with economic conditions.

Some of Nice's findings seem applicable to antiabortion violence that has occurred since his study. According to Risen and Thomas (1998), the murderers who killed doctors who performed abortions felt that the killings were necessary to make a political statement. Killing was a means of communication. Paul Hill was so excited by Gunn's murder that he successfully publicized it by appearing on *The Phil Donahue Show* and confronting Gunn's son. Activists were also prominent in the area where the shootings took place. All these factors created an atmosphere in which the killers sought to make a stronger statement than merely persuading women entering the clinic not to have an abortion.

Other issues have changed since Nice's study. Deana Rohlinger (2002) argues that current media coverage of abortion issues differs from that of the 1980s and early 1990s. She states that organizations favoring a woman's right to an abortion understood two critical aspects of media coverage in the previous decades. They knew how certain news organizations framed the debate and how they would cover a story. They also understood the power of news coverage and were able to attract media coverage for their point of view. Organizations against abortion did not know how to attract media coverage or how to utilize it as a propaganda tool. If Rohlinger is correct, it would be wise to follow Brent Smith's path of empirical analysis. Nice's theory of bombing and frustration could be tested against the ability of the antiabortion movement to affect outcomes by media publicity.

Carol Mason (2004) argues that frustration may be building on the pro-choice side. She believes that the antiabortion movement has not only effectively conveyed a message but glorified apocalyptic violence. Antiabortion terrorists become heroes in the antiabortion movement, even though their actions are publicly denounced. She uses the case of **Eric Rudolph** to illustrate her point. Wanted for a string of violent antiabortion acts, Rudolph was finally captured after years of being a fugitive. Rudolph was allowed to play the role of right-wing folk hero, Mason says, after he was taken into custody. She believes that such glorification could lead to a backlash.

Laws protecting access to abortion have not resulted in a backlash. Studies by William Pridemore and Joshua Freilich (Freilich and Pridemore, 2007; Pridemore and Freilich, 2007) found that laws protecting access to abortion had little effect. They neither reduced attacks nor caused a backlash from groups opposing abortions. They found that extremists who attack clinics and providers are more concerned with their cause than with obeying the law.

Pridemore and Freilich also found that about 40% of the clinics in the United States had experienced some form of attack, vandalism, or harassment. Incidents ranged from murder to vandalism against property. The study of self-reported victimization revealed that extremists practiced several methods of attack. Employees reported that they had been harassed, subjected to picketing at home, stalked, threatened, received nuisance telephone calls, and had their property damaged. They also had personal data and their pictures distributed on "wanted" posters and displayed on the Internet.

After the murder of a physician in the vestibule of a Lutheran church in Wichita, Kansas, Amanda Robb (2010) raised questions about lone wolves in a popular magazine. The doctor, who ran a late-term abortion clinic in Wichita, was murdered just before a Sunday worship service. Robb argues that the murderer was not a lone wolf, but the product of a right-wing mindset that promotes anti-government violence. Critics of positions like this feel that the government and liberals in the media are trying to create an atmosphere of political repression. They argue that the government wants to use individual acts to move against people with conservative political beliefs (*The New American*, 2009).

Examining evidence about the effectiveness of terrorism, James Lutz and Brenda Lutz (2009) found that antiabortion terrorism falls into a unique category. There are a variety of political and tactical debates because the movement is based in religion, but it does not represent a single theological perspective. The vast majority of people in the movement protest with peaceful tactics, causing the violent actors to form their own subcategory. From this perspective, antiabortion violence is effective. It is contagious among the subset, and it is effective. Murders and other violent attacks are designed to frighten health care workers and to change their behavior, and these tactics work. It deters doctors and nurses from performing abortions, and potentially violent people are inspired to take action. Lutz and Lutz conclude that there can be no doubt that violent antiabortion terrorism has made abortions more difficult to obtain in the United States, even though the majority of antiabortion activists denounce violence.

There is no easy solution to the abortion debate, as proponents of each side believe that they are morally correct. Those who are pro-choice feel that they are defending constitutional rights, and those who are pro-life often believe that they are following God's will. The abortion debate represents a political issue in which the positions have been defined by extreme political positions, and this frustrates other people who believe a moral solution lies between the two extremes. The atmosphere surrounding the abortion debate is similar to extremist positions surrounding terrorist conflicts in other parts of the world.

Self-Check

> What types of tactics do ELF, ALF, and SHAC employ?
> What is the goal of violent Puerto Rican nationalist groups?
> Is antiabortion violence terrorism?

Chapter Take Aways

By definition, domestic terrorists must act outside of the law. Therefore, it is better to think about the whole realm of politically motivated criminal extremism than to look for cases of domestic terrorism. Criminal extremism can be described by a typology focusing on political orientation. When domestic terrorism is approached in this manner, the results show extremist activities are currently dominated by anti-government and racist movements. Other forms of extremism reveal differing criminal patterns. Homegrown extremists may make individual attacks or receive training and support from abroad. Single-issue extremists are motivated by one all-encompassing passion. Ecoterrorists tend to favor property damage. Nationalists and antiabortion extremists are more prone to violence.

OBJECTIVE SUMMARY

- As the level of domestic terrorism has increased in recent years, Americans have gained a better understanding of it. State, local, and tribal law enforcement agencies have received training in recognizing indicators of terrorism, and improved intelligence analysis can be used to identify possible cases. Difficulties still arise because definitions change in shifting political environments, interest groups attempt to influence the social definition of terrorism, and some agencies still refuse to share information.
- There are several typologies for classifying domestic terrorism. One effective method is to substitute the phrase "violent criminal extremism" when describing politically motivated violence. This avoids the pejorative nature of

"domestic terrorism." It also allows politically motivated crimes to be classified as: anti-government extremism, racist extremism, homegrown jihadist extremism, and single-issue extremism. It is important to remember that holding extremist beliefs is not a crime, but violating the law when acting out extremist beliefs is. Smith finds declining levels of ideological terrorism and increasing threats from single-issue terrorists. Groups may be moving toward the network structure of international terrorists.

- Right-wing extremism can be traced to the Whiskey Rebellion of 1791–1794. It continued through the next two centuries. Contemporary right-wing extremism is based on the sovereign citizen movement, Christian patriotism, various militia movements, and types of survivalism. Frequently, an individual extremist may belong to more than one phase of the movement.
- Left-wing terrorism dwindled much in the way it did in Europe. Single-issue violent extremists dominate the left-wing movement today. Radical ecologists and animal-rights activists primarily engage in property destruction in the name of their causes. Their goal is economic disruption. There are alliances among these groups today.
- The homegrown jihadist movement involves religious radicals taking criminal action in the name of Islam. There is no standard pattern of radicalization, and it may range from individual unorganized attacks to highly complex operations supported by an international infrastructure. Research shows that this is not an Islamic problem and that most American Muslims do not support criminal violence.
- Single-issue terrorism involves criminal activity in support of one all-consuming ideology. Single-issue terrorism dominates left-wing criminal activities today, and it is exemplified by the anarchist movement.
- Criminal activities in support of ecology movements include ecoterrorism, animal rights, and opposition to generic engineering. Most of the attacks are aimed at property damage, and the most active groups are ELF and ALF. SHAC, an offshoot of ALF, has committed crimes of intimidation and violence.
- Puerto Rican nationalistic groups seek independence from the United States. However, many Puerto Ricans want to either keep commonwealth status or seek statehood.
- Antiabortion violence began with bombing and arson but moved into assault and murder. A number of abortion providers have closed operations in response to violent extremism.

Critical Engagement: Police Operations and the Future

Extremism does not represent a violation of criminal law. Violent behavior does. This presents a delicate problem for American law enforcement. If Brian Jenkins is correct (and most intelligence and law enforcement officers believe he is), the most effective action in preventing terrorism is to gather local criminal intelligence through police agencies committed to community policing models (see Chapter 17 for examples). Agencies still have rivalries and guard their territory, but there are attempts at information sharing. Fusion centers and criminal intelligence units in large police agencies are able to analyze possible violent activities involving potential terrorists and criminals. The effectiveness of criminal analysis increases when officers are routinely gathering information and forwarding it through intelligence channels. The problem comes with the phrase "potential terrorists and criminals." Extremism frequently deals with potential actions and not criminal activities.

In April 2009, the Department of Homeland Security, in conjunction with the FBI, briefly released a report on potential violent extremism from resurgent right-wing groups. The report met a firestorm of criticism, causing an immediate federal retreat instead of rational explanations. The most powerful trigger dealt with the warning that war-zone veterans made attractive recruiting targets for right-wing groups given their lethal skills. Talk show hosts and bloggers took the DHS report to task with claims that the government was afraid of its veterans. The Obama Administration was in full retreat over the issue by the end of April.

Despite the reaction, local police agencies were picking up on the increased potential for violent right-wing activity. Southeast Michigan's JTTF made a series of arrests against a militia that allegedly had plans to assassinate a police officer and then detonate bombs along the funeral route. This spawned a series of media confrontations between conservative and liberal personalities. Supporters believed the JTTF was proactive, and critics claimed it had overreacted. A federal judge dismissed most of the charges in 2012.

Domestic terrorism is difficult to define, and it spawns heated political debates. If informal community norms are the most effective method for controlling crime and if police agencies perform most efficiently when deeply connected to the community and operating within those norms, much of the information gleaned from a community will deal with potential criminal activity. This will always be controversial, and it becomes even more so when words like *extremist* and *terrorist* are used.

Consider these issues in terms of future developments:

- What type of approach toward domestic terrorism could limit political controversy? How is your answer related to preventing international terrorism?
- What is the difference between an actual crime and a potential crime? What issues are involved in proving intent to commit a crime if it has not taken place? How might juries react to cases of potential terrorism versus actual terrorism?
- If law enforcement agencies are deeply embedded in communities, how might they use information about potential terrorism to divert behavior? How might the same techniques be used to divert potential criminals and keep people out of the criminal justice system?

KEY TERMS

Whiskey Rebellion, p. 12-313
Know-Nothings, p. 12-313
Nathan Bedford Forrest, p. 12-314
Knight Riders, p. 12-314
Moorish Nation, p. 12-314
Paper terrorism, p. 12-315
white supremacy movement, p. 12-316
Brady Bill, p. 12-316
Ruby Ridge, p. 12-316

Branch Davidians, p. 12-316
Waco siege, p. 12-316
Vernon Wayne Howell, p. 12-317
survivalist, p. 12-317
Anglo-Israelism, p. 12-318
William Potter Gale, p. 12-318
Richard Butler, p. 12-318
Christian Identity, p. 12-318

Nordic Christianity, p. 12-318
Creativity, p. 12-318
Ben Klassen, p. 12-318
skinheads, p. 12-318
New World Order, p. 12-319
Free-wheeling fundamentalists, p. 12-319
militia movement, p. 12-319
Protocols of Zion, p. 12-319

Third Position, p. 12-320
National Alliance, p. 12-320
Robert Matthews, p. 12-321
Brüder Schweigen, p. 12-321
John Walker Lindh, p. 12-323
Adam Gadahn, p. 12-323
Eric Rudolph, p. 12-328

CHAPTER 13

An Introduction to Homeland Security

AP Photo/Lee Jin-man

LEARNING OBJECTIVES

After reading this chapter you should be able to:

> Define *homeland security* and explain why confusion surrounds the term.

> List the agencies responsible for homeland security and describe their functions.

> Describe the intelligence process.

> Differentiate between criminal and national security intelligence.

> Explain the importance of the National Criminal Intelligence Sharing Plan.

> Describe the functions of fusion centers.

> List some of the organizations responsible for processing intelligence.

> Summarize some of the major issues in homeland security.

> List perceived weaknesses in the homeland security from 9/11 to the present.

> Discuss the aspects of intelligence reform.

omeland security stretches beyond law enforcement and governmental controls. Most of the nation's infrastructure is privately owned and managed. Mark Clayton (2012), reporting for the *Christian Science Monitor*, delivered a shocking report about that infrastructure in May 2012. He said that the American natural gas distribution system was under a cyberattack. Some group or some nation was attempting to manipulate the gas grid.

A series of attacks apparently started in February 2012. The targets were computer systems that controlled natural gas pipelines. There are approximately 200,000 miles of interstate gas pipelines in the United States, and they transport approximately 25 percent of the nation's energy. The network is controlled by computers. Clayton says that the Department of Homeland Security issued a special alert to American gas companies and selected energy companies that were threatened by the attack. It involved a spear-phishing attack from a single source.

Spear-phishing has become one of most common methods of attacking private corporations. It begins with the attackers doing research on employees, generally through social network sites. The attackers devise a strategy to send e-mails to selected targets with lures to get them to open e-mails containing malicious software. The e-mails appear to be sent from close associates of the selected target. When the e-mail is opened, a hacker can enter the system through the portal. According to Clayton's report, once the system has been compromised, the attackers seek to gain control of settings. Cyber experts said that control of gas flow and pressure could lead to disruption of service, systemic failures, and even explosions. The attack indicates that the infrastructure is vulnerable in the age of terrorism.

Defining Homeland Security

In the autumn of 2004, the Department of Defense (DOD) held a conference on special operations that combined the military's counterterrorism efforts with American law enforcement's. Three leading officials from the Bush Administration spoke about homeland security, outlining the national strategy. One of the speakers cited the three major elements of the administration's policy. Another official said that there were five major elements to President Bush's plans, and the last speaker, an advisor from the White House, said that there were four elements to the national strategy. A frustrated US Army officer asked the last speaker if the United States had three, four, or five elements to its counterterrorist policy. The speaker answered that he did not know, but it was not important.

Department of Homeland Security (DHS): A federal agency created in 2003 by Congress from the Office of Homeland Security after the attacks of September 11, 2001.

A few years later in Destin, Florida, several federal agencies sponsored a training session that combined federal law enforcement, military, and intelligence agencies with state, local, and tribal law enforcement. Michael Chertoff (2007), then secretary of the **Department of Homeland Security (DHS)**, spoke of the necessity to operate as a multifaceted team of differing organizations to stop terrorism before it occurred. A retired general in charge of assessing counterterrorist intelligence spoke of fighting international terrorist networks with our own network (Burgess, 2007). Another speaker outlined the changing face of conflict and explained how counterterrorist policy had become a complex network comprising educational, private sector, law enforcement, intelligence, and societal elements (J. White, 2007). Former ABC news analyst John Miller (2007), an FBI deputy director, closed the conference by outlining national policy and the roles of differing levels of government. In terms of policy, there had been a lot of changes in three years.

Searching for Defined Roles

There is a reason for policy transition. It was one thing to transform bureaucracy by reorganization and congressional authorization of a new cabinet position in 2003. It was quite another to define the roles and functions of agencies that would provide homeland security. Agencies have made progress over the last few years, especially in the area of information sharing and cooperation. There is still much to do, but some people believe that the situation is better (Reese, 2007).

The reason for the initial confusion about policy is that America had no common definition of homeland security. Issues surrounding homeland security were confused because the country was dealing with a new concept, a new meaning of conflict, and a change in the procedures used to defend the United States. In the past, military forces protected the homeland, projecting power beyond U.S. borders, but the world has changed with the end of the cold war in 1991. Another reason for confusion lies in the fact that the new DHS was responsible for protecting the borders and the country's interior. Coupled with this state of affairs were bureaucratic efforts to redefine relations among agencies. The situation was further complicated when state and local governments became involved. Finally, a host of private businesses, nonprofit organizations, and health care systems were involved in security efforts. It was not easy to find a common definition for *homeland security*.

Confusion remains. For example, there are debates about the constitutionality of some aspects of governmental functions and laws that followed the 9/11 attacks (Raab, 2006). There are tremendous differences of opinion about the use of the military in the war on terrorism, and this is highlighted in passionate debates about the effectiveness of the Iraq War. Foreign policy relationships and the use of intelligence are also debated as part of the homeland security discussion (Pillar, 2006). Many federal, state, local, and tribal police agencies still search for their mission (J. White, 2007).

Despite the initial confusion, the first steps toward role definition have been taken, and agencies are beginning to understand their roles. Roles are divided into three functions: preventing terrorism, responding to attacks, and providing technical support to local agencies (Chertoff, 2007). Agencies are coming to grips with the concept of homeland security because, in its most rudimentary form, the term means "keeping the country safe." The concept was formed in the wake of a jihadist attack, but it has expanded beyond September 11. Basically, homeland security protects lives, property, and infrastructure. It is designed to secure the United States.

Critics maintain that confusion remains and that the country is not prepared to thwart an attack. Stephen Flynn (2002, 2004a, 2004b) points to weaknesses in port security. Robert Poole (2006) told Congress that aviation security remains inadequate even after the disasters of 9/11. The greatest criticism is aimed at the borders. Although illegal immigration is a hot topic of political debate, the southern border is not secure by any measure. Many counterterrorism experts believe that it will become one of the main infiltration routes for jihadists. The northern border, which does not receive the same amount of attention, is also difficult to secure (Clarke, 2007).

Security Missions

It might be more appropriate to move beyond the confusion about homeland security and to look at the missions of various organizations and their common understanding of the concept. Essentially, *mission* and *understanding of homeland security* mean the same thing, but there are many different understandings of homeland security because agencies have differing missions. For example, the Department of Energy (DOE) is responsible for protecting nuclear materials, power grids, and gas lines. DOE's understanding of homeland security is related to its mission. Customs and Border Protection in the DHS, on the other hand, uses its agents to secure U.S. borders and points of entry, with customs agents collecting revenue. It has a law enforcement mission and defines homeland security within this context. The elements of security expand or contract depending on an organization's mission.

There is confusion, to be sure, but it centers on policy, not mission. The policy guiding homeland security in the United States has not been fully developed, and agency leaders are not quite sure how all the missions of the various agencies fit together. Groups inside and outside government are adjusting to new roles. The intelligence community was criticized after the attacks, and the 9/11 Commission and its supporters were successful in implementing reform in the intelligence community. Critics, however, are not impressed with the commission's version of reform. They maintain that the 9/11 Commission was established to investigate the attacks but that it had neither the expertise nor the capability to reform intelligence gathering (Posner, 2004). This leaves the roles of the various intelligence groups in transition. The law enforcement and military communities are trying to find policies to define their roles. The functions of domestic and international laws have not been fully established. Various levels of government and private industry are trying to figure out where they interact. All of these undertakings take time.

Homeland security also involves civil defense, that is, citizens engaged in homeland security. Civil defense did not develop overnight; rather, it emerged slowly from

civil defense: Citizens engaged in homeland security.

civilian functions during World War II. After 1960, civil defense structures were intended to help government protect citizens in such areas as emergency communications, through private and public broadcasting, direct assistance during emergencies, and designation of evacuation routes and fallout shelters. During the cold war various organizations involved in **civil defense** gradually learned specific missions. The idea of "civil defense" will take on a new meaning in the coming years because the nature of conflict has changed. Homeland security is much more than the sum of the agencies charged with protecting the United States. A major portion of security is a civic responsibility.

 Self-Check

> Why do law enforcement and domestic security agencies search for defined roles?
> Why do they compete with one another?
> How does an agency's mission determine its role definition?

Agencies Charged with Preventing and Interdicting Terrorism

Congress approved the creation of DHS by uniting 22 agencies in 2002, but many other governmental organizations also focus on homeland security. These organizations exist at all levels of government: federal, state, local, and tribal. Two types of private-sector organizations participate in homeland security: businesses providing critical infrastructure and businesses centered on security technology and service. The health care system and energy sector are also part of the infrastructure of homeland security.

The Department of Homeland Security

The DHS was created from the Office of Homeland Security in 2003 as a direct result of the 9/11 attacks. It has several different missions. One group of internal organizations responds to natural and human disasters, and this function is complemented by a group of agencies charged with health and policy. Closely related to this are organizations charged with monitoring science and technology, including the detection of nuclear activities. Other parts of the department are tasked with managing both DHS's internal affairs and some functions external to it. DHS also coordinates its responses with thousands of state, local, and tribal organizations. There are several internal agencies that have security functions directly related to terrorism prevention.

Formerly, the U.S. Coast Guard was under the Department of Transportation (except in time of war, when it is subsumed by the U.S. Navy). It was the first agency to be assigned to the DHS. The Coast Guard has many duties, including the protection of coastal and inland waterways, environmental protection, the interdiction of contraband, and maritime law enforcement. For counterterrorism, its primary mission is to intercept terrorists and weapons on the high seas. Coast Guard personnel also serve wherever U.S. military personnel are deployed under the command of the armed forces.

Other departments inside DHS have counterterrorist responsibilities. Many DHS agencies are involved in intelligence: Its Office of Intelligence and Analysis coordinates intelligence with other agencies. The Transportation Security Administration is responsible for airport security. The U.S. Customs and Border Protection includes customs agents and the Border Patrol. Their work is augmented by an investigative agency, Immigration and Customs Enforcement (ICE), which is DHS's largest investigative arm. The Secret Service also serves under DHS. In addition to providing presidential security, the Secret Service retains its former role in countering financial crime. It is also involved in investigating identity theft, banking practices, and cyber-attacks (Figure 13.1).

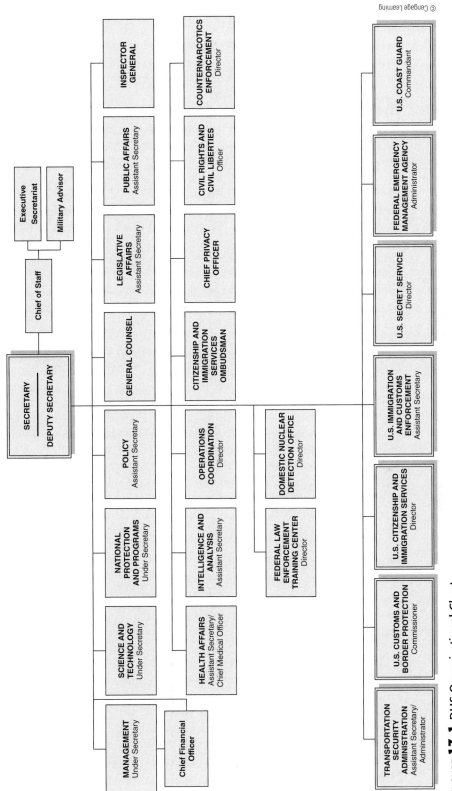

FIGURE **13.1** DHS Organizational Chart

Many DHS employees are employed in law enforcement tasks and have arrest powers. In the new Homeland Security structure, these special agents and federal police officers are trained at the **Federal Law Enforcement Training Center (FLETC)** in Glencoe, Georgia. FLETC instructors also teach basic and advanced classes on terrorism. Before 2003, FLETC was responsible for training all federal law enforcement officers except special agents from the FBI and DEA. These agencies have their own training academies at the Marine Corps base in Quantico, Virginia.

The Department of Justice

The Department of Justice (DOJ) maintains several functions in the realm of counterterrorism. The most noted agency is the FBI (FBI, n.d.). Before 9/11, the FBI was designated as the lead agency for *investigating* cases of terrorism in the United States. After 9/11, Director Robert Mueller maintained that *preventing* terrorism would be the bureau's chief mission. The FBI enhanced its Counterterrorism Division and increased the number of intelligence analysts assigned to it under Mueller's direction. As discussed at other points in this text, the FBI also coordinates state and local law enforcement efforts in Joint Terrorism Task Forces (JTTFs). The bureau also maintains Field Intelligence offices in its local agencies (see "Building Intelligence Systems" later in this chapter).

The DOJ is involved in other areas as well (U.S. DOJ, 2006). U.S. attorneys investigate and prosecute terrorism cases and coordinate intelligence sharing (see "Building Intelligence Systems"). The U.S. Marshals Service (2005) provides protection to federal officials under any type of threat in addition to the roles of securing the courts and apprehending escaped offenders. Marshals are responsible for securing federal courts and officials from terrorist attacks. The Bureau of Alcohol, Tobacco, and Firearms (ATF) has for years played a leading role in counterterrorism. Bombs are one of the most frequently used weapons in terrorism, and the ATF has some of the best explosives experts in the world. It is also charged with federal firearms enforcement. Although the FBI is the lead agency in domestic terrorism, ATF's role in explosives and firearms enforcement is crucial. Many FBI investigations would be less productive without ATF help (ATF, 2007). The Bureau of Justice Assistance (BJA) has trained more than 100,000 state, local, and tribal officers since 9/11 in the BJA State and Local Anti-Terrorism Training (SLATT) program (BJA/ SLATT, 2010). SLATT trainers have also been used by various federal law enforcement agencies and the armed forces.

The Department of Defense

Obviously, in time of war, the military organizations in the DOD play the leading role. The DOD has also assumed counterterrorist functions. It does this in two ways. First, DOD operates the U.S. Northern Command to ensure homeland security. Because the Constitution forbids military forces from enforcing civil law except in times of declared martial law, the Northern Command limits its activities to military functions. It participates in information gathering and sharing, but it is excluded from civil affairs. In times of emergency, however, military forces can provide much-needed assistance to local units of government. This is the second function of DOD. When civilian authorities request and the president approves it, military forces may be used to support civilians in counterterrorism (U.S. DOD, 2005). This power can be used in times of national emergency or to assist in disasters or civil disorders.

The Intelligence Community

The federal intelligence community underwent massive changes after 9/11 and after the invasion of Iraq and the failure to find weapons of mass destruction (WMD). The Office of the Director of National Intelligence (ODNI) began operations in April 2005.

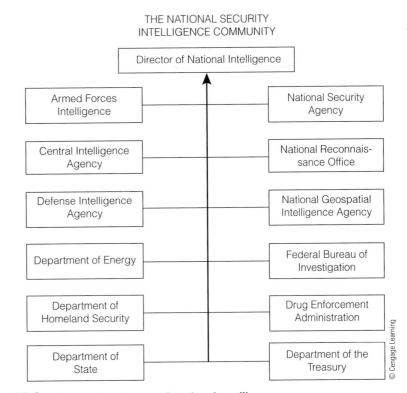

THE NATIONAL SECURITY
INTELLIGENCE COMMUNITY

FIGURE **13.2** Office of the Director of National Intelligence

The purpose of the ODNI is to unite America's national security intelligence under one umbrella. The idea dates back to 1955, when several intelligence experts suggested that the deputy director of the Central Intelligence Agency (CIA) should run day-to-day intelligence operations for the agency and that the director should assume the responsibility of coordinating all national intelligence efforts. The 9/11 Commission report suggested sweeping intelligence reforms, including the creation of a single intelligence director. The ODNI resulted from those recommendations (U.S. Office of the Director of National Intelligence, 2007).

The ODNI is a new concept in intelligence gathering. It coordinates information from national security and military intelligence. These agencies include the CIA, the National Security Agency, the Defense Intelligence Agency, the National Geospatial-Intelligence Agency, and the National Reconnaissance Office. It also includes intelligence operations from the Department of State. Based on the recommendations of the 9/11 Commission, the ODNI has incorporated federal law enforcement intelligence under its umbrella as well. Law enforcement agencies that report to the director of national intelligence include the FBI's National Security Branch, the DOE's Office of Intelligence and Counterintelligence, the DHS's Office of Intelligence and Analysis, the Department of the Treasury's Office of Intelligence and Analysis, and the Drug Enforcement Administration's Office of National Security Intelligence (Figure 13.2).

State, Local, and Tribal Law Enforcement

The federal government also envisions three intelligence roles for local governments. David Carter (2005) explains the first two. State, local, and tribal law enforcement agencies need to collect tactical intelligence for the prevention of terrorism and other crimes. They must also use intelligence for planning and the deployment of resources. Chief Gary Vest (2007) explains the third role. Information sharing is at the heart of local intelligence systems. Vest says that agencies are sharing information at an unprecedented scale but that they need to enhance the process by creating systems governed by policies. Vest believes that agencies need to form associations with governing boards that have the power to enforce rules and regulations. These will regulate intelligence within the law, prevent leaks, and provide routine methods for sharing the information.

Carter (2004, pp. 2–6) says that the role of intelligence and information sharing among state, local, and tribal law enforcement agencies enhances counterterrorism efforts. Large federal systems operate on a global basis, and officers in local communities know their jurisdictions better than anyone else. Community partnerships enhance the amount and quality of information that they can accumulate. The federal government does not have the resources or the community contacts to develop these links. The National Criminal Intelligence Sharing Plan comes to the same conclusion. The ability of state, local, and tribal agencies to share information is at the heart of preventing terrorist strikes within the borders of the United States (Daniels, 2003). When it comes to terrorism, state, local, and tribal agencies are crucial to homeland security.

Self-Check

> What federal departments and agencies are charged with homeland security?
> Why does the intelligence community interface with law enforcement?
> What roles do state, local, and tribal law enforcement agencies have in homeland security?

Building Intelligence Systems

Redirecting military and police forces is an essential part of developing a system to protect the nation. The most important aspect of security, however, is the information that guides security forces. If policies and strategy are important to the overall effort, information is crucial for day-to-day operations. For example, Thomas Barnett's (2004) idea of creating an inclusive geopolitical economic policy in which everybody wins is a long-term strategy for reducing international violence. Somewhere between the current state of affairs and the outcome of such a policy is the everyday world of homeland security. This world is driven by intelligence, and security forces can be no more effective than their ability to gain information and process it in a meaningful way.

The Intelligence Process

Information gathering is comparable to academic research. Before beginning, a researcher needs basic knowledge of a field and an understanding of subdisciplines. Much of this background information has no direct bearing on the actual question a researcher is trying to answer; but, without background preparation, the researcher cannot even address the question. Command of basic information allows the researcher to move toward applying results. Applied information, with the specificity the researcher seeks, requires both in-depth knowledge about a specific topic and the latest information from the discipline. In the sciences and social sciences, this process leads a researcher from general concepts to applied ideas, from abstract principles to glimpses of reality.

For example, if a terrorist threat is coming from a particular country, intelligence analysts need to have a basic understanding of terrorism, crime, and political power before they are able to begin an examination of the problem. They need to have skills in several social sciences, an understanding of communication and language, and the ability to estimate the influence of nationalist and religious influences on behavior. Such basic knowledge comes from a multidisciplinary liberal education.

It may not have a direct bearing on the problem, but basic information provides the skills needed to gather and analyze information about the actual terrorist threat. This is applied information.

Although academic in nature, this process is directly applicable to gathering intelligence. Police intelligence systems can be modeled after academic research. Basic intelligence involves general information about a subject and its subdisciplines. Applied intelligence involves gathering basic information about a target and real-time information about its current activities.

The practical application of this process comes through organizing structures aimed at collecting, analyzing, and forwarding information. Someone in every American law enforcement agency should be assigned to collect and forward terrorist intelligence. In small agencies, this may mean assigning a person who represents several police and sheriff's departments; in moderate-size agencies the function could be performed in the detective bureau or the planning unit. Large metropolitan and state police agencies need full-time intelligence units. At the state and regional levels, efforts must be made to assemble, categorize, and analyze information and place it within national and international contexts.

This results in a four-step process:

- *Basic information:* Analysts begin work after obtaining an in-depth, multidisciplinary education.
- *Applied information:* Analysts gather information about a specific problem.
- *Real-time information:* Analysts receive actual information as it is forwarded from the field.
- *Analyzed information:* Analysts produce intelligence based on analyzed information.

Ideally, steps two through four are repeated with each new piece of information.

National Security and Criminal Intelligence

national security intelligence: A system of agencies and networks that gather information about threats to the country. Any threat or potential threat is examined under the auspices of national defense intelligence. Unlike criminal intelligence, people and agencies gathering defense information do not need to suspect any criminal activity. The FBI is empowered to gather defense intelligence.

As mentioned earlier, in network-to-network conflict, bureaucracies should not change their role. For example, if the CIA were to operate as if gathering evidence for a criminal prosecution, it would not be able to function. The same applies to all levels of law enforcement. Police agencies cannot gather information illegally. If they do, they defeat the society they are trying to protect. Each organization in a network has its own function, and the key to success in a network is sharing information.

This leads to the need for two different types of intelligence. **National security intelligence** is gathered to defend the nation. It is not used in criminal prosecutions, and it is not subject to legal scrutiny. **Criminal intelligence** is gathered by law enforcement and prosecuting attorneys. It cannot be gathered, analyzed, or stored without a reason to believe that a crime is about to take place or has taken place (J. White, 2004b, pp. 73–74).

criminal intelligence: Information gathered on the reasonable suspicion that a criminal activity is occurring or about to occur. It is collected by law enforcement agencies in the course of their preventive and investigative functions. It is shared on information networks such as the Regional Information Sharing System (RISS). Unlike national defense intelligence, criminal intelligence applies only under criminal law. Agencies must suspect some violation of criminal law before they can collect intelligence.

Richard Best (2001) argues that national security differs from law enforcement. In police work, officers react to information provided voluntarily. Police actions are governed by the rules of evidence, and the ultimate purpose is to protect the rights of citizens, including those who have been arrested. National security intelligence, on the other hand, is used to anticipate threats. It uses aggressive methods to collect information, including, at times, operations in violation of the law. National security intelligence is ultimately designed to protect targets, not individuals' rights.

Best quotes Stansfield Turner, a former director of the CIA, to summarize the differences between law enforcement and national security. "Give the FBI a task," Turner once said, "and it will try to complete the mission within the constraints of the law. Give the CIA the same mission, and it tries to complete the task without concern for legality." Law enforcement's prime concern is public service. The American police will lose public trust if they rely on covert illegal operations.

Using Best's insight, law enforcement should plan and develop two channels for information. One channel should be aimed at law enforcement intelligence, that is, the types of information police agencies collect. As Best (2001) describes it, this information is based on criminal activity and the protection of individual rights. It is governed by the rules of evidence. In other words, it must be legally admissible in court. Yet police agencies will inevitably come upon threats to national security involving information that will not be used in a criminal prosecution. At this point, state and local police agencies should be prepared to pass such information along to defense sources. These two paths for information, one for criminal investigation and one for national security, can serve as the basis for dealing with intelligence collected by state and local police agencies. For example, an officer may stop an individual for suspected criminal behavior. After questioning the person, the officer no longer suspects that a crime is being committed, but the person seems to be associated with a known terrorist organization. The officer gathers information about the person and forwards it to a local fusion center. Neither the officer nor the police agency can keep this information because it does not involve a crime. The fusion center, however, has a group of analysts responsible for national security. They will analyze the officer's information, transforming it into national security intelligence. It will not be used in a criminal prosecution, and it will not be stored by a law enforcement agency or used in a criminal prosecution.

A Checkered Past

Law enforcement and intelligence agencies present their systems in a positive light, but critics point to two types of failures. First, intelligence processes have been ineffective. The FBI and CIA have been roundly criticized for failing to gather information before the September 11 attacks and ineffectively analyzing the information they did have (Dillon, 2001; Nordland, Yousafzi, and Dehghanpisheh, 2002). The Bush administration and police agencies expressed disapproval of the FBI's information sharing policies (Fields, 2002).

Second, the government has abused its authority in the past. Civil liberties groups fear growing power in agencies associated with homeland security, and others express concern over expanding executive authority (Herman, 2001; CNN, 2006; Keefer, 2006).

COINTELPRO: An infamous FBI counterintelligence program started in 1956. Agents involved in COINTELPRO violated constitutional limitations on domestic intelligence gathering, and the program came under congressional criticism in the early 1970s. The FBI's abuse of power eventually resulted in restrictions on the FBI.

Rules for collecting criminal and national security intelligence are necessary to prevent such abuses in the future. For example, in the 1950s the CIA tested drugs on Americans without their consent or knowledge; the FBI's counterintelligence program, **COINTELPRO** exceeded the authority of law enforcement in the name of national security. The government, responding to such abuses, began to limit the power of intelligence operations, unintentionally hampering their effectiveness. Law enforcement and national defense intelligence experienced difficult times during the administration of President Jimmy Carter (1976–1980). Carter was not seeking to dismantle intelligence operations; he wanted to protect Americans from their government. The president tried to correct the abuse of power and end the scandal of using covert operations against American citizens.

President Carter's reaction was understandable, but critics believe that he went too far, and no other administration has been able to reconstitute effective intelligence organizations. A *Time* magazine article (Calabresi and Ratnesar, 2002) states the issue succinctly: America needs to learn to spy again. National security intelligence is crucial, but law enforcement has a role, the *Time* authors argue. They also censure bureaucratic structures for failing to share information, and they condemn the system for relying too heavily on machine and electronic information. We need information from people, the *Time* authors state emphatically. Another weak point is the inability to analyze information. Intelligence is fragmented and ineffective. Their opinion has been reflected in other studies (Best, 2001; Betts, 2002; D. Wise, 2002). (See *Another Perspective: Types of Intelligence.*)

☀ ANOTHER PERSPECTIVE

David Carter's Recommendations for Law Enforcement Intelligence

David Carter suggests refocusing law enforcement efforts. Police activity, he argues, should be led by intelligence. In order to accomplish this, police agencies should take an "R-cubed" approach: reassess, refocus, and reallocate.

1. Reassess the following:
   a. calls for service
   b. specialized units
   c. need for new specializations
   d. community resources
   e. potential threats
   f. current intelligence
   g. political mandates from the community

Source: Carter, 2004.

2. Refocus in these ways:
   a. Establish new priorities based on reassessment.
   b. Weigh priorities in terms of criticality.
   c. Actually implement changes.
3. Reallocate: Commit the resources needed to implement changes.

Law enforcement intelligence differs from intelligence gathered for national security. Law enforcement agencies must base their activities on a reasonable suspicion that some criminal activity is taking place or has taken place.

Unlike national defense or security intelligence gathering, police agencies are required to demonstrate a reasonable suspicion of criminal activity before they may collect information. As long as agencies reasonably suspect that the law is being broken or has been broken, law enforcement departments may gather and store criminal intelligence. The USA PATRIOT Act increases the ability of law enforcement and intelligence agencies to share information, but David Carter (2004), one of the foremost academic experts on law enforcement intelligence in the country, solemnly warns that the abuses of the past must not be repeated if police agencies want to develop effective intelligence systems (see also Dreyfuss, 2002). If police agencies improve their intelligence-gathering operations, they will do so under more stringent rules than those required for national security.

☀ ANOTHER PERSPECTIVE

Types of Intelligence

There are different types of intelligence-gathering systems. The differences are crucial when dealing with civil rights (see Chapter 16), but each intelligence system has its own practical methods for assembling information.

Criminal intelligence is gathered by law enforcement agencies investigating illegal activity. State, local, and federal police agencies are not allowed to gather, store, or maintain record systems on general activities. Their information must be based on a reasonable suspicion that some sort of criminal activity is taking place or has taken place. Certain FBI operations may gather noncriminal intelligence if agents are assigned to national security. They do not use this evidence in criminal prosecutions.

National defense or security intelligence is gathered by several organizations in the DOD,

National Security Agency, DOE, DHS, FBI, and CIA. Defense or security intelligence is usually based on one or more of the following sources:

- humint: Human intelligence from spies, informers, defectors, and other people
- imint: Imagery intelligence from satellites and aircraft
- sigint: Signal intelligence from communications
- masint: Measures and signatures intelligence from sensing devices, such as detecting a weapons system based on the amount of heat it is producing

Defense or security intelligence can be gathered whether the targets are involved in a crime or not.

Domestic Intelligence Networks

National Criminal Intelligence Sharing Plan (NCISP): A plan to share criminal intelligence among the nation's law enforcement agencies. It suggests minimum standards for establishing and managing intelligence operations within police agencies.

Shortly after 9/11, the IACP joined with the DOJ to create the **National Criminal Intelligence Sharing Plan (NCISP)**. The plan established norms for collecting, analyzing, and storing criminal intelligence within legal guidelines. It also suggested how information could be shared among agencies. Its primary function was to set minimum standards for criminal intelligence so that every American police agency knew the legal guidelines for using criminal information. It also sought to create standards for using technology and giving police officers access to information. The standards guide intelligence-gathering activities, and a national coordinating group seeks to maintain them (U.S. Bureau of Justice Assistance, 2005; Brooks, 2011).

Regional Informational Sharing System (RISS): A law enforcement network that allows law enforcement agencies to share information about criminal investigations.

David Carter (2004, pp. 123–143) points to a number of criminal-intelligence networks in operation after 9/11. The **Regional Information Sharing System (RISS)** was created in 1973. RISS has six centers—each serving a selected group of states—that share criminal information with investigators working on a variety of criminal activities, including terrorism. RISS expanded operations in April 2003 by creating the Anti-Terrorism Information Exchange (ATIX). Complementing these systems is the FBI's Law Enforcement Online (LEO), which provides FBI intelligence to state, local, and tribal agencies. The Law Enforcement Intelligence Unit (LEIU) was created by a variety of police agencies in 1956. Today, it serves as a venue to share secure information on organized crime and terrorism.

Fusion centers: Operations set up to fuse information from multiple sources, analyze the data, turn it into usable intelligence, and distribute intelligence to agencies needing the information.

Carter notes that the DHS has also created an intelligence system. The Homeland Security Information Network (HSIN) is set up to connect all jurisdictions with real-time communication. It includes state homeland security officials, the National Guard, emergency operations centers, and local emergency service providers. HSIN provides encrypted communications on a secure network. Designed to combine the criminal information of RISS with critical infrastructure protection, HSIN is designed to unite all the different organizations involved in homeland security (see *Another Perspective: Homeland Security Information Network*). Critics maintain that the system is underused and that it duplicates the functions of proven systems like RISS (Jordan, 2005).

Despite the systems and networks that were developed to share information, many agencies still were not part of the information-sharing process. **Fusion centers** came about to correct this. Endorsed by the NCISP, fusion centers were designed to

ANOTHER PERSPECTIVE

Homeland Security Information Network

The Homeland Security Information Network (HSIN) is a computer-based counterterrorism communications system connecting all 50 states, five territories, Washington, D.C., and 50 major urban areas.

The HSIN allows all states and major urban areas to collect and disseminate information among federal, state, and local agencies involved in combating terrorism. It also

- helps provide situational awareness.
- facilitates information sharing and collaboration with homeland security

partners across federal, state, and local levels.

- provides advanced analytic capabilities.
- enables real-time sharing of threat information.

This communications capability delivers to states and major urban areas real-time interactive connectivity with the National Operations Center. This collaborative communications environment was developed by state and local authorities.

Source: U.S. Department of Homeland Security, 2010.

place all intelligence in a single center, combining multiple agencies in a single unit to analyze all types of threats. As a result, a typical fusion center may have analysts and agents from several federal law enforcement and intelligence agencies, military personnel, and local police officers and criminal analysts. It merges information—earning the name *fusion*—into a single process of data analysis. Criminal information is channeled to investigations, and national security intelligence is passed on to the appropriate agency. Once passed on, national security intelligence is not available for criminal analysis or storage in law enforcement files (U.S. DOJ, Office of Justice Programs, 2006).

Fusion Centers

Regional Intelligence Centers: Originally established to gather drug trafficking intelligence, RICs helped provide the basis for fusion centers.

High Intensity Drug Trafficking Area: Specialized RICs in regions experiencing a high level of drug trafficking and drug-related crimes. They evolved from RICs and were the direct predecessor to fusion centers. Some HIDTAs simply expanded to become full fusion centers.

Regional Crime Gun Centers (RCGC): ATF intelligence centers similar to RICs but focused on the illegal use of firearms.

The idea of an intelligence fusion center represents a new concept, but it has actually been developing over the past 35 years. Law enforcement agencies were aware of the need to collect and analyze criminal intelligence long before the attacks of 9/11. David Carter (2008) says that fusion centers evolved from **Regional Intelligence Centers** (RIC) created to counteract drug trafficking in the 1980s. There was no single model for these units, and the structure and organization of RICs differed from state to state. The RICs eventually evolved into **High Intensity Drug Trafficking Area** intelligence centers—HIDTA-RIC.

Carter says the Bureau of Alcohol, Tobacco, and Firearms (ATF) began to centralize its efforts to gather intelligence for reducing gun violence over the next decade, creating **Regional Crime Gun Centers** (RCGC). Realizing the effective operations of the HIDTA-RICs, ATF began coordinating activities with them, and in some jurisdictions both gun and drug intelligence even operated from the same buildings. These specialized intelligence units aimed at specific crimes would become the basis of the fusion centers.

Although the centers were operating by the beginning of the twenty-first century, Carter reports that they had some drawbacks. First, their focus tended to be on local crimes and issues. There were few efforts to share information on a larger, more systematic scale. Second, no funding was available to expand the operation of the centers. These factors combined to produce a third weakness: There was no incentive to expand or increase operations due to the focus on the immediate region. Finally, the centers only focused on specific crimes. The directors of the intelligence centers made no effort to look at exotic crimes like terrorism, and they had no effective method of identifying and passing on national security intelligence. Indeed, the attitudes of the Department of Justice and the attorney general would have prevented such activity.

Despite these weaknesses, cooperation between the HIDTA-RIC and the ATF centers gave law enforcement a new advantage. Information from multiple jurisdictions was being gathered, analyzed, and "fused" into a single intelligence picture of criminal activity. This was the embryo that would grow into a larger intelligence system. David Carter says the intelligence process changed drastically after 9/11, but that the foundation for fusion centers was present well before the event. When the newly created Department of Homeland Security looked for a model to enhance domestic intelligence, it found one in the partnership between HIDTA-RIC and ATF. DHS began funding the centers, and they eventually evolved into fusion centers.

Although each fusion center remains unique and is geared to meet regional needs, the centers follow a common process. Bart Johnson (2007, 2011) describes the model for fusing intelligence. The purpose of fusion centers is to place experts and analysts from a variety of fields and organizations in a single collaborative work environment. The analysts bring diverse skill sets to provide the resources and expertise necessary to evaluate and disperse intelligence. Raw information comes to fusion centers from law enforcement, other government agencies, and the private sector. The raw information is analyzed to reveal patterns of suspicious activity, the behavior habits of known or suspected terrorists, the vulnerability of targets, and the probability

intelligence product: The output of information analysis. Information is analyzed and turned into intelligence. This product is distributed to users.

of an attack. This information, known as an **intelligence product**, is returned to the field on a need-to-know basis. When they were initially created, the primary focus was terrorism, but the mission would expand. Although these models differed, the fusion centers together created the basis for state, local, tribal, and federal intelligence partnerships.

Fusion Center Intelligence

The initial focus on terrorism was understandable given the 9/11 attacks. Yet fusion centers created a vehicle for several types of operations that could be synchronized. The centers provided a link with private corporations, which was critical because most of the infrastructure is under private ownership. National security intelligence agencies and military forces sent their representatives, and their areas of operations were separated from the criminal intelligence gathered by law enforcement. They were placed in a secure, top secret setting inside the fusion centers. When a criminal analyst came upon noncriminal intelligence that had a potential impact on national security, it could be passed through proper legal channels within the center (Kanable, 2011).

total criminal intelligence (TCI): An "all crimes" approach to the intelligence process. The same type of intelligence that thwarts terrorism works against other crimes and community problems.

Fusion centers continued to evolve with an "all crime" or **total criminal intelligence** (TCI) mentality. Carter (2008) shows that fusion centers took the TCI concept one step further by analyzing information about "all threats," and from there analysis went to "all hazards." The primary mission remains analyzing intelligence to identify terrorist threats, but there is a great redundancy in information. In other words, the information that can be used to prevent terrorism is also useful in identifying criminal and public health problems. Carter says the same type of information can also be used to target law enforcement activities for community-based crime control and problem solving. Finally, fusion centers created an opportunity to improve the delivery of emergency and nonemergency services.

Practitioners argue that the new efforts have proven to be successful (Johnson, 2007, 2011). For example, a California town experienced a series of armed robberies at gas stations in 2005. At first, this appeared to be a series of local crimes. Officers investigating the robberies gathered standard criminal information to help identify suspects, and in the routine course of the investigations they forwarded information to a fusion center. Analysts at the fusion center made a startling discovery. The robberies were not being staged for financial gain. The group behind the robberies was trying to collect money to support a campaign of domestic terrorism. The robberies were solved and several planned acts of terrorism were thwarted.

Such incidental evidence indicates that fusion centers have increased the effectiveness of law enforcement and have enhanced domestic security. There is a need for more systematic research and evaluation to determine the overall effectiveness of the fusion centers. Currently, 72 centers collect and analyze information, coordinating that information with DHS. Still, there are squabbles from time to time about information sharing, and there are struggles among the various bureaucracies for control of information. The ideal goal is to distribute information to agencies that have a right to know and need to know. Sometimes the ideal is not attained. The rhetoric is based in information sharing and cooperative analysis. Rigorous research is required to determine if this is actually happening.

The New Jersey Intelligence System

Gathering information within the bounds of criminal intelligence need not bar the path to efficiency. It is possible to build criminal-intelligence systems within the letter and spirit of legal regulations, and several agencies have an excellent track record in doing so. The New Jersey State Police (NJSP), for example, has an extensive intelligence-gathering apparatus (New Jersey State Police, 2002). The NJSP Intelligence

Service Section is made up of three main divisions. The Intelligence Bureau is the largest division, composed of six units. The Analytical Unit is responsible for reviewing data from organized crime families and street gangs. It synthesizes information to produce a broad picture of the entire state, and it also conducts threat assessments for major public events. The Casino Intelligence Unit collects information on gambling affiliations involved in traditional and nontraditional crimes. It also serves as the government's liaison for regulatory agencies and conducts background investigations on contractors working in the casino industry. The Electronic Surveillance Unit conducts court-authorized monitoring and assists federal agencies in national security investigations. Critical information is shared through the Liaison Computerized Services Unit, including the sharing of information with agencies outside New Jersey. The Services Unit also codifies and organizes intelligence reports. Finally, the Street Gang Unit collects information and works with local gang task forces. The NJSP system is a model for gathering, organizing, analyzing, and sharing criminal information.

Two other divisions complete the picture of the NJSP system. The Central Security Division is responsible for New Jersey's counterterrorist mission. Its primary purpose is the prevention of terrorist activities through intelligence operations. In other words, it is a proactive organization designed to prevent terrorism through interdiction. According to its official public statement, the Central Security Division is primarily concerned with maintaining civil peace, protecting dignitaries, and monitoring known hate groups.

The Solid Waste Division, which gathers information about hazardous materials and keeps an eye on organized crime, and the Casino Bureau round out the organization of the NJSP Intelligence Service Section. The key to its organization and its preventive capabilities is the collection, analysis, and sharing of information. Recently, NJSP linked its intelligence service with federal law enforcement, giving it the potential for greater effectiveness.

The California Intelligence System

California also introduced a new concept in statewide intelligence systems, the California Anti-Terrorism Information Center (CATIC). Formed after September 11, this statewide intelligence system was designed to combat terrorism. The center linked federal, state, and local information services in one system and divided operational zones into five administrative areas. The design called for trained intelligence analysts to operate within civil rights guidelines and to use information in a secure communications system (California Department of Justice, 2002). Information was analyzed daily.

CATIC was unique in state and local law enforcement. It combined machine intelligence, that is, the type of information that can be gathered by computers and other automated devices, with information coming from a variety of police agencies. The information was correlated and organized by analysts looking for trends. Future projections were made by looking at past indicators. Rather than simply operating as an information-gathering unit, CATIC was a synthesizing process. It combined public information with data on criminal trends and possible terrorist activities. The processed intelligence produced threat assessments for each area and projected trends outside the jurisdiction.

CATIC developed as a prototypical intelligence fusion center, but it hit a snag. According to records obtained by critics of the system, CATIC collected and maintained records on several individuals and groups that had nothing to do with terrorism. In fact, if critics are correct, it gathered and stored information on political dissidents who engaged in no criminal activity (B. Hoffman, 2003). This is an illegal activity. Despite the initial hopes, CATIC closed its doors.

California created new systems under the tight control of regional law enforcement agencies and in partnership with four regional JTTFs. The State Terrorism Threat Assessment Center now coordinates the activities of regional threat-assessment centers. Modeled after fusion center plans, the system works only with criminal intelligence. The regional centers are staffed with local law enforcement and infrastructure protection personnel, and they work with the local FBI field offices (California Highway Patrol, 2007). The new regional systems have the potential to be more effective as CATIC. The key to their success will be in strict monitoring of the type of information gathered and stored by the analysts.

The NYPD Intelligence System

The New York City Police Department (NYPD) has taken the offensive spirit a step further. Police Commissioner Raymond Kelly created two new units, one for counter-terrorism and one for intelligence. Retired Marine Corps General Frank Libutti heads the counterterrorism section, and a former high-ranking CIA official, David Cohen, was selected to head the intelligence section. Kelly stated that he wanted the NYPD to do a better job of intelligence analysis and to work more closely with the federal government. The International Association of Chiefs of Police (IACP) said that the plan was appropriate for New York City (K. Johnson, 2002).

U.S. Attorneys and JTTFs

The DOJ has created two intelligence systems, one in federal prosecutors' offices and the other in law enforcement. According to the DOJ (U.S. DOJ, 2007), "There are 93 United States Attorneys stationed throughout the United States, Puerto Rico, the Virgin Islands, Guam, and the Northern Mariana Islands. United States Attorneys are appointed by, and serve at the discretion of, the President of the United States, with advice and consent of the United States Senate. One United States Attorney is assigned to each of the judicial districts, with the exception of Guam and the Northern Mariana Islands where a single United States Attorney serves in both districts. Each United States Attorney is the chief federal law enforcement officer of the United States within his or her particular jurisdiction."

Each U.S. attorney's office has an Anti-Terrorist Assistance Coordinator (ATAC). The purpose of the ATAC is to coordinate the collection of criminal intelligence and to share intelligence among federal, state, local, and tribal law enforcement agencies. ATACs hold security clearances, so they can view secret national security intelligence. Although they do not use this information in criminal prosecutions, they are authorized to pass the information to agencies charged with national security.

The various JTTFs operate in a similar manner. Each JTTF is made up of officers from all levels of American law enforcement and from a variety of different types of agencies. This gives each JTTF a wide range of authority because officers from different police agencies have different types of law enforcement authority and power. Every JTTF agent also receives a national security intelligence clearance. Like the ATAC, JTTF agents may not use national security intelligence in criminal prosecutions, but they are allowed to collect and use it for national defense. They may also work with various intelligence agencies. In addition, each regional FBI office has a field intelligence coordinator who works with ATACs and JTTFs (Cumming and Masse, 2004).

Self-Check

> How does raw information become intelligence?

> What is the difference between national security and criminal intelligence?

> How can existing systems be used to create or to expand future intelligence networks?

Issues in Homeland Security

There are many organizational and bureaucratic problems inherent in organizations. These issues are discussed in Chapter 14. Other aspects of homeland security are directly related to homeland security. These issues include understanding the role of law enforcement, the value of symbolic targets, threat analysis, planning, and the ability to create a culture of information sharing.

Law Enforcement's Special Role

If military forces are to transform themselves in the fashion suggested by Thomas Barnett (2004), law enforcement must seek and find new roles. More than half of the DHS agencies have police power, and state and local governments look to law enforcement to prevent attacks and respond to the unthinkable. Interestingly, federal, state, and local officers have taken the lead role in identifying and disrupting terrorism in the United States. Whether terrorists are homegrown or imported from foreign lands, police agencies are responsible for breaking some of America's most formidable terrorist cells. Law enforcement has a key function in homeland security (see Carter, 2004).

American law enforcement has a long tradition of reactive patrol, that is, responding to crimes and calls for assistance. With the advent of radio-dispatched motorized patrol, response time became the measure of police effectiveness. It was assumed that the sooner the police arrived at the scene of a crime, the more likely they were to make an arrest. Like fire departments responding to smoke, police effectiveness was determined by the ability to respond quickly to crime.

The problem of terrorism brings the need for preemptive, offensive policing to a new level. If law enforcement simply responds, it will have little impact on the prevention of terrorism. Defensive reactions alone will not stop terrorism, and no government can afford to fortify all the potential targets in a jurisdiction. Even if all targets could be defended, the goal of asymmetrical warfare is not to destroy targets, but to show that security forces are not in charge. Terrorists are free to strike the least-defended symbolic target. Defensive thinking, like reactive patrol, cannot win a fight in the shadows.

If state and local agencies shift to offensive thinking and action, two results will inevitably develop. First, police contact with potential terrorists will increase, but as Sherry Colb (2001) points out, the vast majority of any ethnic or social group is made up of people who abhor terrorism. This increases the possibility of negative stereotyping and the abuse of power. Second, proactive measures demand increased intelligence gathering, and much of the information will have no relation to criminal activity. If not properly monitored, such intelligence may be misused.

Another issue appears in the private sector. Kayyem and Howitt (2002) find that offensive action begins in the local community. The weakness in local systems occurs, however, because state and local police departments frequently do not think beyond their jurisdictions, and they do not routinely take advantage of potential partnerships inside their bailiwicks. Kayyem and Howitt believe that partnerships are the key to community planning. One of the greatest potential allies is private security organizations. Unfortunately, many law enforcement agencies frown on private security and fail to create joint ventures with the private sector.

On the positive side of the debate, counterterrorism is not a mystical operation. It uses many of the skills already employed in preventive patrol, criminal investigation, and surveillance. With a few tweaks, police intelligence operations and drug enforcement units can add counterterrorism to their agendas, and patrol and investigative units can be trained to look for terrorist activities in the course of their normal duties. If properly managed, these activities need not present a threat to civil liberties.

The Role of Symbols and Structures

symbolic targets: Terrorist targets that may have limited military or security value but represent the power of the state under attack. Terrorists seek symbolic targets to strike fear into society and to give a sense of power to the terrorist group. The power of the symbol also multiplies the effect of the attack.

Asymmetrical war is waged against **symbolic targets**, and homeland security is designed to secure symbols. Just because a target has symbolic significance does not mean it lacks physical reality. The bombing of the Murrah Federal Building in Oklahoma City in 1995, for example, had symbolic value, and the casualties were horrific. Attacks against symbols disrupt support structures and can have a high human toll. Defensive measures are put in place to protect the physical safety of people and property as well as the symbolic meaning of a target (see Juergensmeyer, 2000, pp. 155–163; Critical Incident Analysis Group, 2001, pp. 9–16).

Symbols need not only be considered in the abstract. Blowing up a national treasure would entail the loss of a national symbol, but killing thousands of innocent people becomes a symbol in itself. Grenville Byford (2002) points out that a symbolic attack may simply be designed to inflict massive casualties—killing people has a symbolic value, and thus killing civilians achieves a political purpose for terrorists. Strategies for protection should be grounded in an understanding of the problem. Ian Lesser (1999, pp. 85–144) outlines three forms of terrorism: symbolic, pragmatic, and systematic. Symbolic terrorism is a dramatic attack to show vulnerability; pragmatic terrorism involves a practical attempt to destroy political power; and systematic terrorism is waged over a period of time to change social conditions. Lesser also points to several examples in which symbolic factors enter into the attacks. In other words, terrorists use symbolic attacks, or attacks on symbols, to achieve pragmatic or systematic results.

The University of Virginia's Critical Incident Analysis Group (CIAG) brought law enforcement officials, business leaders, governmental administrators, and academics together to discuss America's vulnerability to symbolic attack (CIAG, 2001). Symbols can have literal and abstract meanings, such as a capitol that serves literally and abstractly as the seat of governmental power. The key to security is to offer protection without destroying abstract meanings. For example, the words of one CIAG participant summed up the problem: "We want to protect the Capitol building," he said, "without making Washington, D.C., look like an armed camp."

All societies create symbols, and American democracy is no different. In a time of asymmetrical war, American symbols demand protection. The key to security, the CIAG concludes, is to enhance protection while maintaining openness. The irony is that every added security measure increases the feeling of insecurity. The CIAG report cites metal detectors at county courthouses as an example. Simply going through the detector before entering a building gives a person the feeling that things might fall apart. The key is to make symbolic targets as secure as possible while giving the illusion that very few security precautions have been taken.

ANOTHER PERSPECTIVE

Community Threat Analysis

Examine the following considerations for defensive planning, or community threat analysis. What other items might be added?

- Find networks in and among communities. Look at transportation, power grids and fuel storage, water supplies, industrial logistics and storage, and the flow of people.

- Think the way a terrorist does. Which targets are vulnerable? Which targets would cause the most disruption? Which buildings are vulnerable? Where is private security ineffective?

- Obtain architectural plans for all major buildings. Protect air intakes, power supplies, and possible points for evacuation.

- Have detailed emergency information for each school.
- Practice tactical operations in each school building after hours.
- Prioritize. Assign a criticality rating to each target, assessing its importance, and rank targets according to comparative ratings.
- Coordinate with health services.
- Discuss triage and quarantine methods. Plan for biological, chemical, and radiological contamination.

- Look at emergency plans for other communities.
- Prepare added security for special events.
- Designate an emergency command post and roles for personnel from other agencies. Practice commanding mock attacks.
- Study past emergencies and determine what law enforcement learned from its shortcomings.

Source: Management Analytics and others, 1995.

Planning for Homeland Security

Everyone knows that planning should take place before a problem emerges. Effective police planning incorporates a description of a goal and methods for achieving it (Hudzik and Cordner, 1983). Planning should be based on the assets available to an agency and a projection of resources needed to meet the goal. A good plan will show how different entities interrelate and may reveal unexpected consequences. Planning brings resources together in a complex environment to manage multiple consequences.

The complexities of terrorism can seem overwhelming, so planning is essential. It enhances the gathering, organizing, and analyzing of information (Bodrero, 2002). Police agencies have long been aware of the need to make reactive plans. Emergency planning, for example, is a tool for dealing with weather disasters and industrial accidents. After riots in Dade County, Florida, in 1980, local agencies developed field-force-deployment plans similar to mutual aid pacts among firefighters. The tragedies of Oklahoma City and September 11 brought several plans to fruition. Successful efforts in planning can be transferred into offensive strategies.

The IACP (2001) believes planning can be guided by looking for threats within local communities. Police agencies should constantly monitor communities to determine whether a terrorist threat is imminent. Indicators such as an increase in violent rhetoric, the appearance of extremist groups, and increases in certain types of crimes may demonstrate that a terrorist threat is on the horizon. Planning is based on the status of potential violence, and law enforcement can develop certain responses based on the threat. Prepared responses, the IACP contends, are proactive (see *Another Perspective: Information for Planning*).

Creating a Culture of Information Sharing

The National Strategy for Homeland Security (Office of Homeland Security, 2002, p. 56; U.S. Department of Homeland Security, 2004b, pp. 3–34) calls for increasing information sharing among law enforcement agencies by building a cooperative environment that enables sharing of essential information. It will be a "system of systems that can provide the right information to the right people at all times." This is an excellent idea in principle.

D. Douglas Bodrero (2002) believes that many of these systems are already in place. The six-part RISS information network, whose policies are controlled by its members, is ideal for sharing intelligence. It has secure intranet, bulletin board, and conference capabilities. The High Intensity Drug Trafficking Areas (HIDTAs) system and the El Paso Intelligence Center (EPIC) are also sources for information sharing. The International Association of Law Enforcement Intelligence Analysts (IALEIA) routinely shares information with member agencies. These established systems are now complemented by HSIN and a host of fusion centers (U.S. DOJ, Office of Justice Programs, 2006). Critics say that these networks are underused. In the past, Robert Taylor (1987) found two primary weaknesses in U.S. systems: (1) Intelligence is not properly analyzed, and (2) agencies do not coordinate information. Today, critics say the same thing. They feel that information sharing is recommended on the highest levels, but it does not take place (Nilson and Burke, 2002).

ANOTHER PERSPECTIVE

Information for Planning

- List available resources.
- Project potential attacks.
- Identify critical infrastructures.

Factors influencing plans, including

- emergency command structures
- coordination among agencies

- mass casualties
- victim and family support
- preservation of evidence
- crime scene management
- media relations
- costs
- training and preincident exercises

Source: International Association of Chiefs of Police, 2001.

intelligence-led policing: A type of law enforcement in which resources are deployed based on information gathered and analyzed from criminal intelligence.

Despite criticism, information sharing is growing into a law enforcement norm. The NCISP has been accepted at all levels of police administration. The systems created after 9/11, older systems such as RISS, fusion centers, and individual agency operations point to a new idea in law enforcement, **intelligence-led policing**. This concept is a continuation of community policing, in which police officers anticipate and solve community problems with citizens before an increase in crime and social disorder occurs. Community policing is based on information gathered from police–citizen partnerships, and intelligence-led policing systematically combines such information with other intelligence data from multiple sources. The purpose of intelligence-led policing is to redeploy resources in areas where they are most needed based on the analysis of criminal information (Duekmedjian, 2006).

David Carter (2004, pp. 39–54) sees intelligence-led policing as the logical outcome of the intelligence process. As police agencies adopted community policing strategies, officers developed skills in problem solving, building community partnerships, and gathering and analyzing the information needed to deal with crime and social problems in a local community. Citing the NCISP, Carter says that these skills have created a reliable and continuous flow of information between the community and the police. It is a gateway to the prevention of terrorism. Intelligence-led policing is an extension of this process. It not only prevents terrorism; it also becomes **total criminal intelligence (TCI)**, and it serves to prevent and address all problems in a community.

total criminal intelligence (TCI): All criminal intelligence gathered and analyzed for intelligence-led policing. Rather than focusing on one type of issue, such as terrorism, agencies focus on gathering information about all potential crimes and social problems.

Intelligence-led policing is part of a process to guide the deployment of law enforcement resources. Carter says that information from citizens defines the parameters of community problems. Law enforcement agencies need to provide information so that citizens can distinguish between normal and suspicious behavior. The law enforcement agencies are to organize community meetings and work with the community to gather information. In addition, they must communicate with the community, working with citizens and advising them of police policy for problems. In this model, the police are to serve as an extension of community needs while advising citizens on the issues that the police see as social problems. All data are scientifically analyzed to guide the distribution of law enforcement resources.

Intelligence-led policing, especially within the framework of counterterrorism, is not without its critics. Critics are afraid that information sharing will lead to massive databases on people who are not subject to criminal investigations. They also fear privacy violations as citizens share information, and they are afraid that anyone who casually encounters a known terrorist suspect will be labeled a terrorist supporter. Critics also say that intelligence-led policing may work in conjunction with national security intelligence gathering, and there will be no oversight of the collection, analysis, and storage of information. They also fear misguided profiling. For example, when a Muslim family moves into a non-Muslim neighborhood, citizens who see the practice of Islam as a suspicious behavior could discriminate against the family (Abramson and Godoy, 2006).

Self-Check

> How do diverse, independent law enforcement agencies assist with homeland security?
> Why is planning an important process in protecting both infrastructure and symbols?
> Explain intelligence-led policing and total criminal intelligence.

Perceived Weaknesses—9/11 to the present

In late 2002, President George W. Bush signed legislation that created a commission to investigate the attacks of September 11. The National Commission on Terrorist Attacks upon the United States, better known as 9/11 Commission, was charged with preparing an investigative report on the circumstances leading up to the attacks, an assessment of the response to the attacks, and recommendations for guarding against future attacks. Ten years later Congress assessed the state of intelligence. Their goal was not to evaluate the 9/11 Commission recommendations, but to assess DHS's capabilities and the information-sharing environment. Others have asked for a thorough assessment of homeland security. Findings reveal perceived weaknesses.

The 9/11 Commission Report Findings

The 9/11 Commission Report stated that the DOJ was geared to gather evidence, prosecute, and convict. It was not designed to look into additional intelligence after a verdict is rendered. DOJ's chief investigative arm, the FBI, measured success by crime rates, arrests, and crime clearances. It did an outstanding job when investigating terrorist incidents, but the bureau did not emphasize the role of intelligence gathering and analysis in order to prevent attacks. The commission criticized the FBI because:

• It did not place resources in intelligence gathering.
• The division established to analyze intelligence faltered.
• The bureau did not have an effective intelligence-gathering system.

Despite these views, the commission did not blame the FBI for all the intelligence failures. It stated that a series of rulings by the attorney general and mandates from Congress limited the FBI's ability to collect domestic intelligence. As a result, DOJ officials were confused about the relationship between criminal investigations and intelligence operations, and this resulted in a complete separation of the FBI's criminal and national security functions. The commission said that the separation was reinforced by several misinterpretations of the Foreign Intelligence Surveillance

Act of 1978 (FISA) by DOJ, the FBI, and the FISA court. (The FISA court approves warrants for surveillance under FISA.) These misinterpretations prevented intelligence agencies from sharing relevant information with FBI criminal investigators.

Other federal law enforcement agencies were not focused on terrorism. The commission pointed to cooperation between the FBI and other agencies in the Department of the Treasury, but agencies such as the Secret Service and ATF were only called in for limited participation in terrorism investigations. The JTTFs were excellent tools; however, they worked on a case-by-case basis under the direction of the commanders of the regional FBI offices. (This executive level of federal law enforcement is similar to a chief of police. The agent is called a Special Agent-in-Charge, or SAC.) State and local agencies were not even included in antiterrorist operations.

Other federal agencies were not directed toward terrorism. The Immigration and Naturalization Service focused on the southwestern U.S. border and did not have enough personnel to deal with terrorism. The Federal Aviation Administration (FAA) had layered defensive measures in place to gather intelligence, single out suspected terrorists, screen passengers, and provide in-flight procedures for emergencies at differing points in the security process. The FAA intelligence division was not adequately staffed, and its no-fly lists did not contain the names of terrorists known to other governmental agencies. Airport security screening performed poorly. In fact, the FAA rejected a ban on small knives, fearing screeners could not find them and searches would create congestion at screening areas. (The 9/11 hijackers used box cutters.) Procedures for in-flight emergencies did not include plans to counter suicide hijackers. The commission acknowledged some of the circumstances surrounding air security. In defense of the FAA, the 9/11 Commission noted that hijackings had diminished for a decade and that they had not seemed to be an immediate threat (Figure 14.3).

The commission believed that America's multiple intelligence agencies did not see the attack coming because of the way the intelligence bureaucracy was structured.

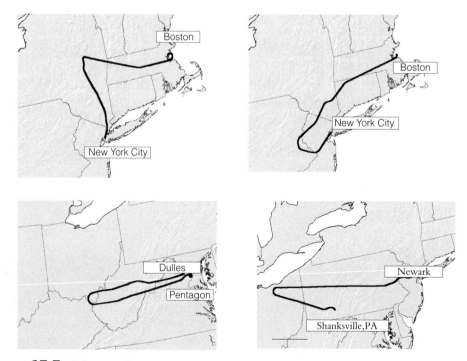

FIGURE **13.3** Flights on 9/11

Source: 9/11 Commission Report

Intelligence agencies, in general, were not prepared to deal with terrorism; the intelligence community remained geared to fight the cold war. The commission criticized the executive branch of government because there was no overall director of intelligence. In addition, intelligence operations were hampered by reduced resources. American universities did not produce scholars with in-depth knowledge of jihadist issues and appropriate foreign-language capabilities.

The findings also pointed to the Department of State. The State Department had lost much of its ability to establish foreign policy because foreign policy planning had been shifting to the National Security Council (NSC) and the DOD since 1960. Former Secretary of State Warren Christopher tried to lump counterterrorism into drug and crime control but was prevented from doing so by Congress. The screening system for visas was full of holes.

The DOD sought to deter terrorism by retaliating against acts of terrorism with limited air strikes. Its record of internal competition among the Army, Navy, Air Force, and Marines for resources, as well as a poor response record for dealing with terrorism, did not prepare the DOD for dealing with unconventional threats. The limited air-strike policy was not effective against a loosely bound international terrorist organization. The DOD needed more intelligence resources and greater flexibility in unconventional operations.

Congress received special attention. The commission said that Congress bore much of the responsibility for the state of affairs in government. It had failed to create an effective mechanism for protecting the country. It had maintained a large bureaucracy with ineffective oversight and communication. Among the issues noted by the 9/11 Commission were the following:

- There were too many committees overseeing intelligence.
- Like the intelligence community, Congress was structured for a cold war enemy.
- Congressional priorities were in areas other than terrorism.
- Congress was slow to react to terrorism and favored local domestic issues over those of national security.

The 9/11 Commission (2004, pp. 340–344) points out that it was easy to develop this critique with hindsight. As the jihadist network developed, only a few people, such as Dale Watson of the FBI and Richard Clarke of the White House staff, were focused on counterterrorism. American institutions and, more important, the American people were not overly concerned with jihadist terrorism. As the jihadist network grew, Americans looked the other way.

The 9/11 Commission Report Intelligence Recommendations

The 9/11 Commission Report (2004, pp. 399–428) suggested several reforms for restructuring government in the wake of the September 11 attacks, and the recommendations became law in December 2004. The recommendations focused on defense, intelligence, information sharing, homeland security, and law enforcement. The most sweeping recommendation came with the creation of a national intelligence director. The 9/11 Commission suggested the following reforms:

1. Create a National Counterterrorism Center.
2. Create a director of national intelligence to oversee intelligence gathering and all the agencies involved in national defense intelligence.
3. Refocus the CIA. Reporting to the director of national intelligence, the CIA director should
   a. Build the analysis capability of the CIA.
   b. Increase information gathered from people.
   c. Develop extensive language capabilities.

    d. Recruit from diverse groups in order to have agents who can blend in with a variety of cultures.

    e. Establish routine communications with other agencies.

4. Paramilitary operations should move to Special Operations in the Defense Department.

    a. Covert operations should move to the Defense Department.

    b. Northern Command should assume responsibility for military threats against the United States.

5. Make the intelligence budget public.

6. Demand that agencies share information.

7. Streamline and strengthen congressional oversight of intelligence and homeland security.

8. Accelerate the appointment of national security administrators during presidential transitions.

9. Introduce new structures in the FBI.

    a. Create career paths for agents and others assigned to intelligence and national security.

    b. Create a culture of cross-fertilization between criminal justice and national defense.

    c. Restructure the budget to emphasize (1) intelligence, (2) counterterrorism and counterintelligence, (3) law enforcement, and (4) criminal justice services.

10. The Department of Homeland Security should

    a. assess threats.

    b. develop and test emergency plans.

    c. protect critical infrastructure.

    d. create a system for response to threats and attacks.

Criticism of the Commission's Recommendation

Critics maintain that the 9/11 Commission did not possess the expertise to reform the homeland security system. Judge Richard A. Posner (2004) argues that the 9/11 Commission Report presents two competing parts. The first, he writes, is an excellent step-by-step analysis of the events that led up to the attacks on September 11 and an explanation of actions after the terrorists struck. The second part of the report is a series of recommendations. Posner says that he paused when he encountered the recommendations because the policies and directions the commission suggested were not altogether consistent with the analysis of the first part of the report.

Posner suggests that the FBI's record of combating terrorism was poor, and restructuring may not improve its capabilities. Combining 17 different intelligence agencies designed to do everything from launching spy satellites to gathering criminal information is illogical, he says. The agencies exist for different reasons and are responsible for different tasks. The national intelligence director, who is supposed to manage the new conglomerated menagerie of agencies, will spend most of his or her time dealing with arguments among the intelligence community, the DOJ, and the secretary of defense. Posner writes that in the aftermath of September 11, governmental agencies have an incentive to work together, but restructuring the bureaucracy will not automatically make the United States safer.

Congressional Review

Rather than focusing on 9/11, Congress reviewed the general state of homeland security a decade later (Meehan, 2012). Testimony in a congressional investigation revealed several concerns with the system. While most of the representatives and witnesses seemed to agree that all levels of law enforcement should gather and share information within the nation's fusion centers, they were unsure about outcomes. In essence, they did not think they could determine if the homeland security network was working and whether or not law enforcement agencies were sharing information. The main problems were lack of assessment and protection of personal privacy.

Discussions revealed that the DHS did not have valid measurements to determine the efficiency of information sharing. The rhetoric was there, but the tools were not. Further, there was a lack of evidence demonstrating the effectiveness of fusions centers, the intelligence community, and the homeland security partnerships. Assessment measures also failed to reveal whether agencies were actually sharing information, and if they were doing so, what amount of intelligence they were sharing. Finally, DHS lacked effective measures to demonstrate that personal privacy was being protected. These issues are discussed in more detail in the next two chapters.

Academic Research

Some academic research reveals criticism similar to the congressional inquiry. Robert Taylor and Amanda Russell (2012) state that the NCISP was essentially a reaction to 9/11 and that it outlined the theoretical plan for developing and utilizing law enforcement intelligence in the wake of disaster. They also agree with Meehan's committee. There is no evidence to show that it is working. Their report goes a step further, suggesting that the nature of the NCISP is at odds with the mission of law enforcement. Indeed, the structure of American law enforcement is based on autonomy and the self-established goals of individual agencies. In other words, chiefs and sheriffs have little incentive to surrender their political authority maintained by the control of information to centralized authority. Again, this is discussed in the next chapter in an analysis of law enforcement bureaucracy.

Torin Monahan and Neal Palmer (2009) also have concerns. They argue that fusion centers have three weaknesses. First, not only is there a lack of evidence demonstrating the efficacy of fusion centers; their research shows the homeland security system is ineffective and expensive. Second, the expansion of responsibility from terrorism prevention to dealing with all hazards represents a task beyond law enforcement's mission. Finally, the massive amount of information centralized in fusion centers threatens civil liberties.

Not all criticism is quite so stinging. Brandon Kramb (2011) is critical of the fusion center mission, *if* it lacks efficacy. His study of a fusion center in Michigan measures the effectiveness of intelligence returned to the field against the goals of intelligence-led policing. If the system is effective, Kramb argues, data should demonstrate greater arrest and clearance rates for criminal activity. He also explored the relationship between the level of crime and the amount of intelligence returned to the field. Agencies utilizing intelligence should be more effective in solving crime and community problems. If the claims of fusion centers are correct, intelligence might also be related to a reduction in crime. Kramb concludes that there is not enough data in Michigan. It was not possible to determine whether the system was working or not.

Intelligence Reform

The *Washington Post* (Priest and Arkin, 2010) ran a series of articles critiquing the intelligence community in the summer of 2010. The project involved a dozen journalists doing research over a two-year period. The *Post* found that the intelligence community had grown so large that no one could account for its costs. In fact, the number of people involved in intelligence and the number of agencies doing the same work were also unknown. It found that over 3,000 public and private organizations operated counterterrorism-related programs at 10,000 locations across the United States. The number of top secret security clearances, numbering about 854,000 people, was astounding. Over 50,000 intelligence reports were published each year, and no one agency had the authority to manage the overall operation. A panel of experts (*Washington Post*, 2010) concluded that the massive endeavor was unmanaged, ineffective, and operated with no clear lines of authority. Its worst characteristic was that the intelligence community did not produce credible information about potential threats.

Moving in the Right Direction?

Nancy Tucker (2008), a former executive in the intelligence community and now a professor at Georgetown University, suggests that the failure of intelligence analysis is evidenced by two factors: the surprise attacks of September 11 and the analysis of the WMD program in Iraq. Congress created the ODNI to address such flaws. The ODNI was intended to be a vehicle for continuous reform, an organization to prevent bureaucratic goal displacement and organizational stagnation; however, its massive restructuring met all types of resistance. First, many people believed that the efficiency and methods of the intelligence community needed to be improved. Restructuring created another level of bureaucracy, but it did not address the need for accuracy and efficiency. Second, the new organization confused traditional lines of authority. Specifically, the director of the CIA was to be the one person who could synthesize information and present an apolitical, objective assessment of data to the executive branch of government.

Tucker, however, believes that the reorganization of intelligence under the ODNI has signaled the beginning of improvement. The ODNI is able to balance the needs for information of all the intelligence agencies. In the past, the CIA director performed this function but was always forced to guard the interests of the CIA. The ODNI is able to avoid this bureaucratic pitfall, producing a better balance in analyzed information. The ODNI has also been able to attack the problem of **group think** by placing analysts in critical thinking training during the first stages of their careers.

group think: Refers to a bureaucratic process in which members of a group work together to solve a problem; however, innovation and deviant ideas are discouraged as the group tries to seek consensus about a conclusion. Powerful members of the group may quash alternative voices. Intelligence groups tend to resist making any risky conclusion lest they jeopardize their individual careers. Peer pressure creates an atmosphere in which every individual comes to the same conclusion.

Even with the initial success, she says, the new structure has just barely started the reforms needed to improve the intelligence community. Tucker argues that because Congress created the ODNI, it is therefore responsible for cleaning its own house. The number of committees and budgetary authority lines from Congress is astronomical. Congress needs to streamline its process, and it needs to be assertive. It is difficult to balance the tasks of intelligence gathering within a democracy, especially when the intelligence community is looking at individuals rather than competing nation-states. Congress needs to assert its authority and rigorously review and restrict intelligence activities. In addition, a single National Intelligence University should be created to train all analysts from every agency. Specific agency training, she says, narrows the scope of analysis and creates a culture that reinforces loyalty to a particular agency. Another needed reform is to base intelligence gathering and analysis techniques on success. Procedures should be based on methods that work. Tucker believes that all analysis should be based on evidence that the outcome is successful. Finally, the intelligence community needs to reach out to nontraditional venues. There are many institutions that have tremendous analytical capabilities, but the intelligence community ignores them. For example, international retail outlets gather tremendous amounts of information, but they are ignored by government.

Tucker concludes that the system of classifying information, the process of making information secret, can be unreasonable. This happens in two primary ways.

First, political actors may classify information to defend their political position. For example, a president can classify information that would be harmful to his party's political position even though the information has nothing to do with national security. Second, bureaucracies hold classified information for power. Overabundant secrecy and manipulation of "need-to-know" information creates power structures among law enforcement and intelligence agencies. Although not cited by Tucker, almost any law enforcement officer who has worked closely with the FBI knows how an agency can hoard information. Information, Tucker says, should be developed and shared to produce outcomes. Classification should be designed to protect sources, not information. Almost all the information is in the public realm anyway.

Redirecting the Focus of Reform

Uri Bar-Joseph and Rose McDermott (2008) suggest that the problem in intelligence is not the structure of the system; the problem can be found with individual analysts. Official intelligence investigations into shortcomings tend to focus on structures and organization, so they miss this point. Certain types of personalities, Bar-Joseph and McDermott argue, are more prone to fall prey to making erroneous judgments. Some people have traits that influence their ability to objectively analyze information. Personality assessment tests are able to screen people for these tendencies, and intelligence agencies should spend more time examining and selecting analysts.

Bar-Joseph and McDermott base their argument on psychological assessment techniques that have been developed over the past 50 years. It is important to identify biases that an analyst brings to the job to help to ensure that internal prejudices do not filter the information under review. Psychological assessments can determine which people would discount information not contained in their personal experiences and which people would interpret ambiguous circumstances only within the framework of previous understandings. Both of these traits create an internal circle; that is, new information is interpreted within existing understandings of reality, discounting any new possibility. When this happens, analysts develop conclusions that they expected to find in the first place. This type of reasoning is susceptible to group think, where groups of similar individuals join together to reinforce their own erroneous conclusions. This leads to a three-part pattern: (1) There is new information about a surprise activity before a terrorist attack develops, (2) analysts ignore new information and focus on their previous experiences with terrorism, and (3) the real-life outcome is a surprise. This is reinforced by a bureaucratic tendency to avoid taking risks. When respected peer group members suggest that information be interpreted in a particular manner, it is difficult to go against the current.

Bar-Joseph and McDermott say that there was tremendous pressure to reform the intelligence community after 9/11, and these calls for reform fell into two broad categories. One approach called for comprehensive reform of the intelligence system. This resulted in the formation of the ODNI and a reshuffling of the agencies of the intelligence community. This approach was also responsible for the reasoning behind the creation of the DHS. The second part of the debate focused on reforming the specific components of the system. This type of reform suggested that analysts develop their material as a product for a consumer. Under this model, the intelligence community is like a business producing goods that consumers want to purchase. Unfortunately, the consumer model sometimes creates a product for a consumer looking for evidence to support a particular position. This distorts objective intelligence. For example, in the Bush administration, some political actors wanted to find WMD in Iraq. Analysts, designing information for the consumer, pointed to where the weapons might be even though the WMD threat never existed.

The key to reform, Bar-Joseph and McDermott conclude, is to shift the unit of analysis away from organizational structures and consumer-driven intelligence products. The entire system needs independent minds that will look at new ways of interpreting data and that will challenge established methods of interpretation. The authors argue that psychological assessment during the selection process will help agencies find the types of people who think in this manner. This change will produce a new method of selecting, training, and promoting analysts. It will also provide, they believe, better information and fewer surprises.

Target-Based Analysis

John Gentry (2008) suggests that the current spate of reform is part of an American tradition. The literature of American intelligence is replete with examples of failures to predict significant events and reform efforts to overcome deficiencies. Gentry believes that most current efforts will fail because they are misdirected. The bureaucracies in the intelligence community have a tremendous stake in preserving the status quo, and employees in each organization believe that they will be blamed for misinterpreting information. This produces a culture that avoids risk taking and reinforces group think.

Reform, if and when it develops, is laboriously slow. Gentry concludes that the intelligence process will work better if local domestic issues and vulnerabilities are lessened. This is based on two questions: What targets are vulnerable? What capabilities exist to address threats? As David Carter (2004) concludes, intelligence works best when information is based on potential threats and there is a sharing of the information among differing levels of government.

Self-Check

> Why is the intelligence and homeland security process so confused?
> What reform efforts look promising?
> How might a focus on both analysts and local targeting issues improve intelligence?

CHAPTER TAKE AWAYS

Homeland security involves a variety of activities at all levels of government, law enforcement agencies, the military, intelligence agencies, and the private sector. Preventing terrorism is the result of gathering and analyzing information. This is accomplished under two sets of laws, one guiding criminal intelligence and the other focused on national security. While this is extremely complicated, the NCISP has provided guidelines and standards for combing the intelligence process. This takes place in 72 regional fusion centers. Homeland security is ever-changing, and the intelligence process must be continually reviewed and changed to meet new threats.

OBJECTIVE SUMMARY

- Americans define *homeland security* in several different ways. It has a variety of meanings to different government agencies, private organizations, and interest groups. The best way to define it is to look at the mission of each particular agency dealing with homeland security.
- After 9/11, several federal agencies were tasked with homeland security. The Departments of Homeland Security, Justice, and Defense have major roles in preventing terrorism. The intelligence community contributes to counterterrorism, and there is a major role for state, local, and tribal law enforcement to play.
- The intelligence process is very close to basic and applied academic research. It involves the legal recognition, collection, analysis, and distribution of information. *Intelligence* is "analyzed information."

- It is important to understand the legal differences between criminal intelligence and national security intelligence when using information. National security intelligence is not meant to be used in criminal prosecutions.
- The International Association of Chiefs (IACP) of police created a committee to develop national standards for criminal intelligence. This resulted in the National Criminal Intelligence Sharing Plan (NCISP). The Department of Justice created the Global Justice Information Sharing Coordinating Council (Global) to address the problems inherent in sharing information among multiple levels of law enforcement.
- Fusion centers developed from Regional Intelligence Centers. The Department of Homeland Security expanded their operations after the 9/11 attacks. Fusion centers take criminal intelligence from multiple sources and blend or "fuse" it together to create a real-time picture of criminal activity. They can also forward national security intelligence without using it in criminal prosecutions.
- Law enforcement has a leading role in homeland security because of its presence in communities and its ability to gather information. Model systems for information gathering can be found in the NJSP and the NYPD. There are several excellent federal networks such as RISS and HSIN. The HIDTA system and EPIC assist in distributing antiterrorism intelligence even though they were designed for drug interdiction. Federal law enforcement agencies and several units in the Department of Homeland Security also gather and analyze information.
- There are several important issues for homeland security. Law enforcement has a special role in terms of recognizing possible terrorist activity and coordinating preventive measures from multiple community partnerships. Planning is a crucial part of the process. While the infrastructure is critical, symbolic targets also have a special significance. Finally, all partners responsible for homeland security must create a culture of information sharing.
- The 9/11 Commission summarized the events that led to the September 11 attacks and recommended a response. Its recommendations included sweeping reforms in the intelligence community, the creation of a national director of intelligence, new roles for the FBI, greater cooperation among law enforcement agencies, increased domestic security safeguards, and reformed congressional oversight. Both governmental and academic critiques question whether this has happened.
- While intelligence has received quite a bit of attention since 9/11, there are areas where it can be improved. The goal of creating a safe homeland should guide intelligence efforts. Analysts must be trained to recognize broad patterns. Finally, intelligence must be based on threats to known or suspected targets.

Critical Engagement: Intelligence Bureaucracies and the Future

Law enforcement and intelligence bureaucracies thrive on information. Control of information represents organizational power, and it creates a path for personal success. In addition, individuals inside each organization have personal rivalries, informal friendship groups, and people they dislike. These internal factors are compounded by external ones. Agency executives have the same types of feelings toward their friends and foes in other agencies. In theory, everyone is supposed to be professional and act as if they are cool, rational bureaucrats. In practice, groups operate in ways that managerial literature has described for years. They cooperate within informal friendship and communication networks. This means that information is not always managed properly and is not always shared.

The number of private think tanks, not-for-profit organizations, and government contracting agencies has grown since 9/11. These companies frequently compete for government projects, and the livelihood of their employees depends on their ability to obtain government money. They have no incentive to share information with other companies, and they want to manage information given to the government. For example, if a company has a contract with a government agency, the incentive is to provide the best possible product with the least amount of sharing of information. In other words, it makes sense to impress the government agency with results but to leave the agency wanting even more products or information. This helps to ensure future contracts. Private organizations have monetary incentives for controlling information.

Political actors have a large stake in the process. This can include keeping information secret when it would damage a political party or even classifying information if a law has been broken. Theoretically, Congress has the power to regulate the information process, but, as noted by the 9/11 Commission, it has a plethora of redundant oversight and budgetary committees. The problem has been exacerbated during the past two decades by heated diatribes between Republicans and Democrats and an unwillingness to work together for compromise. It is no wonder that scholars like John Gentry look at intelligence reform efforts with a hefty dose of skepticism.

Despite these issues, bureaucracies are able to get results in times of national crisis. For example, the United States had almost no army when it entered World War I in April 1917; yet it fielded a massive force that turned the tide on the Western Front. Today, there exist a multitude of competing bureaucracies, yet many critical pieces of information are processed and shared. Granted that sometimes the country just gets lucky, but intelligence gathering and sharing has stopped a number of domestic and international terrorist attacks. The process may not be efficient, but it works more often than it fails. The problem in terrorism is that the government needs to be correct 100 percent of the time. Terrorists only need to succeed once.

Consider these issues in terms of future developments:

- How can managers create environments in which people are rewarded for sharing information? How would this work inside an agency? among agencies? among differing levels of government? Should the federal government create single law enforcement and intelligence agencies?
- Private contractors are forced to compete with one another. This means that they must produce a product in a market environment. How can this hinder—or help—the analysis of information?
- How might the ODNI be used to create cooperative intelligence systems? What impact would this have on providing a direction for homeland security?

KEY TERMS

Department of Homeland Security (DHS), p. 13-334
Civil defense, p. 13-336
Federal Law Enforcement Training Center (FLETC), p. 13-338
National security intelligence, p. 13-341
Criminal intelligence, p. 13-341

COINTELPRO, p. 13-342
National Criminal Intelligence Sharing Plan (NCISP), p. 13-344
Regional Information Sharing System (RISS), p. 13-344
Fusion centers, p. 13-344

Regional Intelligence Centers, p. 13-345
High Intensity Drug Trafficking Area, p. 13-345
Regional Crime Gun Centers (RCGC), p. 13-345
Intelligence product, p. 13-346

Total criminal intelligence (TCI), p. 13-346
Symbolic targets, p. 13-350
Intelligence-led policing, p. 13-352
Total criminal intelligence (TCI), p. 13-352
Group think, p. 13-358

CHAPTER 14

Law Enforcement and Homeland Security

Jeff Greenberg/Alamy

LEARNING OBJECTIVES

After reading this chapter you should be able to:

> Outline law enforcement's bureaucratic challenge.

> Explain the ways homeland security represents Weberian bureaucracy.

> Summarize bureaucratic issues within criminal and national security intelligence agencies.

> Explain issues involved in border protection.

> Discuss the ways the immigration debate impacts homeland security.

> Define and describe infrastructure protection.

> Describe the need for partnerships in homeland security.

> Summarize the critical bureaucratic issues in law enforcement partnerships.

> Outline Flynn's recommendations for effective homeland security.

> Explain how the Joint Terrorism Task Force (JTTF) arrangement might become a model for law enforcement partnerships.

Sometimes a problem can be more complex than it seems. In other cases, a simple problem can become complex because of the way it is handled. Regardless of complexity, logical steps can be taken to face simple and difficult issues in large organizations. It is necessary to define the problem and determine what needs to be done to control it. Once the process for controlling the problem is identified, it needs to be adopted in a policy. In turn, the policy must be reasonable and acceptable. The people responsible for controlling the problem should be trained in the policy and given the tools necessary to implement it. Managers should oversee the implementation of the policy and evaluate it to determine if it provides the intended solution. If it does, the policy should be continued. If it does not, the policy should be modified or a new solution should be implemented.

According to an editorial in the *Los Angeles Times* (2011), federal bureaucracies were in disarray in December 2011 over an important issue that had implications for justice, individual rights, immigration, and homeland security. Sexual assaults in federal prisons were a national problem. Congress became aware of the problem and passed the Rape Elimination Act in 2003. Officials from the U.S. Bureau of Prisons (BOP) conferred with their superiors at the Department of

Justice (DOJ) and developed policies for controlling sexual assault based on the new law. They began implementing the policies according to the mandate from Congress. Then the problem became more complex.

Hundreds of immigrants are held in federal detention facilities. BOP and DOJ officials asked Congress if the new laws applied to these units. The Democrat and Republican co-sponsors of the bill said they did. BOP began to implement the policy in the detention centers, but things came to a halt in late 2011. The Department of Homeland Security (DHS) informed BOP that detention centers were controlled by DHS. As a result, DOJ and DHS began to argue about control. The *Los Angeles Times* editorial complained that the Obama administration was doing nothing to resolve the problem. Such behavior is common when bureaucracies collide.

The Challenge of Bureaucracy

Presentations on information sharing, interagency cooperation, and shared responsibilities abound at conferences of chiefs and sheriffs on the national, state, and local levels. Federal law enforcement executives give speeches laced with references to classified, official, and law enforcement–sensitive information. They pledge to support new bureaucracies designed to share information, and chiefs and sheriffs respond with promises to cooperate in a spirit of seamless interface with their federal partners. Law enforcement agencies have a national plan to share criminal intelligence and new bureaucracies, such as the National Counterterrorism Center, to ensure this will happen. Unfortunately, when everybody goes back to work, they are faced with the realities of organizational management, personal and interagency rivalries, and a host of individualized problems. Homeland security depends on the relationships among thousands of state, local, and tribal law enforcement agencies and the ways they interact with dozens of federal law enforcement and intelligence organizations.

In the realm of terrorism and homeland security, the primary role of law enforcement is prevention. To fulfill their role, every agency involved in homeland security must deal with organization. The creation of the Department of Homeland Security (DHS) involved one of the most massive reorganizations of government in American history. It combined several agencies, ranging from the Secret Service to the Coast Guard. DHS is responsible for protecting almost every facet of American life, but it must coordinate its activities with other federal agencies. It has its own intelligence analysts and capabilities, as do the other federal bureaucracies. DHS also coordinates activities with thousands of other organizations on state, local, and tribal levels as well as in the private sector. Every law enforcement agency—from part-time, one-person police departments to the FBI—has some role in homeland security. All of the roles and relationships must be negotiated among competing bureaucracies.

Control and Cooperation

The federal government undertook massive reforms and reorganizations from 2002 to 2005 in the wake of 9/11. Some officials and terrorism specialists applaud these actions (see Jenkins, 2006). Others say it has not gone far enough (see Flynn, 2004a, 2004b). Still others say that homeland security cannot be tackled until Congress reforms its oversight function and places homeland security under a single committee. Currently, a variety of Senate and House committees are responsible for different aspects of homeland security. Critics believe that the organizational problems involving federal, state, local, and tribal law enforcement cannot be handled

bureaucracy: Governmental, private-sector, and nonprofit organizations. It assumes that people organize in a hierarchy to create an organization that will solve problems.

until the nation's lawmakers restructure their own lawmaking **bureaucracy** (Meese, Robb; Abshire, 2005). There are literally thousands of law enforcement organizations in the United States, and they need to form partnerships with each of tens of thousands of business and community organizations if law enforcement is to have an effective role in homeland security.

The federal government cannot assume that the reforms will carry over into state and local governments. The states may cooperate with the federal government, but they are not mandated to do so. The states and their local governments have entrenched bureaucracies with their own managerial structures and agendas. These organizations will not suddenly change methods of operation simply because centralized executive authority has mandated new policies for homeland defense. In a nutshell, this is the essence of the bureaucratic challenge; yet it does not imply that state and local governments will automatically reject chances to participate. Change can happen, and may even be welcomed, if federal agencies enter into cooperative relationships with their local counterparts (Liptak, 2002; for classic studies see Downs, 1967; Warwick, 1975).

Some advocates believe federal reform has begun. A 1995 attempt to reduce paperwork in the federal government is one example. An earlier effort came in the **1978 Civil Service Reform Act**, which gave special executives managerial authority and placed them in performance-based positions. The most recent overhaul of the federal bureaucracy came with the **Government Management Reform Act of 1994**.

1978 Civil Service Reform Act: A federal law designed to prevent political interference with the decisions and actions of governmental organizations.

Government Management Reform Act of 1994: A federal law designed to prevent political interference in the management of federal governmental organizations and to increase the efficiency of management.

Nevertheless, managing homeland security will still require attention to the issues raised in this chapter. Large organizations are difficult to manage, and problems increase rapidly when organizational effectiveness requires cooperation on several levels. Homeland security calls for new alliances among federal agencies and cooperative relations among local, state, and federal levels of government. All of the issues interact with law enforcement agencies.

If the Department of Homeland Security (DHS) can create effective partnerships with intelligence and law enforcement agencies on the federal level, it could focus attention on these issues. However, in addition to thwarting an attack, homeland security has a duty much larger than merely gathering and analyzing information—responding to events. That is a subject beyond the scope of this book. Response involves massive coordination among agencies. Fortunately, all levels of government have extensive experience in this realm. The difficulty is *preventing* terrorism. Prevention requires bureaucratic change, and powerful bureaucrats and bureaucratic procedures do not change easily.

Scholars who study organizational management have suggested that terrorism presents exceptional emergency situations, but the bureaucracies established to deal with the problem are focused on routine. This can be overcome if organizational leaders focus their attention on exceptions and gather key lower-level managers to join them in solving the problem. The key challenge is to develop structures designed to deal with fluid emergency situations rather than to treat emergencies as disruptions to routine activities (May, Workman, and Jones, 2009). This reflects the ideal projection of bureaucracy: a group of workers focused on solving a critical problem. A famed German sociologist projected this model in the nineteenth century.

Max Weber: (1864–1920) One of the major figures of modern sociological methods, he studied the organization of human endeavors. Weber believed that social organizations could be organized for rational purposes designed to accomplish objectives.

The Weberian Ideal

If you have studied public administration, you have most likely encountered the classic works on bureaucracy. **Max Weber** (1864–1920), one of the founding masters of sociology, coined the term *bureaucracy* to describe professional, rational organizations. For Weber, every aspect of organizational structure was to be aimed at rationally achieving a goal. In other words, people organize for a purpose and their organization should accomplish that purpose.

For example, if your purpose is to keep dirt from washing over an embankment, you gather people who know how to channel dirt. You then select managers who know how to get people to accomplish the task. People who assist in managing are selected because they know how to manage people who can do the job. Managers impersonally direct the organization to build walls, dig trenches, and change drainage patterns. The managers use only people who can accomplish assigned tasks. They do not favor friends, relatives, or tradition. They avoid people who attract others through charisma. When the task is finished, dirt no longer washes over the embankment. The process is rational: There is a problem, people organize to solve it, they work together, and the problem is solved. Weber believed that impersonal, professional human groups (bureaucracies) converge to solve the problems of society. Weber argued that bureaucracy should be designed to accomplish specific purposes.

In Weber's ideal, labor is to be divided into specific functional areas, or bureaus, and all the bureaus of the organization are to assemble logically to produce the whole. The bureaus work together to produce a logical outcome. Management in the organization is rationally oriented and devoid of friendship, family, or political influences. Modern bureaucratic management ideally comes from leaders who excel at leadership. There is no place for inherited leadership or popularly elected managers in Weber's bureaucracy. Every aspect of the organization centers on rational efficiency (Weber, 1947).

More than a century has passed since Weber first outlined the field that would become known as bureaucratic organizational theory. To be sure, hundreds of other scholars have filled myriad books with organizational theories. These works range from highly theoretical psychological treatises to practical business administration guides. The sheer number of these tracts indicates that running an organization is a complicated affair, and the larger and more complex the organization becomes, the more difficult it is to manage.

Bureaucracy and Preventing Terrorism

There are two views concerning the expanded homeland security bureaucracy. Supporters of one position maintain that consolidating power is efficient. They argue that a large bureaucracy with a clear mission will empower the security forces to perform their mission. The decision to create DHS was based on this idea (Office of Homeland Security, 2002). Proponents of the second position suggest that decentralizing power personalizes services and helps develop links to communities. They believe localized, informal offices are more adept at recognizing and handling problems. Support for this position can be found among those who seek to trim the homeland defense concept and those who favor limiting the involvement of state and local governments in a larger organization (see *Another Perspective: Taking Aim at Bureaucracy*). Although both ideas appear to be new in the wake of September 11, they are actually part of a long-time, ongoing debate.

Intelligence and Bureaucracy

The role of law enforcement and intelligence in homeland security is not exempt from the issues surrounding bureaucracy. Whether federal, state, or local, bureaucratic police work is a political process occurring in the context of official, routine procedures. Intelligence agencies, whether involved with the military or not, face the same problems. Both intelligence-gathering and law enforcement organizations operate within the American political system. They reflect governmental power, and their actions have political ramifications. Internally, conflicts arise from personal rivalries, territorial fights, and power struggles. They are as much a part of these services as they are in any organization (Gaines and Cordner, 1999, pp. 179–180; see also Walker, 1992).

ANOTHER PERSPECTIVE

Taking Aim at Bureaucracy

Critics level harsh attacks against public bureaucracies, making the following points:

- Bureaucracies work toward stagnation. Innovation, creativity, and individuality are discouraged.
- Career bureaucrats are rewarded with organizational power. Therefore, they look for activities that provide organizational power instead of solutions to problems.
- Public bureaucracies do not face competition.
- Within a bureaucracy, it is better to make a safe decision than the correct decision.

- Bureaucratic organizations protect themselves when threatened by outside problems.
- Bureaucrats postpone decisions under the guise of gathering information.
- Policies and procedures are more important than outcomes in bureaucracies.
- Centralized bureaucracy increases paperwork.
- As bureaucracies grow, simple problems result in complex solutions.

Whether or not you agree with these criticisms, consider this question: Is there an alternative to classic bureaucracy when organizing state and local police for homeland defense?

National Counterterrorism Center (NCTC): An organization designed to filter information from the intelligence process, synthesize counterterrorist information, and share it with appropriate organizations.

Homeland security involves the use of intelligence and law enforcement. The Bush Administration argued that counterterrorism is mainly a military problem. In the United States, however, the lead agency for counterterrorism is the FBI (Best, 2001). The FBI has several charges in this realm. First, under Director Robert Mueller, its charge is to prevent terrorism. Second, it is to coordinate intelligence-gathering and intelligence-sharing activities with the Border Patrol, Secret Service, and CIA. Third, it is to operate as a partner of state and local law enforcement. Finally, because the FBI is in the Department of Justice (DOJ), it is to coordinate its activities with DHS and the Department of Defense (DOD). Under the intelligence reform law of 2004, all intelligence coordination must take place in the **National Counterterrorism Center (NCTC)** (U.S. Congress, 2004).

This face of homeland security involves a new role for the CIA. When it was originally established at the end of World War II, the CIA was supposed to be the agency that would coordinate all U.S. intelligence data, but the head of the agency, as director of central intelligence, never received the political authority to consolidate the information-gathering power. In addition, the CIA was to operate apart from U.S. criminal law and was not officially allowed to collect data on Americans inside the United States (Best, 2001). Today, the situation is somewhat modified. Chastised

ANOTHER PERSPECTIVE

DHS and Intelligence

The Department of Homeland Security has a large intelligence section, but its effectiveness is open to question. Several factors plague DHS intelligence:

1. It is relatively powerless in the intelligence community.
2. DHS does not maintain terrorist watch lists.

Source: Rood, 2004.

3. The CIA has the leading role at the National Counterterrorism Center (NCTC), formerly the Terrorist Threat Integration Center.
4. The CIA and FBI compile the president's daily intelligence briefing.
5. DHS intelligence has been slow to develop its mission.

by public outcry and by the 9/11 Commission, and with formal orders from the president, the CIA is to cooperate fully with the FBI on counterterrorism intelligence (Office of Homeland Security, 2002; Baginski, 2004). The FBI and CIA are to work jointly on intelligence gathering and sharing inside and outside America's borders.

The DHS was created from the Office of Homeland Security in 2003 and charged with counterterrorism. DHS includes law enforcement agencies, such as the Secret Service, the Border Patrol, the new Immigration and Customs Enforcement (ICE), the U.S. Customs Service, and other agencies. It has its own military force, the U.S. Coast Guard, which has limited law enforcement power. DHS is responsible for port security and transportation systems. It manages security in airports through the massive Transportation Security Administration. It has its own intelligence section (see *Another Perspective: DHS and Intelligence*), and it covers every special event in the United States, from political conventions to football games. It is clearly the largest organization involved in homeland security (DHS, 2004b).

The DOD has a limited but critical role in homeland security. Currently, the main military role in counterterrorism is to project American power overseas. DOD's military forces take the fight to terrorists in other lands, rather than letting terrorists become a problem within America's borders (Barnett, 2004, pp. 299–303). It also augments civilian defense and provides special operations capabilities. In some cases, military intelligence can also be used in counter-narcotics operations. Military forces can be used to protect the borders when ordered by the president.

This is an impressive array of American power. In theory, led by the FBI and the CIA, multiple agencies will work together to gain information, analyze it together, and share the results with every bureaucracy concerned with homeland security. *Cooperation* and *sharing* are the two buzzwords of the day. This is a charge not only to federal bureaucracies but to the FBI and CIA, which are to create a cooperative, sharing atmosphere with thousands of state and local law enforcement agencies. In addition, cooperation does not stop there. DHS calls on the entire system of homeland security bureaucracies to form relations with local communities and private industry. On paper, this is a massive force designed to stop terrorism and protect the United States of America.

The federal bureaucracy is massive, which presents a problem for agency cooperation. Yet the bigger challenge is in coordinating the thousands of state, local, and tribal law enforcement agencies in the United States. They form a network of potential sources of information, and their ability to function and cooperate is crucial to the homeland security mission. If terrorism can be envisioned as a network of terrorists and supporters fighting against a network of security-related agencies and the people they represent, then state, local, and tribal police agencies are a vital element of America's counterterrorist network (J. White, 2007).

Administrators at DHS, DOJ, the FBI, and the Office of the Director of National Intelligence have recognized the importance of state, local, and tribal law enforcement agencies and the value they bring to homeland security. One of the priorities of the federal government is creating a system where information can flow among the various levels of government, from and through America's police agencies. This is the major bureaucratic challenge facing law enforcement (Johnson, 2007).

State, Local, and Tribal Law Enforcement Bureaucracies

As discussed in Chapter 13, American policing is localized. With more than 800,000 state, local, and tribal law enforcement officers in the United States, agencies must cooperate to transform organizations. Any plan for changing so many bureaucracies must allow each agency to have the flexibility to change according to local demands. There are issues to overcome and partnerships with external agencies to be created, but it is not an impossible task. America's law enforcement agencies have overcome these problems to build systems in the past, and they can do the same thing in homeland security (see Bodrero, 2002).

The first issue to overcome is building a consensus among police agencies on the task to be accomplished. **Task orientation** will focus the actions of individual departments as they meet the homeland security needs within their communities. The task is to provide security. This is accomplished by **threat analysis**, information gathering, and information sharing. Individual tasks will vary. As Richard Marquise (2006, pp. 27–29) says, law enforcement tasks differ between Oklahoma City and New York City, but the mission remains the same. For law enforcement, the primary job is to prevent terrorism. Agencies need emergency service plans and comprehensive preparedness to respond to disasters, but their mission is to prevent attacks. When police officers become first responders, counterterrorism has failed.

Task orientation keeps law enforcement focused on the problem of preventing terrorism. By focusing on the goal, law enforcement agencies avoid three common bureaucratic problems: **goal displacement, mission creep,** and **process orientation.** Goal displacement happens when managers begin focusing on issues other than the purpose of the organization. For example, a good manager takes care of employee needs so that employees can accomplish their tasks. Goal displacement occurs if a manager emphasizes employee needs over a unit's purpose. Mission creep refers to adding too many secondary tasks to a group of workers assigned to an important task. Process orientation involves emphasizing the method of accomplishing a task over the completion of a job. All three problems divert a unit or organization from its goal. Unfortunately, these diversions are common at all levels of bureaucracy.

If multiple agencies are to focus on the task of preventing terrorism, then executives must buy into the concept. Chiefs, sheriffs, and directors set the administrative tone for their agencies. When groups of executives are oriented toward prevention, middle managers—captains and lieutenants—implement policies; sergeants, as first-line supervisors, ensure that the work takes place. Preventing terrorism becomes one of many emergency functions that state, local, and tribal law enforcement agencies handle. Homeland security transforms into routine police work (J. White, 2007).

Smith and Roberts (2005) demonstrate that terrorists engage in criminal activities before a planned attack. This gives local agencies an opportunity to prevent attacks. To accomplish this, officers need to become aware of the types of activities that take place before an attack. These are known as **pre-incident indicators**. The indicators for terrorism are known, but they are too sensitive to list in a college textbook. It is enough to be aware that they exist, that officers can learn to recognize them, and that terrorists can be stopped when law enforcement either makes arrests or gathers relevant information.

If terrorism prevention is to be successful on the local level, agencies must participate in systems. Once again, American police agencies have a history of doing this. The Law Enforcement Information Network (LEIN) links agencies to a host of bureaucracies to provide valuable information on everything from vehicle registrations to warrants. The National Crime Information Center (NCIC) maintains information on a nationwide basis. The systems discussed in the intelligence section of the preceding chapter, such as the Regional Information Sharing System (RISS), El Paso Intelligence Center (EPIC), and the numerous High Intensity Drug Trafficking Areas (HIDTAs), attest to the willingness of state, local, and tribal agencies to cooperate in regional and national networks.

Bureaucratic changes present challenges, but they also provide opportunities. Two recent national innovations demonstrate this, and both processes are crucial to homeland security. As discussed in Chapter 13, community policing changed the face of American law enforcement (Chermak and Weiss, 2006; Duekmedjian, 2006). It began as an idea and spread with support from the federal government, research from university criminal justice departments, creation of community associations

task orientation: As used in this text, the ability to stay focused on the primary mission of an organization.

threat analysis: The process of examining a community to determine the areas that might be subject to attack and the criticality of those areas to the functions of the community.

goal displacement: Favoring process over accomplishments. Process should be reasonable and efficient. Too much focus on the process, however, interferes with completion of job tasks.

mission creep: Adding too many secondary tasks to a unit. Too many jobs divert a unit from its primary mission.

process orientation: Paying more attention to the manner of achieving organizational goals than achieving them. Process is important when it focuses on ethical and legal requirements. Process orientation goes beyond legal and moral norms, and it becomes dysfunctional when an organization's goal is conceived as maintaining procedures.

pre-incident indicators: The criminal and social actions of individuals and groups before a terrorist attack.

and partnerships and regional organizations, and participation of law enforcement executives who oriented themselves to the task of increasing police effectiveness. Homeland security presents the same opportunity, and community police networks are ideal for the functions it requires.

The second recent innovation is the National Criminal Intelligence Sharing Plan (NCISP). The concept of information gathering, analysis, and sharing began with the Global Advisory Committee to the U.S. attorney general. It moved to a **working group** of executives from all levels of law enforcement. As the working group developed ideas for carrying the concept out, groups like the International Association of Chiefs of Police (IACP) reviewed and amended the recommendations. Like community policing, it was a national team effort of many different law enforcement agencies. When the NCISP was unveiled and endorsed by the IACP, a multitude of police agencies, law enforcement associations, intelligence organizations, and associated bureaucracies endorsed and adopted it.

The many different organizations that comprise state, local, and tribal law enforcement agencies face a daunting task in transforming bureaucracy, but preventing terrorism requires this transformation. The cooperative efforts of community policing and the NCISP indicate that local law enforcement bureaucracies can meet a challenge and even participate with multiple federal agencies. Such transformation can happen again as agencies develop homeland security missions. In fact, homeland security is an extension of what state, local, and tribal agencies are already doing (see Carter, 2004).

working group: A term used in the federal government for a group of subject matter experts who gather to suggest solutions to common problems.

ANOTHER PERSPECTIVE

Goals of the Working Group

The Global Intelligence Working Group created the National Criminal Intelligence Sharing Plan. It sought to create a system for state, local, and tribal law enforcement that would:

- become a model intelligence-sharing model for all agencies;
- support and promote intelligence-led policing;
- create a blueprint for enhancing or building an intelligence system;

- develop model policies;
- protect privacy and civil rights;
- create technologies for sharing of information;
- set national criminal intelligence training standards;
- promote timely intelligence sharing; and
- allow for innovation and flexibility.

Source: Bureau of Justice Assistance, 2005.

Self-Check
> What is the Weberian ideal and how does it relate to modern bureaucracy?
> Why is terrorism prevention a bureaucratic problem?
> How might bureaucracies cooperate to prevent terrorism?

Border Protection

Aside from the myriad functions related to law enforcement and intelligence, the federal government has another major goal: to protect America's borders. The responsibility falls on the DHS and a group of agencies contained within it. The main agencies responsible for border protection include Customs and Border Protection, ICE, and the Coast Guard. The Transportation Security Administration (TSA) has supporting responsibilities at international airports inside the United

States, and agents from the agencies protecting the border are trained at the Federal Law Enforcement Training Center (FLETC). Many of the agencies coordinate their efforts with local units of government, and many DHS personnel are armed and carry arrest power.

American borders are vulnerable in several areas. Long stretches of unprotected areas along the northern and southern borders are open to infiltration, and more than 300 seaports must be secured. The DHS has agencies responsible for securing entry into the United States at airports, and it is responsible for protecting air travel once the entry points are protected. Border agents are responsible for staffing entry points along the northern and southern borders. This activity is augmented by efforts by the Coast Guard as it patrols the ocean shores and Great Lakes. Finally, another DHS agency has the task of accounting for noncitizens within U.S. borders (DHS, 2005).

Policy Disputes

The scope of activities is daunting, even for an agency as large as DHS, and the variety of functions multiplies the problems. In some cases, such as keeping track of noncitizens, DHS cooperates with the FBI and CIA. DHS has increased the number of people who patrol the border, and it has tried to shift agents to the least secure areas. DHS also uses technology such as biometric measuring—identification systems based on body characteristics such as fingerprints, facial patterns, or DNA—to maintain records on aliens (DHS, 2005).

These functions have not come without problems. Critics say that DHS activities, broad as they may be, are not altogether effective (Flynn, 2004a, 2004b). A union representing DHS employees surveyed 500 border patrol agents and 500 immigration inspectors from the Border Protection and Customs divisions. The union president stated that old bureaucratic procedures leave borders unprotected, and members of the union agreed. Only 16 percent were satisfied with DHS's efforts. The majority of respondents complained of low morale. DHS administrators countered that only rank-and-file personnel completed the survey (Z. Alonso, 2004).

Some DHS policies have not been popular with other countries. For example, DHS implemented a policy of fingerprinting and photographing visitors from some other countries; some of America's closest allies were exempted from the process. This policy met with a storm of criticism from nation after nation. Brazil even retaliated, requiring photographs and fingerprints of U.S. visitors to its land. DHS has also tried more advanced methods of biometric measuring, hoping to create a database of body types. Some have complained that the process was ahead of its time (CNN, 2004a).

Local governments have been asked to assist with border protection, but some of them have balked at the idea. Many local governments feel that they need the trust and cooperation of foreigners living in their areas. If aliens distrust the actions of local governments, governmental functions could be hampered. The education system would be disrupted, aliens would not seek health care, and law enforcement officials would neither get information nor be able to serve people in the jurisdiction (National Immigration Forum, 2004).

The 9/11 Commission Report (2004, pp. 400–407) addressed the issue of border security and suggested sweeping reforms. The commission said that more than 500 million people cross U.S. borders each year, and 330 million of them are foreigners. Bureaucratic reform is essential if these crossings are to be monitored because the system before September 11 was unable to provide security or monitor foreigners coming into the United States. A single agency with a single format, the commission recommended, should screen crossings. In addition, an investigative agency should be established to monitor all aliens in the United States. The commission also recommended gathering intelligence on the way terrorists travel and combining intelligence and law enforcement activities to hamper their mobility. The commission suggested using a standardized method for obtaining identification and passports with biometric measures. In essence, the commission recommended standardizing the bureaucratic response for monitoring the entry of foreigners into the United States.

A more recent empirical examination suggests that all the recommendations from various agencies and the massive reorganization fostered by the creation of DHS has had less of an impact than originally intended (May, Sapotichne, and Workman, 2009). The primary reason is that it is difficult to change large bureaucracies. Peter May and his fellow researchers demonstrated that workers in smaller bureaus under the grand bureaucracy maintain their routines and systems. Even a massive change in structure does not prevent workers from fighting for turf. Even the powerful disruption of the 9/11 attacks did not alter many of the subsystems. This has many implications for relations among levels of government. If DHS is unable to change federal bureaucratic relations, it is doubtful that it will have a major impact on state, federal, and tribal systems in areas such as information sharing, immigration, and implementing a national identity system.

The Immigration Debate

One controversial issue surrounding border protection involves immigration. Many elected officials argue that the United States cannot be secure unless its borders are secure. A few people want to eliminate immigration, but more want to stop only illegal immigration and install tighter controls on immigration from countries that may harbor hostility toward the United States. Other people believe that the immigration debate is overemphasized. They say that the United States is a country based on immigration and that immigrants do not represent a terrorist threat.

Conservative political candidate and pundit Patrick Buchanan (2002, pp. 97–109, 235) summarizes one view. By allowing the unregulated flow of immigrants from the southern border, Buchanan argues, the United States opens the door to terrorist infiltration. The situation is made worse by allowing emigrants from hostile Muslim countries to enter the United States. They can operate as independent terrorists or as agents for a rogue regime. Buchanan takes the argument a step further. By allowing the unregulated influx of Hispanics from the south, the United States risks not only terrorism but the destruction of American culture. Some critics dismiss Buchanan as a right-wing ideologue, but scholars such as Samuel Huntington (2004) make the same argument.

Most of the people concerned with border security make the distinction between legal and illegal immigration, and their primary concern reflects a desire for the rule of law. Kerry Diminyatz (2003) puts forward this idea in a research paper written while training at the U.S. Army War College. The southern border is not secure, and DHS plans for securing the border have not been adequate. This is a security threat, not only in terms of terrorism but from a variety of other criminal activities. Diminyatz argues that it is possible to secure the border but that it will take major reforms. The major issues involve economic, social, and political inequities and corruption on both sides of the border.

Diminyatz says that the failure to protect the southern border presents four major national security threats: (1) terrorism and weapons of mass destruction (WMD), (2) drug trafficking, (3) human smuggling, and (4) infectious disease. The most significant threat of unregulated immigration comes in the form of terrorism and organized crime. Although this has been a problem for decades, no presidential administration has effectively approached the dilemma. Diminyatz argues that all agencies charged with border security need to be brought into a single organization. The multiple bureaucracies responsible for border security are inefficient, and the structure fails to focus all efforts. To correct the situation, U.S. military forces should be deployed along the border until civilian law enforcement can be consolidated and physical and technological barriers can be established to prevent illegal border crossings.

The federal government seeks to form partnerships with local communities so that state, local, and tribal law enforcement officers can act as an extension of agencies charged with border security (Seghetti, Vina, and Ester, 2005). However, these law enforcement officials might not welcome the idea of joining a federal partnership to secure the borders. Sometimes local law enforcement agencies refuse to cooperate because they want to maintain informational relationships with the illegal community (National Immigration Forum, 2004). They need information from both legal and illegal immigrants to protect the community and investigate crime. Successful policing requires information, and crimes cannot be investigated without it.

Other methods of enhancing border security have nothing to do with a reorganization of bureaucracy. Congress has considered a number of methods (Garcia, Lee, and Tatelman, 2005). One tool could be the introduction of national identification cards. Another is a law regulating asylum for those from countries openly hostile to the United States. Some members of Congress have suggested creating special laws or legal reviews for legal immigrants who pose a security threat. Others have advocated holding illegal aliens and not deporting them. These positions represent controversies within the controversy. The problem of border security might be best addressed by enhancing an agency's legal authority to deal with the issue. Civil libertarians are wary of such approaches, believing they will result in the abuse of governmental power.

Janice Kephart (2005), a former legal counsel to the 9/11 Commission, believes that the holes in border security come from lax enforcement of existing law. She says that a study of the activities of 94 foreign-born terrorists who operated in the United States from 1990 to 2004 show the inadequacy of enforcement. Two-thirds of the terrorists engaged in criminal activities before or in conjunction with their terrorist attacks. Note that this reinforces findings from Brent Smith and Paxton Roberts (2005). Terrorists enter the United States with temporary visas and then fail to follow the provisions of entry. They make false statements on applications and lie on other official documents while in the country. They make sham marriages or utilize other loopholes to stay in the country. Kephart believes that border protection starts with rigorous law enforcement and background checks.

Sebastian Mallaby (2007), writing an opinion column for the *Washington Post*, vehemently argues that the focus on illegal immigration is not relevant to homeland security. Undocumented workers commit fewer crimes than natives, and there is no indication that they convert to jihadist ideology. Immigrants come to the United States because they want to live here, Mallaby says. Homeland security has little to do with immigration reform. Mallaby says that security efforts should focus on two types of targets—those most likely to be hit and those that will cause the greatest loss of life. Immigration is not a factor.

The debate about immigration reveals the problems inherent in law enforcement bureaucracy. To begin with, the nature of the problem is under dispute. Some arguments claim that illegal immigration is not a problem, whereas the opposite side maintains that legal, let alone illegal, immigration is destroying civilization. There is confusion about the relationship between local law enforcement and federal agencies. This is complicated by the number of federal agencies that have a role in border security and immigration. Finally, there are concerns with the efficiency of immigration laws. Some people argue that they are not being enforced, some want tougher laws, and still others believe border security is not an issue in preventing terrorism. It is difficult to formulate policy in the face of so many contradictory positions.

The immigration debate has grown more heated as the country continues to be divided over ideological positions. The *New York Times* (Archibald, 2010) summarized the issues through an examination of a controversial Arizona law that empowered state and local officers to investigate the status of suspected illegal immigrants. Although the law had public support throughout the country, critics maintained that it would lead to police profiling of Hispanics. The law spawned a heated national debate, lawsuits, demonstrations, and the deployment of National Guard troops on the border with Mexico. If nothing else, the Arizona controversy indicated the problem of addressing a single issue through multiple layers of bureaucracy and competing interest groups.

Self-Check

> How do political disputes affect border security?
> Why are state, local, and tribal agencies hesitant to enforce border security?
> Summarize the different positions on the immigration debate.

Infrastructure Protection

Another area concerning DHS is infrastructure protection. Information, energy, communication, transportation, and economic systems are vulnerable to terrorist attack. Their vulnerability requires all levels of government to develop new capabilities to provide protection. The DHS (Office of Homeland Security, 2002, pp. xi–xii) states that law enforcement agencies will need to develop cooperative links with public and private bureaucracies, including private security organizations, educational institutions, and health care systems. Fortunately, state and local police agencies are not starting in a vacuum. The IACP (IACP, 2001) issued guidelines to provide for cooperation among all levels of government and private industry and identify threats to the infrastructure to defend against them.

Private versus Governmental Partnerships

Just because some units of government and private industry realize that the infrastructure needs to be protected does not mean that bureaucracies will jump into action. Critics think that too little is being done. Jeanne Cummings (2002) points to two primary weaknesses. As much as a year after September 11, the federal government had failed to provide funding to state and local governments. State emergency planners complain that they received little federal direction and no federal money. Cummings says that the problem is even worse in the private security industry. After a survey of security at America's largest shopping mall, in Minnesota, Cummings concludes that federal law enforcement does little to assist private security. Keeping Americans safe, Cummings says, depends on state and local efforts outside Washington.

Richard Clarke, a former special advisor to the president with an impressive bipartisan service record, testified before the Senate Subcommittee on the Judiciary on February 13, 2002 (Clarke, 2002). He outlined many of the threats facing the nation's infrastructure, painting a grim picture. Most computer systems are vulnerable to viruses, Clarke believes, because computer users will not pay for proper protection. The government has made efforts to partially address this problem, but more protection is needed. Clarke says that the nation's power system and the technological organizations that support it are vulnerable to disruptions. The Internet and other computer networks that support these systems are also vulnerable to attack. Pointing to the railroad industry as an example, Clarke shows how many low-tech organizations have imported high-tech support systems. If you shut down electrical grids and computers, Clarke maintains, you'll shut down transportation and communication (see *Another Perspective: Infrastructure Protection*).

As Clarke stated in his testimony, the FBI should not have been the lead agency for infrastructure protection; that role is more suited to technological specialists. (On November 25, 2002, following Clarke's recommendation, the Bush administration ordered the National Infrastructure Protection Center to move to the DHS.)

Extending Clarke's logic, it can also be argued that state and local law enforcement should not play a lead role in infrastructure protection. The key is to develop relationships so that state, local, and tribal police agencies can support security functions.

Many private corporations have the ability to gather and control information, and it is crucial to their ability to function when they compete for business with other companies. Corporations like Walmart, General Motors, and Apple have excellent information-gathering and security systems, and they often share information with governments for the public good. It is quite another matter to hand corporations analyzed criminal and national security intelligence. The problem is that private industry uses information for competition and profit. When governmental agencies share information, they do so in the public domain for the public good. Government partnerships with private corporations have the potential to give large companies a competitive edge.

The Need for Private Partnerships

All levels of law enforcement are faced with the need for technical specialists and access to privately owned portions of the infrastructure. Protection of the infrastructure does not result automatically with the acquisition of technical expertise equivalent to that of industrial specialists; it comes when specialists in crime fighting and protection establish critical links with the public and private organizations in maintaining America's infrastructure. Connections should be developed in two crucial areas. First, the police should be linked to the security forces already associated with infrastructure functions. The American Society of Industrial Security (Azano, 2003) has made great strides in this area, but more needs to be accomplished. Second, state and local law enforcement agencies must establish formal and informal networks with the organizations in their jurisdictions, and these networks should expand to a cooperative federal system.

Michael Vatis (1999) points to another area: cyber security. Police agencies need to protect their own information infrastructures (see *Another Perspective: Recommendations for Cybersecurity*). Following the trend of most American organizations, police agencies integrate electronic management and records systems in everyday routines. If these systems are disrupted, police agencies could lose their ability to function. Surveying major agencies throughout the country, Vatis argues that infrastructure defense begins at home. He worries that law enforcement agencies are not only unprepared to defend community infrastructure; they are unable even to protect their own support systems.

ANOTHER PERSPECTIVE

Infrastructure Protection

President Clinton issued a directive declaring law enforcement to be part of the nation's critical infrastructure. Shortly after taking office, the Bush Administration published a report based on the directive. Among its points are the following:

- Each law enforcement agency is responsible for the protection of its own infrastructure. The U.S. government mandates federal agencies to develop plans and encourages local agencies to do so likewise.
- Local plans should be flexible, based on the recommended model but applicable to individual needs.

- Because police agencies use information systems, each department is asked to review its infrastructure and assess vulnerabilities. Factors recommended for the threat assessment include evaluating critical missions and capabilities, critical assets, critical interdependent relations, types of threats, and vulnerability to attack.
- Planning for protection should be based on a prioritized listing of critical services and vulnerabilities.

Source: Vatis, 1999.

Self-Check

> Why is the infrastructure under both public and private control?
> What problems are caused by private–public partnerships?
> Why must the government work with private agencies to protect infrastructure?

Governmental Partnerships

One of the most important aspects of DHS operations is communicating with local communities, law enforcement agencies, and private industries as they relate to intelligence-gathering activities and infrastructure protection. DHS (2004) says that local efforts are essential to successful security plans. The IACP (2001) believes that local law enforcement agencies will become the hinge on which all local efforts pivot. It will be the job of local law enforcement, the IACP says, to coordinate activities from a host of agencies throughout local jurisdictions all through the United States.

ANOTHER PERSPECTIVE

Recommendations for Cybersecurity

The Institute for Security Technology Studies at Dartmouth College recommends following the "best practices" of security in the computer industry. Best practices include the following:

- Update software.
- Enforce rigid password security.

- Disable unnecessary services.
- Scan for viruses and use virus protection.
- Utilize intrusion detection systems.
- Maintain firewalls.

Source: Vatis, 2001, p. 19.

The Federal Mission

As envisioned by federal bureaucracy, homeland security entails coordinating efforts of several local organizations, including private industry, public service, health care systems, and law enforcement. Emergency-response planning falls into two broad categories: prevention and reaction (Cilluffo, Cardash, and Lederman, 2001). State and local agencies assume expanded roles in this concept because they are the obvious choice for prevention, and they will be among the first to respond to a domestic attack. If local agencies assume such a role, law enforcement officers will be forced to rethink the ways they do business.

As discussed in Chapter 13, national security intelligence is a function of the federal government. As local agencies become involved in homeland security, they will need to think beyond criminal intelligence. Two new functions become apparent. They must become involved in assessing terrorist threats in their jurisdictions. They must also learn to recognize possible information that may add to national defense intelligence and develop routines to forward such information. This creates a legal problem because law enforcement agencies need to have a reasonable suspicion that criminal activity is taking place or has taken place before they can collect information (see Carter, 2004; O'Conner, 2004).

Expanding Local Roles

If they are to be engaged in homeland security, state and local police agencies will need to expand the role of traditional law enforcement. On the most rudimentary level, officers could be assigned to security tasks and trained to look for information beyond the violation of criminal law. On a more sophisticated level, police intelligence units could be established to gather and pass on intelligence information. The most effective initial practice would be to train patrol officers, investigators, and narcotics officers to look for indicators of terrorism during their daily activities. This would be an effective method of enhancing intelligence, but critics fear governmental infringement on civil liberties (see Chapter 15; Cole and Dempsey, 2002, pp. 186–187).

Assuming that local law enforcement agencies will collect information only within the context of criminal investigations, bureaucratic problems remain. The process of gathering defense intelligence is not readily apparent in American policing. Most law enforcement officers did not enter police ranks thinking that they were joining an army or aspiring to be part of DHS. Their motivation generally focuses on elimination of crime, not national defense. In addition, local police policies and employment incentives reinforce their original notions. Officers are encouraged to maintain a local view, and police managers reinforce pragmatic actions while discouraging abstract thinking. Police work is extremely political, and law enforcement officers think locally. To paraphrase the late Speaker of the House Tip O'Neill, all law enforcement politics is local. The goal is not to alienate constituencies, but to develop strong community ties to help keep information flowing. Information about suspects, crimes, and criminal activity translates into power and successful individual performance in police agencies, and it solves crimes (Manning, 1976, p. 35).

Thinking Internationally

State and local officers are not rewarded for thinking in terms of international issues or national security. Chiefs of police and sheriffs do not usually praise abstract reasoning. In an early critique of collegiate criminal justice programs, Lawrence Sherman (1978) claims that higher education has done little to help this situation. Criminal justice programs do not produce abstract, critical thinkers for law enforcement; instead, Sherman believes, they impart skills. According to a recent survey by *Police: The Law Enforcement Magazine*, graduates steeped in academic preparation are not as welcome in law enforcement agencies as recruits with military experience (July 2002). Discipline and the willingness to obey orders are more important than individual thinking and creativity.

Modern terrorism is an abstract, nebulous concept, which fluctuates according to historical and political circumstances. To combat terrorism, security forces require groups of people with abstract reasoning skills, knowledge of international politics and history, and specialized expertise in particular regions (Betts, 2002). If the police are to participate as full partners in this process, they need outside specialists with skills not typically available in law enforcement organizations. The ethos behind policing, however, rejects this logic. American law enforcement relishes pragmatic information with immediate applicability in practical situations.

Localized attitudes inspire contempt from intelligence agencies. Unlike analysts in defense intelligence, state and local police officers frequently exhibit no concern for in-depth background information, the kind of information needed to understand intelligence. As a result, intelligence bureaucracies frequently question the competence of police. Intelligence analysts know that information is not usually valuable until it is categorized and placed within social and political contexts. If police agencies are unable to engage in this type of examination, intelligence organizations are hesitant to form partnerships with them. These factors present enormous problems as the DHS tries to create a network of information.

 Self-Check

> Why must governmental agencies form homeland security partnerships with each other?

> Why is it necessary to think about international problems at all levels of law enforcement?

> Why might people fear the expansion of state, local, and tribal roles?

New Approaches to Mission

If state and local law enforcement officers were to begin looking for signs of terrorism, they would need to frame basic questions about potential adversaries. For example, in addition to criminal briefings before patrol or investigative tours, officers would need to think of questions such as the following:

• What is the modus operandi of our enemy?
• How does the enemy's organization function?

• What types of tactics will the enemy use?
• What types of weapons will the enemy use?
• How can information be gathered while protecting the source?
• What activities in the community might indicate that terrorists may be operating in a jurisdiction?
• How can information be shared securely with other agencies?

Bureaucratic Problems

Unlike the ideal rational organizations described by Weber, public service organizations have weaknesses that emerge in the everyday social construction of reality. Personalities are important, varying levels of competency limit or expand effectiveness, and organizations tend to act in their own interests. If all the organizations involved in homeland security agree to pool their efforts, several bureaucratic hurdles need to be cleared (see Swanson, Territo, and Taylor, 2001, pp. 643–644; Best, 2001; Bodrero, 2002; Mitchell and Hulse, 2002).

Federal Rivalries

The standard administrative logic is that federal bureaucracies do work together. In reality, this is not always true. Sometimes, federal agencies act more like rivals than partners. The 9/11 Commission criticized agencies for not working together. Anyone who has worked in or with the federal government can relate stories of interagency rivalries. Former FBI Director Louis Freeh (2005, p. 192) says that talking about CIA–FBI rivalries might sell books, but it is not true. Former CIA Director George Tenet (2007, p. 193) admits that the CIA and FBI had a history of contentious relations, but he and Directors Freeh and Robert Mueller worked hard to overcome them.

For example, as American troops were preparing to enter Iraq in 2003, there was a tremendous dispute between the CIA and the military about the validity of intelligence coming out of Iraq (Gordon and Trainor, 2006, pp. 198–199). Another example is that, despite claims to the contrary, individual CIA agents probably refused to share information with the Joint Terrorism Task Force (JTTF) in New York City before 9/11 (L. Wright, 2006, p. 353). Perhaps the best example can be found in the FBI's decision to locate its counterterrorism efforts in its Washington field office. Former FBI executive Richard Marquise (2006, p. 26) says that Washington was the best place to locate counterterrorist headquarters because it positioned the FBI for inevitable turf battles with the CIA and Department of State. Bureaucracies engage in competition, even when they are working toward the same goal.

Unfortunately, federal agencies distrust one another at times, and their failure to cooperate in some circumstances influences local police relationships. Many federal law enforcement agencies openly resent the FBI, and this attitude is frequently reciprocated. In addition, the creation of new bureaucracies, such as the Transportation Security Administration, exacerbates rivalries. Some rivalry is natural because people tend to look at problems from the perspective of the agency where they are employed. In the real world of bureaucracy, organizations on every level frequently act out of self-interest rather than out of concern for the overall mission (Valburn, 2002).

FBI versus Locals

In October 2001, FBI Director Robert Mueller attended the IACP meeting in Toronto, Ontario. According to police chiefs who attended the meeting, it was not a pleasant experience for him. State and local law enforcement executives criticized him for failing to share information. Mueller vowed that the FBI would never allow this failure to happen again. American law enforcement would witness a new FBI. Despite the intentions of the most forceful bureaucratic leaders, however, orders are not always carried out as planned. There have been success stories with information sharing, but there have also been tales of woe. Many American police executives are not convinced that the FBI is in full partnership with them in efforts to stop terrorism (L. Levitt, 2002).

The purpose here is not to condemn the FBI, but to acknowledge a bureaucratic issue. Many state and local police executives believe that the FBI will act only in its own interests, and this attitude extends down through the ranks of law enforcement agencies. Many police officers believe the FBI seems to assist local agencies so they can claim credit for any resulting success, and the FBI has a reputation for gathering information without sharing it. In turn, many FBI agents believe their performance is far superior to other federal, state, local, and tribal officers. Similar attitudes can be seen in rivalries among state and local agencies, such as the way many state troopers and sheriffs' deputies interact. If police in America are to become part of homeland defense, the relationship between the FBI and state and local law enforcement must improve (Riordan and Zegart, 2002).

Local Control and Revenue Sources

Some people feel that cooperation between state and local law enforcement will result in the de facto concentration of police power. This attitude was prevalent at the turn of the twentieth century when state police agencies were forming. Many local governments believed that state police forces had too much power, and many states limited the local agencies to patrolling state highways. Civil libertarians believe that consolidated police power will erode civil rights. Local governmental officials worry that their agendas will be lost in federalization. The bureaucratic arguments extend beyond these interest groups (Hitt and Cloud, 2002).

There is also frustration among local governments with the monetary costs of their homeland security responsibilities. Some local governments want homeland security money to be distributed evenly. Larger jurisdictions, like New York City, argue that money should be distributed according to the likelihood of attacks. Even then, New York City officials complain, federal money does not cover the cost of security (Mintz, 2005). Other people worry that homeland security grants are given to local units of government for strange uses. For example, the state of Kentucky received $36,000 in federal money to keep terrorists from infiltrating bingo halls (Hudson, 2006).

Legal Bureaucracy

Another factor inhibiting police cooperation is the legal bureaucracy of criminal justice. For example, many criminal justice scholars believe that the justice system is actually not a system at all but a multifaceted bureaucracy with intersecting layers— or not. Drawing on earlier research, they refer to the justice system quite humorously as the "wedding cake model." Rather than a smooth flow among police, courts, and corrections, they see a cake in which a large bottom layer represents misdemeanors, a smaller middle layer represents serious crimes, and the smallest tier at the top represents a few celebrated cases. Each layer has differing procedures for dealing with different types of crimes, and police departments, court systems, and correctional agencies work apart from one another even within each layer (see Walker, 1985; Cole and Smith, 2004, p. 8).

Each entity in the criminal justice system is independent, although it interacts with the other parts. There is no overall leader; instead, law enforcement, courts, and correctional agencies refuse to accept single management. From a constitutional perspective, the courts are hardly designed to fit into a criminal justice system. While police and correctional institutions represent the executive branch of government, the courts autonomously belong to the judicial branch (del Carmen, 1991, pp. 275–277). Efforts to increase the efficiency of homeland defense will not change these relationships.

Self-Check

> Describe rivalries among law enforcement agencies.
> What might be done to overcome those rivalries?
> Why does inflexibility hamper an organization's ability to operate?

Bureaucratic Solutions

Successful organizations, whether car manufacturers or universities, overcome problems. Bureaucracies contain inherent problems, but they, too, can work for solutions. Law enforcement, homeland security, and intelligence agencies produce a unique product, but all formal organizations have the same internal and external troubles. Law enforcement bureaucracies will interact to solve problems. The lead panel at the first National Fusion Center Conference focused on this issue (Johnson, 2007). Panel participants from local agencies, the National Guard, the FBI, DHS, and the intelligence community addressed the problem directly. To combat terrorism, every bureaucratic obstacle that hinders the flow of information and action must be directly addressed (Figure 14.1).

Coordination of the activities of many different types of agencies is essential. Panel members stated that agencies had to develop new methods of coordinating and

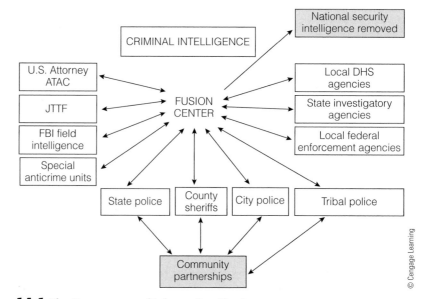

© Cengage Learning

FIGURE **14.1** The Bureaucracy of Information Sharing

communicating ideas. This involved coordination committees and communication among leaders. Every person involved in the intelligence effort needs to understand his or her role in the process. As law enforcement officers collect and forward information, analysts at local fusion centers turn the information into **actionable intelligence**. This intelligence is forwarded to the NCTC, where it is analyzed with information from all other sources in the network. This newly created actionable intelligence is returned to the fusion centers as an **intelligence product**. It can be delivered to patrol officers, deputies, agents, and troopers.

Bureaucracies have problems, but they also offer a process. When law enforcement agencies and the other organizations for preventing terrorism stay focused on the goal, the process can produce results. It is possible to gather and analyze information, assess threats, and mobilize resources to prevent an attack.

Border Security: Critique and Reform

There are problems with border security, to be sure. Stephen Flynn, a senior fellow in national security studies at the Council on Foreign Relations (2002, 2004a, 2004b), believes that the goals of homeland security are crucial and that America's bureaucracies and leadership are squandering the opportunity to really defend the United States. Flynn says that America has made two crucial mistakes. First, homeland security has been separated from national security. Second, the infrastructure is vulnerable to attacks. Despite all the rhetoric and departmental rearrangements for homeland security, the reality is that the United States has not organized its resources for defense.

Flynn vehemently argues that homeland security should be part of a national strategy to defend the United States. America needs to be able to strike a blow as well as to take one. Although both political parties speak of the war on terrorism, terrorism is not something that can be destroyed only by fighting in other areas of the world. There is no central front, Flynn argues, and America cannot always project its power to fight elsewhere. The United States has marshaled its resources to fight overseas while neglecting to protect its home front.

To illustrate the point, Flynn points to the use of WMD. According to the CIA, the most likely route for smuggling WMD into the United States is by sea. It is difficult to inspect all of the cargo containers arriving in seaports; therefore, the oceans represent an opportunity for terrorists. Flynn points out that the Bush Administration did very little to protect the nation's 361 seaports. There was a lot of rhetoric but insufficient action. He finds it hard to believe that in 2004 the United States spent more money every three days to fight the war in Iraq than it did in three years to protect the seaports.

The nation's critical infrastructure remains open to attack, Flynn says. In the 2005 national budget, the DOD was allotted $7.6 billion to enhance the fortification of its bases. In the same budget, the infrastructure for the *entire* nation received only $2.6 billion. Dirty bombs and chemical threats can be developed from hazardous materials; nevertheless, over the past three years funds for secure disposal of such materials have been drastically reduced. Police and firefighter numbers have been cut even though they are crucial for security.

Flynn also sees a problem in strategic thinking in DHS and other agencies. For example, the scientific and medical communities are essential elements of homeland security. Nearly 50 percent of the scientific and medical personnel employed by the federal government retired before 2010. Currently, they are not being replaced quickly enough. The colleges and universities that would produce their replacements are underfunded. In addition, the federal government has virtually ignored private industry, claiming that it is responsible for protecting its own infrastructure. However, Flynn finds that private industry is not doing this.

actionable intelligence: Information that law enforcement agencies, military units, or other security forces can use to prevent an attack or operation.

intelligence product: Any outcome or output of analyzed information that can be used by law enforcement agencies, military units, or security forces to take an immediate action.

Even meeting the need for enhanced border security will not protect America against terrorist attack. Security is a dynamic process that combines intelligence, military, and law enforcement power. It requires international coordination and cooperation to counter the attacks that are planned overseas. Flynn says that America needs an integrated system for defense.

Flynn believes that jihadists are fully aware of the vulnerabilities in our infrastructure. They will not simply let the United States bring the fight to them; they intend to strike, and the safest and most effective way to hit America is to strike its infrastructure. Jihadists understand the economic effect of their actions. For example, Flynn says that if terrorists managed to shut down the closed-container operations of America's shipping industry for just three weeks, the whole world could be thrown into an economic recession.

Flynn urges policy makers to reinvent homeland security. Defense at home is as important as the ability to wage military action overseas. DHS and other federal bureaucracies should think of security from a broad perspective. There are many benefits to doing so. Flynn argues that developing an integrated system against terrorism would reduce the drug trade, contraband smuggling, and theft. These are residual benefits for a strategic program, he believes.

Despite the system's shortcomings, Flynn believes bureaucracies can overcome the problems. We will never have enough security to prevent every attack, he says, but we should follow the path of the aviation industry. Private and public aviation officials have worked together to lower the possibility of airplane accidents and reduce the devastation when they do occur. Although the air industry experiences horrific disasters at times, people continue to fly. Flynn believes that this is because of the faith people have in the air transportation system. They know that failures, although inevitable, are an aberration. They continue to use the system because they believe in its overall safety. Flynn says that homeland security should have the same goal. In a system of civil defense, people have a civic responsibility to maintain the system. When bureaucracies recover from failure after an attack, people will believe life is getting back to normal and they will continue to function. This is the goal of bureaucracy, Flynn says. Americans must be able to absorb a major attack and continue to function. That, Flynn argues, should be the model for homeland security agencies.

ANOTHER PERSPECTIVE

Infrastructure Problems in the DOE

60 Minutes reporter Ed Bradley examined the Department of Energy and its nuclear facilities. It has many problems, including the following concerns:

- Stolen keys to secure facilities that were not replaced for three years.
- Guards were sleeping on duty.

Source: Bradley, August 29, 2004.

- Facilities were penetrated during mock terrorist attacks.

Bradley's report concluded that America's nuclear facilities are protected on paper but that the DOE has not implemented real security measures.

If police departments follow Flynn's suggestions, they will see security as a "work in progress." Flynn says that if policies become a process, attention is focused on how work is accomplished rather than on the results. Law enforcement agencies should look for weaknesses in the system, probe them, and make changes based on the results. Every agency also needs to forge and sustain a variety of nontraditional partnerships with the community, different levels of government, private industry, and the nonprofit sectors. Flynn says that our federal system lends itself to these partnerships because many decision-making functions are reserved for state governments.

Even though Flynn is critical of America's bureaucratic weaknesses, he is optimistic about the future. He believes that bureaucratic leaders, including police executives and managers, will grow to see the problems of terrorism from a more realistic perspective. This will cause them to improve homeland security *before an attack*. Although not every attack can be prevented, most terrorism can be deterred through cooperative partnerships. Prevention demands new skills for law enforcement officers, a culture of information sharing, and new bureaucratic relationships; however, interdiction of terrorism is an attainable goal.

Preparing for Successful Law Enforcement Processes

Imagine the following scene: On a snowy afternoon a road-patrol deputy stops a car on a Nebraska highway. Everything looks routine, and the driver, a foreign national, is exceedingly polite. The deputy notices that the car is registered in South Carolina and that the driver has an operator's permit issued in Colorado. The deputy asks questions about the driver's country of origin, his South Carolina or Colorado residence, and his reason for driving through Nebraska. The answers are smooth—too smooth. Had they been rehearsed? When the deputy rephrases the questions, the driver repeats the same answers without variation and seems to be confused by the deputy's questions.

In the course of the interview, the deputy finds that the car is rented and that the driver's name is spelled one way on his license and another way on the rental agreement. Further questioning reveals the driver's immigration papers with a third spelling. At this point, the deputy begins to ask more in-depth questions. The deputy knows that spelling names in multiple ways and creating false identification are methods mastered by many international terrorists.

Terrorism Screening Center (TSC): A multiagency operation in West Virginia that evaluates information gathered from a variety of governmental sources.

The deputy returns to her vehicle and calls the local fusion center. The analyst puts the deputy in contact with the **Terrorism Screening Center (TSC)** in West Virginia. The TSC tells the deputy to gather as much information as possible but not to make an arrest. The deputy follows instructions and forwards the information. She does not know it, but the driver she has stopped is a suspect in an ongoing JTTF investigation in Florida, and the information she has provided will become valuable in the prevention of a terrorist attack and the arrest of the perpetrators *before* the event can take place.

The foregoing example is only imaginary, but recently a Midwestern police officer stopped a vehicle for speeding on an interstate highway. The car contained two men and a number of other items, objects the officer failed to see. The patrol officer failed to notice weapons and explosives in the car, including two loaded automatic weapons behind the driver and a semiautomatic pistol by the driver's hand. He also missed racist literature advocating violence, and other extremist propaganda lying open in the car. He failed to see a clue when he first approached the car that would have given warning—a Ku Klux Klan symbol on the back window. Failing to do a proper warrant check, he did not know that one of the men was a fugitive. He gave the driver a speeding ticket, never knowing that his life had been in danger or that one of the men in the car was a member of a terrorist group planning a massive attack in Texas. The exact details of the stop are known because the other man in the suspect's car was an undercover police officer working the case (Keathley, 2002).

Law enforcement efforts are improving, and police officers are reporting information. It is also being shared on a number of levels. William Dyson (2011) looked at data from terrorism cases from 2008 to 2011. He found that American law enforcement officers had a tremendous success rate in both investigating terrorism cases and stopping terrorist or extremist attacks. The reason this has happened is twofold. First, law enforcement personnel, through training and awareness, were recognizing possible indicators and warning signs of terrorism. Second, police officers reported this information, and it was being shared by fusion centers and other intelligence agencies. Despite a cumbersome system and all the other problems of bureaucracies, counterterrorism investigations have improved.

New Approaches to the Law Enforcement Mission

The JTTF system might well serve as an outstanding example of law enforcement cooperation. Critics like Cole and Dempsey (2002) believe that gathering security information in the course of criminal investigations is both legal and effective. The JTTF offers a sensible alternative by creating a system that separates criminal and national security intelligence. These units also combine local, state, and various federal police officers, as well as corrections officials and prosecutors, in regional units designed to combat terrorism. Local and state officers are given federal authority, and the presence of such officers gives federal agents the ability to act in local jurisdictions. The JTTFs have been effective in many cases (Watson, 2002).

An alternative for state and local agencies is to combine training in terrorism awareness with specialized training for selected officers. Rather than bringing an entire department into intelligence-gathering operations, select units could engage in counterterrorist activities. Intelligence specialists like David Carter (2004) see the value in this. Rather than bringing police officers into the intelligence process as full partners, police officers could be trained to look for indicators of terrorism in the course of normal operations and to pass the information along. Trained police officers may expand their efforts by creating public and private partnerships through community policing efforts.

On the surface, JTTFs seem tailored to the needs of state and local law enforcement, but in some cases they meet opposition. Local governments have refused to allow their police forces to assist in counterterrorist activities, and some jurisdictions refuse to share criminal intelligence with federal law enforcement. Civil libertarians sometimes see the formation of a JTTF as too great of a consolidation of governmental power. In addition, although academics and governmental officials are fond of using the phrase "criminal justice system," the courts are not part of the system because they do not belong to the executive branch. State and federal courts may well limit the role of local agencies in homeland security, especially in intelligence-gathering activities.

On the other hand, police are in a perfect position to engage in intelligence-gathering activities and expand their role in national defense. Other Western democracies, such as France and Germany, have done this quite successfully. The Canadians and British accomplished the same thing but kept more of a public service model than the French or the Germans. The JTTF model may be a start, but law enforcement efforts need to go further. Partnerships with all types of formal and informal organizations and cooperation among all levels of law enforcement in an environment that rewards information sharing are the ultimate answer to preventing terrorism.

The final aspect of preventing terrorism involves applying crime prevention and detection skills. Patrol officers and investigators encounter many more common criminals in their daily routines than terrorists, but the same techniques work against both sets of criminals. For example, former FBI agents Joe Navarro and John Shafer point out that law enforcement officers need to be able to recognize and intervene when they observe suspicious behavior. They need to be able to tell when people are lying, through verbal or written cues, and they need the interviewing skills to move beyond reasonable suspicion of criminal activity to probable cause. In short, they need the skills to uncover deceptive behavior. It involves routine police work, and this type of law enforcement not only disrupts criminal activity, it can prevent terrorism when officers recognize suspicious circumstances (Shafer and Navarro, 2004; Navarro, 2005; Navarro and Karlins, 2008; Shafer, 2010). In the end, many aspects of counterterrorism involve basic police work.

Self-Check

> What issues impact border security?
> How can law enforcement agencies prepare for success?
> What law enforcement skills are involved in homeland security?

Responding to Disasters

emergency-response plans: Preparations by any agency to deal with natural, accidental, or man-made disasters. They involve controlling the incident through an organized response-and-command system and assigning various organizations to supervise the restoration of social order.

No security system can completely stop terrorism, and law enforcement agencies will be called upon to respond when an attack occurs. The process for response and recovery involves planning. Fire departments, regional disaster teams, the health community, and other agencies have **emergency-response plans**. Law enforcement agencies have roles under these plans. Their primary responsibilities are to respond and restore order, assist emergency and rescue operations, and support health and human services. They are also charged with investigative and prosecutorial actions. With the exception of the last two functions, the procedures are similar to those when responding to natural disasters, civil disorders, or massive infrastructure failures. All of these functions involve reaction.

Response functions are critical and they save lives, but emergency-response planning differs from preventing terrorism. When law enforcement agencies respond to disasters, it does not matter whether the cause was an industrial accident, an act of nature, or a terrorist attack. Multiple agencies, including police departments, respond to emergencies. Plans and actions designed to stop terrorism involve different skills. Gathering information, analyzing it, and sharing findings are part of an intelligence process. Law enforcement's primary role is to prevent terrorism and crime, and its secondary purpose is to react to it to save lives. Reaction to a crisis, although one of the critical missions of police and homeland security agencies, is an emergency function. It has little to do with the cause of the disaster. For example, when a traffic officer responds to a car crash, that is reaction. Preventing automobile accidents is a different function. The same principle applies to preventing terrorism.

Self-Check

> How does prevention differ from emergency-response planning?
> Why do law enforcement roles differ in prevention and response?
> Has law enforcement failed when it engages in a responsive role?

CHAPTER TAKE AWAYS

The vast maze of law enforcement agencies form a complex set of bureaucracies that mix with other governmental and private organizations to form a homeland security network. Ideally, it should operate as a rational bureaucracy. There are many snags, but the system seems to be improving. It is complicated by the national debate about immigration, the large expanse of borders and number of ports of entry, and the sheer size of the infrastructure. Homeland security will only work when law enforcement agencies share information in partnerships with other governmental and private bureaucracies. Bureaucracies can be efficient and effective, but actions require constant reviews to ensure that processes are achieving goals.

OBJECTIVE SUMMARY

- The problem of law enforcement bureaucracy with respect to homeland security and the prevention of terrorism is the sheer number of organizations in multiple layers of government. Bureaucracies can also become stagnant and more consumed with the processes of performing tasks than with the actual goals of the organization.

- Max Weber's ideal bureaucracy rationally organizes people under goal-oriented leaders. Workers and managers are selected only according to their abilities. Most American governmental organizations—the military and some private industry—base their structures on the Weberian ideal of bureaucracy.

- Many bureaucracies are involved in homeland security, and their most important functions center on law enforcement and activities related to intelligence. The federal bureaucracy is massive, which presents a problem for agency cooperation. Yet the bigger challenge is in coordinating the thousands of state, local, and tribal law enforcement agencies in the United States. DHS has assumed many roles in homeland security, but it has relatively little power in the intelligence community.

- Border protection involves ports of entry—seaports, border checkpoints, and ocean shores—and vast expanses of land on our northern and southern borders. Weaknesses in security develop because of the vast size of the borders and the multiple points of entry. Critics maintain that security checks in these areas are ineffective.

- Americans are divided on their approach to immigration policy. This division is exacerbated by the activities of interest groups among immigrant and anti-immigrant communities, and it is also compounded by the large pool of illegal immigrants living in the country. The debate about immigration is heated, interfering with attempts to create sound policies to protect the borders and points of entry.

- Infrastructure protection refers to security provided for the underpinnings of social life, such as roadways, computer networks, bridges, electrical grids, and pipelines. It is protected by government agencies, but most of the assets are owned by private corporations.

- It is not possible to secure the homeland with a single agency or small groups of agencies. Effective security can only come through partnerships among agencies. Barriers that separate bureaucracies need to be minimized. Partnerships also require cooperation between units of government and private corporations.

- If state, local, and tribal law enforcement agencies are to take part in homeland security, the mission needs to be reconceived. Making the needed changes seems to make sense, but several factors work against change.

- Flynn maintains that the focus on homeland security is misplaced. People and products coming into the country need to be checked and monitored. America needs to become resilient to recover from terrorist strikes.

- The JTTF system may serve as a starting point for cooperation among police agencies. In the final analysis, law enforcement agencies will need to create and sustain a variety of new partnerships in the public, private, and nonprofit sectors.

Critical Engagement: Bureaucratic Goal Displacement and Future Change

Ideally, the purpose of a bureaucracy is to solve a problem rationally. However, every bureaucracy has several groups competing for control of organizational processes and outcomes. In Michigan, for example, the automobile industry dominated the state and much of the national economy in the mid-twentieth century, and while it seemed to only need to satisfy consumers, each automotive company had competing constituencies. Consumers wanted cars that performed and met their needs. Government regulators and interest groups demanded greater safety and fuel performance, and workers demanded higher wages and better benefits. Corporate directors and stockholders wanted profits, while professional workers sought advancement and prestige. In reality, there were many more competing interests, and the automakers tried to satisfy them all. By the end of the twentieth century, the big three automakers were in trouble in Michigan. The goal of their bureaucracy was to produce and sell cars at a profit, but competing interests moved them away from their original goal.

This process is called goal displacement. As soon as a bureaucracy is created with the purpose of rationally achieving a goal, a host of internal and external actors begin manipulating or attempting to influence the organization for their own ends. The bureaucracy may end up serving purposes for which it was not designed. Any attempt to create a system to prevent terrorism in the United States will involve literally thousands of different constituencies competing in all branches of government at three different levels: federal, state, and local.

Despite problems and inefficiencies, bureaucratic organizations frequently accomplish their missions. Successful executives keep other managers focused on the main organizational objectives. Managers, in turn, need to maintain support of key actors within the bureaucracy. Executives also need to look outside the bureaucracy. They need to manage the expectations of consumers or constituents, interest groups, competitors, other bureaucracies, and political actors. The process is complicated, but successful management prevents goal displacement.

In law enforcement, the best terrorism prevention programs start when officers have applied successful community-oriented policing strategies. They gather information and pass it forward to centers where it can be analyzed from a broad perspective. Their efforts can become the driving force for state and federal terrorism prevention efforts. If the system is to work, a number of bureaucratic actors must remember that their goal is to prevent terrorism. If they fail to do so, the goal is displaced.

Consider these issues in terms of future developments:

- Peter May and his associates (see both 2009 studies) found that it is necessary for a variety of lower-level bureaucratic managers to embrace a mission if an organization is to accomplish a goal. Do you think this is true or false? How does your answer account for goal displacement?
- Research the Office of Justice Programs (OJP), U.S. Department of Justice. How does OJP seek to connect state, local, and tribal law enforcement with the federal government? How does this prevent multiple agencies from displacing goals?
- Despite complexity, organizations like the JTTF have a solid record of success. Why is this so? How does the JTTF structure help to avoid goal displacement?

KEY TERMS

Bureaucracy, p. 14-365	National Counterterrorism Center (NCTC), p. 14-367	Mission creep, p. 14-369	Intelligence product p. 14-381
1978 Civil Service Reform Act, p. 14-365		Process orientation, p. 14-369	Terrorism Screening Center (TSC), p. 14-383
Government Management Reform Act of 1994, p. 14-365	Task orientation, p. 14-369	Pre-incident indicators, p. 14-369	Emergency-response plans, p. 14-385
	Threat analysis, p. 14-369	Working group, p. 14-370	
Max Weber, p. 14-365	Goal displacement, p. 14-369	Actionable intelligence, p. 14-381	

CHAPTER 15

Homeland Security and Constitutional Issues

Scott J. Ferrell/Congressional Quarterly/Getty Images

LEARNING OBJECTIVES

After reading this chapter you should be able to:

> Explain the dangers of restricting freedom in the name of security.

> Differentiate between civil liberties and human rights.

> Describe the relationship between the idea of defense in depth and civil liberties.

> Summarize the USA PATRIOT Act of 2001 and its renewal in 2011.

> List the constitutional issues that affect homeland security.

> Cite arguments to support and oppose increasing executive power to combat terrorism.

> Describe courts' responses to attempts to counter terrorism with increased governmental executive branch power.

> Describe the role of law enforcement agencies in a social network opposed to terrorism.

> Discuss the dangers of militarizing police work.

> Summarize emerging criminal justice scholarship focusing on governmental power.

There were many reflections about the meaning of 9/11 during the tenth anniversary of the terrorist attack. Adam Liptak (2011) of the *New York Times* wrote an analysis of the change in American law. Criminal law, he writes, has not changed too much in the decade following 9/11. For all the fuss and bluster surrounding the USA PATRIOT Act, it became a relatively benign tool. The USA PATRIOT Act's official name, the Uniting and Strengthening America by Providing Appropriate Tools Required to Intercept and Obstruct Terrorism Act of 2001, became more frightening than the enforcement of its provisions. Liptak expresses little concern about the law.

He has concerns, however, about attitudes. Threats to civil liberties did not emanate from the law. They came from attitudes. He cites the actions of intelligence agencies and military forces, but his main focus is on the executive branch of the federal government. It has assumed pervasive power, he writes, and that attitude has continued through two presidential administrations, both Republican and Democratic. It is based on power. Liptak complains about surveillance of religious and political groups, denial of rights to immigrants, arrests of people loosely associated with terrorism, and the abuse of power in the name of national security. It is an attitude of "arrest early and charge broadly," Liptak writes. He compares the new attitude to other periods of American history when civil rights were threatened under the guise of security.

There is another side to the story, but Liptak captures the emotion of the debate. Law enforcement agencies, fusion centers, and the Department of Homeland Security are keenly aware of civil rights issues, something Liptak addresses at the end of the editorial. There are many official efforts to prevent abuses while protecting the country. On the whole, Liptak's reflective analysis captures the paradox of homeland security. Law enforcement must join the network to prevent terrorism, and function to protect the rights of the people even as it monitors and arrests them. This reflects the ironic role of security forces in a democracy.

The Security Conundrum

September 11 changed the way America views terrorism. The wars in Afghanistan and Iraq claimed the lives of thousands, and massive counterterrorist measures were taken at home. The USA PATRIOT Act of 2001, which made significant changes in the structure of federal law enforcement, was passed within weeks of the September attacks. The act was renewed in 2006, after both the Senate and the House introduced several provisions curbing governmental authority. In 2004, the 9/11 Commission issued a report calling for a complete overhaul of the U.S. intelligence system; in response, a law was passed in December 2004. The National Criminal Intelligence Sharing Plan (NCISP) set standards for a new system of domestic intelligence gathering and analysis. All of these activities generated tremendous controversy, and the debates took place as America waged foreign wars against an enemy who projected no central front. As America's internal debates continued, terrorist events around the world became deadlier.

The Bush Administration underwent a barrage of criticism for many of its policies in the wake of 9/11. People expressed concerns over eavesdropping on telephone calls, the collection of domestic intelligence, the treatment of terrorist suspects, and the rendition of suspected terrorists to countries that openly used torture. One of the most contentious issues dealt with the detention of suspected terrorists. The CIA maintained detention facilities in various foreign countries, military forces ran detention centers in Iraq and Afghanistan, and hundreds of people were detained without warrant. The detention facility at Guantánamo Bay, Cuba, became a lightning rod for domestic and international criticism of Bush policies.

military tribunals: military courts trying combatants outside the civilian court system. Trials take place in front of a board of military officers operating under military law.

While running for president, Barack Obama promised to put a stop to these practices, but his administration continued many of them. Attorney General Eric Holder tried to move a set of trials from **military tribunals** in Guantánamo Bay to New York City, only to back away from efforts to do so. The same thing happened when President Obama sought to close the Cuban detention center. Ironically, the president, who campaigned on promises to move away from Bush's security policies, allowed military tribunals to begin trying cases in 2012. In all fairness to both Presidents Bush and Obama, it is much easier to talk about complexity than it is to manage complex situations.

Security and Liberty

There are always tradeoffs when considering security. This applies to social structures and to physical aspects of security. It is possible to use force to create a social structure in which people can have limited fear of crime and illegal violence. The underside is that people in such a society must often fear the powers of the civil government. Crime can be reduced through aggressive apprehension and punishment of criminals, but when the government goes beyond legal norms, people no longer fear only the criminals—they also fear the government that is supposed to protect their rights (Giroux, 2002).

This is both an ancient and a modern principle. When the Athenians were threatened with invasion, they were often willing to suspend the rules of democracy in favor of protection. They shifted from the structure of open democracy to grant more authoritarian power to leaders in times of crisis, and the power would last until the threat abated (Finley, 1983, pp. 24–25). The Romans would follow a similar course in their republic, creating a dictatorship in times of war (Mackay, 2004, pp. 27–28). During the American Civil War, Abraham Lincoln imprisoned opponents without informing them of charges, suspending the writ of habeas corpus (Goodwin, 2005, pp. 354–355). In times of emergencies, some societies have been willing to sacrifice personal liberty in the name of security.

The question of the suspension of liberty lies at the root of arguments concerning homeland security. Proponents at one end of the spectrum argue that the open nature of democratic societies leaves the social structure open to attack. They argue that some limitation on civil liberties is necessary to preserve the greater good. On the other end of the spectrum, people argue that limiting civil liberties is far more dangerous than the more limited threats posed by terrorism. Like Donald Black (2004), they argue that when governments suppress freedom in the name of counterterrorism, their actions are more violent than the terrorists they are trying to stop. There are many differing positions between these two extremes, and the debate complicates any approach to homeland security (Wise and Nadar, 2002).

Because the dispute is unresolvable, a metaphor might be helpful. More than a century ago, tremendous debates raged in the navies of Japan, Europe, and the United States about the construction of battleships. The problem focused on three critical aspects of battleships: speed, armor, and firepower. Any time engineers increased one of the three, they had to decrease the other two. For example, one set of nations decided to develop fast battle cruisers before World War I. This meant that they had to reduce the number and caliber of big guns on the ships as well as the armor plating. Guns and armor added weight and slowed the cruisers. The battleship debate was a zero-sum game.

The debate about homeland security involves similar factors. Decreasing civil liberties limits individual freedom and increases governmental power. It may increase protection from terrorism, but it increases citizen vulnerability to the abuse of governmental power. Just as it was impossible to build a battleship that had the heaviest guns, the thickest armored protection, and the fastest speed in any navy, so it is impossible to construct a counterterrorist system that ensures complete protection, allows for maximum civil liberty, and protects unrestricted freedom of movement. Issues need to be balanced, and the debate centers on the areas that should be emphasized.

Human Rights and Civil Liberties

civil liberties: Individual rights granted to citizens under the U.S. Constitution.

Civil liberties refers to the individual freedoms people have under a system of law. The Constitution is the law of the land in the United States. It establishes procedures for government and provides for civil liberties. The first ten amendments, known as the **Bill of Rights,** further limit the power of government. Americans enjoy particular freedoms under the Constitution, and the government cannot take these freedoms away. This is civil liberty.

Bill of Rights: The first ten amendments to the U.S. Constitution.

human rights: The basic entitlements and protections that should be given to every person.

Most people believe that all humans enjoy basic rights. They should not be enslaved, exploited, or subjected to arbitrary abuse such as genocide or unwarranted punishment. These are known as human rights, and they have been articulated by many governments as well as the United Nations (1948). **Human rights** focus on the legal right to exist in a society in which people are free from arbitrary coercion.

People have the right to be free, choose their religion, and have a fair trial (see *Expanding the Concept: The UN Universal Declaration of Human Rights*).

Human rights intersect terrorism and homeland security in two controversial areas. First, terrorist attacks on innocent civilians violate the human right of people to exist apart from political violence against innocent people. Second, governments must respect the human rights of their opponents. Ideally, governments are not allowed to act outside the bounds of human decency and law when countering terrorists. Both positions create political and legal firestorms. Terrorists justify murders by stating that civilians are never innocent because they act within the governmental system (Pew Foundation, 2005). Governments frequently justify inhumane actions against terrorists by stating that they have sacrificed the right to humane treatment because they use terrorism (Porteous, 2006).

Debates about terrorism, governmental authority, and homeland security almost always touch on these issues. Those who favor strong security at any cost tend to overlook human rights abuses and de-emphasize civil liberties. Those who favor civil liberties tend to de-emphasize security while emphasizing human rights. Many different positions between these extremes argue that the rule of law serves to mediate between these positions.

Defense in Depth

Changes in how war is fought affect the structure of civil society. For example, jihadist communities believe that their very existence is threatened. To paraphrase their most important philosopher, Sayyid Qutb (1965), jihadists are on a cliff and about to topple over its edge. They are threatened by Muslims who do not accept the jihadist philosophy and by the non-Muslim West. As a result, jihadists believe they can use any method to disrupt their enemies' societies. Stated another way, the target of terrorism is social order. Terrorists fight against the way a group of people lives. Therefore, combating terrorism is not simply a matter of taking a battle to an enemy.

The logic of conflict becomes clear when the method of fighting and the targets of combat are placed together. Terrorism attacks *civil* society and *civilian* targets. Defending against terrorism implies that military force must extend beyond the military. In other words, to defend against terrorism, a nation or culture must use *civil defense*. The idea of **defense in depth** is that all levels of society must become involved in homeland security. Defense in depth is designed to protect a community fighting for its way of life (see Cebrowski and Barnett, 2003; Barnett, 2004).

defense in depth: Using social networks in national defense. It is based on Arthur Cebrowski's idea of operating at all levels of society.

Homeland security makes sense within this logic, but it raises a host of issues. This logic assumes that the community wants to fight for its existence, which implies that all members of the community are committed to a similar goal. Approaching conflict in this manner may solve logical issues, but it asks a society to engage in great sacrifice to achieve its objectives. As Martin van Creveld (1991, pp. 142–156) says, at some point violence serves to justify violence. This style of thought also asks members of a social group to be sufficiently ruthless with enemies to defeat them and to have the political will for rigorous self-examination. In short, defense in depth may require citizens to alter the way they live and sacrifice the comforts of everyday life. For example, Americans have learned to tolerate increased security at airports and public schools.

The ideas of democracy and individual freedom have been developed in the West over the past thousand years. The United States, founded on these principles, struggled with the issues of democracy and civil rights. At the country's birth, property-holding males governed, women were noncitizens, and slavery was acceptable. The rights of citizenship spread slowly for nearly 250 years, and the reality of individual freedom developed in the tension between ideal freedom and state power. Defense in depth alters the balance by emphasizing state power. Laws, military behavior, police power, information gathering, and other aspects of civil existence are altered when an entire society engages in a conflict.

When homeland security is being discussed, the topic of individual rights usually becomes part of the discussion. To engage in a struggle against terrorism, Americans must examine themselves and honestly select a course of action that they will accept. It cannot be imposed by legislative action, military force, or police power. It cannot be defined by self-appointed civil rights guardians. Attorneys and courts are fond of claiming this area for their exclusive jurisdiction, but the issue extends far beyond judicial logic. If Americans want to secure the homeland, they need to engage in a thorough self-examination and decide what they are willing to sacrifice and how they will maintain the most cherished aspects of social freedom (Cole and Dempsey, 2002, pp. 11–12).

This is not an abstract academic exercise. Many jihadists are engaged in a cosmic struggle, what they believe is a life-and-death struggle between good and evil. They believe that they must not lose the battle for God; they also feel bound by no rules in

EXPANDING THE CONCEPT

The UN Universal Declaration of Human Rights

In 1948, the United Nations adopted the Universal Declaration of Human Rights. The provisions include the following:

- All human beings are born free and equal in dignity and rights. They are endowed with reason and conscience and should act toward one another in a spirit of brotherhood.
- Everyone is entitled to all the rights and freedoms in the Declaration; and no distinction shall be made on the basis of the racial, religious, political, jurisdictional or international status of the country or territory to which a person belongs.
- Everyone has the right to life, liberty, and security of person.
- No one shall be held in slavery or servitude; slavery and the slave trade shall be prohibited in all their forms.
- No one shall be subjected to torture or to cruel, inhuman, or degrading treatment or punishment.
- Everyone has the right to recognition everywhere as a person before the law.
- All are equal before the law and are entitled without any discrimination to equal protection of the law.
- Everyone has the right to a legal remedy if human rights are violated.
- No one shall be subjected to arbitrary arrest, detention, or exile.
- Everyone is entitled in full equality to a fair and public trial.
- Every defendant has the right to be presumed innocent until proved guilty according to law in a public trial.
- No one shall be subjected to arbitrary interference with his privacy, family, home, or correspondence. Everyone has the right to the protection of the law against such interference or attacks.
- Everyone has the right to freedom of movement, and the right to leave any country, including his own, and to return to his country.
- Everyone has the right to seek political asylum from persecution.
- No one shall be arbitrarily deprived of his nationality nor denied the right to change his nationality.
- Men and women of full age have the right to marry and to found a family. Marriage shall be entered into only with the free will and consent of the spouses.
- Everyone has the right to own property and no one shall be arbitrarily deprived of his property.
- Everyone has the right to freedom of thought, conscience, and religion.
- Everyone has the right to freedom of opinion and expression.
- Everyone has the right to freedom of peaceful assembly and association.
- Everyone has the right to take part in the government of his country, directly or through freely chosen representatives. The will of the people shall be the basis of the authority of government.

Source: United Nations, http://www.un.org/Overview/rights.html.

the course of this holy war (Ruthven, 2000, p. 398). Killing their enemies—Muslims who disagree with the jihadist philosophy and non-Muslims—is a sacramental act. Death is the ultimate expression of their religion, and killing is horrific and spectacular. If the jihadists obtain weapons of mass destruction (WMD), they will use them. Americans will be better prepared to secure the homeland if they have engaged in a nationwide discussion of defense in depth and its impact on civil liberties before an attack. If the discussion takes place after a population center has been destroyed, emotions and reaction will guide the response. In that case, homeland security itself could become a threat to the American way of life.

Self-Check

> Explain the difference between civil rights and human rights.
> Is it possible to increase security and preserve civil rights?
> How is defense in depth related to civil rights?

Civil Liberties and Federal Power

Federal counterterrorist laws were toughened after the 1995 Oklahoma City bombing. President William Clinton supported legislation to increase the government's power to limit civil liberties in the face of terrorism. Many civil libertarians criticized Clinton and Congress for these actions. President George W. Bush supported similar legislation in 2001 and again in 2005. After heated debate, the president and Congress reached a compromise in 2006; the provisions of the PATRIOT Act stayed intact. President Obama continued the same policies after taking office in 2009, and he supported continuing many of its provisions in May 2011. The pattern was clear: The United States had increased restrictions on civil liberties after each major terrorist attack.

The USA PATRIOT Act of 2001

In the weeks following September 11, the Bush Administration sponsored legislation that contained increased responsibilities for criminal justice and other agencies. The **USA PATRIOT Act** has ten sections, or titles, outlining new powers for governmental operations (for a summary, see Doyle, 2002, and *Expanding the Concept: An Overview of the USA PATRIOT Act*). Title I is designed to enhance domestic security. It creates funding for counterterrorist activities, expands technical support for the FBI, expands electronic intelligence-gathering research, and defines presidential authority in response to terrorism. This section of the law also forbids discrimination against Arabs and Muslims.

Some of the most controversial aspects of the PATRIOT Act appear in Title II, which aims to improve the government's ability to gather electronic evidence. In other words, it gives police officials expanded authority to monitor communications. It also allows intelligence and federal law enforcement agencies to share noncriminal information with each other. In addition, it forces private corporations to share records and data with federal law enforcement agencies during investigations and allows the FBI to seize material when it believes national security is jeopardized. Title II also contains a sunset clause, automatically ending the provisions of the PATRIOT Act unless it is renewed before a certain time limit, and it enacts congressional oversight of the act.

Other sections of the law affect law enforcement and the criminal justice system in a variety of ways. Title III empowers federal law enforcement to interact with banking regulators and provides arrest power outside U.S. borders for U.S. agents investigating terrorist financing and money laundering. Title IV increases border patrols and monitoring of foreigners within the United States and mandates detention of suspected terrorists. Title VII focuses on police information sharing, specifically targeting a nationwide police investigative network known as the Regional Information Sharing System (RISS). Before the PATRIOT Act, RISS was used only in criminal investigations.

USA PATRIOT Act: A law passed in October 2001 that expands law enforcement's power to investigate and deter terrorism. Opponents claim that it adversely affects civil liberties; proponents claim that it introduces reasonable measures to protect the country against terrorists. The act was amended and renewed in 2006, and the ability to collect and analyze domestic intelligence remained part of the law. Provisions for allowing roving wiretaps, increased power to seize evidence, and increasing wiretaps were approved in 2011.

EXPANDING THE CONCEPT

An Overview of the USA PATRIOT Act

Critics of the USA PATRIOT Act say that it infringes on civil liberties. Supporters believe that it provides critical law enforcement tools. Here is an overview of the sections affecting law enforcement.

Title I, Designed to Enhance Domestic Security. Creates a counterterrorism fund, increases technical support for the FBI, allows law enforcement to request military assistance in certain emergencies, expands the National Electronic Task Force, and forbids discrimination against Muslims and Arabs.

Title II, Designed to Improve Surveillance. Grants authority to federal law enforcement agencies to intercept communication about terrorism, allows searches of computers, allows intelligence agencies to share information with criminal justice agencies, explains procedures for warrants, creates new definitions of intelligence, allows for roving wiretaps, and provides for expanding intelligence gathering. The USA PATRIOT Act has a sunset clause: If not renewed by Congress, it will automatically expire.

Title III, Designed to Stop Terrorism Finances. Grants expanded powers to law enforcement agencies to seize financial records, provides access to financial records, forces transactions to be disclosed, and expands investigative power in money laundering.

Title IV, Designed to Protect U.S. Borders. Outlines measures to protect the borders, tightens immigration procedures, allows foreigners to be photographed and fingerprinted, and gives benefits to victims of terrorism.

Title V, Enhances Investigative Powers. Provides a reward program, calls for sharing of investigative findings among law enforcement agencies, extends Secret Service jurisdiction, and forces educational institutions to release records of foreign students.

Title VI, Designed to Compensate the Families of Public Safety Officers Killed during a Terrorist Attack.

Title VII, Designed to Expand the Information-Sharing Network. Provides for the expansion of law enforcement's nationwide information exchange—the Regional Information Sharing System (RISS).

Title VIII, Strengthens Criminal Laws. Defines terrorist attacks, defines domestic terrorism, provides the basis for charging terrorists overseas, criminalizes support for terrorism, criminalizes cyberterrorism, allows investigation of terrorism as racketeering, and expands bioterrorism laws.

Title X, Contains Miscellaneous Addenda.

Supporters of the PATRIOT Act believe that it will increase federal law enforcement's ability to respond to terrorism and that it will create an intelligence conduit to improve communication among local, state, and federal police agencies (U.S. Department of Justice, n.d.). Supporters believe counterterrorism will be strengthened by combining law enforcement and national defense intelligence. Opponents of the law argue that it goes too far in threatening civil liberties and expanding police powers (Cole and Dempsey, 2002, pp. 186–187). Critics are especially concerned about sharing noncriminal intelligence during criminal investigations. The most pressing concern centers on the increased power of the government to monitor the activities of its own citizens.

The Debate about Governmental Power

The most controversial facets of counterterrorism are symbolized by the USA PATRIOT Act, and the most sensitive aspect of the law deals with intelligence gathering and sharing. Many diverse groups across the spectrum of American politics, from constitutional conservatives to civil libertarian activists, worry that the law will encroach on civil freedoms. The American government was founded on the idea

separation of powers:
The distribution of power among the executive, legislative, and judicial branches of government. When powers are separated, there is a balance among the powers. No one branch can control the government.

First Amendment:
Guarantees the rights to speech, assembly, religion, press, and petitioning the government.

Fourth Amendment:
Particularly applicable to law enforcement and homeland security, it limits government search and seizure, including the elements of arrest.

Fifth Amendment:
Protection against arbitrary arrest, being tried more than once for the same crime, and self-incrimination. It also guarantees due process.

Sixth Amendment:
Guarantees the right to an attorney and a speedy public trial by jury in the jurisdiction where an alleged crime occurred. The amendment also requires that a suspect be informed of any changes.

of civil liberties. This means that citizens are free from having their government infringe unreasonably on the freedoms guaranteed in the Constitution and the Bill of Rights. Stated simply, increasing the ability of the government to collect information increases executive-branch power. Therefore, opponents of increased governmental power focus their criticism on the government's intelligence activities, or information gathering. Supporters of increased intelligence activities say that a nation cannot fight terrorism without gathering intelligence (for general comments on intelligence in U.S. law enforcement, see Carter, 2004).

When criminal justice and national security agencies gather information about organizations and people, they do so as an extension of the executive branch of government. Any effort to expand executive power will affect the other branches of government. The U.S. Constitution separates the powers of the three branches of government: executive, legislative, and judicial. This is known as the **separation of powers.** Elected bodies of lawmakers (the legislative branch) pass laws, courts (the judicial branch) rule on them, and law enforcement and correctional agencies (executive branch) enforce them. This separation of powers acts as a check and balance to the amount of power wielded by each branch of government (Perl, 1998; Best, 2001; Cole and Dempsey, 2002, pp. 15–16; Carter, 2004, pp. 8–17).

A quick overview of constitutional issues illustrates points where homeland security policies and the Constitution intersect. The main body of the Constitution separates powers and prescribes duties for each branch of government. Powers not explicitly given to the federal government go to the states. The Bill of Rights also comes into play by protecting free speech and the right to assemble (**First Amendment**), preventing the government from performing illegal search and seizure (**Fourth Amendment**), and preventing self-incrimination (**Fifth Amendment**). The **Sixth Amendment** helps to protect these rights by ensuring that suspects have access to an attorney. Interpretations of the Constitution and its amendments have protected American liberties for more than two centuries.

Constitutional Amendments Important to Law Enforcement

First Amendment—Congress shall make no law respecting an establishment of religion, or prohibiting the free exercise thereof; or abridging the freedom of speech, or of the press; or the right of the people peaceably to assemble, and to petition the government for a redress of grievances.

Fourth Amendment—The right of the people to be secure in their persons, houses, papers, and effects, against unreasonable searches and seizures, shall not be violated, and no Warrants shall issue, but upon probable cause, supported by Oath or affirmation, and particularly describing the place to be searched, and the persons or things to be seized.

Fifth Amendment—No person shall be held to answer for a capital, or otherwise infamous crime, unless on a presentment or indictment of a Grand Jury, except in cases arising in the land or naval forces, or in the Militia, when in actual service in time of War or public danger; nor shall any person be subject for the same offence to be twice put in jeopardy of life or limb; nor shall be compelled in any criminal case to be a witness against himself, nor be deprived of life, liberty, or property, without due process of law; nor shall private property be taken for public use, without just compensation.

Sixth Amendment—In all criminal prosecutions, the accused shall enjoy the right to a speedy and public trial, by an impartial jury of the State and district wherein the crime shall have been committed, which district shall have been previously ascertained by law, and to be informed of the nature and cause of the accusation; to be confronted with the witnesses against him; to have compulsory process for obtaining witnesses in his favor, and to have the Assistance of Counsel for his defence.

The Constitution guides the United States in war and peace, and it allows certain actions in times of emergency—actions that would be prohibited if there were no emergency. This makes terrorism a constitutionally murky subject, a cloudy area obscuring the boundary separating war and peace, because many people disagree about the nature of terrorism. Many legal scholars argue that terrorism is not a continuing emergency (Cole and Dempsey, 2002, pp. 189–201). For example, America's enemies of September 11 used terrorists trained in military-style camps to attack civilian targets. Logically, national security agencies, such as military forces and the CIA, try to prevent attacks whether they are engaged in a war or not. Criminal justice agencies do not take actions for war—they protect individual rights; local, state, and federal courts are not charged with national defense (see del Carmen, 1991, pp. 73–176). Controversy arises when criminal justice systems and the defense establishment begin to blend their activities.

National Public Radio broadcast a special report focusing on constitutional issues in December 2001, and matters quickly lined up along party lines. Attorney General John Ashcroft called for the right to deport suspected terrorists after secret hearings, and Defense Secretary Donald Rumsfeld gave orders to detain accused al Qaeda terrorists without trial. Two such detainees were U.S. citizens. Critics argued that such actions endangered the rights of Americans (Seelye, 2002).

Senate Judiciary Committee Chair Patrick Leahy (D-Vermont) said that the executive orders coming from the Bush Administration were disconcerting. According to Senator Leahy, President Bush's counterterrorist proposals threatened the system of checks and balances, giving the executive branch of government too much power. Attorney General Ashcroft disagreed with Senator Leahy's conclusions, arguing that the proposed guidelines were solely to protect the country from terrorists. One group is skeptical of increased executive power; the other sees it as logically necessary to protect the country.

Several other issues come to the forefront with regard to civil liberties. Civil rights attorney Nancy Chang (2001) criticizes the PATRIOT Act on the basis of democracy. She points out that the act was rushed through the House and Senate, with no public hearings and no time for public debate. There were no conferences or committee reports. No time was allowed for security needs to be examined; the legislation came quickly in the emotional tide after September 11. The most important aspect, she finds, is the increased ability of the government to look into the affairs of its own citizens. By allowing the government to blur the distinction between defense intelligence and criminal evidence, the PATRIOT Act tramples on reasonable expectations of privacy.

Others argue that the PATRIOT Act is an unreasonable attack on electronic communication (Electronic Frontier Foundation, 2001b). According to this line of thought, the government overreacted to September 11. Technological societies are open to attack by subnational groups or even deranged individuals, and protection requires thoughtful, reflective analysis and reaction. Instead, Congress rushed legislation, amending 15 different statutes. The law gives federal law enforcement agencies the right to monitor Internet searches and to keep tabs on individual queries. The government is allowed to conduct roving wiretaps without probable cause in the hope of obtaining information. For many, the provision in Title II forcing Internet service providers to give information on their users to federal law enforcement agencies is not acceptable.

Not everyone believes that the PATRIOT Act represents an attack on individual rights. For example, two senators with strong civil liberties records think that the criticism of the act is premature (Straub, 2002). Senator Dianne Feinstein (D-California) believes that we cannot rush to judgment. Time will show how the act is used in the real world. It may be necessary to revisit the law, but first we need to see how it is implemented. Senator Charles Schumer (D-New York) believes that the law is balanced. It limits personal freedom while reasonably enhancing security. Both senators think that it is necessary to balance civil liberties and social protection.

Championed by the Bush Administration, the PATRIOT Act is a lightning rod in the debate pitting national security against civil liberties. Technological societies are vulnerable to technological attack—whether from individuals engaged in a killing spree, criminal gangs, or terrorist conspiracies—regardless of ideology. The more sophisticated the attackers, the greater the chances for multiple deaths. September 11 exacerbated the issue, but America was vulnerable before the hijackings and remains vulnerable today. Supporters claim that the PATRIOT Act and other governmental actions are necessary for security. Critics believe that the loss of civil liberties in the name of security is unreasonable. This debate continues, and the courts have yet to rule on the issues.

Debate and the 2006 Law

The 2001 PATRIOT Act was scheduled for renewal in 2005. Although the House of Representatives voted to renew the law in December, some members of the Senate believed that the 2001 law had been passed too quickly. They argued that many of the provisions expanded governmental authority too far. In addition, they were leery about making some of the intelligence-gathering practices permanent. Although many Republicans wanted to pass the extension of the PATRIOT Act before the 2006 elections, the Democratic Senate leaders urged caution. Some in the president's own party had reservations about some of the PATRIOT Act's provisions (Holland, 2005).

How the PATRIOT Act had been used in prior years caused these reservations. The Bush Administration contended that law enforcement agencies had employed the provisions carefully, using them only to stop terrorist attacks. In testimony before Congress, officials from the Justice Department assured the nation that no agency had overstepped its bounds. Critics did not agree. They accused the government of having selectively released information and of having hidden unfavorable reports. They also said that agencies were classifying public documents in an effort to hide governmental activities. They were especially critical of "sneak and peek" provisions that had allowed the government to search for information without informing the person who was being investigated (Regan, 2004).

Several lawmakers, both Republican and Democratic, were concerned about provisions for gathering secret information and the original PATRIOT Act stipulations denying legal representation in terrorism investigations. In the spring of 2006, the White House and Congress reached a compromise on some of the controversial articles of the PATRIOT Act, and new provisions were approved. Under the renewed act, when the government seeks information, the request can be challenged in court. When information is requested in a terrorist investigation, suspects and others involved may talk about it. Suspects may also seek counsel from an attorney. The renewal also requires retailers to maintain information on sales of over-the-counter drugs that could be used to produce methamphetamines.

Some of the less controversial articles were renewed. The government has the right to intercept communications. Criminal intelligence can be given to agencies charged with national security, and the security community can openly communicate with the law enforcement community. The renewed law also extends the time suspects can be kept under surveillance and allows the government to seize electronic or other evidence with a warrant. The law also requires Internet and e-mail providers to hand over records. Finally, the renewed law expands the power of federal law enforcement agencies to collect national security intelligence (Associated Press, 2006).

Extending Provisions in 2011

Much of the power of the PATRIOT Act was preserved in 2011 when the Department of Justice argued for the continuation of three key provisions. First, the attorney general asked for permission to continue **roving wiretaps**. These are used when a surveillance target is using disposable phones or intermittent Internet connections. Law enforcement officials may quickly monitor all new transmissions without returning to a court to obtain a new search warrant.

roving wiretaps: A method of quickly intercepting disposable phone or Internet traffic. A roving wiretap allows law enforcement officers to monitor new connections without returning to court for another search warrant.

The second provision deals with evidence. The PATRIOT Act gives law enforcement officials expanded powers to gather evidence in national security cases. When they are making an arrest or serving a search warrant, they may collect all items that might be related to the cases. For example, if a person is taken into custody in a terrorism case, investigators may want to seize all of the electronic equipment in the suspect's home. They may do so.

The final aspect of the law preserved by the Obama Administration deals with eavesdropping. The government has the right to conduct wiretaps of noncitizens who are suspected of acts that threaten national security (*New York Times*, 2012). Leading Democrats in the Senate complained about the president's support for these three provisions, claiming that there were no efforts to ensure that civil liberties would be protected. The attorney general disagreed (D. Taylor, 2011).

Self-Check

> Why is it necessary to limit governmental power even when the nation is threatened by terrorism?

> Describe the most controversial aspects of the 2001 PATRIOT Act.

> How were those aspects addressed in the 2006 renewal?

Terrorism and the Constitution

One of the major contentious issues between civil rights advocates and the government during the Bush Administration was the role of the president. When they came to power in 2000, both President Bush and Vice President Richard Cheney believed that the power of the presidency had been watered down in past presidencies and that Congress and "activist judges" had taken too much authority from the president's office. They sought to increase presidential power (Mayer, 2006). This resulted in a series of confrontations over power, confrontations that spilled over into counterterrorist operations.

Constitutional Concerns

David Cole and James Dempsey (2002) sent out a warning after the 1996 counterterrorist law took effect in the wake of the 1995 Oklahoma City bombing. They reiterated their warning after passage of the 2001 USA PATRIOT Act. Stated simply, they fear that federal law enforcement's power is growing too strong in a wave of national hysteria. Their thesis is that counterterrorist legislation empowers law enforcement agencies to enforce political law. By contrast, terrorists must violate criminal laws to practice terrorism. Therefore, Cole and Dempsey argue, it is best to keep the police out of politics and focused on criminal violations. For example, police agencies should not be allowed to interfere with citizens engaged in political associations, even when they are unpopular. (Cole and Dempsey would probably say *especially* when they are unpopular.) Law enforcement has the right to intervene in a citizen's affairs when officers reasonably suspect that a crime has been committed or if a person may be involved in criminal activity. If terrorists are prosecuted under criminal law, the Constitution will be preserved.

Cole and Dempsey point to four cases that illustrate their fears. In the late 1960s and early 1970s, the FBI trampled the rights of suspects and citizens through COINTELPRO, its counterintelligence program. Second, from 1981 to 1990, the FBI overreacted against U.S. citizens who expressed sympathy for revolutionaries in El Salvador. The FBI even designated friends of activists as "guilty by association." Third, in the 1990s, Muslims and Palestinians were targeted by investigations even though there were no reasonable suspicions that they were involved in a crime. Finally, during the 1990s, political investigations of radical environmentalists and others expanded.

Citing a group of law professors that petitioned Congress to limit political investigations, Cole and Dempsey argue that law enforcement should gather intelligence only when there is reason to suspect criminal activity. They worry that the 1996 counterterrorist legislation and the 2001 PATRIOT Act and its 2006 renewal give the police power to regulate political activity. The real danger is not using reasonable efforts to fight terrorism, they say. There are certain instances when the intelligence community should share information with the criminal justice community. For example, when Osama bin Laden was charged in the bombings of Dar es Salaam and Nairobi, it would have been appropriate for the FBI and CIA to share information. Cole and Dempsey worry that Congress has given these agencies and others too much power to share intelligence without judicial review.

Their argument illustrates the passions involved in counterterrorism. The Cole–Dempsey thesis is endorsed by a host of jurists, civil rights organizations, legal scholars, and die-hard conservatives who support many of the Bush Administration's other efforts. There is even support for their position inside law enforcement, especially within the FBI.

The Cole–Dempsey argument is directly applicable to two critical arguments made during the Bush Administration, and both positions are applicable to the idea of increasing executive power as the primary method for countering terrorism. President Bush and Vice President Cheney maintained that the president has the power to designate certain terrorists as **enemy combatants** and subject them to trial by special military courts. They also contended that the president has the authority to allow national security intelligence agencies to intercept telephone calls that originate in the United States but are directed to suspected terrorists in foreign countries (Savage, 2006). Critics maintain that this is an abuse of power (Leahy, 2006).

The issues around executive power form the crux of the debate about civil rights and security, and it is no different from the examples cited earlier from ancient Greece and Rome and the American Civil War. Some societies give presidents, prime ministers, and other leaders increased power when a nation is threatened. Because leaders sometimes abuse those powers, civil libertarians are almost always suspicious of additional authority. It is the primary issue involved in discussions about the Constitution, the role of executive authority, and the subsequent actions of law enforcement agencies.

Increased Executive Powers

Several constitutional scholars have examined the issue of increasing executive powers to combat terrorism. Lewis Katz (2001) believed in limited government before September 11, but he rethought his position in the wake of the attacks. He finds an analogy in drug enforcement. America launched its "war on drugs" and soon discovered that it could not thwart drug traffickers under constitutional rules of evidence. As a result, police power has been growing since 1971, Katz argues, and citizen protection under the Fourth Amendment has been decreasing.

Leery of government, Katz says that the real test of the Fourth Amendment is **reasonableness**. In normal times, police officers can be held to a higher standard of behavior than in times of emergency. September 11 constituted an emergency.

enemy combatants: A legal term used to describe non-state paramilitary captives from Afghanistan. The term was later applied to all jihadist terrorists by the Bush Administration. The Obama Administration maintained detention centers after ordering the closing of Guantánamo shortly after President Obama took office in January 2009.

reasonableness: The actions an average person would take when confronted with certain circumstances. This is a Fourth Amendment doctrine.

It was not unreasonable to interview Middle Eastern immigrants, Katz concludes, nor was it unreasonable to increase electronic surveillance powers. Although a longtime opponent of a national identification system, Katz now says that such a system would not be unconstitutional, provided citizens were not ordered to produce identification without reasonable suspicion. Actions taken to prevent another September 11, he argues, do not violate the Fourth Amendment when they are reasonable.

Katz does believe that some governmental actions are unreasonable. Eavesdropping on attorney–client conversations, for example, violates the Sixth Amendment, a suspect's right to counsel. Military tribunals deny the presumption of innocence. He argues that we cannot sacrifice the very liberties that we are fighting to preserve. Katz's argument indicates that the balance of powers is a dynamic system, vacillating according to circumstances. In other words, there is no blanket policy of reasonableness, and care must be taken to balance security with civil liberties.

Sherry Colb (2001) of the Rutgers University School of Law also applies a doctrine of reasonableness. Examining the issue of racial profiling (targeting specific groups of people on the basis of race, ethnicity, religion, or other social factors), Colb concedes that police in America are facing a new enemy. Racial profiling has not helped the police control drugs, she argues, and it violates the Due Process Clause of the **Fourteenth Amendment**. Yet the scope of September 11 calls into question previous assumptions about profiling. As police agencies assemble profiles of terrorists, one of the characteristics may be ethnicity.

Fourteenth Amendment: A person cannot be deprived of freedom or property by the government unless the government follows all the procedures demanded for legal prosecution.

Colb believes that any profiling system, including one having ethnicity as a factor, will yield many more investigative inquiries than apprehensions. The reason is that there are only a small number of terrorists in any group, regardless of their profile. For example, the population of people matching the profile is greater than the population of terrorists in the profile group. By the same token, a number of terrorists may fall within a particular ethnic group, and the urgency of September 11 may require action. If a terrorist profile is developed and it includes race as one of the characteristics, Colb suggests that some opponents of ethnic profiling may find that they endorse it in the case of counterterrorism.

The Bush Administration moved quickly in the wake of September 11 (Van Natta, 2002). Wanting to do everything possible to catch terrorists, the Department of Justice (DOJ) scrapped the restrictions it had placed on agents in earlier times. Issuing new guidelines, it freed the FBI from the requirement to rely on reasonable suspicion before launching an inquiry. Unless the courts ruled otherwise or legislative bodies intervened, agents were free to search for indicators of illegal activity in open-source information, including the Internet. They could monitor chat rooms or engage in data mining. Agents could go undercover in political or religious organizations to search for threats to security. No longer required to seek central-office approval, local FBI offices were empowered to launch inquiries based on their own information and initiative. According to the *New York Times* (Savage, 2009), the Obama Administration kept these changes intact.

New guidelines, executive orders, and military tribunals have created strange twists in the criminal justice system. Reporter Katherine Seelye (2002) examines the summer of 2002, when two foreign-born terrorist suspects were arrested on the basis of probable cause and were sent to trial. At the same time, two U.S. citizens, Yaser Esam Hamdi and Jose Padilla, were held by military force without representation. Hamdi was fighting for al Qaeda when he was captured in Afghanistan in November 2001; Padilla was arrested on May 8, 2002, for his alleged involvement in a plot to detonate a dirty bomb in the United States. Hamdi and Padilla, both of whom would have been criminally charged before September 11, were detained much like prisoners of war, whereas two alleged terrorists arrested on U.S. soil were afforded the rights of criminal suspects. Hamdi was released in September 2004.

Ruth Wedgwood (2002), a former federal prosecutor who now teaches law, offers an explanation of the irony of Americans being detained militarily and foreigners being held under civilian arrest. She says that al Qaeda attacked civilian targets, gaining an advantage in the U.S. criminal justice system. Al Qaeda, Wedgwood says, has learned that it is best to recruit U.S. citizens for operations because citizens are not subject to arbitrary arrest. Pointing to Jose Padilla, Wedgwood states that his arrest represents a conundrum between reconciling public safety and the law. The issues surface in the difference between intelligence operations and law enforcement administration. In short, she says, going to trial means exposing intelligence sources for the sake of a criminal conviction.

Wedgwood presents the logic of the two situations. Common sense dictates that the detention of terrorists does not follow the pattern of criminal arrests. Terrorists are detained because no writ, no law, and no court order will stop them from attacking. They must be physically restrained, Wedgwood says. The purpose of detention, she argues, is not to engage in excessive punishment but to keep terrorists from returning to society. She admits that the situation presents a public dilemma for a nation under the rule of law.

Wedgwood argues that indefinite detention by executive order is not the most suitable alternative. Terrorists could be given a military hearing to determine whether they continue to represent a threat. A panel of judges might rule on the danger of releasing suspected terrorists from custody. The Constitution is not a suicide pact, she says, citing a famous court decision. Common sense demands a reasonable solution to the apparent dichotomy between freedom and security.

E. V. Konotorovich (2002) is not as concerned about executive orders as Wedgwood. The stakes are so high, he argues, that the United States must make all reasonable efforts to stop the next attack. Torture is out of the question in this country, but drugs are a viable alternative. Police are allowed to do body-cavity searches for contraband in prison, Konotorovich argues, and the September 11 attacks make abhorrence of such searches pale in the face of massive terrorism. Drugs should not be used for prosecution, he says, but they are acceptable for gaining information. The threat is real, and legal arguments against obtaining information are an illusion. Americans captured by al Qaeda have been quickly executed. Konotorovich believes that Americans must take decisive actions against such terrorists.

Limiting Executive Powers

Susan Herman (2001) of Brooklyn Law School vehemently urges a different approach to counterterrorism, believing that the PATRIOT Act is a law that throws the balance of powers off kilter. She asserts that Congress has relinquished its power to the president and failed to provide any room for judicial review. Congress, Herman argues, chose to fight terrorism by providing funding to the Bush Administration, relinquishing its powers to check the executive branch. Proposals coming from the administration complement congressional actions by increasing the executive power to take actions without judicial review. For Herman, the beginning of the "war on terrorism" translates to a "war on the balance of powers." Herman's argument is based in constitutional law. She compares the USA PATRIOT Act with two previous sweeping pieces of legislation: the 1968 Crime Control and Safe Streets Act and the 1978 Foreign Intelligence Surveillance Act (FISA). Both laws provide guidelines for domestic surveillance.

Title III of the safe-streets act mandates judicial review of police surveillance. Under Title III, criminal evidence cannot be gathered without prior approval from a federal court, and although a judge reviews a request for surveillance in secrecy, the police must prove that wiretaps or other means of electronic eavesdropping will lead to establishing probable cause for a crime. FISA surveillance differs from

Title III warrants. Under FISA, various forms of eavesdropping can be used to gather intelligence. A special judicial review is required before surveillance can be initiated, and any evidence gathered during the investigation cannot be used in a criminal prosecution.

The constitutional concern Herman voices partially focuses on judicial review. The courts have not been as vigilant in protecting individual rights during intelligence cases as they have been in criminal trials. For example, she cites the record of FISA requests. Between 1978 and 2001 federal law enforcement officers applied for 4,275 FISA warrants. They were all granted.

In fairness to the judicial reviewers, it should be remembered that evidence gleaned from these warrants is not used in criminal prosecutions, but this is not the issue bothering Herman. She compares FISA warrants to the type of surveillance proposed under the PATRIOT Act and concludes that the PATRIOT Act allows the government to watch its own citizens with similar rules.

There is no guarantee that such surveillance will exclude evidence from being used in criminal prosecutions. The other part of Herman's argument focuses on the relationship between the executive and legislative branches; she feels that the PATRIOT Act concentrates too much power in the executive branch. The act gives the attorney general power to detain and deport aliens with less judicial review than was required before September 11; the attorney general is required only to have reason to believe that the action is necessary. Courts, she states, would require a much higher standard of proof. The PATRIOT Act also gives the attorney general and the secretary of state the power to designate certain associations as terrorist groups, and they may take actions against people and organizations associated with these groups. Herman believes that Congress has failed to aggressively seek a role in counterterrorism under the PATRIOT Act. The Constitution, she argues, is threatened by these increased executive powers. Her primary fear is that increased executive powers will be used to mask an attack on civil liberties.

The American Civil Liberties Union (ACLU) (2002) voices other concerns over civil liberties. Citing increased executive powers to detain immigrants, the ACLU charges the attorney general with trying to gut the role of immigration courts. The ACLU expresses two concerns. First, after September 11, the attorney general ordered the detention of several hundred immigrants. He refused to openly charge most of the detainees and refused to make the list known for several months. In addition, Attorney General Ashcroft sought to have the rules for detaining and deporting immigrants streamlined. He wanted to make the process more efficient by decreasing the amount of judicial review involved in immigration and naturalization cases. These issues alarmed the ACLU.

During the Bush Administration the ACLU argued that tightened immigration laws were a smoke screen for increasing executive powers at the expense of individual rights. The ACLU believed that the attorney general would rely on political considerations rather than on the rules of evidence when deciding which cases to prosecute. With immigration courts streamlined, there would be no judicial body to oversee executive decisions. The ACLU also believed that President Bush would appoint judges sympathetic to Attorney General Ashcroft's views. This process undermined civil liberties at the expense of the Constitution. The ACLU shifted its focus after the Obama Administration came to power. When Arizona passed a tough new immigration law in 2010, the ACLU supported federal efforts to strike down the state law (ACLU, 2010).

The ACLU's concern can be illustrated by a case shortly after 9/11—the case of Ali Maqtari. Married to a member of the armed forces, Maqtari was driving his wife to Fort Campbell, Kentucky, when police stopped him for questioning and detained him without probable cause to believe he had committed a crime. He was held for eight weeks without formal charges, according to the ACLU. After Maqtari was granted a hearing, a court ruled that the government's position was unjustified and he was released. Without effective judicial review, the ACLU says, Maqtari might not have been released. Coming to grips with terrorism should not involve scrapping personal freedoms protected by the Constitution.

Executive Power and the Courts

While the struggle between Congress and the president continued and legal scholars argued positions about executive authority, the courts began to review some of the issues involved in counterterrorism. One of the first issues involved the detention of enemy combatants at Guantánamo Bay, Cuba. The government contended that it could try the defendants in special military tribunals, apart from normal criminal prosecutions and military law. Judges were not swayed by this argument.

Both civilian and military courts, using similar language, handed down decisions blocking the government's desire to establish special military courts that violate the civil rights established in the American legal system (Bravin, 2007). In the Hamdi case, previously discussed, courts ruled that the defendants were entitled to contest the basis of their arrests. The government cannot hold a person without a hearing in order to ensure that an arrest is justified by probable cause.

There are several other cases in which courts limited executive power. The Supreme Court ruled that the detainees at Guantánamo could contest the charges against them, much in the same manner that the Hamdi case did. In 2006, the courts ordered the government to transfer Jose Padilla, the American originally accused of conspiring to use a dirty bomb, from the military to the civilian criminal court system, where he was convicted of criminal conspiracy in 2007. Later in 2006, the Supreme Court declared that the military tribunal system established for enemy combatants was illegal. In 2007, a military court in Guantánamo dismissed cases against two defendants at Guantánamo Bay on the basis of the earlier Supreme Court decision (Bravin, 2007).

Although the Bush Administration won some of its early battles to gain more power, the courts have been increasingly limiting executive power (see *Expanding the Concept: Court Reversals*). One of the primary reasons is that the president acted without specific congressional authority. The courts have historically supported special laws when Congress has given permission, but they are skeptical when no law is in place. According to an analysis in the *Wall Street Journal* (Bravin, 2007), the Bush Administration did not seek such authorization after 9/11 because it feared that Congress would not grant it.

President Obama issued an executive order closing the Guantánamo facility shortly after taking office in 2009. During the summer Attorney General Eric Holder announced plans to charge some of the leading suspects in the 9/11 plot under federal

EXPANDING THE CONCEPT

Court Reversals

Despite the attempts to increase executive authority in counterterrorism, several court decisions have reversed policies of the White House. These include the following:

June 2004—Two decisions that allow enemy combatants the right to contest their arrests.

April 2006—A decision that prevents U.S. citizens arrested in the United States from being tried outside the criminal court system.

June 2006—The military tribunal system established at Guantánamo is declared illegal because it did not have congressional approval.

June 2007—A military tribunal dismisses charges against two enemy combatants based on the June 2006 Supreme Court decision.

Source: Bravin, 2007.

criminal law. He moved to have the case brought to New York City. Administration officials searched the country for a new detention facility in an effort to move the detainees out of Guantánamo. Both actions met a firestorm of controversy, and the government backed away from holding the criminal trials in New York City. Speaking on National Public Radio in October (NPR, 2009), Attorney General Holder said the January 2010 deadline for closing Guantánamo would be tough to meet, but that it would be done. He also promised that the decision on criminal trials would be made within a month. The government achieved neither objective.

Court decisions and executive power remain an unsettled issue. The United States has not been involved in this type of conflict before. Most analysts think that terrorism should be handled within the bounds of criminal law, but both the Bush and Obama Administrations have failed to provide a clear path for a course of action. This has resulted in legal contradictions that have limited or threatened individual rights. American courts tend to intervene when this happens. If the executive branch of government will not make policy, the judicial branch will begin to do so.

Self-Check

> Why are constitutional scholars concerned with intelligence gathering and the prevention of terrorism?

> Explain the benefits of expanding (or limiting) executive power.

> What effect do courts have on the power of the executive branch to confront terrorism?

Civil Liberties and Police Work

The FBI, with an eye on the court system and a director's promise to fight terrorism within the law, conducted an internal audit to make sure that its actions were legal. The audit found that the FBI might have violated its own rules or federal laws in national security investigations more than 1,000 times since 2002. The vast majority of violations dealt with storing information from e-mails and Internet service providers that agents were not authorized to collect. This indicated a weakness in bureau procedures, and it unveiled something the FBI feared. Its agents did not understand their authority in national security investigations (Solomon, 2007). Critics may point to overreaction, but it should be noted that the FBI performed this audit on its own.

As part of the executive branch of government, law enforcement agencies stand at the forefront of counterterrorism. Whether civil liberties are protected or abused most frequently depends on the way police officers handle their responsibilities. This applies to federal agencies such as the FBI, the Bureau of Alcohol, Tobacco, and Firearms (ATF), and the Secret Service, but it is also applicable to state, local, and tribal law enforcement departments.

Controversies in Law Enforcement

Effective counterterrorist policy is based on intelligence. The 9/11 Commission Report (2004, pp. 339–348) criticizes federal agencies for failing to recognize and share intelligence. The PATRIOT Act, before the commission's findings, was designed to facilitate intelligence gathering and to ensure intelligence sharing. Although this remains controversial on the federal level, sharing is logical because the federal government is constitutionally responsible for national defense. The government can make the argument that *any* federal agency can assist in this process. The problem comes when the federal government requests assistance from state and local governments. When the federal government asks state agencies to collect and forward national defense intelligence, many people take notice.

Any attempt to use state and local law enforcement in intelligence-gathering operations will have constitutional implications. The police may be used in homeland security, but there are strong and logical arguments against this, and equally powerful arguments supporting it. Regardless, even when the executive branch proposes a course of action, police operations will be influenced by court decisions. Local law enforcement's role in homeland defense cannot be developed in a constitutional vacuum.

The criminal justice system collects *criminal* intelligence, not information regarding national security. It collects information when it has reasonable suspicion to believe people are involved in crimes. Although some people may argue about the type of criminal intelligence the police gather, no one questions their right to gather information about criminal activity (see Commission on Accreditation for Law Enforcement Agencies, 1990; Walker, 1992; Radelet and Carter, 2000; Carter, 2004, pp. 8–17).

The dilemma emerges because terrorism moves the police into a new intelligence realm. Criminals engage in crime for economic gain or psychological gratification. Terrorists are political actors using crime to strike their enemies. This causes terrorists to encounter the police, but not from the standpoint of traditional criminals. To gather counterterrorist intelligence, the police are forced to collect political information. If state and local law enforcement agencies are included in national defense, they will collect information having no relation to criminal investigations. No matter which position you might support, this is a dilemma for American democracy. The police are not designed to collect political information (Schmitt, 2002).

Although lacking a defined role, the police in the United States have traditionally been associated with crime control. They respond to crime, prevent crime, and engage in social-maintenance tasks, such as traffic control, within local communities. Although not a formal role, responding to and preventing crime has become the de facto purpose of American law enforcement. Local communities and states have empowered agencies to keep records to assist them in anticrime efforts, but many federal, state, and local laws, as well as civil rights groups, have imposed limits on the types of information the police may gather and retain. Any move to include the police in an intelligence-gathering system alters the expectations local communities have about law enforcement. Communities may decide to empower their police agencies to collect intelligence, but this means changing the focus of police work (see Manning, 1976).

Terrorism, both domestic and international, poses a variety of problems; Richard Best (2001) summarizes well the dilemma over the role for criminal justice. On the one hand, state and local law enforcement agencies are in a unique position to collect and analyze information from their communities. Corrections officials can perform the same role by both incarcerating terrorists and gaining information through jailhouse intelligence. Law enforcement and correctional agencies can become the eyes and ears of domestic intelligence. On the other hand, when the criminal justice system has participated in national defense in the past, abuses have occurred. The primary question is, Does criminal justice have a role in homeland security? Secondary questions are: Do criminal justice agencies want to assume this role? Does the public they serve want them to assume it? There are no easy answers to these questions.

National Security and Crime

Among the controversies surrounding the USA PATRIOT Act is the role of criminal justice, especially law enforcement. The debate comes to a head when the role of intelligence is discussed. There are two general schools of thought about the role of the police in intelligence gathering. One position can be summarized as "eyes and ears." Advocates of this position believe that state and local law enforcement should be used as extensions of, or the eyes and ears of, America's intelligence agencies. They believe the police should collect information and forward it to the appropriate intelligence unit. Extreme proponents of this position would use special police units to collect information beyond potential evidence to be used in criminal investigations. The purpose of such units would be to monitor the activities of political groups that might engage in violence.

Another way of thinking can be called traditional crime response and prevention. Supporters of this perspective fear that police intelligence-gathering activities will interfere with the traditional police missions of fighting crime and providing a social service. They believe that other agencies should gather intelligence. Some other people have a parallel view, fearing expanded police powers.

After September 11, the difference between these two positions became more than an academic debate. Local, state, and federal police agencies began to share information at an unprecedented level. State and local agencies expanded training activities in terrorism, and Attorney General Ashcroft ordered the FBI to create more Joint Terrorism Task Forces (JTTFs). The attorney general also used his prosecutors, the U.S. attorneys who represent the government in the federal court system, to create Anti-Terrorism Task Forces (ATTFs) in all the nation's U.S. attorneys' offices. The name was changed to Anti-Terrorist Assistance Coordinators (ATACs) in 2003. All these federal efforts were based on the assumption that local, state, and federal agencies would work together. The attorney general also called for a seamless interface between law enforcement and defense intelligence. The intelligence role in law enforcement is what frightens civil libertarians.

Intelligence, Networks, and Roles

All levels of law enforcement form nodes in a network opposed to terrorism. Although police agencies have a multitude of other functions, their primary roles in preventing terrorism involve information gathering and sharing, protecting citizens and property, and investigating criminal conspiracies (J. White, 2007). Collecting, analyzing, and storing criminal intelligence requires a criminal predicate. Under the Fourth Amendment, law enforcement personnel cannot collect intelligence without the standard of reasonable suspicion. As stated in federal guidelines (28 CFR Part 23), the police must have a suspicion that a crime is taking place or is about to take place before information can be gathered, analyzed, and stored. Information involved in national security may not meet this test. Law enforcement is not to assume the national security mission. In other words, police officers should continue their assigned role in law enforcement and legally share information (Carter, 2004, pp. 5–18; J. White, 2004b, pp. 73–74). (See *Expanding the Concept: The War on Drugs as an Intelligence Model.*)

Networks encourage the flow of information. Carter (2004, pp. 192–193) argues that when information is not shared it loses its value. It is not enough to maintain community partnerships; agencies need to act in cooperation. Total criminal intelligence (TCI) involves sharing; indeed, TCI does not work unless agencies share criminal intelligence. Sharing information neither poses a threat to civil liberties nor reduces the effectiveness of partnerships. Shared information enhances crime prevention and decreases fear inside a community. It allows the intelligence function to operate effectively when it is accomplished within legal guidelines.

Danger to civil liberties appears when agencies inside a network either act illegally or forget their role. The growth of terrorism has thrown law enforcement into an arena traditionally reserved for national security, but police officers are neither intelligence agents nor soldiers. Confronting a terror network requires resources for a long-term struggle and a solidified national will. It does not and should not require extraconstitutional law enforcement actions. Stated more succinctly, the ideological Salafi jihadist network does not threaten American civil liberties, but an improper police response may (see Jenkins, 2006, pp. 169–177). Law enforcement's role in national defense is to continue efforts at community partnerships.

In testimony before the House Subcommittee on Homeland Security (C-Span, 2007), Brian Jenkins, Frank Cilluffo, and Salam al Marayati offered an interesting assessment of the role of community partnerships in preventing terrorism. Rather than militarizing the problem, they presented terrorism, especially the jihadist movement, as a social idea. It appeals to young people, especially confused and potentially violent young men. There are times when force must be used, but Jenkins, Cilluffo, and al Marayati equated terrorism to other social problems such as child abuse, illegal drug use, gangs, drunk driving, and family fights. Law enforcement agencies became involved in education, intervention, information gathering, and enforcement in each of these areas. As Jenkins said, they play their role without violating civil rights.

EXPANDING THE CONCEPT

The War on Drugs as an Intelligence Model

The war on drugs has produced a national system of police intelligence gathering and dissemination. Combined federal, state, and local law enforcement agencies operate in conjunction with each other to gather intelligence and conduct operations.

Proponents hail this process as a model of sharing resources and intelligence. They point to cooperation among agencies and investigative information-sharing systems as the answer to the intelligence problem (National Drug Intelligence Center, 2002). At the national level, drug intelligence reports are synthesized and disseminated to state and local agencies. On the surface, these multijurisdictional efforts seem to be an effective tool in countering drug traffickers.

Opponents have a different view. Many police administrators believe that the systems are not effective, and they refuse to participate in them (Herman, 2001). Other people outside law enforcement look at the intelligence network and claim that it is both a failure and an assault on the Fourth Amendment. Proponents of this position state that the war on drugs is ineffective, and the real loser in the process is civil liberty. Critics believe that trying to collect drug intelligence merely leads to labeling certain people or groups without making a dent in drug traffic.

War has not changed, tactics have. Terrorism represents a tactical change in conflict. Police work has not changed, nor has the police function. Deeper community relationships will enhance law enforcement's role in national security by preventing crime, reducing fear, solving problems, and increasing the flow of information. Returning to traditional crime-fighting roles or militarizing the police will reduce police effectiveness. Police operating deeply in the community in the service role help to provide for the common defense (J. White, 2007).

Militarization and Police Work

There are roles for law enforcement in homeland security, but there are questions about the necessity of developing these functions along military lines. Some policy makers have responded by increasing the military posture of the police. In other words, some police agencies have developed units that appear more suited for military functions than for police work. On the other hand, some administrators and critics stress the civilian aspect of law enforcement, and they lament the paramilitary approach to controlling social problems. The debate between these two approaches will become more intense as the police role in homeland defense is institutionalized over time.

militarization: Responding to social problems with military solutions. In law enforcement, militarization is usually characterized by martial law.

Before discussing the issue, it is necessary to define **militarization**. Military forces are necessary for national defense, and they are organized along principles of rigid role structures, hierarchies, and discipline. A military posture prescribes unquestioning obedience to orders and aggressive action in the face of an enemy. In Clausewitz's sense, military forces are either at war or at peace, and when engaged in war, their efforts are targeted toward an enemy. Any bureaucracy can be militarized when it adopts military postures and attitudes, and the police are no exception. If the United States is engaged in a war against terrorism, some policy makers will inevitably want the police to look more and more like a military force, especially because the Constitution prevents the U.S. armed forces from enforcing domestic law. In this context, militarization refers to a process in which individual police units or entire agencies begin to approach specific problems with military values and attitudes. They adopt paramilitary dress, behave with military discipline, and, most importantly, prepare to make war with an enemy.

In 1967, the International Association of Chiefs of Police (IACP) discussed the problem of confronting violent demonstrators (International Association of Chiefs of Police, 1967, pp. 307–327). The late 1960s was a time of social change and violent confrontation, and state and local police frequently found themselves facing hostile crowds. In response, the police often adopted military maneuvers to control violent demonstrations, and the tactics were successful. The IACP, however, was not quick to jump on a military bandwagon. Its training manual instructs police officers to use minimal force to solve potential problems. The appearance of paramilitary force should be a last resort, used only when a situation has deteriorated. The IACP, America's largest association of state and local police executives, has traditionally favored the civil role of policing over a militaristic approach.

Terrorism may bring a change in attitudes. For example, because many forms of terrorism require resources beyond the capacity of local police agencies, law enforcement has been forced to turn to the military for assistance. State and local law enforcement agencies have few international resources compared with the defense and intelligence communities. Finally, terrorism demands a team approach. Law enforcement officers exercise considerable individual discretion when on calls or initiating activities, and they generally work alone or in small groups of two and three. Terrorism, like special events, changes the equation, bringing hundreds of officers together in a single function. The temptation may be to militarize the police response to terrorism.

Two trends may be seen in this area. The first comes from violent demonstrations. The Metro-Dade Police Department in Florida developed an effective method, called the field-force technique, for responding to urban riots after a particularly bad riot in 1980. By 1995, hundreds of U.S. police agencies were using the technique, and it now seems firmly established. The technique calls for responding to a growing disorderly crowd, a crowd that can become a precursor to a riot, with a massive show of organized police force. Officers assemble in an area away from the violent gathering. They isolate the area, providing a route for the crowd to disperse. Then they overwhelm it with military riot tactics. A field-force exercise looks as though a small army has moved into an area using nonlethal violence (see Christopher, 1999, pp. 398–407; Kraska and Kappeler, 1999, pp. 435–449).

A second source of militarization comes from police tactical units. These special operations units are called out to deal with barricaded gunmen, hostage situations, and some forms of terrorism. They are also frequently used on high-risk drug raids. Tactical units use military weapons, small-unit tactics, and recognized military small-unit command structures (see Cappel, 1979; Jacobs, 1983; Mattoon, 1987). In the past few years, many of the units have abandoned the blue or brown tactical uniforms of police agencies for military camouflage, making it virtually impossible to distinguish them from military combat units.

Peter Kraska (1996) takes exception to these trends in militarization. He argues that police in America have gradually assumed a more military posture after violent standoffs with domestic extremists, and he fears that terrorism will lead to a further excuse to militarize. This will adversely affect democracy, Kraska argues, because it will lead police to picture their jurisdictions as war zones and their mission as military victory. If the problem of terrorism is militarized, other social problems will see the same fate. Kraska's point is well taken. As Michael Howard (2002) states, calling our struggle with terrorism a "war" creates a variety of conceptual problems. In addition, Americans have become used to military metaphors for other social problems such as "wars" on drugs or poverty.

Most terrorism analysts believe that terrorism is best left to the police whenever possible (see Wardlaw, 1982, pp. 87–102). The difficulty is that the growing potential for devastation in single events sometimes takes the problem beyond local police control. In addition (U.S. Department of Defense, 2001; Perl, 2001), military forces are often targeted, and they must develop forces to protect themselves. Some of the same principles guiding military force protection will eventually spill over into American policing. In the future, state and local police may face subtle social pressure to militarize the terrorist problem and respond to it with paramilitary force.

Emerging Critiques in the Academic Community

Quite a few criminologists, behavioral scientists, and civil libertarians have begun to question the new emphasis on intelligence operations and the role of law enforcement in homeland security. Once again, this illustrates differences between the practice of law enforcement and the academic analysis of the field, and it is indicative of the split between practical and applied criminology. Practitioners tend to develop and/or analyze the processes of homeland security networks, intelligence systems, and partnerships (J. White, 2004; Carter, 2004 and 2007; Johnson, 2007; Carter and Carter, 2009; Straw, 2009). Although some practitioners are critical of the process (Taylor and Russell, 2012), there is a growing body of behavior literature questioning new intelligence structures. These studies go beyond the operational work of practitioners, and such views are important in the democratic control of intelligence.

Anthony Newkirk (2010) examines a controversial case involving the Maryland State Police to argue that the network of homeland security intelligence operations amounts to an assault on civil liberties. Troopers in a Maryland fusion center gathered data on a wide array of groups from 2005 to 2006. They were able to analyze data from the field using a private software system. In addition, the system allowed the troopers to conduct data mining operations on their targets. The groups under examination included community activists, peace advocates, environmentalists, death penalty opponents, and advocates for immigrants. This resulted in a tremendous amount of data that were placed in numerous files. Newkirk argues that these files were not appropriate because there was no criminal predicate for gathering, analyzing, storing, and sharing the information. One antiwar group had data about political activities stored under the heading "Terrorism: Anti-War Protest." Another entry for an environmental group was stored under "Terrorism: Environmental Extremism." The activities of peaceful political groups, however, are neither terrorism nor subject to government control.

Newkirk sees a number of problems with such intelligence. First, the surveillance itself is scandalous. It is not lawful to spy on American citizens engaged in political activity. Second, the fusion of information leads to a threat to civil liberties. Various levels of law enforcement shared this information with intelligence units and private corporations. This was conducted with murky lines of authority and a lack of public accountability. Finally, the government has no right to maintain security files on innocent people. The history of homeland security since 9/11, Newkirk argues, is a story of violations of liberty. The exacerbated information-sharing environment of the homeland security system, as evidenced in Maryland, is but one example of a system of abuse.

Torin Monahan (2009, 2010; and Monahan and Palmer, 2009) of Vanderbilt University argues in a similar vein. Looking at operations during the Obama Administration, Monahan uses case data to demonstrate that the homeland security system is too invasive. Rather than protecting civil rights, it threatens them. The primary vehicle behind the threat is the fusion center concept. Stated simply, Monahan claims that law enforcement officials break laws in fusion center operations. His studies suggest that officials illegally infiltrate political groups and collect data. Since many investigations are based on nationality or ethnicity, the resulting data helps to inject racism into the intelligence system. Worst of all, the network of fusion centers has no public accountability.

The intelligence system is justified under the concept of "predictive policing," that is, the analysis of data to prevent crimes before they occur. The world of fusion centers is akin to the movie *Minority Report*, a futuristic story of a police unit that arrests and detains potential criminals prior to criminal activity. The only protection from such abuses, according to Monahan, is to introduce democratic accountability.

field contacts: People encountered during normal patrol or investigative operations. Law enforcement officers frequently gather information from such people. The Nationwide SAR Initiative standardizes such information.

Suspicious Activity Reporting (SAR), a Department of Justice program designed to systematically analyze information gleaned from law enforcement **field contacts**, is another issue bothering some social scientists. Discussed more fully in the next chapter, the Nationwide SAR Initiative standardizes the manner in which law enforcement information is gathered and stored. Civil rights advocates believe that information should not be gathered and stored based on suspicion alone. In fact, under federal law, such information must be destroyed unless the government can prove that it is directly related a criminal activity. Under terrorism rules, however, information can be stored under the auspices of national security. Kenneth Farrall (2011), New York University, says this is an affront to personal privacy.

Despite such emerging criticism, there are operators within the homeland security system who are keenly aware of civil rights, privacy issues, and civil liberties. Writing for *Security Management*, Joseph Straw (2009) admits that the tremendous amount of information gathered by the national network of fusion centers could expose innocent citizens to unfair scrutiny. This is why policy guidelines are crucial. They must reflect the law and be rigorously enforced. Ron Brooks (2011), the director of a fusion center in northern California, agrees. Policy guidelines must be enforced and coordinated on a national basis. If power is abused, the fusion center concept will be threatened along with security. David and Jeremy Carter (2009) argue that enforceable standards can be used to protect civil liberties.

There is no easy answer to this problem. Technology allows small groups of people to inflict tremendous numbers of casualties, but it can also be used to collect and analyze the information necessary to prevent such destruction. The balance between security and liberty is precarious and will remain so.

✓ **Self-Check**

> Why must civil libertarians be concerned with law enforcement power?
> What might happen if law enforcement agencies move beyond their traditional role and act as an instrument of military force?
> What concerns do some academic analysts have about the intelligence system?

CHAPTER TAKE AWAYS

Law enforcement has a paradoxical role in homeland security. On the one hand, it participates in a system of national defense. On the other hand, law enforcement's key function is to preserve the rights of citizens. It is difficult to balance this power. Many civil libertarians believe that the government in general and law enforcement in particular have gained too much power in the name of homeland security. Positions can be summarized by looking at arguments for and against the PATRIOT Act and the increased power of the executive branch of government. Increased executive power has the potential to separate law enforcement from the public through militarization and surveillance. Such separation is not acceptable in a democracy.

OBJECTIVE SUMMARY

- Increased intelligence activities, homeland security measures, and using governmental power in preventing terrorism must be balanced with the protection of liberty. *Civil rights* refers to protection from governmental power. The basic freedoms and protections that should be granted to all people are known as human rights.
- Changes in the nature of conflict bring about a need to operate deeply in the social structure. This concept can be called *defense in depth*. Because it encompasses civil society, it is not possible to talk about such a concept with regard to homeland security without discussing civil rights.
- The USA PATRIOT Act, first enacted in 2001, enhanced the gathering and sharing of intelligence. It increased executive authority. Several aspects of the PATRIOT Act were modified in 2006. Provisions supporting roving wiretaps, increased powers to gather evidence, and monitoring of noncitizens were renewed in 2011. Supporters of the PATRIOT Act believe that it gives the government tools necessary for combating terrorism. Critics maintain that the PATRIOT Act threatens civil liberties.
- The PATRIOT Act affects the doctrine of the separation of powers by increasing the power of the executive branch of government. It impacts the Bill of Rights, the first ten amendments to the Constitution, by giving the government greater power to monitor communication, search and seize evidence, and detain suspects. It affects the Fourteenth Amendment because the government has more legal methods for denying or removing civil rights.
- An increase in executive-branch powers makes criminal justice more effective, but it threatens civil liberties. There are arguments for both increasing and reducing the power of the executive branch of government in preventing terrorism.
- Recent court decisions have emphasized the importance of (1) balanced power among the branches of government and (2) maintenance of civil rights. Despite the recent increase of executive power, the courts still have the right to review national security laws.
- Criminal justice agencies protect individual civil rights. The key for successful performance is to continue preventing terrorism by completing law enforcement functions and building community partnerships.
- Law enforcement remains a civilian entity. The police are more effective in a democracy when they are embedded in a community and when they reflect its values. The police should be an extension of the community equipped to solve problems and enforce the law. There is a danger when police work becomes militarized. It separates law enforcement agencies from the communities they serve.
- Recent criminal justice scholarship has been taking a more critical view of enhanced governmental powers. It has been focused on the intelligence system and the role of fusion centers. Generally, many researchers feel that law enforcement agencies are collecting too much information beyond criminal intelligence.

Critical Engagement: Detainees and the Future

National security was a contentious issue in the 2008 president election, and it has remained so in subsequent elections. People who believe that September 11 changed the way the United States approaches international conflict tend to favor detention without arrest, military tribunals for suspected terrorists, and denial of civil rights to accused terrorists. Civil libertarians tend to see the other side. They prefer extending constitutional protection to suspected terrorists, trials in civilian courts, and dismantling detention facilities like the one at Guantánamo Bay. Both sides are passionately committed to their positions.

President Obama vowed to end many of the policies of President Bush, and he moved in that direction shortly after taking office. America has a history of governing by law, and President Obama moved to use the criminal justice system to combat terrorism. He ordered the closing of the Guantánamo detention facility within days after his inauguration. Attorney General Eric Holder sought to have Khalid Sheikh Mohammed and other September 11 suspects moved to New York City for a civilian trial. The DOJ also began to look for a new detention facility in the United States. These moves raised a firestorm of opposition and fears that suspected terrorists would use their trials as a propaganda stage and a platform for martyrdom.

In the end, the Obama administration not only backed away from its original intentions, it sought to maintain a variety of security measures started by the Bush administration. It sought continued authority to monitor communications, and it argued for the necessity to delay Miranda warnings in the cases of two jihadist suspects taken into custody after attempted attacks in the United States. It authorized attacks on American citizens who had embraced the jihad in Yemen and Pakistan. While the DOJ opened investigations on prisoner abuses, the administration seemed to hesitantly embrace the Bush doctrine of preemptive strikes by asking NATO to operate beyond its borders to deter international terrorism. The administration continued to argue that detainees could be deported to countries that knowingly violate human rights, and it continued to argue for the right to detain foreign terrorist suspects indefinitely. In many ways, both President Bush and President Obama have used the same policies.

Consider these issues in terms of future developments:

- Does terrorism present a unique set of challenges such that traditional American civil liberties should be denied? If yes, at what points should government actions be limited? If no, how could terrorism be combated within the limits of criminal law? Prosecutors routinely overcharge suspects to obtain a better plea bargaining position. What would happen if they used terrorism charges to enhance plea bargaining power?
- Do civil rights apply equally to any person in America regardless of citizenship? Do they apply to noncitizens taken into military custody in a foreign country?
- Has the problem of terrorism changed the American system of justice? Some countries have developed special legal measures during times of terrorism. If the United States follows this path, what steps could it take to continue legal standards in criminal law?

KEY TERMS

Military tribunals,
  p. 15-389
Civil liberties, p. 15-390
Bill of Rights, p. 15-390
Human rights,
  p. 15-390
Defense in depth,
  p. 15-391

USA PATRIOT Act,
  p. 15-393
Separation of powers,
  p. 15-395
First Amendment,
  p. 15-395
Fourth Amendment,
  p. 15-395

Fifth Amendment,
  p. 15-395
Sixth Amendment,
  p. 15-395
Roving wiretaps,
  p. 15-398
Enemy combatants,
  p. 15-399

Reasonableness,
  p. 15-399
Fourteenth Amendment,
  p. 15-400
Militarization,
  p. 15-407
Field contacts,
  p. 15-410

Security, Terrorism, and the Future

LEARNING OBJECTIVES

After reading this chapter you should be able to:

> Describe the purposes of the DHS quadrennial review.

> Identify the factors that increase the future effectiveness of multiagency antiterrorism operations.

> Explain factors that complicate partnerships between units of government and private industry.

> Describe the importance of foreign policy in homeland security operations.

> Explain the necessity of creating a system that can absorb an attack.

> Identify the value of a liberal education as a means of countering future terrorism.

> Outline probable future methods of terrorist attacks.

> Summarize the developing law enforcement programs designed to prevent terrorism.

> Describe probable future strategic directions in terrorism.

In April 2012 Don Yamamoto, a principal deputy for Africa in the U.S. Department of State, testified in front of the House Committee on Foreign Affairs (U.S. Department of State, 2012). He focused on the nature of political violence in Africa, and this caused him to move beyond regional African problems to the future of terrorism. Specifically, the al Qaeda ideology of central Asia was spawning franchise operations throughout the world. Even though violence in Africa tends to be dominated by local political issues, al Qaeda might establish future footholds in Africa.

Yamamoto pointed to three areas: the Horn, the Maghreb, and the Niger Delta. Al Shabaab signed an alliance with al Qaeda central in Pakistan, Yamamoto testified. This was worrisome because Somalia and the Horn are dominated by regional militias, African peace keepers, and local issues. While mainly symbolic, al Shabaab's action threatened to further destabilize and internationalize the conflict. This was directly related to al Qaeda in the Islamic Maghreb (AQIM). A regional movement that has been unsuccessful in establishing a political base, AQIM has raised quite a bit of money in a kidnapping campaign. Money gives it power and the al Qaeda–al Shabab alliance provides a link to organizations with a political base. Boko Haram in Nigeria has only focused on Muslim–Christian fighting, but the proximity of AQIM and the extremist rhetoric of Boko Haram provide the basis for an expanded alliance. One of the future directions of terrorism may involve establishing franchises of ideology—that is, small regional groups forming networks through a common radical set of beliefs. This is one of many potential threats in the future of terrorism.

Security and the Changing Nature of Terrorism

Terrorism must change constantly. If terrorists fail to change their structures and tactics, they can be dissected, isolated, and destroyed by security forces. Therefore, updating a practical text on terrorism for law enforcement, security, the military, and readers in related fields is difficult. The historical and sociological sections can be modified by reviewing the emerging scholarly material, but contemporary issues present a different problem. When presenting the latest information, much of the data is outdated within weeks of the book's release. At the same time, the discussions remain relevant since they serve as background material for unfolding events. This is true of any work based on current events, and it is particularly applicable to terrorism because terrorist groups and operations change constantly. Terrorists transform for survival. When terrorists remain static, they can be arrested or destroyed.

Speculation about future issues is also difficult, but it is a necessary process. National defense and criminal intelligence operations are based partially on building background information to assess the probability of future pathways. The past helps to identify future trends. This chapter differs from previous chapters that focused on the essential background and current issues. The focus here is on the future. To be sure, a detailed analysis of future probabilities requires not only background information; it also needs to be augmented with real-time field intelligence and tactical assessments. Therefore, no chapter in any book can complete this task. It is possible, however, to look at broad policy areas and identify selected issues that will impact the field. That is the purpose of this final chapter. In essence, each section becomes almost like the exercises you were asked to complete in the *Critical Engagement* sections of the preceding chapters.

The chapter begins with two discussions, one involving emerging issues in homeland security and the other focusing on trends in law enforcement and other security forces. These discussions will be followed by an examination of trends in terrorist tactics, and this section will discuss probable changes that security forces may be forced to face. The chapter will conclude with speculations about the future of international and domestic terrorism.

Emerging Issues in Antiterrorist Security Policy

Homeland Security Act of 2002: A federal law created in 2002 and amended in following years. It established the Department of Homeland Security and reorganized the presidential cabinet. DHS's primary antiterrorism mission is to prevent attacks and respond to them when they occur.

The **Homeland Security Act of 2002** was touted as the biggest reformation of government since World War II, and it certainly changed the organization of the federal government. It also increased potential confusion. In essence, the Department of Justice (DOJ), the Department of Defense (DOD), and the Department of Homeland Security (DHS) were given specific functions in national security, and their missions were to support the overall direction of foreign policy and the Department of State (DOS). Each department also interfaces with the Office of the Director of National Intelligence (ODNI) and the multiple agencies assigned to that organization. Since Congress controls funding for all the departments and since it exercises oversight, it should be expected to ensure that homeland security is guided by an efficient, comprehensive direction in policy (see recommendations from the 9/11 Commission). A comprehensive federal direction in homeland security, in turn, should help to clarify the antiterrorism role for state, local, and tribal police agencies. In practice, actual operations often become duplicative and inefficient. Therefore, some type of assessment is needed to increase future efficiency.

Quadrennial Home-land Security Review (QHSR): A requirement that the secretary of DHS conduct a review of the department's operations every four years. According to the first report, the Homeland Security Act of 2002, as amended, requires the secretary to "delineate and update, as appropriate, the national homeland security strategy," and to "outline and prioritize the full range of the critical homeland security mission areas of the Nation" (DHS, 2010).

9/11 Commission Imple-mentation Act of 2007: A federal law requiring selected recommendations of the 9/11 Commission to be implemented. One of its provisions helped to create regional fusion centers.

Janet Napolitano: (b. 1957) The third secretary of homeland security. President Obama appointed her while she was serving her second term of governor in Arizona.

Although critics maintain that there is no overall direction, Congress tried to create a method for ensuring cooperation rather than confusion at the national level when it passed the Homeland Security Act. It required a **Quadrennial Homeland Security Review (QHSR)**, and the **9/11 Commission Implementation Act of 2007** recommended that the first review be conducted in 2009. The DOD undergoes the same type of review every four years. Such assessments of past activities provide information for future directions, although the first review was complicated because it began with a Republican administration that had different goals from the Democratic administration that replaced it and conducted the evaluation (Hanson, 2009).

The purpose of the four-year review is to try to prevent the type of confusion and duplication that arises from overlapping roles. As a result, the first review described interagency cooperation, the future direction and priorities of security activities, and the actions which ensure that operations will complement the overall direction of national security policy. DHS Secretary **Janet Napolitano** directed that her department focus on five areas: (1) counterterrorism and domestic security management, (2) securing U.S. borders, (3) enforcing immigration laws, (4) disaster prevention and management, and (5) unifying the DHS mission with all the other departments and national policy (Hanson, 2009). Secretary Napolitano created a set of goals after the review (Department of Homeland Security, 2010b).

Multilevel Communication and Sharing

The most complex process in the DHS analysis is the implementation of a comprehensive strategy to ensure effective management of national policies. In addition to the critical issues identified in the four-year review, practical aspects of everyday operations and management become vital for policy success. This implies three important areas for future security. First, all the federal agencies involved in terrorism prevention need to develop procedures to ensure that activities complement one another. But this is not enough.

The people who most frequently encounter terrorism are found in local law enforcement. This means that future antiterrorism activities must operate beyond the federal level and be effective among state, local, and tribal police agencies. Second, agencies need to develop methods for encouraging communication. Although procedures and personal rivalries frequently inhibit communication, organizational leaders

---

ANOTHER PERSPECTIVE

Four-Year Review Findings

Department of Homeland Security

- Threats and Hazards
  - WMD attack
  - Jihadist extremism
  - Cyberattacks
  - Pandemics, accidents, natural hazards
  - Criminal networks and transnational crime
  - Small-scale terrorism

- Future Trends
  - Economic and financial instability
  - Dependence on fossil fuels
  - Threats from climate change
  - Emerging technologies
  - Uncontrolled, illegal, or dangerous movement of people and goods

Source: Quadrennial Homeland Security Review Report, 2010.

need to develop formal and informal connections among agencies and encourage their personnel to use those networks. Third, it is necessary to share information. Policies will not work unless information flows through the system (Wise and Nader, 2008).

These issues may seem overwhelming at first, but obstacles can be circumvented if multiple agencies establish and utilize a network of formal and informal relationships. For example, a study of 500 law enforcement agencies in Illinois revealed that both police executives and local government officials believed that the probability of a terrorist attack was low. They also realized that if an attack were to happen, it would have massive consequences. Therefore, they expanded outreach to other law enforcement agencies and developed methods for sharing criminal intelligence (Giblin, Schafer, and Burruss, 2009). This information, in turn, can be passed on to various federal agencies and incorporated in national policy. Agencies in Illinois developed a formal system of information sharing that resulted in formal and informal communications.

The Private Industry Problem

Another critical policy link in terrorism prevention comes from the private sector. Effective preventive policies can be enhanced by private–public partnerships. This comes with two problems. First, private businesses operate outside government, and they are not subject to the same constitutional rules and regulations. They might use information obtained through open government security networks to gain some type of business advantage or to stop a competitor. Second, and somewhat related, private businesses may use their relations with governments to win government contracts.

Tom Barry (2010) believes that one of the emerging critical issues in antiterrorism policy is the development of homeland security industries by private businesses.

ANOTHER PERSPECTIVE

DHS Security Mission and Goals

Mission 1: Preventing Terrorism and Enhancing Security

- Goal 1.1: Prevent Terrorist Attacks
- Goal 1.2: Prevent the Unauthorized Acquisition or Use of Chemical, Biological, Radiological, and Nuclear Materials and Capabilities
- Goal 1.3: Manage Risks to Critical Infrastructure, Key Leadership, and Events

Mission 2: Securing and Managing Our Borders

- Goal 2.1: Effectively Control U.S. Air, Land, and Sea Borders
- Goal 2.2: Safeguard Lawful Trade and Travel
- Goal 2.3: Disrupt and Dismantle Transnational Criminal Organizations

Mission 3: Enforcing and Administering Our Immigration Laws

- Goal 3.1: Strengthen and Effectively Administer the Immigration System
- Goal 3.2: Prevent Unlawful Immigration

Mission 4: Safeguarding and Securing Cyberspace

- Goal 4.1: Create a Safe, Secure, and Resilient Cyber Environment
- Goal 4.2: Promote Cyber Security Knowledge and Innovation

Mission 5: Ensuring Resilience to Disasters

- Goal 5.1: Mitigate Hazards
- Goal 5.2: Enhance Preparedness
- Goal 5.3: Ensure Effective Emergency Response
- Goal 5.4: Rapidly Recover

Source: Quadrennial Homeland Security Review Report, 2010.

He draws a parallel with national defense industries, saying that the term **military-industrial complex** is no longer applicable to the relationship between big defense contractors and the government. These businesses, he argues, have gone far beyond supplying weapons or goods; they provide command and control systems and perform military services. In other words, they are replacing defense activities traditionally performed by the government. Barry cites the increasing number of operations that corporations perform in the DOD and in the intelligence community.

Barry fears that the future will bring a further expansion as defense contractors move into homeland security. As evidence, he says that industrial contracting amounted to 45 percent of the DOD budget in 1960, but that it consumes about 70 percent today. The relationship with the whole government is greater because defense contractors and subsidiaries have expanded business by providing essential services to other governmental agencies. Several units of government now simply outsource their work to private contractors. Barry says that this has created a "government-industrial complex," and it is expanding into homeland security operations.

Since 9/11, Barry argues, the private incursion into the public sphere has been expanded by the wars in Iraq and Afghanistan, the focus on homeland security, and the technical requirements of governmental communication systems. He believes that this has resulted in a governmental–industrial partnership whose boundaries are difficult to determine. More important, blurring services makes it difficult to determine if the national interests are being served.

After September 11, the nation's ten largest defense contractors immediately created homeland security departments in their companies, and they quickly became the largest contractors under DHS. They offered several security services, including services in information and communication technology. This cemented their position in homeland security because defense contractors possess skills most governmental agencies do not have. This means that private corporations control vast amounts of intelligence data. The situation is magnified by what Barry calls "revolving door security." When government officials leave organizations responsible for homeland security, they are frequently hired by industries in the same business. Other government officials form their own consulting corporations, performing the same tasks that they performed in government. Barry believes that future security will be privatized by corporations unrestrained by constitutional limitations on government power.

Dawn Rothe and Jeffery Ian Ross (2010) share Barry's fears. Analyzing the role of private military contractors from a criminological perspective, they present evidence to show that private companies often circumvent the constraints on government power. This happens in a number of ways. Private companies act within their own operational systems and decide what they will and will not report. Rothe and Ross argue that they frequently act outside of the rules of warfare. At times, the government has even intervened to protect civilian contractors who have broken local laws, giving them the same protection afforded to the U.S. military forces. Logistical contractors have been given even more freedom because the DOD has reduced the number of regulators in support and supply. Private corporations are doing the work of the government.

These arguments point to a dangerous trend in the future of homeland security. As discussed in several previous chapters, information is power. If Barry is correct, private contractors control both quite a bit of the intelligence flowing through the homeland security system and the manner in which it flows. They also control information about their activities, and corporations tend to behave in their own self-interest, as Rothe and Ross demonstrated with military contracting. Corporations do not share their shortcomings with the government agencies that hire them. If these trends continue, a large portion of private industry will control vast portions of anti-terrorist policy. This can be stopped if government agencies hold corporations strictly accountable and if a capacity to replace private functions is readily available.

The United States experienced a major recession beginning in 2007, the worst in 75 years, because several large banks were on the verge of collapsing. The federal government lent billions of dollars to the banking industry, stating that they would devastate the economy if they did, indeed, fail. A similar crisis could develop if private corporations became responsible for homeland security.

Private and public partnerships have produced some positive benefits. These have developed from relations between government agencies and businesses cooperating in physical security. Rather than purchasing systems or services, this approach involves sharing security information to benefit the entire community. This involves such activities as protection of the infrastructure, threat analysis, shared security information, and reducing community vulnerability. When cooperative relationships focus exclusively on community security, the risks posed by government–private industrial relationships are reduced.

Homeland Security and Foreign Policy

New military counterinsurgency policies suggest that approaches to terrorism require partnerships. While this implies intergovernmental relations among DHS, DOJ, DOD, the intelligence community, and local law enforcement, it also means that homeland security will be increasingly determined by foreign policy. In other words, future homeland security depends on the success of U.S. foreign policy. The policy should be comprehensive, moving in effective pragmatic directions, and its counterterrorism efforts should complement other attempts to secure the homeland (see Garfinkle, 2008).

Defense Secretary Robert Gates (2010) addresses these issues from a military perspective. One of the greatest threats in the coming decades, Gates writes, is a city poisoned or reduced to rubble by a terrorist attack. The plan for this type of attack will most likely originate in a state that cannot secure its own territory. He believes that this is the main security problem of our times. The United States must approach this from a comprehensive perspective, combining defense policy with homeland security efforts and a renewed focus on foreign relations. Reestablishing failed states, Gates says, is beyond the capacity of the military.

partner capacity: As used by Robert Gates, the ability of the U.S. military forces to form alliances with security forces and civilian governments inside states threatened with destabilization.

Gates believes that security begins by developing a concept he calls **partner capacity**. The primary goal of this policy is to help countries develop the means to defend themselves and create alliances to support them. It also means that American military forces should be prepared to train, equip, and help secure military forces within counties deemed to be our partners. Gates says that the United States has a long record of performing this type of mission, but it has not fully embraced the potential benefits. The primary reason for falling short is that such an approach to security is beyond the military's capacity. Partnerships extend beyond a government needing assistance. Gates writes that partnerships require new cooperative intergovernmental relationships, assistance from allies, and the pooling of resources to solve security problems. In particular, it takes pooled funding and shared missions from the defense and state departments.

Gates argues that three principles should guide this combined approach to foreign policy and antiterrorism security. First, it must be agile and flexible. Threats from failed states do not match institutional planning goals or the congressional budget cycle. Gates says that the United States needs to be able to respond immediately to emerging threats outside of bureaucratic norms. Second, Congress and the executive branch of government need to develop effective oversight mechanisms. He believes that this would be enhanced by including the judiciary. This would have two effects: it would help to keep policy focused, and it would limit opportunities to abuse power. Third, it requires consistent long-term behavior in American foreign policy. Gates concludes that convincing other countries and leaders to become partners with the United States depends on proving that the United States will be reliable and consistent over a long period of time.

The Israeli–Palestinian Conflict

Given the synergistic nature of the conflict between Israel and Palestine, attempts to secure the homeland must take the Middle East into account. Conflict in this area is one illustration of Gates's thesis. Eventually, most jihadist movements come to embrace the Israeli–Palestinian conflict because it is a source of recruitment and focusing anger. Robert Malley and Peter Harling (2010) argue that future foreign policy should shift from a simplistic separation of anti-American militants and pro-American supporters to a more pragmatic framework that takes into account the complex motivations and interests of the nations involved in regional conflicts. America tends to focus on old policies, they argue, rather than on looking at dynamic trends in the region.

According to Malley and Harling, the United States needs to refocus its peacemaking efforts in three areas. First, it needs to stop combining all militants into a single camp. There is no single militant ideology, and countries supporting the militants are not united either. Second, several countries have interests in Middle Eastern stability, and peacemaking policy should take their views into account. Malley and Harling say that Turkey, Syria, and Iran need to be engaged. A realistic Middle Eastern policy cannot be developed if their interests are ignored. Third, when other interests are taken into account, the United States should encourage Israel to make peace with the other regional actors. It will not be easy for the United States to make these shifts, they conclude, nor will the changes be free of risks. The alternative, however, is to continue the failed policies of the past.

Daniel Byman (2010) and Stephen Kinzer (2010), in separate works, suggest two fairly radical shifts to accomplish the shift proposed by Malley and Harling. Byman says that Israel's future security, and by implication peace in the region, depends on the future of Hamas. Although it is an important player in the Middle East, Israel and its allies have refused to recognize Hamas's role as a power broker and a military force. To date, Hamas's legitimacy has not been recognized, and Israel has responded to its rule in Gaza with military force and a controversial blockade that has the support of Egypt. This is ineffective, Byman argues.

Middle East peace talks can begin without Hamas, Byman writes, but they will not be successful if it remains on the sidelines. The international community needs to engage Hamas where it is possible and exploit its weaknesses and vulnerabilities when it will not be engaged. Hamas's rhetoric is radical and uncompromising, but its political activities are more pragmatic. Byman believes that if Hamas is given an opportunity to achieve some type of favorable outcome for Gaza, it might be willing to create a more stable relationship with Israel. Such an approach is risky. It might alienate moderates who feel that Israel is rewarding violence or allow Hamas to build its future military capacity. Yet, Byman says, Hamas is here to stay. Refusing to deal with it will not enhance regional peace. Since our future homeland security depends on a stable Middle East, Byman's approach seems to suggest that the United States should take a more pragmatic approach to Hamas and encourage its allies, including Israel, to follow the same path.

Stephen Kinzer goes even further, suggesting that the United States should develop a new alliance in the region. He suggests a strategic partnership with Turkey to promote regional peace and democracy and to combat extremism. He believes that the movement should include a new partner, the Islamic Republic of Iran. While this appears counterintuitive on the surface, Kinzer believes that Turkey and Iran represent the region's greatest potential for establishing democracies. Turkey has achieved its first steps and is the most democratic nation in the region. Most of Iran's citizens, long denied democratic institutions, dream of having them.

Kinzer focuses on the long-term future, admitting that this triangular approach would not develop overnight. Turkey needs to make small changes, he says, while Iran would have a longer way to go. The United States must also make major changes.

Turkey and the United States have enjoyed a long alliance based on mutual interests. Although this relationship has been strained in the first part of the twenty-first century, it remains stable. Iran is another issue, but Kinzer bases his argument on pragmatism. Iran has two underlying factors: It is emerging as the major regional power, and its current government, with its overtly hostile rhetoric toward Israel and the West, will not be in power forever. Both the United States and Iran have more to gain by cooperating than they do by competing. The major issue is, will America take a long-term approach to rapprochement with Iran and subdue its anger over the 1979 embassy takeover? If so, Kinzer says, an American–Turkish–Iranian alliance would become a major force for regional peace.

Several years ago, police chief James Ahern (1972) wrote that the president speaks from American police cars. He was referring to civil disturbances that required changes in federal policy, the legal system, and the reformation of American policing. It might seem ironic to discuss military partnerships, failed states, foreign policy, and peace in the Middle East in a criminal justice text focused on terrorism and homeland security, but Ahern provided the proper metaphor. Law enforcement efforts to secure the homeland are part of a complex system of intergovernmental actions needed to prevent terrorism. Although state, local, and tribal police forces are in a position to encounter terrorists inside the country's borders, they are not sufficiently deployed or capable of protecting the United States from terrorist attacks. Foreign policy and regional stability in areas like the Middle East are necessary to reduce future terrorist threats. In this sense, the president speaks from the patrol car and so do the other branches of government involved in homeland security.

Absorbing an Attack

The best antiterrorism efforts will fail at points in the future. The United States will continue to experience low-level attacks, and it probably will suffer from a massive assault with thousands of casualties. When this happens, the country will need to recover socially, psychologically, and economically. Lessons about maintaining infrastructure can be learned by looking at the results of natural disasters. If the suffering of New Orleans in the wake of Hurricane Katrina had been due to a terrorist attack, it would have been deemed a successful strike. The reason is that social order completely broke down (Powers and Shen, 2008). This presents another dilemma in the ability to absorb an attack. Democracies need to develop the ability to maintain social order without destroying the base of the democracy (see Body-Gendrot, 2010). If an American city is devastated by an attack or if a segment of the infrastructure is destroyed, the United States will need to have the capability to maintain social order.

Jakub Grygiel (2009) points to an issue identified shortly after 9/11 by former Coast Guard officer Stephen Flynn (2004). The United States must not only work to prevent terrorist attacks, it must also develop the capacity to absorb a major strike. Grygeil says that this is due to the nature of modern terrorist groups. If a state were to use a WMD on another state, the culprit is readily identifiable and the attacked state could strike back. Therefore, even though a WMD threat is real, it is balanced by the capacity for retaliation. Modern terrorist groups, however, operate outside state structures. In essence, Grygiel says, they have an incentive to exist within the nebulous cloud of a nonstate. If a group launches a major attack when it has no visible geographical or political location, it is partially insulated from reprisal.

Al Qaeda can be used to illustrate Grygiel's point. After the 9/11 attacks, the United States struck back at al Qaeda by launching an attack in Afghanistan. When the first phase of the offensive failed to kill or capture al Qaeda's elusive leadership, America became bogged down in the longest war in its history. Only after al Qaeda leadership could be pinpointed in the tribal regions of Pakistan did American efforts to kill or capture its leadership become more effective.

Grygiel illustrates that nonstate actors have an advantage in not being limited by political boundaries. They are not as vulnerable as recognized states, and the threat of retaliation does not diminish their willingness to engage in a massive attack. Therefore, an effective homeland security policy needs to take another factor into account. The United States needs to develop the capacity to absorb a major attack on one of its cities or on some critical aspect of the infrastructure.

Grygiel proposes a measure to deal with networked decentralized terrorist groups. Homeland security strategies should involve defensive measures based on the assumption that a WMD attack will be successful. He suggests that the infrastructure needs to be decentralized. A central system can be disrupted when its control structure is destabilized. It is vulnerable to an attack. A segmented, dispersed infrastructure might be less efficient than a central system, but it is more likely to survive an attack on one of its control structures. Grygiel illustrates this by pointing to the electrical grid. If it is dependent on a few critical transfer stations, it is vulnerable. On the other hand, if its nodes are dispersed in regional networks, it is difficult to take the entire system off-line by destroying a few critical targets. In addition, it is difficult for stateless groups to launch complicated simultaneous attacks against multiple targets.

Grygiel says an effective homeland security policy should be based on the ability to maintain social, political, and economic functions after a major attack. Conventional military and police forces assigned to security are of little value because they cannot protect all possible targets, and it is difficult for military units to attack an organization operating without a national sponsor. Diffuse threats require diffuse defensive measures. He says that cities and regions need to have greater authority to prevent and, if necessary, to respond to terrorist attacks. He believes that creating regional counterterrorism centers in major cities like Los Angeles and New York City is a good beginning. Segments of the United States need to maintain their functions if one of its major cities suffers a devastating attack.

This comes with a risk, Grygiel says. Distribution of state power cannot be accompanied by a virtual splintering of the political system. It is a matter of balance. Decentralization is necessary to the point that it maintains the function of the infrastructure in the event that a centralized center is destroyed. Grygiel does not present a model for creating such a system, but he does point out the need for one. A centralized state cannot be weakened to the extent that it becomes vulnerable to its neighbors, but the nature of modern terrorism requires a reexamination of centralized systems. The future holds the type of prolonged terrorist conflict, Grygiel concludes, that will force the reconceptualization of centralized security.

Other Critical Issues

The future holds changes for other aspects of homeland security, including some that are more abstract. One of these questions focuses on education and training. The nation needs individuals who are broadly educated to deal with emerging complex security threats. Although a number of colleges and universities are creating new degrees, certificate programs, or other concentrations in homeland security, one of the basic functions of homeland security is to develop a pool of critical thinkers. This requires college graduates schooled in a liberal education. Approaching antiterrorism by specialized programs, such as degrees in homeland security or terrorism, may become popular among colleges and universities seeking to increase their number of students, but they cannot replace the basic aspects of a liberal education. Higher education programs, especially at the undergraduate level, will better provide candidates for law enforcement, intelligence, and security force activities if they develop interdisciplinary, problem-solving–based programs (Steinberg, 2008). People charged with preventing terrorism should have critical thinking skills. Liberally educated people can learn a variety of vocational skills.

Closely related to this is an issue raised by the 9/11 Commission (2004, p. 414). The national intelligence community needs a new generation of analysts and agents who are specifically trained to understand the complexities of terrorism. This can begin with a liberal education, but it should be enhanced by graduate and postgraduate education in defense and intelligence-oriented study programs.

Another aspect of future policy should be aimed at settling the debate over the nature of the terrorism problem. Chapter 1 discussed the problem of approaching terrorism as either a military or a criminal justice issue. Historian Richard Kohn (2009) argues that the United States has become increasingly enamored of militarizing social problems since the 1930s. Never slipping into militarism, American political leaders have embraced the rhetoric of war, and this was true after the attacks of 9/11. Kohn believes that this presents problems for the future. First, by militarizing the problem of terrorism, the United States follows a policy embraced by no other Western democracy. Second, civil liberties will be threatened if the response to a future terrorist attack moves America beyond the rhetoric to the reality of a militarized government. Third, the war metaphor does not work. It causes an overreaction to a problem that can be handled by established legal principles.

Brian Jenkins (2010) offers clarity for future terrorism policy. Terrorism is primarily a problem for law enforcement. Terrorists operate outside the law, and they encounter law enforcement officers in the course of their duties. The country's Joint Terrorism Task Forces (JTTF) are much better equipped to deal with the problem of terrorism than the military force is. Yet massive attacks, foreign activities, and failed states are sometimes beyond the capabilities of law enforcement. Intergovernmental operations require that terrorism be approached as a complex problem demanding military, diplomatic, and intelligence community resources to augment law enforcement. Terrorism is a problem for criminal justice, but there are times when a criminal justice approach does not work. Turning to the military for support does not constitute a declaration of war on terrorism.

A theme related to this debate is the necessity of employing military forces in peacetime operations. The U.S. military forces have experience in responding to disasters, bringing humanitarian aid, and providing peacekeeping and security forces in war-torn areas. In addition to the lethal role they play in making military strikes on terrorist strongholds, the military will be called on to assist domestic and international law enforcement agencies faced with a terrorist threat or a terrorist attack. They will also be involved in police-like operations in **force protection**. This will require rules of engagement that are not applicable to combat situations. It means that military forces will increase the use of nonlethal weapons in the future (Capstick, 2001). This is one of the many reasons the United States Military Academy prepares future officers with a curriculum emphasizing critical thinking skills and a liberal education (Keith, 2010).

Jenkins (2010) points to another future issue. The JTTFs represents the best counterterrorist tools in the legal system, but they have one significant drawback. They are based on criminal prosecution rather than on gaining intelligence. Jenkins suggests that the focus of the JTTFs should be expanded and driven by a focus on gathering criminal and national defense intelligence as well as on launching criminal investigations. Opening criminal cases is important, he says, but the importance of gathering intelligence is just as significant. He believes that the JTTF is equipped to carry out this mission.

force protection: Refers to security operations by military forces engaged in securing bases, ports, other areas of operations, and personnel. Military personnel frequently cooperate with local law enforcement and other civil forces when engaged in force protection.

✔ **Self-Check**

> Why is it necessary to create better relations among differing units and levels of government?

> What problems are posed by public–private homeland security measures? How are domestic homeland security activities related to foreign policy?

> What types of homeland security issues are likely to surface in the future?

Future Tactics

Mumbai: The LeT launched several attacks in Mumbai, India, in November 2008. Terrorists killed dozens of people and took several hostages. The attacks paralyzed the city for several days.

The basic tactics of terrorism remain relatively constant, but terrorists continually develop innovative ways to use them. Such innovation implies that tactics will continue to evolve. Recent innovative methods suggest future tactical trends.

Terrorists may begin attacking multiple targets simultaneously, as Lashkar-e-Taiba (LeT) did in **Mumbai** in 2008, and they will continue to use secondary attacks after security forces respond to an initial attack. Criminal and terror networks will intersect, even though they will probably not form a common front. Ultimately, terrorists want to destabilize society, but criminals need government stability in order to operate. Cyberterrorism has yet to reach its full potential, and the United States remains vulnerable to attack. The future path of radicalization will change, but its direction is open to question. Finally, terrorist operations may bifurcate, or break into two branches. Small attacks will continue as they do today, while sophisticated larger strikes will evolve from large groups with logistical support.

Swarming and Multiple Attacks

swarming attacks: Launching attacks on multiple targets in the same time frame or suddenly bringing several attackers to a single location and rapidly dispersing.

Raymond W. Kelly: (b. 1941) Became commissioner of the New York City Police Department in 2002. A veteran New York City police officer, Kelley previously served as the commissioner from 1992 to 1994. A retired colonel in the United States Marine Corps Reserve, Kelly has served the NYPD for more than three decades.

NYPD Intelligence: After the 9/11 attacks, the New York City Police Department created a new intelligence operation to assess domestic and international threats to the city. Its first administrator was a former executive from the CIA. The NYPD sends officers overseas to gather information and assess terrorist threats.

On November 26, 2008, several gunmen from the LeT slipped off a hijacked fishing boat in the harbor of Mumbai, India. After slitting the boat captain's throat, they broke into separate teams and slipped into various sections of the city. Their destinations had been reconnoitered, photographed, and studied by each group. Their actions were hardly random. Around 9:30 P.M. the small group assigned to the main railway station calmly took assault rifles from their duffle bags and began to shoot into the crowded station. Within minutes, another group shot their way into a hospital while a third group stormed a café. The chaos was just beginning.

The terrorists moved from target to target, even attacking a police station as they drove by. Explosions rumbled through the air as LeT bombs were detonated. After attacking two hotels, some of the members began to take hostages. Mumbai was in chaos, and the police were outgunned and confused. Their response was ineffective. As security forces sought to regain control, they attempted to respond to each emergency and assess the situation. When the attack ended a few days later, 174 people were dead and hundred more were wounded. Small groups of trained terrorists had attacked unarmed civilian targets in a military fashion. It was a new application of an old tactic (BBC, 2008). Europe avoided a similar series of attacks by proactive police and intelligence work in September 2010 (*Der Spiegel*, 2010).

The LeT learned from its success in Mumbai. Four months later, as a convoy carrying the Sri Lankan cricket team moved through Lahore, Pakistan, the LeT struck again. Nine LeT terrorists seemed to appear out of the crowded streets. They attacked the convoy with assault rifles, explosives, and rocket-propelled grenades. Several people were killed, including seven police officers. When the attack ended, the terrorists melted back into the crowd (Page, 2009).

Like the attacks in Mumbai, the violence in Lahore was a copy of an old terrorist tactic. For example, during the Black and Tan War, the IRA attacked a British police station in much the same manner. The LeT attacks represented tactical innovation. Ambushes and assassinations were transformed into small-unit assaults. Bombings were covered by automatic rifle fire and grenades. The **swarming attacks** in Mumbai and Lahore have implications for the future.

Raymond W. Kelly, commissioner of the New York City Police Department (NYPD), testified in a congressional hearing about the nature of the two styles of swarming attacks and the future of terrorism. Multiple attacks will be part of the oncoming wave of terrorism, he said. The **NYPD Intelligence** conducted a detailed tactical analysis of both attacks and found similarities. Mumbai and Lahore involved small-unit assaults in densely populated areas. They were preceded by extensive preparation and surveillance, and the actual attacks were coordinated by communicating through cell phones and small battery-operated radios. After the initial assaults, teams kept breaking down into smaller units, and local police were outgunned at the time of the initial attacks. All of these factors led the NYPD to conclude that terrorist tactics by sophisticated groups like the LeT will shift from emphasizing suicide bombings to focusing on military-style assaults by small, heavily armed teams (Kelly, 2010).

The FBI generally agreed with the NYPD conclusions (McJunkin, 2010). The FBI analysis noted that the level of sophistication of the two assaults differed. Mumbai was extremely complicated and required coordination among multiple units. The Lahore attack was simple, involving an initial assault and a retreat. Despite the differences, the FBI agreed with the NYPD due to the similarity in the outcomes of both terrorist strikes. Terrorists do not need sophisticated weapons or WMD to create massive chaos. Small cadres of conventionally armed terrorists can wreak havoc in an urban environment through multiple random murders.

The FBI concluded that three future responses are warranted from the lessons learned from Mumbai and Lahore. First, it is necessary to prepare for strikes by small groups operating without a central command. Lahore demonstrated that a single unit can launch an effective attack, and an individual motivated by a radical ideology can do the same thing. Mumbai showed that larger groups can launch more complex operations. Security forces must prepare for both types of attacks. Second, deep relationships with a local community will be imperative. Local citizens are the best source of information about potential terrorist violence. They are in the best position to see activities that fall outside normal behavior. Third, since ideology and organizations transcend national boundaries, the FBI concluded that law enforcement agencies need to develop international partnerships and sources of information.

Arjen Boin (2009) places such attacks within the larger context of a future global crisis. He says that the structure of international systems and infrastructures will impact the nature, frequency, and consequences of terrorism and other disasters. He examines the impact of Mumbai on an international level, but compares such terrorist attacks to natural disasters and other forms of violence. Technology and economic and social networks will transform local disasters into transnational crises that will disrupt international systems. A crisis in the past had a beginning and an end, and its effects were generally localized. As interdependent global relations grow, a future crisis will develop its own life by spreading new forms of chaos throughout a system. Boin says that decision makers need to gather information from any emerging crisis and assess its multiple impacts. Future managerial systems must respond to the impact in overlapping infrastructures and international networks. In addition to developing new approaches to crises, officials will need to improve their ability to communicate among multiple organizations and to develop skills to gather and analyze complex information under pressure.

Another future mode of attack will involve employing multiple explosive devices (see Brueckner, 2009; Ewald, 2006; Sweeny, 2005). Setting off simultaneous explosions can have a dramatic impact, if the devices are numerous or large. Secondary devices, explosives timed to go off after security forces have responded to an initial attack, have long been used by lone bombers and terrorist groups. Their popularity increased in Iraq and Afghanistan, and they will probably appear in the future. Variations on this theme involve covering the explosive with small arms fire or using explosives in conjunction with a small-unit attack. Explosives can be used to create their own style of swarming attack, and they can be used to support them. Bombs were present at the beginning of modern terrorism, and they will continue to be an important weapon in the arsenal of terrorism.

Stephen Graham (2009) says that the military overview of conflict has moved from state-to-state confrontations with a beginning and an end to an ideology accepting perpetual warfare in a variety of civilian environments. Shifting terrorist tactics, such as swarming attacks, threaten to turn urban centers into future battlefields. This shift, Graham warns, can lead to increased militarization and efforts to control information. Local issues will become global issues, and the distinction between police, military, and intelligence operations will become blurred. Military models will define criminal justice systems, and command and control structures will be created along military lines. As terrorist tactics shift, state responses will increasingly accept urban environments as war zones. (See Chapter 1 for another opinion.)

Blending Criminal and Terrorist Networks

Michael Stohl (2008) says conventional wisdom suggests that terrorist and criminal organizations are merging into common networks. He says that it is important to keep the distinction between criminal and terrorist behavior in mind if law enforcement tactics are to be effective. The differences are often overlooked because terrorists and criminals use similar tactics. Terrorists use violence for a tactical objective to achieve a particular goal, and they seek to destabilize authority. Criminals operate in a different manner. They benefit when recognized political authority is stable. Criminal networks require infrastructure and services, the types of functions governments supply, and they exploit stable systems to bribe or corrupt public officials. The tactical objectives of terrorist and criminal networks differ, and law enforcement agencies need to understand the dissimilarities.

Stohl says that there are other differences and similarities between terrorists and organized criminals. Terrorists seek media coverage to enhance their aura, and they want their dramatic criminal activities publicized. Criminals avoid the media, seeking to operate under the public radar. Both criminals and terrorists are frequently charged under the same criminal statutes, but this is often because governments seek to discredit the political claims of terrorists. Criminal groups employ terrorist tactics, and terrorists commit crimes. Terrorists may associate with criminal groups to add to their reputation for ruthlessness. Criminals and terrorists may form alliances, use the same underground networks, share operational motivations, and sometimes even combine operations. It seems that similarities outweigh the differences, and many analysts point to this as evidence of growing collusion.

Stohl says the opposite is true. Overlapping aspects of behavior and shared networks do not signify a growing union between terrorists and criminals. No one disputes, he writes, that criminals and terrorists frequently move in the same circles. The important issue, however, is the relationship between networks. Stohl questions whether networks actually share information or permanently join operations. He also questions whether terrorist networks and criminal organizations can ultimately share long-term alliances and goals.

The dynamic structure of networks also impacts the relationship. Networks are dynamic, Stohl argues. The current thought is that they operate according to a set of rules, but Stohl says that they should be understood as ever-changing structures that flow with social fluctuations. The network metaphor is useful when it describes a changing range of linkages among multiple groups. It does not signify a unified hierarchy or a permanent alliance among networked groups.

Different organizational goals, Stohl says, result in two separate organizations within networks. Organizations intersect in short-term relations at the nodes where criminal and terrorist needs intersect. For example, terrorists need weapons and organized criminals may provide them for a profit. Even though the terrorists and criminals are working for different goals, their interests intersect at the point where weapons are exchanged. Stohl says that the exchange represents the node where law enforcement should direct its attention. Police actions should be focused on denying network connections to terrorist groups and utilizing community policing techniques to isolate terrorists from the public. Law enforcement's eventual goal is not to categorize terrorists as criminals but to create justice systems that can end violence and reintroduce them to their communities. Stohl suggests that the nodes where criminal organizations and terrorist groups intersect also provide opportunities to capture terrorists.

One of the most important intersections between criminals and terrorists is in the field of finance. Patrick Hardouin (2009) says that financial institutions will become more critical in the future because they are inevitably used by criminals and terrorists. He also argues that public–private partnerships in this area do not pose risks of unfair competition or private control of governmental functions because each financial institution provides the government with the same type of information. When the banking industry helps law enforcement prevent illegal activities or investigate crimes, they simply serve as a tool for investigations.

John Cassara (2007; Cassara and Jorisch, 2010) agrees with Hardouin, but he suggests that future financial investigations will become more difficult. Terrorists are learning new methods of avoiding financial detection, and lone-wolf terrorist activities require little financing. Cassara believes that law enforcement officials need to develop better forensic accounting skills to counter future financial crimes. The nexus between criminal and terrorist networks will continue to intersect in financial nodes, and Cassara believes that a new generation of law enforcement officials must learn new methods to detect illegal transfers of money, goods, and services.

Mette Eilstrup-Sangiovanni and Calvert Jones (2008) do not dispute the fact that criminal and terrorist networks intersect and that future financing is important. They do suggest, however, that the future power of networks may diminish. The reason is that networks are not as tactically efficient as many analysts believe them to be. The prevailing mood of pessimism about future operations, they argue, is premature. Many terrorism analysts believe that the hidden nature of terror networks automatically gives groups the ability to adapt to future changes. Eilstrup-Sangiovanni and Jones argue that this may not be true. Historical and contemporary research suggests that underground movements are vulnerable. Further, organized crime and terrorist networks are not as adaptable as many analysts believe. They offer a detailed examination of al Qaeda to illustrate the point. As its network expands and intersects with other networks, its ability to act as a single entity is diminished. In other words, the networked command structure is less efficient than a single command system. If this line of logic is correct, the future of networks and the meshing of criminals and terrorists may produce more weaknesses than strengths.

Other Tactical Trends

Other tactical trends appear to be in the offing. Former counterterrorism czar Richard Clarke teamed with Robert Knake of the Council on Foreign Relations (Clarke and Knake, 2010) to focus on the need to secure America's cyber network. Although their primary focus is on military defense, their warning extends to terrorism. They see cyber systems as an infrastructure in need of protection. Pointing to the 2008 war between Georgia and Russia, they note that Georgia's Internet connections were jammed from the start of the war. Nations seeking to attack the United States would achieve a strategic advantage if they could disrupt communications, financial systems, data banks, and the information technology infrastructure. *Security* magazine editor Mark McCourt (2010) supports this conclusion, saying that government systems protect government domains, not the country's infrastructure. The .com, .org, and .edu environments are a matter for the private sector, and they do not enjoy the same protection as the .gov systems. The private cyber network will be subject to hacking and attacks designed to disrupt systems as well as terrorist groups seeking to use the Internet to raise funds.

In late 2010, three dozen of the nation's leading law enforcement experts in terrorism were asked to attend an informational meeting at the request of the **Bureau of Justice Assistance (BJA)**. Analysts were asked to identify emerging trends in

Bureau of Justice Assistance: A division of the United States Department of Justice that assists state, local, and tribal law enforcement agencies.

areas of their expertise. A number of analysts noted the bifurcated nature of terrorist attacks. Complex attacks require a lengthy planning period and sophisticated logistical support, but the future trend is moving toward smaller, individualized attacks. Smaller attacks are more difficult to detect, require shorter planning periods, and appear to be the dominant future trend.

The response from the BJA revealed other emerging tactical trends. Violent radicals are attempting to infiltrate military and law enforcement ranks, and this is primarily a domestic threat. Most of the analysts found that investigations were pointing toward future individual radicalization, again believing that such a process will lead to smaller attacks. Explosive experts pointed to bomb data, demonstrating that "the philosophy of the bomb" will continue to remain a viable terrorist weapon. The most likely future trend is the use of remote detonation devices. Financial experts pointed to increasing fraud to fund operations, and experts on the domestic right wing noted that many **sovereign citizen** fraud schemes were used for economic gain instead of for funding operations. Several of the participants feared swarming attacks. Finally, experts presented data suggesting that law enforcement officers will be increasingly targeted by violent domestic extremists.

One of the greatest fears remains the use of chemical, biological, or radiological weapons. Opinions about the future are varied. Many analysts think that it is inevitable, and others think that it will not happen. The future of WMD security is another issue. Reducing the threat of theft and increasing the security of chemical, biological, and radiological agents are imperative future actions (Bunn, 2009). The framework for international law in preventing the spread of nuclear weapons already exists. These laws need to be updated, and provisions against trafficking should be added (Joyner and Parkhouse, 2009). James Van De Velde (2010) says diversion is the best way to keep terrorists from using megaweapons. He argues that methods should be employed to steer potential recruits into activities other than terrorism and other forms of crime.

sovereign citizen: A citizen who believes that the original citizens of the United States were free from all governmental control. Sovereign citizens think that they were duped by the government in "schemes" like Social Security, driver's licenses, and car registrations. That is, once people participate in those conspiracies, they lose their natural freedom and become citizens of the United States. Sovereign citizens believe that they can renounce those regulations and free themselves from American law. This should be noted: though they free themselves from taxes and fees, they rarely reject government benefits.

 Self-Check

> Why must terrorists continually develop new tactical innovations?
> How might swarming and simultaneous attacks impact future terrorism?
> Where do organized crime and terror networks intersect?
> What other tactical trends seem to be emerging in the future?

Law Enforcement and the Future

There are several aspects of effective antiterrorist activities that affect the future of American law enforcement. Some new challenges are appearing, and these issues present opportunities to improve security. They include initiatives such as the **Smart Policing Initiative (SPI)**, **Communities Against Terrorism (CAT)**, and the **Targeting Violent Crime Initiative (TVCI)**. Unfortunately, some of the old problems of the past will continue into the future. Rivalries remain, such as the dysfunctional competition between the ATF and FBI over explosive investigations. Closely associated with unhealthy competition is the reluctance to share information. A more neutral future trend is the continuing necessity to train law enforcement personnel in recognizing the indicators of terrorism and in developing effective interviewing techniques.

Smart Policing Initiative (SPI): A federal program designed to focus law enforcement resources on a particular type of crime or community problem. Programs are evaluated by external research institutions and modified based on the results of the evaluation.

Overcoming Barriers to Sharing

Despite the necessity to share information, as discussed in Chapter 15, law enforcement agencies are reluctant to do so. This results from issues other than maintaining bureaucratic power. Information security is important to officer safety and police operations. Misused information can compromise investigations or intelligence operations, and it might put officers' lives in danger. Therefore, agencies usually seek

Communities Against Terrorism (CAT): A law enforcement initiative that provides businesses with information about terrorist activities particular to each business or industry. Liaisons from local agencies contact businesses, provide information about the types of pre-incident activities employees might see in that type of business, and leave contact information.

Targeting Violent Crime Initiative (TVCI): A Department of Justice grant program administered through the Bureau of Justice Assistance. Its purpose is to fund multijurisdictional state, local, and tribal law enforcement teams that prevent selected violent crimes through intelligence-led policing.

Nationwide SAR Initiative (NSI): A federal program designed to develop common antiterrorism intelligence-reporting procedures among state, local, and tribal law enforcement agencies. SAR is an acronym for suspicious activity report.

field contacts: Information recorded from contacts during patrol operations or investigations. Police officers come into contact with many people during the course of routine patrol or investigations. They frequently encounter suspicious people or circumstances without enough evidence to make an arrest. Field contacts refer to recorded information about such encounters.

e-Guardian: An FBI system to share information about possible terrorist threats.

National Criminal Intelligence Sharing Plan: A 2005 set of recommendations designed to overcome barriers to sharing criminal intelligence. The plan contains recommended actions, oversight of operations, and standards for protecting privacy and individual rights.

to control intelligence or information about ongoing suspicious activity, even when barriers to information sharing have been minimized. This inhibits efforts to stop criminal activity, including operations aimed at preventing and interdicting terrorism.

A new initiative is being tested, and it will probably dominate law enforcement in national security activities in the coming years. The **Nationwide SAR Initiative (NSI)** is designed to overcome both the danger of and reluctance to share information about activities that might indicate a terrorist attack is in the making. The idea is based on two key factors. First, **field contacts** are reported with standardized information gathered from a variety of law enforcement departments. Second, each agency retains control of the information. Department administrators approve all the data that will be released, and the department retains control of information that might jeopardize operations or personnel safety (U.S. Department of Justice, 2010).

The system works in the following manner. When an officer encounters activity that might be an indicator of potential terrorism, the officer gathers as much information as possible and forwards it in accordance with individual department procedures. The information is first reviewed by an intelligence analyst; then it goes to a supervisor. If the information appears valid, selected portions may be released on a secure computer server outside the agency's own system. Two more reviews take place before the information can be accessed. First, the local JTTF reviews the data to determine if it threatens any ongoing secret investigation. This is followed by a review from **e-Guardian**. If both of these reviews are positive, the information can be reviewed by other agencies. Any investigator or analyst accessing the information is only able to look at material approved and released by the originating agency.

The NSI began with 12 agencies in an experimental effort to see if the concept would work. The sites were evaluated in 2010. According to the review, executives in the selected agencies took "ownership" of the project, and their actions became a critical factor in the experiment's success. When chiefs, sheriffs, and their top executives actively supported SAR procedures, line officers reported more information.

Officials from the Department of Justice feared that the increased gathering and sharing of information would threaten to invade personal privacy. They believed that the NSI would be dismantled if this happened. As a result, DOJ convened a board of civil rights organizations to review the procedures, including the American Civil Liberties Union. No organization was asked to approve the NSI, but the government changed procedures for administering the project based on input from these outside reviews (U.S. Department of Justice, 2010).

DOJ officials also decided that no agency should participate in the SAR process unless it had a publicly approved policy for collecting and sharing criminal intelligence that matched the standards set in the **National Criminal Intelligence Sharing Plan** (IIR, 2010b). If an agency had a public policy matching these standards, it was allowed to submit the policy for further review by the Office of the Director of National Intelligence. If approved in this review, the agency was allowed to join the NSI and participate in SAR (U.S. Department of Justice, 2010).

The evaluation in 2010 demonstrated that SAR was effective, but it also revealed a few areas that needed to be addressed. First, criminal analysts needed to be trained. As information flow increases, analysts need to know how to look at standardized SAR-generated data. Second, patrol officers and investigators received SAR training, but an expansion of the system will require training supervisors. New SAR efforts should also include **field training officers**. Finally, SAR works because it collects specific types of information about criminal activities associated with preparation for terrorist attacks. As tactics change, SAR indicators must reflect those changes. Future information needs to reflect the actual activities of terrorists. All of these issues can be treated with training and supervision. The NSI selected 25 new agencies for expanding SAR, based on the initial evaluation (U.S. Department of Justice, 2010).

field training officers: Experienced senior patrol officers who ride with police academy graduates. They are responsible for on-the-job training. They mentor and evaluate new recruits.

Procedures such as those in e-Guardian and the NSI effectively gather and distribute information, but the human factor remains. Individual competition, agency rivalries, and duplication of effort continue to hamper the effective flow of information (*Washington Post*, 2010). Future efforts to improve cooperation among agencies will need to account for the diverse nature of American law enforcement. This is a strength and weakness at the same time. On the one hand, individual rights are protected when the system of law enforcement is ineffective. The multitude of state, local, tribal, and federal law enforcement agencies produce inefficiency. The strength of this structure means that America does not have a single powerful police agency strong enough to threaten individual freedom. The weakness is that such a system ensures that inefficiencies will continue. The future challenge will be to utilize associations and concepts like SAR and fusion centers to ensure the flow of criminal intelligence.

Total Criminal Intelligence

Terrorism has presented new challenges for law enforcement, but diminishing resources and budget cuts result in fewer units for deployment. Police forces will be expected to do more work with fewer resources in the future. One change that has already begun and that will continue in the future is the deployment of patrol and investigative units based on information from **total criminal intelligence**. Law enforcement agencies are moving away from reactive patrol and investigation-focused models of policing to newer methods of deploying resources based on known patterns of crime and criminal behavior. This will make police agencies more effective in preventing terrorism and increase their importance as part of the nation's security forces (see Carter, 2009).

total criminal intelligence: A concept aimed at gathering information about all potential crimes, the activities of known and suspected criminals, crime patterns, and potential social problems. Information is analyzed and used to prevent crime. Total Criminal Intelligence is redundant; that is, several types of crime can be prevented by acting on single sources of information. There are several variations on the theme, including Problem-Oriented Policing, Intelligence-Led Policing, and the Smart Policing Initiative.

One of the most intriguing managerial concepts in modern law enforcement is the idea of **intelligence-led policing** (ILP). Jerry Ratcliffe (2008) says that the word intelligence is misunderstood. It implies clandestine activities or specialized techniques employed in criminal investigations. When introduced to ILP, many agencies claim that they have been practicing the concept for years, though they have little understanding of the idea and they do not use intelligence in a systematic way. Ratcliffe says that ILP is a method of applying criminal intelligence and data analysis for the deployment of all law enforcement resources. It targets social problems, potential sources of crime, and offenders. The goal is to deploy police forces efficiently, based on information analyzed from a community.

intelligence-led policing: A managerial model which focuses on the collection and analysis of information. After analysis, law enforcement resources are deployed to prevent and disrupt crime and to target specific crimes and offenders. ILP is an alternative to using criminal intelligence to support investigations and other forms of reactive policing.

ILP fits the model of terrorism prevention. Under this concept, officers gather information and forward it for analysis. Managers armed with analyzed information then organize resources to deal with specific issues rather than deploying police power haphazardly or reacting to crimes as they occur. Ratcliffe says that the problem of terrorism after 9/11 fueled international thinking about ILP. If law enforcement agencies only responded to emergency situations, they would be ineffective in combating terrorism. Reactive patrol and investigation-focused activities would not prevent terrorism. ILP is designed to disrupt criminal activities prior to a criminal act, identify community problems, and prevent crime. Promoted by the International Association of Chiefs of Police, it is emerging as the dominant policy for organizing and deploying police resources. Its goal is to prevent crime, including terrorism.

Another concept in the TCI model is the Smart Policing Initiative (Medaris, 2009). This attempts to direct resources toward solving specific criminal and social problems. Law enforcement operations address problem areas, and the results of their actions are evaluated by outside researchers. It began with an experiment to evaluate ten agencies. The Department of Justice required that each agency target specified criminal activities and team with a research partner. SPI is not directed at terrorism, but information from targeted crimes flows through the criminal intelligence system. Terrorism is one aspect of criminal behavior, and TCI utilizes all forms of criminal information. If the SPI works, it may emerge as a future tool for antiterrorist operations in law enforcement.

Another future trend in information gathering and analysis will be expanding community involvement. The Department of Justice created the Communities Against Terrorism program to begin facilitating this trend (IIR, 2010a). The idea is predicated upon extending community partnership to businesses. Businesses in local neighborhoods may have contact with terrorists who purchase services or goods in preparation for a terrorist attack.

The process begins when law enforcement officers visit particular businesses to provide indications of suspicious behavior particular to that industry. For example, landscaping and farm supply stores receive information about potential explosives constructed from gardening supplies. Officers encourage employees to report any suspicious behavior from a list of activities provided for their industry.

❂ ANOTHER PERSPECTIVE

Intelligence-Led Policing

ILP is a concept developed in the United Kingdom. It involves:
- Deploying resources in anticipation of crime and social disorder
- Utilizing deployed resources to gather new information
- Organizing information for analysis
- Analyzing information

- Disseminating information to operational units
- Re-evaluating information with incoming information
- Planning and decision making
- Redeploying resources based on information, and to gather new information

Source: Peterson, 2005.

❂ ANOTHER PERSPECTIVE

The Smart Policing Initiative (SPI)

- The goal of the Smart Policing Initiative (SPI) is to identify law enforcement tactics and strategies that are effective, efficient, and economical.
- SPI seeks to build on offender-based and place-based policing by replicating evidence-based practices or to encourage exploration

of new, unique solutions to public safety problems.
- Grantees described a process to identify crime problems they will address.
- A research partner will assess the project.

Source: http://www.ojp.usdoj.gov/newsroom/pdfs/smart_policing_fact_sheet.pdf.

Najibullah Zazi: (b. 1985) A 1999 immigrant to the United States. Zazi was born in Afghanistan and raised in Pakistan. He was arrested in 2009 for planning suicide attacks in New York City and pleaded guilty to charges of terrorism in 2010.

In 2008, **Najibullah Zazi** flew from Newark to Afghanistan to join the Taliban. Unsuccessful, he ended up receiving rudimentary training in explosives from al Qaeda terrorists. Returning to the United States, he began purchasing large quantities of chemical precursors to explosives from a beauty supply store in Colorado. When an employee commented on the large number of chemicals, Zazi claimed that he was planning on opening a beauty shop (FBI, 2010). The idea behind Communities Against Terrorism is that the employee would have been given a list of suspicious behaviors associated with beauty supplies and contact information for reporting such behavior to a local police agency. In fact, Zazi's actions appear on a list from the brochure designed for beauty supply stores (IIR, 2010). SAR, ILP, TVCI, and SPI train officers to recognize and report information. Communities Against Terrorism involve the business community in the process. All of these activities are likely to increase. Future policing, including terrorism prevention, will be driven by information.

ANOTHER PERSPECTIVE

Smart Policing Initiative (SPI)—First Evaluation Projects

Law Enforcement Agency	Research Partner	Research Initiative
Boston Police Dept.	Harvard University	Robbery, burglary
Glendale Police Dept. (AZ)	Arizona State University	Crime-prone neighborhoods
Lansing Police Dept. (MI)	Michigan State University	Neighborhood drug markets
Memphis Police Dept. (TN)	University of Memphis	Robbery, burglary
Los Angeles Police Dept.	Justice and Security Strategies	Gun violence
Palm Beach Sheriff (FL)	Florida State University	Hispanic victims
Philadelphia Police Dept.	Temple University	Violent crime
Reno Police Dept. (NV)	University of Nevada	Juvenile drug abuse
Savannah Police Dept. (GA)	Savannah State University	Violent repeat offenders
Winston-Salem Police Dept. (NC)	Winston-Salem University	Intelligence-led policing

No SPI project deals directly with terrorism, but each initiative places law enforcement agencies in environments where terrorists commit crimes. Agencies will gather multiple types of information by focusing on total criminal intelligence. If successful, SPI will become a tool for preventing terrorism.

Source: BJA, http://www.ojp.usdoj.gov/newsroom/pdfs/smart_policing_fact_sheet.pdf.

 Self-Check

> How might the NSI and SAR reports help overcome factors that inhibit the flow of information?
> What future changes have been suggested to make SAR more effective?
> How can ILP and TCI be used to reduce the future threat of terrorism?

Probable Strategic Directions

National Intelligence University: An in-service initiative standardizing training for the entire intelligence community.

Proteus USA: A project designed to identify future threats to national security by assembling panels of experts in various fields that might impact national defense. It was developed by the U.S. Army War College and the National Intelligence University.

While assessing the strategic future of terrorism is difficult, there is a body of applied and scholarly literature that attempts to do so. The **National Intelligence University** and the U.S. Army War College teamed together to create **Proteus USA,** an international think tank designed to consider future strategic problems. Futurists Martin Cetron and Owen Davies (2008) produced one of the project's first papers on the future of terrorism. They identified 55 future changes based on current trends.

Proteus USA

Cetron and Davies suggest that terrorism will grow in the future. They believe that jihadist veterans from Iraq will return to their native lands and train future jihadists. This will cause terrorism to spread. They suggest that the United States, France, and the United Kingdom are at the greatest risks, and they predict an attack on the scale of 9/11 by 2018. Emerging technology will impact the effectiveness of security, but it will multiply the force of terrorist groups. New technology will also allow terrorists to strike economic and logistical targets.

They suggest that the three most important courses of future action indicated by current behavior are: (1) growing terrorist ranks, (2) probable access to WMD, and (3) spin-off jihadist movements obtaining legitimate political power. These probabilities, they argue, should guide the Western response to terrorism. The ten most important factors contributing to terrorism are:

> - Western economic growth will spawn resentment and radicalization by populations who believe they are victimized by the West. Muslim countries present the greatest risk.
> - Militant Islam will gain power and spread.
> - Barring nuclear war or some type of global plague, the world's population will reach 9.2 billion in 2050. The United States will continue to prosper, while poverty will increase in poor nations, increasing resentment against the United States. America will remain an attractive terrorist target.
> - Recent technological changes are just the beginning of a revolution that will grow exponentially in the coming decades.
> - Americans will lose almost all privacy.
> - The global economy will continue to grow and multinational corporations will expand. Economic crime and terrorism will continue to expand with the economy.
> - Cities will continue to grow, creating large pockets where religious radicalization will foster and terrorism will grow.
> - Internet growth will slow, but it will remain the most important method for planning and administering terrorist operations. Almost all the world's population will have access to the Internet within 20 years. It will serve as a vehicle for recruiting terrorists and may be used for financial crimes to support operations.
> - Communication technology will continue to expand and impact terrorism in a manner similar to Internet growth.
> - The United States is losing its technical and scientific leadership to other countries. This has caused an increase in the number of technicians and scientists in lands hostile to the United States. Some scientists will be able to supply terrorists with lethal technologies.

Cetron and Davies produced a provocative report. While some of these conclusions provoke controversy, they had a panel of distinguished experts respond to each proposal. While the conclusions have fostered debate, the process they employed was extremely objective. Several points of view and dissenting opinions permeate their paper.

Democratic Accountability

As the United States continues to respond to terrorism, a number of concerns have surfaced that remain to be addressed. One factor is the future role of the massive security system the federal government has developed to protect the United States. Warren Eller and Brian Gerber (2010) argue that the process is so complex that a coherent policy toward terrorism has yet to emerge. Funding, management, and even the goals of homeland security policy are not straightforward. Several competing bureaucracies and managerial structures complicate efforts to develop a consistent policy. Eller and Gerber suggest that bureaucracies are not the problem, however. Bureaucratic organizations were designed to solve complex problems.

One of the things that bureaucrats do well, they argue, is analyze policy. This skill should be applied to homeland security. Eller and Gerber argue that future security policy should be developed within the body of existing theoretical literature. It will be a complex process, they write, but academics and policy specialists know how to analyze policy. Policy goals should be the guides for homeland security. There is much we do not know about terrorism, they say, but that is no excuse for confusion. They call on the scholarly community of policy theorists to improve analytical tools, assess target vulnerability, and develop better methods for forecasting and measuring costs.

Research also points to the growing loss of privacy and the inadequacy of current law. Similar to the 2008 Proteus findings, Paul Rosenzweig (2010), a defense consultant, writes that computer processing and data storage capabilities will continue to increase at an astronomical pace. This will allow for extensive data mining and record storage, and this will interact with the electronic footprints on the Internet. This data can be correlated to show what sites an Internet user has visited and all activities on the site. It can also be used to reconstruct communication. Governments will be able to build dossiers on individuals and point to those most likely to engage in terrorism. Rosenzweig believes that this opportunity will be too tempting for governments and that they will seek to expand surveillance by keeping records on everyone. He believes that the U.S. law needs to be updated to prevent this from happening.

Closely related to privacy is the necessity to protect individual liberty. James Piazza and James Walsh (2010) state that the conventional wisdom is that individual rights must be curtailed to protect the nation from terrorism. After conducting an empirical analysis of several recent terrorist campaigns, they were surprised at their findings. Restricting freedom does not lead to greater protection from terrorism. The relationship between individual liberty and terrorism is much more complex than conventional wisdom suggests. They conclude that future research should be conducted on the relationship between specific abuses of individual rights and a state's susceptibility to terrorism.

enhanced interrogation: A process of questioning suspects by using physical duress. Supporters argue that such actions are necessary to gain information about future terrorism. Opponents argue that such actions constitute torture, thus violating human rights.

Researchers and analysts have pointed to the necessity of clarifying the ways in which suspected terrorists are treated. Brian Jenkins (2010) reiterates the position that most experts hold: Terrorism is a problem for criminal justice. Terrorists should be handled in accordance with criminal law, and this position draws such controversial practices as **enhanced interrogation** into question. Aside from the morality of torture, the effectiveness of such techniques is questionable. In addition, any information gained under duress cannot be used in a criminal prosecution. Several FBI agents observed enhanced interrogation at the detention facility at Guantánamo Bay, Cuba. One agent called his supervisor, wanting to arrest the interrogators. Some agents with the best background in jihadist terrorism left the FBI in disgust after witnessing enhanced interrogations (Mayer, 2008, pp. 327–325). Future policies should point to a single legal solution for dealing with captured terrorists.

Domestic and International Terrorism

The literature on terrorism points to strategic directions in future terrorism. Ethnic and ideological confrontations will continue, and experts debate about the future of religious terrorism. The course of international terrorism will be determined partially by the ability of the West to create alliances that bring regional stability and economic security to unstable regions (see Barnett, 2006). Violent domestic extremism will continue to focus on ideology, and at least one leading expert, Bruce Hoffman (2010), believes that domestic jihadists will base operations in the United States.

Domestically, right-wing violent extremism is growing in popularity (ADL, 2010). Fueled by the immigration debate, the election of President Obama, and a sagging economy, the number of violent groups will grow in the short-term future. Right-wing violence is framed in antigovernment extremism and the reemergence of the sovereign citizen movement. Old racist elements are appearing within extremist groups, but many right-wing extremists have abandoned racial politics for antigovernment fanaticism. Frustrated extremists refuse to recognize the power of the federal government. Their actions seem to point to increasing confrontations with law enforcement officers.

There is a spirited debate about the future of religious terrorism. Defense analyst Thomas McCabe (2010) suggests that the jihadist strategy is ultimately self-defeating. They may conduct brilliant tactical operations, but their strategic weakness will lead to their demise. Al Qaeda and its affiliates made crucial mistakes. They underestimated the strength of the United States, and they widened the war only to encounter a number of other enemies. Their indifference to Muslim casualties has increased their unpopularity. In short, they alienate local populations. McCabe believes that jihadist terrorism will fade away. Religious militants will only be effective if they back away from intolerant millenarianism and appeal to mainstream followers.

Many political leaders state that al Qaeda has become a symbolic organization and the United States has the jihadists on the ropes. Bruce Hoffman (2010) notes that America's political leadership has turned the fight against jihadist violence into a "numbers game." According to this argument, each drone strike further decapitates al Qaeda, suggesting that victory is nearing. Some officials, Hoffman says, have even gone as far as saying that al Qaeda is all but defeated. If these opinions are correct, then religious terrorism will fade away. This view, however, is hotly contested.

Hoffman writes that the Bush and Obama Administrations have championed the idea that eliminating jihadist leadership will bring victory against terrorism. Citing David Galula, Hoffman points out that the French captured five of Algeria's top terrorist leaders during the Algerian War, but it had little effect on the rebellion. Similarly, Israel has engaged in a series of targeted assassinations of terrorist leadership for two decades with no visible reduction in terrorism. Hoffman also notes that after the United States killed al Qaeda's leader in Iraq, the group's violent activities actually increased. The struggle is not over, and future jihads will be lethal.

The United States has created a blind spot. By focusing on operations overseas and failing to account for the complexity of evolving jihadist organizations, the unthinkable has happened. Hoffman says that the jihadists have created bases of operations in the United States. He points to ten jihadist plots or terrorist attacks in America during 2009. Although some of the culprits were incompetent, activities in 2009 represented an unprecedented level of attempts. In addition, the planned attack on Christmas Day 2009 would have been the deadliest incident since 9/11. The secretary of homeland security claimed that the system worked, but Hoffman argues that alert passengers and a failed attempt to detonate the bomb prevented the tragedy. The system failed, and the situation will get worse.

The future requires a reassessment of America's approach to the jihad. Hoffman writes that al Qaeda's strategy is attrition. It increases its network and recruiting power, especially in the United States, while it wears down America's ability to fight. Our security system is overwhelmed with information, but it misses many planned attacks. The country is responding to al Qaeda's moves instead of anticipating them, killing and capturing leaders instead of stopping the processes of recruitment and radicalization.

Hoffman believes al Qaeda's campaign of religious terrorism will continue in the future. He recommends three steps to counter its effectiveness. First, America must seek to understand its enemy. This not only includes tactical operations, it mandates an understanding of the appeal of al Qaeda's message. Second, the campaign to eliminate leaders and terrorists should continue, but it must be complemented with actions based on a more strategic effort. Third, the step that leads to victory will be countering al Qaeda's ability to recruit and radicalize jihadists. Unless the approach to terrorism shifts, Hoffman concludes, America will remain on the defensive.

Self-Check
> Compare the importance of foreign policy to tactical responses to future terrorism.
> What trends seem to be emerging in future terrorism?
> What types of attacks can be expected in the immediate future?

CHAPTER TAKE AWAYS

Terrorism is ever-changing, and counterterrorist methods must be flexible to meet this challenge. It is important to constantly analyze the vast network of homeland security operations to ensure that public–private partnerships are not abused and that operations are effective. New initiatives in law enforcement can be used and analyzed efficaciously. Bureaucratic stagnation and the abuse of power represent current and future threats to the security system. Terrorist tactics and organizations will present new challenges. These will probably include new forms of operations, new technologies, swarm attacks, and franchised ideologies. Alienation and radicalization will probably increase. Despite the interest in international terrorism, right-wing domestic violence will probably increase in the immediate future. New security technologies can be employed to counter future terrorism, but increased technology represents a greater danger to privacy.

OBJECTIVE SUMMARY

- Several federal agencies have functions that could create needless duplication. The functions also complicate federal relations with state local and tribal police agencies. The DHS quadrennial review is supposed to assess the effectiveness of its own operations and the way that it functions with other agencies.
- Three factors will help to ensure the effectiveness of antiterrorism operations. (1) Federal agencies need to ensure that their functions complement one another and that they interface with state, local, and tribal law enforcement. (2) This implies that all agencies involved in antiterrorism need to develop formal and informal communication networks. (3) It also means that agencies must actually share information.
- Private–public partnerships are complicated because the Constitution limits the power of government, but the same rules do not apply to private industry. Companies may use information for economic advantage. They might also become so deeply embedded in defense that they would replace military forces in some aspects of national security.
- Antiterrorism policy begins with united DOS and DOD efforts. The Israeli–Palestinian conflict illustrates this idea. State, local, and tribal law enforcement agencies lead homeland security efforts, and the DHS and other federal departments and agencies coordinate the strategic role of law enforcement. Their efforts are dependent on the success of U.S. foreign policy.
- The United States will continue to experience low-level attacks, and it may experience a massive assault. When any terrorist attack occurs, the infrastructure must be designed to absorb the damage and maintain social, psychological, and economic normality.
- Traditional liberal education programs, interdisciplinary approaches to problem solving, and the development of critical thinking skills are necessary to understand the complexities of terrorism. Simplistic thinking leads to misguided solutions and militarizes social policy.
- Swarming attacks will become popular with large terrorist groups. Criminal and terrorist networks will join each other when they have common objectives, and cyber systems remain vulnerable to terrorist attacks. Domestically, right-wing extremism is growing.
- Law enforcement agencies are developing terrorism prevention measures. The SPI targets specific problems. The NSI is attempting to implement the SAR program. CAT gathers information specific to certain types of businesses. The TVCI identifies violent crime data that may impact terrorism prevention.
- Future terrorism will rely on technology. Radicalization is increasing along with the gap between rich and poor nations. The Internet will continue to be one of the most important vehicles in recruiting terrorists and planning operations. Government surveillance and records from companies and non-government organizations are eliminating privacy. Right-wing domestic extremism is increasing, and homegrown jihadists have created virtual bases in the United States.

Critical Engagement: Emphasizing Antiterrorism and the Future

September 11, 2001, was horrible by any measure. If the Proteus study is correct, something of the same magnitude will happen again. Clearly, this means that the nation must be prepared and take measures to prevent an attack before it happens. Law enforcement agencies are charged with solving problems, and terrorism requires a solution. Military forces must continually adapt to new threats, and the intelligence community will continue to gather and analyze information. Fusion centers will focus on a similar task, primarily collecting and analyzing criminal intelligence. The Department of Homeland Security was created in the major reorganization of the federal government. Its complex functions are part of an extensive system of bureaucracies that is difficult to change. A major part of foreign policy should center on preventing terrorism. One of the central questions for the future is: Should antiterrorism play such a key role in the function of state, local, tribal, and federal governments?

Supporters of strong antiterrorism policies respond to the question with a resounding yes! Terrorism is *the* new form of international conflict. It is a war with consequences no different from those of World War II. Terrorism will dominate our future. The problem is growing, and more terrorists are being radicalized in the homeland. A WMD attack is very likely, but everything must be done to try to prevent it. Massive security efforts are necessary, and we must limit some of our historic freedoms in the name of security. Terrorists are not like the other enemies we have faced. Therefore, they can be held without warrant, sent to countries that openly torture political prisoners, and harshly questioned when in the custody of the United States. It is time, the supporters argue, to take off the gloves.

Critics are warier. We need to be prepared, but antiterrorism is not the primary focus of government. Reorganization of security and intelligence at all levels of government has militarized the criminal problem of terrorism. It suggests that violent domestic extremism and international terrorism can only be solved by military methods. Antiterrorism hysteria causes us to blind ourselves to actual situations. Al Qaeda is being degraded by our killing or capturing its leaders, and law enforcement has thwarted several attacks in Europe and North America. An unrealistic fear of terrorism is responsible for millions upon millions of dollars in wasted expenditures. We divert money from other defense needs and a variety of social problems, all in the name of security from terrorism. Our foreign policy alienates the United States from the world, and it is generating anti-Muslim sentiment at home. We are losing our privacy and liberty because of the overemphasis on security, according to this argument.

Consider these issues in terms of future developments:

- Which parts of each set of arguments seem to make the most sense to you? Why is it not possible to discuss antiterrorism measures by searching for simple either-or solutions?
- Jihadists improperly cloak violence in religious rhetoric. How can their violence be countered without seeming to attack Islam?
- What measure of freedom are you willing to sacrifice for better security from terrorism?

KEY TERMS

Homeland Security Act of 2002, p. 16-414

Quadrennial Homeland Security Review (QHSR), p. 16-415

9/11 Commission Implementation Act of 2007, p. 16-415

Janet Napolitano, p. 16-415

Military industrial complex, p. 16-417

Partner capacity, p. 16-418

Force protection, p. 16-422

Mumbai, p. 16-423

Swarming attacks, p. 16-423

Raymond W. Kelly, p. 16-423

NYPD Intelligence, p. 16-423

Bureau of Justice Assistance (BJA), p. 16-426

sovereign citizen, p. 16-427

Smart Policing Initiative (SPI). p. 16-427

Communities Against Terrorism (CAT), p. 16-427

Targeting Violent Crime Initiative (TCVI), p. 16-427

Nationwide SAR Initiative (NSI), p. 16-428

Field contacts, p. 16-428

e-Guardian, p. 16-428

National Criminal Intelligence Sharing Plan, p. 16-428

Field training officers, p. 16-428

total criminal intelligence, p. 16-429

Intelligence-led policing, p. 16-429

Najibullah Zazi, p. 16-430

National Intelligence University, p. 16-431

Proteus USA, p. 16-431

Enhanced interrogation, p. 16-433

GLOSSARY

1978 Civil Service Reform Act A federal law designed to prevent political interference with the decisions and actions of governmental organizations.

1985 hijacking of a TWA flight The hijacking of TWA Flight 847 by a group believed to have links to Hezbollah while it was en route from Athens to Rome. The plane went to Beirut and then to Algeria, where terrorists tortured and murdered U.S. Navy diver Robert Dean Stethem, a passenger on the flight. The plane returned to Beirut, and passengers were dispersed throughout the city. Terrorists released began releasing hostages as the incident continued. After Israel agreed to release 700 Shiite prisoners, the terrorists released the remaining hostages and escaped.

1993 World Trade Center bombing A carbomb attack by a cell led by Ramzi Youseff. The cell had links to the Egyptian IG.

9/11 Commission The bipartisan National Commission on Terrorist Attacks upon the United States, created after September 11, 2001, in order to investigate the attacks.

9/11 Commission Implementation Act of 2007 A federal law requiring selected recommendations of the 9/11 Commission to be implemented. One of its provisions helped to create regional fusion centers.

Abbas Musawi (1952–1992) A leader of Hezbollah, who was killed with his family in an Israeli attack in 1992.

Abdel Aziz Rantisi (1947–2004) One of the founders of Hamas along with Ahmed Yassin. He took over Hamas after Israeli gunships assassinated Yassin. He, in turn, was assassinated by the Israelis a month after taking charge.

Abdullah Azzam (1941–1989) The Palestinian leader of Hizb ul Tahrir and the spiritual mentor of bin Laden.

Abdullah Ocalan (b. 1948) The leader of the PKK. Ocalan was captured in 1999 and sentenced to death, but his sentence was commuted. He ordered the end of a suicide bombing campaign while in Turkish custody and called for peace between Turkey and the Kurds in 2006.

Abimael Guzmán (b. 1934) A philosophy professor who led the Shining Path from 1980 until his arrest in 1992. Guzmán is serving a life sentence in Peru.

Abu Bakr (circa 573–634) Also known as Saddiq, the first caliph selected by the Islamic community (*umma*) after Mohammed's death in 632. Sunnis believe Abu Bakr is the rightful heir to Mohammed's leadership, and they regard him as the first of the *Rishidun*, or Rightly Guided caliphs. He led military expeditions expanding Muslim influence to the north of Mecca.

Academic consensus definition A complex definition based on the work of Alex Schmid. It combines common elements of the definitions used by leading scholars in the field of terrorism.

Actionable intelligence Information that law enforcement agencies, military units, or other security forces can use to prevent an attack or operation.

Adam Gadahn (b. 1958) The American spokesperson for al Qaeda. His nom de guerre is Azzam the American.

African Cell A French military unit stationed in Africa and France. It retains between 10,000 and 15,000 troops in various African countries and answers directly to the president of France.

Ahmed Yassin (1937–2004) One of the founders and leaders of Hamas. Yassin originally started the Palestinian Wing of the Muslim Brotherhood but merged it into Hamas during the Intifada. He was killed in an Israeli-targeted assassination.

AIDS pandemic Great numbers of people with HIV/AIDS (human immunodeficiency virus/acquired immunodeficiency syndrome). In 2005, Africa had 25.8 million HIV-positive adults and children. Africa has 11.5 percent of the world's population but 64 percent of its AIDS cases. From 1982 to 2005, AIDS claimed 27.5 million African lives (Cook, 2006).

Al Aqsa Intifada An uprising sparked by Ariel Sharon's visit to the Temple Mount with a group of armed escorts in September 2000. The area is considered sacred to Jews, Christians, and Muslims. Muslims were incensed by the militant aspect of Sharon's visit because they felt he was invading their space with an armed group. Unlike the 1987 Intifada, the al Aqsa Intifada has been characterized by suicide bombings.

Al Aqsa Intifiada An uprising sparked by Ariel Sharon's visit to the Temple Mount with a group of armed escorts in September 2000. The area is considered sacred to Jews, Christians, and Muslims. Muslims were incensed by the militant aspect of Sharon's visit.

Al Jazeera An international Arabic television network.

Al Manar Hezbollah's television network.

Al Shabaab (also known as the Harakat Shabaab al-Mujahedeen, the Youth, Mujahedeen Youth Movement, and Mujahedeen Al Shabaab Movement) Formed as a militant wing of a federation of Islamic courts in Somalia in 2006. Its senior leadership is affiliated with al Qaeda.

Alberto Fujimori (b. 1938) President of Peru from 1990 to 2000. He fled to Japan in 2000 but was extradited to Peru in 2007. He was convicted of human rights violations and sentenced to prison.

Ali ibn Talib (circa 599–661) Also known as Ali ibn Abi Talib, the son of Mohammed's uncle Abu Talib and married to Mohammed's oldest daughter Fatima. Ali was Mohammed's male heir because he had no surviving sons. The followers of Ali are known as Shiites. Most Shiites believe that Mohammed gave a sermon while perched on a saddle, naming Ali the heir to Islam. Differing types of Shiites accept authority from diverse lines of Ali's heirs. Sunni Muslims believe Ali is the fourth and last Rightly Guided caliph. Both Sunnis and Shiites believe Ali tried to return Islam to the purity of Mohammed's leadership in Medina.

Alienation Happens when an individual or group becomes lost in the dominant social world. A person or group of people is alienated when separated from the dominant values of society at large.

Altruistic suicide The willingness of individuals to sacrifice their lives to benefit their primary reference group such as a family, military unit, ethnic group, or country. It may involve going on suicide missions in combat, self-sacrifice without killing others, or self-sacrifice and killing others.

Alvaro Uribe (b. 1952) President of Colombia, 2002–2010. He was known for his tough stance against FARC and other revolutionary movements.

American embassy takeover During the Iranian hostage crisis, revolutionary students stormed the U.S. embassy in Tehran with the support of the Iranian government. They held 54 American hostages from November 1979 to January 1981.

Anarchists Those in the nineteenth century who advocated the creation of cooperative societies without centralized governments. There were many forms of anarchy. In the popular understanding of the late nineteenth and early twentieth centuries, anarchists were seen as violent socialist revolutionaries. Today, anti-globalists calling themselves anarchists have little resemblance to their earlier counterparts.

Anders Breivik (b. 1979) A violent right-wing extremist who went on a one-day killing spree in Norway in July 2011. He detonated a bomb in Oslo and went on a shooting spree at a Labor Party youth camp for political reasons.

Anglo-Irish Peace Accord An agreement signed in 1985 that was the beginning of a long-term attempt to stop terrorist violence in Northern Ireland by devising a system of political autonomy and by protecting the rights of all citizens. Extremist Republicans rejected the accord because it did not unite Northern Ireland and the South. Unionists rejected it because it compromised with moderate Republicans.

Anglo-Israelism The belief that the lost tribes of Israel settled in western Europe. God's ancient promises to the Hebrews became promises to the United Kingdom, according to this belief. Anglo-Israelism predated Christian Identity and is the basis for most Christian Identity beliefs.

Anwar al Awlaki (1971–2011) An American-born Muslim cleric who worked to build U.S.-Muslim relations after 9/11. He became increasingly militant and called for attacks on America. He was arrested in Yemen in 2006 and released in 2007. In 2009, he swore allegiance to AQAP.

Arab nationalism The idea that the Arabs could create a European-style nation, based on a common language and culture. idea faded after the 1967 Six Day War.

Argentina in 1992 and 1994 Two bombings in Buenos Aires. Terrorists struck the Israeli embassy in 1992, killing twentynine people, and the Jewish Community Center in 1994, killing eighty-five people. Imad Mugniya his suspected to have been behind the attacks.

Aryan Nations An American antigovernment, antiSemitic, white supremacist group founded by Richard Butler. Until it was closed by a suit from the Southern Poverty Law Center, the group sponsored a Christian Identity Church called the Church of Jesus Christ, Christian.

Asif Ali Zardari (b. 1955) The husband of Benazir Bhutto, Zardari, inherited control of the Pakistan People's Party after Bhutto's assassination in December 2007. He was elected president in 2008.

Ayub Khan (1907–1974) The second president of Pakistan, from 1958 to 1974. Khan seized control of the government in 1958 and then staged elections. He was the first of Pakistan's many military leaders.

Baathist A member of the pan-national Arab Baath Party. Baathists were secular socialists seeking to unite Arabs in a single socialist state.

Bacterial weapons Enhanced forms of bacteria that may be countered by antibiotics.

Badr The site of a battle between the Muslims of Medina and the merchants of Mecca in 624. Mohammed was unsure whether he should resist the attacking Meccans, but decided God would allow Muslims to defend their community.

After victory, Mohammed said that Badr was the Lesser Jihad. Greater Jihad, he said, was seeking internal spiritual purity.

Balfour Declaration A policy statement by the British government in November 1917 that promised a homeland for Jews in the geographical area of biblical Israel. Sir Arthur Balfour was the British foreign secretary.

Baluchistan The largest of four states in Pakistan dominated by the Baloch tribe. Many Balochs are fighting a guerrilla war against the Pakistan Army in a dispute over profits from natural resources. The central government is creating a deepwater port and international trade center in Gwadar, Pakistan's principal seaport, and displacing many Baluchs.

Belfast Agreement Also known as the Good Friday Agreement, an agreement signed in April 1998 that revamped criminal justice services, established shared government in Northern Ireland, called for the early release of prisoners involved in paramilitary organizations, and created a Commission on Human Rights and Equity. Its provisions led to the decommissioning of paramilitary organizations.

Ben Klassen (1918–1993) The founder of the Creativity Movement.

Beslan school A Chechen terrorist attack on the first day of school in September 2004 in North Ossetia. The scene was chaotic and Russian forces were never able to establish a security perimeter. Although details remain unclear, the incident resulted in the murder of nearly 400 people, including more than 100 children.

Big Man An anthropological term to describe an important person in a tribe or clan. *Big Man* is sometimes used by political scientists to describe a dictator in a totalitarian government.

Bill of Rights The first ten amendments to the U.S. Constitution.

Black June The rebel organization created by Abu Nidal in 1976. He changed the name to the Fatah Revolutionary Council after a rapprochement with Syria in 1981. Most analysts refer to this group simply as the Abu Nidal Organization.

Black Market Peso Exchange A method for converting illegal profits in U.S. currency to Colombian pesos in an effort to hide the illegal funds. Terrorists have frequently used the system, although they launder less money than organized crime or drug networks.

Black Widows Chechen female suicide bombers. They are known as Islamic martyrs in the Chechen language.

Blind terrorism Tactic used by the FLN. It included indiscriminant attacks against French outposts, which involved bombing, sabotage, and random assassination.

Bourgeois The middle class. *Bourgeoisie* (plural) in Marxist terminology refers to tradespeople, merchants, artisans, and other nonpeasants excluded from the upper classes in medieval Europe. Marx called the European democracies after the French Revolution Bourgeois governments, and he advocated a democracy dominated by workers.

Brady Bill A law that limits gun ownership, named for President Ronald Reagan's press secretary after he was disabled by a gunshot in a 1981 assassination attempt on Reagan.

Branch Davidians Followers of Vernon Wayne Howell, also known as David Koresh. They lived in a compound outside Waco, Texas.

Brüder Schweigen German for *silent brothers*, the name used by two violent right-wing extremist groups, Brüder Schweigen and Brüder Schweigen Strike Force II. The late Robert Miles, leader of the Mountain Church of Jesus in Michigan, penned an article about the struggle for white supremacy, "When All of the Brothers Struggle."

Bureau of Justice Assistance A division of the United States Department of Justice that assists state, local, and tribal law enforcement agencies.

Bureaucracy Governmental, private-sector, and nonprofit organizations. It assumes that people organize in a hierarchy to create an organization that will solve problems.

Camp David Peace Accord A peace treaty between Egypt and Israel brokered by the United States in 1979.

Capone discovery A term used by James Adams to explain the Irish Republican Army's entry into organized crime.

Carlos Marighella (1911–1969) A Brazilian communist legislator and revolutionary theorist. Marighella popularized urban terrorism as a method for ending repression and eliminating U.S. domination of Latin America. He was killed in a police ambush in São Paulo in 1969.

Cell The basic unit of a traditional terrorist organization. Groups of cells form columns. Members in different cells seldom know one another. In more recent terrorist structures, *cell* describes a tactical group dispatched by the network for selected operations.

CesareBeccaria (1738–1794) One of the founders of the discipline of criminology. His work *Of Crimes and Punishments* (1764) is the classic Enlightenment study of the discipline.

Chain organizations Temporary associations of diverse groups. Groups in a chain come together for a particular operation and disband after it is over.

Charles Taylor (b. 1948) A warlord in the First War of the Liberian Civil War and president of Liberia from 1997 to 2003.

Christian Identity An American extremist religion proclaiming white supremacy. Adherents believe that white Protestants of western European origin are the true descendants of the ancient Israelites. Believers contend that Jews were spawned by Satan and that non-whites evolved from animals. According to this belief, white men and women are the only people created in the image of God.

Civil defense Citizens engaged in homeland security.

Civil liberties Individual rights granted to citizens under the U.S. Constitution.

COINTELPRO An infamous FBI counterintelligence program started in 1956. Agents involved in COINTELPRO violated constitutional limitations on domestic intelligence gathering, and the program came under congressional criticism in the early 1970s. The FBI's abuse of power eventually resulted in restrictions on the FBI.

Colombo The traditional capital of Sri Lanka and the country's largest city, with a population of 5,648,000. The Sri Lankan government moved the capital to Sri Jayawardenapura Kotte, five miles away, in 1982. Colombo remains the economic center of Sri Lanka.

Combined Joint Task Force, Horn of Africa (CJTF-HOA) An American- led counterterrorist unit combining military, intelligence, and law enforcement assets of several nations in the Horn.

Committee of Public Safety Assembled by Maximilien Robespierre (1758–1794) to conduct the war against invading monarchal powers, it evolved into the executive body of France. The Committee of Public Safety initiated the Reign of Terror.

Communists Socialists who believed in a strong centralized economy controlled by a strong central government. Their ideas were summarized in *The Communist Manifesto*, written by Karl Marx and Friedrich Engels in 1848.

Communities Against Terrorism (CAT) A law enforcement initiative that provides businesses with information about terrorist activities particular to each business or industry. Liaisons from local agencies contact businesses, provide information about the types of pre-incident activities employees might see in that type of business, and leave contact information.

Copycats Refers to people who imitate other criminals after viewing, hearing, or reading a story about a crime. A copycat copies the targets and methods of another criminal.

Creativity The deistic religion of the Creativity movement. It claims that white people must struggle to defeat Jews and nonwhite races.

Criminal intelligence Information gathered on the reasonable suspicion that a criminal activity is occurring or about to occur. It is collected by law enforcement agencies in the course of their preventive and investigative functions. It is shared on information networks such as the Regional Information Sharing System (RISS). Unlike national defense intelligence, criminal intelligence applies only under criminal law. Agencies must suspect some violation of criminal law before they can collect intelligence.

Critical media consciousness The public's understanding of the media and the way stories are presented. A critically conscious audience would not simply accept a story presented in a news frame. It would look for the motives for telling the story, how the story affected social constructs and actions, and hidden details that could cause the story to be told in another way.

Cuban guerrilla war A three-step process as described by Che Guevara: (1) Revolutionaries join the indigenous population to form guerrilla *foco*, as Guevara called them; (2) small forces form columns and control rural areas; and (3) columns unite for a conventional offensive to overthrow government.

Cultural Revolution A violent movement in China from 1966 to 1976. Its main purpose was to rid China of its middle class and growing capitalist interests. The Cultural Revolution ended with the death of Mao Zedong.

Cyberterrorism Using computers to attack other networks or to conduct physical attacks on computer-controlled targets. The most frightening scenario involves an attack designed to create catastrophic failure in the economy or infrastructure.

David Galula (1919–1967) French captain who fought in Algeria in 1956–1958. He returned to Paris to analyze the Algerian campaign, producing a critique of the strategy followed in the war. His work inspired the development of counterinsurgency doctrine in the U.S. military.

Defense in depth Using social networks in national defense. It is based on Arthur Cebrowski's idea of operating at all levels of society.

Department of Homeland Security (DHS) A federal agency created in 2003 by Congress from the Office of Homeland Security after the attacks of September 11, 2001.

Desert Shield The name of the defensive phase of the international coalition, created by President George H. W. Bush after Iraq invaded Kuwait on August, 2, 1990, to stop further Iraqi attacks and to liberate Kuwait. It lasted until coalition forces could begin an offensive against Iraq in January 1991.

Desert Storm The military code name for the January– February offensive in the 1991 Gulf War.

Domestic issues Gonzalez-Perez uses domestic issues to refer to groups within a country fighting to change the social or political structure of that nation.

E-Guardian An FBI system to share information about possible terrorist threats.

Embedded reporters Refers to reporters who placed inside military units during a combet operation.

Emergency-response plans Preparations by any agency to deal with natural, accidental, or man-made disasters. They involve controlling the incident through an organized response-and command system and assigning various organizations to supervise the restoration of social order.

Endemic terrorism Terrorism that exists inside a political entity. For example, European colonialists created the nation of Rwanda by combining the lands of two tribes that literally hate each other. The two tribes fight to eliminate each other. This is endemic to political violence in Rwanda. The term was coined by J. Bowyer Bell.

Enemy combatants A legal term used to describe nonstate paramilitary captives from Afghanistan. The term was later applied to all jihadist terrorists by the Bush Administration. The Obama Administration maintained detention centers after ordering the closing of Guantánamo shortly after President Obama took office in January 2009.

Enhanced interrogation A process of questioning suspects by using physical duress. Supporters argue that such actions are necessary to gain information about future terrorism. Opponents argue that such actions constitute torture, thus violating human rights.

Enlightenment An eighteenth-century intellectual movement following the Scientific Revolution. Also called the Age of Reason, the Enlightenment was characterized by rational thought and the belief that all activities could be explained.

Eric Rudolph (b. 1966) A right-wing extremist known for bombing the Atlanta Olympics, a gay night club, and an abortion clinic. Rudolph hid from authorities and became a survivalist hero. He was arrested in 2003 and received five life sentences in 2005.

Ernesto "Che" Guevara (1928– 1967) Fidel Castro's assistant and guerrilla warfare theorist. Guevara advocated guerrilla revolutions throughout Latin America after success in the Cuban Revolution. He was killed in Bolivia in 1967 while trying to form a guerrilla army.

Eschatology (pronounced es-ka-TAW-low-gee) A Greek word used to indicate the theological end of time. In Judaism and Christianity, it refers to God bringing creation to an end. In some Shi'ite Islamic sects and among Christians who interpret biblical eschatological literature literally, believers contend that Jesus will return to lead a final battle against evil. Other major religions also have end-time theology.

Estates General An assembly in pre-evolutionary France consisting of all but the lowest class. The Estates General had not been called since 1614, but Louis XVI assembled them in 1789 in response to demands from the Assembly of Notables, who had been called to address the financial problems of France. Radical elements in the Estates General revolted, and the disruption led the French Revolution.

Expropriation A term used by Carlos Marighella for armed robbery.

Failed state An area outside a government's control. Failed states operate under differing warlords, criminal groups, or competing governments.

Far enemy A jihadist term referring to non-Islamic powers or countries outside the realm of Islam.

Fedayeen Warriors who sacrifice themselves. The term was used differently in Arab history; the modern term is used to describe the secular warriors of Fatah.

Federal Law Enforcement Training Center (FLETC) A law enforcement training academy for federal agencies. Operating in Glencoe, Georgia, FLETC trains agents and police officers for agencies that do not operate their own academy.

Field contacts People encountered during normal patrol or investigative operations. Law enforcement officers frequently gather information from such people. The Nationwide SAR Initiative standardizes such information.

Field contacts Information recorded from contacts during patrol operations or investigations. Police officers come into contact with many people during the course of routine patrol or investigations. They frequently encounter suspicious people or circumstances without enough evidence to make an arrest. Field contacts refer to recorded information about such encounters.

Field training officers Experienced senior patrol officers who ride with police academy graduates. They are responsible for on-the-job training. They mentor and evaluate new recruits.

Fifth Amendment Protection against arbitrary arrest, being tried more than once for the same crime, and self-incrimination. It also guarantees due process.

First Amendment Guarantees the rights to speech, assembly, religion, press, and petitioning the government.

Force multiplier A method of increasing striking power without increasing the number of combat troops in a military unit. Terrorists have four force multipliers: (1) technology to enhance weapons or attacks on technological facilities, (2) transnational support, (3) media coverage, and (4) religious fanaticism.

Force protection Refers to security operations by military forces engaged in securing bases, ports, other areas of operations, and personnel. Military personnel frequently cooperate with local law enforcement and other civil forces when engaged in force protection.

Forensic accounting An investigative tool used to track money used in illegal activities. It can be used in any crime involving the exchange, storage, or conversion of fiscal resources.

Fourteenth Amendment A person cannot be deprived of freedom or property by the government unless the government follows all the procedures demanded for legal prosecution.

Fourth Amendment Particularly applicable to law enforcement and homeland security, it limits government search and seizure, including the elements of arrest.

Francisco Franco (1892–1975) Leader of the nationalist forces during the Spanish Civil War and the fascist dictator of Spain from 1939 to 1975.

Free State The name given to the newly formed Republic of Ireland after Irish independence.

Freedom of Information (FOI) Act A law ensuring access to governmental records.

Free-wheeling fundamentalists White supremacists or Christian patriots who either selectively use Bible passages or create their own religion to further the patriot agenda.

Fusion centers Operations set up to fuse information from multiple sources, analyze the data, turn it into usable intelligence, and distribute intelligence to agencies needing the information.

Globalization A common global economic network ideally uniting the world through production and international trade. Proponents believe it will create wealth. Critics believe it creates corporate wealth and increases distance between the rich and poor.

Goal displacement Favoring process over accomplishments. Process should be reasonable and efficient. Too much focus on the process, however, interferes with completion of job tasks.

Golden Temple The most sacred shrine of Sikhism. Its official name is the Temple of God.

Government Management Reform Act of 1994 A federal law designed to prevent political interference in the management of federal governmental organizations and to increase the efficiency of management.

Group think Refers to a bureaucratic process in which members of a group work together to solve a problem; however, innovation and deviant ideas are discouraged as the group tries to seek consensus about a conclusion. Powerful members of the group may quash alternative voices. Intelligence groups tend to resist making any risky conclusion lest they jeopardize their individual careers. Peer pressure creates an atmosphere in which every individual comes to the same conclusion.

Gulf States Small Arab kingdoms bordering the Persian Gulf. They include Bahrain, Qatar, the United Arab Emirates, and Oman.

Habib Akdas (birth date unknown) Also known as Abu Anas al Turki, the founder of al Qaeda in Turkey. Akdas left Turkey to fight in Iraq after the American invasion. He was killed in a U.S. air strike in 2004.

Hapsburgs The ruling family of Austria (1282–1918), the Austro-Hungarian Empire (1437–1918), and the Holy Roman Empire (1282–1806). Another branch of the family ruled in Spain (1516–1700). Reference here is to the Austrian royal family.

Haqqani network A family in the tribal area of Pakistan that has relations with several militant groups and the ISI. The Haqqani family is involved in organized crime, legitimate businesses, the ISI, and terrorism groups. It is the major power broker in the tribal region.

Hassan al Banna (1906–1949) The founder of the Muslim Brotherhood. He was murdered by agents of the Egyptian government.

Hassan al Turabi (b. 1932) A Sudanese intellectual and Islamic scholar. He served in the Sudanese government during the time bin Laden was in exile in Sudan.

Hassan Nasrallah (b. 1960) The secretary-general of Hezbollah. He took over the leadership of Hezbollah after Musawi's death in 1992. Nasrallah is a lively speaker and charismatic leader.

Hawala system A system of exchanging money based on trust relationships between money dealers. A chit, or promissory note, is exchanged between two hawaladars, and it is as valuable as cash or other traded commodities because the trust between the two parties guarantees its value.

High Intensity Drug Trafficking Area Specialized RICs in regions experiencing a high level of drug trafficking and drug-related crimes. They evolved from RICs and were the direct predecessor to fusion centers. Some HIDTAs simply expanded to become full fusion centers.

Highly enriched uranium (HEU) A process that increases the proportion of a radioactive isotope in uranium (U-235), making it suitable for industrial use. It can also be used to make nuclear weapons. Nuclear weapons are made from either HEU or plutonium.

Hohenzollerns The ruling family of Brandenburg and Prussia that ruled a united Germany from 1871 to 1914.

Homeland Security Act of 2002 A federal law created in 2002 and amended in following years. It established the Department of Homeland Security and reorganized the presidential cabinet. DHS's primary antiterrorism mission is to prevent attacks and respond to them when they occur.

Human rights The basic entitlements and protections that should be given to every person.

Hussein ibn Ali (626–680) Also known as Hussein ibn Ali, Mohammed's grandson and Ali's second son. He was martyred at Karbala in 680. The majority of Shiites believe that Hussein is the Third Imam, after Imam Ali and Imam Hasan, Ali's oldest son.

Ibn al Khattab (1969– 2002) Also known as Emir Khattab or the Black Wahhabi, a Saudi international jihadist who went to fight in Chechnya. He tried to move the Chechen revolt from a nationalistic platform to the philosophy of religious militancy. He was killed the Russian secret service in 2002.

Imad Mugniyah (1962–2008) The leader of the international branch of Hezbollah. He has been implicated in many attacks, including the 1983 U.S. Marine and French paratrooper bombings. He is also believed to have been behind bombings of the U.S. embassy in Beirut and two bombings of Israeli targets in Argentina. He was assassinated in Damascus in February 2008.

Independent Monitoring Commission (IMC) A commission created in 2004 to investigate paramilitary actions and alleged governmental abuses during the Irish peace process.

Infotainment telesector A sarcastic term to describe cable news networks. It refers to news organizations producing stories to entertain their audiences under the guise of presenting objective information.

Intelligence product The output of information analysis. Information is analyzed and turned into intelligence. This product is distributed to users.

Intelligence product Any outcome or output of analyzed information that can be used by law enforcement agencies, military units, or security forces to take an immediate action.

Intelligence-led policing A type of law enforcement in which resources are deployed based on information gathered and analyzed from criminal intelligence.

Intelligence-led policing A managerial model which focuses on the collection and analysis of information. After analysis, law enforcement resources are deployed to prevent and disrupt crime and to target specific crimes and offenders. ILP is an alternative to using criminal intelligence to support investigations and other forms of reactive policing.

International focus Gonzalez-Perez uses international focus to refer to terrorist groups operating in multiple countries.

Interservice Intelligence Agency (ISI) The Pakistani domestic and foreign intelligence service, created by the British in 1948. Supporters claim that it centralizes Pakistan's intelligence. Critics maintain that it operates like an independent state and supports terrorist groups.

Intifada The first spontaneous uprising against Israel, lasting from 1987 to 1993. It began with youths throwing rocks and creating civil disorder. Some of the violence became more organized. Many people sided with religious organizations, abandoning the secular PLO during the Intifada.

Iranian Revolution The 1979 religious revolution that toppled Mohammed Pahlavi, the shah of Iran, and transformed Iran into an Islamic republic ruled by Shi'ite religious scholars.

Iran–Iraq War A war fought after Iraq invaded Iran over a border dispute in 1980. Many experts predicted an Iraqi victory, but the Iranians stopped the Iraqi army. The war produced an eight-year stalemate and more than a million casualties. The countries signed an armistice in 1988.

Islamic Courts Union (ICU) A confederation of tribes and clans seeking to end violence and bring Islamic law to Somalia. It is opposed by several neighboring countries and internal warlords. Some people feel that it is a jihadist organization, but others see it as a grouping of clans with several different interpretations of Islamic law.

Izz el Din al Qassam Brigades The military wing of Hamas, named after the Arab revolutionary leader Sheik Izz el Din al Qassam (1882–1935), who led a revolt against British rule.

James W. von Brunn (1920–2010) An American white supremacist and anti-Semite. He entered the Holocaust Museum on June 10, 2009, and began shooting. He killed a security officer before he was wounded and subdued. He died in federal custody while awaiting trial.

Jammu and Kashmir A mountainous region in northern India claimed by India and Pakistan. It has been the site of heavy fighting during three wars between India and Pakistan in 1947–1948, 1971, and 1999. Kashmir is artificially divided by a line of control (LOC), with Pakistani forces to the north and India's to the south. India and Pakistan made strides toward peace after 2003, but many observers believe that the ISI supports jihadist operations in the area.

Janet Napolitano (b. 1957) The third secretary of homeland security. President Obama appointed her while she was serving her second term of governor in Arizona.

John Walker Lindh (b. 1981) An American captured while fighting for the Taliban in 2001 and sentenced to 20 years in prison.

Joseph Kony (b. 1961) The leader of the Lord's Resistance Army in Uganda. His group has branched out to several other nations in central Africa. He is wanted by the International Criminal Court for crimes against humanity.

Joseph Stalin The dictator who succeeded Lenin. Stalin solidified communist control of Russia through a secret-police organization. He purged the government of all suspected opponents in the 1930s, killing thousands of people.

Khalid Meshal (b. 1956) One of the "outside" leaders of Hamas, in Damascus, Syria, Meshal became the political leader of Hamas in 2004. After the 2006 election he continued to lead in exile.

King Gyanendra (b. 1947) King of Nepal from 2001 to 2008. After the attack and murder of several members of the royal family, Gyanendra became king of Nepal in 2001. He took complete power in 2005 to fight the Maoist rebellion. In the spring of 2006, he was forced to return power to parliament, and he was removed from power in 2008.

King Hussein (1935–1999) King of Jordan. King Hussein drove the PLO from Jordan in September 1970. After his death his son Abdullah assumed the throne.

Knight Riders The first terrorists of the Ku Klux Klan. Donning hoods and riding at night, they sought to keep newly freed slaves from participating in government and society.

Know-Nothings Different groups of American nationalists in the early nineteenth century who championed native-born whites over immigrants.

Leila Khalid (b. 1944) Was a member of the Popular Front for the Liberation of Palestine. In 1969, she was part of a team that hijacked four aircraft that were destroyed after the passengers and crews disembarked. Arrested in 1970 after another attempted hijacking, she was released as part of a prisoner exchange.

Leon Trotsky A Russian revolutionary who led foreign affairs in Stalin's government and later became the commander of the Red Army. He espoused terrorism as a means for spreading White revolution. He was thrown out of the Communist Party for opposing Stalin and was assassinated by communist agents in Mexico City in 1940.

Liberian Civil War Two episodes of conflict involving rebel armies and militias as well as neighboring countries. The First War, 1989–1996, ended when a rebel army brought Charles Taylor to Monrovia, the capital. The Second War, 1999–2003, toppled Charles Taylor from power. Both wars were characterized by village massacres and conscription of child soldiers.

Liberians United for Reconciliation and Democracy (LURD) A revolutionary movement founded in 1999 in western Africa. LURD was instrumental in driving Charles Taylor from power in 2003.

Longitudinal studies In social science, these studies involve examinations of the same subjects over long periods of time.

Lord's Resistance Army Ugandan guerrilla force opposing the government since 1987. The LRA has conscripted thousands of children, forcing them into its ranks or mutilating and killing them. Dropping all pretense of political activity, it roams through Uganda, southern Sudan, the Democratic Republic of the Congo, and the Central Africa Republic. Its primary tactics are mass murder, mass rape, theft, and enslavement of children. Uganda has referred the LRA to the International Criminal Court.

Made-for-TV dramas Refers to news stories that will keep viewers' attention. H. H. A. Cooper was among the first analysts to recognize the drama that terrorism presented for television.

Madrassas Islamic religious schools.

Mahmud Abbas (b. 1935) The president of the Palestinian Authority since 2005, founding member of Fatah, and an executive in the PLO.

Majilis council The Islamic name given to a religious council that advises a government or a leader. Some Islamic countries refer to their legislative body as a majilis.

Mandate of Palestine The British Mandate of Palestine was in effect from 1920 to 1948. Created by the League of Nations, the mandate gave the United Kingdom the right to extend its influence in an area roughly equivalent to modern Jordan, Israel, and the Palestinian Authority.

Margherita Cagol (1945–1975) Also known as Mara Cagol, the wife of Renato Curcio and a member of the Red Brigades. She was killed in a shoot-out with Italian police a few weeks after freeing her husband from prison.

Mark Sykes (1879–1919) A British diplomat who signed a secret agreement with Francois Georges-Picot in May 1916. The Sykes-Picot Agreement divided the Middle East into spheres of French, British, and Russian influence.

Marwan Barghouti (b. 1969) A leader of Fatah and alleged leader of the al Aqsa Martyrs Brigades. A Brigades statement in 2002 claimed that Barghouti was their leader. He rose to prominence during the al Aqsa Intifada, but he is currently held in an Israeli prison.

Max Weber (1864–1920) One of the major figures of modern sociological methods, he studied the organization of human endeavors. Weber believed that

social organizations could be organized for rational purposes designed to accomplish objectives.

Meaning The subjective interpretation people give to events or physical objects. Meanings are developed by individuals and groups, and different meanings can be attributed to the same event or physical object because the definitions are always influenced by interpretation. Social scientists in this tradition believe that meanings cause actions.

Meaning framework The definitional boundaries for a particular social meaning. Individuals and groups create boundaries around their experiences and perceptions, and they define issues within them. Meaning frameworks are the social boundaries surrounding those definitions. Juergensmeyer sees the clash between modern values and traditional culture as one of the reasons for terrorism. Religious terrorists look at the modern world and reject it. This world is evil in the meaning framework of religious terrorists, and they refuse to accept the boundaries of the secular modern world.

Militarization Responding to social problems with military solutions. In law enforcement, militarization is usually characterized by martial law.

Military tribunals military courts trying combatants outside the civilian court system. Trials take place in front of a board of military officers operating under military law.

Military-industrial complex A term coined by President Dwight D. Eisenhower (1890–1969) to describe the relationship between American military forces and private industry.

Militia Movement A political movement started in the early 1980s, possibly spawned from survivalism. Militias maintain that the Second Amendment gives them the right to arm themselves and form paramilitary organiztions apart from governmental control and military authority.

Mission creep Adding too many secondary tasks to a unit. Too many jobs divert a unit from its primary mission.

Mogadishu The capital of Somalia. This note is a reference to "Black Hawk Down." U.S. troops moved into Mogadishu during Operation Restore Hope from December 9, 1992, until May 4, 1993, when the United Nations took over the operations. American forces were involved in a major battle in October 1993 involving a downed U.S. Army helicopter.

Mohammed Ali Jinnah (1876–1948) The leader of the Muslim League and the founder of modern Pakistan. He served as Governor-General until his death in 1948.

Mohammed Fneish (age unknown) A Hezbollah politician and minister of energy in the Lebanese prime minister's cabinet.

Mohammed ibn Abdul Wahhab (1703–1792) Also known as Abdul Wahhab; a religious reformer who wanted to purge Islam of anything beyond the traditions accepted by Mohammed and the four Rightly Guided caliphs. He conducted campaigns against Sufis, Shi'ites, and Muslims who made pilgrimages or who invoked the names of saints.

Mohammed Reza Pahlavi (1919–1980) Shah of Iran from 1941 to 1979. The shah led a rigorous program of modernization that turned Iran into a regional power. He left the throne and accepted exile as a result of the 1979 Iranian Revolution.

Moorish Nation An African American group that does not recognize the validity of the United States government.

Moscow theatre (Theatrical Center, Dubrovka, Moscow, 2002) The site of a Chechen attack where approximately 40 terrorists took 850 hostages. Russian forces stormed the theater on the third day of the siege, killing 39 terrorists and at least 129 hostages.

Mossad The Israeli intelligence agency, formed in 1951. It is responsible for gathering foreign intelligence. Shin Beth is responsible for internal security.

Mullah Omar (b, 1959) The leader of the Taliban. After the collapse of the Taliban government in 2001, Omar went into hiding.

Mumbai The LeT launched several attacks in Mumbai, India, in November 2008. Terrorists killed dozens of people and took several hostages. The attacks paralyzed the city for several days.

Muqtada al Sadr (b. 1974) An Iraqi ayatollah. Al Sadr leads the Shi'ite militia known as the Mahdi Army.

Musa Abu Marzuq (b. 1951) The "outside" leader of Hamas, who is thought to be in Damascus, Syria. He is believed to have controlled the Holy Land Foundation.

Muslim Brotherhood An organization founded by Hassan al Banna, designed to recapture the spirit and religious purity of the period of Mohammed and the four Rightly Guided caliphs. The Brotherhood seeks to create a single Muslim nation through education and religious reform. A militant wing founded by Sayyid Qutb sought the same objective through violence. Hamas, a group that defines itself as the Palestinian branch of the Muslim Brotherhood, has rejected the multinational approach in favor of creating a Muslim Palestine.

Najibullah Zazi (b. 1985) A 1999 immigrant to the United States. Zazi was born in Afghanistan and raised in Pakistan. He was arrested in 2009 for planning suicide attacks in New York City and pleaded guilty to charges of terrorism in 2010.

Narcoterrorism A controversial term that links drugs to terrorism in one of two ways: Either drug profits are used to finance terrorism or drug gangs use terrorism to control production and distribution networks.

Nasir al Wuhayshi (age unkown) The spiritual leader of AQAP and a former aide to Osama bin Laden. Wuhayshi escaped from a Yemeni prison in 2006 to form AQY. In 2009, he joined his group with dissidents in Saudi Arabia to form AQAP.

Nathan Bedford Forrest (1821–1877) A famed and gifted Confederate cavalry commander who founded the Ku Klux Klan in Pulaski, Tennessee. Forrest tried to disband the KKK when he saw the violent path that it was taking.

National Alliance The white supremacist organization founded by the late William Pierce and headquartered in Hillsboro, West Virginia.

National Convention Elected in 1792, it broke from the Estates General and called for a constitutional assembly. The White Convention served as the major legislative body of France until it was replaced by the Directory in 1795.

National Counterterrorism Center (NCTC) An organization designed to filter information from the intelligence process, synthesize counterterrorist information, and share it with appropriate organizations.

National Criminal Intelligence Sharing Plan A 2005 set of recommendations designed to overcome barriers to sharing criminal intelligence. The plan contains recommended actions, oversight of operations, and standards for protecting privacy and individual rights.

National Criminal Intelligence Sharing Plan (NCISP) A plan to share criminal intelligence among the nation's law enforcement agencies. It suggests minimum standards for establishing and managing intelligence operations within police agencies.

National Intelligence University An in-service initiative standardizing training for the entire intelligence community.

National Liberation Movement The Tupamaros' official name.

National security intelligence A system of agencies and networks that gather information about threats to the country. Any threat or potential threat is examined under the auspices of national defense intelligence. Unlike criminal intelligence, people and agencies gathering defense information do not need to suspect any criminal activity. The FBI is empowered to gather defense intelligence.

Nationwide SAR Initiative (NSI) A federal program designed to develop common antiterrorism intelligence-reporting procedures among state, local, and tribal law enforcement agencies. SAR is an acronym for suspicious activity report.

Near enemy A jihadist term referring to forms of Muslim governments and Islamic law (*sharia*) that do not embrace the narrow- minded philosophy of Sayyid Qutb.

Netwar One network fighting another network.

Networks Organizations of groups, supplies, weapons, and any structure that supports an operation. Much like a traffic system or the World Wide Web, networks do not have central leadership, and they operate under a variety of rules.

New economy of terrorism A term used by Loretta Napoleoni to describe the evolution of terrorist financing from the beginning strategies of the cold war to the present. Economic support and antiterrorist policies interact to form the new economy.

New World Order A phrase used by President George H. W. Bush to describe the world after the fall of the Soviet Union. Conspiracy theorists use the phrase to describe what they believe to be Jewish attempts to gain control of the international monetary system and, subsequently, to take over the U.S. government.

News frames Visual, audible, or written packages used to present the news. Communication scholars do not agree on a single definition, but news frames generally refer to the presentation of the news story. They contain a method for beginning and ending the story, and they convey the importance of characters and actions as the story is told.

News media As used in this text, refers to television, radio, and print journalism. It also refers to newer sources on the Internet, including news reporting services, the blogosphere, website pages, and propaganda broadcasts.

Nidal Malik Hasan (b. 1970) an American soldier of Palestinian descent. Hasan was an Army psychiatrist who apparently White became self-radicalized, embracing militant Islam. He went on a shooting spree at Fort Hood, Texas, on November 5, 2009, killing 13 people and wounding almost three dozen others. He was wounded, arrested, and charged with several counts of murder.

Nodes In counterterrorist or netwar discussions, the points in a system where critical components arestored or transferred. The importance of a node is determined by its relationship to the network.

No-go areas An informal term to describe geographical areas that the duly empowered government cannot control. Security forces cannot routinely patrol these places.

Nordic Christianity A religion that incorporates the ancient Norse gods in a hierarchy under the Christian triune deity. It is similar to Odinism, but it does not completely abandon Christianity.

North-West Frontier Province (NWFP) One of four Pakistani states, inhabited primarily by ethnic Pashtuns. Several areas of the NWFP are controlled by tribes, and jihadists operate in the area. Peshawar, NWFP's capital, served as a base for organizing several mujahedeen groups in the Soviet-Afghan War.

Nuclear black market When the Soviet Union collapsed, it was difficult to account for all the nuclear weapons that were in the control of military officials and the newly independent states. People feared that these weapons would be sold to terrorists. Similar fears exist for Pakistan's nuclear bombs and nuclear development programs in North Korea and Iran.

NYPD Intelligence After the 9/11 attacks, the New York City Police Department created a new intelligence operation to assess domestic and international threats to the city. Its first administrator was a former executive from the CIA. The NYPD sends officers overseas to gather information and assess terrorist threats.

Omar Hammami (b. 1984) An American leader of Al Shabaab, under the name of Abu Mansoor al-Amriki.

Ottoman Empire A Turkish empire that lasted for 600 years, until 1924. The empire spanned southeastern Europe, North Africa, and southwest Asia, and reached its zenith in the fourteenth and fifteenth centuries.

Panga A heavy-bladed machete used in agricultural work. It was the weapon favored by people who took the Mau Mau oath.

Paper terrorism Using false documents to clog legal, financial, or bureaucratic processes.

Partner capacity As used by Robert Gates, the ability of the U.S. military forces to form alliances with security forces and civilian governments inside states threatened with destabilization.

Peace dividend A term used during President William Clinton's administration (1992—2000) to describe reducing defense spending at the end of the Cold War.

People Power Revolution A mass Philippine protest movement that toppled Ferdinand Marcos in 1986. Marcos ruled as dictator after being elected as president in 1965 and declaring martial law in 1972. When Gloria Macapagal-Arroyo (president, 2001–2010) assumed the presidency January 2001, her government proclaimed a second People Power Revolution.

Pervez Musharraf (1943–) The president of Pakistan (2001–2008). A career army officer, Musharraf took power in a 1999 military coup and declared himself president in 2001. After 9/11 he sought closer relations with the United States, while trying to mollify sources of domestic religious strife.

Philosophy of the bomb A phrase used by anarchists around 1848. It means that social order can be changed only through violent upheaval. Bombs were the first technological force multiplier.

Plan Colombia A joint effort by the United States and Colombia to reduce violence and illegal drugs. It began in 1999.

Police Service of Northern Ireland (PSNI) The police force created in November 2001 to replace the Royal Ulster Constabulary.

Postmodern Describing the belief that modernism has ended; that is, some events are inexplicable, and some organizations and actions are naturally and socially chaotic and defy explanation. A postmodern news frame leaves the consumer thinking there are many possible conclusions.

Pre-incident indicators The criminal and social actions of individuals and groups before a terrorist attack.

Process orientation Paying more attention to the manner of achieving organizational goals than achieving them. Process is important when it focuses on ethical and legal requirements. Process orientation goes beyond legal and moral norms, and it becomes dysfunctional when an organization's goal is conceived as maintaining procedures.

Profiling A practical criminological process designed to identify the behavioral attributes of certain types of criminals.

Proteus USA A project designed to identify future threats to national security by assembling panels of experts in various fields that might impact national defense. It was developed by the U.S. Army War College and the National Intelligence University.

Protocols of Zion A forged document written in czarist Russia allegedly explaining a Jewish plot to control the world. It was popularized in the United States by Henry Ford. It is frequently cited by the patriot and white supremacy movements. Jihadists also use it as evidence against Jews.

Provisionals The nick-name for members of the Provisional Irish Republican Army. They are also known as Provos. The name applies to several different

Republican paramilitary terrorist groups.

Pyramid An illustration of the way terrorists organize themselves into hierarchies. It is an analogy showing a large base of support culminating in a small group of terrorists at the top.

Quadrennial Homeland Security Review (QHSR) A requirement that the secretary of DHS conduct a review of the department's operations every four years. According to the first report, the Homeland Security Act of 2002, as amended, requires the secretary to "delineate and update, as appropriate, the national homeland security strategy," and to "outline and prioritize the full range of the critical homeland security mission areas of the Nation" (DHS, 2010).

Racial terrorism A dominant group using violence to intimidate a racial minority. Tactics would include lynching, murder, beatings, and other forms of violence against a minority group. For example, the Ku Klux Klan historically has practiced racial terrorism.

Radiation sickness Caused by exposure to high doses of radiation over a short period of time. It is characterized by nausea, diarrhea, headaches, and fever. High doses produce dizziness, weakness, and internal bleeding. It is possible to treat patients who have been exposed to doses of radiation, but higher doses are usually fatal. Other than the two nuclear bombs used in World War II, most radiation sickness has been caused by industrial accidents.

Radical democrats Those who tried to bring democracy to all classes. They sought a more equitable distribution of wealth throughout all economic classes, believing that concentrated wealth and class inequities prevented societies from becoming truly democratic.

Radicalization As used in this context, refers to the psychological process of adopting extremist positions.

Rajiv Gandhi (1944–1991) Prime Minister of India from 1984 until 1991, when he was assassinated by an LTTE suicide bomber.

Ranasinghe Premadasa (1924–1993) President of Sri Lanka from 1989 until 1993, when he was killed by an LTTE suicide bomber.

Raúl Sendic (1926–1989) A Uruguayan revolutionary leader. Sendic founded the National Liberation Movement (MLN), popularly known as the Tupamaros.

Following governmental repression in 1973, he fled the country. Sendic died in Paris in 1989.

Raymond W. Kelly (b. 1941) Became commissioner of the New York City Police Department in 2002. A veteran New York City police officer, Kelley previously served as the commissioner from 1992 to 1994. A retired colonel in the United States Marine Corps Reserve, Kelly has served the NYPD for more than three decades.

Reasonableness The actions an average person would take when confronted with certain circumstances. This is a Fourth Amendment doctrine.

Red Army Faction a West German Marxist group modeled as Marighel-lastyle urban guerrillas. They were the most violent and active revolutionary group during the heyday of left-wing European terrorism. After German re-unification, the records of the former East German secret police led to the demise of the RAF. It was also known as the Baader-Meinhof Gang when it first formed.

Red Brigades An Italian Marxist terrorist group that had its most effective operations from 1975 to 1990. It amended the centralized Tupamaro model by creating semiautonomous cells.

Red Corridor The area of Naxalite violence in India. The corridor runs from Nepal through southern India, and from India's east coast to the central regions.

Red Mosque *Lal masjid*, located in Islamabad, with a madrassa and a school for women. It taught militant theology. The government ordered the mosque closed in 2007. This resulted in a shootout and a standoff. Government forces stormed the mosque on July 2007, killing more than 100 students. One of the leaders, Abdul Rashid Ghazi, was killed. His brother Maulana Abdul Aziz, the mosque's other leader, was captured while trying to escape in women's clothing.

Regional Crime Gun Centers (RCGC) ATF intelligence centers similar to RICs but focused on the illegal use of firearms.

Regional Informational Sharing System (RISS) A law enforcement network that allows law enforcement agencies to share information about criminal investigations.

Regional Intelligence Centers Originally established to gather drug trafficking

intelligence, RICs helped provide the basis for fusion centers.

Reign of Terror The name given to the repressive period in France, 1794–1795. The revolutionary government accused thousands of French nobles and clergy of plotting to restore the monarchy. Executions began in Paris and spread throughout the countryside. Large mobs attacked and terrorized nobles in rural areas. Summary executions (executions on the spot without a trial) were quite common.

Renato Curcio (b. 1941) The founder and leader of the Red Brigades in Italy.

Reporting frame The simplest form of a news frame. It is a quick, fact-driven report that summarizes the latest information about a story. It does not need to contain a beginning or an end, and it assumes that the consumer understands the context of the facts.

Revolutionary Guards The militarized quasi-police force of the revolutionary government during the Iranian Revolution.

Reza Shah Pahlavi (1878–1944) Shah of Iran from 1925 to 1941. He was forced from power by a British and Soviet invasion.

Richard Butler (1917–2004) A self-made millionaire and white supremacist. Butler founded the Aryan Nations in Hayden Lake, Idaho.

Robert Matthews (1953–1984) The leader of The Order, killed in a shootout with the FBI.

Routes to terrorism As used by John Horgan, refers to the psychological and social factors that motivate people to join and remain in terrorist groups.

Roving wiretaps A method of quickly intercepting disposable phone or Internet traffic. A roving wiretap allows law enforcement officers to monitor new connections without returning to court for another search warrant.

Royal Irish Constabulary (RIC) The police force established by the United Kingdom in Ireland. It was modeled after the London Metropolitan Police, but it represented British interests. After the Free State was formed, the RIC became the Royal Ulster Constabulary (RUC). In turn, the RUC gave way to the Police Service of Northern Ireland (PSNI) as part of Irish and British attempts to bring peace to Northern Ireland after 1995.

Ruby Ridge The location of a 1992 standoff between survivalists and U.S. federal law enforcement officers in Idaho during which a U.S. marshal and survivalist Randy Weaver's wife and son were killed.

Ruhollah Khomeini (1900–1989) The Shi'ite grand ayatollah who was the leading figure in the 1979 Iranian Revolution. Khomeini toppled the shah's government and consolidated power by destroying or silencing his enemies, including other Shi'ite Islamic scholars. Iran was transformed into a theocracy under his influence.

Sabri al Banna (1937–2002) The real name of Abu Nidal. Al Banna was a founding member of Fatah but split with Arafat in 1974. He founded militias in southern Lebanon, and he attacked Western and Israeli targets in Europe during the 1980s. In the 1990s, he became a mercenary. He was murdered in Iraq, probably by the Iraqi government.

Salafi movement Used by orthodox Muslims to follow the Prophet and the elders of the faith. Militants narrow the use of the term and use it to justify violence. The Salafi movement refers to those people who impose Islam with force and violence.

SAVAK Mohammed Pahlavi's secret police, established after the 1953 downfall of the democratic government.

Sayyid Imam al Sharif (b. 1951) Also known as Dr. Fadl, one of Egypt's leading militants in the 1970s. While jailed, he embraced Islam and renounced the violence of al Qaeda–style militancy. He is viewed as a traitor by violent jihadists. He has provided much of the information about religious militancy, and he continues to publish works denouncing it. Still maintaining anti-Western and anti-government views, he sees jihad as a necessary part of Islam. Al Qaeda's version, he claims, violates the morality of Islamic law.

Sayyid Qutb (1906–1966) An Egyptian educator who called for the overthrow of governments and the imposition of purified Islamic law, based on the principles of previous puritanical reformers. Qutb formed a militant wing of the Muslim Brotherhood.

Selective terrorism A term used by Michael Collins during the Irish War of Independence (1919–1921). Collins did not launch indiscriminate terror attacks.

Rather, he selectively targeted the British military, the police force it sponsored, and the people who supported the United Kingdom.

Separation of powers The distribution of power among the executive, legislative, and judicial branches of government. When powers are separated, there is a balance among the powers. No one branch can control the government.

Shaba farm region A small farming region in southwest Lebanon annexed by Israel in 1981. When Israel withdrew from southern Lebanon in 2000, it remained in the Shaba farm region, creating a dispute with Lebanon, Hezbollah, and Syria.

Shamil Basayev (1965–2006) A jihadist leader in Chechnya, Basayev engineered several operations resulting in mass civilian casualties.

Sheik Mohammed Hassan Fadlallah (1935–2010) A grand ayatollah and leader of Shi'ites in Lebanon. The spiritual leader of Hezbollah. He was the target of a 1985 U. S.-sponsored assassination plot that killed 75 people.

Sheik Omar Abdel Rahman (b. 1938) A Sunni Islamic scholar linked to the Egyptian IG. He came to the United States in 1990 even though his name was on a State Department watch list. He was arrested and convicted of conspiracy after the 1993 World Trade Center bombing. He is currently serving a life sentence in the American federal prison system.

Shell state A political situation where a government nominally controls its own state but where large regions are either anarchic or under the control of others. A government is unable to enforce law or provide for other forms of social order in a shell state.

Sinn Fein The political party of Irish Republicans. Critics claim it represents terrorists. Republicans say it represents their political interests. Despite the debate, Sinn Fein historically has close connections with extremism and violence.

Six Day War A war between Israel and its Arab neighbors fought in June 1967. Israel launched the preemptive war in the face of an Arab military buildup, and it overwhelmed all opposition. At the end of the war, Israel occupied the Sinai Peninsula, the Golan Heights, and the West Bank of the Jordan River. It

also occupied the city Jerusalem, or al Quds to Muslims.

Six tactics of terrorism As defined by Brian Jenkins: (1) bombing, (2) hijacking, (3) arson, (4) assault, (5) kidnapping, and (6) hostage taking.

Sixth Amendment Guarantees the right to an attorney and a speedy public trial by jury in the jurisdiction where an alleged crime occurred. The amendment also requires that a suspect be informed of any changes.

Skinheads Young people or groups who embrace racial hatred and white supremacy.

Smart Policing Initiative (SPI) A federal program designed to focus law enforcement resources on a particular type of crime or community problem. Programs are evaluated by external research institutions and modified based on the results of the evaluation.

Social construct The way people view reality. Groups construct a framework around a concept, defining various aspects of their lives through the meanings they attribute to the construct.

Social context The historical, political, and criminological circumstances at a given point in time. The social context affects the way terrorism is defined.

Social geometry As used by Donald Black, the social space occupied by a structure and the direction in which it moves.

Social process As used in this discussion, social process is the way individuals and groups structure themselves, interpret reality, and take action based on those interpretations.

Socialists Radical democrats who sought wealth equality in capitalist societies. Some socialists sought governmental guarantees of living standards. Others believed that the state should control industry and divide profits among all members of society. Others believed that people would form cooperative relationships on their own with no need of a government.

South Lebanese Army A Christian militia closely allied with and supported by Israel. It operated with Israeli support from 1982 to 2000.

Sovereign citizen A citizen who believes that the original citizens of the United States were free from all governmental control. Sovereign citizens think that they were duped by the government in "schemes" like Social Security, driver's licenses, and car registrations. That is, once people participate in those conspiracies, they lose their natural freedom and become citizens of the United States. Sovereign citizens believe that they can renounce those regulations and free themselves from American law. This should be noted: though they free themselves from taxes and fees, they rarely reject government benefits.

Spain in 1807 The Peninsular War (1808–1814) began when Spanish and French forces divided Portugal in 1807. Napoleon, whose army entered Spain in 1807, attempted to use his forces to capture the Spanish throne in 1808. British forces under Sir Arthur Wellesley, later Duke of Wellington, joined Spanish forces White loyal to the king of Spain and Spanish partisans to fight the French.

Spanish Civil War >(1936–1939) A war that pitted pro-communist Republicans against pro-fascist Nationalists. The war ended with a Nationalist victory and a fascist dictatorship under Franco.

Steganography Refers to embedding a hidden encoded message on an Internet site.

Structural framework The idea that social constructs are based on systems that provide order. The systems are social structures that accomplish functions necessary to survive. Human activity occurs to accomplish the functions required to maintain the social structure of the system.

Structure The manner in which a group is organized and its purpose. Social scientists from this tradition feel that a group's structure and purpose cause it to act. They also believe that groups are created for specific functions.

Supreme Council of the IRB The command center of several Republican terrorist organizations, including the Irish Republican Army, the Official Irish Republican Army, and the Provisional Irish Republican Army. The name was transposed from the Irish Republican Brotherhood.

Survivalist A person who adopts a form of right-wing extremism advocating militant rejection of society. The members advocate a withdrawl from society in preparation for a coming internal war. Secluded in armed compounds, they hope to survive the coming collapse of society.

Swarming attacks Launching attacks on multiple targets in the same time frame or suddenly bringing several attackers to a single location and rapidly dispersing.

Sweet crude A type of oil with less than 0.5 percent sulfur content. Nigeria sits on a large sweet crude field, giving the country potential wealth. The people who live above the oil, however, are povertystricken, and oil production has been harmful to the environment.

Symbolic targets Terrorist targets that may have limited military or security value but represent the power of the state under attack. Terrorists seek symbolic targets to strike fear into society and to give a sense of power to the terrorist group. The power of the symbol also multiplies the effect of the attack.

Taliban The Islamicist group that governed Afghanistan from 1996 to 2001.

Tamils An ethnic minority in southern India and Sri Lanka. The Tamils in Sri Lanka are primarily Hindu, and the Sinhalese majority, mostly Buddhist. Ethnicity, however, not religion, defines most of the conflict between the two groups.

Taqi al Din ibn Taymiyyah (c. 1269–1328) Also known as ibn Taymiyya; a Muslim religious reformer in the time of the Crusades and a massive Mongol invasion.

Targeting Violent Crime Initiative (TVCI) A Department of Justice grant program administered through the Bureau of Justice Assistance. Its purpose is to fund multijurisdictional state, local, and tribal law enforcement teams that prevent selected violent crimes through intelligence-led policing.

Task orientation As used in this text, the ability to stay focused on the primary mission of an organization.

Terrorism Screening Center (TSC) A multiagency operation in West Virginia that evaluates information gathered from a variety of governmental sources.

Theory of action A social science theory that assumes human beings take action based on the subjective meanings they attribute to social settings.

Theory of suicide terrorism A theory developed by Robert Pape that states that a group of people occupied by a democratic power are likely to engage in suicide attacks when there are

differences between the religions of the group and the democratic power and when the occupied religious community supports altruistic suicide.

Thermobaric bomb A twostage bomb. The first stage spreads either a fuel cloud or finely ground powder through the air. The explosive material mixes with the oxygen present in the atmosphere. The second stage detonates the explosive material, which explodes in all directions in a series of shock waves. The cloud can penetrate a number of barriers. A person breathing the material explodes from the inside out when the material is ignited.

Third Position A movement started after the Branch Davidian standoff at Waco. It attempts to unite left- wing, right-wing, and single- issue extremists in a single movement.

Threat analysis The process of examining a community to determine the areas that might be subject to attack and the criticality of those areas to the functions of the community.

Tony Blair (b. 1953) The Labour Party prime minister of the United Kingdom from 1994 to 2007.

Total criminal intelligence A concept aimed at gathering information about all potential crimes, the activities of known and suspected criminals, crime patterns, and potential social problems. Information is analyzed and used to prevent crime. Total Criminal Intelligence is redundant; that is, several types of crime can be prevented by acting on single sources of information. There are several variations on the theme, including Problem- Oriented Policing, Intelligence- Led Policing, and the Smart Policing Initiative.

Total criminal intelligence (TCI) An "all crimes" approach to the intelligence process. The same type of intelligence that thwarts terrorism works against other crimes and community problems.

Total criminal intelligence (TCI) All criminal intelligence gathered and analyzed for intelligenceled policing. Rather than focusing on one type of issue, such as terrorism, agencies focus on gathering information about all potential crimes and social problems.

Transitional Federal Government (TFG) A group established to govern Somalia in 2004 until a permanent government could be established. It was backed by the United Nations, with

American support, and the African Union.

Tribal areas Refers to Federally Administered Tribal Areas (FATA) in Pakistan along the Afghan border. Seven different Pashtu tribes have control of the region by agreement with the central government.

Triborder region The area where Brazil, Paraguay, and Argentina join. The major city is Cuidad del Este.

Triborder region The area where Brazil, Paraguay, and Argentina join. The major city in the area is Cuidad del Este.

Tupac Amaru (?–1572) An Inca chieftain who led a revolt against Spain in the sixteenth century. His story has inspired many liberation and democratic movements in South America.

Uighar nationalists China's ethnic Turkmen. Some Uighar nationalists organized to revive an eighteenth-century Islamic state in China's Xinjiang province. Using Kyrgyzstan and Kazakhstan as a base, they operate in China.

Ulricke Meinhof (1934–1976) Co-created the Red Army Faction with Andreas Baader in 1970. She was the co-leader of the group. Arrested in 1972, she committed suicide in prison.

Ulster Volunteer Force One of a number of militant Unionist organizations. Such groups wage terrorist campaigns against Catholics and militant Republican organizations.

Umar (circa 580–644) Also known as Umar ibn al Khattab, the second Rightly Guided caliph, according to Sunnis. Under his leadership, the Arab empire expanded into Persia, the southern part of the Byzantine empire, and Egypt. His army conquered Jerusalem in 637.

Umar Farouk Abdulmutallab (b. 1986) According to a federal indictment, smuggled a chemical bomb and chemical igniter in a syringe onto a Northwest flight from Amsterdam to Detroit on December 25, 2009. He was born into a family that practiced Islam but became radicalized while attending school in the United Kingdom. He was allegedly trained by terrorists in Yemen, who supplied the explosive compound.

Umayyads The first Arab and Muslim dynasty ruling from Damascus from 661 to 750. The Umayyads were Uthman's family.

Umbrella A group that shelters, supports, and inspires smaller terrorist groups. The RAND Corporation refers to this as a hub.

USA Patriot Act A law passed in October 2001 that expands law enforcement's power to investigate and deter terrorism. Opponents claim that it adversely affects civil liberties; proponents claim that it introduces reasonable measures to protect the country against terrorists. The act was amended and renewed in 2006, and the ability to collect and analyze domestic intelligence remained part of the law. Provisions for allowing roving wiretaps, increased power to seize evidence, and increasing wiretaps were approved in 2011.

USS Cole A U.S. Navy destroyer attacked by two suicide bombers in the port of Aden, Yemen, on October 12, 2000. Seventeen American sailors were killed in the attack.

Uthman (circa 580–656) Also known as Uthman ibn Affan, the third Rightly Guided caliph, according to Sunnis. He conquered most of the remaining parts of North Africa, Iran, Cyprus, and the Caucasia region. He was assassinated by his own soldiers for alleged nepotism.

Velupillai Pirapaharan (1954–2009) Founder and leader of the LTTE. Pirapaharan's terrorists conducted more successful suicide bombings than any other terrorist group in the world.

Vernon Wayne Howell (or David Koresh, 1959–1993) The charismatic leader of the Branch Davidian cult.

Violent radicalization Refers to the process of adopting extremist positions and engaging in violence based on a new set of beliefs.

Viral weapons Enhanced forms of viruses. The virus is "hardened" so that it can live for long periods and enhanced for deadlier effects.

Virtual organizations Associations that develop through communication, financial, and ideological links. Like a network, a virtual organization has no central leadership.

Vladimir Lenin The Russian revolutionary who led a second revolution in October, bringing the communists to power. Lenin led the communists in a civil war and set up a dictatorship to enforce communist rule in Russia.

Vladimir Putin (b. 1952) a former KGB officer and second president of the Russian Federation from 1999 to 2008. He began serving as Russia's prime minister after the end of his presidential term.

Waco Siege The 1993 standoff between members of the Branch Davidian cult and federal law enforcement officers. The standoff ended when FBI agents tried to bring the siege to an end, but Branch Davidian leaders set fire to their compound killing eighty-two of the followers.

War of the Spanish Succession (1702–1714) The first global war exported from Europe, pitting the French and Austrians against each other for familial control of the Spanish throne. Although it involved myriad political factors, it set the stage for the evolution of modern Spain. There are several dates given for the end of the war due to the many peace treaties that ended military operations in Europe and around the world.

Waziristan Literally, the land of the Waziris, a tribal region between the North-West Frontier Province and Baluchistan. Waziri tribes clashed with the Pakistan Army from 2004 to 2006, and they support several jihadist operations in Afghanistan and Pakistan. Al Qaeda and Taliban forces operate in Waziristan.

Whiskey Rebellion The uprising that took place in 1791 when a group of Pennsylvania farmers refused to pay a federal tax on corn used to make alcohol. The rebellion ended when President George Washington sent troops to stop the rebellion.

White Supremacy A political philosophy claiming that white people are superior to all other ethnic groups.

William Potter Gale (1917–1988) An American military leader who coordinated guerrilla activities in the Philippines during World War II. Gale became a radio preacher and leader of the Christian Identity movement after returning home.

Workers Councils (or Soviets) The lowest-level legislative body in the Soviet Union following the October

Revolution. *Soviet* is the Russian word for "council."

Working group A term used in the federal government for a group of subject matter experts who gather to suggest solutions to common problems.

World Islamic Front against Jews and Crusaders An organization created in 1998 by Osama bin Laden and Ayman al Zawahiri. It represents a variety of jihadist groups that issued a united front against Jews and the West. It is commonly called al Qaeda.

Yasser Arafat (1929– 2004) The name assumed by Mohammed al Husseini. Born in Cairo, he was a founding member of Fatah and the PLO. He merged the PLO and Fatah in 1964 and ran a terrorist campaign against Israel. After renouncing terrorism and recognizing Israel's right to exist, Arafat was president of the Palestinian National Authority from 1993 to 2004.

Yom Kippur War A war between Israel and its Arab neighbors fought in October 1973. Also known as the Ramadan War, hostilities began with a surprise attack on Israel. After initial setbacks, Israel counterattacked and regained its positions.

9/11 Commission Report. *See* National Commission on Terrorist Attacks Upon the United States.

ABA. (2011). Obama Signs Patriot Act Extension with Autopen. *ABA Journal*. Online: http://www.abajournal.com/news/article/obama_signs_patriot_act_extension_with_auto_pen_legal_opinons_finds_no_pres/

Abbey, E. (1975). *The Monkey Wrench Gang*. Salt Lake City: Roaming the West.

ABC News. (1998). "John Miller-Interview with Osama bin Laden." Online: http://abcnews.co.com/sections/world/DailyNews/terror 1st person 980612.html.

ABC News. (2004). "Al Qaeda Has 18,000 Militants for Raid—Think Tank." May 25. Online: http://abcnews.go.com/sections/world/Investigation/Insider_DTR_040525.html.

Abinales, P. N. (2008). "ThePhilippines: Weak State, Resilient President." *Southeast Asia Affairs:* pp. 291–312.

Abinales, P. N., and D. J. Amoroso. (2006). "The Withering of Philippine Democracy." *Current History* (September): pp. 190–195.

Aboul-Enein, Y. H. (2004). "Ayman al-Zawahiri: The Ideologue of Modern Islamic Militancy." Maxwell Air Force Base, AL:United States Air Force, Air University. Online: http://www.au.af.mil/ awcgate/cpc-pubs/ward2.pdf.

Abrahamsen, R. (2004). "A Breeding Ground for Terrorists? Africa and Britain's War on Terrorism."*Review of African Political Economy* 31 (102): pp. 677–684.

Abramson, L., and M. Godoy. (2006). "The Patriot Act: Key Controversies." National Public Radio. Online: http://www.npr.org/news/specials/patriotact/patriotact provisions.html.

Abuza, Z. (2003a). "Funding Terrorism in Southeast Asia: The Financial Network of al Qaeda and Jemaah Islamiya." *Contemporary Southeast Asia* 25 (2) (August):pp. 169–200.

Abuza, Z. (2003b). *Militant Islam in Southeast Asia: Crucible of Terror.* Boulder, CO: Lynne Rienner.

Abuza, Z. (2006a). "JI Moneyman and Top Recruiter: A Profile of Noordin Mohammed Top." *Terrorism Focus* 3 (29)(July 25). Online: http://www. jamestown.org/single/?no_cache=1&tx_ttnews[tt_news]=850.

Abuza, Z. (2006b). "A Breakdown of Southern Thailand's Insurgent Groups." The Jamestown Foundation. *Terrorism Monitor* 4 (17). Online: http://www.jamestown.org/single/?no_cache=1&tx_ttnews[tt_news]=893.

Acharya, A.(2011). "Nizam, la Tanzim (System, not Organization): Do Organizations Matter in Terrorism Today? A Study of the November 2008 Mumbai Attacks."*Studies in Conflict and Terrorism*, Vol. 34: pp. 1-16.

ACLU. (2010). "Immigrants' Rights: No Human Being Is Illegal." *ACLU*, July 22. Online: http:// www.aclu.org/immigrants-rights.

Adams, B. (2005). "Nepal at the Precipice." *Foreign Affairs* 84(5): pp. 112–134.

Adams, D. (2003). "Narcoterrorism Needs Attention." *St. Petersburg Times*, March 10. Online: http://www.sptimes.com/2003/03/10/Columns/_Narcoterrorism_need.shtml.

Adams, J. (1986). *The Financing of Terror*. New York: Simon & Schuster.

ADL. (2010). "The Sovereign Citizens Movement." Chicago:ADL.

AFP. (2010). "Ex-guard Says Bin Laden Wants to Use Nukes." Online: http://www.news.com.au/breaking-news/ex-guard-says-bin-laden-wants-to-use-nukes/story-e6frfku0-1225859703802.

Afsar, S.,C. Samples,and T. Wood. (2008). "The Taliban: An Organizational Analysis." *Military Review* 88 (3): pp. 58–73.

Agbese, A., Mahmud, and A.B. Muhktur. (2012). "Nigeria: 10 Killed in Jos after Church Bomb." *All Africa*, March 12. Online: http://allafrica.com/stories/201203121075.html.

Agence France Presse. (2004). "Basque ETA Separatists Call for Unconditional Dialogue." Online: http://www.elkarri.org/en/pdf/Agence_France_Pres_28_10_04.PDF.

Ahern, J. F. (1972). *Police in Trouble*. New York: Hawthorne Books, Inc.

Albright, M. (2003). "Bridges, Bombs, or Bluster." *Foreign Affairs* 82 (September/October): pp. 2–19.

Alcohol, Tobacco, and Firearms (ATF), U.S. Department of the Treasury. (1995). *Violent White Supremacist Groups*. Washington, DC: ATF.

Algazy, J. (2004). "Amnesty: IDF Killed 100 Children Last Year." Online: http://www.fromoccupiedpalestine .org/.

Ali, F. (2007). "Dressed in Black: A Look at Pakistan's Radical Women." *Global Terrorism Analysis*. The Jamestown Foundation. Online: http://www.jamestown .org/programs/gta/single/?tx_ttnews [tt_news]=4114&tx_ttnews [backPid]=182&no_cache=1.

Ali, T. (2008). *The Duel: Pakistan on the Flight Path of American Power*. New York: Scribner.

Al Jazeera. (2006). "Timeline: Lebanon Conflict." English edition, August17. Online: http://english.aljazeera. net/ English/archive/archive? ArchiveId= 24660.

Alonso, R. (2001). "The Modernization in Irish Republican Thinking toward the Utility of Violence." *Studies in Conflict and Terrorism* 24 (2): pp. 131–144.

Alonso, Z. (2004). "Border Guards Divided on Security Adequacy." *Los Angeles Times*, reported in *The Grand Rapids Press*, August 29: p.A5.

Al-Shishani, M. B. (2010). "AQAP'sNew Strategy: Targeting Westerners and Promoting the Individual Jihad." *Terrorism Monitor* 8(24). Online: http://www.jamestown.org/ programs/gta/single/? tx_ttnews[tt_ news] =36513&tx_ttnews[backPid] =457&no_cache=1.

Althaus, S. L. (2002). "American News Consumption during Times of National Crisis." *Political Science and Politics* (September): pp. 517– 521. Online: http://www .apsanet.org/imgtest/AmericanNews-Consumption-Althaus.pdf.

Altheide, D. L. (2006). "Terrorism and the Politics of Fear." *Cultural Studies <=>Critical Methodologies* 6 (4): pp. 415–439. Online: http://csc .sagepub.com.ezproxy.gvsu. edu:2048/cgi/reprint/6/4/415.

Altheide, D. L. (2007). "The Mass Media and Terrorism." *Discourse and Communication* 1 (3): pp. 287– 308. Online: http://dcm. sagepub. com/cgi/content/refs/1/3/287.

American Civil Liberties Union. (2002). "ACLU Decries Ashcroft Scheme to Gut Immigration Courts." March 20. Online: http://www.aclu.org/ immigrants-rights/ aclu-decries-ashcroft-scheme-gut-immigration-courts.

Amon, M. (2004). "Can Israel Survive the West Bank Settlements?" *Terrorism and Political Violence* 16 (Spring): pp. 48–65.

Anderson, B. C. (2005). *South Park Conservatives: The Revolt against Liberal Media Bias*. Washington, DC: Regnery.

Anderson, D. (2005). *Histories of the Hanged: The Dirty War in Kenya and the End of Empire*. New York:W. W. Norton and Company.

Animal Liberation Front. (2000). Homepage. Online: http://www .animalliberationfront.com/.

Anti-Defamation League (ADL). (2010). "The Lawless Ones." ADL. Online: http://www.adl.org/learn/sovereign_ movement/sovereign_citizens_ movement_report.pdf.

Aplin, D. (2010). "FBI Routinely Skirted ECPA Protections to Obtain Phone Records, Justice IG Reports." *The Criminal Law Reporter*86 (16): p. 484.

Appleby, R. S. (2000). *The Ambivalence of the Sacred*. New York: Rowman & Littlefield.

Arbatov, A., A. Pikaev, and V. Dvorkin. (2008). "Nuclear Terrorism: Political, Legal, Strategic, and Technological Aspects." *Russian Politics and Law* 46 (1):pp. 50–78.

Archibold, R. C. (2010). "Judge Blocks Arizona's Immigration Law." *New York Times*, July 28. Online: http:// www.nytimes.com/2010/07/29/us/ 29arizona.html.

Arena, M. P., and B. A. Arrigo. (2005). "Identity and the Terrorist Threat: An Interpretive and Explanatory Model." In L. L. Snowden and B. C. Whitsel (eds.), *Terrorism: Research, Readings, and Realities*. Upper Saddle River, NJ: Prentice Hall.

Armstrong, K. (2000a). *Islam: A Short History*. New York: The Modern Library.

Armstrong, K. (2000b). *The Battle for God*. New York: Random House.

Army of God. (n.d.). "The Army of God Manual." Online: http:// www.armyofgod.com/AOGhistory .html.

Arquilla, J., and D. Ronfeldt. (1996). *The Advent of Netwar*. Santa Monica, CA: RAND.

Arquilla, J., and D. Ronfeldt (2001). *Networks and Netwars: The Future of Terror, Crime, and Militancy*. Santa Monica, CA: RAND.

Arquilla, J., D. Ronfeldt, and M. Zanini. (1999). "Networks, Netwar, and Information-Age Terrorism." In Ian O. Lesser et al. (eds.), *Countering the New Terrorism*. Santa Monica, CA: RAND.

Asprey, R. B. (2002). *War in the Shadows: The Guerrilla in History*. Lincoln, NE: iUniverse.

Associated Press. (2006). "Provisions in the USA Patriot Act." *The San Francisco Chronicle*. May 7. Online: http://sfgate.com/cgi-bin/ article.cgi?f=/n/a/2006/03/07/ national/w134940S84.DTL.

Associated Press. (2007a). "Thousands Protest in Turkey against an Islamic-Based Government." *The International Herald Tribune*, May 20. Online: http://www.iht.com/ articles/2007/05/20/africa/ankara .php.

Associated Press. (2007b). "Spain Arrests 15 on Terror Recruitment Charges." *MSNBC*, May 28. Online: http://www.msnbc.msn .com/id/18903462/.

ATF. *See* Alcohol, Tobacco, and Firearms.

Avilés, W. (2009). "Despite Insurgency: Reducing Military Prerogatives in Colombia and Peru." *Latin American Politics and Society*51 (1): pp. 57–86.

Awad, N. (2003). "Written Testimony of Nihad Awad before the Senate Subcommittee on Terrorism, Technology, and Homeland Security." September 10. Online: http:// www.anti-cair-net.org/awad Testimony2003.html.

Azam, J. P. (2005). "Suicide Bombing as an Inter-Generational Investment." *Political Choice* 122: pp. 177–198.

Azani, E. (2009). *Hezbollah: The Story of the Party of God*. New York: Palgrave MacMillan.

Azano, H. J. (2003). "Can Security Help with Civil Defense?" *Security Management* (February). Online: http://www.securitymanagement .com/.

Azmanova, A. (2004). "The Mobilisation of the European Left in the Early Twenty-First Century." *European Journal of Sociology/Archives Europeénnes de Sociologie* 45(2): pp. 273–306.

Badey, T. J. (2003). "Defining International Terrorism: A Pragmatic Approach." In T. J. Badey (ed.), *Annual Editions—Violence and Terrorism 2003/2004*. New York: McGraw-Hill.

Baginski, M. (2004). "Statement of Maureen A. Baginski before the House of Representatives Select Committee on Homeland Security." August 22. Online: http://www .gov/congress/congress 04baginsky081704.htm.

Bajoria, J. (2010). "Pakistan's New-Generation of Terrorists." *Council on Foreign Relations*. Online: http://www.cfr.org/publication/15422/pakistans_new_generation_of_terrorists.html?breadcrumb=%2Fissue%2F135.

Bakier, A. H. (2006a). "JihadisProvide Internet Training for Female Suicide Bombers." *Terrorism Focus* 3 (40). Online: http://www.jamestown.org/terrorism/news/article.php?issue_id=3890.

Bakier, A. H. (2006b). "Lesson from al Qaeda's Attack on the Khobar Compound." *Terrorism Monitor*. Online: http://jamestown.org/terrorism/news/article.php?issue_id=3830.

Bakunin, M. (orig.1866; 1987). "Revolution,Terrorism, Banditry." Reprint 1987in Walter Laqueur and Yonah Alexanderm *The Terrorism Reader*. New York: Meridian: pp. 65–68.

Ballard, J. D. (2003). *Nuclear Waste Transportation*. Reno: State of Nevada. Online: http://www.state.nv.us/nucwaste/news2003/pdf/nas_ballard.pdf.

Banerjee, S. (2009). "Reflections of a One-Time Maoist Activist." *Dialectical Anthropology* (33): pp. 253–269.

Baniela, S. I. (2010). "Piracy at Sea: Somalia an Area of Great Concern." *Journal of Navigation* 63 (2): pp. 191–206.

Barber, B. R. (1996). *Jihad vs. McWorld: How Globalism and Tribalism Are Reshaping the World*. New York: Ballantine Books.

Barclay, J. (2010). "Can al-Qaeda Use Islam to Justify Jihad in the United States? A Debate in Progress." *Terrorism Monitor* 8 (26). Online: http://www.jamestown.org/programs/ gta/single/?tx_ttnews [tt_news] =36562&tx_ttnews [backPid]=457&no_cache=1.

Bar-Joseph, U., and R. McDermott. (2008). "Change the Analyst and Not the System: A Different Approach to Intelligence Reform." *Foreign Policy Analysis* 4 (2): pp. 127–148.

Barkan, J. D. (2004). "Kenya after Moi." *Foreign Affairs* 83 (1): pp. 87–100.

Barkun, M. (1997a). *Religion and the Racist Right: The Origins of the Christian Identity Movement*. Chapel Hill: University of North Carolina Press.

Barkun, M. (1997b). "Leaderless Resistance and Phineas Priests: Strategies of Uncoordinated Violence on the Far Right." Paper presented at the American Society of Criminology, San Diego.

Barnett, T. P. M. (2005). *The Pentagon's New Map: War and Peace in the Twenty-First Century*. New York: Putnam's.

Barnett, T. P. M. (2006). *Blue Printfor Action: A Future Worth Creating*. Toronto: The Berkley Publishing Group.

Baron, D. P. (2004). "Persistent Media Bias." Online: http://www.wallis.rochester.edu/conference11/mediabias.pdf.

Barry, T. (2010). "Synergy in Security: The Rise of the National Security Complex." *Dollars and Sense*287 (March–April): pp. 11–16.

Basile, M. (2004). "Going to the Source: Why al Qaeda's Financial Network Is Likely to Withstand the Current War on Terrorist Financing." *Studies in Conflict and Terrorism* 27 (3): pp. 169–185.

Bassiouni, M. C. (1981). "Terrorism and the Media." *Journal of Criminal Law and Criminology* 72: pp. 1–55.

BBC. (1998). "World: Europe. Spain's State-Sponsored Death Squads." *BBC News*, July 29. Online: http:// news.bbc.co.uk/2/hi/europe/141720.stm.

BBC. (2010a). "Mumbai Attacks." *BBC News*. Online: http://news.bbc.co.uk/2/hi/in_depth/south_ asia/2008/mumbai_attacks/default.stm.

BBC. (2010b). "Nepal Country Profile." *BBC News*, January 20. Online: http://news.bbc.co.uk/2/hi/ south_asia/country_profiles/1166502.stm.

BBC News. (2000). "Turkish Hezbollah: 'No State Links.'" January 23. Online: http://news.bbc.co.uk/1/hi/world/europe/615785.stm.

BBC News. (2001). "TimeLine: India Targeted Attacks." December 13. Online: http://news.bbc.co.uk/2/hi/south_asia/1708861.stm.

BBC News. (2002). "Challenge to Israel's 'Assassination Policy.'" January 24. Online: http://news.bbc.co.uk/1/hi/world/middle_east/1780051.stm.

BBC News. (2003). "Profile: Al Aqsa Martyrs' Brigades." *BBC New World Edition*, July 1. Online: http://news.bbc.co.uk/2/hi/ middle_east/1760492.stm.

BBC News. (2004). "Timeline: Madrid Investigation." April 28. Online: http://news.bbc.co.uk/1/hi/world/europe/3597885.stm.

BBC News. (2005a). "Arrest after Stabbing Victim Dies." January 30. Online: http://news.bbc.co.uk/1/hi/northern_ireland/4221599.stm.

BBC News. (2005b). "Murder Witnesses 'Facing Threats.'" March 9. Online: http://news.bbc. co.uk/1/hi/northern_ireland/4332747.stm.

BBC News. (2005c). "IRA Weapons Report Handed Over." Online: http://news.bbc.co.uk/1/hi/northern_ireland/4281104.stm.

BBC News. (2006). "Turkey Seizes 'al Qaeda Members.'" December 9. Online: http://news.bbc.co.uk/2/hi/europe/6164789.stm.

Beck, J. M., and J. D. Markusse. (2008). "Basque Violence: A Reappraisal of Culturalist Explanations." *European Journal of Sociology* 49 (1): pp. 91–118.

Beebe, K. (2006). "The Air Force's Missing Doctrine: How the U.S. Air Force Ignores Counterinsurgency." *Air and Space Power Journal* 20 (1): pp. 27–34.

Beirich, H. (2010). "Hate Groups Donate to Arizona Law's Defense." Southern Poverty Law Center. Online: http://www.splcenter.org/blog/2010/07/13/hate-groups-donate-to-arizona-laws-defense/.

Bell, D. A. (2007). *The First Total War: Napoleon's Europe and the Birth of War as We Know It*. New York: Houghton Mifflin Company.

Bell, J. B. (1974). *The Secret Army: A History of the IRA, 1916–1970.* Cambridge, MA: MIT Press.

Bell, J. B. (1975). *Transnational Terror.* Washington, DC: American Enterprise Institute.

Bell, J. B. (1976). "Strategy, Tactics, and Terror: An Irish Perspective." In Y.Alexander (ed.), *International Terrorism.* New York: Praeger.

Bell, J. B. (1998). "Ireland: The Long End Game." *Studies in Conflict and Terrorism* 21: pp. 5–28.

Bell, J. B., and T. R. Gurr. (1979). "Terrorism and Revolution in America." In H. D. Graham and T. R. Gurr (eds.), *Violence in America.* Newbury Park, CA: Sage.

Benedetta, B. (2009). "Colombia's FARC and the Basque ETA: Exploring the Tactical and Economic Partnership." *Terrorism Monitor* 7 (2)(January 23). Online: http://www.jamestown. org/articles-by-author/?no_cache=1&tx_cablanttnewsstaffrelation_pi1%5Bauthor%5D=491.

Benini, A. A., and L. H. Moulton. (2004). "Civilian Victims in an Asymmetrical Conflict: Operation Enduring Freedom, Afghanistan." *Journal of Peace Research* 41 (4): pp. 403–422.

Benjamin, D., and S. Simon. (2002). *The Age of Sacred Terror.* New York: Random House.

Benjamin, D., and S. Simon. (2003). "The Real Worry: In Iraq We Have Created a New Field of Jihad." *Time* 162 (September 1): p. 35.

Bergen, P., and P. Cruickshank. (2007). "Al Qaeda-on-Thames: UK Plotters Connected." *Washington Post*, April 30. PostGlobal.com. Online: http://newsweek.washingtonpost.com/postglobal/needtoknow/2007/04/al_qaedaonthames_plotters_well.html.

Bergen, P., and K. Tiedemann. (2010). "The Almanac of al Qaeda." *Foreign Policy* 179 (May/June).

Bergen, P. L. (2001). *Holy War, Inc.: Inside the Secret World of Osama bin Laden.* New York: Free Press.

Berger, C. R., J. T. Johnson, and E. J. Lee. (2003). "Antidotes for Anthrax Anecdotes: The Role of Rationality and Base-Rate Data in Assuaging Apprehension." *Communication Research* 30: pp. 199–223.

Online: http://crx. sagepub.com/cgi/content/abstract/30/2/198.

Berkeley, B. (2001). *The Graves Are Not Yet Full: Race, Tribe, and Power in the Heart of Africa.* New York: Basic Books.

Berlet, C., and M. N. Lyons. (2000). *Right-Wing Populism in America: Too Close for Comfort.* New York: Guildford.

Berman, E. (2009). *Radical, Religious, and Violent: The New Economics of Terrorism.* Boston: MIT Press.

Berthelsen, J. (1996). "Room with No View." *Far Eastern Economic Review* (May 9):p. 159.

Best, R. A., Jr. (2001). *Intelligence and Law Enforcement: Countering Transnational Threats to the U.S.* Congressional Reference Service. CRS Report for Congress, December 3. Online: http://www. fas.org/irp/crs/RL30252.pdf.

Betts, R. K. (2002). "Fixing Intelligence." *Foreign Affairs* 81: pp. 43–59.

Bhatt, C. (2010). "The 'British Jihad' and the Curves of Religious Violence." *Ethnic and Racial Studies* 33 (1): pp. 39–59.

Biddle, S., M. E. O'Hanlon, and K. M. Paul. (2008). "How to Leave a Stable Iraq." *Foreign Affairs* 87 (5): pp. 40–58.

Biersteker, T. J., and S. E. Eckert. (2007). *Countering the Financing of Terrorism.* New York: Routledge.

Bisharat, G. E., T. Crawley, S. Elturk, C. James,; R. Mishaan, A. Radhakrishnan, and A. Sanders. (2009). "Israel's Invasion of Gaza in International Law." *Denver Journal of Law and International Policy* 38 (1): pp. 41–114.

BJA/SLATT. (2010). "State and Local Anti-Terrorism Training Program." Online: https://www.slatt. org/default.aspx.

Black, D. (2004). "The Geometry of Terrorism." *Sociological Theory* 22 (1): pp. 14–25.

Black, I. (2003). "EU Hits Out at Israeli Fence." *The Guardian*, November 18. Online: http://www.guardian. co.uk/israel/Story/0,2763,1087396,00.html.

Blair, D. (2012). "Anders Breivik's Norway Shooting Spree Relived in Chilling Detail." *The Telegraph*, April 24. Online: http://www

.telegraph.co.uk/news/worldnews/europe/norway/9217315/Anders-Behring-Breiviks-Norway-shooting-spree-relived-in-chilling-detail.html.

Blank, S. (2003). "Terrorism in Asia and the Pacific." Testimony—Committee on International Relations, Subcommittee on the Middle East and Central Asia, U.S. House of Representatives. *Congressional Quarterly*, December 29. Online: http://homeland.cq.cm/hs/display.do?dockey=/usr/local/ cqonline/docs/html.

Blee, K. M. (2005). "Women and Organized Racial Terrorism in the United States." *Studies in Conflict and Terrorism* 28:pp. 421–433.

Blomberg, S. B.,G. D. Hess, and A. Weerapana (2004). "An Economic Model of Terrorism." *Conflict Management and Peace Science* 21: pp. 17–28.

Bodansky, Y. (1999). *Bin Laden: The Man Who Declared War on America.* Rocklin, CA: Forum.

Bodrero, D. D. (2002). "Law Enforcement's New Challenge to Investigate, Interdict, and Prevent Terrorism." *The Police Chief* (February): pp. 41–48.

Body-Gendrot, S. (2010). "European Policies of Social Control Post 9/11." *Social Research* 77 (1): pp. 204–228.

Boin, A. (2009). "The New World of Crises and Crisis Management: Implications for Policymaking and Research." *Review of Policy Research* 26 (4):pp. 367–377.

Bond, C. S., and L. M. Simons. (2009). "The Forgotten Front: Winning Hearts and Minds in Southeast Asia." *Foreign Affairs* 88 (6): pp. 52–63.

Borum, R. (2004). *Psychology of Terrorism.* Tampa: University of South Florida.

Boustany, N. (2005). "Spain Keeps a Vigilant Eye on al Qaeda Threat." *Washington Post*, April 20. Online: http://www.washingtonpost.com/wp-dyn/articles/A2944-2005Apr19.html.

Bowers, S. R., and K. R. Keys. (1998). "Technology and Terrorism: The New Threat for the Millennium." *Conflict Studies*, May. Paper presented by Research Institute for the Study of Conflict and Terrorism.

Bowman, B. L. (2005). "Realism and Idealism: US Policy Toward Saudi Arabia, from the Cold War to Today." *Parameters* 35 (4): pp. 91–106.

Bozek, J. (2009). *Sayyid Qutb: Analysis of Jihadist Philosophy*. Saarbru[the u needs an umlaut]cken, Germany: VDM Verlag.

Bozell, L. B. (2005). *Weapons of Mass Distortion: The Coming Meltdown of the Liberal Media*. New York: Three Rivers Press.

Brachman, J. "Al Qaeda's Dissident." *Foreign Policy* 176(December): pp. 40–42.

Brachman, J. M., and W. F. McCants. (2006). "CTC Report: Stealing Al-Qaida's Playbook." West Point, NY: United States Military Academy. Online: http://www.ctc.usma.edu.

Brackett, D. W. (1996). *Holy Terror: Armageddon in Tokyo*. New York: Weatherhill.

Bradley, E. (2004). *60 Minutes*. CBS.

Bradshaw, B. (1978). "Sword, Word, and Strategy in the Reformation in Ireland." *The Historical Journal* 21 (3): pp. 475–502.

Branche, R. (2008). "The French State Faced with the Algerian Nationalists (1954–1962): A War against Terrorism?" In S. Cohen (ed.), *Democracies at War with Terrorism*. New York: Palgrave Macmillan.

Brar, S. S. (2003). "The Sikhism Homepage." Online: http://www.sikhs.org/.

Bravin, J. (2007). "Terror War Legal Edifice Teeters." *Wall Street Journal*, June 13: p.A4.

Bronson, R. (2005). "RethinkingReligion: The Legacy of the U.S.-Saudi Relationship." *The Washington Quarterly* 28 (4): pp. 121–137.

Brookbank, J. (2006). "Understanding the Terrorism Threats Posed to Medical Technology." *Biomedical Instrumentation & Technology* 40 (2): pp. 94–95.

Brooks, R.E. (2011). "Improving Criminal Intelligence Sharing: How the Criminal Intelligence Coordinating Council Supports Law Enforcement and Homeland Security." *The Police Chief* 78 (February): pp. 34–38.

Brown, I. (2009). "Terrorism and the Proportionality of Internet Surveillance." *European Journal of Criminology* 6 (2):pp. 119–134.

Bruce, S. (2001). "Terrorism and Politics: The Case of Northern Ireland's Loyalist Paramilitaries." *Studies in Conflict and Terrorism* 13 (2): pp. 27–48.

Bruechner, S. A. (2009). "Swarming Geographic Event Profiling, Link Analysis, and Prediction." *Vector Research Center*. Online: http://www.newvectors.net/staff/brueckners/publications/2009/ gp34SASO_cameraReady.pdf.

Bruil, B. C. O., and R. Rozema. (2009). "Fatal Imaginations: Death Squads in Davao City and Medellin Compared." *Crime, Law, and Social Change* 52: pp. 405–424.

Bruton, B. (2009). "In the Quicksands of Somalia: Where Doing Less Helps More." *Foreign Affairs* 88 (6): pp. 79–94.

Buchanan, P. J. (2002). *The Death of the West: How Dying Populations and Immigrant Invasions Imperil Our Country and Civilization*. New York: Thomas Dunn.

Bunker, R. J. (1998). "Information Operations and the Conduct of Land Warfare." *Military Review*(September–November): pp. 4–17. Online: http://www.iwar.org.uk/war/resources/milrev/bunker/pdf.

Bunn, M. (2009). "Reducing the Greatest Risks of Nuclear Theft and Terrorism." *Daedalus* 138 (4): pp. 112–124.

Bureau of Justice Assistance. (2005). *National Criminal Intelligence Sharing Plan*. Bureau of Justice Assistance. Online: http://www.it.ojp.gov/documents/National_Criminal_Intelligence_Sharing_Plan.pdf.

Bureau of Justice Assistance. (2010). *Threats to Law Enforcement Officers and Communities from Ideological Extremists*. Washington, DC: Bureau of Justice Assistance.

Burgess, C. A. (2007). "OpeningRemarks." First National Fusion-Center Conference, Destin, FL (unpublished).

Burgess, M. (2002). "In the Spotlight: The Islamic Movement of Uzbekistan (IMU)." Center for Defense Information. Online: http://www.cdi.org/terrorism/imu.cfm.

Burke, J. (2004). "Al Qaeda." *Foreign Policy* 142 (May/June): pp. 20–26.

Burleigh, M. (2009). *Blood and Rage: A Cultural History of Terrorism*. New York: Harper.

Burns, J. (2010). "Cameron Says 1972 Killings in N. Ireland Were Unjustified." *New York Times*, June 10. Online: http://www.nytimes.com/2010/06/16/world/europe/16nireland.html.

Burns, J.F. (2011). "Basque Separatists Halt Campaign of Violence." *New York Times*, October 20. Online: http://www.nytimes.com/2011/10/21/world/europe/eta-basque-separatists-declare-halt-to-violence-in-spain-and-france.html.

Burton, A. (1976). *Urban Terrorism*. New York: Free Press.

Bustamante, M., and S. Chaskel. (2008). "Colombia's Precarious Progress." *Current History* (February):pp. 77–84.

Butler, P. (2002). "Terrorism and Utilitarianism: Lessons from, and for, Criminal Law." *Journal of Criminal Law and Criminology* 93: pp. 1–22.

Butler, R. E. (1976). "Terrorism in Latin America." In Y.Alexander (ed.), *International Terrorism*. New York: Praeger.

Byford, G. (2002). "The Wrong War." *Foreign Affairs* 81 (July/August): pp. 34–43.

Byman, D. (1998). "The Logic of Ethnic Terrorism." *Studies in Conflict and Terrorism* 21: pp. 149–169.

Byman, D. (2003). "Should Hezbollah Be Next?" *Foreign Affairs* 82(6): pp. 54–66.

Byman, D. (2006). "Do Targeted Killings Work?" *Foreign Affairs*85 (2): pp. 95–111.

Byman, D. (2010). "How to Handle Hamas: The Perils of Ignoring Gaza's Leadership." *Foreign Affairs* 89 (3): pp. 45–62.

Cahill, T. (2003). *How the Irish Saved Civilization: The Untold Story of Ireland's Heroic Role from the Fall of Rome to the Rise of Medieval Europe*. New York: Bantam/Doubleday.

Calabresi, M., and R. Ratnesar. (2002). "Can We Stop the Next Attack?" *Time*(March 11):pp. 24–37.

Calhoun, C. (1989). "Classical Social Theory and the French Revolution of 1848." *Sociological Theory* 7(2): pp. 210–225.

California Department of Justice, Office of the Attorney General. (2002). *Anti-Terrorist Information Center*. Online: http://caag.state.ca.us/antiterrorism/index.htm.

California Highway Patrol. (2007). "State Terrorism Threat Assessment Center." Online: http://www.chp.ca.gov/offices/sttac.html.

Cancian, M. (2008). "Capitalizing on al Qaeda's Mistakes." *U.S. Naval Institute Proceedings* 134 (4) (April).

Cappel, R. P. (1979). *S.W.A.T. Team Manual*. Boulder, CO: Paladin Press.

Capstick, P. R. (2001). "Non-Lethal Weapons and Strategic Policy Implications for 21st Century Peace Operations." Carlisle Barracks, PA: U.S. Army War College. Online: http://smallwarsjournal.com/documents/capstick.pdf.

Carmichael, P., and C. Knox. (2004). "Devolution, Governance, and the Peace Process." *Studies in Conflict and Terrorism* 16 (Autumn): pp. 593–621.

Carmichael, P., and C. Knox. (2005). "The Law Enforcement Intelligence Function: State, Local, and Tribal Agencies." *The FBI Law Enforcement Bulletin* (June). Online: http://findarticles.com/p/articles/mi_m2194/is_6_74/ai_n15966184.

Carter, D.L. (2008). *The Intelligence Fusion Process*. East Lansing: Michigan State University.

Carter, D. L. (2009). *Law Enforcement Intelligence: A Guide for State, Local and Tribal Agencies*, 2nd ed. United States Department of Justice. Online: https://intellprogram.msu.edu/CARTER_Intelligence_Guide_2d.pdf.

Carter, D.L., and J.G. Carter. (2009). "The Intelligence Fusion Process for State, Local, and Tribal Law Enforcement." *Criminal Justice and Behavior* 36 (12): pp.1323–1339.

Cassara, J. A. (2006). *Hide and Seek: Intelligence, Law Enforcement, and the Stalled War on Terrorist Finance*. Dulles, VA: Potomac Books.

Cassara, J. A., and A. Jorisch. (2010). *On the Trail of Terror Finance: What Law Enforcement and Intelligence Officials Need to Know*. Washington, DC:Red Cell IG.

Cassidy, R. M. (2006). *Counterinsurgency and the Global War on Terrorism: Military Culture and Irregular War*. Westport, CT: Praeger Security International.

Casteel, S.W. (2003). "Narco-Terrorism: International Drug Trafficking and Terrorism—A Dangerous Mix." Testimony, Committee on the Judiciary, U.S. Senate. May 20. Online: http://www.judiciary.senate.gov/testimony.cfm?id=764&wit_id=2111.

Cavanaugh, T. (2004). "Meet Hizbollah." *Reason Online*, March 11. Online: http://reason.com/interview/hizbollah.shtml.

CBS News. (2004). "Chicago Bomb Plot Stopped." August 5. Online: http://www.cbsnews.com/stories/2004/08/05/terror/main634270.shtml.

Cebrowski, A. K. (2004). "Netwar." Assistant Secretary of Defense Conference on Special Operations, September, Alexandria, VA (unpublished speech).

Cebrowski, A. K., and T. P. M. Barnett. (2003). "The American Way of War." *Proceedings U.S. Naval Institute* (January): pp. 42–43.

Cebrowski, A. K., and J. J. Gratska. (1998). "Network-Centric Warfare: Its Origins and Future." *Proceedings of the U.S. Naval Institute* (January): pp. 28–35.

Center for Consumer Freedom. (2004). "Non-Violent Protests with Guns?" September 4. Online: http://www.consumerfreedom.com/news_detail.cfm/headline/1561.

Center for Strategic and International Studies. (2004). *Cybercrime, Cyberterrorism, and Cyberwarfare*. Forward and Recommendations. Online: http://www.csis.org/pubs/cyberfor.html.

Center of Excellence—Defence against Terrorism. (2007). *Suicide as a Weapon*. Ankara, Turkey: IOS Press.

Cetron, M. J., and O. Davies. (2008). "55 Trends Now Shaping the Future of Terrorism." Proteus USA. Online: http://www.au.af.mil/au/awc/awcgate/army/proteus-55-terror.pdf.

Chalk, P. (2010). "Lashkar-e-Taiba's Growing International Focus and Its Links with al-Qaeda." *Global Terrorism Analysis*. The Jamestown Foundation. Online: http://www.jamestown.org/programs/gta/single/?tx_ttnews[tt_news]=36683&tx_ttnews[backPid]=26&cHash=fc945260f6.

Chalk, P. (2012). "Profiles of Mexico's Seven Major Drug Trafficking Organizations." *CTC Sentinel* 5 (1): pp. 5–8.

Chamberlain, G., and M. Tran. (2009). "Sri Lankan Troops Mop Up Tigers as Leader Said to Have Died in Bunker." *Guardian* (Manchester,UK), May 17. Online: http://www.guardian.co.uk/world/2009/may/17/tamil-surrender-sri-lanka/print.

Chang, N. (2001). "The USA Patriot Act: What's So Patriotic about Trampling on the Bill of Rights?" Center for Constitutional Rights. Online: http://www.ccr-ny.org/whatsnew/usa_patriot_act.asp.

Chatain, P.-L. (2009). *Preventing Money Laundering and Terrorism Financing: A Practical Guide for Bank Supervisors*. The World Bank.

Chermak, S., and A. Weiss. (2006). "Community Policing in the News Media." *Police Quarterly* 9(2): pp. 135–160.

Chermak, S. L., and J.A. Greunewald (2006). "The Media's Coverage of Domestic Terrorism." *Justice Quarterly* 23 (4): pp. 428–461.

Chermak, S.M., J.D. Freilich, and Z. Shemtob. (2009). "Law Enforcement Training and the Domestic Far Right." *Criminal Justice and Behavior* (36): pp. 1305–1322. Online: http://cjb.sagepub.com/content/36/12/1305.

Chertoff, M. (2007). "Keynote Address." First National Fusion Center Conference, Destin, FL, February (unpublished).

Chomsky, N. (2002). "Who Are the Global Terrorists?" Online: http://www.chomsky.info/articles/200205–02.htm.

Chomsky, N. (2006a). "Noam Chomsky on 'The Clash of Civilizations.'" YouTube. Online: http://www.youtube.com/watch?v=qT64TNho59I.

Chomsky, N. (2006b). "On the U.S.-Israeli Invasion of Lebanon." *Znet*, August 23. Online: http://www.zmag.org/content/showarticle.cfm?ItemID=10811.

Chouvy, P. A. (2004). "Narco-Terrorism in Afghanistan." *Terrorism Monitor: In-Depth Analysis of the War on Terror* 2 (6) (March 25). Online: http://www.jamestown.org/single/?no_cache=1&tx_ttnews%5Btt_news%5D=26379

Christia, F., and M. Semple. (2009). "Flipping the Taliban: How to Win in Afghanistan." *Foreign Affairs* 88 (4): pp. 34–45.

Christopher, W. (1999). "Report of the Independent Commission on the Los Angeles Police Department." In L.K. Gaines and G.W. Cordner (eds.), *Policing Perspectives: An Anthology*. Los Angeles: Roxbury.

Chung, C.-P. (2002). "China's 'War on Terror.'" *Foreign Affairs* 81 (4): pp. 8–12.

Cilliers, J. (2003). "Terrorism and Africa." *African Security Review* 12 (4): pp. 91–103. Online: http://www.iss.org.za/pubs/ASR/12No4/Cilliers.pdf.

Cilluffo, F. J., S. L. Cardash, and G. N. Lederman. (2001). *Combating Chemical, Biological, Radiological, and Nuclear Terrorism: A Comprehensive Strategy: A Report of the CSIS Homeland Defense Project*. Washington, DC: Center for Strategic and International Studies.

Ciovacco, C. J. (2010). "The Contours of al Qaeda's Media Strategy." *Studies in Conflict and Terrorism* 32 (10): pp. 853–875. Online: http://dx.doi.org/10.1080/10576100903182377. [I failed to update this from my notes. This is entered under M.S. Doran in the correct spot.]

Clark, C. (2006). *Iron Kingdom: The Rise and Downfall of Prussia, 1600–1947*. London: Oxford University Press.

Clark, J. K. (1988). "Guevara." *Global Security*. Online: http://www.globalsecurity.org/military/library/report/1988/CJK.htm.

Clark, K. (1998). *Petersburg: Crucible of Cultural Revolution*. Cambridge, MA: Harvard University Press.

Clark, R. (1979). *The Basques*. Reno: University of Nevada Press.

Clark, R. (1984). *The Basque Insurgents*. Madison: University of Wisconsin Press.

Clark, W. K. (2001). *Waging Modern War*. New York: Public Affairs.

Clarke, R. (2002). "U.S. Senate Subcommittee on the Judiciary." Testimony on Cyberspace Security. Washington, DC: U.S. Senate, recorded from C-Span, February 13.

Clarke, R. (2010). *Lashkar-i-Taiba: The Fallacy of Subservient Proxies and the Future of Islamist Terrorism in India*. Ft. Leavenworth, KS: U.S. Army War College. Online: http://www.strategicstudiesinstitute.army.mil/pubs/display.cfm?pubID=973.

Clarke, R. A. (2007). "A Back Door for Terrorists." *New York Times*, June 1. Opinion, Editorial.

Clarke, R. A., and R. K. Knake. (2010). *Cyber War: The Next Threat to National Security and What to Do about It*. New York: Ecco/Harper Collins.

Clausewitz, C. (1831). *On War*. M. Howard and P. Paret (trans.). Reprint, Princeton, NJ: Princeton University Press, 1984.

Clayton, M. (2005). "Is Black-Market Baby Formula Financing Terror?" *The Christian Science Monitor*, June 29. Online: http://www.csmonitor.com/2005/0629/p01s01-usju.html.

Clayton, M. (2012). "Alert: Major Cyber Attack Aimed at Natural Gas Pipeline Companies." *Christian Science Monitor*, May 5. Online: http://www.csmonitor.com/USA/2012/0505/Alert-Major-cyber-attack-aimed-at-natural-gas-pipeline-companies.

Cloward, R., and L. Ohlin. (1960). *Delinquency and Opportunity*. New York: Free Press.

Clutterbuck, L. (2004). "The Progenitors of Terrorism: Russian Revolutionaries or Extreme Irish Republicans?" *Terrorism and Political Violence* 16 (Spring): pp. 154–181.

Clutterbuck, R. C. (1975). *Living with Terrorism*. London: Faber & Faber.

CNN. (2002). "Russian Troops Storm Moscow Theater." October 26. Online: http://archives.cnn.com/2002/WORLD/europe/10/25/moscow.siege/index.html.

CNN. (2004a) "Most Will Miss Biometric Passport Deadline." January 29. Online: http://www.cnn.com/2004/US/01/28/biometric.passports/.

CNN. (2004b). "Cyanide, Arsenal Stirs Domestic Terror Fear." January 30. Online: http://www.cnn.com/2004/US/Southwest/01/30/cynaide.probe.ap/index.html.

CNN. (2006). "House Approves Patriot Act." CNN.com. Online: http://www.cnn.com/2006/POLITICS/03/07/patriot.act/.

CNN. (2012). "Report: Hostages Held by Shining Path freed after clashes in Peru." Online: http://articles.cnn.com/2012-04-14/world/world_peru-hostages_1_hostages-rebel-group-kepashiato?_s=PM:WORLD.

Cochrane, P. (2004). "Is Al-Hurra Doomed?" Worldpress.org. Online: http://www.worldpress.org/Mideast/1872.cfm.

Cohen, A. (2003) "Terrorism in Asia and the Pacific." Testimony—Committee on International Relations, Subcommittee on the Middle East and Central Asia, U.S. House of Representatives. *Congressional Quarterly*, October 29. Online: http://homeland.cq.cm/hs/display.do?dockey=/usr/local/cqonline/docs/html.

Colb, S. F. (2001). "The New Face of Racial Profiling: How Terrorism Affects the Debate." *Find Law's Legal Commentary*, October 10. Online: http://writ.news.findlaw.com/200111010.html.

Cole, D. (2003). *Enemy Aliens: Double Standards and Constitutional Freedoms in the War on Terrorism*. New York: The New Press.

Cole, D., and J. X. Dempsey. (2002). *Terrorism and the Constitution: Sacrificing Civil Liberties in the Name of National Security*. New York: Free Press.

Cole, G. F., and C. E. Smith. (2004). *The American System of Justice*. Belmont, CA: Wadsworth.

Collin, B. (2004). "The Future of Cyber Terrorism: Where the Physical and Virtual Worlds Converge." Online: http://afgen.com/terrorism1.html.

Commission of Inquiry. (2007). "Terrorism, Intelligence, and Law Enforcement: Canada's Response to Sikh Terrorism." Commission of Inquiry into the Investigation of the Bombing of Air India Flight 182. Online: http://www.major-comm.ca/documents/dossier2_ENG.pdf.

Commission on Accreditation for Law Enforcement Agencies. (1990). *Accreditation Program Overview*. Fairfax, VA: CALEA.

Commission on the Prevention of Weapons of Mass Destruction Proliferation and Terrorism. (2010). "Report Card: Government Failing to Protect America from Grave Threats of WMD Proliferation and Terrorism." Online: http://www.preventwmd.org/1_26_101/.

Conetta, C. (2001). "Strange Victory: A Critical Appraisal of Operation Enduring Freedom and the Afghan War." Cambridge, MA: Project on Defense Alternatives.

Online: http://www.comw.org/pda/0201strangevic.pdf.

Cook, N. (2006). "AIDS in Africa." *CRS Reports for Congress*. Online: http://fas.org/sgp/crs/row/IB10050.pdf.

Cooley, J. (2002). *Unholy Wars: Afghanistan, America, and International Terrorism*. London: Pluto Press.

Coolidge, S., and J. Prendergast. (2003). "Police Shut Down Crime Ring." *The Cincinnati Enquirer*, October 3. Online: http://www.enquirer.com/editions/2003/10/03/loc_crimering03.html.

Cooper, H. H. A. (1977a). "Terrorism and the Media." In YAlexander and S.Finger (eds.), *Terrorism: Interdisciplinary Perspectives*. New York: John Jay.

Cooper, H. H. A. (1977b). "What Is a Terrorist? A Psychological Perspective." *Legal Medical Quarterly* 1: pp. 8–18.

Cooper, H. H. A. (1978). "Terrorism: The Problem of the Problem of Definition." *Chitty's Law Journal* 26: pp. 105–108.

Cooper, H. H. A. (2001). "Terrorism: The Problem of Definition Revisited." *American Behavioral Scientist* 44 (February):pp. 881–893.

Cooper, H. H. A., et al. (1976). *Task Force Report on Disorders and Terrorism*. Washington, DC: National Advisory Committee on Criminal Justice Standards and Goals.

Cordesman, A. H. (2005). "Escalating to Nowhere: The Israeli-Palestinian War." Center for Strategic and International Studies. Online: http://csis.org/files/media/csis/pubs/ch08.pdf.

Cordesman, A. H. (2006). "Preliminary 'Lessons' of the Israeli-Hezbollah War." Center for Strategic and International Studies. Online: http://csis.org/files/media/csis/pubs/060817_isr_hez_lessons.pdf.

Cordesman, A. H. (2009). "CSIS: 'The Gaza War': A Strategic Analysis." Council on Foreign Relations. Online: http://www.cfr.org/publication/18527/csis.html.

Corley, F. (2004). "Ruslan Gelayev: Feared Chechen Rebel-Turned-Bandit." *Independent News*, March 4. Online: http://news.independent.co.uk/people/obituaries/story.jsp?story=497568.

Corman, S. R., and J. S. Schiefelbein (2006). "Communication and Media Strategy in the Jihadi War of Ideas." Phoenix: Arizona State University. Online: http://www.asuzz.edu/clas/communication/about/csc/ publications/jihad_comm_media.pdf.

Cornell, S. E. (2005). "Narcotics, Radicalism and Armed Conflict in Central Asia: The Islamic Movement of Uzbekistan." *Terrorism and Political Violence* 17 (4): pp. 577–597.

Coronel, S. S. (2007). "The Philippines: Democracy and Its Discontents." *Asian Survey* 47 (1):pp. 175–182.

Corrado, R., and R. Evans. (1988). "Ethnic and Ideological Terrorism in Western Europe." In M. Stohl (ed.), *The Politics of Terrorism*. New York: Dekker.

Costigan, G. (1980). *A History of Modern Ireland*. Indianapolis, IN: Bobbs-Merrill.

Cottle, S. (2006). "Mediatizing the Global War on Terror." In A. P. Kavoori and T. Fraley (eds.), *Media, Terrorism, and Theory: A Reader*. Lanham, MD: Rowman & Littlefield.

Council on Foreign Relations. (2002). "Basque Fatherland and Liberty (ETA)." Online: http://cfrterrorism.org/groups/eta.html.

Council on Foreign Relations. (2004). "Al-Asqa Martyrs Brigades." Online: http://www.cfr.org/publication/9127/ alaqsa_martyrs_brigade.html.

Council on Foreign Relations. (2005). "Terrorism Havens: Pakistan." Online: http://www.cfr.org/publication/9514/#3.

Council on Foreign Relations. (2006). "Kashmir Militant Extremists." Online: http://www.cfr.org/publication/9135/.

Council on Foreign Relations. (2007). "November 17, Revolutionary People's Struggle, Revolutionary Struggle (Greece, Leftists)." Online: http://www.cfr.org/publication/9275/november_17_revolutionary_peoples_struggle_revolutionary_struggle_greece_leftists.html.

Council on Foreign Relations. (2009). "Hamas: Backgrounder." Online: http://www.cfr.org/publication/8968/hamas.html.

Countdown with Keith Olberman. (2004). "Interview with Steven Emerson." MSNBC.

Cowen, T. (2006). "Terrorism asTheater: Analysis and Policy Implications." *Public Choice* 128 (1): pp. 233–244.

Coyle, D. J. (1983). *Minorities in Revolt: Political Violence in Ireland, Italy, and Cyprus*. East Brunswick, NJ: Associated University Presses.

CQ Researcher. (2010). "Homegrown Jihadists: Can Muslim Terrorists in the U.S. Mount Serious Attacks?" *CQ Researcher* 20 (30): pp. 701–724. Online: http://library.cqpress.com/cqresearcher/getpdf.php?file=cqr20100903C.pdf.

CQ Researcher. (2010). "Prosecuting Terrorists." *CQ Researcher* 20 (10): pp. 217–240. Online: http://library.cqpress.com/cqresearcher/getpdf.php?file=cqr20100312C.pdf.

Craig, G. A. (1968). *The Politics of the Prussian Army, 1640–1945*. New York: Oxford University Press.

Cram, I. (2006). "Regulating the Media: Some Neglected Freedom of Expression Issues in the United Kingdom's Counter-Terrorism Strategy." *Terrorism and Political Violence*18 (2): pp. 335–355.

Creativity Movement. (n.d.). "The Creativity Movement." Online: http://www.creativitymovement.net/.

Creed, R. D., Jr. (2002). "Eighteen Years in Lebanon and Two Intifadas: The Israeli Defense Force and the U.S. Army Operational Environment." Fort Leavenworth, KS: U.S. Army Command and General Staff College.

Crenshaw, M. (1972). "The Concept of Revolutionary Terrorism." *The Journal of Conflict Resolution* 16 (3): pp. 383–396.

Crenshaw, M. (ed.). (1983). *Terrorism, Legitimacy, and Power*. Middletown, CT: Wesleyan University Press.

Creveld, M. V. (2008). "Bottling the Nuclear Demon." *Nature* 452 (April): pp. 694–695.

Creveld, M. van. (1991). *The Transformation of War*. Cambridge, MA: Harvard University Press.

Crile, C. (2003). *Charlie Wilson's War*. New York: Grove Press.

Criminal Law Reporter. (2007). "News: Judicial Check on Government's Assertion of State Secrets Privilege Needed, ABA Says." *Criminal Law Reporter*81 (20): p. 611.

Criss, N. B. (1995). "The Nature of PKK Terrorism in Turkey." *Studies in Conflict and Terrorism* 18: pp. 17–38.

Cristiani, D. (2010). "Algeria's AQIM Becomes a Regional Threat Despite Surrender of Senior Leaders." *Terrorism Monitor* 8 (35). Online: http://www.jamestown.org/ programs/gta/single/?tx_ttnews [tt_news]=36527&tx_ttnews [backPid]=457&no_cache=1.

Critical Incident Analysis Group. (2001). *Threats to Symbols of American Democracy*. Charlottesville: University of Virginia.

Croft, A., and J. Heller. (2010). "Lebanon Warns of 'Dangerous' Situation with Israel." Reuters, February 10. Online: http://www .reuters.com/ article/idUSTRE6191P120100210.

Crone, M., and M. Harrow. (2011). "Homegrown Terrorism in the West." *Studies in Conflict and Terrorism* (23): pp. 521–536.

Cronin, A. K. (2003). "Al Qaeda after the Iraq Conflict." Congressional Reference Service. *CRS Report for Congress*, Order Code RS21529, May 23. Online: http://www.fas.org/ irp/crs/RS21529.pdf.

Cronin, S. (1984). *Irish Nationalism: A History of Its Roots and Ideology*. Dublin: University Press of Ireland.

C-Span. (2007). "Testimony: Brian Jenkins, Frank Cilluffo, and Salam al Marayati." House Subcommittee on Homeland Security, June 14.

Cumming, A., and T. Masse. (2004). "FBI Intelligence Reform Since September 11, 2001: Issues for Congress." Congressional ReferenceService. Online: http:// www.fas.org/irp/crs/RL32336. html.

Cummings, J. (2002). "States Mend Homeland Security Blanket." *Wall Street Journal*(August 13):p. A4.

Curtis, E. (2000). *A History of Ireland from the Earliest Times to 1922*. London: Routledge. (Orig. pub. 1936.)

Dagne, T. (2002). "Africa and the War on Terrorism." *CRS Report for Congress*. Online: http://fpc.state.gov/ documents/organization/7959.pdf.

Dahl, E.J. (2011). "The Plots That Failed: Intelligence Lessons Learned from Unsuccessful Terrorist Attacks Against the United States." *Studies in Conflict and Terrorism* (34): pp. 621–648.

Daily Mail. (2007). "Olmert: No Option but to Strike Hezbollah Immediately." *Daily Mail Online*, May 10. Online: http://www. daily mail.co.uk/pages/live/articles/ news/worldnews.html?in_article_ id=453922&in_page_id=1811.

Daily News and Analysis. (2010). "Government to Install Radiation Monitoring Portals at Ports." *Daily News and Analysis, India*, April25. Online: http://www.dnaindia. com/india/report_govt-to-install-radiation-monitoring-portals-at-ports_1375392.

Dakroub, H. (2004). "Beheading Condemned by Hamas and Hizbollah." *Independent News*. Online: http:// www.independent. co.uk/news/ world/middle-east/ beheading-condemned-by-hamasand-hizbollah-563351.html.

Dalgaard-Nielsen, A. (2010). "Violent Radicalization in Europe: What We Know and Don't Know." *Studies in Conflict and Terrorism* (33): pp. 797–814.

Daly, J. C. K. (2006a). "Saudi Oil Facilities: Al Qaeda's Next Target?" *Terrorism Monitor*. Online: http://jamestown.org/ terrorism/ news/article.php?articleid= 2369910.

Daly, J. C. K. (2006b). "The Baloch Insurgency and Its Threat to Pakistan's Energy Sector." *Terrorism Focus*. Online: http:// jamestown.org/terrorism/news/article. php?issue_id=3660.

Damphousse, K. R., and B. L. Smith. (2004). "Terrorism and Empirical Testing: Using Indictment Data to Assess Changes in Terrorism Conduct." In M. DeFlem (ed.), *Terrorism and Counter-Terrorism: Criminological Perspectives*. Amsterdam: Elsevier.

Daniels, D. A. (2003). "Breaking Barriers: Sharing Information in a Changing World." Law Enforcement Information Sharing Symposium, Office of Justice Programs, U.S. Department of Justice, Arlington, VA. Online: http://www.ojp.usdoj. gov/aag/speeches/deainfosharing. htm.

Danitz, T., and W. P. Strobel. (1999). "The Internet's Impact on Activism: The Case of Burma." *Studies in Conflict and Terrorism* 22: pp. 257–269.

Dawisha, A. (2003). *Arab Nationalism in the Twentieth Century: From Triumph to Despair*. Princeton, NJ: Princeton University Press.

Dawkins, R. (1998). *Unweaving the Rainbow: Science, Delusion, and the Appetite for Wonder*. Boston: Houghton Mifflin Company.

de Silva, M. (1996). "Sunshine over Jaffna." *Far Eastern Economic Review*(May 5):p. 159.

Debray, J. R. (1967). *Revolution in the Revolution?* Westport, CT: Greenwood.

del Carmen, R. (1991). *Civil Liberties in American Policing: A Textfor Law Enforcement Personnel*. Englewood Cliffs, NJ: Prentice Hall.

Della Porta, D. (1995). "Left-Wing Terrorism in Italy." InM. Crenshaw (ed.), *Terrorism in Context*. State College: Pennsylvania State University.

Denson, B., and J. Long. (1999). "Ecoterrorism Sweeps the American West." *Oregonian*, September 26; "Ideologues Drive the Violence," September 27; "Terrorist Acts Provoke Change in Research, Business, Society," September 28; "Can Sabotage Have a Place in a Democratic Community?" September 29. Online: http://www .oregonlive. com/cgi-bin/printer/ printer.cgi.

Department of Homeland Security. (2009). "Rightwing Extremism: Current Economic and Political Climate Fueling Resurgence in Radicalization and Recruitment." Extremism and Radicalization Branch, Homeland Environment Threat Analysis Division. Originally FOUO. Online: http://www.fas.org/ irp/eprint/rightwing.pdf.

Department of Homeland Security. (2010). "Executive Summary: Quadrennial Homeland Security Review Report." Online: http://www.dhs. gov/xlibrary/assets/qhsr_executive_summary.pdf.

Der Spiegel. (2010). "Western Officials Concerned about Attack in Europe." *Spiegel Online*, September 29. Online: http://www .spiegel.de/ international/world/ 0,1518,720206,00.html

DHS. *See* U.S. Department of Homeland Security.

Diamond, L. (2004). "What Went Wrong in Iraq." *Foreign Affairs* 83 (September/October): pp. 34–56.

Dickey, C. (2010). "A Thousand Points of Hate." *Newsweek*(January 11): pp. 34–36.

Dillon, S. (2001). "A Forum Recalls Unheeded Warning." *New York Times*(October 4): p. A16.

Diminyatz, K. L. (2003). "Providing for the Common Defense: Securing the Southwest Border." Paper presented at United States Army War College. Online: http://stinet.dtic.mil/cgi-bin/GetTRDoc?AD=ADA414219&Location=U2&doc=GetTRDoc.pdf.

Discovery Times Channel. (2005). *Media Jihad*.

Dixon, P. (2004). "Peace within the Realms of the Possible? David Trimble, Unionist Ideology, and Theatrical Politics." *Terrorism and Political Violence* 16 (Autumn): pp. 462–482.

Dobbins, J. (2005). "Iraq: Winning the Unwinnable War." *Foreign Affairs* 84 (January/February):pp. 16–25.

Dobson, C., and R. Payne. (1982). *The Terrorists*. New York: Facts on File.

Donnelly, J. (2005). "Oil in Africa: A Special Report by the Boston Globe." *The Boston Globe*. Online: http://www.boston.com/ news/specials/oil_in_africa/.

Donner, H. (2009). "Radical Masculinity: Morality, Sociality, and Relationships through Recollections of Naxalite Activists." *Dialectical Anthropology* 33: pp. 327–343.

Donovan, M. (2002). "Palestinian Islamic Jihad." Center for Defense Information. Online: http://www. cdi.org/terrorism/pij.cfm.

Doran, M. S. (2002). "Somebody Else's Civil War." *Foreign Affairs* 81(January/February).

Dower, J.W. (2010). *Cultures of War*. New York: W.W. Norton.

Downs, A. C. (1967). *Inside Bureaucracy*. Boston: Little, Brown.

Doyle, A. (2010). "Blast May Signal Rise of Greek Insurgents." *National Post* (Canada), (June 26): p. A16.

Doyle, C. (2002). "The USA Patriot Act: A Sketch." Congressional Reference Service.*CRS Report for Congress*. Online: http://www.fas.org/irp/crs/RS21203.pdf.

Drakos, K., and A. M. Kutan. (2003). "Regional Effects of Terrorism on Tourism in Three Mediterranean Countries." *Journal of Conflict Resolution* 45 (5):pp. 621–641.

Dreyfuss, R. (2002). "The Cops Are Watching You." March 23. Online: http://www.ccmep.org/ hotnews2/cops_are_watching052302.htm.

Duekmedjian, J. E. (2006). "From Community to Intelligence: Executive Realignment of the RCMP Mission." *Canadian Journal of Criminology and Criminal Justice* 48 (4): pp. 523–542.

Duffy, H. (2005). *The War on Terror and the Framework of International Law*. Cambridge, UK: Cambridge University Press.

Duku, J., D. and G. Ogunwale, and Abuja. (2011). "Boko Haram: Exedos in Yobe as Death Toll Reaches 150." *The Nation*, November 7. Online: http://www.thenationonlineng.net/2011/index.php/news/25500-boko-haram-exodus-in-yobe-as-death-toll-hits-150.html

Dunn, S., and V. Morgan. (1995). "Protestant Alienation in Northern Ireland." *Studies in Conflict and Terrorism* 18: pp. 175–185.

Durham, F. D. (1998). "News Frames as Social Narratives: TWA Flight 800." *Journal of Communication* 48 (4): pp. 100–117.

Duyvesteyn, I. (2004). "How New Is the New Terrorism?" *Studies in Conflict and Terrorism* 27 (2): pp. 439–454.

Dymond, J. (2004). "U.S. and Turkey to Hit PKK." BBC News, October2. Online: http://news.bbc.uk/2/hi/europe/3158686.stm.

Dyson, W. (2011). "Connecting the Dots." Tallahassee, FL: IIR.

Dyson, W. E. (2008). *Investigating Terrorism: An Investigator's Handbook*, 3rd ed. Cincinnati, OH: Anderson.

Economist. (2003). "Al Qaeda Operations are Rather Cheap." *Economist* (October 4):p. 45.

Economist. (2008). "Turkey Invades Northern Iraq." *The Economist*, February 28. Online: www.economist.com/displaystory.cfm?story_id=10766808.

Economist. (2009). "DyingSpasms." *The Economist* 392 (8643) (August 8).

Economist. (2010). "Europe: Gone Fishing; Spain and ETA." *The Economist* 394 (8672): p. 69.

Edgley, C. (2003). *Handbook of Symbolic Interactionism*. Lanham, MD: AltaMira.

Egerton, F. (2011). "Alienation and its Discontents." *European Journal of International Relations*17: pp. 453–474. Online: http://ejt.sagepub.com/content/17/3/453.

Ehlen, P. (2001). *Frantz Fanon: A Spiritual Biography*. New York: Crossroad 8th Avenue.

Ehrenfeld, R. (2003). *Funding Evil: How Terrorism Is Financed and How to Stop It*. Chicago: Bonus Books.

Eilstrup-Sangiovanni, M., and C. Jones. (2008). "Assessing the Dangers of Illicit Networks: Why al-Qaida May Be Less Threatening Than Many Think." *International Security* 33 (2): pp. 7–44.

Elbe, P. (2000). "The Orange Order in the Wake of Drumcree: Parity of Esteem, Protest, and Propaganda in Northern Ireland, 1995–98." *Archive: A Journal of Undergraduate History*. Online: http://www.sit.wisc.edu/~uwho/Archive/Archive%204%20orange%20order.pdf.

Elbe, P. (2001). "EFF Analysis of the Provisions of the USA Patriot Act." Online: http://www.eff.org/Privacy/Surveillance/Terrorism_militias/20011031_efft_usa_Patriot_analysis.html.

Elkins, E. (2003). "Detention, Rehabilitation, and the Destruction of Kikuyu Society." In Lonsdale andE. S. Odhiambo (eds.), *Mau Mau and Nationhood: Arms, Authority, and Narration*. Athrns, OH: Ohio University Press.

Eller, W. S., and B. J. Gerber. (2010)."Contemplating the Role of Precision and Range in Homeland Security Policy Analysis: A Response to Mueller." *Policy Studies Journal* 38 (1): pp. 23–46.

Ellingsen, S. A. (2008). "Safeguards against Nuclear Terrorism: HEU v. Plutonium." *Defense and Security Analysis* 24 (2): pp. 129–146.

Ellingsen, T. (2005). "Toward a Revival of Religion and Religious Clashes?" *Terrorism and Political Violence* 17 (3): pp. 305–332.

Elliot, A. (2010). "The Jihadist Next Door." *New York Times Magazine* (January 31): pp. 26–35,42–47.

Emerson, S. A. (1994). *Jihad in America*. Public Broadcasting System.

Emerson, S. A. (2002). *American Jihad: The Terrorist Living among Us.* New York: Free Press.

Emerson, S. A. (2006). *Jihad Incorporated: A Guide to Militant Islam in the U.S.* Amherst, NY: Prometheus.

Emerson, S. A., and C. Del Sesto. (1991). *Terrorist: The Inside Story of the Highest Ranking Iraqi Terrorist Ever to Defect to the West.* New York: Villard.

Emerson, S. A., and J. Levin. (2003). "Terrorism Financing: Origin, Organization, and Prevention: Saudi Arabia, Terrorist Financing and the War on Terror." Testimony, United States Senate, Committee on Governmental Affairs, July 31.

Enteshami, A. (1995). *After Khomeini: The Iranian Second Republic.* London: Routledge.

Epstein, B. (2001). "Anarchism and the Anti-Globalism Movement." *Monthly Review* 53 (4): pp. 1–14.

Eriksson, M. (2006). "Islamic Extremism in Uzbekistan: Is It a Threat?" *Stanford's Student Journal of Russian, East European, and Eurasian Studies* (Spring). Online: http://zhe.stanford.edu/spring06/extremism.pdf.

Esposito, J. (1999). *The Islamic Threat: Myth or Reality.* New York: Oxford University Press.

Esposito, J. L. (2002). *Unholy War: Terror in the Name of Islam.* New York: Oxford University Press.

Ewald, S. (2006). "Twisted Rail WMD: An ARES Response." *QST* 90(5): pp. 78–82.

FAIR. (1999). "Extra!'s Report on Steven Emerson: Setting the Record Straight." *Fairness and Accuracy in Reporting*, February 2. Online: http://www.fair.org/press-releases/emerson.html.

Fairfield, R. P. (1959). "Cyprus: Revolution and Resolution." *Middle East Journal* 13 (3): pp. 235–248.

Fanon, F. (1980). *A Dying Colonialism.* London: Writers and Readers. (Orig. pub. 1965.)

Fanon, F. (1982). *The Wretched of the Earth.* New York: Grove.

Farah, C. (2000). *Islam.* Hauppage, NY: Baron's.

Farrall, K. (2011). "Suspicious Activity Reporting: U.S. Domestic Intelligence in the Postprivacy Age?" *Research in Social Problems and Public Policy* 19: pp. 247–276.

Farrell, W. R. (1990). *Blood and Rage: The Story of the Japanese Red Army.* Lexington, MA: Lexington Books.

FBI. (1999). *Terrorism in the United States: Special Report—Thirty Years of Terrorism.* Washington, DC: FBI.

FBI. (2000). "U.S. Embassy Bombings Summary." Online: http://www.fbi.gov/majcase/eastafrica/summary.htm.

FBI. (2004). "Counterterrorism Website." October 12. Online: http://www.fbi.gov/terrorinfo/terrorism.htm.

FBI. (2005). "Crime in the United States 2005." Online: http://www.fbi.gov/ucr/05cius/.

FBI. (2008). "Crime in the United States." Online: http://www.fbi.gov/ucr/cius2008/index.html.

FBI. (2010). "Najibullah Zazi Pleads Guilty to Conspiracy to Use Explosives against Persons or Property in U.S., Conspiracy to Murder Abroad, and Providing Material Support to al Qaeda." FBI, New York, Press Release. Online: http://newyork.fbi.gov/dojpressrel/pressrel10/nyfo022210.htm.

FBI. (n.d.). "Counterterrorism." Online: http://www.fbi.gov/terrorinfo/counterrorism/waronterrorhome.htm.

Federation of American Scientists. (2010). "Types of Chemical Weapons." Online: http://www.fas.org/programs/bio/chemweapons/cwagents.html.

Feickert, A. (2005). "U.S. Military Operations in the Global War on Terrorism: Afghanistan, Africa, the Philippines, and Colombia." *CRS Reports for Congress.* Online: http://www.law.umaryland.edu/marshall/crsreports/crsdocuments/RL3275802042005.pdf.

Ferguson, J. (2004). "Al Qaeda's Threat to Japan: Tokyo's Wake Up Call to the War on Terrorism." The Jamestown Foundation. *Terrorism Monitor* 2 (2) (January 30). Online: http://www.jamestown.org/terrorism/news/article.php?articleid=23504.

Felix, B. (2010). "Sarkozy Vows to Punish Qaeda Killers of Frenchman." Reuters, July 26. Online: http://www.reuters.com/article/idUSTRE66P3QH20100726.

Fernandez, R. (1987). *Los Macheteros: The Wells Fargo Robbery and the Violent Struggle for Puerto Rican Independence.* Upper Saddle River, NJ: Prentice Hall.

Fernandez, R. (1996). *The Disenchanted Island: Puerto Rico and the United States in the Twentieth Century.* Westport, CT: Greenwood.

Ferrero, M. (2002). "Radicalization as a Reaction to Failure: An Economic Model of Islamic Extremism." DIW workshop on The Economic Consequences of Global Terrorism, Berlin, June.

Fesperman, D. (2004). "Link between Hamas, al-Qaida Feared." *The Baltimore Sun.* Online: http://www.baltimoresun.com/news/local/balte.md.hamas25aug25,1,934840.story?coll=bal-local-headlines.

Fields, G. (2002). "U.S. Probe of Intelligence Lapses to Go beyond CIA and FBI." *Wall Street Journal* (May 3): p. A4.

Findlay, M. (2007). "Terrorism and Relative Justice." *Crime, Law, and Social Change* 37 (1): pp. 57–68.

Findlay, P. (2001). *Silent No More: Confronting America's False Images of Islam.* Beltsville, MD: Amana.

Finley, M. I. (1983). *The Politics of the Ancient World.* Cambridge, UK: Cambridge University Press.

Firestone, R. (1999). *Jihad: The Origins of Holy War in Islam.* New York: Oxford University Press.

Fisher, M. (2007). "Abbas Calls Emergency as Hamas Routs Fatah." *The Gazette* (Montreal), June 15.

Fitzpatrick, S. (2001). *The Russian Revolution.* New York: Oxford University Press.

Flemming, P. A., M. Stohl, and A. P. Schmid. (1988). "The Theoretical Utility of Typologies of Terrorism: Lessons and Opportunities." In M. Stohl (ed.), *The Politics of Terrorism.* New York: Dekker.

Fletcher, H. (2008). "Mujahadeen-e-Khalq (MEK) (aka People's Mujahedin of Iran or PMOI)." Council on Foreign Relations. Online: http://www.cfr.org/publication/9158/mujahadeenekhalq_mek_aka_peoples_mujahedin_of_iran_or_pmoi.html.

Flynn, S. (2002). "America the Vulnerable." *Foreign Affairs* 81: pp. 60–74.

Flynn, S. (2004a). *America the Vulnerable.* New York: Harper Collins.

Flynn, S. (2004b). "The Neglected Home Front." *Foreign Affairs.* 83 (September/October): pp. 20–33.

Foote, S. (1986a). *The Civil War: A Narrative. Volume I: Fort Sumter to Perryville*. New York: Vintage Books.

Foote, S. (1986b). *The Civil War: A Narrative. Volume III: Red River to Appomattox*. New York: Vintage Books.

Foreign Policy Association. (2004). "Great Decisions Guides: Terrorism—The Basque ETA." Online: http://www.fpa.org/newsletter_info2478/newsletter_info_sub_list.htm?section=The%BasqueETA.

Foster, R. F. (2000). "Ascendancy and Union." In R. F. Foster (ed.), *The Oxford Illustrated History of Ireland*. New York: Oxford University Press.

Foster, R. F. (2001). *The Oxford History of Ireland*. New York: Oxford University Press.

Fraley, F., and E. L. Roushanzamir. (2006). "Critical Media Theory, Democratic Communication, and Global Conflict." In A. P. Kavoori and T. Fraley (eds.), *Media, Terrorism, and Theory: A Reader*. Lanham, MD: Rowman & Littlefield.

Fraser, B. (2007). "No Longer Silent: Women and Children Who Survived Peru's Civil War FindHope, Strength Together." *National Catholic Reporter*, March 16.

Fraser, J., and I. Fulton. (1984). *Terrorism Counteraction*. FC 100-37. Fort Leavenworth, KS: U.S. Army Command and General Staff College.

Freedman, R. O. (2009). "Goldstone Reports Ugly Politics." *Baltimore Jewish Times*310 (5) (October 2): pp. 48–49.

Freeh, L. J. (2005). *My FBI: Bringing Down the Mafia, Investigating Bill Clinton, and Fighting the War on Terror*. New York: St. Martin's Press.

Freilich, J.(2007). "Surveying American State Police Agencies about Terrorism Threats, Terrorism Sources, and Terrorism Definitions." *Law and Human Behavior* 31 (6): pp. 611–627.

Freilich, J.D., and W. A. Pridemore. (2007). "Politics, Culture, and Political Crime: Covariates of Abortion Clinic Attacks in the United States." *Journal of Criminal Justice*35 (3): pp. 323–336

Friedman, T. (2012). "A Middle East Twofer." *New York Times*, April 3. Online: http://www.nytimes.com/2012/04/04/opinion/a-middle-east-twofer.html.

Friedman, T. L. (2000). *From Beirut to Jerusalem*. New York: Harper Collins.

Friedman, T. L. (2004). "War of Ideas, Part 2." *New York Times*(January 11): Sec. 4, p. 15.

Fromkin, D. (2001). *A Peace to End All Peace: The Fall of the Ottoman Empire and the Creation of the Modern Middle East*. New York: Owl Books, Henry Holt.

Frontline. (1999). "Hunting bin Laden." PBS. Online: http://www.pbs.org/wgbh/pages/frontline/ shows/binladen/.

Frontline. (2002). "Interview: JihadJa'Aire, Al Asqa Martyrs Brigade Leader." PBS. Online: http://www.fromoccupiedpalestine.org/node.php?id=745.

Gaines, L. K., and G W. Cordner. (1999). *Policing Perspectives: An Anthology*. Los Angeles: Roxbury.

Galula, D. (1963). *Pacification in Algeria 1956–1958*. Santa Monica, CA:RAND. (Reprint 2006 with forward by B. Hoffman.)

Galula, D. (1964). *Counterinsurgency Warfare: Theory and Practice*. Westport, CT: Praeger Security International. (Reprint 2006 with foreword by J. A. Nagel.)

Gambetta, D. (2005). *Making Sense of Suicide Missions*. Oxford, UK: Oxford University Press.

Gambill, G. C., and Z. K. Abdelnour. (2002). "Hezbollah: Between Tehran and Damascus." Online: http://www.meib.org/articles/0202_11.htm.

Ganguly, S. (2009). "India in 2008: Domestic Turmoil and External Hopes." *Asian Survey* 49 (1): pp. 39–52.

Ganor, B. (2011). "An Intifada in Europe? A Comparative Analysis of Radicalization Processes among Palestinians in the West Bank and Gaza versus Muslim Immigrants in Europe." *Studies in Conflict and Terrorism*34: pp. 587–599.

Garcia, M. J., M. M. Lee, and T. Tatelman. (2005). "Immigration: Analysis of the Major Provisions of the REAL ID Act of 2005." Congressional Research Service.

Online: http://www.mipt.org/pdf/CRS_RL32754.pdf.

Garfinkle, A. (2008). "Comte's Caveat: How We Misunderstand Terrorism." *Orbis* 52 (3): pp. 403–421.

Garrison, A. H. (2004). "Defining Terrorism: Philosophy of the Bomb, Propaganda by Deed, and Change through Fear and Violence." *Criminal Justice Studies* 17 (3): pp. 259–279.

Gartenstein-Ross, D. (2009). "The Strategic Challenge of Somalia's al Shabab: Dimemsions of Jihad." *Middle East Quarterly* 16 (4): pp. 25–36.

Gartenstein-Ross, D., and L. Grossman. (2009). *Homegrown Terrorists in the U.S. and U.K.: An Empirical Analysis of the Radicalization Process*. Washington, DC: Foundation for the Defense of Democracies.

Gates, R. M. (2010). "Helping Others Defend Themselves: The Future of U.S. Security Assistance." *Foreign Affairs* 89 (3): pp. 2–6.

Gato, P., and R. Windrem. (2007). "Hezbollah Builds a Western Base." NBC News, MSNBC. Online: http://www.msnbc.msn.com/id/17874369.

Gause, F. G., III. (2005). "Can Democracy Stop Terrorism?" *Foreign Affairs* 84 (5): pp. 62–76.

Gauthier-Villars, D. (2007). "Colonial-Era Ties to Africa Face a Reckoning in France." *Wall Street Journal*(May 16):p. A1.

Gentry, J. A. (2008). "Intelligence Failure Reframed." *Political Science Quarterly* 123 (2): pp. 247–262.

Gerges, F. A. (2005). *The Far Enemy: Why Jihad Went Global*. New York: Cambridge University Press.

Gerges, F. A. (2006). *Journey of the Jihadist: Inside Muslim Militancy*. Orlando, FL: Harcourt.

Giblin, M. J., J. A. Schafer,and G. W. Burruss. (2009). "Homeland Security in the Heartland: Risk, Preparedness, and Organizational Capacity." *Criminal Justice Policy Review* 20 (3): pp. 274–289. Online: http://cjp.sagepub.com/content/20/3/274.

Gil-Alana, L. A., and Carlos P. Barros. (2010). "A Note on the Effectiveness of National Anti-Terrorist Policies: Evidence from ETA." *Conflict Management and Peace Science* 27 (1): pp. 28–46. Online: http://cmp.sagepub.com/cgi/content/abstract/27/1/28.

Gilboa, E. (2005). "Global Television News and Foreign Policy: Debating the CNN Effect." *International Studies Perspectives* 6 (3): pp. 325–341.

Giles, L. (2000). Sun Tzu, *The Art of War. The Internet Classics Archive.* Online: http://classics.mit.edu/Tzu/artwar.html.

Gilio, M. E. (1972). *The Tupamaros.* London: Secker & Warburg.

Gill, P., J. Horgan, and J. Lovelace. (2011). "Improvised Explosive Device: The Problem of Definition." *Studies in Conflict and Terrorism* 34 (9): 732–748.

Gips, M. A. (2006). "Do al Qaeda Tapes Augur Attacks?" *Security Management* 50 (5): pp. 24–25.

Giraldo, J. K., and H. A. Trinkunas (eds.). (2007). *Terrorism Funding and State Responses: A Comparative Perspective.* Stanford, CA: Stanford University Press.

Giroux, H. A. (2002). "Democracy and the Politics of Terrorism: Community, Fear, and the Suppression of Dissent." *Cultural Studies Critical Methodologies* 2 (3): pp. 334–342.

Glantz, K.M., and A. Turner. (2009). "Threat, Risk, and Vulnerability Methodology." *Sheriff* 61 (January/February): pp. 14–18.

Glasser, S. B., and S. Coll. (2005). "The Web as a Weapon." *Washington Post*, August 1. Online: http://www.washingtonpost.com/wpdyn/content/article/2005/08/08/AR2005080801018.html.

Global Security.org. (n.d.). "Sikhs in Punjab." Online: http://www.globalsecurity.org/military/world/war/punjab.htm.

Global Witness. (2003). *For a Few Dollars More: How al Qaeda Moved into the Diamond Trade.* London: Global Witness.

Goffman, E. (1959). *The Presentation of Self in Everyday Life.* Garden City, NY: Doubleday.

Goldberg, B. (2003). *Bias: A CBS Insider Exposes How the Media Distort the News.* New York: Perennial Editions (HarperCollins).

Goldberg, J. (2002). "In the Party of God: Hezbollah Sets up Operations in South America and the United States." *The New Yorker*, October 28.

Goldman, S. D. (2007). "Russian Political, Economic, and Security Issues and U.S. Interests." *CRS Reports for Congress.* Online: http://www.fas.org/sgp/crs/row/RL33407.pdf.

Gongloff, M. (2012). "European Debt Crisis Flares Again amid Violent Protests in Spain." Huffington Post, March 29. Online: http://www.huffingtonpost.com/2012/03/29/european-debt-crisis_n_1388251.html.

González, F. E. (2009). "Mexico's Drug Wars Get Brutal." *Current History* (February): pp. 72–76.

Gonzalez-Perez, M. (2008). *Women and Terrorism: Female Activity in Domestic and International Terror Groups.* New York: Routledge.

Goodman, A. (2003). "Basque Question: Spain's Pressing Problem." CNN. Online: http://www.cnn.com/SPECIALS/201/basque/stories/overview.html.

Goodwin, C. (2010). "The Blonde's Bombshell: Nuclear Armageddon Is Closer Than We Think, Warns a Terrifying New Documentary by Lucy Walker." *The Sunday Times* (London), May 16. Online: http://entertainment.timesonline.co.uk/tol/arts_and_entertainment/film/article7125512.ece.

Goodwin, D. K. (2005). *Team of Rivals: The Political Genius of Abraham Lincoln.* New York: Simon & Schuster.

Gordon, M. R., and B. E. Trainor. (2006). *Cobra II: The Inside Story of the Invasion and Occupation of Iraq.* New York: Pantheon Books.

Gordon, N. (1999). "Terrorism in the Arab-Israeli Conflict." South Bend, IN: University of Notre Dame, Joan B. Kroc Institute for International Peace Studies, Occasional Paper.

Gorritti, G. (2006). "The Fog of Forgetting: Thirteen Years and Two Trials after First Sentencing, the Leader of Peru's Shining Path Is Back in Court." *Index on Censorship* 3: pp. 6–15.

Graber, D. (2003). "Styles of Image Management during Crises: Justifying Press Censorship." *Discourse and Society* 14 (5): pp. 539–557. Online: http://das.sagepub.com.ezproxy.gvsu.edu:2048/cgi/content/abstract/14/5/539.

Graham, S. "The Urban Battlespace." *Theory, Culture & Society* 26 (7–8): pp. 278–288.

Green, D. (2007). "Counterinsurgency Diplomacy: Political Advisors at the Operational and Tactical Levels." *Military Review* 87(3): pp. 24–30.

Greer, S. (1995). "De-Centralised Policing in Spain: The Case of the Autonomous Basque Police." *Policing and Society* 5 (1): pp. 15–36.

Grob-Fitzgibbon, B. (2004). "From the Dagger to the Bomb: Karl Heinzen and the Evolution of Political Terror." *Terrorism and Political Violence* 16 (Spring): pp. 97–115.

Groseclose, T., and J. Milyo. (2005). "A Measure of Media Bias." *Quarterly Journal of Economics* 4 (November): pp. 1191–1239. Online: http://www.polisci.ucla.edu/faculty/groseclose/Media-Bias.8.htm.

Grossman, M. (1999). "Cyberterrorism." *Computer Law Tip of the Week.* Online: http://www.mgrossmanlaw.com/articles/1999/cyberterrorism.htm.

Gruen, M. (2004). "Demographics and Methods of Recruitment." In Z. Baran (ed.), *The Challenge of Hizb ut Tahrir: Deciphering and Combating Islamist Ideology.* The Nixon Center. Online: http://www.nixon-center.org/Program%20Briefs/PB%202004/confrephiztahrir.pdf.

Grygiel, J. (2009). "The Power of Statelessness." *Policy Review* 154 (April–May): pp. 35–50.

Guardian. (2010). "Russia Terror Attacks Timeline." Guardian.co.uk. Online: http://www.guardian.co.uk/world/2010/mar/29/russian-terror-attacks-timeline.

Guevara, E. (1968). *Reminiscences of the Cuban Revolutionary War.* New York: Monthly Review Press.

Guha, R. (2007). "A War in the Heart of India." *The Nation* (July/16): pp. 28–31.

Gunaratna, R. (1998). "International and Regional Implications of the Sri Lankan Tamil Insurgency." *Institute for Counter-Terrorism.* Online: http://www.ict.org.il/.

Gunaratna, R. (2000). "Suicide Terrorism: A Global Threat." *Jane's Intelligence Review.* Online: http://www.janes.com/security/international_security/news/usscole/jir001020_1_n.s.html.

Gunaratna, R. (2002). *Inside al Qaeda: Global Network of Terror.* New York: Columbia University Press.

Gunaratna, R. (2004). "Links with Islamist Groups: Ideology and Operations." In Z. Baran (ed.), *The Challenge of Hizb ut Tahrir: Deciphering and Combating Islamist Ideology*. The Nixon Center. Online: http://www.nixoncenter. org/Program%20Briefs/PB%20 2004/confrephiztahrir.pdf.

Gunaratna, R., and M.B. Ali. (2009). "De-Radicalization Initiatives in Egypt: A Preliminary Insight. *Studies in Conflict and Terrorism*32: pp. 277–291.

Gunter, B. (2008). "Media Violence: Is There a Case for Causality?" *American Behavioral Scientist* 51: pp. 1061–1122. Online: http:// abs.sagepub.com/cgi/content/ abstract/51/8/1061.

Gurr, T. R. (1988a). "Political Terrorism in the United States: Historical Antecedents and Contemporary Trends." In M. Stohl (ed.), *The Politics of Terrorism*. New York: Dekker.

Gurr, T. R. (1988b). "Some Characteristics of Political Terrorism in the 1960s." In M. Stohl (ed.), *The Politics of Terrorism*. New York: Dekker.

Haahr, K. (2006). "Authorities Break Up GSPC Cells in Italy." *Terrorism Focus* 3 (30) (August 1). Online: http://www.jamestown. org/terrorism/news/article. php?articleid=2370090.

Hacker, F. J. (1976). *Crusaders, Criminals, and Crazies*. New York: Norton.

Hadar, L. (2002). "Pakistan in America's War on Terrorism: Ally or Unreliable Client?" The Cato Institute. Online: http://www.cato.org/pubs/ pas/pa436.pdf.

Haddad, S. (2006). "The Origins of Popular Support for Lebanon's Hezbollah." *Studies in Conflict and Terrorism* 29: pp. 21–34.

Hagby, M.,A. Goldberg,S. Becker,D. Schwartz,and Y. Bar-Dayan. (2009). "Health Implications of Radiological Terrorism: Perspectives from Israel." *Journal of Emergencies, Trauma, and Shock* 2 (2): pp. 117–123.

Haleem, I. (2004). "Micro Target, Macro Impact: The Resolution of the Kashmir Conflict as a Key toShrinking al-Qaeda's International Terrorist Network." *Journal of Terrorism and Political Violence* 16 (Spring): pp. 18–47.

Halm, H. (1999). *Shi'a Islam: From Religion to Revolution*. Princeton, NJ: Marcus Wiener.

Halversheid, S., and E. W. Witte. (2008). "Justification of War and Terrorism: A Comparative Case Study Analyzing Ethical Positions Based on Prescriptive Attribution Theory." *Social Psychology* 39 (1): pp. 26–36.

Hamas. (1988). "Hamas Character." Translated and copied by MidEastWeb. Online: http://www .mideastweb.org/hamas.htm.

Hambling, D. (2004). "Experts Fear Terrorists Are Seeking Fuel-Air Bombs." *New Scientist*. Online: http://www.newscientist.com/news/ news.jsp?id=ns99994785.

Hamilton, C. (2007). *Women and the ETA: The Gender Politics of Radical Basque Nationalism*. Manchester, UK: Manchester University Press.

Hamilton, I. (1971). "From Liberalism to Extremism." *Conflict Studies* 17: pp. 5–17.

Hamm, M. (ed.). (1994). *Hate Crime: International Perspectives on Causes and Control*. Cincinnati, OH: Anderson.

Hamm, M. (1996). *American Skinheads: The Criminology and Control of Hate Crime*. New York: Praeger.

Hamm, M. S. (2007). *Terrorist Recruitment in American Correctional Institutions: An Exploratory Study of Non-Traditional Faith Groups*. National Institute of Justice. Online: www.ncjrs.gov/pdffiles1/nij/ grants/220957.pdf.

Hamm, M. S. (2009). "Prison Islam in the Age of Sacred Terror." *British Journal of Criminology* 49: pp. 667–685. Online: http://bjc. oxfordjournals.org/cgi/content/ abstract/49/5/667.

Hanauer, L. S. (1995). "The Path to Redemption: Fundamentalist Judaism, Territory, and Jewish Settler Violence in the West Bank." *Studies in Conflict and Terrorism* 18: pp. 245–270.

Hanson, M. A. (2009). "Homeland Security QDR: Defense No Longer Has a Monopoly on QuadrennialReviews."*The Officer* (November):p. 16.

Hanson, S. (2009). "FARC, ELN: Colombia's Left-Wing Guerrillas." *Council on Foreign Relations*. Online: http://www.cfr.org/publication/9272/farc_eln.html.

Hanson, V. D. (2000). *The Western Way of War: Infantry Battle in Classical Greece*. Berkeley, CA: University of California Press.

Hanzich, J. (2003). "Dying for Independence." *Harvard International Review* 25 (2): pp. 32–36.

Harel, A., and A. Issacharoff. (2008). *34 Days: Israel, Hezbollah, and the War in Lebanon*. New York: Palgrave MacMillan.

Harik, J. P. (2004). *Hezbollah: The Changing Face of Terrorism*. London: I. B. Taurus.

Harris, E. (1995). *Guarding the Secrets: Palestinian Terrorism and a Father's Murder of His Too-American Daughter*. New York: Scribner.

Harris, M. (1991). *Our Kind: Who We Are, Where We Came from, and Where We Are Going*. New York: HarperCollins.

Harris, R. (2010). "Private Briefing to Assistant U.S. Attorney General." July 14, Washington, D.C. (unpublished).

Harris, W. (1998). *Burglary for the Patrol Officer*. Longview, TX: Rough Edge Publications.

Hart, M. J. (2008). "Al Qaeda: Refining a Failed Strategy." *Joint Forces Quarterly* 51 (4): pp. 117–124.

Hastings, M. (1970). *Barricades in Belfast*. New York: Taplinger.

Hauser, C., and A. O'Connor. (2007). "Arrested in Plot to Attack Fort Dix." *The New York Times*, May8. Online: http://www.nytimes. com/2007/05/08/us/08cnd-dix. html?ex=1336276800&en= 85a2795016f8037f&ei=5088&partner=rssnyt&emc=rss.

Heilman, J. P. (2010). "Family Ties: The Political Genealogy of Shining Path's Comrade Norah." *Bulletin of Latin American Research* 29 (2): pp. 155–169.

Helms, R.,S.E. Constanza, andN. Johnson. (2012). "Crouching Tiger or Phantom Dragon: Examining the Discourse on Global Cyber-Terror." *Security Journal*25 (1): pp. 57–75.

Henderson, D. (2006). "Former Detectives Arrested in McCord Probe." *The Independent*, August 9. Online: http://news.independent.co.uk/uk/ ulster/article1217930.ece.

Hereen, M. W., and S. A. Brown. (2002). *Christ in Celtic Christianity: Britain and Ireland from the Fifth to the Tenth Century*. Rochester, NY: Boydell Press.

Herman, E. S. (1983). *The Real Terror Network*. Boston: South End Press.

Herman, E. S. (1999). *The Myth of the Liberal Media: An Edward Herman Reader*. New York: Peter Lang.

Herman, M. (2008). "Protagonists and Victims: Women Leading the Fight for a Democratic Colombia." *Feminist Review* 88: pp. 122–127.

Herman, S. (2001). "The USA Patriot Act and the U.S. Department of Justice: Losing Our Balances." *Jurist*, December 3. Online: http://jurist.law.pitt.edu/forum/forum new40.htm.

Hewitt, C. (1984). *The Effectiveness of Anti-Terrorist Policies*. Lanham, MD: University Press of America.

Hewitt, C. (2003). *Understanding Terrorism in America: From the Klan to al Qaeda*. New York: Routledge.

Higgins, A. (2006). "Hezbollah Fund-Raiser's Mission: Money for Bullets and Loans." *Wall Street Journal*, December 26.

Hill, F. (2003). "Terrorism in Asia and the Pacific." Testimony, Committee on International Relations, Subcommittee on the Middle East and Central Asia, U.S. House of Representatives. *Congressional Quarterly*, October 29. Online: http://homeland.cq.cm/hs/display.do?dockey=/usr/local/cqonline/docs/html.

Hinnen, T. M. (2004). "The Cyber-Front in the War on Terrorism: Curbing Terrorist Use of the Internet." *The Columbia Science and Technology Law Review*. Online: www.stlr.org/html/volume5/ hinnen.pdf.

Hinton, H. L. (1999). *Combating Terrorism: Observations on Biological Terrorism and Public Health Initiatives*. Washington, DC: General Accounting Office.

Hiro, D. (1987). *Iran under the Ayatollahs*. London: Routledge & Kegan Paul.

History Channel. (2000). "100 Years of Terror." Four-part series. New York: A&E Television Networks.

Hitt, G., and D. S. Cloud. (2002). "Bush's Homeland Security Overhaul Faces Obstacles." *Wall Street Journal*, June 10, p. A4.

Hobijn, B. (2002). "How Much Will Homeland Security Cost?" Federal Reserve Bank of New York. Online: http://www.security management.com/library/Bart_Homeland0203.pdf.

Hocking, J. (2004). *Terror Laws: ASIO, Counter-Terrorism, and the Threat to Democracy*. Sydney: University of South Wales Press.

Hoffman, B. (1995). "Holy Terror: The Implications of Terrorism Motivated by a Religious Imperative." *Studies in Conflict and Terrorism* 18: pp. 271–284.

Hoffman, B. (1998). "Old Madness, New Methods." Santa Monica, CA: RAND. Online: http://www.rand.org/publications/randreview/issues/rr.winter98.9/methods.html.

Hoffman, B. (2006a). "Forward." In D. Galula (ed.), *Pacification in Algeria, 1956–1958*. Santa Monica, CA: The RAND Corporation.

Hoffman, B. (2006b). *Inside Terrorism: Revised and Expanded*. New York: Columbia University Press.

Hoffman, B. (2008a). "The Myth of Grass-Roots Terrorism." *Foreign Affairs* 87 (3): pp. 133–138.

Hoffman, B. (2008b). "Hoffman Replies." *Foreign Affairs* 87(4): pp. 165–166.

Hoffman, B. (2009). "Radicalization and Subversion: Al Qaeda and the 7 July 2005 Bombings and the 2006 Airline Bombing Plot." *Studies in Conflict and Terrorism* 32: pp. 1100–1116.

Hoffman, B. (2010). "American Jihad." *The National Interest* (May/June): pp. 17–27.

Hoffman, F. G. (2008). "Al Qaeda's Demise or Evolution?" *United States Naval Institute Proceedings* 134 (9): pp. 18–22.

Hoffman, S. (2003). "The High and the Mighty: Bush's National-Security Strategy and the New American Hubris." *The American Prospect* 13 (January 13): pp. 28–32.

Holden, R., and J. White. (2010). "Elements of Radicalization." Bureau of Justice Assistance. Online: https://www.slatt.org.

Holland, J. J. (2005). "House Approves Extension of Patriot Act." Associated Press, December 14. Online: http://news.yahoo.com/s/ap/20051214/ap_on_go_co/patriot_act.

Homer-Dixon, T. (2002). "The Rise of Complex Terrorism." *Foreign Affairs* 81 (January/February): pp. 52–62.

Hooper, I. (2000). "WSJ Rejects Muslim Reply to Steven Emerson." Council on American-Islamic Relations, November 15. Online: http://www.musalman.com/islam-news/amjwsjrejectsmuslimreply.html.

Horchem, H. J. (1986). "Terrorism in West Germany." *Conflict Studies* 186.

Horgan, J. (2005). *The Psychology of Terrorism*. New York: Routledge.

Horgan, J. (2009). *Walking Away from Terrorism*. New York: Routledge.

Horgan, J., and K. Braddock.(2010). "Rehabilitating the Terrorists? Challenges in Assessing the Effectiveness of De-Radicalization Programs." *Terrorism and Political Violence* 22: pp. 267–291.

Hosenball, M., M. Isikoff, and E. Thomas. (2010). "The Radicalization of Umar Farouk Abdulmutallab." *Newsweek* (January 11): pp. 37–41.

Hourani, A. (1997). *A History of the Arab Peoples*. Cambridge, MA: Belknap Press.

Hourdin, P. (2009). "Banks, Governance, and Public-Private Partnership in Preventing and Confronting Organized Crime, Corruption, and Terrorism Financing." *Journal of Financial Crime* 16 (3): pp. 199–209.

Howard, M. (1988). *Clausewitz*. New York: Oxford University Press.

Howard, M. (2002). "What's in a Name? How to Fight Terrorism." *Foreign Affairs* 81 (January/February): pp. 43–59.

Howard, R. D. (2004). "Understanding Al Qaeda's Application of the New Terrorism." In R. Howard and R. Sawyer (eds.), *Terrorism and Counterterrorism: Understanding the New Security Environment*. New York: McGraw-Hill.

Howden, J., and J. Ryan. (2009). "Hiding in Plain Site: Community Organization, Naïve Trust, and Terrorism." *Current Sociology* 57 (3): pp. 323–343.

Hudson, A. (2006). "Antiterror Grant to Probe Bingo Halls Criticized." *Washington Times*, April 12. Online: http://washingtontimes.com/national/20060411-115930-6028r.htm.

Hudzik, J., and G. Cordner. (1983). *Planning in Criminal Justice Organizations and Systems*. New York: Macmillan.

Huffman, I. (2003) "Lockyer's Spying Reforms Not Enough, Activists Say." *Oakland Tribune Online*, April 12. Online: http://findarticles.com/p/articles/mi_qn4176/is_20030803/ai_nl4555774.

Hughes, J., and C. Donnelly. (2004). "Attitudes to Community Relations in Northern Ireland: Signs of Optimism in the Post Cease Fire Period?" *Terrorism and Political Violence* 16: pp. 567–592.

Huntington, S. P. (1993). "The Clash of Civilizations." *Foreign Affairs* 72: pp. 22–49.

Huntington, S. P. (1996). *The Clash of Civilizations and the Remaking of World Order*. New York: Simon & Schuster.

Huntington, S. P. (2004). "The Hispanic Challenge." *Foreign Policy*(March/April): 30–45.

Hutchcroft, P. D. (2008). "The Arroyo Imbroglio in the Philippines." *Journal of Democracy* 19 (1): pp. 141–155.

Hutt, M. (ed.). (2004). *Himalayan People's War: Nepal's Maoist Rebellion*. Bloomington, IN: University of Indiana Press.

IACP. *See* International Association of Chiefs of Police.

Ibrahim, R. (2007). *The al Qaeda Reader*. New York: Broadway Books.

Ihsanoglu, E. (2005). "Speech of H. E. Professor Ekmeledin Ihsanoglu." The International Conference on Combating Terrorism. Riyadh, Saudi Arabia. Online: http://www.oicoci.org/press/english/2005/feb%202005/SG-terrrorism.htm.

IIR. (2010a). "Communities against Terrorism." Tallahassee: IIR. Available for public review. Public site online: https://www.slatt.org/default.aspx.

IIR. (2010b). "National Criminal Intelligence Sharing Plan." *Institute for Intergovernmental Research*. Online: http://www.iir.com/global/ncisp.htm.

Imperial Knights of the Ku Klux Klan of America. Online: http://www.k-k-k.com/items.html.

Institute for Counter-Terrorism. (2001). *Countering Suicide Terrorism*. Herzliya, Israel: Institute for Counter-Terrorism.

Institute for Counter-Terrorism. (2004). "Hamas." *ICT*. Online: http://www.ict.org.il/inter_ter/orgdet.cfm?orgid=13.

Institute for the Study of War. (2011). "Haqqani Network." ISW. Online: http://www.understandingwar.org/themenode/haqqani-network.

International Association of Chiefs of Police. (2001). *Terrorism Response*. Alexandria, VA: IACP.

International Crisis Group. (2004). "Indonesia Backgrounder: Jihad in Central Sulawesi." February 3. Online: http://www.crisisgroup.org/library/documents/asia/indonesia/074_jihad_in_central_sulawesi_mod.pdf.

International Crisis Group. (2005a). "Recycling Militants in Indonesia: Dural Islam and the Australian Embassy Bombing." February 22. Online: http://www.crisisgroup.org/library/documents/asia/indonesia/074_jihad_in_central_sulawesi_mod.pdf.

International Crisis Group. (2005b). "Islamist Terrorism in the Sahel: Fact or Fiction?" March 31. Online: http://www.crisisgroup.org/library/documents/africa/west_africa/092_islamist_terrorism_in_the_sahel_fact_or_fiction.pdf.

International Crisis Group. (2005c). "Uzbekistan: The Andijon Uprising." May 25. Online: http://www.crisisgroup.org/library/documents/sia/central_asia/b038_uzbekistan_the_andijon_uprising_edited.pdf.

International Crisis Group. (2005d). "Somalia's Islamists." December12. Online: http://www.crisisgroup.org/library/documents/africa/horn_of_africa/100_somalia_s_islamists.pdf.

International Crisis Group. (2006a). "Fuelling the Niger Delta Crisis." Online: http://www.crisisgroup.org/home/index.cfm?id=4394&l=1.

International Crisis Group. (2006b). "Pakistan: The Worsening Conflict in Balochistan." Online: http://www.crisisgroup.org/home/index.cfm?id=4373&l=1.

International Crisis Group. (2006c). "The Swamps of Insurgency Nigeria's Delta Unrest." August 3. Online: http://www.crisisgroup.org/en/regions/africa/west-africa/nigeria/115-the-swamps-of-insurgencynigerias-delta-unrest.aspx.

International Crisis Group. (2006d). "Bangladesh Today." October 23. Online: http://www.crisisgroup.org/library/documents/asia/south_asia/121_bangladesh_today.pdf.

International Crisis Group. (2006e). "Cote d'Ivoire: Stepping Up the Pressure." September 7. Online: http://www.crisisgroup.org/home/index.cfm?id=4365&l=1.

International Crisis Group. (2006f). "Sri Lanka: The Failure of the Peace Process." November 28. Online: http://www.crisisgroup.org/library/documents/asia/south_asia/sri_lanka/124_sri_lanka_the_failure_of_the_peace_process.pdf.

International Crisis Group. (2006g). "Pakistan's Tribal Areas: Appeasing the Militants." December 11. Online: http://www.crisisgroup.org/library/documents/asia/south_asia/125_pakistans_tribal_areas_appeasing_the_militants.pdf.

International Crisis Group. (2007a). "Discord in Pakistan's Northern Areas." April 2. Online: http://www.crisisgroup.org/home/index.cfm?id=4748&l=1.

International Crisis Group. (2007b). "Nepal's Maoists: Purists or Pragmatists?" May 18. Online: http://www.crisisgroup.org/home/index.cfm?id=4842&l=1.

International Crisis Group. (2009). "Women and Radicalization in Kyrgyzstan." September 3. Online: http://www.crisisgroup.org/~/media/Files/asia/central-asia/kyrgyzstan/176_women_and_radicalisation_in_kyrgyzstan.ashx.

International Crisis Group. (2010a). "Improving Security in Colombia." International Crisis Group, *Policy Briefing*, June 29. Online: http://www.crisisgroup.org/~/media/Files/latin-america/colombia/B23%20Improving%20Security%20Policy%20in%20Colombia.ashx.

International Crisis Group. (2010b). "Somalia's Divided Islamists." ICG, *Policy Briefing*, May 18. Online: http://www.crisisgroup.org/~/media/Files/africa/horn-of-africa/somalia/B74%20Somalias%20Divided%20Islamists.ashx.

International Crisis Group. (2010c). "The Tamil Diaspora after the LTTE." February. Online: http://www.crisisgroup.org/en/regions/asia/south-asia/sri-lanka/

186-thesri-lankan-tamil-diaspora-after-the-ltte.aspx.

Isikoff, M., and M. Hosenball. (2004). "Paying for Terror." *Newsweek* Web Exclusive, March 12. Online: http://www.msnbc.msn.com/id/4963025/.

Israel, J. I. (2001). *Radical Enlightenment: Philosophy and the Making of Modernity*. New York: Oxford University Press.

Isseroff, A. (2004). "A History of the Hamas Movement." MidEastWeb. Online: http://www.mideastweb.org/hamashistory.htm.

Jaber, H. (1997). *Hezbollah: Born with a Vengeance*. New York: Columbia University Press.

Jackson, G. (1972). *Peoples' Prison*. London: Faber & Faber. (Published in the United States in 1974 as *Surviving the Long Night*. New York: Vanguard.)

Jackson, R. (2005). *Writing the War on Terrorism: Language, Politics, and Counter-Terrorism*. Manchester, UK: Manchester University Press.

Jacobs, J. (1983). *S.W.A.T. Tactics*. Boulder, CO: Paladin Press.

Jamal, A. (2010). "The Asian Tigers—The New Face of the Punjabi Taliban." *Terrorism Monitor* 8 (20). Online: http://www.james town.org/programs/gta/single/?tx_ttnews[tt_news] =36398&tx_ttnews[backPid] =457&no_cache=1.

Jamestown Foundation. (2010). "Will India Deploy Its Army against Maoist Terrorists?" *Terrorism Monitor*, June 17. Online: http://www.jamestown.org/programs/gta/single/?tx_ttnews[tt_news] =36502&tx_ttnews[backPid] =457&no_cache=1.

Jamestown Foundation. (2012). "Shining Path Faces Leadership Vacuum in Upper Huallaga Valley." *Militant Leadership Monitor*, March 12. Online: http://mlm.jamestown.org/single/?tx_ttnews%5Btt_news%5D=39201&tx_ttnews%5BbackPid%5D=539&cHash=a6028a2 2ae8ad466650d6ad5a2c5cdf0.

Jamwal, N. S. (2002). "Hawala—The Invisible Financing System of Terrorism." *Strategic Analysis* 26 (2): pp. 181–198.

Jane's. (2007). "United Nations Office of Drugs and Crime." Terrorism Definition. *Jane's Military and Security Assessments*. Online: http://jtic.janes.com/public/jtic/terrorism_definition_noscript.shtml.

Jarboe, J. (2002). "FBI Testifies to House Ecoterror Hearing." Testimony before the U.S. House of Representatives, House Resource Committee, Subcommittee on Forests and Forest Health, February 12. Online: http://www.furcommission.com/news/newsF04f.htm.

Jenkins, B. (1987). "Will Terrorists Go Nuclear?" In W. Laqueur and Y. Alexander (eds.), *The Terrorism Reader*. New York: Meridian.

Jenkins, B. M. (1983). *New Modes of Conflict*. Santa Monica, CA: RAND.

Jenkins, B. M. (1984). "The Who, What, When, Where, How, and Why of Terrorism." Paper presented at the Detroit Police Department Conference on Urban Terrorism: Planning or Chaos? November, Detroit.

Jenkins, B. M. (2004a). "The Operational Code of the Jihadists." Briefing prepared for the Army Science Board, RAND, April 1 (unpublished).

Jenkins, B. M. (2004b). "Where I Draw the Line." *Christian Science Monitor*. Online: http://www.csmonitor.com/specials/terrorism/lite/expert.html.

Jenkins, B. M. (2006). *Unconquerable Nation: Knowing Our Enemy, Strengthening Ourselves*. Santa Monica, CA: RAND.

Jenkins, B. M. (2009). "Outside Expert's View." In D. Gartenstein-Ross and L. Grossman (ed.), *Homegrown Terrorists in the U.S. and U.K.: An Empirical Analysis of the Radicalization Process*. Washington, DC: Foundation for the Defense of Democracies.

Jenkins, B. M. (2010). "Would-Be Warriors: Incidents of Jihadist Terrorist Radicalization in the United States Since September 11, 2001." *RAND Corporation*. Online: http://www.rand.org/pubs/occasional_ papers/2010/RAND_OP292.pdf.

Jenkins, P. (2009). "Terror Begins at Home." *The American Conservative* 8 (6): pp. 16–17.

Jensen, R. B. (2004). "Daggers, Rifles, and Dynamite: Anarchist Terrorism in Nineteenth Century Europe." *Terrorism and Political Violence* 16 (Spring): pp. 116–153.

John, B.R. (2011). "Fusion Centers: Strengthening the Nation's Homeland Security Enterprise." *The Police Chief* 78 (February): pp. 62–68.

John, W. (2005). "The Roots of Extremism in Bangladesh." The Jamestown Foundation. *Terrorism Monitor* 3 (1) (January 13). Online: http://www.jamestown.org/publications_details.php?volume_id=411&issue_id=3196&article_id=2369092.

Johnson, B. R. (2007a). Panel chair for "Information Sharing between State, Local, and Tribal Agencies and the Federal Government—Discussion of the Common Framework." First National Fusion Center Conference, Destin, FL, March.

Johnson, B.R. (2007b). "A Look at Fusion Centers: Working Together to Protect America." *FBI Law Enforcement Bulletin* 76 (12): pp. 28–32.

Johnson, D., and B. Brunner. (2004). "Timeline of Key Events in Chechnya, 1830–2004." Online: http://www.infoplease.com/spot/chechnyatime1.html.

Johnson, K. (2002). "NYPD Adds CIA, Military Experts." *USA Today*, January 29. Online: http://www.usatoday.

Johnson, T. (2011). "Boko Haram." Council on Foreign Relations. Online: http://www.cfr.org/africa/boko-haram/p25739.

Jones, D., and M. L. R. Smith. (2010). "Beyond Belief: Islamist Strategic Thinking and International Relations Theory." *Terrorism and Political Violence* 22 (2): 242–266.

Jones, S. (2010). "It Takes the Villages." *Foreign Affairs* 89 (3): pp. 120–127.

Jones, S. G., and M. C. Libicki. (2008). *How Terrorist Groups End: Lessons for Countering al Qa'ida*. Santa Monica, CA: RAND Corporation. Online: http://www.rand.org/pubs/monographs/MG741-1/.

Jordan, J., and R. Wesley. (2006). "The Madrid Attacks: Results of Investigations Two Years Later." The Jamestown Foundation, May 9. Online: http://jamestown.org/terrorism/news/article.php?articleid=2369921.

Jordan, L. J. (2005). "Homeland Security Information Network Criticized." *Washington Post*,

May 10. Online: http://www .washingtonpost.com/wp-dyn/ content/article/2005/05/09/ AR2005050901076.html.

Joshi, M. (1996). "On the Razor's Edge: The Liberation Tigers of Tamil Eelam." *Studies in Conflict and Terrorism* 19: pp. 19–42.

Josson, P. (2006). "New Profile of the Home-Grown Terrorist Emerges." *Christian Science Monitor*, June 26.

Joyner, C. C., and A. I. Parkhouse. (2009). "Nuclear Terrorism in a Globalizing World: Assessing the Threat and Emerging Management Regime." *Stanford Journal of International Law* 45 (2): pp. 203–242.

Juergensmeyer, M. (1988). "The Logic of Religious Violence." In D.C. Rapoport (ed.), *Inside Terrorist Organizations*. New York: Columbia University Press.

Juergensmeyer, M. (2003). *Terror in the Mind of God: The Global Rise of Religious Violence*. Berkley, CA: University of California Press.

Juergensmeyer, M. (2009). *Global Rebellion: Religious Challenges to the Secular State from Christian Militias to al Qaeda*. Berkeley: University of California Press.

Kafala, T. (2001). "Israel's Assassination Policy." BBC News, August 1. Online: http://news.bbc.co.uk/1/hi/ world/middle_east/1258187.stm.

Kagan, R. (2004). "America's Crisis of Legitimacy." *Foreign Affairs* 83 (March/April): pp. 65–87.

Kahan, D. M. (1997). "Social Influence, Social Meaning, and Deterrence." *Virginia Law Review* 83 (2): pp. 349–395. Online: http://heinonline. org/HOL/LandingPage?collection =journals&handle=hein.journals/ valr83& div=19&id=&page=.

Kanable, R. (2011). "Fusion Centers Grow Up." *Law Enforcement Technology* (September): pp. 8–16.

Kaplan, D. E. (2003). "The Saudi Connection: How Billions in Oil Money Spawned a Global Terror Network." *U.S. News & World Report*, December 15. Online: http://www.usnews/issue/031215/ usnews/15terror.htm.

Kaplan, D. E. (2005). "Paying for Terror." *U.S. News & World Report*, December 5. Online: http:// www.usnews.com/usnews/news/ articles/051205/5terror.htm.

Kaplan, E. (2006). "The Al-Qaeda-Hezbollah Relationship." Council on Foreign Relations. Online: http://www.cfr.org/publication/ 11275/alqaedahezbollah_ relationship.html.

Kaplan, E. H., A. Mintz, S. Mishal, and C. Samban. (2005). "What Happened to Suicide Bombings in Israel? Insights from a Terror Stock Model." *Studies in Conflict and Terrorism* 28: pp. 225–235.

Karam, P. A. (2005). "Radiological Terrorism." *Human and Ecological Risk Assessment* 11: pp. 501–523.

Karim, K. H. (2001). *Islamic Peril: Media and Global Violence*. Ottawa: Black Rose Books.

Kariuki, J. M. (1963). *Mau Mau Detainee*. Baltimore: Penguin Books, Ltd.

Karman, E. (2000). "Hamas' Terrorism Strategy: Operational Limitations and Political Constraints." *Middle East Review of International Affairs* 4 (1) (March). Online: http:// meria.idc.ac.il/journal/2000/issue1/ jv4n1a7.html.

Karon, T. (2003). "Why Turks and Kurds Prize Kirkuk." *Time*, May 10. Online: http://www.time.com/time/ world/article/0,8599,425230,00. html.

Karyotis, G. (2007). "Securitization of Greek Terrorism and Arrest of the 'Revolutionary Organization November 17.'" *Cooperation and Conflict* 42 (3): pp. 271–293. Online: http://cac.sagepub.com/ content/42/3/271.

Katel, P. (2008). "Mexico's Drug War: Background." *CQ Researcher* 18 (43).

Katersky, A. (2010). "Faisal Shahzad Pleads Guilty in Times Square Car Bomb Plot, Warns of More Attacks." ABC News, June 21. Online: http://abcnews.go.com/ Blotter/faisal-shahzad-pleads-guilty-times-square-car-bomb/ story?id=10970094.

Katz, L. R. (2001). "Anti-Terrorism Laws: Too Much of a Good Thing." *Jurist*, November 24. Online: http:// jurist.law.pitt.edu/forum/forum-new39.htm.

Kayyem, J., and A. M. Howitt (eds.). (2002). *Beyond the Beltway: Focusing on Hometown Security*. Cambridge, MA: Harvard University.

Keathley, J. (2002). "Conducting Undercover Terrorism Investigations." Tallahassee, FL: IRR (unpublished).

Keats, A. (2002). "In the Spotlight: Al Jihad (Egyptian Islamic Jihad)." Center for Defense Information. Online: http://www.cdi.org/terrorism/ aljihad.cfm.

Keefer, W. J. (2006). "The Patriot Act Reauthorized." *The Jurist*. Online: http://jurist.law.pitt.edu/forumy/ 2006/03/patriot-act-reauthorized. php.

Keegan, J. (1993). *A History of Warfare*. New York: Vintage Books.

Keegan, J., and A. Wheatcroft. (1976). *Who's Who in Military History*. New York: William Morrow.

Keinon, H. (2004). "Israel Preparing for Wave of Terror." *Jerusalem Post*, May 21.

Keith, B. (2010). "The Transformation of West Point as a Liberal Arts College." *Liberal Education* 96 (2). Online: http://www.aacu.org/liber-aleducation/le-sp10/LESP10_Keith. cfm.

Keller, D. (2006). "September 11, Social Theory, and Democratic Politics." In A. P. Kavoori and T. Fraley (eds.), *Media, Terrorism, and Theory: A Reader*. Lanham, MD: Rowman & Littlefield.

Kellner, D. (2002). "September 11, the Media, and War Fever Television." *New Media* 3 (May): pp. 143–151.

Kellner, T., and F. Pepitone. (2010). "Inside Mexico's Drug War." *World Policy Journal* 27 (1): pp. 29–39.

Kelly, R. W. (2010). "Statement of Raymond W. Kelly, Commissioner, New York City Police Department." The Mumbai Attacks: A Wakeup Call for America's Private Sector. Hearing before the Subcommittee on Transportation Security and Infrastructure Protection of the Committee on Homeland Security, U.S. House of Representatives. Online: http://www.gpoaccess.gov/congress/ index.html.

Kelly, R.W. (2011). "9/11: 10 Years Later." *The Police Chief* 78 (September): pp. 20–25.

Kenney, M. (2011). "Hotbed of Radicalization or Something Else? An Ethnographic Exploration of a Muslim Neighborhood in Ceuta." *Terrorism and Political Violence* (23): pp. 537–559.

Kepel, G. (2002). *Jihad: The Trail of Political Islam*. Cambridge, MA: Belknap Press.

Kepel, G. (2004). *The War for Muslim Minds: Islam and the West*. Cambridge, MA: Belknap Press.

Kephart, J. L. (2005). "Immigration and Terrorism: Moving Beyond the 9-11 Staff Report on Terrorist Travel." Center for Immigration Studies. Center Paper 24. Online: http://www.cis.org/articles/2005/kephart.pdf.

Kershaw, S. (2010). "The Terrorist Mind: An Update." *New York Times*, "Week in Review," January 10.

Ketcham, C. C., and H. J. McGeorge. (1986). "Terrorist Violence:Its Mechanics and Countermeasures." In N. C. Livingstoneand T. E. Arnold (eds.),*Fighting Back*. Lexington, MA: Heath.

Keyer, D., and L.W. Miller III. (2011). "Nationwide SAR Initiative Delivers Value to Fusion Centers."*The Police Chief* 78 (February): pp. 40–44.

Khashan, H. (2003). "Collective Palestinian Frustration and Suicide Bombings." *Third World Quarterly* 24 (6): pp. 1049–1067.

Khatami, S. (1997). "Between Class and Nation: Ideology and Radical Basque Ethnonationalism." *Studies in Conflict and Terrorism* 20: pp. 395–417.

Kimery, A. (2009). "Rejection of Jihadist, War on Terrorism Terms Draws Fire, Debate." *Homeland Security Today*. Online: http://www.hstoday.us.

King, A. (2009). "Islam, Women, and Violence." *Feminist Theology* 17: pp. 292–328. Online: http://fth.sagepub.com/cgi/content/abstract/17/3/292.

King, C., and R. Menon. (2010). "Prisoners of the Caucasus: Russia's Invisible Civil War." *Foreign Affairs* 89 (4): pp. 20–34.

King, M., and D.M. Taylor. (2011). "The Radicalization of Homegrown Jihadists: A Review of Theoretical Models and Social Psychological Evidence." *Studies in Conflict and Terrorism*23: pp. 602–622.

Kinzer, S. (2010). "The Next Power Triangle." *The American Prospect* 21 (6): pp. 27–30.

Klite, P. (2000). "Media Can Be Antibiotic for Violence." *The Quill* 88 (3): pp. 32–34.

Kohlman, E. F. (2004). *Jihad in Europe: The Afghan-Bosnian Network*. New York: Berg.

Kohlmann, E. (2005). "Spreading Terrorist Dogma." MSNBC. Online: http://www.msnbc.msn.com/id/13848605.

Kohn, R. K. (2009). "The Danger of Militarization in an Endless 'War' on Terrorism." *Journal of Military History* 73 (1):pp. 177–208.

Kolar, J. (2006). "What We Now Know about the Alleged 9-11 Hijackers." In P. Zarembka (ed.), *The Hidden History of 9-11-2001*. San Diego, CA: Elsevier.

Kometer, M. W. (2004). "The New Terrorism: The Nature of the War on Terrorism." Maxwell Air Force Base, AL: Air War College. Online: http://www.maxwell.af.mil/au/aul/aupress/SAAS_Theses/SAASS_Out/Kometer/Kometer.pdf.

Konotorovich, E. V. (2002). "Make Them Talk." *Wall Street Journal*(June 18): p. A12.

Korn, A. (2004). "Israeli Press and the War against Terrorism: The Construction of the 'Liquidation Policy.'" *Crime, Law, and Social Change* 41: pp. 209–234.

Korn, D. A. (1995). "Interview with Abdullah Ocalan." Online: http://kurdstruggle.org/index.shtml.

Kosterlitz, J. (2008). "Touting 'Terrorists.'" *National Journal* 40 (3).

Kramb, B. (2011). "Does Intelligence-Led Policing Close the 'Demand Gap' between Recorded Crimes and Arrests? Preliminary Evidence from the State of Michigan." Master's thesis, Grand Valley State University, Allendale, MI.

Kransoboka, N. (2002). "Real Journalism Goes Underground: The Internet Underground." *International Journal for Communications Studies* 64 (5): pp. 479–499.

Kraska, P. B. (1996). "Enjoying Militarism: Political/Personal Dilemmas in Studying U.S. Police Paramilitary Units." *Justice Quarterly* 13: pp. 405–429.

Kraska, P. B., and V. Kappeler. (1999). "Militarizing American Police: The Rise and Normalization of Paramilitary Units." In L. K. Gaines and G. W. Cordner (eds.), *Policing Perspectives: An Anthology*. Los Angeles: Roxbury.

Krasna, J. S. (1997). "Narcotics and the National Security Producer States." *Texas Law Review*. Online: http://www.lib.unb.ca/Texts/JCS/s96/articles/krasna.html.

Krauthammer, C. (2004). "U.N. Will Go to Any Length to Condemn Israel." *Jewish World Review*, July16. Online: http://www.jewishworldreview.com/0704/krauthammer_2004_07_16.php3.

Kruglanski, A. W.,M. Crenshaw, J. M. Post,and J. Victoroff. (2008). "What Should This Fight Be Called? Metaphors of Counterterrorism and Their Implications." *Psychological Science in the Public Interest* 8 (3): pp. 97–133.

Kunnath, G. J. (2006). "Becoming a Naxalite in Rural Bihar: Class Struggle and Its Contradictions." *Journal of Peasant Studies* 33 (1): pp. 89–123.

Kurz, A. (1994). "Palestinian Terrorism—The Violent Aspect of a Political Struggle." In Y. Alexander (ed.), *Middle Eastern Terrorism: CurrentThreats and Future Prospects*. New York: Hall.

Kurzman, C. (2001). "Critics Within: Islamic Scholars' Protest against the Islamic State of Iran." *International Journal of Politics, Culture and Society* 15 (2): pp. 341–359.

Kurzman, C. (2004). *The Unthinkable Revolution in Iran*. Cambridge, MA: Harvard University Press.

Kushner, H. W., and B. Jacobson. (1998). "Financing Terrorist Activities through Coupon Fraud and Counterfeiting." *Counterterrorism and Security International* 5 (Summer): pp. 10–12.

Kutschera, K. (1996). "Algeria's Fighting Women." Online: http://www.chris-kutschera.com/A/algeria_women.htm.

Kuusisto, A.-K. (2001). "Territoriality, Symbolism, and the Challenge." *Peace Review* 13 (1): pp. 59–66.

Kux, D. (2002). "India's Fine Balance." *Foreign Affairs* 81 (3):pp. 93–106.

Labeviere, R. (2000). *Dollars for Terror: The United States and Islam*. New York: Algora.

Laffan, M. (1999). *Resurrection of Ireland: The Sinn Fein Party, 1916–1923*. Port Chester, NY: Cambridge University Press.

Lake, E. (2004). "Hamas Agents May Be Lurking in U.S.: Fears

Rantisi's Vow to Attack May Awaken Operatives Here." *New York Sun*, April 29.

Lamloum, O. (2009). "Hezbollah's Media: Political History in Outline." *Global Media and Communication* 5 (3): pp. 353–357.

Lang, P. (2006). "Of Other Things: Al Qaeda and the Jihadis." *America* (October 2): pp. 20–21.

Langguth, A. J. (1978). *Hidden Terrors*. New York: Pantheon.

Lappin, Y. (2010). "West Bank Terrorist Who Killed Soldier Was a PA Officer." *Jerusalem Post*. Online: http://www.jpost.com/Israel/Article.aspx?id=168332February 10.

Laqueur, W. (1987). *The Age of Terrorism*. Boston: Little, Brown.

Laqueur, W. (1999). *The New Terrorism: Fanaticism and the Arms of Mass Destruction*. New York: Oxford University Press.

Laqueur, W., and Y. Alexander. (1987). *The Terrorism Reader*. Boston: Little Brown.

Latora, V., and M. Marchioni. (2004). "How the Science of Complex Networks Can Help Developing Strategies against Terrorism." *Chaos, Solutions, and Fractals* 20 (1): pp. 69–75.

Lau, S. (2003). "An Analysis of Terrorist Groups' Potential Use of Electronic Steganography." SANS Institute. Online: http://www.sans.org/reading_room/whitepapers/steganography554.php.

Leahy, P. (2006). "Statement of Senator Patrick Leahy." Senate Committee of the Judiciary, United States Senate. Online: http://judiciary.senate.gov/member_statement.cfm?id=2048&wit_id=3984.

Lee, A. M. (1983). *Terrorism in Northern Ireland*. New York: General Hall.

Lee, G. D. (2005). *Conspiracy Investigations: Terrorism, Drugs and Gangs*. Upper Saddle River, NJ: Prentice Hall.

Leiter, M. (2009). "Eight Years after 9/11: Confronting the Terrorist Threat to the Homeland." Testimony of the Director of the National Counterterrorism Center, Hearing before the Senate, Homeland Security and Governmental Affairs Committee. Online: http://docs.google.com/viewer?a=v&q=cache:-4A9_

bTY-0MJ:hsgac.senate.gov/public/index.cfm?FuseAction=Files.

LeMelle, G. (2009). "African Policy Outlook 2009." *Foreign Policy in Focus* 4 (4).

Lesser, I. O. (1999). "Changing Terrorism in a Changing World." In I. O. Lesser, B. Hoffman, J. Arquilla, D. Ronfeldt, M. Zanni, and B. M. Jenkins (eds.), *Countering the New Terrorism*. Santa Monica, CA: RAND.

Levi, M. (2007). *On Nuclear Terrorism*. Cambridge, MA: Harvard University Press.

Levin, B. (2007). "Trials for Terrorists: The Shifting Legal Landscape of the Post-9/11 Era." *Journal of Contemporary Criminal*23: pp. 195–218. Online: http://ccj.sagepub.com/content/23/2/195.

Levin, D. (2003). "Structure of News Coverage of a Peace Process." *Press/Politics* 8 (4): pp. 27–53.

Levin, M. (2003). "John Stuart Mill: A Liberal Looks at Utopian Socialism in the Years of Revolution 1848–49." *Utopian Studies* 14 (2): pp. 68–82.

Levit, L. (2006). *Hamas: Politics, Charity, and Terrorism in the Service of Jihad*. New Haven, CT: Yale University Press.

Levitas, D. (2002). *The Terrorist Next Door: The Militia Movement and the Radical Right*. New York:St. Martin's Press.

Levitt, L. (2002). "A Fed-Friendly NYPD? Not Yet." *Newsday*, January 28. Online: http://nypdconfidential.com/columns/2002/020128.html.

Lewis, B. (1966). *The Arabs in History*. London: Hutchinson University Press.

Lewis, B. (1993). *Islam and the West*. New York: Oxford University Press.

Lewis, B. (1995). *Cultures in Conflict: Christians, Muslims, and Jews in the Age of Discovery*. New York: Oxford University Press.

Lewis, B. (2002). *What Went Wrong? The Clash between Islam and Modernity in the Middle East*. New York: Oxford University Press.

Lewis, B. (2003a). *The Crisis in Islam: Holy War and Unholy Terror*. New York: Random House.

Lewis, B. (2003b). *What Went Wrong? The Clash between Islam and Modernity in the Middle East*. New York: Perennial.

Lewis, B. (2003c). *The Assassins: A Radical Sect in Islam*. New York: Basic Books.

Lewis, B. (2004). *From Babel to Dragomans: Interpreting the Middle East*. New York: Oxford University Press.

Lichtblau, E. (2001). "Impassioned Letter Left Behind by Hijackers Urges Them to Stay the Course in Return for Paradise." *Los Angeles Times*, September 29. Online: http://www.latimes.com/news/ nationworld/nation/la-092901letter.story.

Liddell Hart, B. H. (1967). *Strategy*. New York: Praeger.

Liff, S., and A. S. Laegren. (2003). "Cybercafes: Debating the Meeting and Significance of Internet Access in a Café Environment." *New Media & Society* 5 (3): pp. 307–312.

Lindeman, M. (2010). "Laboratory of Asymmetry: The 2006 Lebanon War and the Evolution of Iranian Ground Tactics." *Military Review* 90 (3): pp. 105–116.

Linn, B. M. (2000). *The U.S. Armyand Counterinsurgency in the Philippine War, 1899–1902*. Chapel Hill: University of North Carolina Press.

Linstone, H. (2003). "The 21st Century: Everyman as Faust—Technology, Terrorism, and the Multiple Perspective Approach." *Technological Forecasting and Social Change* 70 (3): pp. 283–296.

Linstroth, J. P. (2002). "History, Tradition, and Memory and the Basques." *History and Anthropology* 13 (3): pp. 159–189.

Lippman, T. W. (1995). *Understanding Islam: An Introduction to the Muslim World*. New York: Meridian.

Liptak, A. (2002). "Changing the Standard." *New York Times*, May31. Online: http://nytimes.com/2002/05/31/national/31ASSE.html.

Liptak, A. (2010). "Court Affirms Ban on Aiding Groups Tied to Terror." *New York Times*, June 21. Online: http://www.nytimes.com/2010/06/22/us/politics/22scotus.html?sq=pkk&st=cse&adxnnl=1&scp=5&adxnnlx=1277326830-HE9VnglcrJmh/Z3oVX1iNQ.

Liptak, A. (2011). "Civil Liberties Today." *New York Times*, Sept 7. Online: http://www.nytimes.com/2011/09/07/us/sept-11-reckoning/civil.html?pagewanted=all.

Livingstone, N. C., and T. E. Arnold (eds.). (1986). *Fighting Back*. Lexington,MA: Heath.

Llora, F., J. M. Mata, and C. L. Irvin. (1993). "ETA: From Secret Army to Social Movement: The Post-Franco Schism of the Basque Nationalist Movement." *Terrorism and Political Violence* 5: pp. 106–134.

Lonsdale, J. (2003). "The War within Mau Mau's Fight for Land and Freedom." In Lonsdale and E. S. Odhiambo (eds.), *Mau Mau and Nationhood: Arms, Authority, and Narration*. Athens, OH: Ohio University Press.

Lopez, G. A., and D. Coright. (2004). "Containing Iraq: Sanctions Worked." *Foreign Affairs* 83 (July/August): pp. 90–103.

Los Angeles Times. (2011). "Editorial: Protect Detainees, Too." December 12. Online: http://articles.latimes .com/2011/dec/12/opinion/ la-ed-prea-20111212.

Luft, G., and A. Korin. (2004). "Terrorism Goes to Sea." *Foreign Affairs* 83 (November/December): pp. 61–71.

Lufti, A. (2004). "Uyghur Separatism and China's Crisis of Creditability in the War on Terror." The Jamestown Foundation. *China Brief* 4 (3) (February 4). Online: http://www.jamestown.org/ single/?no_cache=1&tx_ttnews [tt_news]=3624.

Lunch, M. (2006). "Al-Qaeda's Media Strategies." *The National Interest* (Spring): pp. 50–56.

Lutz, B. J., and J. M. Lutz. (2008). *Global Terrorism*. London: Routledge.

Lyew, B. H. (2010). "An Examination of the Philippine Anti-Terror Law, *Suaviter in Modo, Fortiter in Re*." *Pacific Rim Law and Policy Journal Association* 19 (1): pp. 188–216.

Lyman, P. N., and J. S. Morrison. (2004). "The Terrorist Threat in Africa." *Foreign Affairs* 83(1): pp. 75–86.

Lynch, D. (2004). *Engaging Eurasia's Separatist States: Unresolved Conflicts and De Facto States*. Washington, DC: United States Institute of Peace.

Lynch, M. (2003). "Taking the Arabs Seriously." *Foreign Affairs* 82 (September/October): 81–94.

MacDermott, J. (2009). "Colombia's ELN Rebels Show New Vigor." BBC News, November 5. Online: http://news.bbc.co.uk/2/hi/ 8341093.stm.

MacDonald, A. [William Pierce]. (1985). *The Turner Diaries*. Arlington, VA: National Vanguard.

MacDonald, A. [William Pierce]. (1989). *Hunter: A Novel*. Hillsboro, WV: National Alliance.

MacDonald, R. (1972). "Electoral Politics and Uruguayan Political Decay." *International Economic Affairs* 26: pp. 24–45.

Mackay, C. S. (2004). *Ancient Rome: A Military and Political History*. New York: Cambridge University Press.

Mackey, R. (2010). "Another Middle-Class Terror Suspect." *New York Times*, May 4. Online: http://the-lede.blogs.nytimes.com/2010/05/05/ another-middle-class-terror-suspect/?scp=1&sq=mackey%20 &st=cse.

Macleod, S. (2008). "Who Killed Imad Mugniyeh?" *Time*, February 13. Online: http://mideast.blogs.time. com/2008/02/13/who_killed_imad_ mughniyeh/.

Maier, T. (2003). "Counterfeit Goods Pose Real Threat." *Insight on the News*(November 10):p. 21.

Maise, M., and H. Burgess. (n.d.). "Extremist/Spoilers." BeyondIn-tractability.org. Online: http://www.intractableconflict .org/m/extremists.jsp.

Makarenko, T. (2002). "Terrorism and Transnational Organized Crime: The Emerging News." In P.Smith (ed.), *Transnational Violence and Seams of Lawlessness in the Asia-Pacific: Linkages to Global Terrorism*. Honolulu: Asia Pacific Centre for Security Studies.

Mallaby, S. (2007). "The Low Risk of Immigrants." *Washington Post*, May 28. Online: http://www.cfr.org/ publication/13462/low_risk_from_ immigrants.html.

Mallesh, N., and M. Wright. (2011). "An Analysis of the Statistical Disclosure Attack and Receiver-Bound Cover." *Computers and Security* 30 (8): pp. 597–612.

Malley, R., and P. Harling. (2010). "Beyond Moderates and Militants: How Obama Can Chart a New Course in the Middle East." *Foreign Affairs* 89 (3): pp. 18–29.

Management Analytics et al. (1995). "Sun Tzu: The Art of War." Online: http://www.all.net.books/tzu/html.

Manchanda, R. (2004). "Maoist Insurgency in Nepal: Radicalizing Gendered Narratives." *Cultural Dynamics* 16 (2/3): pp. 237–258. Online: http://cdy.sagepub.com/ content/16/2-3/237.

Manning, P. K. (1976). *Police Work: The Social Organization of Policing*. Cambridge, MA: MIT Press.

March, A. (2005) "Guerrilla War, a Method." *Che Guevara Studies Center and Ocean Press*. Online: http://www.marxists.org/archive/ guevara/1963/misc/guerrilla-war-method.htm.

Marighella, C. (1969). *The Minimanual of the Urban Guerrilla*. U.S. Army Military Intelligence School (unpublished). Online: http://www.marxists.org/ archive/marighellacarlos/1969/06/ minimanual-urban-guerrilla/.

Marighella, C. (1971). *For the Liberation of Brazil*. J. Butt and R. Sheed (trans.). Harmondsworth, UK: Pelican.

Marquise, R. A. (2006). *Scotbom: Evidence and the Lockerbie Investigation*. New York: Algora.

Marshal, M. A. (2009). "Domestic Terrorism: Veterans Are the Focus of Reports on Extremism." *The Officer* 85 (6): pp. 16–17.

Marshall, A. (2008). "Lost Girls of the Jungle." *Marie Claire* 15 (2): pp. 108–112.

Martin, M. (2007). "Jailhouse Conversion takes 'Extreme' Turn." National Public Radio, Interview with Mark Hamm, August 8. Online: http:// www.npr.org/templates/story/story. php?storyId=12587106.

Martindale, D. (1965). *Functionalism in the Social Sciences: The Strength and Limits of Functionalism in Anthropology, Economics, Political Science, and Sociology*. Philadelphia: American Society of Political Science.

Martinez, J. S. (2008). "Process and Substance in the War on Terror." *Columbia Law Review* 108(5): pp. 1013–1092. Online: http:// www.columbialawreview.org/assets/ pdfs/108/5/Martinez.pdf.

Marx, K., and F. Engels. (1848). *The Communist Manifesto*. Online: http://www.marxists.org/archive/

marx/works/1848/communist-manifesto/index.htm.

Mason, C. (2004). "Who's Afraid of Virginia Dare? Confronting Anti-Abortion Terrorism after 9-11." *Journal of Constitutional Law* (April): pp. 796–817. Online: http://64.233.179.104/scholar?hl=en&lr=&q=cache:wXS6hyrjQHUJ:www.law.upenn.edu/conlaw/issues/vol6/num4/mason.pdf+%22eric+rudolph%22+abortion.

Massie, R. K. (1991). *Dreadnought: Britain, Germany and the Coming of the Great War*. New York: Random House.

Masters, D. (2008). "The Origin of Terrorist Threats: Religious, Separatist, or Something Else?" *Terrorism andPolitical Violence* 20 (3): pp. 396–414.

Matinuddin, K. (1999). *The Taliban Phenomenon*. New York: Cambridge University Press.

Matthews, M. M. (2008). *We Were Caught Unprepared: The 2006 Hezbollah-Israeli War*. Fort Leavenworth, KS: U.S. Army Combined Arms Center, Combat Studies Institute Press. Online: http://www.cgsc.edu/carl/download/csipubs/matthewsOP26.pdf.

Mattoon, S. (1987). *S.W.A.T. Training and Deployment*. Boulder, CO: Paladin Press.

Matusitz, J. (2010). "Cyberterrorism: Postmodern State of Chaos." *Journal of Digital Forensics* 3 (2–4): pp. 115–123.

May, P. J.,J. Sapotichne,and S. Workman. (2009). "Widespread Policy Disruption: Terrorism, Public Risks, and Homeland Security." *Policy Studies Journal* 37 (2): pp. 171–194.

May, P. J.,S. Workman,and B. D. Jones. (2009). "Organizational Attention: Responses of the Bureaucracy to Agenda Disruption." *Journal of Public Administration Research and Theory* 18 (4): pp. 517–541.

Mayer, J. (2006). "The Hidden Power." *The New Yorker*, July 3.

Mayer, J. (2008). *The Dark Side*. New York: Anchor Books.

Mazur, A. (1982). "Bomb Threats and the Mass Media: Evidence for a Theory of Suggestion." *American Sociological Review* 47: pp. 407–410.

Mazzei, J. (2009). *Death Squads or Self-Defense Forces? How Paramilitary Groups Emerge and Challenge Democracy in Latin America*. Chapel Hill: University of North Carolina Press.

McBride, M. "The Logic of Terrorism: Existential Anxiety, the Search for Meaning, and Terrorist Ideologies." *Terrorism and Political Violence* 23 (4): 560–581.

McCabe, T. R. (2010). "The Strategic Failures of al Qaeda." *Parameters* (Spring): pp. 60–71.

McCauley, C. R. (accessed 2010). "The Psychology of Terrorism." *Social Science Research Council*. Online: http://essays.ssrc.org/sept11/essays/mccauley.htm.

McClintock, C. (2006). "An Unlikely Comeback in Peru." *Journal of Democracy* 17 (4): pp. 95–109.

McCormick, D. W. (2009). "Dramaturgical Analysis of Organizational Change and Conflict." *Journal of Organizational Change* 20 (5): pp. 685–689.

McCourt, M. (2010). "Is Cyber Your Biggest Threat?" *Security* 47(8): p. 12.

McCoy, A. W. (2006). *A Question of Torture: CIA Interrogation from the Cold War to the War on Terror*. New York: Henry Holt Company.

McGee, R. (2010). "Is Yemen Contemplating a Military Offensive in the Secessionist South?" *Terrorism Monitor* 8 (25). Online: http://www.jamestown.org/programs/gta/single/?tx_ttnews[tt_news]=36525&tx_ttnews[backPid]=457&no_cache=1.

McGinn, D. (2006). "IRA Has Changed Drastically." *The Independent*, October 4. Online: http://news.independent.co.uk/uk/ulster/article1794267.ece.

McGreal, C. (2006). "Fatah Struggles with Tainted Image." *The Guardian*, January 24. Online: http://www.guardian.co.uk/world/2006/jan/24/israel.

McGregor, A. (2010). "Tribal Resistance and al-Qaeda: Suspected Airstrike Ignites Tribes in Yemen's Ma'rib Governorate." *Terrorism Monitor* 8 (28). Online: http://www.jamestown.org/programs/gta/single/?tx_ttnews[tt_news]=36623&tx_ttnews[backPid]=457&no_cache=1.

McJunkin, J. W. (2010). "Statement of James W. McJunkin, Deputy Assistant Director, Counterterrorism Division, Federal Bureau of Investigation." The Mumbai Attacks: A Wakeup Call for America's Private Sector,Hearing before the Subcommittee on Transportation Security and Infrastructure Protection of the Committee on Homeland Security, U.S. House of Representatives. Online: http://www.gpoaccess.gov/congress/index.html.

McPherson, J. M. (1988). *Battle Cry of Freedom: The Civil War Era*. New York: Ballantine.

Meehan, P. (2012). "Representative Patrick Meehan Holds a Hearing on Sharing Intelligence with Law Officials after 9/11." Washington, DC: House Committee on Homeland Security, Subcommittee on Counterterrorism and Intelligence.

Meese, E.,C. Robb,and D. Abshire. (2005). "Reform Congress, Improve Homeland Security." *The Heritage Foundation*. Online: http://www.heritage.org/Press/Commentary/ed010505b.cfm.

Melton, J. V. H. (2001). *The Rise of the Public in Enlightenment Europe*. Cambridge, UK: Cambridge University Press.

Memorial Institute for the Prevention of Terrorism. (n.d.). "Group Profile: Tupamaros." MIPT. Online: http://www.tkb.org/Group.jsp?groupID=235.

Miko, F. T. (2004). "Removing Terrorist Sanctuaries: The 9/11 Commission Recommendations and U.S. Policy." *CRS Reports for Congress*. Online: http://www.fas.org/irp/crs/RL32518.pdf.

Military.com. (2004). "Palestinian Islamic Jihad." Military.com. Online: http://www.military.com/Resources/ResourceFileView?file=PIJ-Organization.htm.

Military Technology. (2009). "Combating Piracy off Somalia." *Military Technology* 33 (3): pp. 38–40.

Miller, A. (1982). *Terrorism, the Media, and the Law*. New York: Transnational.

Miller, J. (2007). "Plenary Session." First National Fusion Center Conference, Destin, FL (unpublished).

Miller, J.,S. Engelberg,and W. Broad. (2001). *Germs: Biological Weapons and America's Secret War*. New York: Simon & Schuster.

Miller, L. (2006). "The Terrorist Mind, II: Typologies, Psychopathologies, and Practical Guidelines for Investigation." *International Journal of Offender Therapy and Criminology* (50): 255–268. Online: http://ijo.sagepub.com/cgi/content/abstract/50/3/255?rss=1.

Miniter, R. (2005). *Disinformation: 22 Media Myths that Undermine the War on Terror*. Washington, DC: Regnery.

Mintz, J. (2005). "Security Spending Initiates Disputes." *Washington Post*, March 13. Online: http://www.washingtonpost.com/wp-dyn/articles/A47964-2005Apr12.html.

MIPT. *See* Memorial Institute for the Prevention of Terrorism.

Mitchell, A., and C. Hulse. (2002). "Accountability Concern Is Raised over Security Department." *New York Times*, June 27. Online: http://www.nytimes.com/2002/06/27/national/27RIDG.html.

Moeller, S. D. (2009). *The Packaging of Terrorism: Co-opting the News for Power and Profit*. Chichester, UK: Wiley-Blackwell.

Momen, M. (1985). *An Introduction to Shi'a Islam*. New Haven, CT: Yale University Press.

Monaghan, R. (2004). "An Imperfect Peace: Paramilitary Punishments in Northern Ireland." *Terrorismand Political Violence* 16:pp. 439–461.

Monahan, T. (2009). "The Murky World of 'Fusion Centers.'" *Criminal Justice Matters* 75 (1): pp. 20–21.

Monahan, T. (2010). "The Future of Security? Surveillance Operations at Homeland Security Fusion Centers." *Social Justice* 37 (2/3): pp. 84–98.

Monahan, T., and N.A. Palmer. (2009). "The Emerging Politics of DHS Fusion Centers." *Security Dialogue*40 (6): pp. 617–636.

Montlake, S. (2007). "The Philippines Fights Leftists, Fair or Foul."*Far Eastern Economic Review* 170 (3): pp. 2–5.

Montpetit, J. (2008). "Tricky to Track Terrorist Cash." *Toronto Star*, April 28: p. A13.

Moore, R. F. (2006). "Deep Inside City Jails, Top Cops Keep a Watchful Eye Out for Terror." *New York Daily News*, August 13.

Online: http://www.nydailynews.com/front/story/443116p-373179c.html.

Moss, R. (1972). *Urban Guerrillas*. London: Temple Smith.

Moxon-Browne, E. (1987). "Spain and the ETA." *Conflict Studies* 201.

MSNBC. (2007). "DOJ Statement on JFK Airport Plot Arrests." MSNBC, June 2. Online: http://www.msnbc.msn.com/id/ 19002569/.

Muir, A. M. (1999). "Terrorism and Weapons of Mass Destruction: The Case of Aum Shinrikyo." *Studies in Conflict and Terrorism* 22: pp. 79–91.

Mullendore, K., and J. R. White. (1996). "Legislating Terrorism: Justice Issues and the Public Forum." Paper presented at the Academy of Criminal Justice Sciences Annual Meeting, March, Las Vegas, NV.

Mullerson, R. (2005). "Being Tough on Terrorism or Respecting Human Rights: A False Dilemma of Authoritarian and Liberal Responses." *American Behavioral Scientist* (48): pp. 1626–1656. Online: http://abs.sagepub.com/content/48/12/1626.

Munck, R. (1992). "The Making of the Troubles in Northern Ireland." *Journal of Contemporary History* 27 (2): pp. 211–229.

Munson, Z. (2008). "Terrorism." *Context* 7 (4): pp. 78–79.

Muro, D. (2009). "The Politics of War Memory in Radical Basque Nationalism." *Ethnic and Racial Studies* 32 (4): pp. 659–678.

Murphy, J. (2005). "The 9-11 Files." *The Village Voice* (December 13): p. 30.

Murphy, P. (2004). *The Wolves of Islam: Russia and the Faces ofChechen Terrorism*. Washington, DC: Brassey's.

Murray, J. (2005). "Policing Terrorism: A Threat to Community Policing or Just a Shift in Priorities?" *Police Practice and Research* 6 (4): pp. 347–361.

Murray, N. (2010). "Profiling in the Age of Total Information Awareness." *Race and Class*52 (2): pp. 3–24. Online: http://rac.sagepub.com/content/52/2/3.

Nacos, B. L. (2000). "Accomplice or Witness? The Media's Role in Terrorism." *Current History* (April):pp. 174–178.

Nacos, B. L. (2002). *Mass-Mediated Terrorism: The Central Role of the Media in Terrorism and Counterterrorism*. Lanham, MD: Rowman &Littlefield.

Nacos, B. L. (2005). "The Portrayal of Female Terrorists in the Media: Similar Framing Patterns in the News Coverage of Women in Politics and in Terrorism." *Studies in Conflict and Terrorism* 28: pp. 435–451.

Nacos, B. L. (2008). "The Central Role of Media in Terrorism and Counterterrorism." In M. J. Rozell and J. D. Mayer (eds.), *Media Power, Media Politics*, 2nd ed. Lanham, MD: Rowman &Littlefield.

Nance, M. W. (2003). *The Terrorist Recognition Handbook*. Guilford, CT: Lyons Press.

Napoleoni, L. (2003). *Modern Jihad: Tracing the Dollars behind the Terror Networks*. London: Pluto.

Nasr, K. B. (1997). *Arab and Israeli Terrorism*. Jefferson, NC: McFarland.

National Commission on Terrorist Attacks upon the United States. (2004). *The 9/11 Commission Report: Final Report of the National Commission on Terrorist Attacks upon the United States*. New York: Norton. Online: http://www.9-11commission.gov/report/911Report.pdf.

National Conference of State Legislatures. (2003). "Cyberterrorism." http://www.ncsl.org/programs/lis/CIP/cyberterrorism.htm.

National Counterterrorism Center. (2010a). "Revolutionary Armed Forces of Colombia (FARC)." *Counterterrorism Calendar 2010*. Online: Http://www.nctc.gov/site/groups/farc.html.

National Counterterrorism Center. (2010b). "The National Counterterrorism Center Calendar 2010." Washington, DC: National Counterterrorism Center. Online: www.ntc.gov.

National Counterterrorism Center. (2010c). *Counterterrorism Calendar: Profiles, Groups, Methods and Tactics*. Washington, DC: U.S. Department of Justice, 2010. Online: http://www.nctc.gov.

National Immigration Forum. (2004). "State and Local Police Enforcement Backgrounder: Immigration Law Enforcement by State and

Local Police." Online: http://www.immigrationforum.org/DesktopDefault.aspx?tabid=572.

National Post. (2010). "Chechnya: A Timeline." Online: http://www.nationalpost.com/Chechnya+timeline/2741009/story.html.

National Public Radio. (2001). "Liberty vs. Security: An NPR Special Report." December 6. Online: http://www.npr.org/programs/specials/liberties/index.html.

National Strategy for Combating Terrorism. (2006). "National Strategy for Combatting Terrorism." Online: http://www.whitehouse.gov/nsc/nsct/2006/.

Navarro, J. (2005). *Hunting Terrorists: A Look at the Psychopathology of Terror*. Springfield, IL: Charles C. Thomas.

Navarro, J., and M. Karlins. (2008). *What Every BODY Is Saying: An ex-FBI Agent's Guide to Speed Reading People*. New York: Harper.

Navarro, P. (2010). "A Maoist Counterpoint: Peruvian Maoism beyond Sendero Luminoso." *Latin American Perspectives* 37 (1): pp. 153–171. Online: http://lap.sagepub.com/cgi/content/abstract/37/1/153.

Navias, M. S. (2002). "Financial Warfare as a Response to International Terrorism." *Political Quarterly* 73 (August): pp. 57–79.

NBC/*Wall Street Journal*. (2004). "War on Terrorism." Polling Report.com, August 23–25. Online: http://www. pollingreport.com/terror.htm.

Nechaev, S. (1987). "Catechism of the Revolutionist." In W. Laqueur and Y. Alexander (eds.), *The Terrorism Reader*. New York: Meridian.

Nellis, A.M. (2009). "Gender Differences in Fear of Terrorism." *Journal of Contemporary Criminal Justice* 25 (3): pp. 322–340.

Nelson, K. B. "Enhancing the Attendee's Experience through Creative Design of the Event Environment: Applying Goffman's Dramaturgical Perspective." *Journal of Convention and Event Tourism* 10(2): pp. 120–133.

Ness, C. D. (2005). "In the Name of the Cause: Women's Work in Religious and Secular Terrorism." *Studies in Conflict and Terrorism* 28: pp. 353–373.

Netanyahu, B. (1997). *Terrorism: How the West Can Win*. New York: Avon.

Neuberger, L.C., and T. Valentini. (1996). *Women and Terrorism*. New York: St. Martin's Press.

Neuman, P. R. (2007). "Negotiating with Terrorists." *Foreign Affairs* 86 (3): pp. 128–138.

New American. (2003). "9-11 Report Suppressed." *The New American* (June 30): p. 13.

New American. (2009). "New Push to Criminalize Dissent." *The New American* 25 (14) (July 6):p. 6.

New Jersey State Police. (2002). Intelligence Service Section. Online: http://www.state.nj.us/lps/njsp/about/intel.html.

New York Times. (2009). "Shining Path." *New York Times*, March 18. Online: http://topics.nytimes.com/topics/reference/timestopics/organizations/s/shining_path/index.html.

New York Times. (2010). "Umar Farouk Abdulmutallab." *New York Times*, February 10. Online: http://topics.nytimes.com/top/reference/timestopics/people/a/umar_farouk_abdulmutallab/index.html?scp=1-spot&sq=umar%20farouk%20abdulmutallab&st=cse.

New York Times. (2012). "Times Topics: USA Patriot Act." *New York Times*, May 15. Online: http://topics.nytimes.com/top/reference/timestopics/subjects/u/usa_patriot_act/index.html.

New York TimesInternational. (2004). "World Briefing: Middle East." July 29. Online: http://www.nytimes.com/2004/07/29/international/29brie.html?ex=1093752000&en=2ddc52a32376a2a2&ei=5070&page wanted=all.

Newkirk, A.B. (2010). "The Rise of the Fusion-Intelligence Complex: A Critique of Political Surveillance after 9/11." *Surveillance and Society* 8 (1): pp. 43–60.

Ng, K.Y.K., and M.N. Lam. (2009). "The Canadian Forces' Information and Intelligence Fusion Center: A Preliminary Capacity Planning Study." *Defense and Security Analysis* 25 (1): pp. 69–79.

Nicas, B. (2005). "The Portrayal of Female Terrorists in the Media: Similar Framing Patterns in the News Coverage of Women in Politics and Terrorism." *Studies in Conflict andTerrorism*, 28: pp. 435–451,

Nicas, B.L.,Y.Bloch-Elkon.and R.Y. Shapiro. (2008). "Prevention of Terrorism in Post 9/11America: News Coverage, Public Perceptions, and the Politics of Homeland Security." *Terrorism and Political Violence* 20 (1): pp. 1–25.

Nice, D. C. (1988). "Abortion Clinic Bombings as Political Violence." *American Journal of Political Science* 32: pp. 178–195.

Nilson, C., and T. Burke. (2002). "Environmental Extremists and the Eco-Terrorism Movement." *ACJS Today* 24: pp. 1–6.

Nima, R. (1983). *The Wrath of Allah: Islamic Revolution and Reaction in Iran*. London: Pluto.

Noble, R. K. (2003). "Intellectual Property Piracy." *Intellectual Property and Technology Law Journal* 15 (10): pp. 21–22.

Non-State Armed Groups. (2008). "Palestinian Islamic Jihad or Islamic Jihad Movement in Palestine." Harvard University Graduate Institute, Geneva. Online: http://www.armed-groups.org/6/section.aspx/ViewGroup?id=69.

Nordland, R.,S. Yousafzi,and B. Dehghanpisheh. (2002). "How al Qaeda Slipped Away." *Newsweek*(August 19):pp. 34–41.

Northern Ireland Office. (2007). "The Agreement." Northern Ireland Office. Online: http://nio.gov.uk/the-agreement.

Norton, A. R. (2009). *Hezbollah: A Short History*. Princeton, NJ: Princeton University Press.

Novikov, E. (2004). "The Recruiting and Organizational Structure of Hizb ut Tahrir." Jamestown Foundation. *Terrorism Monitor* 2 (22) (September 18). Online: http://jamestown.org/terrorism/ news/article.php?articleid=2368890.

NPR. (2009). "Holder: Guantánamo Detainee Decision Soon." National Public Radio, October 15. Online: http://www.npr.org/templates/story/story.php?storyId=113840271.

Nuclear Threat Initiative. (2009). "Civilian Uses of HEU." Nuclear Threat Initiative. Online: http://www.nti.org/db/heu/civilian.html.

Nydell, M. K. (2002). *Understanding Arabs: A Guide for Westerners*. Yarmouth, MN: Intercultural Press.

Nzwili, F. (2006). "Leadership Profile: Somalia's Islamic Courts Union."

The Jamestown Foundation,June13. Online: http://jamestown.org/news_details.php?news_id=184.

O'Conner, T. (2004). "Civil Liberties and Domestic Terrorism." North Carolina Wesleyan College,November 2. Online: http://faculty.ncwc.edu/toconnor/429/429lect19.htm.

O'Conner, T. (2006). "Latin America." Online: http://faculty.ncwc.edu/toconnor/areas/latin.htm.

O'Connor, A. S. (2007). "Picked Last: Women and Terrorism." *Joint Force Quarterly* 44:pp. 95–100.

O Corrain, D. (2000). "Prehistoric and Early Christian Ireland." In R. F. Foster (ed.), *The Oxford Illustrated History of Ireland*. New York: Oxford University Press.

Oetken, J. (2009). "Counterinsurgency against the Naxalites in India." In S. Ganguly and D. P. Fidler (eds.), *India and Counterinsurgency: Lessons Learned*. New York: Routledge.

Office of Homeland Security. (2002). *National Strategy for Homeland Security*. Washington, DC: Office of Homeland Security.

Oliver, H. J. (2002). *The Wahhabi Myth: Dispelling Prevalent Fallacies and the Fictitious Link with bin Laden*. Birmingham, UK: Salafi Publications.

Oliver, M. (2004). "Israel Targeting Entire Hamas Leadership." *The Guardian*, May 23. Online: http://www.guardian.co.uk/israel/Story/0,2763,1175986,00.html.

Oliverio, A., and P. Lauderdale. (2005). "Terrorism as Deviance or Social Control." *International Journal of Comparative Sociology* 46 (1–2): pp. 156–169.

O'Neill, K. M., J. M. Calia, C. Chess, and L. Clarke. (2007). "Miscommunication during the Anthrax Attacks: How Events Reveal Organizational Failures." *Research in Human Ecology* 14 (2). Online: http://www.human ecologyreview.org/pastissues/her142/oneilletal.pdf.

Organization for the Prohibition of Chemical Weapons. (2000). "Nerve Agents: Lethal Organo-Phosphorus Compounds Inhibiting Cholinesterase." http://www.opcw.nl/chemhaz/nerve.htm.

Osborn, R. (2007). "On the Path of Perpetual Revolution: From Marx's

Millenarianism to Sendero Luminoso." *Totalitarian Movements and Political Religions* 8 (1): pp. 115–135.

Osterholm, M. T., and J. Schwartz. (2000). *Living Terrors*. New York: Delta.

Ostovsky, S., D. Beliakov,and M. Franchetti. (2004). "Death of Mercy." *Sunday Times* (London): Features Section, pp. 14–16.

Outram, D. (1995). *The Enlightenment*. New York: Oxford University Press.

Page, J. (2009). "Sport in Line of Fire as Terrorists Target Sri Lankan Cricket Team." *The Sunday Times*, March 4. Online: http://www.timesonline.co.uk/tol/news/world/asia/article5841980.ece.

Palestine Monitor. (2004). "Israel Emptying Jerusalem of Palestinians by Bulldozing Their Homes." *Palestine Monitor*, April 29. Online: http://www.palestinemonitor.org/updates/israel_emptying_jerusalem_of_palestinians.htm.

Palmer, M., and P. Palmer. (2004). *At the Heart of Terror: Islam, Jihadists, and America's War on Terrorism*. Lanham, MD: Rowman & Littlefield.

Pan, E. (2005a). "Europe: Integrating Islam." Council on Foreign Relations,July 13. Online: http://www.cfr.org/publication/8252/.

Pan, E. (2005b). "Turkey's EU Bid." Council on Foreign Relations, September 30. Online: http://www.cfr.org/publication/8939/turkeys_eu_bid.html.

Pantucci, R. (2010). "Europol Report Suggests Separatism Rather Than Islamism Constitutes Biggest Terrorist Threat to Europe." *Terrorism Monitor* 8 (22): June 4. Online: http://www.jamestown.org/articles-by-author/?no_cache=1&tx_cablanttnewsstaffrelation_pi1%5Bauthor%5D=473.

Pape, R. A. (2003). "The Strategic Logic of Suicide Bombing." *American Political Science Review* 97 (3): pp. 1–19. Online: http://www.danieldrezner.com/research/guest/Pape1.pdf.

Pape, R. A. (2005). *Dying to Win: The Strategic Logic of Suicide Terrorism*. New York: Random House.

Parachini, J. (2003). "Putting WMD Terrorism into Perspective." *Washington Quarterly* 26 (4): pp. 37–50.

Online: http://www.twq.com/03 autumn/docs/03autumn_parachini .pdf.

Parent, B., and J. J. Onder (2001). "Response to Terrorism through the Media." *Sheriff* 53 (6): pp. 13–16.

Parker, L. (2002). "A Frenzied Race for Answers, Antibiotics." *USA Today*, January 23.

Parsons, T. (1951). *The Social System*. Glencoe, IL: Free Press.

Patai, R. (reprint, 2002). *The Arab Mind*. New York. Hetherleigh Press.

Patriquin, M. (2009). " Hearts and Minds: Israel's Been Winning the PR War over Gaza, but Can That Last?" *Maclean's* (January 19): pp. 34–39.

Patterns of Behavior, Investigation, and Prosecution of American Terrorists, Final Report. U.S. Department of Justice. Online: http://www.ncjrs.gov/pdffiles1/nij/grants/193420.pdf.

Paul, J., and M. Spirit. (2008). "War and Politics." *Britain's Small Wars*. Online: http://www.britains-small-wars.com/cyprus/war.html.

Payne, S. (1971). "Catalan and Basque Nationalism." *Journal of Contemporary History* 6 (1): pp. 15–33.

Paz, R. (2000). "Hamas's Lesson from Lebanon." Institute for Counter-Terrorism. Online: http://www.ict.org.il/ home.htm.

Paz, R. (2004). "Hamas' Solidarity with Muqtada al-Sadr: Does the Movement Fall under the Control of Hizbollah and Iran?" Herzliya, Israel: PRISM Series of Special Dispatches on Global Jihad, No. 4/2.

Peacetalk. (2003). "Politics and Markets." http://www.peaktalk.com/archives/2003_07.php.

Pearce, S. (2005). "Religious Rage: A Quantitative Analysis of the Intensity of Religious Conflicts." *Terrorism and Political Violence* 17 (3): pp. 333–352.

Pedahzur, A.,A. Perliger,and L. Weinberg. (2003). "Altruism and Fatalism: The Characteristics of Palestinian Suicide Terrorists." *Deviant Behavior* 24 (4):pp. 405–423.

Percox, D. A. (2003). "Mau Mau and the Arming of the State." In J. Lonsdale and E. S. Odhiambo (eds.), *Mau Mau and Nationhood: Arms, Authority, and Narration*. Athens, OH: Ohio University Press.

Perl, R. F. (1998). *Terrorism: U.S. Response to Bombings in Kenya* and Tanzania: A New Policy Direction? Congressional Reference Service, *CRS Report for Congress*. Online: http://usinfo.state.gov/topical/pol/terror/crs96091.htm.

Perl, R. F. (2001). *National Commission onTerrorism: Background and Issues for Congress*. February 6. Online: news.findlaw.com/cnn/docs/crs/natlcomterr206010.pdf.

Perlinger, A. (2006). *Middle Eastern Terrorism*. New York: Chelsea House.

Perry, M. (2010). *Talking to Terrorists: Why America Must Engage with Its Enemies*. New York: Basic Books.

Peters, R. (1996). *Jihad in Classical and Modern Islam*. Princeton, NJ: Marcus Wiener.

Peterson, M. (2005). *Intelligence-Led Policing: The New Intelligence Architecture*. U.S. Department of Justice. Online: http://www.ncjrs.gov/pdffiles1/bja/210681.pdf

Petraeus, D. H. (2006). "Learning Counterinsurgency: Observations from Soldering in Iraq." *Military Review* (January/February). Online: http://usacac.army.mil/CAC/milreview/English/JanFeb06/Petraeus1.pdf.

Petraeus, D. H., and J. F. Amos. (2006). *The United States Army and Marine Corps Counterinsurgency Manual*. Chicago: University of Chicago Press. Online: http://www.fas.org/irp/doddir/army/fm3-24fd.pdf.

Petraeus, D. H., and J. N. Mattis. (2006). "Forward." In D. A. Petraeus andJ. F. Amos (ed.), *The United States Army and Marine Corps Counterinsurgency Manual*. Chicago: University of Chicago Press. Online: http://www.fas.org/irp/doddir/army/fm3-24fd.pdf.

Petrou, M. (2009). "Hosted by Terrorists?" *Maclean's*122 (10/11) (March 23): pp. 24–26.

Pew Foundation. (2005). "Pew Global Attitudes Project." Online: http://pewglobal.org/reports/pdf/248.pdf.

Pfau, M., M. Haigh, M. Gettle, M. Donnelly, G. Scott, D. Warr, and E. Wittenberg. (2004). "Embedding Journalists in Military Combat Units: Impact on Newspaper Story Frames and Tone." *Journal of Mass Communication Quarterly* 81 (1): pp. 74–89.

Philips, S. (2010). "Breaking Yemen Apart: Al-Qaeda Exploits Social Divisions to Further Its Agenda."

Terrorism Monitor 8 (19). Online: http://www.jamestown.org/programs/gta/single/?tx_ttnews[tt_news]=36387&tx_ttnews[backPid]=457&no_cache=1.

Phillips, K. (1999). *The Cousins' War: Religion, Politics, and the Triumph of Anglo-America*. New York: Basic Books.

Philp, C., and M. Evans. (2009). "Fear and Mistrust on Both Sides:Analysis." *The Times* (London),October 20.

Piazza, J. A., and J. I. Walsh. (2010). "Physical Integrity Rights and Terrorism." *Political Science and Politics* 43 (3): pp. 411–414.

Pieth, M. (2006). "Criminalizing the Financing of Terrorism." *Journal of International Criminal Justice* 4 (5): pp. 1074–1086.

Pillar, P. R. (2004). "Counterterrorism after al Qaeda." *Washington Quarterly* 27 (3): pp. 101–113.

Pillar, P.R. (2005). "Perceptions of Terrorism: Continuity and Change." U.S. Army War College. Online: htpp://www.carlisle.army.mil/ssi.

Pillar, P. R. (2006). "Intelligence, Policy, and the War in Iraq." *Foreign Affairs* 85 (2): pp. 15–27.

Pipes, D. (2003). *Militant Islam Reaches America*. New York: Norton.

Pisano, V. S. (1987). *The Dynamics of Subversion and Violence in Contemporary Italy*. Stanford, CA: The Hoover Institute.

Pitcavage, M. (1999a). "Anti-Government Extremism: Origins, Ideology, and Tactics." Tallahassee, FL: Institute for Intergovernmental Research.

Pitcavage, M. (1999b). "CurrentActivities and Trends." Tallahassee, FL: Institute for Intergovernmental Research.

Pitcavage, M. (1999c). "Old Wine, New Bottles: Paper Terrorism,Paper Scams, and Paper Redemption." *Militia Watch Dog*, November 8. Online: http://www.adl.org/mwd/redemption/asp.

Pizam, A., and A. Fleischer. (2002). "Severity versus Frequency of Acts of Terrorism: Which Has a Larger Impact on Tourism Demand?" *Journal of Travel Research* 40(3): pp. 337–339. Online: http://jtr.sagepub.com/cgi/content/abstract/ 40/3/337.

Plet, B. (1999). "World: bin Laden Behind Luxor Massacre." BBC

News, May 13. Online: http://news.bbc.co.uk/1/hi/world/middle_east/343207.stm.

Pluchinsky, D. (1982). "Political Terrorism in Western Europe: Some Themes and Variations." In Y. A. and K. A. Myers (eds.), *Terrorism in Europe*. New York: St. Martin's.

Pluchinsky, D. (1993). "Germany's Red Army Faction: An Obituary." *Studies in Conflict and Terrorism* 16: pp. 135–157.

Polack, R. J. (2004). "Social Justice and the Global Economy: New Challenges for Social Work in the 21st Century." *Social Work* 49 (2): pp. 281–291.

Police: The Law Enforcement Magazine. (2002). "Survey." July. Online: http://policemag.com/t_homt.cfm.

Pollinger, Z. A. (2008). "Counterfeit Goods and their Potential Financing of International Terrorism." *Michigan Journal of Business* 1 (1): pp. 85–102.

Poole, R. (2006). "New Study Calls for Rethinking TSA's Role." *Aviation Security Newsletter* 17 (January). Online: http://www.reason.org/aviationsecurity17.shtml.

Porath, N. (2010). "Civic Activism Continued through Other Means: Terror-Violence in the South of Thailand." *Terrorism and Political Violence* 22 (4): pp. 581–596.

Porteous, T. (2006). "The al Qaeda Myth." TomPaine.com. Online: http://www.tompaine.com/articles/2006/04/12/the_al_qaeda_myth.php.

Porter, P. (2009). "Long Wars and Long Telegrams: Containing al Qaeda." *International Affairs* 85 (2): pp. 285–305.

Porzecanski, A. C. (1973). *Uruguay's Tupamaros*. New York: Praeger.

Posner, R. A. (2004). "The 9-11 Report: A Dissent." *New York Times*, August 29. Online: http://www.nytimes.com/2004/08/29/books/review/29POSNERL.html?ex=1094787860&ei=1&en=b755-f3ccc383aefd.

Post, J. M. (1984). "Notes on a Psychodynamic Theory of Terrorist Behavior." *Terrorism* 7:pp. 241–256.

Post, J. M. (1987). "Rewarding Fire with Fire: Effects of Retaliation on Terrorist Group Dynamics." *Terrorism* 10: pp. 23–36.

Post, J. M. (2007). *The Mind of the Terrorist: The Psychology of Terrorism from the IRA to Al-Qaeda*. New York: Palgrave Macmillan.

Powers, M. R., and Z. Shen. (2008). "Social Stability and Catastrophe Risk: Lessons from the Stag Hunt." *Journal of Theoretical* 20 (4): pp. 477–497.

Pratt, D. (2010). "Religion and Terrorism: Christian Fundamentalism and Extremism." *Terrorism and Political Violence* 22: pp. 438–456.

Preidmore, W.A., and J.D. Freilich. (2007). "The Impact of State Laws Protecting Abortion Clinics and Reproductive Rights on Crimes Against Abortion Providers: Deterrence, Backlash, or Neither?" *Law and Human Behavior* 31 (6): 611–627.

Prendergast, J., and C. Thomas-Jensen. (2007). "Blowing the Horn." *Foreign Affairs* 86 (2): pp. 59–74.

Priest, D., and W. M. Arkin. (2010). "Top Secret America." *Washington Post*, July 19. Online: http://projects. washingtonpost.com/topsecret-america/articles/a-hiddenworld-growing-beyond-control/.

Protor, C. E. (1990). *Women, Equality, and the French Revolution*. Westport, CN: Greenwood Press.

Pruitt, D. G. (2007). "Readiness Theory and the Northern Ireland Conflict." *American Behavioral Scientist* 50 (11): pp. 1520–1541.

Qutb, S. (1965). *Milestones*. Reprint, Indianapolis: American Trust Publications, 1990.

Raab, C. P. (2006). "Fighting Terrorism in an Electronic Age: Does the Patriot Act Unduly Compromise Our Civil Liberties?" *Duke University Law and Technology Review*. Online: http://www.law.duke.edu/journals/dltr/articles/2006dltr0003.html.

Rabasa, A., P. Chalk, K. Cragin, S. A. Daly, H. S. Gregg, T. W. Karasik, K. A. O'Brien, and W. Rosenau. (2006). *Beyond al Qaeda: Part II—The Outer Rings of the Terrorist Universe*. Santa Monica, CA: RAND.

Radelet, L., and D. Carter. (2000). *Police and the Community*, 7th ed. New York: Macmillan.

Raghavan, S. (2010). "Yemen's Internal Divide Hampers U.S. Fight." CBS News and *Washington Post*, January 8. Online: http://www .cbsnews.com/stories/2010/01/08/ politics/washingtonpost/ main6070619.shtml.

Ralph, D. (2006). "Islamophobia and the 'War on Terror': The Continuing Pretext for U.S. Imperial Conquest." In P. Zarembka (ed.), *The Hidden History of 9-11-2001*. San Diego, CA: Elsevier Ltd.

Raman, B. (2002). "Islamic Terrorism in India: The Hydra-Headed Monster." *South Asia Analysis Group*. Online: http://www.saag.org/ papers6/ paper526.html.

Raman, B. (2003). "Istanbul: The Enemy Within." *Asia Times*. Online: http://www.atimes.com/atimes/ Middle_East/EK22Ak01.html.

Raman, B. (2004, March 3). "Massacres of Shias in Iraq and Pakistan—The Background." South Asia Analysis Group. Online: http://www.saag. org/papers10/paper941.html.

Randal, J. (2004). *Osama: The Making of a Terrorist*. New York: Andrew A. Knopf.

Ranstorp, M. (1994). "Hizbollah's Command Leadership: Its Structure, Decision-Making Relationship with Iranian Clergy and Institutions." *Terrorism and Political Violence* 6 (3) (Autumn). Online: http://www.st-andrews. ac.uk/academic/intrel/research/cstpv/ pages/terrorism.html.

Ranstorp, M. (1996). *Hizb'Allah in Lebanon: The Politics of the Western Hostage Crisis*. New York: St. Martin's Press.

Ranstorp, M. (1998). "Interpreting the Broader Context and Meaning of Bin-Laden's Fatwa." *Studies in Conflict and Terrorism* 21: pp. 321–330.

Rao, S., and P.N. Weerasinghe. (2011). "Media Coverage: Examining Social Responsibility in South Asian Journalism." *Journalism Practice* 5 (4): pp. 414–428.

Rapoport, D. (1984). "Fear and Trembling: Terrorism in Three Religious Traditions." *American Political Science Review* 78 (3): pp. 658–677.

Rapoport, D. (1988). *Inside Terrorist Organizations*. New York: Columbia University Press.

Rashbaum, W. (2010). "Qaeda Leader Indicted in New York Subway Plot." *New York Times*, July 7. Online: http://www.nytimes. com/2010/07/08/nyregion/08terror. html?_r=1&ref=najibullah_zazi.

Rashid, A. (2002). *Jihad: The Rise of Militant Islam in Central Asia*. New Haven, CT: Yale University Press.

Rasler, K. (1996). "Concessions, Repression, and Political Protest in the Iranian Revolution." *American Sociological Review* 61 (February): pp. 132–152.

Ratcliffe, J. H. (2008) *Intelligence-Led Policing*. Cullompton, Devon, UK: Willan Publishing.

Rauf, F. A. (2004). *What's Right with Islam: A New Vision for Muslims*. San Francisco: Harper.

Raufer, X. (1993). "The Red Brigades: Farewell to Arms." *Studies in Conflict and Terrorism* 16: pp. 313–325.

Raymond, C. Z. (2006). "The Threat of Maritime Terrorism in the Malacca Straits." *Terrorism Monitor* 4(3) (February 9). Online: http:// jamestown.org/terrorism/news/ article.php?issue_id=3614.

Read, C. (1996). *From Tsar to Soviets: The Russian People and Their Revolution, 1917–21*. New York: Oxford University Press.

Reese, S. (1999). *The New Jackals: Ramzi Youseff, Osama bin Laden, and the Future of Terrorism*. Boston: Northeastern University Press.

Reese, S. (2007). "State and Urban Homeland Security Plans and Exercises: Issues for the 110th Congress." Congressional Reference Service. Online: http://www.fas.org/ sgp/crs/homesec/RS22393.pdf.

Regan, T. (2004). "New Skirmishes in the Patriot Act Battle." *Christian Science Monitor*, July 14. Online: http://www.csmonitor. com/2004/0714/dailyUpdate.html.

Reiff, M. R. (2008). "Terrorism, Retribution, and Collective Responsibility." *Social Theory and Practice* 34 (2): pp. 209–242.

Renard, T. (2009). "Europol Report Describes Afghanistan-Pakistan Connection to Trends in European Terrorism." *Terrorism Monitor* 7 (12): May 8. Online: http:// www.jamestown.org/articles-by-author/?no_cache=1&tx_ cablanttnewsstaffrelation_ pi1%5Bauthor %5D=539.

Reuters. (1996). "Israel Arch Foe Hizbollah Tough Nut to Crack."

April12. Online: http://www.nando.net/newsroom/nt/412/r/whoiz.html.

Richardson, L. (2007). *What Terrorists Want: Understanding the Enemy, Containing the Threat*. New York: Random House.

Ricks, T. E. (2006). Fiasco: The American Military Adventure in Iraq. New York: Penguin.

Riedel, B. (2008). "Pakistan: The Critical Battlefield." *Current History* 107 (712): pp. 355–361.

Riley, K. J., and B. Hoffman. (1995). *Domestic Terrorism*. Santa Monica, CA: RAND. Online: http://www.rand.org/publications/MR/MR505/MR505.pdf.

Rinehart, C.S. (2009). "Volatile Breeding Grounds: The Radicalization of the Egyptian Muslim Brotherhood." *Studies in Conflict and Terrorism* 32: pp. 953–988.

Ringmar, E. (2009). "Francis Lieber, Terrorism, and the American Way of War." *Perspectives on Terrorism* 3 (4): pp. 53–61.

Riordan, R. J., and A. B. Zegart. (2002). "City Hall Goes to War." *New York Times*, July 5 Online: http://www.nytimes.com/2002/0.7/05/opinion/05RIOR.html.

Risen, J., and J. L. Thomas. (1998). "Pro-Life Turns Deadly: The Impact of Violence on America's Anti-Abortion Movement." January 26. Online: http://www.rick-ross.com/reference/a-abortion/a-abortion2.html.

Ritchey, D. (2010). "Public and Private Security: Bridging the Gap." *Security* 47 (6): pp. 18–24.

Rivera, M. (n.d.). "Welcome to Puerto Rico: History." Online: http://welcometopuertorico.org/history6.shtml.

Robb, A. (2010). "Not a Lone Wolf." *Ms. Magazine* 20 (2): pp. 26–32.

Roberts, A. (2002). "The Changing Faces of Terrorism." BBC News, August 27. Online: http://www.bbc.co.uk/history/war/sept_11/changing_faces_01.shtml.

Roberts, D. E. (1999). "Race, Vagueness, and the Social Meaning of Order-Maintenance Policing." *Journal of Criminal Law and Criminology* 89 (3): pp. 775–836.

Rogers, M. (2012, February). Private conversation with Congressman Michael Rogers (R-Michigan), Chair of the United States House Permanent Select Committee on Intelligence.

Rohlinger, D. A. (2002). "Framing the Abortion Debate: Organizational Resources, Media Strategies, and Movement-Countermovement Dynamics." *Sociological Quarterly* 43 (4): pp. 479–507.

Rojahn, C. (1998). "Left-Wing Terrorism in Germany: The Aftermath of Ideological Violence." *Conflict Studies* 313 (October): pp. 1–21.

Rollins, J. (2010). "Al Qaeda and Affiliates: Historical Perspective, Global Presence, and Implications for U.S. Policy." Congressional Research Service. Online: http://fpc.state.gov/documents/organization/137015.pdf.

Rood, J. (2004). "Memo to New DHS Secretary: With Intel, Smaller Is Better." *Page Fifteen: Congressional Quarterly*. Online: http://page15.com/2004/12/memo-tonew-dhs-secretary-with-intel.html.

Rosenzweig, P. (2010). "Privacy and Counter-Terrorism: The Pervasive Data." *Case Western Reserve Journal of International Law* 42 (3): pp. 625–646.

Ross, J. I. (1999). "Beyond the Conceptualization of Terrorism: A Psychological-Structural Model of the Causes of This Activity." In C.Summers and E.Markusen (eds.), *Collective Violence: Harmful Behavior in Groups and Governments*. New York: Rowman & Littlefield.

Ross, J. I. (2007). "Deconstructing the Terrorism News Media Relationship." *Crime, Media, Culture* 3 (2): pp. 215–225. Online: http://cmc.sagepub.com/cgi/content/refs/3/2/215.

Rotar, I. (2004a). "Hizb ut Tahrir in Central Asia." Jamestown Foundation. *Terrorism Monitor* 2(4) (February 26). Online: http://jamestown.org/terrorism/news/article.php?articleid=23567.

Rotar, I. (2004b). "Hizb ut TahrirToday." Jamestown Foundation. *Terrorism Monitor* 2 (5) (March 11). Online: http://www.jamestown.org/terrorism/news/article.php?articleid=23608.

Rothe, D. L., and J. I. Ross. (2010)."Private Military Contractors, and the Terrain of Unaccountability." *Justice Quarterly* 27 (4): pp. 593–617.

Rothem, D. (2002). "In the Spotlight: al-Asqa Martyrs Brigades." Center for Defense Information. Online: http://www.cdi.org/terrorism/asqa.cfm.

Rothmyer, K. (2009). "Misreading the Somali Threat." *The Nation* 288 (18): pp. 23–24.

Roul, A. (2010). "Little-Known Ghazi Brigade Now a Major Player in the Punjabi Jihad?" *Terrorism Monitor* 8 (28). Online: http://www.jamestown.org/programs/gta/single/?tx_ttnews[tt_news]=36621&tx_ttnews[backPid]=457&no_cache=1.

Ruane, M. E. (2009). "The Life ofJames W. von Brunn." Washingtonpost.com, July 6. Online: http://www.cbsnews.com/stories/2009/07/06/politics/washingtonpost/main5136822.shtml.

Rubenstein, R. E. (1987). *Alchemists of Revolution*. New York: Basic Books.

Rubin, B. (2003). "Lessons from Iran." *Washington Quarterly* 26 (3): pp. 105–115.

Rubin, B., and J. C. Rubin. (2002). *Anti-American Terrorism and theMiddle East: A Documentary Reader*. New York: Oxford University Press.

Rubin, J. (2003). "Stumbling into War." *Foreign Affairs* 82 (September/October): pp. 46–66.

Russell, C. A., and B. H. Miller. (1983). "Profile of a Terrorist." In L. Z. Freedman and Y. Alexander (eds.), *Perspectives on Terrorism*. Wilmington, DE: Scholarly Resources.

Ruthven, M. (2000). *Islam in the World*. New York: Oxford University Press.

Ryan, J. (2007). "The Four P-Words of Militant Islamist Radicalization and Recruitment: Persecution, Precedent, Piety, and Perseverance." *Studies in Conflict and Terrorism* 30: pp. 985–1011.

Sachs, J. D.,J. W. MacArthur,G. Schmidt-Truab,M. Kruk,C. Bahadar,M. Faye,and G. McCord. (2004). "Ending Africa's Poverty Trap." The Brookings Institute. Online: http://www.sociologia.unimib.it/wcms/file/materiali/2635.pdf.

Saeed, A., and H. Saeed. (2004). *Freedom of Religion, Apostasy, and Islam*. Aldershot, UK: Ashgate.

Sageman, M. (2004). *Understanding Terror Networks*. Philadelphia: University of Pennsylvania.

Sageman, M. (2008a). *Leaderless Jihad: Terror Networks in the Twenty-First Century*. Philadelphia: University of Pennsylvania Press.

Sageman, M. (2008b). "The Reality of Grass-Roots Terrorism." *Foreign Affairs* 87 (4): pp. 163–165.

Said, E. W., and C. Hitchens. (1990). *Blaming the Victims: Spurious Scholarship and the Palestinian Question*. New York: Verso.

Salem, P. (2006). "The Future of Lebanon." *Foreign Affairs* 85(6): pp. 13–22.

Sallot, J. (2006). "Auto Thefts Help Finance Terrorism, Day Says." *The Globe and Mail* (Canada) (June 9): p. A15.

Sanger, D. E. (2010). "U.S. Efforts Helps Militants Overseas Focus Efforts." *New York Times*, May 8.

Saradzhyan, S. (2004). "Cult of the Black Widows." *Moscow Times*, February 4. Online: http://www.themoscow-times.com/stories/2004/02/04/011.html.

Saupp, K. (2010). "Fusion Liaison Officer Programs: Effective Sharing of Information to Prevent Crime and Terrorism." *Police Chief* 77(2) (February). Online: http://policechiefmagazine.org/magazine/index.cfm?fuseaction=print_display&article_id=2013&issue_id=22010.

Saux, M. S. (2007). "Immigration and Terrorism: A Constructed Connection—The Spanish Case." *European Journal of Criminal Policy Research* 13 (1/2): pp. 57–72.

Savage, C. (2006). "Hail to the Chief: Dick Cheney's Mission to Expand—or Restore—the Power of the Presidency." *Boston Globe*, September 26. Online: http://www.boston.com/news/globe/ideas/articles/2006/11/26/hail_to_the_chief/.

Savage, C. (2009). "Obama's War on Terror May Resemble Bush's in Some Areas." *New York Times*, February 17. Online: http://www.nytimes.com/2009/02/18/us/politics/18policy.html.

Sawyer, R., and M. Foster. (2008). "The Resurgent and Persistent Threat of al Qaeda." *Annals of the American Academy of Political and Social Science* 618 (270): 197–211.

Scarman, L. (1972). *Violence and Civil Disturbance in Northern Ireland in 1969*. London: Her Majesty's Stationary Office.

Scaruffi, P. (2007). "A Time Line of the Indian Subcontinent." Online: http://www.scaruffi.com/politics/indian.html.

Schabner, D. (2004). "ELF Making Good on Threat." ABCNews.com, January 30. Online: http://abc-news.go.com/sections/us/DailyNews/elf010130.html.

Schachter, J., Y. Guzansky, and Y. Schweitzer. (2010). "Nuclear Terrorism: Threat to the Public or to Credibility." Tel Aviv: Institute for National Security Studies, April 29. Online: http://canadafreepress.com/index.php/article/22594.

Scherer, J. L. (2009). "Has al Qaeda Been Beaten?" *USA Today Magazine* (September): pp. 14–16.

Scheuer, M. (2006). *Through Our Enemies' Eyes: Osama bin Laden, Radical Islam, and the Future of America*. Washington, DC: Potomac Books.

Schmaus, W. (1999). "Functionalism and the Meaning of Social Facts." *Philosophy of Science* 66: pp. S314–S323.

Schmid, A., and J. deGraaf. (1982). *Violence as Communication*. Newbury Park, CA: Sage.

Schmid, A. P. (1992). "The Response Problem as a Definition Problem." *Terrorism and Political Violence* 4 (4) (Winter): pp. 7–25.

Schmid, A. P., and A. J. Jongman. (2005). *Political Terrorism: A New Guide to Actors, Authors, Concepts, Data Bases, Theories, and Literature*. Somerset, NJ: Transaction Books.

Schmitt, E. (2002). "Administration Split on Local Role in Terror Fight." *New York Times*, April 29. Online: http://www.nytimes.com/2002/04/29/politics/29IMMI.html.

Schneider, F. (2002). "Money for Terrorism—The Hidden Financial Flows of Islamic Terrorist Organisations: Some Preliminary Results from an Economic Perspective." Paper prepared for the workshop on The Economic Consequences of Global Terrorism, organized by DIW Berlin, June 14–15.

Schoof, M., and G. Fields. (2002). "Anthrax Attack Summary." *Wall Street Journal*, March 25.

Schramm, M., and M. Taube. (2002). "The Institution Foundations of al Qaida's Global Financial System." Related papers not presented at The Economic Consequences of Global Terrorism, Berlin, June 14–15.

Schroeder, M. (2010). "The Push against Pirates in Somalia." Stratfor, May 4. Online: http://www.stratfor.com/analysis/20100504_video_dispatch_push_against_pirates_somalia.

Schuster, H. (2006). "In Pakistan, Signs of al Qaida All Around." CNN.com, September 7. Online: http://edition.cnn.com/2006/WORLD/asiapcf/09/05/tracking.terror/index.html.

Schutz, A. (1967). *The Phenomenology of the Social World*. Evanston, IL: Northwestern University Press.

Schweitzer, Y. (2000). "Suicide Terrorism: Development and Characteristics." Institute for Counter-Terrorism. Online: http://www.ict.org.il/_home.htm.

Scott-Joynt, J. (2003). "Charities in Terror Fund Spotlight." BBC News, October 15. Online: http://news.bbc.co.uk/2/hi/business/3186840.

Seale, P. (1992). *Abu Nidal: A Gun for Hire*. New York: Random House.

Security. (2010). "U.S. Flunks Preparation for Biological Terrorism." *Security* (April): p. 17. Online: securitymagazine.com.

Sedgwick, M. (2010). "The Concept of Radicalization as a Source of Confusion." *Studies in Conflict and Terrorism* 22: pp. 479–494.

Seelye, K. Q. (2002). "War on Terror Makes for Odd Twists in Justice System." *New York Times*, June 23. Online: http://www.nytimes.com/2002/06/29/national/23SUSP.html.

Segaller, S. (1987). *Invisible Armies: Terrorism into the 1990s*. San Diego, CA: Harcourt Brace Jovanovich.

Seghetti, L. M., S. R. Vina, and K. Ester. (2005). "Enforcing Immigration Law: The Role of State and Local Law Enforcement." Congressional Reference Service. Online: http://www.ilw.com/immigdaily/news/2005, 1026-crs.pdf.

Seib, P. (2008). "The al Qaeda Media Machine." *Military Review* 88(3): pp. 74–80.

Seixas, X.-M. N. (2005). "Nation in Arms against the Invader: On Nationalist Discourses during the Spanish Civil War." In C. Ealham and M. Richards (eds.), *The Splintering of Spain: Cultural History and the Spanish Civil War—1936–1939*. Cambridge, UK: Cambridge University Press.

Semati, M. (2002). "Imagine the Terror Television." *New Media* 13 (May): pp. 213–218.

Sepper, E. (2010). "Democracy, Human Rights, and Intelligence Sharing." *Texas International Law Journal* 46 (1): pp. 151–207.

Serafino, N. M. (2002). "Combating Terrorism: Are There Lessons to Be Learned from Foreign Experiences?" Congressional Reference Service. Online: http://fpc.state.gov/documents/organization/7957.pdf.

Serrao, S. (2009). "5 Issues Shaping Intelligence Sharing." *Law and Order* 4 (April): pp. 83–88.

Service, R. (1995). *Lenin: A Political Life*, Vol.3: *The Iron Ring*. Bloomington: Indiana University Press.

Service, R. (2005). *A History of Modern Russia: From Nicholas II to Vladimir Putin*. Cambridge, MA: Harvard University Press.

Sever, I., E. Somer, A. Ruvio, and E. Soref. (2008). "Gender, Distress, and Coping in Response to Terrorism." *Affilia: Journal of Women and Social Work* 23 (2): pp. 156–166.

Shafer, J. R. (2010). *Psychological Narrative Analysis: A Professional Method to Detect Deception in Written and Oral Communications*. Springfield, IL: Charles C. Thomas.

Shafer, J. R., and J. Navarro. (2004). *Advanced Interviewing Techniques: Proven Strategies for Law Enforcement, Military, and Security Personnel*. Springfield, IL: Charles C. Thomas.

Shahar, Y. (1997). "Information Warfare." Institute for Counter-Terrorism. Online: http://www.ict.org.il/_articles/articledet.cfm?articleid=13.

Shahar, Y. (1998). "Osama bin Laden: Marketing Terrorism." Institute for Counter-Terrorism. Online: http://www.ict.org.il/articles/articledet.cfm?articleid=42.

Shahar, Y. (2002). "The al-Asqa Martyrs Brigades: A Political Tool with an Edge." Institute for Counter-Terrorism. Online: http://www.ict.org.il/articles/articledef.cfm?articleid=430.

Shahid, L. (2002). "The Sabra and Shatila Massacres: Eye-Witness Reports." *Journal of Palestine Studies* 3 (1): pp. 36–58. Online: http://links.jstor.org/sici?sici=0377-919X%28200223%2932%3A1%3C36%3ATSASME%3E2.0.CO%3B2-5&size=LARGE&origin=JSTOR-enlargePage.

Shaikh, F. (2008). "Pakistan's Perilous Voyage." *Current History* 107 (712): pp. 362–368.

Sharma, D. (2006). "Historical Traces of Hundi, Sociocultural Understanding, and Criminal Abuses of Hawala." *International Criminal Justice Review* 16 (12): pp. 99–121. Online: http://icj.sagepub.com/cgi/reprint/16/2/99.pdf.

Shay, S. (2002). *The Endless Jihad: The Mujahidin, the Taliban, and Bin Laden*. Herzliya, Israel: Institute for Counter-Terrorism.

Shepard, W. S. (2002). "The ETA: Spain Fights Europe's Last Active Terrorist Group." *Mediterranean Quarterly* (Winter): pp. 55–68.

Sherewell, P., and A. Spillius. (2009). "Fort Hood Shooting: Texas Army Killer Linked to September 11 Terrorists." *Daily Telegraph*, November 7 Online: http://www.telegraph.co.uk/news/worldnews/northamerica/usa/6521758/Fort-Hood.

Sherman, L. (1978). *The Quality of Police Education*. San Francisco: Jossey-Bass.

Shlaim, A. (2001). *The Iron Wall: Israel and the Arab World*. New York: Norton.

Shneidermann, S., and M. Turin. (2004). "The Path to Jan Shakar in the Dolakha District: Towards an Ethnography of the Maoist Movement." In M. Hutt (ed.), *Himalayan People's War: Nepal's Maoist Rebellion*. Bloomington, IN: University of Indiana Press.

Shoshoni, A., and M. Sloan. (2008). "The Drama of Media Coverage of Terrorism: Emotional and Attitudinal Impact on the Audience. *Studies in Conflict and Terrorism* 31: pp. 627–640.

Shpiro, S. (2002). "Conflict Media Strategies and the Politics of Counter-Terrorism." *Politics* 22 (2): pp. 76–85.

Shumway, J. (2005). "A Strategic Analysis of the Maneuver Enhancement Brigade." Carlyle, PA: U.S. Army War College. Online: http://www.strategicstudiesinstitute.army.mil/pdffiles/ksil213.pdf.

Siegal, P.C. (2012). "French Counterterrorism Policy in the Wake of Mohammed Merah's Attack." *CTC Sentinel*, April 23. Online: http://www.ctc.usma.edu/posts/french-counterterrorism-policy-in-the-wake-of-mohammed-merahs-attack.

Silke, A. (2001). "The Devil You Know: Continuing Problems with Research on Terrorism." *Terrorism and Political Violence* 13 (4): pp. 1–14.

Simms, K. (2000). "The Norman Invasion and Gaelic Recovery." In R. F. Foster (ed.), *The Oxford Illustrated History of Ireland*. New York: Oxford University Press.

Simon, S. (2009). "Can the Right War Be Won?" *Foreign Affairs* 88(4): pp. 130–137.

Simon, S., and J. Stevenson. (2004). "The Road to Damascus." *Foreign Affairs* 83 (May/June): pp. 110–119.

Simpson, C., and S. Gorman. (2009). "Suspected Fort Hood Shooter Believed to Be Self-Radicalized." *Wall Street Journal*, November 18.

Simpson, G. R., D. Crawford, and K. Johnson. (2004). "Crime Pays, Terrorist Finds." *Wall Street Journal*, April 14.

Singer, P. W. (2001). "Caution: Children at War." *Parameters* 31 (Winter). Online: http://www.brookings.edu/views/articles/fellows/20011203singer.pdf.

Singh, R.K., and R. Popeski. (2012). "Nepal Maoist Leave Camps: First Step to Reintegration." Reuters. Online: http://www.reuters.com/article/2012/02/03/us-nepal-maoists-fighters-idUSTRE81219J20120203.

Sinha Roy, M. (2009). "Magic Moments of Struggle: Women's Memory of the Naxalbari Movement in West Bengal, India (1967–1975)." *Indian Journal of Gender Studies* 16 (2): pp. 205–232.

Sjoberg, L. (2009). "Feminist Interrogations of Terrorism/Terrorism Studies." *International Relations* 23 (1): pp. 69–74. Online: http://ire.sagepub.com.

Slisli, F. (2000). "The Western Media and the Algerian Crisis." *Race and Class* 41 (3): pp. 43–57.

Smith, B. L. (1994). *Terrorism in America: Pipe Bombs and Pipe Dreams*. Albany: State University of New York Press.

Smith, B. L., and K. R. Damphousse. (1998). "Terrorism, Politics, and Punishment: A Test of Structural Contextual Theory and the Liberation Hypothesis." *Criminology* 36 (1): pp. 67–92.

Smith, B. L., and K. R. Damphousse. (2002). *American Terrorism Study: Patterns of Behavior, Investigation,and Prosecution of American Terrorists,Final Report*. U.S. Departmentof Justice. Online: http://www.ncjrs.gov/pdffiles1/nij/grants/193420.pdf.

Smith, B. L., K. R. Damphousse, F. Jackson, and A. Sellers. (2002). "The Prosecution and Punishment of International Terrorists in Federal Courts: 1980–1998." *Criminology & Public Policy* 1 (3): pp. 311–338.

Smith, B. L., and P. Roberts. (2005). "Pre-Incident Indicators of Terrorist Activities: The Identification of Behavioral, Geographic, and Temporal Patterns of Preparatory Conduct." National Institute of Justice. Online: http://www.ojp.usdoj.gov/nij/maps/savannah2005/ papers/Smith.ppt#397.

Snow, N. (2006). "Terrorism, Public Relations, and Propaganda." In A.P. Kavoori and T. Fraley (eds.), *Media, Terrorism, and Theory: A Reader*. Lanham, MD: Rowman & Littlefield.

Sofer, K., and J. Addison. (2012). "The Unaddressed Threat of Female Suicide Bombers: Women Terrorists Are an Increasing Problem." Center for American Progress. Online: http://www.americanprogress.org/issues/2012/01/female_suicide_bombers.html.

Solomon, J. (2007). "FBI Finds It Frequently Overstepped in Collecting Data." *Washington Post*, June 14. Online: http://www.washingtonpost.com/wp-dyn/content/article/2007/06/13/AR2007061302453_pf.html.

Sonmez, S. F., and Graefe, A. R. (1998). "Influence of Terrorism Risk on Foreign Tourism Decisions." *Annals of Tourism Research* 25 (1): pp. 112–144.

Soussi, A. (2004). "The Enigma That Is Lebanon's Hezbollah." *World Press Review Online*, June 14. Online: http://www.worldpress.org/Mideast/1873.cfm.

Spechard, A., N. Tarabrina,V. Krasnov,and K. Akhmedova. (2004). "Research Note: Observations of Suicidal Terrorists in Action." *Terrorism and Political Violence* 16: pp. 305–327.

Spencer, A. T., and S. M. Croucher. "Basque Nationalism and the Spiral of Silence: An Analysis of Public Perceptions of ETA in Spain and France." *International Communication Gazette* 70 (2): pp. 137–153. Online: http://gaz.sage-pub.com/cgi/content/abstract/70/2/137.

Stanek, R.W. (2011). "It Can and Does Happen Here: Somali Youth with Terrorist Ties in the Twin Cities." *Police Chief* 78 (February): pp. 48–52.

Stanton, B. (1991). *Klanwatch: Bringing the Ku Klux Klan to Justice*. New York: Grove Weidenfeld.

START. (2008). "Palestinian Islamic Jihad (PIJ)." National Consortium for the Study of Terrorism and Responses to Terrorism, University of Maryland. Online: http://www.start.umd.edu/start/data/tops/terrorist_organization_profile.asp?id=82.

Staub, E. (2002). "Preventing Terrorism: Raising Inclusively Caring Children in the Complex World of the Twenty-First Century." In C. E. Stout (ed.), *The Psychology of Terrorism*. Westport, CT: Praeger Publishers.

Steinberg, R. J. (2008). "Interdisciplinary Problem-Based Learning: An Alternative to Traditional Majors and Minors." *Liberal Education* 94 (1): pp. 12–18.

Sterling, C. (1986). *The Terror Network*. New York: Dell.

Stern, J. (1999). *The Ultimate Terrorists*. Cambridge, MA: Harvard University Press.

Stern, J. (2003a). "When Bombers Are Women." *Washington Post*, December 18. Reprint, Harvard University, John F. Kennedy School ofGovernment. Online: http://www.ksg.harvard.edu/news/opeds/2003/stern_women_bombers_wp1121803.htm.

Stern, J. (2003b). *Terror in the Name of God: Why Religious Militants Kill*. New York: Harper Collins.

Stern, K. S. (1996). *A Force on the Plain: The American Militia Movement and the Politics of Hate*. New York: Simon & Schuster.

Steuter, E., and D. Wills. (2010). "The Vermin Have Struck Again: Dehumanizing the Enemy in Post 9/11 Media Representations." *Media, War & Conflict*3(2): pp. 152–167.

Stevenson, J. (2003). "How Europe and America Defend Themselves." *Foreign Affairs* 82 (March/ April): pp. 75–90.

Stewart, J. (2009). "Europe's Oldest Terrorist Organization: The Basque ETA Marks 50 Years of Operations." *Terrorism Monitor* 7 (14): May 29. Online: http://www.jamestown.org/programs/gta/single/?tx_ttnews%5Btt_news%5D=35032&tx_ttnews%5BbackPid%5D=26&cHash=426a617a14c.

Stohl, M. (2008). "Networks, Terrorists and Criminals: The Implications for Community Policing." *Criminal Law and Social Change* 50 (1–2): p. 59–72.

Stone, J. (2009). "Al Qaeda, Deterrence, and Weapons of Mass Destruction." *Studies in Conflict and Terrorism* 32: pp. 763–775. Online: http://dx.doi.org/10.1080/10576100903109693.

Storey, I. (2007). "Malaysia's Role in Thailand's Southern Insurgency." The Jamestown Foundation. *Terrorism Monitor* 5 (5) (May15). Online: http://www.jamestown.org/terrorism/news/article.php?articleid=2370279.

Storm, K. J., and J. Eyerman. (2008). "Interagency Coordination: Lessons Learned from the 2005 London Train Bombings." U.S. Department of Justice. Online: http://www.ojp.usdoj.gov/nij/journals/261/coordination.htm.

Stout, D. (2009). "Museum Gunman a Longtime Foe of Government." *New York Times*, June 10. Online: http://www.nytimes.com/2009/06/ 11/us/11shoot.html.

Straub, N. (2002). "USA Patriot Act Powers Prompt Second Look." *The Hill*, May 1. Online: http://www.thehill.com/050102/patriot.shtm.

Straw, J. (2009). "Connecting the Dots, Protecting Rights." *Security Management* 53 (8): pp. 22–24.

Strieff, D. (2006). "Inside Islam's Insurgency in Europe." MSNBC, April 10. Online: http://www.msnbc.msn.com/id/11989895/.

Study of Terrorism and Responses to Terrorism. *See*START

Sud, H. (2004). "End Muslim Terrorism by Ending Wahhabi Influence in Saudi Arabia." South Asia Analysis Group,January 26. Online: http://www.saag.org/papers10/paper903.html.

Sugg, J. F. (1999). "Steven Emerson'sCrusade: Why Is a Journalist Pushing Questionable Sources behind the Scene?" *Extra!* http://www.fair.org/extra/9901/emerson.html.

Sun, I. Y., Y. Wu, and M. Poteyeva. (2011). "Arab Americans' Opinion on Counterterrorism Measures: The Impact of Race, Ethnicity, and Religion."*Studies in Conflict and Terrorism* 34 (7): 540–555.

Suskind, R. (2008). *The Way of theWorld: A Story of Truth and Hope in the Age of Terrorism*. New York: Harper Collins.

Sutter, D. (2001). "Can the Media Be So Liberal? The Economics of Media Bias." *The Cato Journal*20 (3): 431–451. Online: http://cato.org/pubs/journal/cj20n3/cj20n3-7.pdf.

Swanson, C. R., L. Territo, and R. W. Taylor. (2001). *Police Administration: Structures, Processes, and Behavior*, 5th ed. Upper Saddle River, NJ: Prentice Hall.

Sweeny, E. M. (2005). "The Patrol Officer: America's Intelligence on the Ground." *FBI Law Enforcement Bulletin* 74 (9): pp. 14–22.

Taber, R. (2002). *The War of the Flea: The Classic Study of Guerilla Warfare*. Dulles, VA: Potomac Books.

Taheri, A. (1987). *Holy Terror*. Bethesda, MD: Adler & Allen.

Talkleft. (2003). "Victory Act: Redefining Drug Crimes as Terrorism." August 20. Online: http://www.w3c.org/TR1999/REC-html1401-19991224/loose.dtd.

Tamas, G. M. (2001). "The Decay of Terrorism." *East European Constitutional Review* 10 (4). Online: http://www.law.nyu.edu/vol10num4/features/tamas.html.

Tamborini, R.,J. Stiff,and C. Heidl. (1990). "Reacting to Graphic Horror: A Model of Empathy and Emotional Behavior." *Communication Research* 17: pp. 616– 640. Online: http://crx.sagepub.com/cgi/content/abstract/17/5/616.

Tamil Eelam. (n.d.). "Tamil Eelam Homepage." http://www.eelam.com/.

Taylor, D.G. (2011). "Revise the Patriot Act to Increase Government Oversight of Surveillance." Politifact.com .Online: http://www.politifact.com/truth-o-meter/promises/obameter/promise/179/revise-the-patriot-act-to-increase-oversight-on-go/.

Taylor, L. (2006). *Shining Path: Guerrilla War in Peru's Northern Highlands, 1980–1997*. Liverpool, UK: Liverpool University Press.

Taylor, R. W. (1987). "Terrorism and Intelligence." *Defense Analysis* 3: pp. 165–175.

Taylor, R.W., and A.L. Russell. (2012). "The Failure of 'Fusion' Centers and the National Criminal Intelligence Sharing Plan." *Police Practice and Research* 12 (2): pp. 184–200.

Tenet, G. (2007). *At the Center of the Storm: My Years at the CIA*. New York: Harper Collins.

Tetlock, P. E. (2002). "Social Functionalist Frameworks for Judgment and Choice: Intuitive Politicians, Theologians, and Prosecutors." *Psychological Review* 100 (1): pp. 451–471.

Thachik, K.,M. E. Bowman,and C. Richardson. (2008). "Homegrown Terrorism: The Threat Within." National Defense University. Online:http://www.dtic.mil/cgi-bin/GetTRDoc?AD=ADA482139

Tharu, S. (2007). "Insurgency and the State in India: The Naxalite and Khalistan." *South Asian Survey* 14 (1): pp. 83–100.

Theidon, K. (2006). "The Mask and the Mirror: Facing up to the Past in Post War Peru." *Anthropologica* 48 (1): pp. 87–100.

Thompson, D. (2003). "Target: Zarqawi." ABC News, October16. Online: http://abcnews.go.com/sections/world/WorldNewsTo-night/zarqawi_030224.html.

Thorpe, T. (1996). "Black Hebrew Israelites." Online: http://www.blackomahaonline.com/blkheb.htm.

Throup, D. W. (1988). *Economic and Social Origins of Mau Mau, 1945– 1953*. London: James Currey, Ltd.

Thussu, D. (2006). "Televising 'The War on Terrorism': The Myths of Morality." In A. P. Kavoori andT. Fraley (eds.), *Media, Terrorism, and Theory: A Reader*. Lanham, MD: Rowman & Littlefield.

Tilly, C. (2004). "Terror, Terrorism, and Terrorists." *Sociological Theory* 22 (1): pp. 5–13.

Time Europe. (2004). "DefenselessTargets." September 5. Online: http://www.time.com/time/europe/html/040913/story.html.

Times(London). (2009). "New Terror Network." *The Times* (London), February 16.

Times of India. (2003). "Dawood, Osama Share Smuggling Routes." November 19. http://timesofindia. indiatimes.com/cms.dll/html/uncomp/articleshow?msid=291478.

Tosini, D. (2009). "A Sociological Understanding of Suicide Attacks." *Theory, Culture, Society* 26 (4): pp. 67–96. Online: http://tcs.sagepub.com/cgi/content/abstract/26/4/67.

Tota, A. L. (2005). "Terrorism and Collective Memories: Comparing Bologna, Naples, and Madrid 11 March." *International Journal of Comparative Sociology* 46 (1–2): pp. 55–78. Online: http://cos.sage-pub.com.ezproxy.gvsu.edu:2048/cgi/reprint/46/1-2/55.

Trojanowicz, R. C., B. Busqueroux,V. E. Kappeler,and L. K. Ganines. (1998). *Community Policing: A Contemporary Perspective*. Cincinnati, OH: Anderson.

Trujillo, H., J. Jordan, J.A. Gutierrez,and J. Gonzalez-Cabrera. (2009). "Radicalization in Prisons? Field Research in 25 Spanish Prisons." *Terrorism and Political Violence* (21): pp. 558–579.

Trundle, R. C., Jr. (1996). "Has Global Ethnic Conflict Superseded Cold War Ideology?" *Studies in Conflict and Terrorism* 19: pp. 93–107.

Tucker, N. B. (2008). "The Culture Revolution in Intelligence: Interim Report." *Washington Quarterly* 31 (2): pp. 47–61.

Turbiville, G. H., Jr. (2005). "Foreign SOF." *Special Warfare* (February): pp. 42–43.

Turks.US. (2004). "Chechnya's Fighting Not Terror: U.S. Ambassador."

February 29. Online: http://www .turks.us/article.php?story= 20040229232835832.

Turvey, B. E., D. Tamlyn, and W. J. Chisum. (1999). *Criminal Profiling: An Introduction to Behavioral Evidence Analysis*. San Diego, CA: Academic Press.

http://www.nctc.gov/docs/pl108_458. pdfUlph, S. (2004). "Top EgyptianTerrorist under Pressure." The Jamestown Foundation. December9. Online: http://www.jamestown.org/ publications_details.php?volume_ id=403&issue_id=3171&article_ id=2368986.

Ulph, S. (2006a). "Internet Mujahadeen Intensify Research on U.S. Economic Targets." *Terrorism Focus* 3 (2). Online: http://www.james-town.org/terrorism/news/article. php?issue_id=3588.

Ulph, S. (2006b). "Internet Mujahideen Refine Electronic Warfare Tactics." *Terrorism Focus* 3 (5). Online: http://www.jamestown.org/terror-ism/news/article.php?issue_id=3611.

Ulph, S. (2010). *Towards a Curriculum for the Teaching of Jihadist Ideology*. Washington, DC: The Jamestown Foundation.

Unger, C. (2007). "From the Wonderful Folks Who Brought You Iraq." *Vanity Fair*, March. Online: http://www.vanityfair. com/politics/features/2007/03/ whitehouse200703.

United Kingdom, House of Commons. (2001). *Operation Enduring Freedom and the Conflict in Afghanistan: An Update*. Online: http://www. parliament.uk/com-mons/lib/research/rp2001/rp01-081 .pdf.

United Kingdom, House of Commons. (2006). "Report of the Official Account of the Bombings in London on 7 July 2005." Online: http:// news.bbc.co.uk/1/shared/bsp/hi/ pdfs/11_05_06_narrative.pdf.

United Kingdom, Intelligence and Security Committee. (2006). "Report into the London Terrorist Attacks on 7 July 2005." Online: http:// news.bbc.co.uk/1/shared/bsp/hi/ pdfs/11_05_06_isc_london_ at-tacks_report.pdf.

United Nations. (1948). "Universal Declaration of Human Rights." Online: http://www.un.org/ Overview/rights.html.

U.S. Army. (2003). "Cultural Guide to Iraq." Fort Riley, KS: United States Army, First Infantry Division.

U.S. Bureau of Justice Assistance. (2005). *National Criminal Intelligence Sharing Plan*. Online: http:// www.it.ojp.gov/documents/ National_Criminal_Intelligence_ Sharing_Plan.pdf.

U.S. Congress. (2004). "Intelligence Reform and Prevention of Terrorism Act of 2004." December. Online: http://www.nctc.gov/docs/ pl108_458.pdf

U.S. Congress, Office of Technology Assessment. (1995). *Environmental Monitoring for Nuclear Safeguards*. Washington, DC: Government Printing Office.

U.S. Court of Appeals. (1996). Eleventh Circuit, No. 92-4473. *United States of America, Plaintiff-Appellee v. Robert Louis Beasley et al.* Online: http://www.law.emory.edu.11circuit/ jan96/92-4773.man.html.

U.S. Department of Defense. (2001). "DOD USS *Cole* Commission Report." January 9. Online: http://www.defenselink.mil/pubs/ cole20010109.html.

U.S. Department of Defense. (2005). *Homeland Security*. United States Joint Chiefs of Staff. Online: http:// www.dtic.mil/doctrine/jel/new_-pubs/jp3_26.pdf.

U.S. Department of Defense. (2010). "Website Index." Online: http:// www.dhs.gov/index.shtm.

U.S. Department of Homeland Security. (2004a). "Homeland Security andthe National Academies Highlight the Role of the Media in Terrorism Response." http://www. dhs.gov/dhspublic/display?theme=4 3&content=3549&print=true.

U.S. Department of Homeland Security. (2004b). *Securing Our Homeland*. Online: http://www.dhs.gov/inter-web/assetlibrary/DHS_StratPlan_ FINAL_spread.pdf.

U.S. Department of Homeland Security. (2004c). "Homeland Security and the National Academies Highlight the Role of the Media in Terrorism Response." May 11. Online: http:// www.dhs.gov/dhspublic/display? theme=43&content=3549&print= true.

U.S. Department of Homeland Security. (2005). "Border and Transportation Security: Securing Our Borders."

http://www.dhs.gov/dhspublic/ display?theme=50&content=875.

U.S. Department of Homeland Security. (2006). "Homeland Security Information Network." http://www .dhs. gov/xinfoshare/programs/ gc_1156888108137.shtm.

U.S. Department of Justice. (2003). "Members of the Palestinian Islamic Jihad Arrested, Charged with Racketeering and Conspiracy to Provide Support for Terrorists." Press Release, February 20. Online: http://www.usdoj.gov/opa/pr/2003/ February/03_crm_099.htm.

U.S. Department of Justice. (2006). "Combat Terrorism." Online: http://www.usdoj.gov/whatwedo/ whatwedo_ct.html.

U.S. Department of Justice. (2007). "United States Attorneys." Online: http://www.usdoj.gov/usao/index. html.

U.S. Department of Justice. (2010). "The Nationwide SAR Initiative." Online: http://nsi.ncirc.gov/.

U.S. Department of Justice. (n.d.). "Preserving Life and Liberty." Online: http://www.lifeandliberty .gov/.

U.S. Department of Justice, Office of Justice Programs. (2006). *Fusion Center Guidelines*. Online: http:// it.ojp.gov/documents/fusion_center_ guidelines_law_enforcement.pdf.

U.S. Department of State. (1999). *Patterns of Global Terrorism: 1999*. Online: http://www.state.gov/www/ global/terrorism/1999report/appb .html.

U.S. Department of State. (2004a). "The Washington File—MID-EAST." Online: http://usinfo.state.gov/ usinfo/products/washfile.html.

U.S. Department of State. (2004b). *Patterns of Global Terrorism 2003*. Online: http://www.state.gov/s/ct/ rls/pgtrpt/2003/.

U.S. Department of State. (2004c). "Helsinki Groups Issue Three Reports on Human Rights Violations in Russia." August 4. Online: http:// usinfo.state.gov/xarchives/display. html?p=washfile-english&y=2004& m=August&x=200408041344401 CJsamohT0.2353632&t=livefeeds/ wf-latest.html.

U.S. Department of State. (2007). *Country Reports on Terrorism*. Online: http://www.state.gov/s/ct/ rls/crt/2006/.

U.S. Department of State. (2008). "Colombia: An Opportunity for Lasting Success." December. Washington, DC: The DISAM Journal.

U.S. Department of State. (2012). "LRA, Boko Haram, al-Shabaab, AQIM and Other Sources of Instability in Africa." Testimony of Principal Deputy Assistant Secretary Don Yamamoto, Bureau of African Affairs, U.S. Department of State before the House Foreign Affairs Committee, February 25, 2012. Online: http://foreignaffairs.house. gov/112/HHRG-112-FA00-wstate-YamamotoD-20120425.pdf.

U.S. Department of State, Overseas Security Advisory Council. (2006). "U.S. Embassy Damascus Attack, September 12, update number 1" (unpublished briefing).

U.S. Department of the Treasury. (2003). "Informal Value Transfer Systems." Online: http://www .fincen.gov/ advis33.pdf.

U.S. Immigration and Customs Enforcement. (2005). "Two Dearborn Residents Plead Guilty to Document and Visa Fraud." Online: http:// www.ice.gov/pi/news/newsreleases/ articles/050714detroit.htm.

U.S. Marshals Service. (2005). *Monitor*. Online: http://www.usdoj.gov/ marshals/monitor/autumn05.pdf.

U.S. Navy. (2008). "Palestinian Islamic Jihad (PIJ)." Naval Post Graduate School. Online: http://www.nps.edu/ Library/Research/SubjectGuides/ SpecialTopics/TerroristProfile/ Current/PalestineIslamicJihad.html.

U.S. Office of the Director of National Intelligence. (2007). "An Overview of the United States Intelligence Community." http://www.dni.gov/ who_what/061222_DNIHand-book_Final.pdf.

U.S. Senate, Committee on Foreign Relations. (2009). "Confronting al Qaeda: Understanding the Threat in Afghanistan and Beyond." Senate Hearing 111-363. Online: http:// frwebgate.access.gpo.gov/ cgi-bin/ getdoc.cgi?dbname=111_senate_ hearings&docid=f:55931.pdf.

United States of America v. Mohamad Youseff Hammoud, et al. (March 2002). U.S. District Court, Western District of North Carolina, Charlotte Division. Docket No. 3:00CR147-MU.

United States of America v. Mousa Mohammed Abu Marzook, et al. (2003). U.S. District Court, Northern District of Illinois, Eastern Division. Docket No. 03 CR 978.

University of Singapore. (2007). "Contemporary Post-Colonial and Post-Imperial Literature in English— Frantz Fanon." Online: http:// www.scholars.nus.edu.sg/post/ poldiscourse/fanon/fanonov.html.

Upreti, B. R. (2009). "External Links of the Maoist Insurgency in Nepal." In J. Saikia and E. Stepanova (eds.), *Terrorism: Patterns of Internationalization*. New Delhi: Sage.

Uris, L. (1977). *Trinity*. New York: Bantam Books.

Valburn, M. (2002). "Air Marshal Program Drains Other Agencies." *Wall Street Journal*(February 4): p.A18.

Valdeon, R. (2009). "Discursive Constructions of Terrorism in Spain: Anglophone and Spanish Media Representations of ETA." *International Journal of Applied Linguistics* 19 (1): pp. 66–85.

Van De Velde, J. R. (2010). "The Impossible Challenge of Detering 'Nuclear Terrorism' by Al Qaeda." *Studies in Conflict and Terrorism* 33 (8): pp. 682–699.

Van Dongen, T. (2012). "The Naxalite Insurgency in India: No End in Sight." The Aspen Institute Italia. Online: http://www.aspeninstitute. it/aspenia-online/article/naxalite-insurgency-india-no-end-sight.

Van Natta, D., Jr. (2002). "Government Will Ease Limits on Domestic Spying." *New York Times*, March30. Online: http://www.nytimes. com/2002/03/30.html.

Vasilenko, V. I. (2004). "The Concept and Typology of Terrorism." *Statutes and Decisions* 40 (5): pp. 46–56. Online: http:// mesharpe.metapress.com/link. asp?id=rj98031ck9y4b41h.

Vatis, M. A. (1999). *Emergency Law Enforcement Services Vulnerability Survey*. Quantico, VA: Federal Bureau of Investigation.

Vatis, M. A. (2001). *Cyber Attacks during the War on Terrorism: A Predictive Analysis*. Hanover, NH: Institute for Security Technology Studies, Dartmouth College.

Verhoeven, C. (2009). *The Odd Man Karakozov: Imperial Russia, Modernity, and the Birth of Terrorism*. Ithaca, NY: Cornell University Press, 2009.

Vest, G. (2007). "Ohio Local Law Enforcement Information Sharing Network: Policy Issues in Data Exchange." *Police Chief* 72 (6). Online: http://policechief-magazine.org/mag-azine/index.cfm?fuseaction=display_ arch&article_id=612&issue_ id=62005.

Vice President's Task Force on Terrorism. (1986). *The Public Report of the Vice President's Task Force on Terrorism*. Online: http://www. population-security.org/bush_ report_on_terrorism/bush_report_ on_terrorism.htm.

Victoroff, J. (2005). "The Mind of a Terrorist." *Journal of Conflict Resolution* 49 (1): pp. 3–42.

Vidino, L. (2009). "Homegrown Jihadist Terrorism in the United States: A New and Occasional Phenomenon?" *Studies in Conflict and Terrorism* 32 (1): pp. 1–17.

Vidino, L. (2011). "The Buccinasco Pentiti: A Unique Case Study of Radicalization." *Terrorism and Political Violence*23: pp. 398–418.

von Hippel, K. (2002). "The Roots of Terrorism: Probing the Myths." *Political Quarterly*. Online: www. blackwell-synergy.com/doi/ pdf/10.1111/1467-923X.73.s1.4.

von Knop, K. (2007). "The Female Jihad: Al Qaeda's Women." *Studies in Conflict and Terrorism* 30: pp. 397–414.

Wade, S. J., and D. Reiter. (2007)."Does Democracy Matter? Regime Type and Suicide Terrorism." *Journal of Conflict Resolution* 51 (2): pp. 329–348.

Waldmann, P. (1986). "Guerrilla Movements in Argentina, Guatemala, Nicaragua, and Uruguay." InP. Merkle (ed.), *Political Violence and Terror*. Berkeley: University of California Press.

Walker, E. W. (2001). "Roots of Rage: Militant Islam in Central Asia." University of California, Berkeley. Online: http://ist-socrates.berkeley. edu/~bsp/caucasus/articles/walker_ 2001-1029.pdf.

Walker, S. (1985). *Sense and Nonsense about Crime: A Policy Guide*. Pacific Grove, CA: Brooks/Cole.

Walker, S. (1992). *The Police in America*. New York: McGraw-Hill.

Wallach, J., and J. Wallach. (1992). *Arafat in the Eyes of the Beholder*. Rocklin, CA: Prima.

Wall Street Journal. (2010). "Time Line: The Red Terror." Lounge, Livemint. com and the *Wall Street Journal*, April 6. Online: http://www.live-mint.com/2010/03/22111550/ timeline-red-terror.html.

Wall Street JournalResearch Staff. (2005). "A Chronology of Violence." *Wall Street Journal*(November 11): p. A16.

Walter, J. (1995). *Every Knee Shall Bow: The Truth and Tragedy of Ruby Ridge and the Randy Weaver Family*. New York: HarperCollins.

Walter, J. P. (2002). "National Drug Control Strategy: Combating Narcoterrorism." May 2. Online: http://fpc.state.gov/9908.htm.

Ward, R., and S. Hill. (2002). Institute for the Study of Violent Groups. Sam Houston State University, College of Criminal Justice. On-line: http://www.isgv.org/index. php?option=com_content&task= view&id=29&Itemid=61.

Wardlaw, G. (1982). *Political Terror-ism: Theory, Tactics, and Counter-Measures*. London: Cambridge University Press.

Warwick, D. P. (1975). *A Theory of Public Bureaucracy: Politics, Person-ality, and Organization in the State Department*. Cambridge, MA: Har-vard University Press.

Washington Post. (2010). "Experts Discuss the Government's Growing Intelligence Network: Is It Too Big?" *Washington Post*, July 25. Online: http://www.washington-post.com/ wp-dyn/content/article/ 2010/07/24/ AR2010072400164.html.

Washington Post.(2010)."Top Secret America." *Washington Post*, July 19. Online: http://projects.wash-ingtonpost.com/top-secret-america/ articles/a-hidden-world-growing-beyond-control/.

Watson,D. L. (2002). *TheTerrorist Threat Confronting the United States*. Washington, DC: Federal Bu-reau of Investigation. Online: www .fbi.gov.

Waxman, D. (1998). "The Islamic Re-public of Iran: Between Revolution and Realpolitik." *Conflict Studies* (April).

Weatherston, D., and J. Moran (2003). "Terrorism and Mental Illness: Is There a Relationship?" *International Journal of Of-fender Therapy and Comparative Criminology* 47(6): pp. 698–713. Online: http://ijo.sagepub.com. ezproxy.gvsu.edu/2048/cgi/content/ abstract/47/6/698.

Weber, M. (1947). *The Theory of Social and Economic Organization*. New York: Free Press.

Wedgwood, R. (2002). "The Enemy Within." *Wall Street Journal* (June 14): p.A12.

Wege, C. A. (1994). "Hizbollah Organization." *Studies in Conflict and Terrorism* 17 (2): pp. 151–164.

Weimann, G. (2008). "The Psychol-ogy of Mass-Mediated Terrorism." *American Behavioral Scientist* 52: pp. 69–86. Online: http:// abs.sagepub.com/cgi/content/ abstract/52/1/69.

Weimann, G., and K. von Knop. (2008). "Applying the Notion of Noise to Countering Online Terrorism." *Studies in Conflict and Terrorism*31 (10): pp. 883–902.

Weinberg, L., A. Pedhahzur, and S. Hirsh-Hoefler. (2004). "The Challenges of Conceptualizing Terrorism." *Terrorism and Po-litical Violence* 16 (4) (Winter): pp. 777–794.

Weitz, R. (2004). "Storm Clouds over Central Asia: Revival of the Islamic Movement of Uzbekistan (IMU)?" *Studies in Conflict and Terrorism* 27 (6): pp. 505–530.

West, D. L. (2005). "Combatting Terror-ism in the Horn of Africa." Harvard University, Belfer Center for Science and International Relations. Online: http://bcsia.ksg.harvard.edu/BC-SIA_content/documents/Yemen%20 Report%20BCSIA.pdf.

Westcott, K. (2000). "Who Are Hamas?" BBC News Online, October 19. Online: http://news .bbc.co.uk/1/hi/world/middle_east/ 978626.stm.

Westphal, K. (2003). "Steganography Revealed." Online: http://www .securityfocus.com/infocus/1684.

Wexler, M. N., and G. Havers. (2002). "Conspiracy: A Dramaturgical Explanation." *International Jour-nal of Group Tensions* 31 (3): pp. 247–266.

Wheeler, W. (2003). "Second End to Major Hostilities." Center for De-fense Information. December 20.

Online: http://www.cdi.org/pro-gram/document.cfm?DocumentID =1967&StartRow=1&ListRows=1 0&appendURL=&Orderby=D.Da teLastUpdated&ProgramID=39&f rom_page=index.cfm.

Whine, M. (1999). "Cyberspace: A New Medium for Communication, Command, and Control by Extrem-ists." Institute for Counter-Terrorism. Online: http://www.ict.org.il/ articles/ articledet.cfm?articleid=76.

Whitbeck. J. V. (2010). "Zionism, Anti-Semitism, and a Better Future." *Washington Report on Middle East-ern Affairs* 29 (2): p. 41.

White, J. R. (1986). *Holy War: Terrorism as a Theological Construct*. Gaithersburg, MD: International Association of Chiefs of Police.

White, J. R. (1997). "Militia Mad-ness: Extremist Interpretations of Christian Doctrine." *Perspectives: A Journal of Reformed Thought* 12: pp. 8–12.

White, J. R. (2000). *The Religious Roots of Criminal Behavior*. Tallahassee, FL: Institute for Intergovernmental Research.

White, J. R. (2001). "Political Eschatol-ogy: A Theology of Antigovernment Extremism." *American Behavioral Scientist* 44:pp. 937–956.

White, J. R. (2002). *Political Violence*. Tallahassee, FL: Institute for Intergovernmental Research.

White, J. R. (2004a). *Defending the Homeland: Domestic Intelligence, Law Enforcement, and Security*. Belmont, CA: Wadsworth/Thomson Learning.

White, J. R. (2004b). *International Terrorism in Transition*. Tallahassee, FL: Institute of Intergovernmental Research.

White, J. R. (2007). "Networks and Netwars." Destin, FL: First National Fusion Center Conference, February (unpublished).

White, J. R. (2010). "Paths to Radical-ization." Tallahassee, FL:Institute for Intergovernmental Research (unpublished).

White, R. W. (1989). "From Peaceful Protest to Guerrilla War: Micro-mobilization of the Provisional Irish Republican Army." *American Journal of Sociology* 94 (6): pp. 1277–1302.

White, R. W. (1993). *Provisional Irish Republicans: An Oral and*

Interpretative History. Westport, CT: Greenwood Press.

Wickham-Crowley, T. P. (1992). *Guerrillas and Revolution in Latin America: A Comparative Study of Insurgents and Regimes since 1956.* Princeton, NJ: Princeton University Press.

Wieviorka, M. (1993). *The Making of Terrorism.* Chicago: University of Chicago Press.

Wikas, S. (2002). "The Hamas Ceasefire: Historical Background, Future Foretold?" Peacewatch. Online: http://www.washingtoninstitute.org/watch/Peacewatch/peacewatch2002/357.htm.

Wilber, D. Q. (2010). "Von Brunn, White Supremacist Holocaust Museum Shooter Dies." *Washington Post*, January 7. Online: http://www.washingtonpost.com/wpdyn/content/article/2010/01/06/AR2010010604095.html?sid=ST2010010604659.

Wilcox, P., M.M. Ozer, M. Gunbeyi, and T. Gundogdu. (2009). "Gender and Fear of Terrorism in Turkey." *Journal of Contemporary Criminal Justice* 25 (3): pp. 341–357.

Wilkinson, P. (1974). *Political Terrorism.* New York: Wiley.

Wilkinson, P. (2006). *Terrorism versus Democracy.* New York: Routledge.

Williams, B. G., and F. Altindag. (2004). "El Kaide Turka: Tracing an al-Qaeda Splinter Cell." Jamestown Foundation. *Terrorism Monitor* 2 (22) (November18). Online: http://www.jamestown.org/print_friendly.php?volume_id=400&issue_id=3148&article_id=2368888.

Williams, P. (2007). "Warning Indicators and Terrorist Finances." In J. K. Giraldo and H. A. Trinkunas (eds.), *Terrorism Funding and State Responses: A Comparative Perspective.* Stanford, CA: Stanford University Press.

Willis, C. (2005). *The I Hate Ann Coulter, Bill O'Reilly, Rush Limbaugh, Michael Savage, Sean Hannity Reader.* New York: Thunder's Mouth Press.

Wilner, A. S., and C.-J. Dubouloz. (2011). "Transformative Radicalization: Applying Learning Theory to Islamist Radicalization." *Studies in Conflict and Terrorism* 34: pp. 418–438.

Wilson, E. O. (1999). *Consilience: The Utility of the Unknown.* New York: Vintage Press.

Winchester, S. (1974). *Northern Ireland in Crisis.* New York: Holmes & Meier.

Windrem, R., and C. Gubash. (2004). "Many Signs Point to al-Qaida." MSNBC News, March 11. Online: http://msnbc.msn.com/id/4507855/.

Wingate, J. E. (2006). "Steganography: Threat or Hype?" *Homeland Security Report* 167. Online: http://www.terrorisminfo.mipt.org/pdf/hsr167.pdf.

Wise, C. R., and R. Nadar. (2002). "Organizing the Federal System for Homeland Security: Problems, Issues, and Dilemmas." *Public Administration Review* 62 (s1): pp. 44–57.

Wise, C. R., and R. Nader (2008). "Developing and Homeland Security System: An Urgent and Complex Task in Intergovernmental Relations." In T. J. Conlon and P. L. Posner (eds.), *Intergovernmental Management for the Twenty-First Century.* Washington, DC: Brookings Institution Press.

Wise, D. (2002). "Spy Game: Changing the Rules so the Good Guys Win." *New York Times*, June 2. Online: http://www.nytimes.com/2002/06/02/weekinreview/02WISEhtml.

Witty, D. M. (2008). "Attacking al Qaeda's Operational Centers of Gravity." *Joint Forces Quarterly* 48 (1st Quarter): pp. 98–103.

Wojdakowski, W. (2007). "Counterinsurgency Operations (Commander's Note)." *Infantry Magazine* (September–October): p. 1.

Wolf, J. B. (1981). *Fear of Fear.* New York: Plenum.

Wolfowitz, P. (2004). "Ask the White House." The White House. Online: http://www.whitehouse.gov/ask/20040625.html.

Wolfsfeld, G. (2001). "The News Media and the Second Intifada: Some Initial Lessons." *Press/Politics* 6 (4): pp. 113–118.

Stern, J. (2003). "When Bombers are Women. *Washington Post*, December 13: p. A 35.

Woodcock, G. (2004). *Anarchism: A History of Libertarian Ideas and Movements.* Peterborough, ON: Broadview Press, Broadview Encore Editions.

Woodworth, P. (2001). *Dirty Wars, Clean Hands: ETA, the GAL, and Spanish Democracy.* Cork, Ireland: Cork University Press.

Wright, J., and K. Bryett. (2000). *Policing and Conflict in Northern Ireland.* New York: Palgrave Macmillan.

Wright, L. (2002). "The Man behind bin Laden: How an Egyptian Doctor Became a Master of Terror." *The New Yorker*, September 16. Online: http://www.newyorker.com/archive/2002/09/16/020916fa_fact2?currentPage=all.

Wright, L. (2006). *The Looming Tower: Al Qaeda and the Road to 9-11.* New York: Knopf.

Wright, M. (2008). "Technology and Terrorism." *Forensic Examiner* 17 (4): pp. 13–21.

Wright, R. (1986). *Sacred Rage.* New York: Touchstone.

Wright, R. (1989). *In the Name of God: The Khomeini Decade.* New York: Simon & Schuster.

Wright, R. (2000). *The Last Great Revolution: Turmoil and Transformation in Iran.* New York: Knopf.

Young, J. A. T., and J. Collier. (2002). "Attacking Anthrax." *Scientific American* (March): pp. 48–59.

Young, J.K., and L. Dugan. (2011). "Veto Players and Terror." *Journal of Peace Research* 48: pp. 19–33. Online: http://jpr.sagepub.com/content/48/1/19.

Yousef, A.-E. (2008). "The Arab Perspective on the 2006 Israeli War with Hezbollah." *Infantry* 97(2): pp. 11–15.

Zakaria, F. (2009). "They May Not Want the Bomb." *Newsweek*, May23. Online: http://www.newsweek.com/2009/05/22/they-may-not-want-the-bomb.html.

Zakaria, F. (2010a). "Don't Scramble the Jets." *Newsweek*, February 19. Online: http://www.newsweek.com/2010/02/18/don-t-scramble-the-jets.html.

Zakaria, F. (2010b). "The Fantasy of an Iranian Revolution." *Washington Post*, June 21. Online: http://www.washingtonpost.com/wpdyn/content/article/2010/06/20/AR2010062002366.html?hpid=opinionsbox1.

Zarembka, P. (ed.). (2006a). *The Hidden History of 9-11-2001.* San Diego, CA: Elsevier.

Zarembka, P. (2006b). "Initiation of the 9-11 Operation, with Evidence of Insider Trading Beforehand." In P. Zarembka (ed.), *The Hidden History of 9-11-2001.* San Diego, CA: Elsevier.

Zassoursky, Y. N. (2002). "Media and Communications as the Vehicle of the Open Society." *International Journal for Communication Studies* 64 (5): pp. 425–432.

Zenko, M. (2006). "Intelligence Estimates of Nuclear Terrorism." *Annals of the American Academy of Political and Social Science* 607: pp. 87–102. Online: http://ann.sagepub.com/cgi/content/abstract/607/1/87.

Zimmerman, P. R. (2007). "Public Domains: Engaging Iraq through Experimental Digitalities." *Framework* 48 (2): pp. 66–84.

Zirakzadeh, C. E. (2006). *Social Movements in Politics: A Comparative Study.* New York: Palgrave Macmillan.

Zissis, C. (2006). "The Sri Lankan Conflict." Council on Foreign Relations, September 11. Online: http://www.c`fr.org/publication/11407/sri_lankan_conflict.html?breadcrumb=%2Fregion%2F289%2Fsri_lanka.

Zissis, C. (2007). "Terror Groups in India." Council on Foreign Relations, March 5. Online: http://www.cfr.org/publication/12773/terror_groups_in_india.html#4.

Zulaika, J. (2003). "Anthropologists, Artists, Terrorists: The Basque Holiday from History." *Journal of Spanish Cultural Studies* 4 (2): pp. 139–150.